REMINISCENCES

REMINISCENCES

GENERAL OF THE ARMY

Douglas MacArthur

BLUEJACKET BOOKS

Naval Institute Press
Annapolis, Maryland

Naval Institute Press
291 Wood Road
Annapolis, MD 21402

First Bluejacket Books printing, 2001

Library of Congress Cataloging-in-Publication Data
MacArthur, Douglas, 1880–1964.
     Reminiscences / Douglas MacArthur.
          p.   cm.
     Originally published: New York : McGraw-Hill, [1964]
     Includes index.
     ISBN 1-55750-483-0 (acid-free paper)
     1. MacArthur, Douglas, 1880–1964. 2. Generals—United States—Biography. 3. United States. Army—Biography. 4, United States—History, Military—20th century. I. Title.
E745.M28   2001
355'.0092—dc21
[B] 00-051530

Printed in the United States of America on acid-free paper ∞
08 07 06 05 04 03 02 01   8 7 6 5 4 3 2 1

Preface

These reminiscences are neither history, biography nor a diary, although they comprise something of each of these categories. What is presented is far from a complete account even of all the incidents in which I had a part, but merely my recollections of events, refreshed by a reference to my own memoranda and a free use of staff studies and historical records made under my direction and supervision. It may assist the future historian when he seeks to account for the motives and reasons which influenced some of the actions in the great drama of war. It is also my hope that it will prove of some interest to the rising generation, who may learn therefrom that a country and government such as ours is worth fighting for, and dying for, if need be.

The greatest difficulty confronting me was that of recounting my share in the many vital events involved without giving my acts an unwarranted prominence.

In preparing this record, penned by my own hand, of my life and my participation in our great struggles for national existence, human liberty and political equality, I make no pretence to literary merit. The motive that induces me is not that of authorship. The import of the subject matter of my narrative is my only claim to attention. The statements of facts are a matter of documentary evidence. The comments are my own and show how I saw the matters treated of, whether others saw them in the same light or not.

Respectfully dedicating this work to the millions of armed men and devoted women who participated in the great wars of this country, I leave it as a heritage to my wife and son.

Douglas MacArthur
March, 1964

Contents

PART ONE   *Early Years, 1880–1912*   *1*

PART TWO   *Washington and Veracruz, 1912–1917*   *37*

PART THREE   *World War I, 1917–1919*   *49*

PART FOUR   *In Defense of Peace, 1919–1941*   *75*

PART FIVE   *World War II: Retreat from the Philippines,*
      1941–1943   *115*

PART SIX   *World War II: The Allied Offensive, 1943–1944*   *149*

PART SEVEN   *World War II: Conquest of Japan, 1944–1945*   *219*

PART EIGHT   *The Occupation of Japan, 1945–1950*   *267*

PART NINE   *Frustration in Korea, 1950–1951*   *325*

PART TEN   *Soldier's Return, 1951–1964*   *397*

      Index   *427*

viii   CONTENTS

MAPS

Boundaries of the Southwest Pacific Area and the
Extent of the Japanese Advance   *118–119*

Westward Drive along New Guinea   *186*

Landings on Leyte   *213*

Battle of Leyte Gulf   *223*

The Envelopment of Manila   *243*

Map of Korea   *329*

Inchon and Its Harbor: Low Tide   *347*

ILLUSTRATIONS   *1880–1936 Boyhood in Texas · Vera Cruz*
· World War I and the Rainbow Division
· Bonus March · West Point   *following 184*

1937–1945 Corregidor · New Guinea ·
Leyte · Luzon · Manila · Japanese Sur-
render aboard the U.S.S. Missouri   *following 280*

1946–1964 Tokyo · Korea · Wake Island ·
San Francisco · New York · Washington ·
West Point   *following 376*

PART ONE

Early Years
1880–1912

Lhe MacArthurs are of Scottish descent. A branch of the Clan Campbell, the traditions of the family are linked with the heroic lore of King Arthur and the Knights of the Round Table. Their antiquity is measured by the ancient Scottish adage: "There is nothing older, except the hills, MacArtair and the devil."

Seven centuries ago the Campbells were divided into two warring factions, one group led by the Argyle, the other by the MacArtair. By virtue of fire and sword, MacArtair maintained its position as head of the clan until its defeat during the reign of James I in the fifteenth century. Subsequently, the remnants of the clan became located on the shores of Loch Awe, in the general vicinity of Glasgow.

The tartan of the clan is green, black, and gold:

> " 'Tis Green for the sheen o' th' pines
> And Black for the gloom o' th' glen
> 'Tis Gold for the gleam o' th' gorse
> The MacArtair tartan, ye ken."

Its badge is wild myrtle; its motto *Fide et Opera* (with faith and by work); its battle cry "Listen! O Listen."

> "O the bags they are piping on banks of Loch Awe,
> And a voice on Cruachau calls the Lairds of Lochaw;
> 'MacArtair, Most High, where the wild myrtles glisten,
> Come, buckle your sword belt, and Listen! O Listen!' "

During my long national service, I have, like the clansman of Loch Awe, had to listen and listen, and listen.

My American forebear sought this land early in its days of struggle for the rights of man. My grandfather, Arthur MacArthur, was brought to these shores by his widowed mother in 1825 not long after the defeat of Napoleon at Waterloo.

In him, the vigor of the old clan and the hope of a new land were joined. Both of his parents, Arthur and Sarah, were named MacArthur and there has been an Arthur MacArthur in each succeeding generation.

They settled in Chicopee Falls, Massachusetts. Arthur attended Wesleyan, then studied law in New York, where he was admitted to the bar in 1840.

The times were unsettled. Indian wars were frequent and, as befitted a warrior clan, Arthur joined the militia forces of Massachusetts. He became a captain and later Judge Advocate of the Western Military District of the state.

In those days the frontiers of the country were being pushed ever westward by hardy pioneers in Conestoga wagons and canal boats. Law was needed in the expanding territories and so the thirty-five-year-old attorney, with his wife, the former Aurelia Belcher, and four-year-old son, Arthur, left their home in Massachusetts for a new life in the rich lands of the Great Lakes country. Shortly afterwards a second son, Frank, was born.

Arthur's legal experience and abilities earned him marked success and within two years he became city attorney for Milwaukee. In 1855, after a bitter campaign, William A. Barstow, of Waukesha, and Arthur MacArthur were elected governor and lieutenant governor, respectively, of Wisconsin. However, the newly organized Republicans charged Barstow with fraud and he immediately resigned, turning the governorship over to my grandfather. No question was raised about the honesty of his election and Arthur Mac-Arthur was suddenly the governor of Wisconsin.

He was in office for five days when the Supreme Court of Wisconsin ruled that Coles Bashford, the Republican candidate, had been elected, but upheld the election of MacArthur and his tenure of office as governor. This is probably the record for the shortest term ever served by a governor of one of our states.

He returned to the practice of law and in 1857 was elected judge of the Second Judicial Circuit, the most important in the state. "His course," says the record, "was so upright, his decisions so just and courageous, and his bearing so blameless that after the expiration of his first six-year term he was re-elected unanimously."

In 1870 President Grant, the great strategist and victor of the Civil War, then in his first term of office, summoned my grandfather to the White House to appoint him associate justice of the Supreme Court of the District of Columbia.

Arthur MacArthur became one of the first of the criminologists and penologists whose efforts have so revolutionized our judicial processes. His inborn sense of justice and his deep understanding of human nature were the motivating forces in his verdicts. Yet, the records show that in cases where the evidence produced criminal intent and wanton disregard of law, his sentences were severe.

During his stay on the bench, my grandfather lent himself to many benevolent and educational causes. He served as president of the Washington Humane Society, as president and chancellor of the Board of Regents of the National University, and as president of the Associated Charities of the District of Columbia. In an age of conservatism, his efforts to alleviate poverty and privation marked the liberal ideals now common to mankind.

I have many recollections of my grandfather. He was a large, handsome man, of genial disposition and possessed of untiring energy. He was noted for his dry wit and I could listen to his anecdotes for hours. One I shall never forget was a patent case with Daniel Webster and Henry Clay as the opposing attorneys. Webster pleaded that a certain machine violated the patent rights of his client. Clay denied this, and his eloquence held the court breathless for hours until one would have thought that the two machines no more resembled each other than day and night. When Webster rose to answer, the stillness was profound, the excitement intense. Millions of dollars hung in the balance. He gravely placed the two machines before the jury, saying, "There they are. If you can see any difference between them it is more than I can," and sat down. He won the case. And my grandfather had illustrated a lesson which, unhappily, I have not always emulated: "Never talk more than is necessary."

It was he who taught me to play cards and, incidentally, the game of poker. The last hand I ever played with him I held four queens and in my elation bet every chip I had. I can still feel the shock when he laid down four kings. And I have never forgotten his words, "My dear boy, nothing is sure in this life. Everything is relative."

His son Frank graduated from Harvard in 1876, and was admitted to the bar in 1890. Following in his father's footsteps, he began to practice law in New York City, when he died suddenly on December 1, 1890.

Justice MacArthur served on the Supreme Court for eighteen years, resigning in 1888 at the age of seventy-four. Eight years later, on August 24, 1896, he died while vacationing at Atlantic City, watching the surging sea break on the beach, and perhaps—who knows?—dreaming of the placid waters of Loch Awe as they lapped the heathered banks so far away in Scotland.

At the time the Civil War broke out, my father was not yet sixteen years old. His boyhood had been spent in Milwaukee reading and devouring stories of the debates between his hero, Abraham Lincoln, and Stephen Douglas. When the call-to-arms sounded, my father begged to be permitted to join the Union Army.

"Dad," he said, "I'm going to volunteer."

"Not yet," was the reply. "I'll send you to a military school for a year—and then, God be with you."

Attending a private military academy, he so impressed his teachers with his innate grasp and mastery of tactics and strategy that they insisted he should go to the United States Military Academy. Armed with a letter from the governor of Wisconsin to the President of the United States, and escorted by Senior Senator Doolittle of Wisconsin, he called at the White House on a May day in 1862, only to be told that all Presidential vacancies had been filled for the coming June. But there was a definite promise of appointment for the next year. President Lincoln greatly esteemed the boy's father and, placing his arm around the lad's shoulders, told of his own boy, who wanted to go to the front at once. But young Arthur did not wait. Perhaps he could hear the roll of the war drums and the old clan war cry "Listen! O Listen!"

He was seventeen years old when, on August 4, 1862, he left his home as first lieutenant and adjutant of the 24th Wisconsin Volunteer Infantry—the Milwaukee regiment destined for bloody glory on so many battlefields of long ago.

It came first at Perryville, in the heart of Kentucky, on October 8, 1862. The regiment, commanded by Brigadier General Philip Sheridan, was inexperienced and only partially trained. The enemy attacked fiercely, but the raw soldiery held and finally drove them back. Conspicuous at the front was the "boy adjutant." He was cited for "gallantry in action" and awarded the brevet of captain. In those days, except for the Medal of Honor, brevets, not medals, were given. For Arthur MacArthur it was the beginning of Sheridan's esteem for him.

After Perryville the division went into camp at Mill Creek, a short distance from Nashville.

General Sheridan understood that adequate training of troops was essential to victory in war. From the beginning of time professional soldiers have tried to impress their governments with this vital factor. With it comes success, without it disaster. It has been said, with some extravagance it must be admitted, that "Battles are won on the drill field, not the battlefield." In Sheridan's own words:

All worked unremittingly in the camp at Mill Creek in preparing for the storm, which now plainly indicated its speedy coming. Drills, parades, scouts, foraging expeditions, picket and guard duty, made up the course in this school of instruction, supplemented by frequent changes in the locations of the different brigades, so that the division could have opportunity to learn to break camp quickly and to move out promptly on the march. Foraging expeditions were particularly beneficial in this respect, and when sent out, though absent sometimes for days, the men went without tents or knapsacks, equipped with only one blanket and their arms, ammunition and rations, to teach them to shift for themselves with slender means in the event of necessity. The number of wagons was cut down to the lowest possible figure, and everything made compact by turning in all surplus transportation and restricting the personal baggage of officers to the fewest effects possible.

The results of this careful training were repaid a hundredfold in the bloody struggle in Tennessee—beginning on New Year's Eve and lasting three days into 1863—, called Murfreesboro by the North, Stone River by the South. Sheridan's division held the right of the Union line, with General Sill's First Brigade on the outer flank and the 24th Wisconsin at its extremity. The line was a prepared one with rifle entrenchments and supporting artillery. The enemy, in full force, struck the flank in early morning, hoping to envelop and roll up the entire Union line. The struggle was one of the fiercest of the war. In overwhelming numbers the enemy endeavored to encircle the right. But Sheridan pivoted again and again to fend off the blow. Fourteen times that day the Wisconsin regiment changed front until, at the end, it was facing directly toward the rear of its original line of battle—and, strange as it may seem, occupying its original breastworks in the opposite direction. The carnage was merciless. The regiment lost nearly 40 percent of its strength. General Sill was killed. Every mounted officer of the 24th was down except the adjutant. In effect, he became its commander. He was everywhere, rallying the ranks, reorganizing the companies, holding on with tooth and nail. The indomitable Sheridan was roaring in his ears, "Pivot, Arthur, pivot! Roll with the punch! He must not turn you!" And when Sheridan rode up that night he patted the lad and with a grin, when he saw the 24th in its original rifle pits facing the other way, said, "Arthur, my boy, congratulations. You haven't lost a foot of ground."

Shortly after Murfreesboro, Adjutant MacArthur was invalided with typhoid fever and missed the bloody engagement of Chickamauga. The regiment missed him too. It became disorganized in the desperate fighting and was badly mauled. He recovered, however, and rejoined it in time for the engagement at Missionary Ridge.

On the day of the battle, November 25, 1863, the Confederate Army under General Braxton Bragg organized a defensive line of rifle pits beginning at the foot of the ridge, with successive lines up its rugged face. It was a broken, ragged slope difficult of ascent even under peaceful conditions. Jagged boulders jutted out, deep gullies scarred its surface, twisted underbrush barred the way.

Sheridan was ordered to take the rifle pits at the foot of the ridge. Under a storm of shot and shell, the troops pressed forward through the timber and carried the line at the point of the bayonet. But their position was desperate, exposed as it was to the concentrated fire from the slopes and crest. Should they go forward or back?

No one seems to know just what orders may have been given, but suddenly the flag of the 24th Wisconsin started forward. With it was the color sergeant, the color guard of two corporals, and the adjutant. Up they went, step by step. The enemy's fire was intense. Down went the color bearer. One of the corporals seized the colors as they fell, but was bayoneted before he could move. A shell took off the head of the other corporal, but the adjutant grasped the flag and kept on. He seemed to be surrounded by nothing but gray coats. A Confederate colonel thrust viciously at his throat, but even as he lunged a bullet struck and the deflected blade just ripped a shoulder strap. No movement yet from the Union lines. And then, above the roar of battle, sounded the adjutant's voice: "On, Wisconsin!"

They come then; they come with a rush and a roar, a blue tide of courage, a whole division of them. Shouting, cursing, struggling foot by foot, heads bent as in a gale! Gasping breath from tortured lungs! Those last few feet before the log breastworks seem interminable! Men tumble over like tenpins! The charge is losing momentum! They falter! Officers are down! Sergeants now lead! And then, suddenly, on the crest—the flag! Once again that cry: "On, Wisconsin!" Silhouetted against the sky, the adjutant stands on the parapet waving the colors where the whole regiment can see him! Through the ragged blue line, from one end of the division to the other, comes an ugly roar, like the growl of a wounded bear! They race those last few steps, eyes blazing, lips snarling, bayonets plunging! And Missionary Ridge is won.

The adjutant suddenly falls to the ground exhausted, his body retching, racked with pain. He is a terrible sight—covered with blood and mud, hatless, his smoke-blackened face barely recognizable, his clothes torn to tatters. Sheridan, the division commander, utters not a word—he just stares at him—and then takes him in his arms. And his deep voice seems to break a little as he says: "Take care of him. He has just won the Medal of Honor."

Wrote Captain E. B. Parsons, the senior captain in the regiment, to Judge MacArthur:

Arthur was magnificent. He seems to be afraid of nothing. He'd fight a pack of tigers in a jungle. He has become the hero of the regiment. As you know, vacancies among the officers are now filled by vote and Arthur, by unanimous agreement, has been elevated to the rank of Major.

Arthur MacArthur later took command of the regiment and led it for the rest of the war. He was subsequently appointed lieutenant colonel and colonel—at nineteen the youngest officer of his rank in the entire Union Army.

In an ill-considered Union attack at Kenesaw Mountain, eleven regiments, including the 24th Wisconsin, each in full line, one behind the other, attempted to storm that frowning hill. The night before, the eleven colonels, on receiving the order, had met, and all felt it was a suicidal task. Each wrote out a farewell message. All fell. MacArthur was shot through the arm and chest. It was thought he was dead, but a wallet, containing a package of letters from home, a small Bible, and his farewell message, stopped the bullet just short of his heart.

After Atlanta was captured, Sherman was off on his Georgia campaign and Thomas was left in command. Newton had been wounded and was replaced by General Stanley, and the battles for Nashville commenced.

In 1864, an amusing incident occurred while Lincoln was running for re-election. Commissioners were sent to the camps in the field to gather the soldier vote. Colonel MacArthur collected his regiment and led them to the polling booth. But to his amazement his vote was challenged because of his youth. The whole regiment was shocked and the situation grew tense. But the colonel would have none of it. "If the Colonel can't vote," he said, "nobody in the regiment can. So, Mr. Commissioners, get out of my camp." A roar of approval came from the men. The commissioners expostulated, tried to explain, but when a bearded sergeant bellowed out, "Let's ride the rascals out on a rail," they beat a hasty retreat.

On November 30, 1864, at Franklin, the young colonel fought his last fight of the Civil War. Captain Edwin Parsons, who had become the 24th Wisconsin's adjutant, described the battle as follows:

We had been the rear guard of the army in its night march to Franklin. We were posted as a reserve near the Carter House, behind the center of our line which was its weakest spot. The Colonel and I were taking supper, if you can call hardtack and coffee by so formal a name, with the men of "A" Company. At about four o'clock, the Confederates, Cheatham's division of Tennesseeans, suddenly hit and broke through immediately in front of us. Not an instant could be lost. The whole army was imperilled unless the breach could be closed. I saw the Colonel swing into his saddle and heard his yell, "Up Wisconsin." There was no time to form lines. We just rushed pell mell to meet the enemy in a desperate hand to hand melee. I saw the Colonel sabering his way toward the leading Confederate flag. His horse was shot from under him, a bullet ripped open his right shoulder, but on foot he fought his way forward trying to bring down those Stars and Bars. A Confederate Major now had the flag and shot the Colonel through the breast. I thought he was done for but he staggered up and drove his sword through his adversary's body, but even as the Confederate fell he shot our Colonel down for good with a bullet through the knee.

The other regiments of the reserve were now up and we drove the enemy back and healed the breach. When I returned to the Carter House, where they had brought the Colonel, I saw four dead Generals lying on the porch side by side.

Said General David S. Stanley, citing the regiment and its Colonel:

It is rare in history that one can say a certain unit saved the day. But this was the case at Franklin when the 24th Wisconsin, with no orders from higher up, by its spontaneous action, repelled the enemy and rectified our lines. In this it was bravely led by its young Colonel, Arthur MacArthur.

He was invalided for several months, but rejoined the regiment in time to bring it home at the end of the war. I recall so well an anecdote told me by my father which occurred when he had recovered from his wounds and was on his way back to rejoin his regiment. He had been ordered to serve on a military court held in New Orleans.

Cotton, the Confederacy's staple growth, was in much demand in England for its manufacture into textiles. The cotton was in the fields, but all wagons and animal teams were controlled by the district commander, who had resisted every effort to coerce him into letting the cotton be brought to the wharves for loading.

The commander, an attractive young man in his thirties, was a close friend of my father, who had called to pay his respects. As the two old friends were chatting, the orderly, in some perturbation, broke in to say that two Southern ladies were insisting upon speaking personally with the general. He had been unable to get rid of them. My father rose to go, but his host asked him to stay. "With ladies as my visitors, Arthur," he said, "I would like to have witnesses present."

The two women were ushered in and were impressive, indeed. The eldest was a "grande dame" of the Southern aristocracy, and the younger was the loveliest woman my father had ever seen—but one. (My mother was present when he told me the story, and my father was no fool.)

The general seemed fascinated. He could not take his eyes from that beautiful face.

The stillness of the dingy office was broken by the voice of the older woman. "I will at once come to the point. We must have the temporary use of transport facilities to move our cotton. Your country has no wish to antagonize the British to the point of joining the South in the war, and consequently allows blockade running. It would accordingly not regard with dissatisfaction the use of your wagons. In return, here is two hundred and fifty thousand dollars in gold certificates. And, if you need other inducements," she added with a smile, "this young lady will supply them." And with a bow they walked out, leaving the young lady's address on the desk.

My father said his knees were knocking together as they had never done in battle. But the general's voice was crisp and clear as he turned to him and dictated the following dispatch:

To the President of the United States:
I have just been offered two hundred and fifty thousand dollars and the most beautiful woman I have ever seen to betray my trust. I am depositing the money with the Treasury of the United States and request immediate relief from this command. They are getting close to my price.

The war ended, and the 24th Wisconsin, led by its young colonel, marched triumphantly through the streets of Milwaukee before the cheering crowds. But there was many a sob and tear in that great gathering. The regiment had lost more than two-thirds of its officers and men. They were mustered out on June 10, 1865, and Arthur MacArthur was again a civilian.

For a year he studied law, but the call of the West was in his blood and in February 1866, he accepted a commission as second lieutenant in the 17th Regular Infantry. He was promoted at once to first lieutenant and on July 28th to captain in the 36th Infantry.

For the next seven years he was engaged in the onerous task of pushing Indians into the arid recesses of the Southwest and of bringing the white man's brand of law and order to the Western frontier.

And what a dazzling area it was. A frontier where the plains broke off and the land gets rough and unruly—a lonely land of sun and silence. Not yet had the plough turned over the grass, nor the land been spanned by ribbons of steel; not yet tamed by the snorting iron horses, frightening off the buffalo herds; not yet the barbed wire to choke off the endless acres.

Over the East and South hung the smoke and bitterness left by civil war. But here, in the West, was a bright land of promise scarred only by wind and weather—a land with unknown mountains to be climbed, alluring trails to be ridden, streams to be navigated by the strong and vigorous—a land of water holes, of dusty sagebrush, of sturdy ponies.

There lived the indigenous redmen, the Sioux and the Crow, the Blackfoot and the Cheyenne, proud and colorful tribes of most ancient ancestry and descent, the original Americans, whose religion and philosophy of life were little known and less appreciated.

But all this is now changed; the vital vestiges of that blazing era have disappeared. Plowed under are the vast plains and prairies. Cut down or burned in large part are the great expanses of primeval forests. Harnessed are the swift rivers to create power more imposing than the most imaginative Indian medicine man ever conjured for his fascinated braves. In the feverish search for minerals, mountain shapes have been altered. The great herds of wild animals—buffalo, antelope, moose, elk—are gone. Gone, too, are the primitive majesty and stealthy terror of the Indian. Gone are the scalp dances and the warpath, the village circles of buffalo-skin tepees. Defeated and humbled, the redman is herded into overcrowded reservations. The unshaven, buckskin-clad frontiersman, the trapper, trader, trooper, and pioneer homeseeker are no more. The West of old is gone, quite beyond recall. We now seek a new and limitless frontier in the vast spaces of the universe.

But it was the Old West of frontier days, with its thrilling adventures, into which Captain MacArthur plunged. He engaged in the Indian wars around Fort Rawlins in Utah Territory. He served at Fort Bridges and Camp Stanbough, at Fort Fred Steele and Camp Robinson in Wyoming Territory, where life was governed by the rifle and pistol.

He knew the badmen of those days—the James boys, the Youngers—

and the picturesque scouts and lawmen such as "Wild Bill" Hickok and "Buffalo Bill." He was at the center of the disorder, the violence, the fighting involved in this drama of undisciplined and untamed men. Other wide-open spaces, other vast underdeveloped areas there are and still remain, but nowhere else has there been the savage turbulence, the striking vitality, and the raucous glamour of the struggle for law and order in the American West.

He manned guard over the advancing Union Pacific Railroad as it crept forward to join the Central Pacific from the West Coast. He was there when the great drought of the late 1870s ruined the cattle industry and sent thousands of unemployed cowboys out onto the range to shift for themselves. He was present when General Sheridan met with the Indian chiefs in an effort to stop hostilities.

At that meeting, after smoking the pipe of peace, the General endeavored to impress the redmen with the uselessness of trying to compete with the whites. He told them that in contrast to their canoes, the white man had great steamboats traversing the mighty Mississippi River, and asked the interpreter what impression it made on the chiefs. And that buckskinned worthy replied, "General, they don't believe you."

Sheridan then expostulated upon the capacity of the railroad systems spanning the continent, in contrast with primitive pony travel. And again the interpreter translated, "General, they don't believe you."

Finally, Sheridan, fully aware of the limited capabilities of the telephone, played his trump card, saying, "I can talk into a little black box and the Great White Father in Washington will hear me and answer." This time the interpreter remained silent. Impatiently, Sheridan directed him to translate what he had said. But the interpreter still uttered not a word. Sheridan angrily snapped, "What's the matter with you?" And, slowly rolling his quid of tobacco into his cheek, the interpreter explained, "Well, General, now *I* don't believe you."

After these seven years of frontier service, Captain MacArthur was ordered to Jackson Barracks near New Orleans, and there at the Mardi Gras he met his fate.

Mary Pinkney Hardy came from an old Virginia family dating back to Jamestown days. Her ancestors had fought under George Washington and Andrew Jackson, and her brothers, products of the Virginia Military Institute, had followed Robert E. Lee's flag on Virginia's bloody fields. A Hardy was at Stonewall Jackson's elbow that dark night when he fell on the sodden Plank Road near Chancellorsville.

Her father, Thomas Hardy, was a wealthy cotton merchant who built the stately mansion called "Riveredge" in Berkley, on the banks of the Elizabeth River. This locality is now a part of downtown Norfolk.

It was at "Riveredge" that "Pinky" Hardy was born on May 22, 1852. She was nine years old when the Civil War engulfed their Norfolk home. It was taken over by the Union Army as a hospital, and later as Major General Benjamin Butler's headquarters. Safely ensconced in their summer home near Henderson, North Carolina, she and her sisters were removed from the scene of actual fighting until the closing stages of the war, when General Sherman, on his march from Atlanta, camped at "Burnside," much to their dismay and disgust.

When the war ended, the Hardys moved for a time to Baltimore, where "Pinky" was graduated from Mount de Sales Academy. She was awarded its highest honor: "a crown and a gold medal for uniform excellence of conduct." In the winter of 1874, now a young lady, she visited New Orleans, where she met young Captain Arthur MacArthur, and then, for the first time, the dashing "Boy Colonel" had the good sense to surrender. It was love at first sight, a love which lasted throughout their lives—thirty-seven years of perfect union.

They were married at "Riveredge" on May 19, 1875. Their first child, Arthur, was born on August 1, 1876, and then Malcolm in October of 1878. Each time "Pinky" came home to Norfolk for the big event, Captain MacArthur's station was changed, first to Baton Rouge, Louisiana, then to Little Rock, Arkansas. A third child was on the way and, as usual, arrangements were made to bring him into the world at "Riveredge," but something went awry and the birth took place in 1880 at the Arsenal Barracks of Little Rock. But Virginians are nothing if not loyal, and the Norfolk papers covered me beautifully with headlines reading, "Douglas MacArthur was born on January 26, while his parents were away."

Five months later, Captain MacArthur, in command of "K" Company of the 13th Infantry, was on the way to distant Fort Wingate in New Mexico. In 1883 tragedy struck and Malcolm died. They brought him back to Virginia soil and buried him in the old Hardy plot in Norfolk. His loss was a terrible blow to my mother, but it seemed only to increase her devotion to Arthur and myself. This tie was to become one of the dominant factors of my life.

We numbered but four in our little family when orders came in 1884 for "K" Company to march overland 300 miles from Fort Wingate to tiny Fort Selden, some 60 miles above El Paso, to guard the fords of the Rio Grande River from the ever-present danger of Geronimo's marauding Indians. My first memories are of that march.

How well I recall veteran First Sergeant Peter Ripley as I trudged with him at the head of the column. At each halt a big Irish recruit named Moriarity would come complaining of sore feet and ask to ride in the ambulance. Each time the sergeant would refuse. At last the Irishman insisted on speaking to the captain, and Ripley brought him to my father. The recruit was a glib talker with his Irish wit and blarney, and seemed to me to have a good case until my father closed the matter decisively. "Moriarity," he said, "growl you may, but march you must."

And there was the native rancher of whom we asked, "How far to the next water hole?" "About ten miles," he replied. On we labored for nearly three long, hot, dusty hours when we met another homesteader. "How far," asked Ripley again, "to the next water hole?" And again the reply, "About ten miles." And Ripley, turning to the sweating men listening anxiously on the rough trail, said, "It's all right, boys. Thank God, we're holding our own."

The little outpost at Fort Selden became our home for the next three years. Company "K," with its two officers, its assistant surgeon, and forty-six enlisted men comprised the lonely garrison, sheltered in single-story, flat-roofed adobe buildings. It was here I learned to ride and shoot even before I could read or write—indeed, almost before I could walk and talk. My mother, with some help from my father, began the education of her two boys. Our teaching included not only the simple rudiments, but above all else, a sense of obligation. We were to do what was right no matter what the personal sacrifice might be. Our country was always to come first. Two things we must never do: never lie, never tattle.

Life was vivid and exciting for me. In addition to my brother, there was William Hughes, the son of the first lieutenant of the company. We were inseparable comrades then, but little did we dream that years later we would be comrades-in-arms on the far fields of France. He was my operations officer, G-3, and later my chief of staff in the Rainbow Division during the First World War.

We found much to divert us. There were the visiting officers and mounted details from the cavalry post at Fort Stanton to the east guarding the nearby Mescalero Reservation. There were the bumpy rides on the mule-drawn water wagon that would make the daily trip to the Rio Grande several miles west of the post. And toward twilight each evening, the stirring ceremony of retreat, when we would stand at attention as the bugle sounded the lowering of the flag.

One day, while on herd the horses and mules panicked at the sight and smell of a strange new animal moving along the sandy wastes like some shaggy ghost out of the pages of wonderland. It was a camel, lonesome survivor of a herd that in 1855 Jefferson Davis, then Secretary of War, had brought from Egypt to serve as pack animals to supply the chain of isolated forts in this vast desert country.

An educational system for officers was being introduced into the Army, and the Cavalry and Infantry School had been established at Fort Leavenworth, Kansas. Selected companies from the various regiments were concentrated there for the purpose of training the officers. "K" Company was one of that chosen group, and late in 1886 we moved eastward.

For the first time, I attended a regular school and was exposed to the regimen of studies, to the competition between classmates. It opened new vistas for me.

It was a never-ending thrill for me to watch the mounted troops drill and the artillery fire on the practice range. I learned there the vital value of "hits per minute." There was extra excitement when my father commanded the afternoon parade, with the cavalry on their splendid mounts, the artillery with their long-barreled guns and caissons, and the infantry with its blaze of glittering bayonets.

But the freedom and lure of the West was still in my blood and I was a poor student. When my father was temporarily detached to command the troops guarding the "Boomer Line" of the new territory of Oklahoma, I begged to go along. But my father just pointed to my report card, saying I needed the schooling.

Promotion in the Army was very slow. Our country was following its usual postwar custom of reducing its armed forces below the security level of safety. My father had been a captain for twenty-three years when Major General Alexander McCook recommended him for promotion to a vacant majority in the Adjutant General's Department. His endorsement read, "He is beyond doubt the most distinguished Captain in the Army of the United States for gallantry and good conduct in war. He is a student, a master of his profession, has legal ability which fits him for the position, is exceptional in habit, temperate at all times, yet modest withall." He received the appointment.

Washington was different from anything I had ever known. It was my first glimpse at that whirlpool of glitter and pomp, of politics and diplomacy, of statesmanship and intrigue. I found it no substitute for the color and excitement of the frontier West. I entered the Force Public School on Massachusetts Avenue, and there completed my grade school courses. I was only an average student.

My brother Arthur received an appointment from the Oshkosh district of Wisconsin to the Naval Academy at Annapolis in 1892. He was an excellent scholar and graduated in 1896, one of the youngest midshipmen in his class. A good athlete, Arthur won the coveted "N" by breaking the Academy record for the half-mile run. He went on to a most promising Navy career, advancing in grade through the ranks to captain in 1918. He saw action at Santiago on the gunboat *Vixen* when Cervera's Spanish fleet was destroyed, during the insurrection in the Philippines, and the Boxer Rebellion in China. Arthur later became a submarine commander, and was one of the original developers of underwater tactics and strategy. A member of the War College and the General Board of the Navy, he saw many years of sea duty in battleships and destroyers. During World War I he commanded the light cruiser *Chattanooga* against German submarines, for which he received the Navy Cross and the Distinguished Service Medal. The Army awarded him its Commendation Citation for his ability and untiring energy in convoy duty in the Atlantic. He died suddenly on December 2, 1923. I loved my brother dearly and his premature death left a gap in my life which has never been filled. One of his sons, my namesake Douglas, has risen to prominence in our Foreign Service as Ambassador to Japan and later to Belgium.

In September 1893, my father was ordered to Texas. I hailed this move with delight. Housing the largest garrison I had ever seen, Fort Sam Houston guarded our southern borders and was one of the most important posts in the Army. It was here that a transformation began to take place in my development. I was enrolled in the West Texas Military Academy headed by the Reverend Allen Burlesoa, rector of the Army chapel. There came a desire to know, a seeking for the reason why, a search for the truth. Abstruse mathematics began to appear as a challenge to analysis, dull Latin and Greek seemed a gateway to the moving words of the leaders of the past, laborious historical data led to the nerve-tingling battlefields of the great captains, Biblical lessons began to open the spiritual portals of a growing faith, literature to lay bare the souls of men. My studies enveloped me, my marks went higher, and many of the school medals came my way. But I also learned how little such honors mean after one wins them.

I had always loved athletics and the spirit of competition moved me to participate in as many sports as possible. I became the quarterback on the eleven, the shortstop on the nine, the tennis champion of the campus.

On May 26, 1896, my father was promoted to the grade of lieutenant colonel, and the following January he was assigned to the Department of the Dakotas, with station at St. Paul. It was a wrench to leave San Antonio. My four years there were without doubt the happiest of my life. Texas will always be a second home to me.

Always before me was the goal of West Point, the greatest military academy in the world. Situated between the lofty Crow's Nest of New York's Bear Mountain and the venerable Storm King Mountain of the Highlands, the setting is inspiring. Below its noble heights flows the Hudson River, guarded since Revolutionary days by Fort Putnam, termed, in General Washington's orders, as "the citadel and its dependencies." History records that "a great wrought-iron chain with protecting log boom was stretched across the Hudson to block British ships." Its old links are still preserved at Trophy Point. Here, too, just to the south, lies Stony Point with its unforgettable memory of that July midnight in 1779 when Anthony Wayne revived America's drooping cause by storming through to rout the British garrison at bayonet point.

A competitive examination was to be held for a West Point vacancy which would occur the following year in Congressman Theabold Otjen's Fourth District of Milwaukee in the spring of 1898. I decided to try for it.

In Milwaukee, my mother and I lived at the Plankinton House while Dad went on to St. Paul. Every weekend he would join us. I entered classes at the West Side High School under the guidance of its principal, Professor McLanagan. Every school day I trudged, there and back, the two miles from the hotel to the school. I never worked harder in my life.

The night before the examination, for the first time in my life I could not sleep, and the next morning when I arrived at the city hall I felt nauseated. But the cool words of my mother brought me around. "Doug," she said, "you'll win if you don't lose your nerve. You must believe in yourself, my son, or no one else will believe in you. Be self-confident, self-reliant, and even if you don't make it, you will know you have done your best. Now, go to it." When the marks were counted, I led. My careful preparation had repaid me. It was a lesson I never forgot. Preparedness is the key to success and victory.

On April 24, 1898, war with Spain was declared. It was a momentous step. It meant that America's policy of comparative isolation was ended. This country had entered the arena of world politics.

My father was ordered to Chickamauga Park as chief of staff of the IIIrd Army Corps under concentration for the invasion of Cuba. But the complete victory of Admiral George Dewey in the Bay of Manila, when he scorned hidden torpedoes and open foes, and swept the vessels of Montojo's fleet from the face of the water, focused the eyes of the nation upon the Philippines.

Philippine history is blotted with the blood of martyrs and patriots who have sacrificed their lives in the hope that their country might be free. Many flags have flown over Manila. Though Spain had held dominion from the day Magellan first saw the islands twenty-seven years after Columbus discovered America, China, Holland, and England all have launched periods of adventure with Manila as the central scene. But for Filipino leaders, their goal never changed. The taste of freedom is a heady wine that ultimately no human being can resist. America now planned to send its troops into the Philippines to help against Spain. Originally, there was little thought of long occupation; our one desire was to help those seeking independence.

On June 1, 1898, my father was appointed a brigadier general of volunteers and ordered to the Philippines. I was anxious to pass up my coming cadetship and enlist, but his wise counsel prevailed. "My son," said he, "there will be plenty of fighting in the coming years, and of a magnitude far beyond this. Prepare yourself." My mother, too, just scoffed at the idea. As usual, they were right, although I did not think so then. At eighteen one wonders how little parents understand; years later, the wonder is how wise they were.

On July 31st, my father arrived in the Philippines and was assigned to command the Second Brigade of the 1st Division, then, in conjunction with the Filipino Army, besieging Manila.

The resistance in front of the Second Brigade was tenacious, and the fighting along the Singalong Road, with its strong blockhouses, was severe. The city, however, shortly capitulated and a treaty of peace with Spain was negotiated.

My father was at once promoted to be a major general of volunteers and assigned to the command of the 2nd Division of the VIIIth Army Corps.

Under the terms of the Treaty of Paris, Spain ceded the Philippines to the United States, the United States agreeing in return to pay 20-million dollars. The question of the possession of this distant land by our country was hotly debated. The Republican Administration under President McKinley favored expansion; the Democrats led by Grover Cleveland and William Jennings Bryan were, for the most part, convinced that our previous policy of isolationism would best secure American interests.

President McKinley appraised the situation as follows:

The future of the Philippine Islands is now in the hands of the American people, and the Paris Treaty commits the free and franchised Filipinos to the

But the insurrection was far from over. Guerrilla warfare was initiated at the suggestion of General Aguinaldo, who organized his own guerrilla unit in the mountains near Benguet. The remnants of the insurgent forces took to the field and formed the nuclei for guerrilla units that sprung up at various points of the country. In the manner of all guerrilla organizations, these bands maintained themselves through the material support and co-operation of the local civilian communities.

The Filipinos have always been adept at applying guerrilla tactics against a superior enemy. They had shown their mettle in numerous revolts against the Spaniards. Their tenacity and courage, applied against my father and his Americans, was forty years later to be used to good advantage for my father's son and in support of his Americans—and even later, after Philippine independence, by Communist dissidents against their own nation's armed forces.

My father felt that the guerrilla movement could only be stopped by the capture of Aguinaldo—the symbol of the resistance. Violent and repressive measures then in use against the Filipinos would only, in his opinion, intensify the resistance and retard the peaceful administration of the islands. As military governor he put a stop to such action and intensified the search for Aguinaldo's hideout.

The opportunity came when an intercepted letter revealed Aguinaldo to be at Palanan. General MacArthur sent a small force, composed largely of Macabebe Scouts, under General Frederick Funston to make the capture.

Aguinaldo was brought to Manila and treated like an honored guest rather than a prisoner. The guerrilla leaders could not believe that their idol had been captured. They thought it part of a plan to dishearten and induce them to surrender. Manuel Quezon, then a young major in the insurgent army and later my good friend, told me the story. He had been summoned by General Tomas Mascardo and told to surrender to the Americans in order to ascertain whether or not Aguinaldo had been captured.

I surrendered at Marivales to Lieutenant Miller, the first American with whom I had ever come into personal contact. Lieutenant Miller told me that I could consider myself free and could keep my revolver and my dagger. I handed Lieutenant Miller my dagger as a present. This same dagger he sent back to me soon after I was elected President of the Commonwealth, thirty-five years later. I told Lieutenant Miller of the special mission which General Mascardo had confided to me. Lieutenant Miller said, "Of course it is true that General Aguinaldo has been captured. He is now a prisoner of war, but he is living in Malacanan Palace where the Military Governor, General Arthur MacArthur lives, and where he is treated with the utmost courtesy and consideration. I will inform Manila of your mission at once, and perhaps they will let you see Aguinaldo with your own eyes."

On the afternoon of the following day, a small launch carried me from Marivales to Manila and I was conducted directly to Malacanan Palace—the holy place from which Spanish Governors-General had ruled the Philippines, and which I had never seen before. I was ushered into the office of General Arthur Mac-Arthur. Fred Fisher, who in after years became a member of the Supreme Court of the Philippines, acted as interpreter. He told General MacArthur in English what I had said in Spanish, namely that I was instructed by General Mascardo to find out if General Aguinaldo had been captured.

The American General, who stood erect and towered over my head, raised his hand without saying a word and pointing to the room across the hall made a motion for me to go in there. Trembling with emotion, I slowly walked through the hall toward the room, hoping against hope that I would find no one inside. At the door two American soldiers in uniform, with gloves and bayonets, stood on guard. As I entered the room I saw General Aguinaldo—the man whom I had considered as the personification of my own beloved country, the man whom I had seen at the height of his glory surrounded by generals and soldiers, statesmen and politicians, the rich and the poor, respected and honored by all. I now saw that same man alone in a room, a prisoner of war! It is impossible for me to describe what I felt, but as I write these lines, forty-two years later, my heart throbs as it did then. I felt that the whole world had crumbled.

It took me some time before I could collect myself, but finally I was able to say in Tagalog, "I have been sent by General Mascardo to receive your instructions whether he should continue fighting or surrender." General Aquinaldo replied, "I have taken the oath of allegiance to the United States and I have no right to advise you to go on fighting."

That settled it. Mascardo and the others laid down their arms. General MacArthur proclaimed an amnesty and a bounty of 30 pesos for weapons turned in, and the resistance movement was at an end.

With the cessation of hostilities, the U.S. was faced with not only the rehabilitation of the war-torn country, but its preparation for future independence. My father felt that sovereignty was the only possible solution for this freedom loving people—sovereignty with a special friendship binding our own country with theirs. The greatest difficulty would be to convert the hatreds engendered by the war into mutual respect and good will.

Speaking of the purpose of the American occupation, he said:

The grand central idea of our presence in the Philippines is the fact that we are carrying to that people those imperishable ideas which have slowly evolved through many centuries of human aspirations. There are two things that lie close to the human heart. The one is the hope for a degree of personal liberty, and the other is for immortality. The first has slowly evolved and emerged from the strife of centuries and has found its full development in the United States. The idea of personal liberty allows a citizen to do within just limits whatever tends to his own happiness. That idea we are planting in the Orient. Wherever the American flag goes that idea goes. The fruition of that idea in the Philippines is merely a matter of evolution; and to my mind, a brief one. The Filipinos want precisely what we can give them. People ask us what we are going to accomplish in a money way. The planting of liberty—not money—is what we seek. The human race has propagated its higher ideals in a succession of waves, and now its waves are passing beyond the Pacific.

Almost overnight the hatred disappeared, and as equals the natives joined in a program to lay the firm foundations for civil administration and economic development. These foundations might roughly be classified as education, law, defense, and prosperity.

In education, a free public-school system with a normal school, a school of arts and trades, and even a school for the deaf and blind was established. The natives were astounded at the American Army displaying such an interest in the affairs of education. It has always seemed to me that the educational work under the American military occupation of the Philippines is one of the most romantic chapters in Philippine history. While some countries conquered by means of the Cross, and others subjugated by means of the sword, it remained for the United States to colonize through the agency of education.

In law, the old medieval and antiquated code, with its totalitarian injustice and cruelty, was replaced by a civil procedure which is still the basis of present day Philippine jurisprudence. It established for the first time the writ of *habeas corpus*. Civil courts were created, including a supreme court consisting of nine justices, six of whom were Filipino jurists and three American officers. From its earliest conception no jurisdictional system in the world has functioned with more justice and dignity.

In defense, the policy, regarded as very doubtful at the time, of training the Filipino in the arts of war so that ultimately his own shores would be protected by his own troops, was adopted. The foundation was laid in the Macabebe Scouts whom General MacArthur had employed so successfully in the insurrection. The program was broadened and extended to the Philippine Scouts of the American Army who so distinguished themselves by their bravery and devotion during the Japanese invasion.

To promote prosperity, a gold standard was adopted, a public road policy inaugurated, harbors and ports improved, a civil service planned, a bureau of health organized, national industries encouraged, tariff restrictions modified, and local government started through elections.

With the satisfactory accomplishment of these diversified efforts, the logical time for transfer from a military to a civil government arrived, and my father sailed for home on July 4, 1901.

On June 13, 1899, I enrolled at the United States Military Academy. Life at West Point is rigid discipline in an atmosphere of culture and learning. But all is not drudgery in this world apart from all other worlds. There was the thrill of high competition on the athletic field, the dances and excitement and gay hours with beautiful ladies. I worked hard and I played hard. There are some incidents of my happy four years there I still recall. One nearly ended my career as a cadet.

Conditions in those days were different from today. Much of the discipline of new cadets was left in the hands of the upper classes. Hazing was practiced with a worthy goal, but with methods that were violent and uncontrolled. President McKinley at Congress' insistence ordered a special court of inquiry which convened in December 1900 to investigate both an incident of alleged hazing, which had occurred a year prior to my entrance, and also the extent to which plebes were subject to hazing. I was summoned to appear before the court as a principal witness in a case in which I had been the so-called victim.

Under questioning I fully explained all the circumstances, but refused to divulge the names of the upper classmen involved. My father and mother had taught me those two immutable principles—never to lie, never to tattle. But here was a desperate situation for me. If the court insisted and ordered me to reveal the names, and I refused to obey the order, it would in all likelihood mean my dismissal and the end of all my hopes and dreams. It would be so easy and expedient to yield, to tell, and who would blame me?

My mother, who was at West Point at the time, sensed the struggle raging in my soul and sent me this message during a recess of the court:

> Do you know that your soul is of my soul such a part
> That you seem to be fiber and core of my heart?
> None other can pain me as you, son, can do;
> None other can please me or praise me as you.
> Remember the world will be quick with its blame
> If shadow or shame ever darken your name.
> Like mother, like son, is saying so true
> The world will judge largely of mother by you.

> Be this then your task, if task it shall be
> To force this proud world to do homage to me.
> Be sure it will say, when its verdict you've won
> She reaps as she sowed: "This man is her son!"

I knew then what to do. Come what may, I would be no tattletale.

Although more than sixty years have come and gone since then, I can still feel the beads of sweat on my brow, still feel my knees giving way under me and that dreadful nausea that I had felt once before when I faced my competitive examination at the city hall in Milwaukee. I did my best to fend off the question, to dodge the issue, but I was no match for the shrewd old heads who sat in judgment. And then the order came, short, peremptory, unequivocal. At the end I grew weak and pleaded for mercy: that my whole life's hope lay in being an officer; that always I had been with the colors; that my father, then on the battleline 10,000 miles away, was their comrade-in-arms of the Civil and Indian wars; that I would do anything in the way of punishment, but not to strip me of my uniform. And then—I could not go on—I heard the old soldier who presided say, "Court is recessed. Take him to his quarters."

For hours I waited for that dread step of the adjutant coming to put me in arrest. But it never came. The names were obtained through other means. And never again was I to be in doubt about doing what I thought to be right, never again were my knees to knock in trepidation as to my fate, only once again was the old nausea to strike.

Those four years at West Point held so much of those glories of youth that mean so little in the lexicon of later life. I remember the first baseball game ever to be played with the midshipmen of the Naval Academy at Annapolis on May 18, 1901. I was in left field for the cadets, with the Navy stands right next to me. It was a period of great prominence for my father as governor general of the Philippines. It was an overcast day and the Middies carried raincoats. I shall never forget the blast that razzed me when the Army took the field. Every raincoat was swinging, every Navy voice joining the ribald ditty:

> "Are you the Governor General
>   Or a hobo?
> Who is the boss of this show?
> Is it you or Emilio Aguinaldo?"

But I squared it up. With two out and the score tied at three-all, I worked the Navy pitcher for a base on balls. The umpire had been more than generous to me and the Navy catcher was, to put it mildly, understandingly upset by the call. I was no Ty Cobb, but in those days I could run. I went down on the first pitch and, sure enough, the catcher threw wild, allowing me to go on to third. The throw from the outfield went over the third baseman's head, and I trotted home with what proved to be the winning run in a 4-3 contest. They are fine sportsmen, those Navy files, and when the game was over they treated me as though I really were the governor general. I was far from a brilliant ballplayer, even by the limited standards of college baseball, but that game will always stand out as one of my happiest memories.

And that awful moment when a tactical officer caught me on Flirtation Walk publicly kissing a girl, and instead of reporting me for unbecoming conduct, just grinned and said, "Congratulations, Mister MacArthur."

And the day we went to the horseshow in New York, when my roommate, Charles Severson, and "Dotty" Laurson, the Cadet Captain of "E" Company, and myself slipped away and swaggered into Rector's on Broadway, shook hands with "Diamond Jim" Brady, and called for nine martinis. The astounded bartender asked, "Where are the other six?" and "Dotty," striking a Napoleonic posture, bellowed out, pointing to the six waiting glasses, "Their spirits are here." And then we swanked out to a burlesque show. We loved it!

And that day in classroom when the first section was studying the space-time relationship later formulated by Einstein as his Theory of Relativity. The text was complex and, being unable to comprehend it, I committed the pages to memory. When I was called upon to recite, I solemnly reeled off almost word for word what the book said. Our instructor, Colonel Feiberger, looked at me somewhat quizzically and asked, "Do you understand this theory?" It was a bad moment for me, but I did not hesitate in replying, "No, sir." You could have heard a pin drop. I braced myself and waited. And then the slow words of the professor, "Neither do I, Mister MacArthur. Section dismissed." I still do not understand the theory.

I won my "A," became First Captain of the Corps, and to my amazement recorded the highest scholastic record in twenty-five years. This rating has always astonished me and I have never understood it. There were a number of my classmates who were smarter than I, and I am sure there were even a greater number in the preceding twenty-four classes. I studied no longer nor harder than others, and can only account for such a result by my having, perhaps, a somewhat clearer perspective of events—a better realization that first things come first.

I graduated on June 11, 1903, as a second lieutenant of Engineers with the words of Secretary of War Elihu Root, ringing in my ears: "Before you leave the Army, according to all precedents in our history, you will be engaged in another war. It is bound to come, and will come. Prepare your country for that war."

To my great delight, my first assignment was in the Philippine Islands. My father now commanded on the Pacific Coast, with headquarters in San Francisco. I spent my graduation furlough there. It was a pleasant summer, indeed, in a city whose charm extends to all who have enjoyed its hospitality.

Two incidents that occurred during this period are indelibly impressed on my memory. I had dropped in at my father's office quite unexpectedly and found a distinguished group of Californians deep in discussion of the state's future. My father insisted that I stay and listen. The governor of the state, George C. Pardee, was disturbed by the lack of a port on California's southern coast which could harbor sufficient sea traffic to insure the handling and distribution of cargoes coming from and going to its lower areas. He was vigorously supported by E. H. Harriman, the head of the Southern Pacific Railroad, and a number of other prominent executives. My father then proposed what seemed to me a breathtaking plan. It was to carve out an artificial harbor contiguous to Los Angeles, which at that time had a population of slightly less than 300,000. It was his belief that within fifty years such a port would become one of the leading handlers of commerce in the country. He felt that engineering skill could provide what nature had failed to do. His plan was received with the greatest enthusiasm and was placed in effect. The results are well-known. When I was last there and saw that massive metropolis with its limitless growth and potential, I could but marvel. They named the fort which was built to protect the harbor in my father's honor—Fort MacArthur.

The other instance was not so savory. A prisoner engaged in work at Fort Mason, where we lived, had escaped. He was a burly fellow armed with a scythe, and great consternation reigned in the post and the adjacent homes on Van Ness Avenue. Search parties were organized throughout the neighborhood, and women and children warned to stay indoors. The fort is situated on a high bluff sloping down to the harbor line. The slope was rough and covered with tangled underbrush. It was none of my business, but I had tracked trails too often with the Apaches not to pick up this one. His hiding place was easy to locate, and I had him covered before he had a chance to make a move. When I turned him over to the guard, he just spat at me and snarled, "You damn West Pointers!"

I arrived in Manila after a thirty-eight-day voyage aboard the transport *Sherman*. The Philippines charmed me. The delightful hospitality, the respect and affection expressed for my father, the amazingly attractive result of a mixture of Spanish culture and American industry, the languorous laze that seemed to glamorize even the most routine chores of life, the fun-loving men, the moonbeam delicacy of its lovely women, fastened me with a grip that has never relaxed.

During my tour of a year I engaged in typical engineering duties in many parts of the islands. I worked on surveys at Tacloban, harbor improvement in Manila Bay, fortification installations off Corregidor, traverses over the steaming wooded hills of Bataan.

While attempting to construct piers and docks at Guimaris Island, located at the mouth of Iloilo Harbor, I had to procure my own piling, and took a small detachment to cut timber in the jungle forests. The place was dangerous, being infested with brigands and guerrillas. In spite of my early frontier training, I became careless and allowed myself to be waylaid on a narrow jungle trail by two of these desperadoes, one on each side. Like all frontiersmen, I was expert with a pistol. I dropped them both dead in their tracks, but not before one had blazed away at me with his antiquated rifle. The slug tore through the top of my campaign hat and almost cut the sapling tree immediately behind me. My foreman, a Regular Army sergeant and veteran of long years of service, came rushing up. He looked long and hard at the two dead men sprawled on the trail, at my crownless hat still smoking from the blast, at the broken tree behind me. And then, rolling his quid of tobacco into the hollow of his cheek, he slowly drew himself up to his full six feet of height, his heels clicking together, saluted, and drawled in his rich Irish brogue, "Begging thu Loo'tenant's paddon, but all the rest of the Loo'tenant's life is pure velvut."

The old sergeant is dead and gone these many long years, but the pier and dock were still there forty years later when we landed in the harbor of Iloilo to drive out the Japanese.

The islands were policed for internal law and order by a force known as the Constabulary, headed at this time by American officers. From its inception, it has covered itself with honor and glory. I was asked to prepare textbooks on scouting and engineering for its use. Captain James G. Harbord, who held the Constabulary rank of colonel, in expressing thanks invited me to dinner at the Army and Navy Club, then located in the walled city just outside of Manila. He said he wanted me to meet two young Filipinos about my own age, Manuel Quezon and Sergio Osmena, both recent law graduates of Santo Tomas University. Little did I realize that our host would become chief of staff to an American Expeditionary Force on the opposite side of the globe, and that the other two would become presidents of the Philippine Commonwealth. Had we known, perhaps the party might not have been so gay—or would it have been gayer?

In April 1904, I was promoted to be a first lieutenant, and in October I sailed for San Francisco on the transport *Thomas*.

I was assigned to the Golden Gate harbor defenses, and to the California Debris Commission, which was charged with supervision of placer mining for gold. These duties were pleasant ones, especially the stagecoach trips through the Strawberry Valley that recalled my early days in the West.

Early in October I was suddenly ordered to join my father in Japan, where he had been sent to observe the Russo-Japanese War. The purpose of our observations was to measure the strength of the Japanese Army and its methods of warfare. In Washington there was a growing uneasiness. In January 1905, President Roosevelt wrote, "If Japan is careful, and is guided by the best minds in her Empire, she can become one of the leaders of the family of great nations; but if she is narrow and insular, if she tries to gain from her victory in the Russo-Japanese War more than she ought to have, she will array against her all the great powers, and however determined she may be she cannot successfully face an allied world." And two months later he addressed the Chairman of the House Committee on Military Affairs, Representative J. A. T. Hull, as follows: "It may be that the Japanese have designs on the Philippines. I hope not. I am inclined to believe not. But I believe we should put our naval and military preparations in such shape that we can hold the Philippines against any foe."

I met all the great Japanese commanders: Oyama, Kuroki, Nogi, and the brilliant Admiral Heihachiro Togo—those grim, taciturn, aloof men of iron character and unshakeable purpose. It was here that I first encountered the boldness and courage of the Nipponese soldier. His almost fanatical belief in and reverence for his Emperor impressed me indelibly.

Nothing illustrates this devotion better than the following incident.

The Second Japanese Army under General Yasukata Oku was afflicted by the dread disease of beriberi. The surgeon prescribed a prophylactic put up in a small tin can with the inscription, "To prevent beriberi take one pill three times a day." Soldiers are much the same throughout the world: they took the pill once, spat it out, then dumped the can into the mud. The surgeon was at his wits' end until some bright young officer suggested that the cans be marked, "To prevent beriberi, *the Emperor desires you* to take one pill three times a day." The result was instantaneous. Not a pill was wasted. Nothing but death itself could stop the soldiers from taking the medicine.

I asked one of their signal officers what type of codes were used in transmitting their operational messages. Typically, he was evasive, but later, over a bowl of *sake,* he laughingly confided to me that the most secret messages were sent without dilution in the Japanese language. No foreigner, he said, could understand it.

I was deeply impressed by and filled with admiration for the thrift, courtesy, and friendliness of the ordinary citizen. They seemed to have discovered the dignity of labor, the fact that a man is happier and more contented when constructing than when merely idling away time. But I had the uneasy feeling that the haughty, feudalistic samurai who were their leaders, were, through their victories, planting the seed of eventual Japanese conquest of the Orient. Having conquered Korea and Formosa, it was more than evident that they would eventually strike for control of the Pacific and domination of the Far East.

The reports my father submitted to Washington from Japan went beyond battle tactics and strategy. He was aware that Japanese victory over Russia did not mean Russia's elimination from the Far East. This vast, complex area, restless under the boot of European domination, might well be the arena of future world struggle. As a result, he was ordered to extend his comprehensive evaluations to the colonial lands of the Orient, Southeast Asia, and India. His itinerary would take him from Yokohama to Calcutta, by way of Hong Kong, Singapore, and Rangoon. From Calcutta, he would investigate the Northwest Frontier at Peshwar and Quetta, thence to Bombay, Hyderabad, Bangalore, Madras, and Colombo. He was then to return north through Java, Siam, and Indo-China to Shanghai. Several months were to be devoted to China. I was to accompany him as an aide-de-camp.

We were nine months in travel, traversing countless miles of lands so rich in color, so fabled in legend, so vital to history that the experience was without doubt the most important factor of preparation in my entire life. We discussed defense plans behind closed doors and inspected military fortifications and critical areas on the spot. We sat in the charmed circles of the chancelleries of the strong and the weak. Kings and viceroys and high commissioners lay bare their hopes and fears. We listened to both sides of the famous Curzon–Kitchener feud—that age-old struggle between the civil and the military to fix the exact line of demarcation between executive control and the professional duty of the soldier. We traversed the path to Afghanistan with the "King of the Khyber," Sir Bindon Blood; we rode the Grand Trunk Road of Kipling's *Kim;* we reached out from Darjeeling in trace of Sir Francis Younghusband's penetration of Tibet in search of the Grand Llama. We saw the strength and the weakness of the colonial system, how it brought law and order, but failed to develop the masses along the essential lines of education and political economy. We rubbed elbows with millions of the underprivileged who knew nothing of the difference between the systems of the free world and the slave world, but were interested only in getting a little more food in their stomachs, a little better coat on their backs, a little stronger roof over their heads.

It was not without its quaint moments. At a dinner given by King Chulalongkorn of Siam, a progressive monarch devoted to raising the stand-ard of living of his people, the lights suddenly went out and there was much confusion. I had noticed a fuse box near where I was seated and promptly replaced the burned-out fuse. The King (his father, King Mongkut, the sub-ject of Margaret Landon's book *Anna and the King of Siam,* had ninety-two wives and seventy-seven children) was so delighted he proposed to decorate me there and then. Happily, I had the common sense to decline.

The true historic significance and the sense of destiny that these lands of the western Pacific and Indian Ocean now assumed became part of me. They were to color and influence all the days of my life. Here lived almost half the population of the world, with probably more than half of the raw products to sustain future generations. Here was western civilization's last earth frontier. It was crystal clear to me that the future and, indeed, the very existence of America, were irrevocably entwined with Asia and its island outposts. It was to be sixteen years before I returned to the Far East, but al-ways was its mystic hold upon me.

In the fall of 1906, I became a student at the Engineer School of Application located at Washington Barracks, now re-named Fort McNair. In addition, to my great surprise, I was assigned as an aide-de-camp to President Roosevelt. The assignment proved of the greatest interest to me since I came into close contact for the first time with the leading political figures of the country.

I greatly admired Theodore Roosevelt. His prophetic vision of Asian politics marked him as a statesman of brilliant imagination. Assuming the office of President he found a government subordinant in the councils of the world, and now, five years later, had firmly established it in the first rank. The U.S. was admired and respected, its favor sought after, its citizenship esteemed in the remotest corners of the globe. To an unprecedented degree, regardless of party, he had the support of the public. His vigor, courage, abounding vitality, his lack of Presidential pomposity, his familiarity with all manner of men, even his loudness of action and utterance, stimulated all to raise themselves above the ordinary level of their ability and their desires.

He was greatly interested in my views on the Far East and talked with me long and often. I once asked him to what single factor did he attribute his extraordinary popularity with the masses. He replied, "To put into words what is in their hearts and minds but not their mouths. You must listen to the grass grow." When I became angered at an utterly unfounded criticism of him, dreamed up in the editorial room of a local paper, he said, "I like to have them talk well of me, but I would rather have them talk badly than not talk at all."

Another person who attracted my closest attention was the Speaker of the House of Representatives, Joe Cannon. He was the last to rule that august body with the autocracy of a czar. I would sit in the gallery and watch him with fascinated eyes as he wheedled, cajoled, bullied, and dominated the legislative leaders. But he was kindness, itself, when I pleaded for more consideration for our native Indian tribes. One night I was on special duty at the White House during a dinner the President gave for the Speaker. The procedure was to gather the guests in the Red Room, then bring them in to meet the President in the Green Room. I brought the President to his accustomed place, then prepared to bring in the guests. The Speaker was surrounded by an eager group to whom he was declaiming in the most violent way. I knew the President was waiting and three times tried to break in without success. Finally, in desperation, I shoved aside a couple of ambassadors and a Senator or two, and, touching the Speaker's elbow, said, "Mr. Speaker, the President will receive you now." He just glared, looked me up and down, then, blowing the smoke from the big black cigar that was always in his mouth, barked in my face, "The hell he will!", and, to the delight of everyone but myself, continued his harangue. That night I lost any standing I might have had as a social arbiter.

After graduating from the Engineer School, I served for a short time on river and harbor duties in Wisconsin, and in 1908 was ordered to Fort Leavenworth for duty with the Third Battalion of Engineers. As the junior company commander, I was assigned to Company "K," which was the lowest-rated of the twenty-one companies at the post. But I soon recognized the inherent potentials in its personnel, provided I could keep them sober enough while on duty. I had watched my father and First Sergeant Ripley too long not to have learned the trick. By praising them when they were good and shaming them when they were bad, by raising their pride and developing their sense of self-respect, I soon began to convince them they were the best of the lot. I hiked them 25 miles a day, made them break all speed records in pontoon bridge building, taught them to be demolition experts, lauded their natural ability to shoot and ride, and, when the general inspection came, they were the champions. I could not have been happier if they had made me a general. They did make me adjutant of the battalion, and I became a lecturer in the General Service Schools and the Cavalry School at Fort Riley. On February 27, 1911, I was promoted to the grade of captain.

My years of service at Fort Leavenworth were filled with various details that tended to complete my military education as a combat engineer officer. Not the least of these was a tour of duty, at my request, in the Panama Canal Zone, to study the vast engineering project being brought to completion under Colonel George Goethals. I studied the principles of mass sanitation from Colonel William C. Gorgas, and learned much of the complexities of large-scale supply from an old West Point friend of the class of 1900, Robert E. Wood, who later, as the head of Sears, Roebuck and Company, so revolutionized the system of retail sales.

In the spring of 1911, I was ordered to San Antonio with a so-called maneuver division which had been called up because of tension along the Mexican border. No sooner had we pitched camp just outside the city than I hastened toward the old campus. There were the playing fields, and I fancied my scarred desk still stood in the far corner of the assembly hall. They would greet me, I felt, one of the original old grads, with the enthusiasm of warm handclasps and friendly slapping on the back. As I reached the grounds, the students came tearing out, bubbling with the unlimited vitality of youthful play. They looked at me, that look of keen appraisal which seems to leave us as we grow older, and then began to snicker and laugh, and finally burst out into mockery and raillery. It was my hat. Army regulations had just been changed so that, instead of being creased in cowboy fashion, it was peaked into a nondescript sort of pyramid. When they began to chant, "Where did you get that hat?" I turned and left.

But that night I came back to the lower post to see again the home I had loved so well. It was a glorious night of moonshine, with the haunting melody of guitar and mandolin floating in the air, lending a tingle to the blood. As I drew close to the beflowered porch, with its scent of the attar of old-fashioned roses, a young girl suddenly stepped out from its shadowy portals. She startled me, with her blonde head thrown back, a picture of youthful loveliness. I stood spellbound, speechless. But there was nothing lovely in her sharp query, "What are you doing here?" I stuttered and stammered, and tried to explain, but she cut me short: "I believe you're drunk. Get out or I'll call the guard." I never knew who she was. But in the four months we camped there, I never went back again. I had learned one of the bitter lessons of life: never try to regain the past, the fire will have become ashes.

Shortly after returning to Fort Leavenworth, I was relieved from duty with the Third Battalion and appointed head of the Department of Engineering at the Service Schools. It was a wrench to leave these troops, and I bade them farewell with a heavy heart. But the tribute Sergeant Major Corbett paid me is the one which, perhaps, I prize more than any other. "Boys," he said as I left, "there goes a soldier."

Before my father had returned from the Orient, he had, by special act of Congress, been promoted to lieutenant general with a provision that the rank should be abolished with his retirement. Not until the First World War was the proscription lifted, the highest rank being that of major general. He thus became the senior officer of the Army in personal rank. He reached the retirement age of sixty-four on June 2, 1909, and returned to his home in Milwaukee.

On September 5, 1912, his old regiment, the 24th Wisconsin, was to hold its fiftieth and last reunion. My father had been ill and had sorrowfully sent his regrets at being unable to attend. The day proved to be the hottest of the season. The governor and senators had promised attendance, but the heat caused them to cancel the engagement. In this emergency they begged their old commander to attend and, in spite of my mother's earnest remonstrances, he went.

There were but ninety of them left as they sat around the table in Grand Army Hall retelling the old war stories and singing again the old war songs. Then the toastmaster called on my father. Still straight and command-ing, he recalled the old days—they were again changing front at Murfrees-boro, crossing Peach Tree Creek at Atlanta, closing the gap at Franklin. "Your indomitable regiment," he continued, and then he faltered; his face grew ashen white; then he was down for good. Dr. William J. Cronyn, the regimental surgeon, rushed once more to his side.

"Comrades, the General is dying," he said simply.

In the middle of the room the Reverend Paul B. Jenkins began to repeat the Lord's Prayer. And then those ninety old men who had followed him up Missionary Ridge and into the blazing fire of a dozen battlefields knelt by the side of their old commander and joined in. When the prayer ended, he was dead. The adjutant, Captain Edwin Parsons, took from the wall the battle-torn flag that he had so gallantly carried and wrapped it around the General. Captain Parsons stood in silence for a moment, gazing at his dead com-mander, then fell forward over the body and, within two weeks, passed on.

My whole world changed that night. Never have I been able to heal the wound in my heart.

PART TWO

Washington and Veracruz

1912–1917

S hortly after my father's death, I was relieved from duty at Fort Leavenworth and ordered to Washington as a member of the Engineer Board. My mother came to live with me. In September 1913, I was selected to be a member of the General Staff. The General Staff consisted of thirty eight officers, and was supposed to be the brains of the Army in planning operations and deciding matters of highest importance. My selection as its junior member brought me into intimate contact with the senior officers of the Army and Navy, and afforded me the rare opportunity of participating in highest command without the burden of final responsibility. More important, it afforded the chance of close relationship with the chief of staff.

Leonard Wood was no stranger to me. I had seen him as a child when he rode through with Captain Henry Ware Lawton's troop of cavalry in close pursuit of Geronimo. He won the Medal of Honor there. I knew of his gallant service in the war with Spain and of his memorable accomplishments as a military governor in the rehabilitation of Cuba. Originally a physician, and graduate of the Harvard Medical School, it was under his expert supervision that Major Walter Reed conducted the great research which led to the control of yellow fever. But what attracted me most was working as Wood's assistant in his indefatigable crusade for military preparedness. The work was long and confining, and left me little time for relaxation, but it was rewarding.

At this time our relations with Mexico were rapidly deteriorating. General Victoriano Huerta had shot his way to power below the border, and began arresting and molesting Americans legally on Mexican soil. His studied insults toward this country finally forced President Wilson to take counter-measures. A United States fleet blockaded the port of Veracruz, and on April 21, 1914, American sailors and marines seized the city. War fever mounted and the General Staff dispatched to Veracruz a small expedition-ary force, the Fifth Brigade, commanded by Major General Frederick Fun-ston. If necessary, a field army under General Wood was to follow.

On April 22, four days before Funston landed, the Secretary of War, Lindley Garrison, conferred with General Wood and decided to send me to Veracruz to study the lay of the land, and observe and report on all matters that might be useful to General Wood and the War Department. General Wood called me to his office and asked me how soon I could leave. I told him I would be off in an hour. He said that if war exploded I was to be the operations officer, G-3, of the field army.

On my arrival I found that the lack of animal transportation rendered the army almost completely immobile. It was essential, in my opinion, to remedy this condition so that the field army, if it arrived, would not be tied to Veracruz. The railroad seemed to offer a solution to the problem. Freight and passenger cars were in abundance, but where were the locomotives? The all-important initial operations of the command might well depend upon locating them. I felt the very essence of my mission depended on my doing so.

Through the maudlin talk of a drunken Mexican, I received an inkling that a number of engines were hidden somewhere on the line connecting Veracruz and Alvarado. This man was sobered up and found to be a rail-road fireman on the Veracruz and Alvarado Railroad.

Taking the provost marshal, Captain Constant Cordier, into my con-fidence, I proposed the idea of a personal reconnaissance to determine whether or not the fireman was speaking the truth. Captain Cordier was enthusiastic and recommended the plan to Captain William G. Ball, General Funston's aide, and Captain W. A. Burnside, who commanded the outpost line through which the tracks of the railroad ran. I did not approach General Funston, sus-pecting that his confidential orders limited him to the city and its immediate environs. But his inspector general, Major Alexander Dade of the cavalry, whom I had known since childhood, advised against the plan. "It would be too dangerous, Douglas," he said. "Washington does not want war and would not like it. If successful, it would be wonderful information in the event war broke out, but the guerrillas would almost certainly kill anyone attempting it. And," he added with a wry sort of smile, "if they didn't, Washington would. Those gents there in the War Department are rough. You know that."

But it seemed to me that, as the object of the reconnaissance was not aggressive, but merely for the purpose of obtaining vital information, my general instructions seemed to cover this very contingency. I made my plans and confided them in detail to Captain Cordier alone. My Mexican friend, for a certain financial inducement, consented to assist me in locating the engines.

I still preserve the memorandum notes I made at the time on the details of what occurred. Here they are:

My general plan was to leave Vera Cruz alone on foot at dusk and to join my Mexican engineer who was to have a hand car on the main line. There was to be another hand car at Paso del Toro on the Alvarado line manned by two other Mexicans. From Paso del Toro we were to push along the Alvarado line until the engines were located and their condition ascertained. All three of the Mexicans were railroad men and their affiliations and experience enabled them to obtain the hand cars and have them at their appointed places. For their services I agreed to give them one hundred and fifty dollars gold, payable only after my safe return to Vera Cruz.

The night was squally and overcast. At dusk I crossed our line unseen near the wireless station, where a detachment of the 7th Infantry was encamped. I was in military uniform with no attempt at disguise and with absolutely nothing on me in addition to my clothes, except my identification tag, a small Bible and my pistol belt. I found my engineer with a hand car in the appointed place. I searched him and after some demur on his part removed his weapons, a .38 caliber revolver and a small dirk knife. As a further precaution against his possible treachery I had him search me so that he might better realize that there being nothing of value on me my death would afford him no monetary return. The essence of the transaction for him, therefore, became my safe return to Vera Cruz when he could receive his pay.

We proceeded as far as Boca del Rio without incident, but at the Jamapa River found the railroad bridge down. I decided to leave the hand car, concealing it as well as possible. After searching the bank of the river for a short distance, we discovered a small native boat on which we paddled across, landing well above the town so as to escape observation. On landing we located, after some search, two ponies near a small shack and mounted upon them followed the trail along the railway until near Paso del Toro. We then made a detour and hit the Alvarado line below the town. The two Mexican firemen were awaiting us with the hand car.

We hid our ponies and after I had searched the two newcomers and found them unarmed, pushed on. Mile after mile we covered with no sign of the engines. The line was studded with bridges and culverts and my crew protested violently at crossing them without investigating their condition. Time was so short, however, I dared not stop for such steps, and had to take them in our stride. I was obliged to threaten my men at the first bridge, but after that I had no further trouble with them. In fact, after getting into the spirit of the thing their conduct was most admirable. At every town we reached I took one man and left the car which was run through to the far side by the other two. I fastened myself by a lashing to the man acting as my guide so as to insure us against separation, and together we made a circuit of the town, joining the car on the far side. This took time, but was the only way I could avoid detection.

We reached Alvarado shortly after one o'clock and there found five engines. Two of them were switch engines and of little use for our purposes. The other three were just what we needed—fine big road pullers in excellent condition except for a few minor parts which were missing. I made a careful inspection of them and then started back.

At Salinas, while moving around the town with one of my men, we were halted by five armed men. They were on foot and wore no uniforms. They were not soldiers and were evidently one of the marauding bands that infest the country with brigandage as a trade. We started to run for it and they opened fire and followed us. We outdistanced all but two and in order to preserve our own lives I was obliged to fire upon them. Both went down. I was fearful lest the firing might have frightened away my hand car men, but after some search we found them waiting for us beyond the town.

At Piedra, under somewhat similar circumstances and in a driving mist, we ran flush into about fifteen mounted men of the same general type. We were among them before I realized it and were immediately the center of a melee. I was knocked down by the rush of horsemen and had three bullet holes through my clothes, but escaped unscathed. My man was shot in the shoulder, but not seriously injured. At least four of the enemy were brought down and the rest fled. After bandaging up my wounded man we proceeded north with all speed possible.

Near Laguna we were again encountered and fired upon by three mounted men who kept up a running fight with the hand car. I did not return their fire. All but one of these men were distanced, but this one, unusually well mounted, overhauled and passed the car. He sent one bullet through my shirt and two others that hit within six inches of me, forcing our return fire. His horse fell on the track across the front of the car and we had to remove the carcass before proceeding.

At Paso del Toro we abandoned the hand car, found the ponies where we had left them and made our way back to Boca del Rio where we left the animals near the shack where we had found them.

We found the boat where we had left it and started to cross the Jamapa River, but when near the shore the boat struck a snag in the darkness and sank. Fortunately the water at this point was something less than five feet deep, for in our exhausted physical condition I do not believe we would have been capable of swimming. As it was, I was hard put to keep my wounded man's head above water. Day was breaking when we reached the bank. We located our first hand car and ran in close to Vera Cruz where we crossed the lines.

General Wood recommended me for the Medal of Honor. The War Department disagreed. As Major Dade predicted, "Those gents in the War Department are rough." In deciding to make the reconnaissance I may have been right or I may have been wrong. War did not materialize and the utility of our exploits would never be known, but even my old frontier friends would have agreed that it was a wild night under the Southern Cross.

I was promoted to major shortly after my return to Washington and again chosen for detail on the General Staff. Perhaps those "gents in the War Department" were not so rough after all.

It might be well to note here that the Veracruz expedition of April 1914 was a separate and distinct action from the local punitive campaign into North Mexico, against the marauding Pancho Villa, led by General John J. Pershing in 1916. Aside from my staff duties at the War Department, I had nothing to do with the latter action.

Meanwhile, all was not well within the Administration. A clash had developed between President Wilson and his Secretary of War over the issue of preparedness for war. It culminated in February 1916 with the resignation of Secretary Lindley M. Garrison and Assistant Secretary Henry Breckinridge. Three weeks later, Newton D. Baker was appointed Secretary of War. The announcement created a political sensation, and Baker was denounced by the anti-Administration press as a pacifist. Nothing could have been farther from the truth.

I had never previously met Secretary Baker, but knew him by reputation. He had recently been the mayor of Cleveland for two terms, where he was noted for his municipal reforms. It was said of him that he was a "reliable radical and a prudent progressive." Others called him a "genial conservative with an open mind." He styled himself "so much of a pacifist that he would fight for peace." I found him to be diminutive in size, but large in heart, with a clear, brilliant mind, and a fine ability to make instant and positive decisions. He was to become one of our greatest War Secretaries.*

I spent much time with Secretary Baker trying to match his swift and

---

* Newton Baker died on Christmas Day, 1937. I wrote from Manila:

The death of Newton D. Baker marks the passing of one of America's greatest sons and one of the world's most outstanding citizens. He was of those rare characters who outstripped the civilization of their day and lived many decades ahead of their time. His contribution in many fields of endeavor has tended to materially advance the development of the human race. He will perhaps be best remembered historically for his services as Secretary of War during the Wilson Administration. As an organizer of America's war resources he had no superior—perhaps no equal. His unparalleled efficiency along this line and his indomitable prosecution of America's efforts in 1917 and 1918 constituted one of the greatest factors in American victory. He was of those rare few who thought out and understood the realities of that most confusing and confused of all subjects —the related questions of peace, war and defense. He believed that war was the poorest solution for international quarrels but he understood the frailties of human nature and the mechanics of human force. He loved peace but a peace of self-respect and self-reliance—a peace of preparedness, not a peace at any price. To those so intimately associated with him, as I have been, his death is not only a national but a personal tragedy.

uninhibited mind, and answer the innumerable questions of a purely military nature that were constantly cropping up. The imponderables of war and military preparation on a national scale were subjects of constant discussion. He experienced some difficulties in personally handling the press, and on June 30, 1916, in addition to my other duties, I was detailed as military assistant to the Secretary of War, and placed in charge of the Bureau of Information of the War Department. A week later I was made press censor and became the liaison link with the newspaper men who covered the War Department. Through these correspondents and the special writers who dropped in, I was expected to explain our national military policy to the country and to shatter the prevailing delusion of a world living in security.

During this time, the General Staff, in considering the pivotal question of the effective reliability of the National Guard for possible combat service abroad voted predominantly against the use of the Guard. I was the exception, believing that the Guard's strength could be increased by voluntary enlistments and its expanded units trained to combat effectiveness. I steadfastly shared my father's long-held belief in the citizen-soldier. When war with Germany came, as I was certain that it would, National Guard divisions should be able to fight proudly with the Regular Army.

Congress declared war against Germany on April 6, 1917.* It was the inevitable result of more than two years of indiscriminate sinking of American ships by German submarines. The loss of American lives in the torpedo-

* Two days before our declaration of war, the correspondents and writers with whom I had dealt did an unprecedented thing, something never done before and never repeated afterwards. They sent a spontaneous letter to the Secretary of War praising the censorship he had established. It was signed by all twenty-nine men who were the most distinguished representatives of their profession in Washington. It read:

"It seems quite likely that the days of action before us will see many changes in the corps of newspaper correspondents who have been assigned to the War Department for many months past. Some of us will go a-soldiering and others into fields of activity connected with the war. Changes will come, too, in the assignment of Army officers whom we have learned to know here in the Department, and before that time comes, we of the Fourth Estate wish to address to you, and through you to Major Douglas MacArthur, our appreciation of the way he has dealt with us for all these months in his trying position of military censor.

We feel no doubt of what the future holds for Major MacArthur. Rank and honors will come to him if merit can bring them to any man; but we wish to say our thanks to him for the unfailing kindness, patience and wise counsel we have received from him in the difficult days that are past.

Our needs have compelled us to tax that patience at all hours of the day and night. We have never failed to receive courteous treatment from him. Although the censorship imposed was but a voluntary obligation upon the press, it has been kept faithfully, and we feel that it has been largely because of the fair, wise and liberal way in which Major MacArthur exercised his functions that this was possible. He has put his own personality into the task.

No man can ever know to what extent the cordial relations the Major has maintained with the press may have influenced national thought on military matters. It is unquestionable that his hours given to our conferences have never been wasted; they have borne fruit in what we in our turn have written and if wise decisions are reached eventually as to the military policy of our country, we can not but feel that the Major has helped, through us, to shape the public mind."

ing of the *Lusitania* had aroused the righteous wrath of the American people. President Wilson had done everything in his power to keep America out of the war, but Germany's threat to the freedom of the world forced Congress to throw America's gigantic industrial might and manpower into the conflict.

The problem of the scope and nature of American troops for Europe became acute when a staff study was circulated to the effect that the ultimate strength to go was 500,000 and all Regulars. When the paper came to me, I was tired from overwork and indiscreetly endorsed it saying that I completely disagreed with its conclusions, but would not attempt to detail my reasons, as I felt no one would give them the slightest attention. It was a discourteous remark and I regretted it almost immediately, but thought no more of it when I learned that the chief of staff, Major General Hugh Scott, had approved the majority conclusions and sent them to the Secretary of War.

A day later, Sam, the old Negro messenger, knocked at my door. I had known him for years, as he had served my father in the Adjutant General's Department. As a boy it had been my custom after school to call for my father and go home with him. Many a game I had played with Sam while I was waiting in the hall. He looked solemn when he opened the door and said, "Mar'sa Douglas, the Secretary wants to see you at once." "What about, Sam?" I asked. "Don't know," he replied, "but that little feller didn't smile at me."

When I entered the Secretary's office my heart sank. He was squatted deep down in his chair, puffing his pipe and reading that policy paper. He said not a word for a full minute, just sat there smoking his pipe and reading what I felt sure was my brusque endorsement. It was one of my bad moments. Finally he looked up and said in that slow, precise way of his, "Major, I have just read your endorsement," and stopped. I braced myself and cleared my throat to express my regret and apology, but before words came, he suddenly rose saying, "I agree with you in this matter. Get your cap. We are going to the White House to place the whole question before the President for his decision." I felt like walking on air.

I had seen President Wilson on a number of occasions and he had always spoken to me in the most kindly way. This was no exception. For over an hour, the Secretary and I took turns in advancing our arguments for the use of unlimited force and the employment of the National Guard to its full capacity. With grave courtesy the President said, "I am in general accord with your ideas. Baker, put them into effect. And thank you, Major, for your frankness."

Later on, Secretary Baker sent for me. "What is the best way," he said, "to give maximum effect to the President's decision?" I suggested that we take units from the different states so that a division would stretch over the whole country like a rainbow;—from that time on it was known as the Rainbow Division. He selected the chief of the Militia Bureau, Brigadier General William A. Mann, to be its commander and asked what other steps were necessary. As General Mann was approaching retirement age, I said I thought it essential he should have the best colonel of the General Staff as his divisional chief of staff. The Secretary at once replied, "I have already made my selection for that post." And then, putting his hand on my shoulder, added, "It is you." I was flabbergasted, but managed to stammer out that however grateful I felt, being only a major I was not eligible. "You are wrong," he said. "You are now a colonel. I will sign your commission immediately. I take it you will want to be in the Engineer Corps." But, dazed as I was, I could think only of the old 24th Wisconsin Infantry, and answered, "No, the Infantry." And that is how I became a doughboy.

Before all this happened, I was inadvertently drawn into one of the sad incidents in Army annals. It was February 19 1917, and I had the night watch for the General Staff. My old friend, Peyton March, a lieutenant colonel in the Adjutant General's Department, had a similar duty in that office. Secretary Baker was giving a formal dinner that night for the President and left word not to be disturbed unless something of importance took place. About ten o'clock March brought up a wire that General Funston, who had been informally selected to command an American Expeditionary Force if we entered the war, had just dropped dead in the St. Anthony Hotel in San Antonio. We agreed that the Secretary should be told at once. When I reached the Secretary's home, the butler refused to let me enter, saying that he had orders to admit no one. The dining room looked out on the entrance hall and I could see it plainly. It was a gay party, with lights and laughter, the tinkle of glasses, the soft music from an alcove, the merry quips and jokes of a cosmopolitan group. I finally pushed by the butler and tried to attract the attention of the Secretary so I could report to him privately what had occurred. But the President saw me and sang out in the most jovial manner, "Come in, Major, and tell all of us the news. There are no secrets here." There was a general clapping of hands at this, and I knew I was in for it. So I clicked my heels together, saluted him, and barked in a drill-sergeant tone, "Sir, I regret to report that General Funston has just died." Had the voice of doom spoken, the result could not have been different. The silence seemed like that of death itself. You could hear your own breathing. Then, I never saw such a scattering of guests in my life. It was a stampede.

The President and the Secretary took me into an adjacent room and dictated a message of sympathy to Mrs. Funston. Mr. Wilson then turned to the Secretary and said, "What now, Newton, who will take the Army over?" The Secretary paused a moment and then, instead of a direct reply, asked me, "Whom do you think the Army would choose, Major?" It was a poser, but I had my own positive views and replied, "I cannot, of course, speak for the Army, but for myself the choice would unquestionably be General Pershing." The President looked at me, a long inquisitive look, and then said quietly, "It would be a good choice."

I first met General Pershing, then a captain of Cavalry, in my father's office in downtown San Francisco. I had just graduated from West Point, and I shall never forget the impression he made on me by his appearance and bearing. He was the very epitome of what is now affectionately called the "Old Army." As Pershing left, he turned to my father and said, "General MacArthur, I am sure Douglas and I will meet again." How true and how often!

I recall vividly one of our early critical days in France when General Pershing was in the Rainbow Division's sector. A messenger handed me a dispatch for him from General Headquarters. It was Douglas Haig's famous signal, "With our back to the wall, and believing in the justice of our cause, each one of us must fight to the end! The safety of our homes and the freedom of mankind depends alike upon the conduct of each one of us at this critical moment." I looked at Pershing questioningly, but he was expressionless. And then, as he turned to leave, he said with that hoarseness in his voice, which we knew indicated that he was troubled: "We old First Captains, Douglas, must never flinch." He had been the First Captain at West Point in the class of 1886. When he later made me a division commander, the corps commander, a great fighting soldier, Charles Pelot Summerall, had also been First Captain, of the class of 1892. When someone jokingly said, "This makes it three of a kind, a great poker hand," the "Old Man" did not like it and said sharply, "I don't want gambling terms used with reference to this army. The Expeditionary Force is here not to play cards, but to fight." I have never shuffled a deck except for solitaire since that day.

When I became Chief of Staff of the Army in 1931, it was in succession to General Summerall and the long-retired General Pershing. In the vital problems which faced me, the reorganization and revitalization of the Army for World War II, I consulted and advised with him long and often. His wise old head helped me over many a troubled spot. One of the most drastic renovations was the change from horse to armor, from the saddle to the tank.

I broached it to him with some anxiety, as I knew his complete devotion to the conventional cavalry. He listened with scowling brows, and then silence; but the blow made him wince. I then reminded him of that day fifteen years earlier on the blood-soaked fields of France, "We old First Captains must never flinch." He burst into a hearty laugh and replied, "I will back you to the hilt," and there was no harshness now in his voice.

General Pershing's fame rests largely upon his personal character. He was not a genius at strategy and his tactical experience was limited, but in his indomitable will for victory, in his implacable belief in the American soldier, in his invincible resistance to all attempts to exploit or patronize American arms, he rose to the highest flights of his profession. He inspired a self-respect for our national forces and a foreign recognition of our military might which has properly placed us fully equal to the best of the human race. My memories of him sustained and strengthened me during many a lonely and bitter moment of the Pacific and Korean Wars. I could almost feel his warm hand on my back. He was indeed the *beau sabreur*—a "First Captain" in every sense of the term.*

* When he died in July of 1948, I made the following statement: "General Pershing was the embodiment of all that is best in the American soldier. To those of us who followed his victorious banners thirty years and more ago he represented a legendary ideal of a past era. His indomitable qualities of leadership, his lofty principles of personal conduct, and his invincible patriotism will indelibly be stamped on our Army for all time. Through the dim mist of fifty years of affectionate friendship I reverently sorrow as he passes on."

PART THREE

World War I
1917–1919

The 42nd Division was assembled at Camp Mills near Garden City on Long Island, New York, with Major General William A. Mann as commander and myself as chief of staff. The roll of its components listed twenty-six states: infantrymen from New York, Ohio, Iowa, and Alabama; artillerymen from Illinois, Indiana, and Minnesota; engineers from South Carolina, California, and North Carolina; machine-gunners from Pennsylvania, Wisconsin, and Georgia; trench mortarmen from Maryland; military police from Virginia; signalmen from Missouri; ammunition men from Kansas; supply trainmen from Texas; ambulance and field hospital men from New Jersey, Tennessee, Oklahoma, Michigan, Oregon, Nebraska, Colorado, and the District of Columbia; and cavalrymen from Louisiana.

The caliber of both officers and men was excellent. From their ranks came many of the great names that enrich the tablets of military fame. Weapons in modern warfare are a vital factor, but of even greater importance is the human element—the troops who fight the battles, and the personnel who supply, transport, feed, house, and doctor them. In the Rainbow Division the human equation was strikingly expressed by the splendid relationship that existed between the officers and enlisted men, and in the comradeship between the men themselves—a relationship which may have been matched in other military organizations, but certainly was never surpassed. From the division commander down to the private, there was that mutual respect and understanding which made for the accomplishment of objectives. The outfit soon took on a color, a dash, a unique flavor that is the essence of that elusive and deathless thing called soldiering. It has always held a special place in my affection, and to this day I feel a thrill whenever I see the Rainbow's colorful patch.

During August and September the division worked day and night to whip into shape the 27,000 men who had arrived in different stages of training. No frills and fancy gadgets were employed (such as had been over-propagandized by the trench-warfare methods of the Western Front), but the sound basic principles which for time immemorial have laid the solid foundations for victory. There were no leaves, passes were limited, officers and men fared alike. By the time ships were ready, so were we.

On October 18, I sailed on the *Covington,* formerly the Hamburg-American liner *Cincinnati,* one of the many German ships seized in American waters at the beginning of the war. We sailed in convoy from Hoboken. Life on board a troopship was a new and somewhat unnerving experience for the uninitiated. There were endless drills and efforts made to properly exercise the men. Space was cramped and each man was allowed forty-five minutes time a day on deck. Lifebelts were worn all the time. The ship was dark at night, with no smoking allowed in the open. In a running sea it is a real sensation to grope around decks in the darkness.

The convoy sailed under sealed orders, opened up each day, with ships' positions designated for the following afternoon. All lifeboats were let down to deck level, and all rafts unlashed and placed along the rail. Ships were constantly holding target practice with their 6-inch guns. The targets, resembling periscopes, were towed.

After being at sea for ten days we were within four days of our destination—St. Nazaire. From then on all officers remained constantly at their posts. The air was like winter and the sea ice cold. We moved into an acute submarine and mine zone. All ships were zigzagging at a loss of a knot an hour. Captain Hasbrouk never left the bridge. Three days ticked off— long days that seemed like weeks. We had twenty-four hours more to safety when the wireless informed us that we had been spotted by enemy submarines who were moving in for the kill.

As night fell I went up on the bridge, but could see nothing in the black of an unknowing night. All we could hear was the deep voice of the skipper: "Rudder right, rudder left." It was bleak and nerve-racking, but I felt a glow in my heart knowing that the *Chattanooga,* commanded by my brother, Captain Arthur MacArthur, was out there in the escort watching over us. At long last, thank God, I saw the lights of Belle Isle. We steamed up the Loire and docked at St. Nazaire—our first glimpse of France.

By skillfully changing course 45 degrees the *Covington* had evaded the submarines, but on the way out they sank her.

The infantry regiments of the division were immediately disembarked and shipped in the little "40 and 8" French boxcars to training areas south of Toul, in eastern France. The artillery brigade was sent to the artillery training center at Coetquidon in the Breton peninsula, site of the French Military School, where it was to receive its quota of French 75's and 155 heavies. Division headquarters was established at Vaucouleurs in the Lorraine country of Joan of Arc.

Except for artillery pieces, we had been completely equipped at Camp Mills—new machine guns, new uniforms, a full set of blankets, tin hats, gas masks, rolling kitchens, food, and munitions, and I had brought with us sufficient clothing and supplies to last for six months. But a large part of these maintenance items which I had so carefully garnered, including 50,000 pairs of heavy marching shoes, were promptly taken over by G.H.Q. to supply deficiencies in other divisions. We suffered greatly later on from a lack of replacement equipment and supplies.

For the general good we were to suffer locally even greater losses. In organizing the division I had carefully selected for its staff only officers from the flower of the regular service. Of the thirty-three officers of the staff all but two were ordered away. I had, however, from the beginning provided understudies for all important positions and these younger officers met the emergency flawlessly.

But I was not prepared for the heaviest blow. An American Corps was being organized by Chaumont, general headquarters, to consist of three divisions, for which the 42nd was to be broken up as replacements. General Mann protested without avail that the Rainbow had been a uniting force as the nation began to mobilize for war, and that its elimination would be a shock to the country, that replacements could easily come from the troops constantly arriving from the United States. I then decided to go to Pershing's chief of staff, my old Manila friend, Brigadier General James G. Harbord. I asked him to come and see the division and judge himself on the merits of the situation whether such a splendid unit should be relegated to a replacement status. He came and saw, and revoked the order. My action was probably not in strict accord with normal procedure and it created resentment against me among certain members of Pershing's staff.

After a short stay in the Vaucouleurs area, the division moved to Rolampont, where it spread out into the farms and villages of the Meuse River valley. The billets were crowded, miserable affairs for the poorly clothed men who, without even enough blankets, were to face the coldest winter France had known in many years.

At this time, the British and French desperately needed reinforcements, so four infantry regiments of the division were placed under the command of General Georges de Bazelaire of the French VII Army Corps to be battle-trained with four French divisions. As a result, the 42nd moved, in February 1918, to a combat sector in the Lunéville-Baccarat area. General Mann had been replaced by Major General Charles T. Menoher, a regular colonel in the field artillery, who had been a classmate of General Pershing's at West Point. He was an able officer, an efficient administrator, of genial disposition and unimpeachable character. He preferred to supervise operations from his command headquarters, where he could keep in constant touch with the corps and army, relying upon me to handle the battle line. After the war he was to be placed at the head of the fast developing Air Corps. We became great friends, and thirty-two years later his son was to be one of my assistant division commanders in Korea.

On February 26th I had my first contact with German troops. I had long felt it was imperative to know by personal observation what the division had to face. It is all very well to make a perfect plan of attack, to work out in theory a foolproof design for victory. But if that plan does not consider the caliber of troops, the terrain to be fought over, the enemy strength opposed, then it may become confused and fail. I went to see General de Bazelaire, but he was reluctant to authorize me to join a French raiding party out to capture Boche prisoners. I told him frankly, "I cannot fight them if I cannot see them." He understood, and told me to go.

It was an overcast night, but the *poilous'* faces were daubed with black so that the faint light would not gleam on their white features. Carrying pliers to cut the enemy wire, they crawled through the barbed wire and over the bleak piles of war refuse that lay between the German and the Allied trenches. Just short of the trench they intended to raid, a German guard heard them. His gun flashed in the night. The alarm spread through the trench, across the front. Flares soared and machine guns rattled. Enemy artillery lay down a barrage in front of the lines, trapping the party. But the raid went on. They leaped into the trenches, and the fight was savage and merciless. Finally, a grenade, tossed into a dugout where the surviving Germans had fled, ended it. When we returned with our prisoners those veteran Frenchmen crowded around me, shaking my hand, slapping me on the back, and offering me cognac and absinthe. I was probably the first American soldier they had seen. General de Bazelaire pinned a Croix de

Guerre on my tunic and kissed me on both cheeks. I was now one of them. For this small but savage action near Réchicourt the American command awarded me the Silver Star, for "extraordinary heroism and gallantry in action." The award seemed a bit too much to me, but I was, of course, glad to have it.

Early in March it was decided that the Rainbow Division was ready for its acid test—the attack. It had withstood an enemy raid, endured a night gas attack, and had conducted itself well in trench duties, but what our Allies wanted to know, indeed, what the Germans wanted to know, was how the Yanks would do when they met the Boche hand to hand. Millions of people, friend and foe, waited breathlessly for the first news of an American attack. The target was a section of German trench on the Salient du Feys. I received permission from General Menoher to accompany the battalion of the 168th Infantry assigned to make the raid.

Zero hour was five o'clock plus five minutes. The French had moved in their artillery, preparing to commence fire at five minutes short of zero hour. There was a cold drizzle, the air was sharp with coming storm, the mud ankle-deep. The Germans sensed the operation, and forty batteries of their guns opened with a deadly accurate fury. Our casualties began to mount. I began to feel uneasy. You never really know about men at such a time. They were not professionals. Few of them had ever been under fire. I decided to walk the line, hoping that my presence might comfort the men.

Behind our lines, a few scattered batteries had been sporadically trying to hold down the enemy fire. They had not been successful. But as my watch hit zero hour minus five, the night trembled with the thunderous belch of sixty batteries. As fast as sweating gunners could throw in the shells, the guns flashed their fire. In the fast graying twilight I could see pillars of smoke and flame shoot skyward from the German salient.

Our officers and sergeants stood poised and ready, whistles in their teeth, counting off the minutes past five. Two minutes. Three. And now five. Our roaring guns suddenly lowered sights, and laced a blanket of exploding shells just in front of our line.

"All ready, Casey?" I yelled into the ear of "F" Company's battalion commander, Captain Charles J. Casey. "Okay, Colonel," he said, and the whistles blew. "Up you go," I heard his ringing voice. "Keep alignment. Guide is right. Don't rush or you'll get your own barrage on your neck."

I went over the top as fast as I could and scrambled forward. The blast was like a fiery furnace. For a dozen terrible seconds I felt they were not following me. But then, without turning around, I knew how wrong I was to have doubted for even an instant. In a moment they were around me, ahead of me, a roaring avalanche of glittering steel and cursing men. We carried the enemy position.

From then on the Rainbow was rated by both friend and foe as a fighting ace. Major Casey and I were awarded the Distinguished Service Cross, second only to the Medal of Honor as a battle decoration.

The Germans were ready to launch their great attack against the British and French to the north and west in a desperate attempt to end the war before the American Army was fully ready. At 4:40 on the morning of Thursday, March 21st, the German offensive fell on the British Fifth Army about 170 miles to the Rainbow's left. A second German strike, aimed ultimately at the Marne and Paris, immediately followed, causing the four French divisions then serving with the 42nd to be withdrawn. This left the Rainbow to guard the entire Baccarat section on the Lorraine front. For eighty-two days the division was in almost constant combat. When we were relieved on June 21st, French General Pierre-Georges Duport, under whose corps command we had served, cited the 42nd for its "offensive ardor, the spirit of method, the discipline shown by all its officers and men."*

The division's rest was of short duration. It had become evident that the group of German armies under Imperial Crown Prince Wilhelm, with General Erich von Ludendorff in direct charge of operations, was about to launch an all-out attack in the chalk plains of Champagne in a desperate effort to split the British and French armies. The 42nd Division on July 4th was pivoted westward in a series of forced marches to join the French

---

* The courage and devotion of the men who served during these eighty-two days should be noted in full. The complete citation of General Duport reads as follows:

"At the moment when the 42nd U.S. Infantry Division is leaving the Lorraine front, the Commanding General of the 6th Army Corps desires to do homage to the fine military qualities which it has continuously exhibited, and to the services it has rendered in the Baccarat sector.

"The offensive ardor, the sense for the utilization and the organization of terrain as for the liaison of the arms, the spirit of method, the discipline shown by all its officers and men, the inspiration animating them, prove that at the first call, they can henceforth take a glorious place in the new line of battle.

"The Commanding General of the 6th Army Corps expresses his deepest gratitude to the 42nd Division for its precious collaboration; he particularly thanks the distinguished commander of this division, General Menoher, the officers under his orders and his staff so brilliantly directed by Colonel MacArthur.

"It is with a sincere regret that the entire 6th Corps sees the 42nd Division depart. But the bonds of affectionate comradeship which have been formed here will not be broken; for us, in faithful memory, are united the living and the dead of the Rainbow Division, those who are leaving for hard combats and those who, after having nobly sacrificed their lives on the land of the East, now rest there, guarded over piously by France.

"These sentiments of warm esteem will be still more deeply affirmed during the impending struggles where the fate of Free Peoples is to be decided.

"May our units, side by side, contribute valiantly to the triumph of Justice and of Right."

Fourth Army. We were inserted into the middle of the French line to defend the sector north of the village of Suippes on the direct road to Chalons—the enemy's prime objective.

Our new commander was the French General Henri Gouraud. His fame was well known to me. His Algerian exploits had won him the soubriquet of *le lion d'Afrique,* and his Gallipoli campaign had become almost a classic. But I was not prepared for the heroic figure to whom I reported. With one arm gone, and half a leg missing, with his red beard glittering in the sunlight, the jaunty rake of his cocked hat and the oratorical brilliance of his resonant voice, his impact was overwhelming. He seemed almost to be the reincarnation of that legendary figure of battle and romance, Henry of Navarre. And he was just as good as he looked. I have known all of the modern French commanders, and many were great measured by any standards, but he was the greatest of them all. Pétain and Foch rank with the best of any era, but Pétain always exaggerated the enemy potential and thereby failed to exploit fully his successes, and Foch was too inflexible once he had outlined a plan, and consequently missed opportunities. But Gouraud was without a weakness. I spent much time with him in his headquarters at the Ferme de Suippes and the more I saw of him the more I liked him. It became a mutual friendship that lasted until his death many years later.

When I reported, he had already worked out a complete new theory of a defense against the German tactic of breaking through and then by-passing strong points to exploit the lightly held rear areas. He would vacate his first line of trenches except for skeleton "suicide squads" who would warn with rocket flares when the enemy's gray-clad infantry began their assault. Gouraud would wait until the attack reached his now evacuated first line, then lay down a withering fire, thus destroying the enemy's momentum and solidarity. By the time our main line would be reached, the enemy would be spent and ready for destruction. It was an entirely new concept of trench warfare—a defense-in-depth which became a death trap for the attack.

Early in June we became aware of German preparation for a massive attack on the Fourth Army's front. Indications of an increase in circulation on the railroads, the growth of munition dumps, the aviation fields being prepared, announced the imminence of the attack. Our patrols increased their activity and finally, on July 14th, a French detachment penetrated the German frontlines, and, drifting far to the rear, captured a Prussian officer who had the written orders for the enemy attack. The artillery preparation would commence at ten minutes past midnight on July 15th. At 4:15 A.M. the infantry would leave their trenches under cover of a rolling barrage.

Gouraud, acting on the instant, ordered his batteries to commence firing forty minutes before the planned German bombardment. No Boche target, whether road, artillery placement, or concentrating area, was to escape the relentless shelling. The violence of this counter-offensive fire from a thousand guns caught the enemy completely by surprise, and badly disconcerted him. The minute clockwork of this too-precise German machine was suddenly thrown out of gear. But at 12:15 A.M. his guns opened with a concentration of power such as the world had never known. The artillery fire could be heard in Paris, nearly 100 miles away. France was again in peril.

I was watching from our main line of defense and at exactly 4:15 A.M. the warning rockets of our isolated lookouts exploded in the red skies of the breaking dawn. As the enemy stormed our now abandoned trenches, our own barrage descended like an avalanche on his troops. The ease with which their infantry had crossed this line of alert, so thinly occupied by our suicide squads, had given them the illusion of a successful advance. But when they met the dikes of our real line, they were exhausted, unco-ordinated, and scattered, incapable of going further without being reorganized and reinforced.

"Their legs are broken," I told our sweating cannoneers. In a few spots they broke through, but in the main were repulsed and driven back. We launched counterattacks and by afternoon the outcome was clear—the German's last great attack of the war had failed, and Paris could breathe again.

General Gouraud cited the division in the following words:

We have in our midst in the most perfect fraternity of arms the 42nd American Division. We esteem it an honor to rival them in courage and nerve. Its men went under fire as at a football game, in shirtsleeves, with the sleeves rolled up over nervous biceps.

I was awarded the Silver Star for the second time.

A few nights later a group of us toasted our victory in Chalons. We drank to the petite barmaids and sang of "Mademoiselle of Armentières," but I found something missing. It may have been the vision of those writhing bodies hanging from the barbed wire or the stench of dead flesh still in my nostrils. Perhaps I was just getting old; somehow, I had forgotten how to play.

With the failure of the Crown Prince's attack, the initiative passed to the Allies. They opened a relentless offensive which never ceased until the

Armistice on November 11. The 42nd Division was suddenly withdrawn from the Champagne front and ordered to join the French Sixth Army under the command of General Jean Degoutte.

There was heavy congestion on all highways, and late at night my rickety, patched-up automobile was blocked by a fine new Rolls Royce car stalled squarely across the road. It bore the well-known four red stars of the commander-in-chief. I immediately went forward to see if I could be of any assistance. The car was empty except for the driver. General Pershing was famous for his gallantry, and many were the quips and ribald jokes about his conquests. There was, of course, not the slightest foundation for such talk, but such is the tradition of the veteran soldier. I asked the sergeant-chauffeur what seemed to be the trouble. He squinted hard at me, then replied, "Don't know, General, but it might be a hairpin in the clutch." It was Eddie Rickenbacker.

On July 25th, in a black, drizzling night, the division unloaded from its buses in front of Chateau Thierry to relieve the units of the exhausted 26th Division. The Germans were pulling back, and our orders were to press him. Instead of a swift retreat, covered by small rearguards, the German tactic was to position troops on rugged slopes and in protecting woods for a desperate defense. They massed machine guns and mortars behind rugged stone walls and in scattered farm buildings. Our artillery was not in sufficient strength to silence this death blaze of Germany. Death beckoned the bravest and the strongest in the deceptive fields of that bright green countryside. It was to be six of the bitterest days and nights of the war for the Rainbow.

We reverted to tactics I had seen so often in the Indian wars of my frontier days. Crawling forward in twos and threes against each stubborn nest of enemy guns, we closed in with the bayonet and the hand grenade. It was savage and there was no quarter asked or given. It seemed to be endless. Bitterly, brutally, the action seesawed back and forth. A point would be taken, and then would come a sudden fire from some unsuspected direction and the deadly counterattack. Positions changed hands time and again. There was neither rest nor mercy.

Step by step, we fought forward: La Croix Rouge Ferme Beauvardes, Forêt de Fère, Villers-sur-Fère. Kilometer by kilometer, we reached the south bank of the Ourcq River. Across the river on the north bank was the enemy's main line of resistance: Meurcy Ferme on his right flank, Sergy his left, Seringes his center. We forced a passage the evening of July 28th, and took Meurcy Ferme in a hand-to-hand fight. I borrowed two battalions from the 4th Division, which was coming up in reserve, and with their help we stormed Sergy at bayonet point, but were thrown out almost immediately. Eleven times it changed hands before we finally held its smoking ruins. The center at Seringes still held. It looked like a small Gibraltar, with its flanking guns and its barricaded streets and houses swarming with troops. I formed our infantry on the south bank of the stream and rushed the town. Their artillery concentrated, their machine guns east and west of the town raked us fore and aft, but nothing could stop the impetus of that mad charge. We forded the river. We ascended the slopes. We seized Hill 184. We killed the garrison in the town to a man. At dusk on July 29th we were in sole possession.

Shortly after midnight, while reconnoitering in front of our outposts, I thought I could hear unusual sounds from the German lines—explosions, the rumbling of many vehicles on the move. Certain the German was withdrawing, I determined to move in on him at once. If I pressed him close enough, he would be unable to reform his line of battle until he reached the Vesle River, many kilometers away. He would have to abandon his piled-up supply dumps. It could not but save us many thousands of precious lives. There was no time to consult division or corps headquarters. I had to rely upon my own judgment and assume all responsibility.

Our front was about 4 kilometers in length. I decided to traverse this line and direct each regiment to move out with one battalion in line of battle, followed by a second in support, and the third in column as reserve. All were to move out simultaneously so that the whole would present an integrated front. I sent a message to the artillery to at once "advance with audacity."

It was 3:30 that morning when I started from our right at Sergy. Taking runners from each outpost liaison group to the next, moving by way of what had been No Man's Land, I will never forget that trip. The dead were so thick in spots we tumbled over them. There must have been at least 2,000 of those sprawled bodies. I identified the insignia of six of the best German divisions. The stench was suffocating. Not a tree was standing. The moans and cries of wounded men sounded everywhere. Sniper bullets sung like the buzzing of a hive of angry bees. An occasional shellburst always drew an angry oath from my guide. I counted almost a hundred disabled guns of various size and several times that number of abandoned machine guns.

Suddenly a flare lit up the area for a fraction of a minute and we hit the dirt, hard. Just ahead of us stood three Germans—a lieutenant pointing with outstretched arm, a sergeant crouched over a machine gun, a corporal feeding a bandolier of cartridges to the weapon. I held my breath waiting for the burst, but there was nothing. The seconds clicked by, but still nothing. We waited until we could wait no longer. My guide shifted his poised grenade to the other hand and reached for his flashlight. They had not moved. They were never to move. They were dead, all dead—the lieutenant with shrapnel through his heart, the sergeant with his belly blown into his back, the corporal with his spine where his head should have been. We left them there, just as they were, gallant men dead in the service of their country.

When I reached our flank regiment just before dawn, I found Colonel Frank McCoy and the gallant chaplain, Father Duffy, just returned from burying Sergeant Joyce Kilmer under the stump of one of those trees he had immortalized.

I went at once to division headquarters. The Corps Commander, that fine old soldier, Hunter Liggett, was there with General Menoher. I explained what I had done. I had not slept for four days and nights, and was so drowsy everything was beginning to black out. I heard General Liggett saying something about the artillery not attempting to cross the river until the infantry had moved sufficiently forward to insure its safety from any counterattack, but that was all. I fell sound asleep. They told me afterward that General Liggett just looked down at me and said, "Well I'll be damned! Menoher, you better cite him." My fourth Silver Star.

The division, tired and worn as it was, moved forward, led by our 117th Regiment of Engineers under Colonel William Kelly, acting as infantry, with a precision and speed that prevented the enemy from making a stand until he reached the Vesle. By that time it had been relieved by the 4th U.S. Division. France made me a Commander in the Legion of Honor, with a second Croix de Guerre.

At this time I was assigned to the command of the 84th Infantry Brigade of the division. I left the staff with a deep feeling of admiration and affection for it, not only as a body, but for each one individually. I was replaced by my old friend and comrade of Fort Selden days, Billy Hughes. He had been with the division from the beginning and had been one of the two staff officers left when we were decimated at Vaucouleurs. No one could possibly have excelled him in his new assignment. The staff nearly moved me to tears when they presented me with a gold cigarette box with the inscription: "The bravest of the brave." It was, of course, an extravagant statement which defied all realities, but the sentiment moved me almost to tears.

In the bloody Ourcq battles the division had lost nearly half of its effective combat personnel. When we arrived at a rest area, we received thousands of replacements. Their spirit was high, but their training and experience were lacking. During August, we built up depleted stores, physical and spiritual, and were in reasonably good condition when we received orders to move to the St. Mihiel front, southeast of Verdun.

The Germans had captured St. Mihiel in 1914 and had held it for four years. The salient was a thorn in the Allied side; jutting across the Meuse, it impeded communications from Paris and Verdun to the Lorraine front and also lay athwart the invasion route toward southern Germany. But now for the first time a ready American Army was to throw its might against this important salient. As part of the IV Army Corps, First American Army, we moved by night marches to the area under the skillful direction of the Army chief of staff, Colonel Hugh A. Drum. Years later, as a major general, he was to be my first assistant when I became the Army Chief of Staff.

Late in the afternoon of September 10th we received our battle orders. We were to relieve the 89th U.S. Division, so as to be in position for the assault at daybreak on September 12th. "The 42nd Division," it read, "will attack in the center and deliver the main blow." My brigade was to be supported by the 151st Artillery Regiment of the division commanded by a most able officer, Colonel George E. Leach. He was critical of the G.H.Q. order, and as it was impossible at that late date to get higher authority, I authorized him to make such changes in the artillery concentration as he thought desirable. Such a procedure was not in accordance with the strict letter of the book, but as I felt it would save many a life, I accepted the risk of the ire of my superiors in command. Later events proved Leach to be unquestionably correct and I was never put on the carpet.

On the 11th, I established my command post at our jumping off trench on the Metz road. The afternoon and evening were quiet, but as night fell the Germans started shelling it heavily and continued until midnight. Since this was the only spot under fire, it aroused not only my curiosity, but my suspicion of local espionage. A few days later, when we captured Chateau St. Benôit, which had been the German Army headquarters, we found a map, and on it was indicated the exact location of my C.P., with a penciled notation, "Infantry Brigade Headquarters. Most important."

At 1:00 A.M. on September 12th, we commenced our artillery preparation, which continued for four hours. As dawn broke I led my assault line forward. We were followed by a squadron of tanks, which soon bogged down in the heavy mud. The squadron was commanded by an old friend who in another war over this same terrain was to gain world-wide fame, Major George Patton.

I had fought the German long enough to know his technique of defense. He concentrated to protect his center, but left his flanks weak. The field of action, the Bois de la Sonnard, lent itself to maneuver, and we were able with little loss to pierce both flanks, envelop his center, and send his whole line into hurried retreat. By nightfall we had the village of Essey and were out in the open in the broad plain of the Woëvre, on the far side of which was the fortress of Metz—a stronghold since the days of Caesar.

In Essey I saw a sight I shall never quite forget. Our advance had been so rapid the Germans had evacuated in a panic. There was a German officer's horse saddled and equipped standing in a barn, a battery of guns complete in every detail, and the entire instrumentation and music of a regimental band. The town was still occupied by civilians, mostly old men, women, and children. They had been there for four years, and when we came in we had great difficulty in getting them to come out of their cellars. They did not know that United States soldiers were in the war, and it was necessary for us to explain to them that we were Americans. They were started at once to the rear. Men, women, and children plodded along in mud up to their knees carrying what few household effects they could. It was one of the most forlorn sights I have ever seen. On other fields in other wars, how often it was to be repeated before my aching eyes.

We turned in 10,000 prisoners and, although my brigade had pierced further than any other unit, and been the spear point of the American advance, it suffered fewer casualties than any other. I was proud, indeed, and even more so at being cited for my fifth Silver Star.*

The next day I pushed the brigade forward to the St. Benôit line. The opposition was so light that it aroused speculation in my mind as to the German defenses in Metz, now only 20 kilometers away. I decided to find out just what was the situation, and that night, accompanied by my adjutant Major Walter Wolfe, sneaked through the Mars-la-Tour battle-ground of the Franco-Prussian War into the outskirts of the city. As I had suspected, Metz was practically defenseless for the moment. Its combat garrison had been temporarily withdrawn to support other sectors of action. Here was an unparalleled opportunity to break the Hindenburg Line at its pivotal point. There it lay, our prize wide open for the taking. Take it and we would be in an excellent position to cut off south Germany from the rest

* General Pershing praised the IV Corps for its action on September 12, saying in his Order of the Day, "The courageous dash and vigor of our troops has thrilled our countrymen and invoked the enthusiasm of our Allies." Sir Douglas Haig signalled, "All ranks of British Armies in France welcome with unbounded admiration and pleasure the victory which has attended the united offensive of the great American Army." And Marshal Foch radioed General Pershing: "The First American Army has won a magnificent victory by a maneuver as skillfully prepared as it was valiantly acted. I extend to the officers and the troops my deep compliments."

of the country; it would lead to the invasion of central Germany by way of the practically undefended Moselle Valley. Victory at Metz would cut the great lines of communication and supply behind the German front, and might bring the war to a quick close.

I recommended as forcibly as I could that my brigade immediately attack the town, promising that I would be in its famous city hall by nightfall. I emphasized that the tactical success of the last two days meant little in itself unless fully exploited, that to tie us down now would be "like a cavalry horse on a lariat tied to a picket piece. It can go so far and no farther, no matter how much richer the grass is beyond its reach." Division, Corps, and Army agreed with me, but the high command disapproved. Other plans had been made—the Meuse-Argonne drive—and while my ideas were deeply appreciated, no change would be made. I have always thought this was one of the great mistakes of the war. Had we seized this unexpected opportunity we would have saved thousands of American lives lost in the dim recesses of the Argonne Forest. It was an example of the inflexibility in the pursuit of previously conceived ideas that is, unfortunately, too frequent in modern warfare. Final decisions are made not at the front by those who are there, but many miles away by those who can but guess at the possibilities and potentialities. The essence of victory lies in the answer to where and when.

The enemy lost no time. He brought up thousands of troops from Strasbourg and other sectors, and within a week the whole Allied army could not have stormed Metz. I was directed to organize a line of defense and I established my headquarters in the chateau at St. Benôit. I was promptly shelled out. In order to confuse the enemy, I was ordered to stage, on the night of September 25, a powerful double raid against the center of his line to make him think we were about to resume our advance, whereas the real attack was to be in the Argonne.

The raid was to be made on two German strongpoints, one a fortified farm—which in France meant a group of buildings with walls connecting them—and the other a village of stone buildings with trenches and strong barbed wire entanglements. My artillery support was to be the 75's of Colonel Henry J. Reilly's 149th Regiment and the 150's of Colonel Robert H. Tyndell's 150th Regiment, both from the division. The fire from these ninety guns was so accurate and so overwhelming that both German garrisons were practically annihilated. I maneuvered the infantry carefully so as to make a lot of noise and much display, but not to bring it into the line of fire. I actually lost fewer than twenty men killed and wounded. Shortly afterward, the division was relieved and went into preparation for what became the final drive of the war. I was cited for the St. Benôit actions—my sixth Silver Star.

On October 1st, the division was moving toward the vast shifting battlefield along the 80-mile front of the Meuse-Argonne. A million American soldiers were to attempt a breakthrough in the center of the Western Front to Sedan, a breakthrough which would mean the collapse of the powerful Hindenburg Line and the defeat of Germany. We slipped and slithered over the battered highways and roads, through dripping patches of forest and by stricken villages and farms. At Montfaucon we were held for several days in its soaked and crowded woods, as a reserve for the 79th Division. I watched its frontal and unsuccessful attack from the old churchyard on the hill. Without warning, a squadron of German planes dived out of nowhere and shot down every one of the dozen or more observation balloons the Army had in the air. In leaving, they flew not a hundred feet above me and I recognized the flowing yellow scarfs of the Richthofen Squadron—the famous "flying circus" created by the German ace, Manfred Baron Von Richthofen.

In 1914, when the great German armies first marched to conquest, they had come through the Argonne, seized it, and had never been dislodged. The terrain was so difficult, so easily defended, that the French had never attempted to attack. It was so powerfully fortified over four years that doubt existed in Allied high circles that any troops in the world could drive out the Germans. The Germans, themselves, boasted they would drown an American attack in its own blood.

Into this red inferno the Americans had jumped off on September 26th, and foot by foot, over scarred and wooded hill and valley, had fought their bloody way from trench to trench to the enemy's main line of resistance. The Germans, alive to the threat, had a machine gun nest behind every rock, a cannon behind every natural embrasure. Here was the key sector of the famous Hindenburg Line, known as the *Krunhilde Stalling*. Here was the last line of the mighty German defenses in the Argonne. Breach it and there would be laid bare Sedan and Mezieres, the two huge German rail centers, through which all the German armies as far away as the North Sea at Ostend were supplied. Take Sedan and every German army to the west would be outflanked. The railroads by which they could withdraw such large masses of troops would be either in American hands or under fire from American guns. It would mean the capture of troops running into the hundreds of thousands. It would mean the end of the war.

Our troops had paid a fearful price in their advance, and particularly at the group of hills known as the Côte-de-Châtillon, the pivot of the entire *Krunhilde Stalling*. Our hard-hitting 32nd Division had ploughed bravely forward only to fall back bleeding and decimated. The 91st Division suffered the same fate. And the famous 1st Division, the Big Red, pride of the

Regulars, had bled itself white before the deep trenches, endless wire, and innumerable cannon and machine guns. The Rainbow was brought in to relieve the 1st Division, which had driven a deep salient into the German lines. This salient was dominated by the Côte-de-Châtillon stronghold which raked the Allied flank and thus stopped the advancing line of the American attack. Every effort to go forward had been stopped cold by this flanking fire.

I carefully reconnoitered the desolate and forbidding terrain that confronted my brigade. There were rolling hills, heavily wooded valleys of death between the endless folds of ridges. Puffs of gas and shellfire broke like squalls of wind. I saw at once that the previous advances had failed because it had not been recognized that the Côte-de-Châtillon was the keystone of the whole German position; that until it was captured we would be unable to advance. I proposed to capture the Côte-de-Châtillon by concentrating troops on it, instead of continuing to spread the troops along a demonstratedly unsuccessful line of attack. Both the division and corps commanders approved.

The night of October 11th was wet and black, and I had just completed plans for the attack when Major General Charles P. Summerall, the V Corps commander, entered the candle-lit C.P. He was tired and worn, and I made him drink a cup of steaming black coffee, strong enough to blister the throat.

"Give me Châtillon, MacArthur," he suddenly said, his voice strained and harsh. "Give me Châtillon, or a list of five thousand casualties." His abruptness startled me.

"All right, General," I assured him, "we'll take it, or my name will head the list."

While making a further reconnaisance, I was wounded, but not incapacitated, and was able to continue functioning. I discovered that, as usual, while the German center, where the 1st Division had spent its blood, seemed impregnable, the flanks were vulnerable. His deep belt of wire entanglement and trench dribbled out at the ends. There was where I planned to strike with my Alabama cotton-growers on the left, my Iowa farmers on the right. I planned to use every machine gun and every artillery piece as covering fire.

We moved out in the misty dawn, and from then on little units of our men crawled and sneaked and side-slipped forward from one bit of cover to another. When the chance came we would close in suddenly to form squads or platoons for a swift envelopment that would gain a toehold on some slope or deadly hillock. Death, cold and remorseless, whistled and sung its way through our ranks, but by nightfall Hill 288 was in Iowa hands. That night I readjusted and reorganized, and the following day we fought up Hill 282, a frowning height of 900 feet, and fought around and skirted Hill 205 to take the Tuilieres Ferme.

The last defenses of the Côte-de-Châtillon were still before us, but as dusk was falling the First Battalion of the 168th under Major Lloyd Ross moved from the right, while a battalion of the 167th under Major Ravee Norris stalked stealthily from the left toward the gap in the wire. The two battalions, like the arms of a relentless pincer, closed in from both sides. Officers fell and sergeants leaped to the command. Companies dwindled to platoons and corporals took over. At the end, Major Ross had only 300 men and 6 officers left out of 1,450 men and 25 officers. That is the way the Côte-de-Châtillon fell, and that is the way those gallant citizen-soldiers, so far from home, won the approach to final victory.

General Menoher* and General Summerall cited me to General Pershing for promotion, which was favorably endorsed by Secretary Baker. His words, "the greatest front-line general of the war," were quite unrealistic and partial. I have always cherished the great friendship they evidenced.

I was also recommended for the Medal of Honor, but the Awards Board at Chaumont disapproved. It awarded me, however, a second Distinguished Service Cross, the citation of which more than satisfied my martial vanity.†

After Côte-de-Châtillon, the 42nd Division was assigned to the I Corps for the final drive toward Sedan. Our line of battle consisted of the French 40th Division connected with the left of the American

---

* The brigade was cited by the corps commander in the following terms: "This brigade under the command of Brigadier General Douglas MacArthur has manifested the highest soldierly qualities and has rendered services of the greatest valor during the present operations. With a dash, courage and a fighting spirit worthy of the best traditions of the American Army, this brigade carried by assault the strongly fortified Hill 288 on the Krunhilde Stalling and unceasingly pressed its advance until it captured the Tuilieres Fèrme and the Bois de Châtillon. During this advance the enemy fought with unusual determination with first class divisions and in many instances resorted to hand-to-hand fighting when our troops approached his rear. The conduct of this brigade has reflected honor upon the division, the army and the states from which the regiments came. For his field leadership, generalcy and determination during three days of constant combat in front of the Côte-de-Châtillon, I am happy to recommend to you for the second time that he be made a Major General."

† "As brigade commander General MacArthur personally led his men and by the skillful maneuvers of his brigade made possible the capture of Hills 288, 282, and the Côte-de-Châtillon. He displayed indomitable resolution and great courage in rallying broken lines and reforming attacks, thereby making victory possible. On a field where courage was the rule, his courage was the dominant factor."

line, which from left to right comprised the 42nd and 77th U.S. Divisions of the I Corps commanded by General Joseph T. Dickman, and the 1st, 2nd, and 89th Divisions of the V Corps under General Summerall. The strongest enemy resistance was on the front of the 42nd Division, which was the nearest to Sedan.

At First Army headquarters, miles to the rear, Colonel George C. Marshall, operations officer of the First Army, wrote out the general directive under the prompting of General Fox Connor. The order read:

> Memorandum for Commanding Generals, I Corps, V Corps.
> Subject: Message from the Commander-in-Chief.
> 1. General Pershing desires that the honor of entering Sedan should fall to the First American Army. He has every confidence that the troops of the 1st Corps, assisted by the 5th Corps, will enable him to realize this desire.
> 2. In transmitting the foregoing message, your attention is invited to the favorable opportunity now existing for pressing our advantage throughout the night. Boundaries will not be considered binding.
> By command of Lieutenant General Liggett.
> Official:
> G. C. Marshall,
> A.C. of S., G-3

The ambiguous and extraordinary final sentence, "Boundaries will not be considered binding," precipitated what narrowly missed being one of the great tragedies of American history. It is probable that the intent of the order was merely to clear the use of the crooked supply road assigned each division. These roads zigzagged back and forth, and meandered at times across divisional borders, causing confusion. Without informing the I Corps, orders were issued by the V Corps to its division to change course almost 90 degrees and cross squarely in front of the divisions of the I Corps. This made its route of advance almost perpendicular to that of the other divisions. In five columns, stripped of its artillery and supply impedimenta, the division outraced the 77th Division and entered the zone of the 42nd along the road paralleling the river. The stage was set for tragic consequences.

Here is my written record of what happened on the front of the 84th Brigade:

Drove the brigade hard all the night of the fifth and cleared the forest. Had a sniper's bullet through the sleeve of my coat. Close shave but did not even scratch me. These Germans never give up. Have orders to strike the Meuse just below Sedan. Reached the river the evening of the sixth and at nightfall disposed the brigade in line of regiments on the heights dominating the river road and a few hundred yards west thereof, the line facing generally eastward. Found a little patched-up inn in the village of Bulson, located at the foot of the heights, and asked for a meal. Proprietor had nothing but potatoes but what a feast he laid before me. Served them in five different courses—potato soup, potato fricassee, potatoes creamed, potato salad and finished with potato pie. It may be because I have not eaten for thiry-six hours, but that meal seems about the best I ever had. Gave the proprietor ten dollars and told him in my broken French he was a genius. He just about wept with delight. Am in bad shape physically. Have decided to establish my headquarters in Bulson for the night. Awakened just before daybreak by an aide with the startling information that a brigade commander of the 1st Division had just entered Bulson, coming from the south, a direction practically perpendicular to that over which we had advanced. This officer proved to be Colonel Erickson who showed me the orders issued by General Parker, commanding the 1st Division, indicating that the 16th Infantry of his brigade was advancing along the river road. This would bring that regiment under the fire of my brigade. Feeling that in the obscurity of early morning the 16th Infantry might be mistaken by my men for the enemy, I at once hastened to the right of my line to inform Colonel Tynley, commanding the 168th Infantry, of the circumstances and to caution him against any debacle. I had hardly reached his position when in the distance I say troops moving up the river road. Guessing it was the 16th Infantry, I pushed out in front of my line, accompanied by Major Wolfe, my executive and one of my aides. We suddenly stumbled on a patrol of American troops of the 1st Division under the command of Lieutenant Black. He recognized me at once and told me that the troops I saw were the leading battalion of the 16th Infantry, under the command of Colonel Harrell. Harrell was a classmate of mine at West Point. Explained the situation to Lieutenant Black and directed him to return at once and contact Colonel Harrell and explain to him the position of my troops and the danger involved in the situation. As I finished talking to Lieutenant Black I noticed that one of the soldiers in the patrol was looking at me in a rather wishful way. I was smoking a Camel cigarette and presumed he was envying me what was then a rare possession at the front—American tobacco. So I offered him one from the rather dilapidated pack I was using. He thanked me and as he lit it said, "I was thinking, if you had just a'bin a Boche general 'stead of an American one we would all of us got the D.S.C." I laughed and gave him the pack saying, "If you don't get a medal in any event you do get a package of cigarettes." He grinned and blurted out, "To tell the truth, sir, I would rather have the cigarettes than the medal." As they disappeared down the hill he was the rear point of the patrol. He turned and waved his musket and I raised my cap to him as he disappeared in the morning mist. That afternoon the 16th Infantry and the troops of the 42nd were together engaged in bitter fighting at the gates of Sedan. I was told my patrol friend had been killed. Cited today, my seventh Silver Star.

The Rainbow held its ground as General Liggett, angered by the tangled situation, ordered the 1st Division to withdraw. Higher circles then overruled General Pershing and decided that the French Army, after its defeat in the Franco-Prussian War, should have the honor of recapturing Sedan. While this aroused some recriminations, it seemed to me a most proper recognition of the magnificent courage, efficiency, and devotion of the French troops throughout the entire war.

Meanwhile, without my knowledge, criticism of the fact that I failed to follow certain regulations prescribed for our troops, that I wore no helmet, that I carried no gas mask, that I went unarmed, that I always had a riding crop in my hand, that I declined to command from the rear, were reported to G.H.Q. All of this was entirely specious, as senior officers were permitted to use their own judgment about such matters of personal detail. I wore no iron helmet because it hurt my head. I carried no gas mask because it hampered my movements. I went unarmed because it was not my purpose to engage in personal combat, but to direct others. I used a riding crop out of long habit on the plains. I fought from the front as I could not effectively manipulate my troops from the rear. But someone at headquarters foolishly sent an officer to conduct confidential interviews of my comrades, with reference to my actions. One of my former staff officers who had been taken away from us at Vaucouleurs for service at headquarters sent me some of the reports. They were so laudatory that it took out all the sting of the investigation.*

When the matter was referred to General Pershing, he replied in typical fashion: "Stop all this nonsense. MacArthur is the greatest leader of troops we have, and I intend to make him a division commander."†

---

* From a veteran who had been with us from the beginning: "I think he has no superior as an officer in the world. As a soldier if I wanted somebody whom I could utterly rely upon to lead me into battle, that man would be MacArthur. If I were a regimental commander and wanted a divisional general I could depend upon to map my plan of attack, that man would be MacArthur. If I were a father and had my choice of the man to lead my sons, that man would be MacArthur."

From a non-commissioned officer of Colonel Hough's 166th Ohio Regiment: "He's a hell-to-breakfast baby, long and lean, kind to us and tough on the enemy. He can spit nickel cigars and chase Germans as well as any doughboy in the Rainbow."

From General Menoher: "MacArthur is the bloodiest fighting man in this army. I'm afraid we're going to lose him sometime, for there's no risk of battle that any soldier is called upon to take that he is not liable to look up and see MacArthur at his side. At every advance MacArthur, with just his cap and his riding crop, will go forward with the first line. He is the source of the greatest possible inspiration to the men of this division who are devoted to him."

Said General Gouraud: "The most remarkable officer I have ever known."

† "I have just finished reading a report from Menoher. It says, 'MacArthur had just been placed in command of his brigade. He went forward to the battalion that was to lead the way. He said to the Major in command, "Now, when that barrage lifts, I want you to go forward with your men and lead the way. Don't stand back. They will follow you. You can't take it by standing back and telling them to go ahead, but you show the way and you can take it—right up to the top. You do this and I will see that you get the Distinguished Service Cross." Then MacArthur stepped back and looked at him and said, "I see you are going to do it. You've got it now," took off his own Distinguished Service Cross decoration, pinned it on him as the barrage lifted. It is one of the greatest cases of intelligence, psychological leadership and direction I have ever encountered.' "

And he did just that. On November 6th he gazetted me to command the 42nd Division. It was a great moment for me. At the same time, General Menoher was advanced to take over one of the new corps in process of organization. On leaving the Rainbow, he dispatched a most laudatory letter to General Pershing regarding my service under him and sent a copy to my mother.* She cherished it to the day of her death, saying it was the greatest gift she had ever received.

The fighting was ended on November 11th by an armistice that found the division at Buzancy. We were selected with three other divisions for the occupation of Germany, and marched through Belgium and Luxembourg to the Rhine. Late in November, I received a personal letter from General Pershing saying that all promotions of general officers had been discontinued by Washington due to the signing of the armistice, and regretting that in consequence I would not receive promotion to the grade of major general. Major General Clement Flagler, my former battalion commander of Leavenworth days, assumed command of the division and I reverted to the 84th Brigade. I established my headquarters at Sinzig overlooking the river. It was a beautiful spot filled with the lore and romance of centuries.

Shortly afterwards, I fell desperately ill with a throat infection—too much gas during the campaign—but the brigade surgeon and good luck pulled me through. The division thoroughly enjoyed those days of rest and relaxation. The warm hospitality of the population, their well-ordered way of life, their

* "I do not feel that my duty with the 42nd Division has been completed and that I am free to assume another command without recording the services rendered by the former Chief of Staff and one of the present infantry brigade commanders of the division, General Douglas MacArthur, throughout the period during which I commanded the 42nd Division. These services, rendered constantly, for over a year, and in the large part amidst active operations in the field, have been so soundly, brilliantly and loyally performed that in the recognition of them I see only a fair appraisal of the example of energy, courage, and efficiency which General MacArthur has set to the 42nd Division and to our entire army in France. The contributions made to our military establishment by this general officer while under my command have already had far-reaching effects. He has stood for the actual physical command of large bodies of troops in battle, not of a day but of days' duration, and I believe has actually commanded larger bodies of troops on the battleline than any other officer in our army, with, in each instance, conspicuous success. He has developed, combined and applied the use of the infantry and correlated arms with an effect upon the enemy, a husbandry of his own forces and means and a resourcefulness which no other commander in the field has.

"This record represents the unremitting endeavor of a very brilliant and gifted officer who has, after more than a year's full service in France without a day apart from his division or his command, and although twice wounded in action, filled each day with a loyal and intelligent application to duty such as is, among officers in the field and in actual contact with battle, without parallel in our army."

thrift and geniality forged a feeling of mutual respect and esteem. We had often dreamed and boasted during the fighting of "watering our horses in the Rhine," but now that we were there the exhaltation seemed to have disappeared. In its place came a realization of the inherent dignity and stature of the great German nation. When we received our orders to return to the United States, the tearful departure looked more as though we were leaving instead of returning home. We had been away from the States exactly eighteen months to the day the first convoy departed from Hoboken.

I was awarded the United States Distinguished Service Medal by General Pershing and, by the French, an Honorary Corporal of the 8th Regiment of the Line with Legion of Honor Fourragere, and Honorary First Class Private of the *Battaillon de Chasseurs Alpins* with Medal Militaire Fourragere. Many other foreign decorations came my way.

The details of my return are perhaps best expressed in a letter I wrote to one of my former aides who was contemplating matrimony and was mustered out in Paris.

Washington, D.C.
May 13,

My dear Weller:

I have just received the package and your nice letter and thank you most sincerely. You failed to complete the mission in not sending the bill—so I am enclosing a check for you to fill out.

We had a great trip over on the *Leviathan*. I gracefully occupied a $5,000.00 suite consisting of four rooms and three baths. It filled me with excitement to change my bed and bath each evening.

We reached New York on the 25th but where-oh-where was that welcome they told us of? Where was that howling mob to proclaim us monarchs of all we surveyed? Where were those bright eyes, slim ankles that had been kidding us in our dreams? Nothing—nothing like that. One little urchin asked us who we were and when we said—we are the famous 42nd—he asked if we had been to France. Amid a silence that hurt—with no one, not even the children, to see us—we marched off the dock, to be scattered to the four winds—a sad, gloomy end of the Rainbow. There was no welcome for fighting men; no one wanted us to parade; no one even seemed to have heard of the war. And profiteers! Ye gods, the profiteers! He who has no Rolls Royce is certainly ye piker. And expensive living! Paris is certainly a cheap little place after all. I judge, too, that clothes are very, very high, for at the play the girls were absolutely unable to wear any. They looked well.

Poor old Bunch of the 168th was killed shortly after we arrived. Run over by an automobile while on his way to visit the hospital. It distressed me beyond words.

I finally received orders to report to the Chief of Staff for duty. He wasn't here when I arrived and nobody knew wherefore I had been summoned. After about a week both he and the Secretary arrived and I was told to prepare myself to go to West Point as its Superintendent.

I hold my rank and hope to continue to do so. Rumor has it that all the other general officers of the 42nd are to be demoted. They are all out at demobilization camps.

We are wondering here what is to happen with reference to the peace terms. They look drastic and seem to me more like a treaty of perpetual war than of perpetual peace. I feel sorry for our friends at Sinzig who must have been hard hit.

If you and Mrs. Weller are coming to America on your honeymoon, you must come and visit us at West Point. We have a big old house that can accommodate you without the slightest inconvenience to us, and I am counting on you to come.

Remember me to Louis and to the old friends of war days and present my sincerest salutations to the young lady.

Cordially yours,
MacArthur

And thus it came to an end.

PART FOUR

*In Defense
of Peace*

1919–1941

When I assumed the command at West Point on June 12, 1919, the entire institution was in a state of disorder and confusion. Due to wartime demands for officers, the normal four-year course had been shortened to one year. The necessity was pressing for creating a new generation of officers for the coming army, as 9,119 had been killed in action or wounded in France.

"West Point is forty years behind the times," General Peyton March, the Chief of Staff, said flatly, on giving me the assignment. Even the proud spirit of the Academy had flagged. In every way, West Point would have to be revitalized, the curriculum re-established.

The atmosphere of public opinion in the United States at that time was not propitious for such an enterprise. It is a singular habit in this country to raise high the military when war threatens, but to ignore security needs in the pleasanter times of peace. If, said many, this was the war to end wars, the war to save democracy for all time, why go on training, at great expense, officers who would never have to fight? Why have a West Point at all? The thing to do is to abolish West Point and install reserve officer training schools at the colleges—in the remote chance that this war might not be the last war, after all.

Congress, too, was in an economic mood and threatened to strip the school to a skeleton. "Back to normalcy" became the slogan of those who professed to be shocked at what they claimed to be the frightful waste of money for war preparation. "Never again," they protested: "economy."

My first move was to go to Washington and contact the leaders in

Congress, many of whom I had known previously. Many people in this free country of ours constantly criticize this great body for every woe and trouble that assails them, but I had always found its members patient, courteous, and efficient. When the true facts had been presented to them, they had always acted with patriotic courage and fearless determination, irrespective of party affiliation. And so it was in this case.

I explained:

The government's expenditures for military needs are a form of national insurance from which come dividends year by year. Premiums must be paid to correspond with the needs of our country in peace or in war. A comparatively small outlay by the United States will serve in future to lessen the tremendous expense and the loss of blood for which no money can repay when the unforeseen tragedy is upon us. West Point, together with the United States Naval Academy, represents the apotheosis of the public school system, and in its development there should be that spirit of generous foresight that has marked the educational systems of the nation for the past century.

Congress had passed a compromise bill fixing a three-year course, and later accepted my recommendation to return to a four-year course.

But the greatest problems I found were internal ones. My first report sets them forth as follows:

My assumption of the command of the United States Military Academy synchronized with the ending of an epoch in the life of this institution. With the termination of the World's War the mission of West Point at once became the preparation of officer personnel for the next possible future war. The methods of training here have always been largely influenced by the purpose of producing the type of officer which the Army at large dictated. The excellence with which the Academy's mission has been carried out in the past has been testified on the battlefields of the world for a hundred years and more. The problem which faced the authorities was, therefore, this: Have new conditions developed, have the lessons of the World War indicated that a changed type of officer was necessary in order to produce the maximum of efficiency in the handling of men at arms? West Point, existing solely as a source of supply and a feeder to the Army, if a new era faces the latter, must of necessity train its personnel accordingly.

In meeting this problem those who were charged with the solution undertook the task with a full realization of its seriousness. It was well understood that it was no light affair to attempt even in moderate degree to modify a status which had proved itself so splendidly for a century and more. It was understood that change under the guise of reconstruction was destructive unless clearly and beyond question it introduced something of added benefit. It was recognized that reform to be effective must be evolutionary, and not revolutionary. It was evident that many sources of help, in the nature of advice and consultation, lay outside of the Military Academy in the persons of distinguished officers of the Army at large and of professional educators throughout the country.

Careful analysis yielded the following conclusions: Until the World War, armed conflicts between nations had been fought by a comparatively small fraction of the population involved. These professional armies were composed very largely of elements which frequently required the most rigid methods of training, the severest forms of discipline, to weld them into a flexible weapon for use on the battlefield. Officers were, therefore, developed to handle a more or less recalcitrant element along definite and simple lines, and a fixed psychology resulted. Early in the World War it was realized to the astonishment of both sides that the professional armies, upon which they had relied, were unable to bring the combat to a definite decision. It became evident, due largely to the elaborate and rapid methods of communication and transportation which had grown up in the past generation, that national communities had become so intimate, that war was a condition which involved the efforts of every man, woman and child in the countries affected. War had become a phenomenon which truly involved the nation in arms. Personnel was of necessity improvised, both at the front and at the rear; the magnitude of the effort, both of supply and of combat, was so great, that individuals were utilized with the minimum of training. In general result, this was largely off-set by the high personal type of those engaged. Discipline no longer required extreme methods. Man generally needed only to be told what to do, rather than be forced by the fear of consequence of failure. The great numbers involved made it impossible to apply the old rigid methods which had been so successful when battlelines were not so extensive. The rule of this war can but apply to that of the future. Improvisation will be the watchword. Such changed conditions will require a modification in type of the officer, a type possessing all of the cardinal military virtues as of yore, but possessing an intimate understanding of his fellows, a comprehensive grasp of world and national affairs, and a liberalization of conception which amounts to a change in his psychology of command. This standard became the basis of the construction of the new West Point in the spirit of Old West Point.

To hold fast to those policies typified in the motto of the Academy, "Duty, Honor, Country," to cling to thoroughness as to a lodestar, to continue to inculcate the habit of industry, to implant as of old the gospel of cleanliness—to be clean, to live clean, and to think clean—and yet to introduce a new atmosphere of liberalization in doing away with provincialism, a substitute of subjective for objective discipline, a progressive increase of cadet responsibility tending to develop initiative and force of character rather than automatic performance of stereotyped functions, to broaden the curriculum so as to be abreast of the best modern thought on education, to bring West Point into a new and closer relationship with the Army at large, has been the aim and purpose of my administration.

But it was one thing to say what was wanted and quite another to do it. General March had not exaggerated. Conditions with respect to the course of study were chaotic. Under the stress of war, the educational qualifications for admission had been drastically lowered. The morale of the cadet body was low.

The traditional disciplinary system, so largely built around the prestige and influence of the upper classmen was impossible in a situation where there were no upper classmen. Cadet officers had never known the example of cadet officers before them, and the body of the Corps had a most imperfect idea of the standards of bearing and conduct which have been characteristic of the cadet for over a century. The Old West Point could not be recognized as it appeared in June 1919. It had gone; it had to be replaced.

We had however many things in our favor: the buildings and equipment for a great military institution; the traditions of the Old West Point implanted in the character of its graduates; the experience of the World War to point the way; the assurance of loyal and devoted service from the fine corps of officers on duty here; and we soon had a point of departure in the legal establishment of a four-year course of study and training. Our problem was to build upon these foundations, and, with these guides and aids, a new West Point which would continue the fine tradition of the old and would give the most thorough preparation of officer personnel for possible future war. To deliver a product trained with a view to teaching, leading, and inspiring the modern citizen in crises to become an effective officer or soldier.

Our plan was fundamentally based upon what might be euphemistically called democracy-in-action. It has ever been a source of pride to those interested in West Point that the democracy of the Corps assured every individual cadet a standing won by his character and personality, irrespective of his social or financial position outside the walls of the institution. Every member of the student body throughout his four-year course wears the same clothes, eats the same food, passes through the same course of study, rises and retires at the same hours, receives the same pay, and starts always without handicap in the same competition.

The highest standards of honor were to be demanded as the only solid foundation for a military career—a code of individual conduct which would maintain the reputation and well-being of the whole—a personal responsibility to his mates, to his community, and above all to his country. In many businesses and professions the welfare of the individual is the chief object, but in the military profession the safety and honor of the state becomes paramount. In the final analysis of the West Point product, character is the most precious component.

Much criticism of narrowness and provincialism had been directed at the military academy in the past due to the restrictive range of interests possible for cadets during four important, formative years of their lives. They had no opportunity to familiarize themselves with the mores and standards of people in the world without, so that when they graduated and mingled freely with their fellows, they had no common background of knowledge and awareness. They were thrust out into the world a man in age, but as experienced as a high school boy. They were cloistered almost to a monastic extent.

It was felt that this vacuum could be filled by allowing certain privileges common to all higher institutions of learning. This would serve both as a relaxation from the rigid grind of study and training, and as a means of keeping touch with life outside the walls of the institution. They no longer were to be walled up within the Academy limits, but were to be treated as responsible young men.

An important change in the military training system was the removal of the cadets from West Point to a regular army encampment for the summer period. Until this time, summer encampment had been limited to a week's artillery practice for first classmen. Under this new system, the cadets were brought into direct contact with actual service conditions during this important period of their military training. They gain in those qualities of self-confidence and assurance which are so valuable to efficient leadership. They learn more of human nature, acquire understanding, sympathy, and tact. The entire experience both broadens and deepens their character.

The problem of athletic training was one close to my heart. For many years, athletics at West Point had consisted of an excellent system of military gymnastics, but it was apparent from the experiences of the World War that a course of training should be planned not only to fit future officers physically for the rigors of military service, but also to qualify them as physical directors and instructors for their future commands. They must learn, not only how to perform themselves, but how to teach others. They must understand the means by which they can most speedily and efficiently bring their men to the necessary physical condition. They must appreciate the practical details of physical instruction and be qualified to stimulate and inspire, as well as perform.

In the old course, athletics was a voluntary activity. Only those cadets engaged in sports who were spurred by the ambition to gain a place on the team, or who played simply for pleasure. But the war had shown the value of organized group athletics in creating and maintaining morale. The effect upon the army at large of an extensive system of competitive sports, controlled by competent and well-prepared officers, cannot be overestimated. Troops in poor physical condition are worthless. It was evident that the problem of creating a model course in physical training and athletics at this great military school was vital. And it was equally evident that such a project could not fail to have a marked influence on the broad question of the physical qualifications of the youth of the nation.

Accordingly, it was decided that every cadet would be required to participate in all major sports under the supervision of qualified instructors. Mass athletics was to be taught and practiced in the sports of football, baseball, basketball, soccer, lacrosse, track, tennis, golf, and hockey as part of the regular curriculum. Cadets were first divided into small sections of twenty-five for preliminary training, and intramural contests between companies and battalions followed. Nothing brings out the qualities of leadership, mental and muscular co-ordination, aggressiveness, and courage more quickly than this type of competition. Physical qualities may well determine the destiny of the intellect. To emphasize these truths I had carved on the stone portals of the gymnasium these words:

> "Upon the fields of friendly strife
> Are sown the seeds
> That, upon other fields, on other days
> Will bear the fruits of victory"

Day after day, for long hours, I huddled with the Academic Board in formulating and applying these plans of revitalization. We consulted with the leading university and military figures of the country. We sent our instructors to take courses in the greatest colleges throughout the land; adapted military courses to modern needs; scientific courses were brought up to date; classical courses were used as cultural foundations; a new course on economics and government was added; increased emphasis on history and world trends; studies into European conditions and the Far East; modern science, chemistry, electricity, aerodynamics, mechanics, languages, and a course of physical, mental, and moral training which we believed unexcelled by any institution in the world.

If the policies conceived and the means taken for their application were to be successful, if West Point was to incorporate the new without displacing the proven good of the old, it was necessary to submit our plans to the best critics the country could offer. The press, without exception, expressed enthusiastic approval of the changes. The Secretary of War was in accord. The majority of the senior officers of the Army approved. Ninety-one distinguished educators studied the plans, and from none came adverse criticism of the new foundations we were laying. The Board of Visitors, composed of seven members of the United States House of Representatives, reported: "The Board desires to emphasize its strong approval of the splendid service that General MacArthur and the officers associated with him are rendering to the country by constructing a new West Point, founded on the lessons and experiences and the sacrifices of the World War, and in the spirit of Old West Point."

In January 1920, I was appointed a brigadier general in the Regular Army. Late in 1922, being at the top of the roster of general officers for foreign service, I was relieved as superintendent and ordered to the Philippine Islands. Before leaving, I recommended an increase in the size of the Corps of Cadets. I said:

By superior organization, system and efficiency, West Point can turn out annually for its country's service twice the number of qualified men it is now graduating. With the peacetime demand for trained officers, the number of officers is certain to fall far short of requirements. And if this condition holds in time of peace how much greater will be the insufficiency in time of national emergency. West Point has been reconstructed upon the same ideals of public service which it has held from its inception. Its graduates will be a bulwark to the nation in the future as they have been in the past. I can but hope that the dictates of wisdom will prevail and that their number will be steadily increased to correspond with the urgent needs of our country in peace or in war.

This was eventually done and the Corps enlarged from 1,334 to its present strength of approximately 2,500.

It has been a source of deepest satisfaction to me to know how successful have been the cadets who were at the academy during my tour as superintendent. Of those handsome, slim boys in gray, two, Lyman Lemnitzer and Maxwell Taylor, became chairman of the Joint Chiefs of Staff; two others, Hoyt Vandenberg and Thomas White, became chiefs of staff of the Air Corps, and so many became general officers that it would be in vain to attempt to recount them. The worth of such men to the country is without price.

In February 1922 I entered into matrimony, but it was not successful, and ended in divorce years later for mutual incompatibility.

It was early in October 1922 when the transport *Thomas* docked at Pier Five in Manila, and once again the massive bluff of Bataan, the lean gray grimness of Corregidor were there before my eyes in their unchanging cocoon of tropical heat.

It was good to be back after eighteen years and to see the progress that had been made. Home government, under the inspired guidance of Manuel Quezon, now speaker of the Philippine House of Representatives, was moving forward. New roads, new docks, new buildings were everywhere. But there was a change for the worse, too. The Philippine goal of independence was being challenged by foreign forces within the country, as indeed was the goal of equal social status. Attitudes die hard and the old idea of colonial exploitation still had its vigorous supporters. As a result of my friendly relations with the Filipinos, there began to appear a feeling of resentment and even antagonism against me. It is strange how personal abstract national issues can become, how bitter can be the feeling engendered against one of whom there is no actual knowledge, or even acquaintance.

General Leonard Wood, now retired from the Army, was the governor general and the department commander was General George Reed, whom I had known since early Leavenworth days.

I was first assigned to command the Military District of Manila and later the Philippine Scout Brigade. These were excellent troops, completely professional, loyal, and devoted. I was directed to make a thorough study of Bataan, and to draw up a plan of defense for this mountainous and wooded peninsula lying a scant 3 miles across the sea channel from the island of Corregidor, at the mouth of Manila Bay. In the ensuing weeks I covered every foot of rugged terrain, over its trails, up and down its steep mountainous slopes, and through its bamboo thickets.

On January 17, 1925, I was promoted to major general and assigned to the command of the 23rd Infantry Brigade, the Philippine Division, in relief of General Omar Bundy. He was an old friend of Milwaukee days and had commanded the II Corps Area. Shortly thereafter, I was ordered to Atlanta to command the IV Corps Area. Kennesaw Mountain and Peach Tree Creek, where the 24th Wisconsin had served in the Civil War, became daily sights to me. How I longed to have my father there and to listen to his wise counsel with reference to the perceptible crisis which the world was beginning to face.

In the summer of 1925 I was assigned to Baltimore to command the III Corps Area. My service there was the usual routine of a senior commander, broken by two special incidents, one most disagreeable, one most pleasant. The first was the court-martial of my fellow townsman, Billy Mitchell. He was an officer who had greatly distinguished himself as our outstanding combat air commander of the war. A strong proponent of the predominance of air power and of a unified control of all air forces, Billy challenged the concept of the Navy as a first line of defense, and mobilized Congressional and public opinion to permit bombing tests against old battleships. In these tests, the former German dreadnaught, *Ostfriesland,* was hit and sunk along with a German submarine, destroyer, light cruiser, and two obsolete American warships. Our Navy, from that time on, began to build its forces around the air carrier.

Mitchell's friction with the military hierarchy continued to increase. Because of the government's failure to develop the air service, he became an outspoken critic of the country's aviation policy. For months he figured in the newspaper headlines almost daily. The crisis came when the loss of the Navy dirigible *Shenandoah* during an electrical storm caused him to publicly state that such accidents are the result of "incompetency, criminal negligence and almost treasonable administration of the National Defense by the War and Navy Departments."

I was detailed a member of the court, one of the most distasteful orders I ever received. I was thoroughly in accord with the concept of the massive power of the air and that its development should be greatly accelerated. I had publicly stated, "Neither ground nor sea forces can operate safely unless the air over them is controlled by our own air power." It is part of my military philosophy that a senior officer should not be silenced for being at variance with his superiors in rank and with accepted doctrine. I have always felt that the country's interest was paramount, and that when a ranking officer, out of purely patriotic motives, risked his own personal future in such opposition, he should not be summarily suppressed. Superior authority can, of course, do so if it wishes, but the one thing in this world that cannot be stopped is a sound idea. The individual may be martyred, but his thoughts live on.

In such a court-martial as Mitchell's only a two-thirds vote is necessary to convict. When the verdict was reached, many believed I had betrayed my friend, and certain rabid and irresponsible columnists even assailed me for joining "in the persecution of Mitchell." Nothing could be further from the truth. I did what I could in his behalf and I helped save him from dismissal. That he was wrong in the violence of his language is self-evident; that he was right in his thesis is equally true and incontrovertible.

Mitchell was court-martialed for this violent personal attack and sentenced to suspension from duty for two and a half years. He promptly resigned his commission as an officer, and devoted the remaining ten years of his life to propagating his gospel of the air. He died in 1936 and did not witness the vindication of much that he advocated. Had he lived through World War II, he would have seen the fulfillment of many of his prophecies of air warfare: strategic bombardment, mass airborne operations, the military importance of Alaska and the polar areas, and the eclipse of the battleship by the airplane. His governmental redress came from Congress, which in 1946 authorized a special gold medal in his honor.

The agreeable interlude in my Baltimore command dealt with the Olympic Games. William C. Prout, president of the American Olympic Committee, died suddenly in 1927. A deadlock developed in the naming of his successor which threatened to disrupt the entire organization. The emergency was acute due to the imminence of the games. I had never lost my keen interest in sports, and attention had been attracted by the intramural system of athletic training which had been installed at West Point during my tour as superintendent. This system had been largely adopted by the leading colleges of the country, and throughout the garrisons and the camps of the Army. I was elected to fill the gap caused by Prout's death, and charged with the active directorship of our Olympic team. The chief of staff, General Charles P. Summerall, agreed to place me on detached service.

The outlook was not bright for our entrants, but I was determined that the United States should win at Amsterdam. I rode them hard all along the line. Athletes are among the most temperamental of all persons, but I stormed and pleaded and cajoled. I told them we represented the greatest nation in the world, that we had not come 3,000 miles just to lose gracefully, that we were there to win, and win decisively. Due to a splendid team effort, we finished in first place with Germany the runner-up.

The hospitality, courtesy, and warmth of the Dutch captivated us all. The prince consort, Prince Henry of Mecklenburg-Schwerin, became one of our boon companions. Queen Wilhelmina invited me to dine with her. At the dinner the table was decorated with a profusion of the beautiful Mac-Arthur red roses, named by the famous horticulturist, Luther Burbank, for my father. She was anxious to discuss the situation in the Far East, where so much of her domain lay. An extraordinary woman, her grasp of world affairs was complete and her prophetic vision foresaw much of the momentous changes about to take place. She was progressive in thought and solicitous about liberalizing the methods of colonial government in the East Indies. She referred with warmth to the early colonization of our Hudson River Valley by Dutch settlers and once inadvertently called New York City by its original name of New Amsterdam.

Our victorious team returned to New York with the plaudits of the country ringing in our ears. The team was feted from coast to coast, both the press and my superiors * being most generous.

Back in Baltimore, I publicly expressed my fears that pacifist and other alien ideologies were causing America to repeat the errors of the past.

With the Red menace in Russia, Poland in disorder, Romania threatened with secession, France fighting in Morocco, Nicaragua in revolution, Mexico in confusion, and civil war in China, it did not seem unlikely that our streets would again be filled with marching men and our country again have need of our military services. I advocated that provisions for our defense should be fully carried out, that total unilateral disarmament was unthinkable. No one would take seriously the equally illogical plan of disbanding our fire department to prevent fire, or doing away with our police department to stop crime.

Our nation had shrunk from enforced military service, yet had evolved the concept of the citizen-soldier. It was my belief that the life blood of our country would depend on the measures taken at this time, not when the threat of a foreign invader menaced our shores.

My firm belief in the necessity for adequate military preparation gained for me, in those uneasy days of the '20s and early '30s, the lasting hostility of two powerful groups in the United States, the Communists and the pacifists.

I was shortly ordered back to the Philippines as department commander, in charge of all our troops in the islands. No assignment could have pleased me more.

---

* "I can best voice what is universally recognized that you alone are responsible for cementing the bonds between disorganized and factional organizations, infusing a spirit and resolution and will to win in the contestants, and maintaining before the world the noblest ideals of American citizenship. You have not only maintained the reputation that Americans do not quit, but that Americans know how to win.

"With my own warm and deepest gratitude

"Faithfully your friend,
"Charles P. Summerall."

I found Manila as bright and lively as ever. I lived in a spacious set of quarters with my inspector general, Colonel Charles H. Patterson, a West Point classmate; my two aides, First Lieutenant Thomas J. Davis and First Lieutenant Ford Trimble; and an old friend of former days, Colonel Reddy. They formed a gay and lively group, and were a source of constant pleasure to me.

Manuel Quezon was now the undisputed leader of the Filipinos, and I saw much of him. We discussed freely the growing threat of Japanese expansion. Thousands of Japanese were pouring into Davao, in the great southern island of Mindanao. There were dark patches of warning hovering over both Europe and Asia. Germany was beginning to rearm, Japan building up her empire in Manchuria, China threatened from the same source. By subversive measures, Communist Russia had made great gains in the restless, insecure Far East. The stage was being set for a vast political and social upheaval, vitally affecting every land and race in East Asia. By evolution, or by revolution, nationalism was on its way.

With the possibility that the Philippines could easily be caught in the middle of a struggle for power, we trained and maneuvered such forces as we had. They were, however, pitifully inadequate, and Washington apparently had no clear-cut idea with reference to Philippine defense.

The governor general was Henry L. Stimson. I had known him slightly during the war, when, as a colonel of field artillery, he visited my brigade for observation and training. He had a broad and tolerant attitude toward the Filipinos, and was regarded by them with respect and esteem. He was a preparedness man, and supported my military training program with understanding and vigor. We became fast friends.

Late in July 1929, I was awakened just before daybreak by the adjutant general of the department, Colonel Eddie Brown, a West Point classmate, with a decoded cable marked "Secret. For MacArthur's Eyes Only." It read:

The President desires to appoint you as Chief of Engineers. He desires a reorganization of the Engineer Corps administration along broad lines to conform to the magnitude and diversity of its activities, greatly increased by the flood control and inland waterway projects. I have assured the Secretary of War and the President of your unswerving loyalty and cooperation in executing his wishes. He is convinced of your organizing ability and professional qualifications. The President desires to know whether you are willing to accept the appointment. Keep this in strictest confidence. Reply in same code. Summerall. Chief of Staff.

I was very proud to have been in the Engineer Corps, but, having cast my lot with the line, never envisaged being at its head. Eddie Brown was all for my acceptance. But, although it was difficult to turn down such a suggestion from the President, I knew it was the right thing to do. Following the great Mississippi River floods of 1927, a new Flood Control Act placed this problem under the Corps of Engineers, and I had little experience in handling such problems. I thanked President Hoover, but said the position required someone possessing two basic qualifications—outstanding engineering ability, and that ability must be of such general recognition as to give him the complete confidence of the engineering profession at large. I had neither of these qualifications. I called attention to the fact that General Lytle Brown of the Engineers was ideal for the position. Eddie Brown was disgusted. He said Washington would never forgive me, that I had dug my own professional grave. But it was a wise decision I took, both for me and what was much more important, for the government. General Lytle Brown was appointed and, as I predicted, became one of the greatest chiefs the Engineer Corps ever had.

Eddie Brown was wrong, too, about Washington. On August 5, 1930, I received a radiogram saying: "President has just announced your detail as Chief of Staff to succeed General Summerall." I did not want to return to Washington, even though it meant the four stars of a general, and my first inclination was to try and beg off. I knew the dreadful ordeal that faced the new Chief of Staff, and shrank from it. I wished from the bottom of my heart to stay with troops in a field command. But my mother, who made her home in Washington, sensed what was in my mind and cabled me to accept. She said my father would be ashamed if I showed timidity. That settled it.

I returned to the United States in October, and was temporarily assigned to the command of the IX Corps Area in San Francisco. I was back again in the old home my father had occupied at Fort Mason. I spent the next month, however, visiting our principal military establishments throughout the country. On November 21st, I was sworn in as Chief of Staff.

I had been in military service for thirty-one years, years of receiving orders and following policies I had not promulgated, of heeding the motto of my old Scot clan—"Listen! O Listen!" Now the responsibility of making the decisions and giving the orders was mine. The Secretary of War was Patrick Hurley. He was a veteran officer of the war, and both he and President Hoover were keenly solicitous of national security. They invariably supported me in my professional recommendations.

With my mother, I moved into quarters No. One at Fort Myer and prepared to face the music. I did not have to wait long.

All across the country there was loud and persuasive talk to the effect that war could come no more—that it was a vanished art and a dead monstrosity. Congress was bored and annoyed by the Army, which kept on croaking that war would come again and sooner, perhaps, than expected. It became my duty as Chief of Staff to predict the character of this inevitable war, to make the people believe, and to conceive, describe, shape, and build a modern American Army. A speech given at the University of Pittsburgh on June 8, 1932, reflected my anxiety that the American people be apprised of the situation:

Pacifism and its bedfellow, Communism, are all about us. In the theaters, newspapers and magazines, pulpits and lecture halls, schools and colleges, it hangs like a mist before the face of America, organizing the forces of unrest and undermining the morals of the working man.

Day by day this canker eats deeper into the body politic.

For the sentimentalism and emotionalism which have infested our country, we should substitute hard common sense. Pacific habits do not insure peace or immunity from national insult and aggression. Any nation that would keep its self-respect must be prepared to defend itself.

Every reasonable man knows that war is cruel and destructive, and yet very little of the fever of war will melt the veneer of our civilization. History has proved that nations once great, that neglected their national defense are dust and ashes. Where are Rome and Carthage? Where Byzantium? Where Egypt, once so great a state? Where Korea, whose death cries were unheard by the world?

The reaction against these concepts was prompt and tremendous. I was roundly denounced not only by pacifists and Communists, but even on the floor of Congress itself. A small group in that august body fancied themselves far better strategists than any general. I was harassed ceaselessly in the effort to force me into acceptance of their appeasement views. I was slandered and smeared almost daily in the press. The propaganda spared neither my professional attributes nor my personal character. It was bitter as gall and I knew that something of the gall would always be with me.

But little by little, step by step, my main purpose of formulating the basic outline of a broad plan for the United States to meet an inevitable war took shape.

I had the research staff and laboratories. I had the Army's schools, which had been kept in vigorous health. I had an able General Staff and I had my own ideas. It was plain to see that modern war would be a war of massive striking power, a war of lightning movement, a war of many machines, yet a war with its cutting edge in the hands of but a few skilled operatives. We had learned at bitter price the lesson of the last war, that one new innovation, the perfected machine gun, had foiled plans and planners, and had driven great armies into a stalemate of mud and trench. It was easy for the professional mind to foresee the armored task force of bombing planes, tanks, and supporting motorized columns reviving mobile war.

We brought out an Industrial Mobilization Plan and a plan for General Mobilization of Manpower encompassing all citizens, both still in effect. We redesigned the military defense of the United States—the "Four Army Plan"—the basic principles of which still prevail. We evolved the independent striking air arm which became the forerunner of our present Air Force. We forecast the independent armored land force and developed a school for it at Fort Knox. Today, Fort Knox is headquarters for an Armored Force, which, amoeba-like, breeds one armored division upon another and splits them off to flow into the Army system wherever needed. The regrouping of all our land forces under one commander, our air forces under another, and the service of supply into a third, with the three commanders reporting to the Chief of Staff, proved itself successfully in World War II.

But most important was the spirit of change that came over the Army as a whole. Apathy and fear were replaced by a new surge of vitality. At a time when Hitler was still popularly regarded as a windbag, Japan publicized as a fake, and our government promising it would forever keep us out of war, we formed the central character of the United States Army of World War II.

Efforts to reduce military effectiveness continued. A proposal was made in Congress to cut the officer corps of 12,255 by 2,000. I replied:

An army can live on short rations; it can be insufficiently clothed and housed; it can even be poorly armed and equipped; but in action it is doomed to destruction without the trained and adequate leadership of officers. An efficient and sufficient corps of officers means the difference between victory and defeat. There is nothing more expensive than an insufficient army. To build an army to be defeated by some other army is sheer folly, a complete waste of money. If you are defeated you will pay a billion dollars for every million you save on inadequate preparation. There is no such thing in war any more as a glorious defeat. If you lose you will not only pay in money, but you will be a slave in every other way. You will lose that nebulous thing—liberty—which is the very essence of all for which we have stood ever since George Washington and his followers made us what we are. If we had in the treasury of the United States only sufficient money to preserve our integrity against foreign aggression, that is the first use that should be made of it.

The vote was close, 175-154, but we won.

Congress also proposed that no officer's retired pay should be in excess of $2,400 a year, and that the special pension of General of the Armies Pershing of approximately $21,000 a year be drastically reduced. I appeared before the Senate Appropriations Committee and spoke of the tribute accorded General Douglas Haig in England. Haig was Pershing's British counterpart during World War I. After the war, Haig was promoted to field marshal and received, in addition to a life trust of nearly $9,000 a year, a trust fund of nearly half a million dollars yielding an income of about $30,000 a year. This income would be received by his family for three succeeding generations. Happily, Congress realized the contribution made by its military, and vetoed the proposal.*

The most poignant episode during my role as Chief of Staff was the so-called Bonus March. The country was in the third year of the great Depression, and heartache and hunger haunted the millions of unemployed. Men lost faith, and the spirit of the country sank to a low that had not been experienced since the financial panic of 1892. Late in May, an army of disillusioned and lost men who had served in the war, the vanguard of a starved band, arrived in Washington, seeking desperately to influence the Congress to grant an immediate cash bonus for veterans. For two fruitless months they lived in abject squalor, making their daily marches to the Capitol, to the White House, and to all of the other sacrosanct federal buildings where they hoped to loosen the pursestrings of government. In the end, their frustration, combined with careful needling by the Communists, turned them into a sullen, riotous mob.

In these days of wholehearted national unity, it is hard to believe that thirty years ago the President of the United States lived in danger, and that Congress shook with fear at the sight and sound of the marchers. It is hard to believe, too, that government employees and other citizens of Washington

* Shortly thereafter, I received a personal note from General Pershing, now seventy-two years old. He wrote: "Please allow me to send you my warmest congratulations upon the way you have succeeded in overcoming opposition in Congress to the Army. I think you have much to be thankful for, as we all have. And may I also express my appreciation for the way you have defended the Retired List and especially your reference to me."

who bore witness to the tawdry street battles cheered the stoning of the Washington police force.

The movement was actually far deeper and more dangerous than an effort to secure funds from a nearly depleted federal treasury. The American Communist Party planned a riot of such proportions that it was hoped the United States Army, in its efforts to maintain peace, would have to fire on the marchers. In this way, the Communists hoped to incite revolutionary action. Red organizers infiltrated the veteran groups and presently took command from their unwitting leaders.

Walter W. Waters, a persuasive ex-serviceman from Oregon with a gift for public speaking, was the leader of the Bonus Marchers. I conferred with him and reached an agreement that if the Army was called in, he would withdraw the veterans without violence. Many of them were bedded down in partly demolished buildings along Pennsylvania Avenue. To provide further shelter, I issued tents and camp equipment to be set up on the Anacostia Flats. I also ordered out a number of rolling kitchens to relieve any acute suffering. This latter step raised an outburst in Congress. A leader in the House of Representatives said from the floor:

If they come to Washington, sit down and have three meals furnished free every day, then God knows what will happen to us. There are more than 8,500,000 persons out of work in the United States, most of them with families. If the Government can feed those that are here, then we can expect an influx that will startle the whole country.

The rolling kitchens were withdrawn.

Senator J. Hamilton Lewis inspected the tired and, in some cases, shoeless veterans lying around the Capitol Building and then told his colleagues in the Senate that, "By abandoning the plea for justice and adopting in its place threat and coercion, veterans are causing fellow countrymen to wonder whether their soldiers served for patriotism or merely for pay."

Through the month of June the tension mounted. The camps now occupied by an estimated 17,000 spread out to every sizeable vacant lot. At night, morose men squatted by burning campfires listening silently to the endless speeches, always tinged with the increasing violence of Communist propaganda. The privations, the punishing heat, the unsanitary living conditions, and the interminable hours of wishful waiting for the slightly more than one thousand dollars which was to be each man's share—if Congress relented—took its toll.

During June, the governor of New York, Franklin D. Roosevelt, informed New Yorkers among the Bonus Marchers that the state would pay their railroad fares if they left Washington immediately and returned to New York. President Hoover got a bill through Congress authorizing loans for transportation, and most of the real veterans left. But the hard core of the Communist bloc not only stayed, but grew. The Federal Bureau of Investigation reported that an examination of the fingerprints of 4,723 Bonus Marchers showed that 1,069 of them were men who had criminal records ranging from drunkenness to murder and rape. Not more than one in ten of those who stayed was a veteran. By this time Waters had been deposed and the Communists had gained control.

As the violence increased, Pelham Glassford, commander of the Washington police, twice consulted with me about calling on the Army for assistance. Both times I advised against it. But on July 28th, the crisis was reached. A mob 5,000 strong began to move up Pennsylvania Avenue toward the Treasury Building and the White House. The police were outnumbered five to one. Glassford was mauled and stripped of his police superintendent's gold badge, gunfire broke out, two men were killed and a score or more badly injured. It was evident that the situation had gotten beyond the control of the local authorities.

A request was immediately made through the Board of Commissioners of the District of Columbia for federal troops. Commissioner Richelderfer, in requesting such assistance from the President, stated that it would "be impossible for the police department to maintain law and order except by the free use of firearms. The presence of federal troops in small number will obviate the seriousness of the situation, and it will result in far less violence and bloodshed."

The President then conferred with Patrick Hurley, the Secretary of War, who was immediately placed in charge. Hurley issued the following order:

To: General Douglas MacArthur
    Chief of Staff, U.S. Army.
    The President has just now informed me that the civil government of the District of Columbia has reported to him that it is unable to maintain law and order in the District.
    You will have United States troops proceed immediately to the scene of disorder. Cooperate fully with the District of Columbia police force which is now in charge. Surround the affected area and clear it without delay.
    Turn over all prisoners to the civil authorities.
    In your orders insist that any women or children who may be in the affected area be accorded every consideration and kindness. Use all humanity consistent with the due execution of the order.

Patrick J. Hurley,
Secretary of War.

Six hundred soldiers under the command of General Perry L. Miles had been drawn from units close to Washington. General Miles' orders to his unit commanders were as follows:

We are acting on the order of the President of the United States. The cavalry will make a demonstration down Pennsylvania Avenue. The infantry will deploy in line of skirmishers in the rear of the cavalry. You will surround the area and evict the men in possession there. Use care and consideration toward all women and children who may be in the area.

In accordance with the President's request, I accompanied General Miles and brought with me two officers who later wrote their names on world history: Major Dwight D. Eisenhower and Major George S. Patton.

Not a shot was fired. The sticks, clubs, and stones of the rioters were met only by tear gas and steady pressure. No one was killed and there were no serious injuries on either side. By 9:30 P.M. the area was cleared as far as the Anacostia Flats. The show of force, the excellent discipline of the troops, and the proper use of tear gas had turned the trick without serious bloodshed. At Anacostia Flats I received word from the Secretary of War, as we were in the midst of crossing the river, to suspend the operation at my discretion. I halted the command as soon as we had cleared the bridge, but at that moment the rioters set fire to their own camp. This concluded the proceedings for the night.

I personally reported to the President and Secretary Hurley at the White House about eleven o'clock, and they expressed gratification at what had been accomplished. Secretary Hurley asked me to give a statement to the waiting newspaper men. After explaining the events of the preceding day, I continued:

If President Hoover had not acted when he did he would have been faced with a serious situation. Another week might have meant that the government was in peril. He had reached the end of an extraordinary patience and had gone to the very limit to avoid friction before using force. Had the President not acted when he did he would have been derelict in his duty.

The day following the riot, the police rounded up thirty-six of the leaders, including James Ford, the American Communist Party candidate for Vice-President; Emmanuel Levin, a leading New York Communist; and John T. Pace, an acknowledged former Communist. This broke up the organization, and its remnants disappeared.

The most extravagant distortions of what had occurred were widely circulated. I was violently attacked, and even blatantly misrepresented before

Congress. Speeches pictured me in full dress uniform astride a fiery white charger, bedecked with medals, waving a bloody saber, and leading a mad cavalry charge against unarmed and innocent citizens. Of course there was absolutely no foundation for such statements. There was no cavalry charge. There was no fiery white charger. There was no saber. There was no full-dress uniform. There were no medals. I wore the same uniform as the troops. When I challenged such distortions, they were merely shrugged off with the expression, "it was only politics." Franklin Roosevelt once said to me, "Douglas, I think you are our best general, but I believe you would be our worst politician." With his rare sense of humor, I wonder which side of that remark he thought was the compliment.

Three days after the uprising, *The New York Times,* in a front-page account, reported:

The Communist Party, at its Headquarters here, accepted responsibility yesterday for the demonstration that resulted in the bonus-army riots in Washington.

"We agitated for the bonus and led the demonstration of the veterans in Washington," a spokesman for the party said at the headquarters at 50 East 13th Street. "We stand ready to go to Washington again and fight for the working men. We started the march from here for Washington and we will lead the way again!"

In 1948, more of the Communist conspiracy was revealed when Benjamin Gitlow, an admitted Communist, wrote in his book, *The Whole of Their Lives:*

On July 5 Earl Browder declared that the veterans were the shock troops of the unemployed. Said he, "The Bonus revolutionary force in Washington is the most significant beginning of the mass struggle against the deepening consequences of the crisis."

On July 28 the government went into action. General Douglas MacArthur, Chief of Staff of the United States Army, stepped in to prevent serious bloodshed after a fight between communist led veterans and police resulting in the death of one veteran and the shooting of an innocent bystander. It was just what the communists wanted. It is what they had conspired to bring about. Now they could brand Hoover as a murderer of hungry unemployed veterans. They could charge that the United States Army was Wall Street's tool with which to crush the unemployed and that the government and the Congress of the United States were bloody Fascist butchers of unarmed American workmen.

In 1949, John T. Pace testified under oath before a Congressional committee:

I feel responsible in part for the oft repeated lie about President Hoover and General MacArthur.

I led the left wing or communist section of the bonus march. I was ordered by my Red superiors to provoke riots. I was told to use every trick to bring about bloodshed in the hopes that President Hoover would be forced to call out the army. The communists didn't care how many veterans were killed. I was told Moscow had ordered riots and bloodshed in the hopes that this might set off the revolution. My communist bosses were jumping with joy on July 28 when the Washington police killed one veteran. The Army was called out by President Hoover and didn't fire a shot or kill a man. General MacArthur put down a Moscow directed revolution without bloodshed, and that's why the communists hate him.

During the Bonus March communist threats continued to be made against responsible officials. I was to be publicly hanged on the steps of the Capitol. It was the beginning of a definite and ceaseless campaign that set me apart as a man to be destroyed, no matter how long the Communists and their friends and admirers had to wait, and no matter what means they might have to use. But it was to be nineteen years before the bells of Moscow pealed out their glee at my eclipse.

During my tour as Chief of Staff I made two trips to Europe, meeting military and political leaders, inspecting their armies, and discussing portents of future wars. Much valuable information was gained, especially about Germany and Russia. As a representative of the U.S., I was received with affection and honor all over Europe.

The first of my journeys to Europe in September 1931 was at the express invitation of the French government to witness the yearly grand maneuvers. The French Army was experimenting with big, fast, heavily armored tanks to replace horse cavalry. As our own army had just passed through a similar phase, the French minister of war, Andre Maginot, was desirous of profiting by our experiences. The two senior French officers—General Maxime Weygand, who had been Marshal Foch's chief of staff, and General Maurice Gamelin, who had commanded a division neighboring the Rainbow—were wartime comrades of mine.

At the termination of the maneuvers, held on the old Champagne front, I was invited to sit in on a meeting at Rheims with Maginot, Weygand, and Gamelin. The subject was possible war with Germany. I was asked what were the conclusions I had drawn from my recent observations. I stated frankly that I was of the opinion that sooner or later Germany would try again. The Frenchmen then threshed out the problem of how, with a smaller population, France could take the offensive in such a contingency. They wished to have a force sufficient to envelop the German right by striking through Belgium from their own left. To do this, they must be able to contain the German onslaught in front and still have a reserve of thirty-five divisions to make their turning movement. It was their opinion that the only way to do it was to hold the Vosges front with a swift moving mobile unit, requiring only a small fraction of the total force. This would enable them to have an ample force for their counterattack. Such was the inception and purpose of the so-called Maginot Line. It was built to enable the French to attack, not in pursuance of a policy of static defense.

But when the war actually came, the French made the fatal mistake of not carrying out an envelopment maneuver, and remained in passive resistance only. The Maginot Line came to be the universal symbol of static defense, whereas it was meant to be the pivot of a bold offense. History has a strange way, at times, of making white look black.

On my second trip to France in 1932 I saw that, just as in the United States, the French were mechanizing their infantry. They foresaw the day when the foot soldier would advance to the line of battle in motor vehicles. No more slogging columns, marching all night to arrive at the jump-off point of attack weary and haggard, with brain so dulled that clear thinking was impossible. It coincided exactly with my pleas to Congress: "They will be carried to the front in trucks. The approach march will be shorter. They will be fresh in every sense of the word. And if a breakthrough is achieved, they can be rushed by car through the gap to destroy and harass the enemy's rear."

Germany was beginning to rearm. Men like General Erich Ludendorff and General Hans von Seeckt were writing of a war of movement. Herman Goering was advocating air supremacy as the key to world power. President Paul von Hindenburg stated that: "The most vulnerable targets will be the great industrial centers with their fixed populations. I predict that ultimately victory in war will depend on the ability of civilian populations to withstand attack. It will be a question of nerves. That nation will lose whose nerves snap first."

In Yugoslavia, King Alexander's mouth tightened as he showed me his stalwart Serbian divisions being supplied by oxcart.

In Turkey, I talked with that indomitable leader, Mustapha Kemal Ataturk, about his firm determination to rebuild his antiquated armed forces.

In Romania, King Carol II complained that fun and frolic, not preparedness, was predominant.

In Hungary, I heard its regent, Admiral Miklos Horthy, gloomily predict impending disaster.

In Poland, I saw a hundred thousand superb cavalrymen, measured by the standards of fifty years before, and Marshal Józef Pilsudski, its premier, at his wits' end trying to figure a way to avoid certain disaster, caught up geographically as he was between Germany and Russia.

In Czechoslovakia, there was a feverish building of plants that were adaptable for munitions purposes.

And from Russia came the growling mutter of that menacing offspring of Bolshevism and nihilism known as Sovietism.

It was indeed a troubled and confused Europe. What the swift collapse of many of these nations would be before the smash of dive bombers and tanks was startlingly evident. I reported to the Secretary of War: "The next war is certain to be one of maneuver and movement. Even the Lord, Himself, cannot save those who do not move fast. The nation that does not command the air will face deadly odds. Armies and navies to operate successfully must have air cover." He agreed, but Congress remained inert and skeptical.

I stormed, begged, ranted, and roared; I almost licked the boots of certain gentlemen to get funds for motorization and mechanization and air power. I humbled myself seeking allotments to replace leaking, slum-like barracks housing our soldiers. I called for increased speed, increased fire power, fast machines, airplanes, tanks, guns, trucks, and ammunition. "We will be dependent on our air force," I warned, "to defend our coastlines, for attack against hostile ground forces, for bombardment of sensitive points in the enemy's supply organization."

In my five years as chief of staff these are the amounts we received to support both the Army and Air Force:

1931	$347,000,000
1932	335,000,000
1933	304,000,000
1934	277,000,000
1935	284,000,000

Compare this with the fifty billions we now spend for national defense.

Franklin Roosevelt succeeded Herbert Hoover as President. He had greatly changed and matured since our former days in Washington. His political star had risen to its zenith, but poliomyelitis struck him painfully. He became the leading liberal of the age. Whether his vision of economic and political freedom is within the realm of fruition, only future history can tell. That his means for accomplishment won him the almost idolatrous devotion of an immeasurable following is known to all. That they aroused bitterness and resentment in others is equally true. In my own case, whatever differences arose between us, it never sullied in slightest degree the warmth of my personal friendship for him.

His Secretary of War was George Dern. A successful mining executive and former governor of the state of Utah, this sixty-year old Westerner brought to the office a keen interest in military affairs. During the war he had been on the Utah State Council of Defense and was, in consequence, well-versed in matters of national security. He was in thorough agreement with Army plans and was a pillar of support for the military. My esteem for him grew daily.

With the advent of the new Administration, two additional efforts were made to reduce the effectiveness of the military. One was an attempt by the pacifist element in Congress to cut the officer corps of the Regular Army drastically. A bill was introduced to place a large number of officers on a forced furlough list and to reduce their pay by half. Appearing before the House Military Affairs Committee in rebuttal, I pointed out:

The foundation of our National Defense system is the Regular Army, and the foundation of the Regular Army is the officer. He is the soul of the system. If you have to cut everything out of the National Defense Act the last element should be the officer corps. If you had to discharge every soldier, if you had to do away with everything else, I would still professionally advise you to keep those 12,000 officers. They are the mainspring of the whole mechanism; each one of them would be worth a thousand men at the beginning of a war. They are the only ones who can take this heterogeneous mass and make it a homogeneous group.

Congress, however, was not fooled by the false effort at economy and the bill was ultimately tabled.

The second effort at so-called "economy" was, surprisingly enough, from the Executive Branch, and consisted of an announcement from the Bureau of the Budget that in order to balance the budget the Regular Army appropriation, as compared with a normal appropriation, would be cut 51 per cent, the National Guard 25 per cent, the Organized Reserves 33 per cent, the Reserve Officers Training Corps 32 per cent, the Citizens Military Training Corps 36 per cent, and the Rifle Practice Promotion 75 per cent.

The Secretary of War became so alarmed that he requested a private conference with the President. Besides myself, he took with him the Assistant Chief of Staff, General Hugh Drum, and the Chief of Engineers, General Lytle Brown.

The world situation had become too dangerous to allow a weakening of our defense. Germany and Italy were arming in Europe, and in the Orient Japan continued its conquests in Manchuria and China. To economize on our strength at this time could prove a fatal error. But the President was obdurate, and the quiet spoken phrases of Dern were no match for the biting diction of Roosevelt. Under his lashing tongue, the Secretary grew white and silent.

I felt it my duty to take up the cudgels. The country's safety was at stake, and I said so bluntly. The President turned the full vials of his sarcasm upon me. He was a scorcher when aroused. The tension began to boil over. For the third and last time in my life that paralyzing nausea began to creep over me. In my emotional exhaustion I spoke recklessly and said something to the general effect that when we lost the next war, and an American boy, lying in the mud with an enemy bayonet through his belly and an enemy foot on his dying throat, spat out his last curse, I wanted the name not to be MacArthur, but Roosevelt. The President grew livid. "You must not talk that way to the President!" he roared. He was, of course, right, and I knew it almost before the words had left my mouth. I said that I was sorry and apologized. But I felt my Army career was at an end. I told him he had my resignation as Chief of Staff. As I reached the door his voice came with that cool detachment which so reflected his extraordinary self-control, "Don't be foolish, Douglas; you and the budget must get together on this."

Dern had shortly reached my side and I could hear his gleeful tones, "You've saved the Army." But I just vomited on the steps of the White House.

Neither the President nor I ever spoke of the meeting, but from that time on he was on our side. He sent for me frequently and often asked my comments on his social programs, but almost never again on military affairs. One evening, during dinner, curiosity and perhaps some measure of pique prompted me to ask him, "Why is it, Mr. President, that you frequently inquire my opinion regarding the social reforms under consideration, matters about which I am certainly no authority, but pay little attention to my views on the military?" His reply took all the wind out of my sails. He said: "Douglas, I don't bring these questions up for your advice but for your reactions. To me, you are the symbol of the conscience of the American people."

Perhaps the pleasantest memory of that period was my relationship with the Navy. There is no greater myth than the stories of the bitter rivalry between the Army and Navy. Sensational extravagances are so publicized that one would think the two were deadly enemies instead of faithful partners in a common cause. I sat on the Joint Board, a body similar to the present chiefs of staff, and for three years was its chairman, and there was never a question in which the views of all parties were not given full consideration by every member. My brother and nephew died in the uniform of the Navy, and I have always held that magnificent arm in the same admiration and affection I feel for my own branch. In my long association with it, both in war and in peace, it has shown me a loyalty, a devotion, and an efficiency that could not be surpassed. Whenever I have had its components under my command, I have always been astonished at how much better was their performance than I had demanded or had a right to expect.

When my four-year tour as Chief of Staff was ended in 1934, to my surprise, I was retained in the post by President Roosevelt for an additional year. As the end of this additional year approached, Manuel Quezon, now the president-elect of the about-to-be Philippine Commonwealth, arrived in Washington. He had come to discuss the problem of Philippine national defense after his country attained its independence. He bluntly asked me if the islands were defensible. I told him any place could be defended if sufficient men, munitions, and money were available, and above all sufficient time to train the men, to provide the munitions, and to raise the money. He then inquired if I would undertake the task and I told him I would. I emphasized that it would take a full ten years and much help from the United States if it were to be successful. As it turned out, neither was forthcoming. War came in five years, and American help came too late and too little.

Shortly after my talk with Quezon, President Roosevelt called me to Hyde Park. He stated that with the inauguration of the Philippines into a Commonwealth, the governor-generalship would lapse and be replaced by a high commissioner. He offered me the position. It was a flattering proposal but involved my retirement from the Army. So I declined, stating that I had started as a soldier and felt that I should end as one.

No action taken by me while I was chief of staff gave me greater satisfaction than re-establishing the Order of the Purple Heart. It had not been in use for a century and a quarter.

This decoration is unique in several ways: first, it is the oldest in American history, and antedates practically all of the famous military medals of the world; second, it comes from that greatest of all Americans, George Washington, and thereby carries with it something of the reverence which haloes his great name; and third, it is the only decoration which is completely intrinsic in that it does not depend upon approval or favor by any-one. It goes only to those who are wounded in battle, and enemy action alone determines its award. It is a true badge of courage and every breast that wears it can beat with pride.

Before leaving Washington, to my delight, I was awarded a second Distinguished Service Medal. The citation repaid me for much that I had gone through in the frustrating turmoil of those five long years.*

I sailed from San Francisco in the fall of 1935, on the *President Hoover,* accompanied by my mother and a small staff. I was bound again for the Philippines. It was my fifth tour in the Far East—but this one was for keeps.

Within two months after our arrival in Manila my mother died, and our devoted comradeship of so many years came to an end. Of the four of us who had started from the plains of New Mexico, three now were gone, leaving me in my loneliness only a memory of the households we had shared, so filled with graciousness and old-fashioned living. I later brought her remains home to Virginia, where she rests beside my father in the soil of Arlington.

My plan for building a defense for the Philippines was a simple one, patterned after the citizen-soldier system of conscription effectively established in Switzerland. The country was divided into ten military areas, each of which was to train 4,000 men yearly. There was to be a small professional force which would be charged with their development. One hundred and twenty-eight camps were constructed, and trainees were assigned to those nearest their homes. Each camp's permanent training cadre consisted of four

* "As Chief of Staff since November 21, 1930, he has performed his many and exacting duties with signal success. He devised and developed the organization of our land forces; he conceived and established the General Headquarters Air Force, thus immeasurably increasing the effectiveness of our air defenses; he initiated a comprehensive program of modernization in the army's tactics, equipment, training and organization. The professional counsel he has continuously rendered to the President, to the Secretary of War, and to the Congress has been distinguished by such logic, vision, and accuracy as to contribute markedly to the formulation of sound defense policies and the enactment of progressive laws for promoting the nation's security." Equally pleasing was General Pershing's accolade: "I have only praise for General MacArthur as Chief of Staff. He has fully measured up to that high position. He has the clear conception rarely found of the functions of the Chief of Staff and the General Staff, itself. He thoroughly comprehends the requirements necessary to develop the Army, the National Guard and the Reserves into a unified fighting force for National Defense. He is progressive without being radical. His courageous presentations to high authority of his sound views and recommendations have been admirable. By his administration of his office he has won the entire confidence of the Army and Country."

officers and twelve enlisted men. The initial instructional groups were from the Constabulary, which was to become an integral part of the regular army. In addition to the purely military side of the camps, there was a broad effort to build up the health and economic well-being of the trainees, the great majority of whom were from backward rural homes and surroundings. A military academy built on the lines of West Point was established. Supplementing the ground forces, there was to be a naval arm, the backbone of which would be a fleet of fifty small, high-speed, torpedo-throwing craft, and an air force of 250 planes. Eight million dollars a year was the limiting budget. By 1946, when the commonwealth would become independent, the nation would have a trained military force of forty divisions, comprising about 400,000 men. These divisions, whose equipment and weapons were more-or-less obsolete American loans, would be stationed strategically throughout the islands. In the event of crisis, the hope and expectation was that modern weapons would be supplied by the United States. Obstructions arose from the very beginning. A movement of some proportions arose to cancel complete independence and rely solely on the protection of the United States. In addition, as the plan progressed, Japan became concerned, and its propaganda went into high gear to discredit the Quezon-MacArthur team. To quote from a staff report of the period:

"The Philippines are overrun with Japanese political spies—businessmen, sidewalk photographers and bicycle salesmen in every small town and hamlet. One is sure to see them." And secret influences, managed by Soviet Russia, were busy prejudicing the Far East against the United States.

Quezon went before the public to combat the growing doubt and apathy:

The purpose of the plan is to prevent war. Its object is peace without battle. Its possibility of attainment is based upon an adequate defense establishment. This is to be of such strength as to impose such a sort of conquest upon a potential invader as would exclude any hope he might logically entertain of political or economic advantage to be gained by victory. By thus removing any possibility of conquest representing an economic shortcut, the chance of predatory attack would be greatly lessened.

The prospect of peace for the Philippines is properly a hope and ideal for the world, because it would constitute one of the strongest guarantees of tranquility in the Pacific. It is an ideal that can and should be supported by every civilized nation of the world. The Philippine Islands, for obvious reasons, can never be a threat to any other nation in the world.

The difficulties besetting us are great. Defeatists are everywhere. But General MacArthur's faith and hope in the Filipino people have never varied. They have matched even my own faith in my country and in my countrymen.

But his eloquence accomplished little. The quota of trainees was cut by more than half and the budget dropped to $6 million dollars. Opposition grew as propaganda swelled. The United States did nothing.

In vain I pleaded to my countrymen:

The Philippine Army represents one of the most heroic efforts a liberated people has ever made to maintain independence and national integrity. It threatens no one. Its sole purpose is to preserve its country's peace, its democratic principles and its Christian faith. It deserves the complete support of public opinion in the United States and wherever freedom is the guiding spirit of men's lives.

Nothing was forthcoming. On the contrary, the most fantastic statements were falsely attributed to me, such as: "I will make the Philippines impregnable," or "I will turn the Philippines into the Gibraltar of the Pacific." I was charged in high quarters with being a warmonger and threatening the peace of the Far East. All this aroused fear in our State Department that Japan might use them as an excuse to strike. Fred Howe, a trusted advisor to the White House, was asked to investigate and report. Here is what he said:

When I came out here I had been bombarded with statements regarding President Quezon, about the American Army, about a two million man Philippine Army that was being created by General MacArthur, until I hesitated about coming. Much of this came from papers and magazines and friends of a radical sort with whom I have long been associated. And now to my mental amazement I find the same propaganda being made by the imperialists that is being made by portions of the press and my friends back home. I am wondering if our friends are not being used, as they have been used before, to pull the chestnuts out of the fire, for those who want the United States to hold on to the islands, to scuttle President Quezon and discredit General MacArthur, who has won my confidence as few men I have met. Instead of an army of two million I find successive militia groups of twenty thousand men being given six months training with the ultimate objective of an army of four hundred thousand in ten years. Also that the training that they get is in hygiene, in agriculture, in handicraft, and in making them ready to take up homesteads and establish themselves as self-respecting citizens.

But it is the success of President Quezon as an administrator, and of General MacArthur in building a citizen army, designed as a defensive army only, that stands in the way of an imperialistic policy. If President Quezon can be discredited and the trainee system, similar to the Swiss Army, be halted, almost the only alternative is American military and naval protection of the islands. And judging by what I hear from home and the attitude of the imperialistic interests in Manila, that would seem to be the present insidious line of attack; a line of attack in which the pacific minded persons are working hand in glove with the very forces they most fear.

In 1937, I accompanied Quezon when he visited Japan, the United States, and Mexico. Cooped up within the narrow land mass of their four main islands, the Japanese were barely able to feed their burgeoning population. Equipped with a splendid labor force, they lacked the raw materials necessary for increased productivity. They lacked sugar, so they took Formosa. They lacked iron, so they took Manchuria. They lacked hard coal and timber, so they invaded China. They lacked security, so they took Korea. Without the products these nations possessed, their industry could be strangled, millions of their laborers thrown out of work, and an economic disaster precipitated that might easily lead to revolution. They still lacked the nickel and minerals of Malaya, the oil and rubber of the Dutch East Indies, and the rice and cotton of Burma and Siam. It was easy to see that they intended, by force of arms if necessary, to establish an economic sphere completely under their own control. There was nothing in the Philippines they coveted except its strategic position, and Quezon was hopeful to the very end that his country might escape the blow. He was cordially received in Tokyo, but the old friendship toward me had been replaced by a thinly veiled hostility.

Despite a warm welcome in Mexico, Quezon was practically ignored in the United States. My request for supplies and equipment went unheeded by the War Department. But happily, at the Navy Department, when I asked for fast torpedo-carrying motorboats, both Admiral Harold Stark and Admiral William Leahy listened sympathetically, and promised the development of such a craft. It was the beginning of the PT boats in the United States which were later to play a decisive role in the Pacific war.

On the morning of April 30, 1937, I married Jean Marie Faircloth at the Municipal Building in New York. It was perhaps the smartest thing I have ever done. She has been my constant friend, sweetheart, and devoted supporter ever since. How she has managed to put up with my eccentricities and crotchets all these years is quite beyond my comprehension. Jean is from an old aristocratic Southern family of Murfreesboro, Tennessee. Her grandfather, Captain Beard, was a Civil War officer of the 5th Confederate Regiment, of Cleburn's Tennessee Division, which swarmed the 24th Wisconsin at Franklin. Four of her great-uncles were in the Confederate service, one of whom became a distinguished chief justice of the state of Tennessee. Her brothers fought for the Union in both World Wars and Korea. She was a rebel when we were married and still is. I met her on the trip to Manila at a cocktail party given by the skipper of the *President Hoover* for Mayor James M. Curley of Boston. She was with me during Bataan and Corregidor, and the campaigns of the Southwest Pacific Area, and the officers and men were devoted to her. Our son, Arthur, was born on February 21, 1938, and with my little family I would be lonely no more.

New complications began to arise for me. I was under two masters, one the American government, and the other the Philippine government. The growing coolness between Roosevelt and Quezon made my position almost untenable. Roosevelt had become concerned about Hawaii, and wished me to return and take command of both the island and the West Coast. I had, however, given my word to Quezon that I would remain as the military advisor for his full six-year term as president. Moreover, I felt I was blocking promotion by staying on the active list. Generalships being scarce in those days, I settled both problems by retiring from the Army as a four-star general. I had previously been appointed field marshal of the Philippines by the Philippine government, and had received the thanks of the Philippine Congress for my services to the commonwealth.

President Roosevelt sent me a very gracious note, as follows:

Dear Douglas:

With great reluctance and deep regret I have approved your application for retirement effective December 31. Personally, as well as officially, I want to thank you for your outstanding services to your country. Your record in war and in peace is a brilliant chapter of American history.

About a year later I was informed that all financial help to our shipping lines across the Pacific Ocean would be stopped. I could not believe it, but the Dollar Steamship Line servicing the Philippines from the West Coast presented supposedly incontrovertible evidence that the proposal was being seriously studied. As the very life of our military position in the Pacific depended upon keeping open our lines of sea supply, I decided to write the Maritime Commission advising them of the drastic results which would surely follow such action.

As I anticipated, the reply was completely reassuring. It read:

February 1, 1938

My dear General MacArthur:

I want to apologize for my delay in replying to your radiogram of January 5th, but I had so much to do on the West Coast, and since my return this is the first opportunity I have had to write. I want to assure you that the United States Maritime Commission will spare no effort to carry out the mandate outline in the Merchant Marine Act of 1938, under which it is charged with the responsibility not only of maintaining all existing American steamship services engaged in foreign trade, but also of improving and expanding them.

As you may by this time know, all existing services sailing from the Pacific Coast, which have applied for operating subsidies, are now operating under such subsidies, either temporary or permanent, which have been granted by the Commission, and the arrangement arrived at on January 7th, whereby the Commission agreed to grant a temporary subsidy to the Dollar Steamship Line for six months, will make it possible for the continuation of this line during this period in an unimpaired manner. Before the end of that period we shall hope to have worked out some plan whereby this very important service may be placed on a much more stable basis.

For some time the other members of the Maritime Commission, as well as myself, have been acutely conscious of the difficulties which have in the past, and which still do, beset the American Merchant Marine, and it was with a view to obtaining some first hand personal knowledge of those difficulties which are peculiar to the Pacific Coast that I made this trip. I can well appreciate your interest in a matter which is of serious import to you and I pledge the United States Maritime Commission to an earnest endeavor to place the American Merchant Marine in a far more enviable position than that which it now enjoys.

Cordially yours,
Joseph P. Kennedy,
Chairman

By 1939, I had been back in Manila nearly four years, but Washington had not, during this time, offered any meaningful assistance to Filipino defense plans. The Sino-Japanese war had raged openly for two years, the invaders having occupied cities in the interior of China as well as important coastal regions. War clouds, too, hung heavily over Europe. On September 1, 1939, Hitler attacked and successfully overran Poland. The summer and fall of 1940 were filled with disturbing events: the air blitz on England; the uncertainty of the Soviet position after the German spoliation of Poland; our transfer of fifty destroyers to Britain; and the ever-growing threat of Japan.

On May 29, 1941, I received a letter from General George C. Marshall, the American Army chief of staff. It read:

Both Secretary of War Stimson and I are much concerned about the situation in the Far East. During one of our discussions about three months ago it was decided that your outstanding qualifications and vast experience in the Philippines make you the logical choice for the Army Commander in the Far East should the situation approach a crisis. The Secretary has delayed recommending your appointment as he does not feel the time has arrived for such action. However, he has authorized me to tell you that, at the proper time, he will recommend to the President that you be so appointed. It is my impression that the President will approve his recommendation.

On July 27th, I received a second cable from Marshall:

Effective this date there is hereby constituted a command designated as the United States Army Forces in the Far East. This command will include the Philippine Department, forces of the Commonwealth of the Philippines called into the service of the armed forces of the United States for the period of the existing emergency, and such other forces as may be designated to it. Headquarters of the United States Army Forces in the Far East will be established in Manila, Philippine Islands. You are hereby designated as Commanding General, United States Army Forces in the Far East.

I was given the rank of lieutenant general, although my retired rank was that of a full general. Bureaucracy has a strange way of working sometimes, but I had reached a stage of life when I cared little for the reasons of administrators.

We began an eleventh-hour struggle to build up enough force to repel an enemy. The ten-year period so essential for the successful completion of my basic plan was evidently going to be cut in half. Too late, Washington had come to realize the danger. Men and munitions were finally being shipped to the Pacific, but the crucial question was, would they arrive in time and in sufficient strength?

In the meantime, all possible use was being made of available resources. On August 15th, I inducted the Philippine Air Force into the service of the United States. On September 1st, twelve Filipino infantry regiments were also sworn into federal service, and occupied newly enlarged training camps. I pressed Washington hard, and it was clear that the War Department had at last recognized to some extent at least the needs and position of the Philippines.

My weakest element was the air. To correct this deficiency, I sought to develop and equip an efficient air arm, which, with both light and heavy bombers, and adequate protective fighters, would be based on a string of airfields stretching from lower Mindanao northward the 800 miles to upper

Luzon. A supply line was to be established which would run north from Australia, through the Dutch East Indies and Malaya, to Mindanao and Manila. If this could be done, it might change the whole complexion of Philippine strategy from defense to offense. It would place our air power on the flank of Japan's vital sea lanes to the south and, by stifling her raw supplies, cripple her munitions output to such an extent as to disrupt her plans for conquest. But the great factor in all this was time.

The plan met with enthusiastic co-operation from the United States Army Air Corps. In October, nine new B-17 bombers arrived at Clark Field, followed by fifty pursuit planes. But by December our operational force had only reached a strength of thirty-five bombers and seventy-two pursuit planes, less than half the strength originally planned for the Philippine defense force. Airfields, accessories, and munitions were almost entirely lacking.

By December, our ground forces consisted of fewer than 12,000 American troops, about the same number of Filipino Scouts, and 110,000 of the Citizen National Army. Of these, fewer than half were on Luzon, one-third of them had had three months regimental training, one-third two months, and one-third less than one month. They had little artillery, few tanks, and only old Enfield rifles that had been discarded early in the First World War.

Our naval forces, including a regiment of Marines, was not under my command or control. The entire fleet comprised only three cruisers, thirteen destroyers, eighteen submarines, and six PT boats.

For some time Harold Ickes, the Secretary of the Interior, had been interfering in the civil affairs of the commonwealth. The Bureau of Insular Affairs in the War Department had been abolished and its functions taken over by the Interior Department. Secretary Ickes did not believe in early independence for the Philippines, and had unsuccessfully attempted to place an American representative in every branch of the commonwealth government. The issue came to a head on November 27th, with this letter to me from the high commissioner, Francis Sayre:

My dear General MacArthur: In accordance with our conversation of this morning, I am enclosing a copy of a letter of October 7, 1941 from Fiorello La Guardia, the United States Director of Civilian Defense, in which he says, "Confirming our recent conversation, I hereby appoint you Director of Civilian Defense for the Philippine Islands."

As I told you this morning, there must be some mistake, since I have had neither recent conversation nor correspondence with La Guardia. It is apparent that he has not taken into consideration special circumstances obtaining in the Philippine Islands and the progress already achieved in emergency defense measures under the primary responsibility of the Commonwealth Government in conjunction with the advice and cooperation of the military authorities.

I shall appreciate having your views as to what reply should be made to Washington. So that the Director and President Roosevelt may obtain a clear understanding of the situation here, I should appreciate your setting forth in your letter the present status of civilian defense and plans for future activities.

I replied immediately:

I have received your cordial note of November 27th and I concur fully with your thought that the communication from Mr. La Guardia was sent through mistake. The executive power in the Philippine Islands for peace time execution of measures involving extraordinary controls of the civil population are vested in the Commonwealth Government. With the Tydings-McDuffie Act as a basis it enacted emergency laws placing such authority in the hands of its Chief Executive. Accordingly, local measures for civilian defense were initiated several months ago after coordinated discussion between the High Commissioner, the President of the Commonwealth, and the military authorities. A Civilian Emergency Administration for this purpose was constituted operating under the direct control of the President of the Commonwealth. This agency, while a responsibility of the Commonwealth Government, functions with the constant advice and observation of both the High Commissioner's office and the military authorities. It has operated successfully within the natural limitations imposed by local conditions. It would be most unfortunate if any attempt were made to change the present arrangement. The cooperation and complete understanding which now exists between all agencies involved should not be disturbed especially at this critical time.

As the signs of impending conflict became unmistakably clear, I prepared my meager forces, to counter as best I might, the attack that I knew would come from the north, swiftly, fiercely, and without warning.

The Japanese strategic objectives (later determined by captured war records) were complete hegemony in Asia and unchallenged supremacy in the western Pacific. This involved the immediate conquest and subjugation of the Philippines and the capture of the immense natural resources of the Netherlands East Indies and Malaya. The islands represented America's single hope of effective resistance in Southeast Asia, and, given the time and resources, the Philippine Defense Plan would accomplish its long-range objective of making them too costly in men and dollars to attack. Lieutenant General Torashiro Kawabe, deputy chief of the Japanese general staff, joined by Lieutenant General Akira Muto, director of the military affairs bureau of the war ministry, and Lieutenant Colonel Hikaru Haba, intelligence staff, Fourteenth Army, stated that

... an important factor in Japan's decision to invade the Philippines was the fear on the part of the Japanese General Staff of the ten-year plan for the defense of the Philippines. The plan was in its sixth year and a potential menace to Japan's ambitions. The Japanese had to intervene before it was too late.

During one of my staff conferences I had once called the Philippines "the Key that unlocks the door to the Pacific." The Japanese understood this completely, for the Philippines, although not economically necessary to Japan's grandiose scheme, were close to South China and the island stronghold of Formosa, forming not only an obstacle to Japan's international ambitions, but depriving the Rising Sun of a powerful strategic springboard for their drive south and eastward. Flanking the vital sea routes to the south, they were the hub of the transportation system to Southeast Asia and the Southwest Pacific and a direct line of communication to Java, Malaya, Borneo, and New Guinea.

The Japanese planned to isolate the region by destroying Allied naval power in the Pacific and Far Eastern waters, thus severing British and American lines of communication with the Orient. The unsupported garrisons of the Far East would then be overwhelmed and the areas marked for conquest quickly seized. Air attacks launched from progressively advanced airfields would prepare the way for amphibious assaults.

The first major operation would be a crippling attack against the American fleet at Pearl Harbor, followed immediately by advances directed against the Philippines and Malaya, with the invasion of British Borneo following as soon as possible. In the early stages of these campaigns, other striking forces were to seize objectives in Celebes, Dutch Borneo, and southern Sumatra, enabling the forward concentration of aircraft to support the invasion of Java. After the fall of Singapore, northern Sumatra would be occupied, and operations would also be carried out against Burma at an appropriate time in order to cut the Allied supply routes to China. Singapore, Soerabaja, and Manila were expected to become major bases.

The Japanese plan involved the capture of other strategic areas where advance posts could be established, and an outer barrier raised against an Allied counter-offensive. Their scheme of conquest envisaged control of the Aleutians, Midway, Fiji and Samoa, New Britain, New Guinea, points in the Australian area, and the Andaman Islands in the Bay of Bengal. All these would be seized or neutralized when operational conditions permitted.

If the offensive succeeded, the United States would be forced back to Hawaii, the British to India, and China's lifeline would be cut. With this eminently favorable strategic situation and control of the raw materials which they required, the Japanese felt they would be in a position to prosecute the war to a successful conclusion and realize their ambition to dominate the Far East.

My forces were grouped into a number of major commands. The North Luzon Force, under the command of General Jonathan Wainwright, was the most important, being responsible for the defense of the landing beaches at Aparri and Vigan, and the exposed shores of Lingayen Gulf, some 110 miles north of Manila. The South Luzon Force, under General Jones, covered the coast from Batangas to Legaspi. The Lucena Force, under General Parker, defended the Bicol Peninsula. The Visayan Force, under General Chenoy-with, had the central island group, and the Mindanao Force, under General William F. Sharpe, was responsible for that entire island. Corregidor and the harbor defenses were commanded by General Moore, and the Air Force by Major General Lewis H. Brereton. The chief of artillery was General King.

My staff was unsurpassed in excellence, and comprised such outstanding figures as Sutherland, the chief of staff; Marshall in Supply; Casey of the Engineers; Willoughby in Intelligence; Aiken in Communications; Marquat in Artillery. No commander was ever better served.

On November 21st, upon the recommendation of General Brereton, our Bombardment Group of B-17s was moved from Clark Field to Delmonte Field in Mindanao, in order to place it beyond the range of attack from Formosa. Actually, only half of them were withdrawn. I never learned why these orders were not promptly implemented. I realized only too well how small the protecting force of fighters was and how helpless practically undefended Clark Field, with no dispersal areas, would be against heavy air attack.

My orders from Washington were not to initiate hostilities against the Japanese under any circumstances. The first overt move in the Philippine area must come from the enemy. There was apparently some hope that the somewhat indeterminate international position of the commonwealth might eliminate it from attack. This possibility had support not only from Quezon, but from the American chief of staff.

Our pursuit interceptor planes began night patrols on December 4th in territorial waters which extended well out to sea. Each night they located Japanese bombers from 20 to 50 miles out, but these presumed enemy planes turned back before the international line was reached. The last of these night flights was intercepted and turned back at the exact time of the attack on Pearl Harbor.

Whatever might come, we were as ready as we possibly could be in our inadequate defenses, on the night of December 7th. Every disposition had been made, every man, gun, and plane was on the alert.

PART FIVE

*World War II:
Retreat from
the Philippines*

1941–1943

At 3:40 on Sunday morning, December 8, 1941, Manila time, a long-distance telephone call from Washington told me of the Japanese attack on Pearl Harbor, but no details were given. It was our strongest military position in the Pacific. Its garrison was a mighty one, with America's best aircraft on strongly defended fields, adequate warning systems, anti-aircraft batteries, backed up by our Pacific Fleet. My first impression was that the Japanese might well have suffered a serious setback.

We had only one radar station operative and had to rely for air warning largely on eye and ear. At 9:30 A.M. our reconnaissance planes reported a force of enemy bombers over Lingayen Gulf heading toward Manila. Major General Lewis H. Brereton, who had complete tactical control of the Far East Air Force, immediately ordered pursuit planes up to intercept them. But the enemy bombers veered off without contact.

When this report reached me, I was still under the impression that the Japanese had suffered a setback at Pearl Harbor, and their failure to close in on me supported that belief. I therefore contemplated an air reconnaissance to the north, using bombers with fighter protection, to ascertain a true estimate of the situation and to exploit any possible weaknesses that might develop on the enemy's front. But subsequent events quickly and decisively changed my mind. I learned, to my astonishment, that the Japanese had succeeded in their Hawaiian attack, and at 11:45 a report came in of an overpowering enemy formation closing in on Clark Field. Our fighters went up to meet them, but our bombers were slow in taking off and our losses were heavy. Our force was simply too small to smash the odds against them.

Boundaries of the Southwest Pacific Area and the Extent of the Japanese Advance

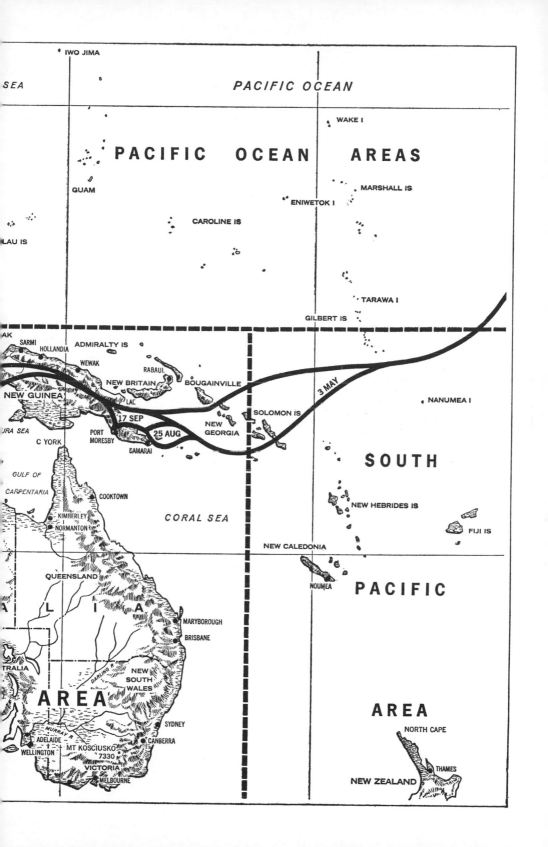

Due to the lack of dispersal fields, the shortage of fighter protectors, and scant supplies, General Brereton recommended that the bombers, the 19th Bombardment Group, under his personal command, be withdrawn to Australia and Java, where they were shortly engrossed in the struggle for the Dutch East Indies. Back in the Philippines, our fighters, with the greatest persistency and many successes, under the brilliant leadership of General George, maintained the unequal struggle before succumbing to inevitable attrition. George's final strike in Subic Bay, sinking an enemy transport with reinforcements aboard, was made with his last four planes.

Sometime in the morning of December 8th, before the Clark Field attack, General Brereton suggested to General Sutherland a foray against Formosa. I know nothing of any interview with Sutherland, and Brereton never at any time recommended or suggested an attack on Formosa to me. My first knowledge of it was in a newspaper dispatch months later. Such a suggestion to the Chief of Staff must have been of a most nebulous and superficial character, as there was no record of it at headquarters. The proposal, if intended seriously, should certainly have been made to me in person. He has never spoken of the matter to me either before or after the Clark Field attack.

As a matter of fact, an attack on Formosa, with its heavy air concentrations, by our small bomber force without fighter cover, which because of the great distance involved and the limited range of the fighters was impossible, would have been suicidal. In contrast, the enemy's bombers from Formosa had fighter protection from their air carriers, an entirely different condition from our own.

A number of statements have been made criticizing General Brereton, the implication being that through neglect or faulty judgment he failed to take proper security measures, resulting in the destruction of part of his air force on the ground. While it is true that the tactical handling of his command, including all necessaries for its protection against air attack of his planes on the ground, was entirely in his own hands, such statements do an injustice to this officer. His fighters were in the air to protect Clark Field, but were outmaneuvered and failed to intercept the enemy. Our air force in the Philippines contained many antiquated models, and were hardly more than a token force with insufficient equipment, incompleted fields, and inadequate maintenance. The force was in process of integration, radar defenses were not yet operative, and the personnel was raw and inexperienced. They were hopelessly outnumbered and never had a chance of winning.

Actually, the ultimate usefulness of our air arm in the Philippines had become academic because of the crippling of the American fleet at Pearl

Harbor. We were operating under the provisions of a basic plan known as Rainbow 5. It provided that our supply lines—the sea lanes—should be kept open by the Navy, and our ground forces should hold out for from four to six months. The Pacific Fleet would then move in with massive force, escorting relieving ground troops. The Navy, being unable to maintain our supply lines, deprived us of the maintenance, the munitions, the bombs and fuel and other necessities to operate our air arm. Our original supplies were meager and were soon exhausted. This naval weakness enabled the enemy to establish a blockade of the Philippines which, without other effort on his part, would shortly render our air power helpless. The stroke at Pearl Harbor not only damaged our Pacific Fleet, but destroyed any possibility of future Philippine air power. Our sky defense died with our battleships in the waves off Ford Island. It cancelled Rainbow 5, and sealed our doom.

Although Admiral King felt that the fleet did not have sufficient resources to proceed to Manila, it was my impression that our Navy deprecated its own strength and might well have cut through to relieve our hard-pressed forces. The Japanese blockade of the Philippines was to some extent a paper blockade. Mindanao was still accessible and firmly held by us. The bulk of the Japanese Navy, operating on tight schedules, was headed south for the seizure of Borneo, Malaya, and Indonesia. American carriers, having escaped destruction at Pearl Harbor, could have approached the Philippines and unloaded planes on fields in Mindanao. The Navy fought the next two years and had great victories without any new ships. They had broken the Japanese code and knew the location of their ships. There was a great reservoir of Allied naval power in the Atlantic Ocean and Mediterranean Sea. A serious naval effort might well have saved the Philippines, and stopped the Japanese drive to the south and east. One will never know.

A top-level decision had long before been reached that the Atlantic war came first, no matter what the cost in the Far East. President Roosevelt and Prime Minister Churchill, in a Washington conference after the Japanese attack on Pearl Harbor, reaffirmed a policy to concentrate first on the defeat of Germany. Until victory was won in Europe, operations in the Pacific would be directed toward containing the Japanese with the limited resources available. General Marshall, the Army Chief of Staff, supported this policy. Unhappily, I was not informed of any of these vital conferences and believed that a brave effort at relief was in the making.

On December 10 the only two Allied capital ships in the whole Western Pacific, the British battleship *Prince of Wales* and the battle cruiser *Repulse,* both commanded by my friend Vice Admiral Sir Tom Phillips, were sunk off the Malayan coast. Sir Tom went down with the *Prince of Wales;* and a whole naval era went down with him. Never again would capital ships venture into hostile waters without air power; Billy Mitchell had been right. Then, after a week's assault, Hong Kong crumbled and surrendered on Christmas Day.

Singapore fell on February 15, 1942. The British were unprepared for a land attack in which Japanese battalions skillfully maneuvered through the formidable jungle growth to bypass and surround strong points; and thus encircled, Lieut. General Sir Arthur Percival surrendered.

Nazi Germany, Japan's ally, had already conquered a large part of Europe, and in the Middle East General Erwin Rommel's armored divisions were attacking the British and Australian troops defending Egypt. But the German armies driving deep into Russia had been stopped before Moscow, and a massive countermove by Russia was beginning to function. I, therefore, recommended that the Soviet Union strike Japan from the north. Such pressure, I felt, supplemented by United States air concentrations in Siberia, would limit the range of Japan's striking power, counter her initial successes, and give time to strengthen the Philippines and the Netherlands East Indies. I believed it would throw Japan from the offensive to the defensive and that it would save the enormous outlay in blood, money, and effort necessary to regain lost ground. I was as insistent on the Russian entrance into the Pacific war at this time as I was against it when we had victory in our grasp.

I dispatched the following message to General Marshall on December 10:

URGENT—SECRET

The mass of enemy air and naval strength committed in the theatre from Singapore to the Philippines and eastward, established his weakness in Japan proper and definite information available here shows that entry of Russia is enemy's greatest fear. Most favorable opportunity now exists, and immediate attack on Japan from north would not only inflict heavy punishment but would at once relieve pressure from objectives of Jap drive to southward. Heavy air attack on Jap objectives would not only pull in much of present widely dispersed air strength but could destroy much of their exposed oil supply. A golden opportunity now exists for a master stroke while the enemy is engaged in over-extended initial air effort.

I received no answer, and, whatever may have transpired, it became evident that the Soviet Union did not elect to engage in hostilities with Japan for the present.

On December 10th, the Japanese began their ground offensive against Luzon. Twelve transports with naval escorts landed troops at Aparri in the north and Vigan on the west coast. Our air force attacked these transports, sinking four and damaging three others. I realized that these landings were only preliminary. The enemy had not yet shown himself in sufficient force for these two operations to be anything but diversionary attacks or security actions to protect the flanks of the main effort yet to come. On December 12th, the Japanese landed in the south at Legaspi under strong naval escort, but again I held back my main forces. At the end of the first week of war there had been many widely scattered actions, but the all-out attack had not yet come. The enemy had carried out fourteen major air raids, but paid dearly in the loss of transports, planes, and troops, and at least two major warships damaged. He had attempted a landing in the Lingayen area, but was repulsed with severe loss by a Philippine Army division. At Aparri, Vigan, and Legaspi there had been only local activity.

I was greatly concerned by the needs of the stricken civilian population, and President Roosevelt authorized me to make available 200-million pesos for relief purposes. I at once turned this amount over to President Quezon.

The second week of war came to a close without the major attack for which I was holding my reserves in readiness. The pattern of the enemy's plans and the direction of his main thrust were not yet revealed. Except for a Japanese landing at Davao in some force, no large-scale operations had taken place, and aerial activity still predominated. The enemy launched twelve major air raids during the week, but for the most part damage was not serious and our casualties were light. Our air force sank two transports at Legaspi, and at Vigan destroyed twenty-five enemy planes which were caught on the ground. By December 21st, the ground fighting was growing in intensity.

I kept a close watch on the low, sloping beaches of Lingayen Gulf, where I had stationed the 11th and 21st Divisions of the Philippine Army at beach defenses. In the deceptive quiet of the gray dawn of December 22nd, the great enemy blow fell at last. A huge invasion force entered Lingayen Gulf in three transport echelons. The first was composed of twenty-seven transports from Takio under the command of Rear Admiral Kensaburo Hara, the second of twenty-eight transports from Mako under Rear Admiral Yoji Nishimura, the third of twenty-one transports from Keelung under Rear Admiral Sueto Hirose. This force of seventy-six transports was supported by three escort units of cruisers, destroyers, and auxiliary craft. The troops convoyed were the Fourteenth Army, commanded by Lieutenant General Masaharu Homma, comprising the 4th, 5th, 16th, 21st, 48th, and 65th Divisions of the Japanese line, a total strength of approximately 80,000 combat troops. This was about twice my own strength on Luzon.

The Japanese knew where to strike. Strength, location, and routes of the American main groupings were accurately plotted on their war maps. More than a year before their invasion, they had made extensive aerial surveys of Northern Luzon, selecting the areas of strategic importance and the points they could best attack. Their objective was the prompt and complete annihilation of the defending forces so as to clear without delay the way to the rich areas that lay to the south.

Two days after the mass landings at Lingayen Gulf, another large Japanese force in twenty-four transports landed at Atimonan, on Lamon Bay, on the east coast of southern Luzon. This was much closer to Manila and central Luzon than the original Japanese elements that had landed far to the south at Legaspi.

With these landings, the strategy of General Homma became immediately apparent. It was obvious he sought to swing shut the jaws of a great military pincer, one prong being the main force that had landed at Lingayen, the other the units that had landed at Atimonan. If these two forces could effect a speedy junction, my main body of troops would have to fight in the comparatively open terrain of central Luzon, with the enemy to the front and to the rear. The Japanese strategy envisaged complete annihilation of the Luzon defense force within a short period. With the principal island of the archipelago under their control, they could look forward to an easy conquest of the remainder of the islands. It was a perfect strategic conception. It would split the South Luzon Force under General Jones from the North Luzon Force under General Wainwright, thus dividing my forces and subjecting them to destruction in detail.

To allow my main bodies to be compressed into the central plain in defense of Manila by an enemy advancing from both directions could only mean early and complete destruction. By retiring into the peninsula, I could exploit the maneuverability of my full forces to the limit and gain our only chance of survival. Our plan of defense, therefore, was that Wainwright would fight a delaying action on successive lines across the great central plain from Lingayen Gulf on the north to the neck of the Bataan Peninsula in the south. Under cover of these delaying actions, Jones with his troops from Manila, in the south, and from the central plain would all be withdrawn into Bataan, where I could pit my own intimate knowledge of the terrain against the Japanese superiority in air power, tanks, artillery, and men.

On Bataan, the main line of resistance would run from Moron, on the coast of the China Sea, to Abucay, on the shore of Manila Bay. If this line was breached, we could drop back to a reserve line some 7 miles to the rear. A third line crossed the Marivales Mountains, the highest part of the peninsula. Still further to the rear, Corregidor, separated from Bataan by 2 miles of water, would serve as the supply base for the Bataan defense and deny the Japanese the use of Manila Harbor, even though they had the city of Manila itself.

The imminent menace of encirclement by greatly superior numbers forced me to act instantly. The problem was to sideslip my troops westward by a series of rapid maneuvers and holding actions to the rocky peninsula and Corregidor forts before their path would be cut off from the north. The crux of the problem was the successful passage of a famous tactical defile—the bridge at Calumpit, just south of San Fernando, where the highway from northern Luzon to Manila joined the highway leading into Bataan. The movement of the southern Luzon force had to be through Manila, a difficult operation in itself. It had then to proceed along the highway to Calumpit, cross the bridge, and pass through San Fernando before it would be safely on the road to Bataan.

The lack of military transportation was solved by using commercial buses and motor vehicles, which were commandeered to speed up the movement of the Southern Luzon Force. Day and night, endless columns of motor transportation moved goods, ammunition, equipment, and medical supplies from Manila to Bataan. Day and night, General Parker, acting as a guard, fended off the pressing enemy.

Bataan itself was quickly organized for a protracted defense by the construction of depot areas in the forests west of Lanao, the development of docks at Cabcaben, Limay, and Lanao, the construction of two general hospitals, and the improvement of the road net, especially along the west coast.

In the north, I designated lines of defense across the central plain for delaying actions, cautioning against possible envelopment and consequent destruction. General Wainwright quickly developed a pattern of defense to cause the maximum of delay to the enemy. He would hold long enough to force the Japanese to take time to deploy in full force, when he would slowly give way, leaving the engineers under General Casey to dynamite bridges and construct roadblocks to bar the way. Again and again, these tactics would be repeated. Stand and fight, slip back and dynamite. It was savage and bloody, but it won time.

The Japanese discovered too late the strategy underlying the movements of my forces behind the curtain of the rearguard actions in both the north and south. Driving with reckless fury, they strove desperately to cut the vulnerable road junction at San Fernando and the bridge defile at Calumpit. At this critical point, I threw in my last reserve supported by a small light tank force under Brigadier General James R. N. Weaver. In a series of costly counter-attacks this force held the enemy long enough for the Southern Force to reach Bataan. When the North Luzon Force reeled back, bruised and battered, it reformed behind the bristling line of battle of the South Luzon Force. It was close—just by a split second—but split seconds are what win battles. Pat Casey's dynamiters, led by Colonel Harry A. Skerry, blew the Calumpit bridge as the Japanese were marching out upon it.

The hazardous timing of this movement was its most notable feature; one slip in the co-ordinated maneuver, and the motor columns from southern Luzon would have been cut off and cornered in Manila. The success of this operation enabled the assembly and reorganization on Bataan of the bulk of my forces, and made possible the subsequent defense of the peninsula. No trained veteran divisions could have executed the withdrawal movement more admirably than did the heterogeneous force of Filipinos and Americans.

On December 24th, Christmas Eve, I evacuated Manila, moving head-quarters to Corregidor, and issued a proclamation on December 26th, declaring Manila an open city:

> In order to spare the metropolitan area from ravages of attack either by air or ground, Manila is hereby declared an open city without the characteristics of a military objective. In order that no excuse may be given for a possible mistake, the American High Commissioner, the Commonwealth Government and all com-batant military installations will be withdrawn from its environs as rapidly as possible. The Municipal Government will continue to function with its police force, reinforced by constabulary troops, so that normal protection of life and property may be preserved. Citizens are requested to maintain obedience to con-stituted authorities and continue the normal processes of business.

Manila, because of the previous evacuation of our forces, no longer had any practical military value. The entrance to Manila Bay was completely cov-ered by Corregidor and Bataan, and, as long as we held them, its use would be denied the enemy. He might have the bottle, but I had the cork.

The Japanese had not expected that our forces would be withdrawn from Manila, intending to fight the decisive battle of the campaign for control of the city. The devastating attack on Pearl Harbor and the subsequent thrusts in Asia left only this one important obstacle in the path of the Japanese on-slaught in the Southwest Pacific. Our tenacious defense against tremendous odds completely upset the Japanese military timetable, and enabled the Allies to gain precious months for the organization of the defense of Australia and the vital eastern areas of the Southwest Pacific. Bataan and Corregidor became a universal symbol of resistance against the Japanese and an inspiration to carry on the struggle until the Allies should fight their way back from New Guinea and Australia, liberate the Philippines, and thus press on to the Japanese homeland itself.

The Japanese themselves realized the important effect of protracted resistance in the Philippines. Their historical records state: "There was an influence, a spiritual influence, exerted by the resistance on Bataan. Not only did the Japanese at home worry about the length of the period of resistance on Bataan, but it served to indicate to the Filipinos that the Americans had not deserted them and would continue to try to assist them."

As for myself, I have always regarded my decision as not only my most vital one of the Philippine defense campaign, but in its corollary consequences one of the most decisive of the war.*

In response to our requests, General Marshall radioed information advising that every effort would be made to send air and troop replacements and reinforcements. But during the year-end conference in Washington again reaffirmed the Allied "Hitler first" strategy, I received this message: "It now appears that the plans for reaching you quickly with pursuit plane support are jeopardized. Your plans and orders are fully approved by the Secretary of War."

My rank was raised to that of full general. I could not but recall that Fort Selden march a half century before, when the next watering hole was always "about ten miles away" and old Sergeant Ripley caustically exploded: "Thank God, Captain, we're holding our own."

On December 28th, I inaugurated guerrilla warfare in the central and southern group of islands. At this time, despite my pleas to Washington, supplies of food and weapons were running dangerously low. General Marshall

---

* During the month of December many congratulatory and encouraging messages were received.

From President Roosevelt:

"My personal and official congratulations on the fine stand you are making. All of you are constantly in our thoughts. Keep up the good work. Warmest regards."

From General Marshall a series of messages:

"The resolute and effective fighting of you and your men, ground and air, has made a tremendous impression on the American people, and confirms confidence in your leadership."

And still later:

"Your reports and those of press indicate splendid conduct of your command and troops. The President and Secretary of War and quite evidently the entire American people have been profoundly impressed with your resistance to Japanese endeavors."

And from *Time* and *Life*, formerly among my most skeptical commentators:

"How right you were. The whole country is with you and for you."

had promised to expend every effort to insure that reinforcements would be sent, and it was upon this promise that I was able to sustain both the civilians and the military.

On January 10th, and again on January 17th, I wired Washington explaining the seriousness of the situation. We had been on half rations for some time now, and the result was becoming evident in the exhausted condition of the men. The limited area occupied by our forces did not offer any means of obtaining food, and we were therefore dependent upon communication by sea, the responsibility for which had passed out of my control. Since the blockade was lightly held, many medium-sized ships could have been loaded with supplies and dispatched along various routes. It seemed incredible to me that no effort was made to bring in supplies. I cannot overemphasize the psychological reaction on the Filipinos. They were able to understand military failure, but the apparent disinterest on the part of the United States was incomprehensible. Aware of the efforts the Allies were making in Europe, their feelings ranged from bewilderment to revulsion.

No one will ever know how much could have been done to aid the Philippines if there had been a determined will-to-win. There was certainly an effort made by the War Department to obtain supply ships and crews. My old friend, Major Pat Hurley, now a brigadier general, was sent to Australia, and Colonel John A. Robenson to Java, but the results were negative. Only three cargo ships reached the Philippines, two at Cebu and one at Anakan, on the north coast of Mindanao.

The crux of the problem lay in the different interpretation given to local problems by Admiral Thomas C. Hart, the naval commander, and myself. He strongly advocated that all air missions be under his command when over water. His criticism of the air force was very sharp, especially after its defeat at Clark Field. Apparently, he was certain that the islands were doomed and made no effort to keep open our lines of supply. In addition to his refusal to risk his ships in resisting the landings made on Luzon, he made no effort to oppose the Japanese blockade. On Christmas Day, he withdrew the bulk of his forces to the Dutch East Indies, where his surface craft were largely destroyed in a series of hopeless naval actions. The naval wireless station on Corregidor, the experienced 4th Regiment of Marines, three gunboats, three minesweepers, six PT boats, and a few other craft, all under Admiral Rockwell, then passed to my command.

During this period, President Roosevelt expressed the debt owed the people of the Philippines for their fight against the aggressor, and pledged Allied efforts for the freedom and independence of the islands. On Corregidor, Manuel Quezon was sworn in for his second term as president of the commonwealth.

Since no significant naval effort was forthcoming, I regrouped my forces on Bataan into two corps. The North Luzon Force now became the I Corps under General Wainwright and occupied the left perimeter, and the II Corps, formerly the South Luzon Force under General Jones came under the command of General Parker, and held the right.

The 4th Marine Regiment, which was under the control of the Navy, was not committed to the heavy fighting on Bataan, being held in reserve for the actual defense of Corregidor, itself. Fighting became heavy along the entire front and the attacks by enemy bombers almost ceaseless. My anti-aircraft ammunition began to dwindle alarmingly, and I was forced to reduce this type of firing to little more than a token effort, with occasional bursts for purposes of deception. The water system and mains on Corregidor and our adjacent fortified islands were practically destroyed, and I had to institute rationing. It was apparent that the enemy was setting up a prepared attack in maximum strength.

On January 10th I received the following epistle:

To: General Douglas MacArthur
    Commander-in-Chief
    United States Army Forces in the Far East
Sir:
    You are well aware that you are doomed. The end is near. The question is how long you will be able to resist. You have already cut rations by half. I appreciate the fighting spirit of yourself and your troops who have been fighting with courage. Your prestige and honor have been upheld.

However, in order to avoid needless bloodshed and to save the remnants of your divisions and your auxiliary troops, you are advised to surrender.

In the meantime, we shall continue our offensive as I do not wish to give you time for defense. If you decide to comply with our advice, send a mission as soon as possible to our front lines. We shall then cease fire and negotiate an armistice. Failing that, our offensive will be continued with inexorable force which will bring upon you only disaster.

Hoping your wise counsel will so prevail that you will save the lives of your troops, I remain,

> Yours very sincerely,
> Commander-in-Chief,
> The Japanese Expeditionary Force

When I failed to respond, they showered our lines with a leaflet reading:

The outcome of the present combat has been already decided and you are cornered to the doom. But, however, being unable to realize the present situation, blinded General MacArthur has stupidly refused our proposal and continues futile struggle at the cost of your precious lives.

Dear Filipino Soldiers!

There are still one way left for you. That is to give up all your weapons at once and surrender to the Japanese force before it is too late, then we shall fully protect you.

We repeat for the last!

Surrender at once and build your new Philippines for and by Filipinos.

Every foxhole on Bataan rocked with ridicule that night.

My food situation had been increasingly prejudiced by the great number of civilians who had fled into Bataan with our army forces. The Japanese had craftily furthered this movement by driving the frightened population of the province of Zambales, just north of Bataan, into our lines, knowing full well we would feed them—a humanitarian measure which cut deeply into our food stocks. I had to establish refugee camps back of our defense positions for many thousands of these forlorn people, mostly old men, women, and children. It forced me to cut the soldiers' ration not only in half, but later to one-quarter of the prescribed allowance. At the end we were subsisting on less than a thousand calories a day. Everywhere was that poignant prayer, "Give us this day our daily bread." The slow starvation was ultimately to produce an exhaustion which became the most potent factor in the destruction of the garrison.

Our headquarters, called "Topside," occupied the flattened summit of the highest hill on the island. It gave a perfect view of the whole panorama of the siege area. As always, I had to see the enemy or I could not fight him effectively. Reports, no matter how penetrating, have never been able to replace the picture shown to my eyes. The Filipinos, even as the smoke pillars of their burning villages dotted the land, were being told that Europe came first. Angry frustration, for citizens and soldiers alike, irritated bruised nerves and increased the sense of heartache and loss. And the enemy, night after night, in the seductive voice of "Tokyo Rose," rubbed raw the wounds by telling them over the radio that defeat and death were to be their fate while America's aid went elsewhere. President Quezon was stunned by the reports of the huge amounts of American supplies now being sent to Russia. His expression of bewildered anger was something I can never forget. As an evidence of assurance to these people suffering from deprivation, destruction, and despair, I deemed it advisable to locate headquarters as prominently as possible, notwithstanding exposure to enemy attack.

They came in a perfect formation of twin-engine bombers, glittering in the brilliant blue sky. Far-off, they looked like silver pieces thrown against the sun. But their currency was death and their appearance a deceit. These were deadly weapons of war and their bomb bays contained a terrible force of destruction. The long white main barracks, a concrete straight line, cracked and splintered like a glass box. The tin edges of the overhanging roof, under the impact of a thousand-pounder, were bent upward like the curvature of a Chinese pagoda. Pieces of the metal whirled through the air like bits of macabre confetti. A 500-pound burst took off the roof of my quarters. Telephone lines snapped and coiled to the ground. The sturdy rails and ties of the local streetcar line were loosed and looped up into meaningless form. The lawn became a gaping, smoking crater. Blue sky turned to dirty gray.

Then came strafing, and again the bombing. Always they followed the same pattern. Their own orders could not have enlightened me more. What I learned, I used to advantage later. They kept it up for three hours. The din was ferocious. The peaceful chirping of birds had been replaced by the shrill scream of dive bombers. The staccato of strafing was answered by the pounding of the anti-aircraft batteries. Machine guns chattered everywhere and ceaselessly. Then they left as shaking earth yielded under this pulverizing attack, and there rose a slow choking cover of dust and smoke and flame.

My new headquarters was located in an arm of the Malinta Tunnel. Carved deep in the rock, the central tunnel was actually the terminal point of a streetcar line. Other passages had been hewn out of the rock and these now housed hospital wards, storerooms, and ammunition magazines. The headquarters was bare, glaringly lighted, and contained only the essential furniture and equipment for administrative procedure. At the sound of the air alarm, an aide and I would make our way out through the crowded civilians seeking shelter in the main passageway, huddled silently in that hunched-down, age-old Oriental squat of patience and stolid resignation, onto the highway to watch the weaving pattern of the enemy's formations.

There was nothing of bravado in this. It was simply my duty. The gunners at the batteries, the men in the foxholes, they too were in the open. They liked to see me with them at such moments. The subtle corrosion of panic or fatigue, or the feeling of just being fed up, can only be arrested by the intervention of the leader. Leadership is often crystallized in some sort of public gesture. For example, in peace, such a gesture might be the breaking of bread as a symbol of hospitality, or with native Indians, the smoking of a peace pipe to show friendship. But in war, to be effective it must take the form of a fraternity of danger welded between a commander and his troops by the common denominator of sharing the risk of sudden death.

I was nevertheless deeply moved by a letter from Quezon:

My dear General MacArthur:

I am writing this letter as the best friend you have ever had and as the President of the Philippines, and I hope you will understand the spirit in which it is written.

I heard from a personal witness the great danger to which you exposed yourself during the raid this afternoon. I hasten to remind you that you owe it to your government and your people, as well as to my government and people, to take no unnecessary risks because if something should happen to you the effect upon the armed forces and the civilian population of the Philippines would be, to say the least, most demoralizing. I am, therefore, appealing to you both as President and friend to save us from that misfortune. And may I add that you have personal obligations to your wife and your boy which require you to be careful of your safety when duty does not compel you to do otherwise.

Devotedly yours,
Manuel Quezon

On January 12th, the Japanese struck in full force. In headlong attacks of unabated fury they tried to break the 20-mile peninsula de Fengo line from Abucay to Mauban. But our intimate knowledge of every inch of that bewildering area paid off. Our artillery, accurately placed in concealed positions for interdiction and flanking fire, completely stopped the bull-like rushes with such heavy slaughter as to leave their infantry, in spite of its great superiority in numbers, baffled and infuriated. They concentrated first on Abucay, our eastern anchor, and for a fleeting moment penetrated. But our counterattack promptly threw them out. They came again five days later, further to the west, but again failed. Again, three days later, in conjunction with a blind assault on Mauban, the western anchor of our line, they struck still further to the west. It was in vain. Attack and counterattack serrated the opposing lines in the bloodiest of hand-to-hand fighting.

Constantly, fresh Japanese troops arrived by transport to replace the enemy's losses. But I could only bury my dead. In all, nearly 100,000 replacements kept their original strength intact. At a critical moment, 150 guns of heavy caliber came in one shipment from Hong Kong. The pressure finally forced us to give ground. My men were beginning to feel the effects of malnutrition, and malaria was taking its toll of their vitality. They were unable to prevent the Japanese from infiltrating across the steep jungle-covered slopes of Mount Natib in the center of the defense line, and by the evening of January 25 General Wainwright had withdrawn from Mauban. We withdrew to our second line from Orion west to Bagac. They tried to storm this line, but were stopped in their tracks. By the end of January, General Homma had to temporarily cease major operations to await substantial reinforcements.

During this waiting period, minor penetrations were attempted into and throughout I Corps sector, but the raiding forces were pinched off and annihilated. A serious attempt to land from the sea on the west coast behind our lines was sealed in and liquidated. All such attacking forces were completely destroyed.

A broadcast from President Roosevelt was incorrectly interpreted, because of poor reception in the Philippines, as an announcement of impending reinforcements. This was published to the troops and aroused great enthusiasm, but, when later corrected, the depression was but intensified.

For the next six weeks the line successfully resisted all attempts at displacement. The enemy ceased his bloody frontal attacks, and Japanese records show that General Homma was on the point of giving up the effort to overwhelm us and substitute a plan to by-pass the islands, merely containing any war effort we might attempt. If only help could have reached the Philippines, even in small form, if only limited reinforcement could have been supplied, the end could not have failed to be a success. It was Japan's ability to continually bring in fresh forces and America's inability to do so that finally settled the issue.

Encouraging and laudatory messages poured in on me from the Allies.*

---

* From President Roosevelt:

"Congratulations on the magnificent stand that you and your men are making. We are watching with pride and understanding and are thinking of you."

From the King of England:

"The magnificent resistance of the forces under your command to the heavy and repeated attacks of an enemy much superior in numbers has filled your allies in the British Empire with profound admiration. Your countrymen must indeed be proud of the United States and Philippine troops who are fighting with such dauntless heroism. I send my congratulations and best wishes to you all. George, R.I."

From Secretary of War Stimson:

"We all think of you. Everyone of us is inspired to greater efforts by the heroic and skillful fight which you and your men are making."

And later:

"The superb courage and fidelity of you and Quezon are fully recognized by the President and everyone of us."

From General Pershing:

"Heartiest congratulations to you and the brave members of your command for the splendid fight you are making."

From General Marshall:

Many of our state legislatures voted the "Thanks of the State." Cities and mayors and civic organizations all voiced deep acclaim. I was awarded the Distinguished Service Star of the Philippine government, the counterpart of our Distinguished Service Cross.

There was one radio broadcast, however, which disturbed me greatly. It was from General Aguinaldo, who spoke as follows:

As one of your loyal friends, I wish to open my heart to you and make this appeal at this critical moment confronting our people. It was, and still is, my earnest desire to spare the Philippines from the ravages of war and let my countrymen continue enjoying peace and prosperity.

It is to my great regret that the present war broke out between Japan and the United States with the result that the Philippines has become a battleground. Loss has been heavy to both life and property. Numerous families were driven away from their homes, suffering hunger, misery and all sorts of untold hardships. Many costly public improvements, including bridges, roads, railroads, shipyards, docks, piers, airdromes, have been destroyed. In some instances even private houses have been reduced to ashes. Hundreds and thousands of Filipinos, civilians as well as those in active military service, have paid dearly with their lives, their tribute to the war. My countrymen had to take up arms against the Japanese Army for the simple reason that the Philippines was under the American flag. Now conditions are changed. With most of the country already occupied by the Japanese Army, the fate of the Philippines is definitely decided. To continue fighting against the Japanese Army is not only futile, it will also bring about more useless sacrifices and disaster on the part of the Filipinos. It will compel American soldiers under your command to continue fighting a hopeless war.

My dear General: You have so often said that you are always desirous of promoting the welfare of the Filipinos; you have so often expressed your affection for my people. You declared Manila an open city in order to avoid unnecessary loss of the lives and property of innocent civilians. I am firmly convinced of your affection for the Philippines and your humanitarian attitude to all. Now that most of the Philippines is occupied by Japanese forces, it is beyond my comprehension why resistance should be continued. Such resistance would exact further sacrifice on the Filipinos, without any effect to the Americans.

I honestly recommend, as one of your old friends, that you pay due consideration to humanity and stop this useless fighting against the Japanese Army and thereby avoid wanton loss of life and property not only to Filipinos but to Americans as well, if you really feel, as I believe you do, sincere affection for the

---

"The magnificent fight of American and Filipino soldiers under your dynamic leadership already has become an epic of this war and an inspiration to the nation. The successes of your troops and your name headline the news of the day. You are rendering a service of incalculable value to the country. The Japanese Army you are holding in check is prevented from reinforcing the enemy's attacks to the southward which gives us the fighting chance to build up the concentrations necessary to break through his widely overextended operations. May the good Lord watch over you and your devoted men."

soldiers under your command, both Filipino and American. As one of your sincere friends, I honestly urge you to stop this useless resistance against the Japanese Army. Surrender with honor, such as that made by the defenders of Hong Kong, Wake Island, and Guam after heroic resistance. You will not affect your brilliant military record. On the contrary, your humanitarian sentiment, which is not incompatible with military valor, will stand out and receive the fullest appreciation.

Japan, through her prime minister, has promised us prompt independence with honor, declaring in the Diet of January 21, 1942: "Japan will gladly grant the Philippines its independence so long as it cooperates and recognizes the Japanese program of establishing a greater East Asia co-prosperity sphere suspensive points."

We Filipinos want independence. It is our earnest desire to restore the peace destroyed by this war. I hope that you will understand that I have no other motive than the well-being of our people and other nationals living in the Philippines. I now appeal to you frankly, from one soldier to another, and express my true sentiments, believing that in your heart of hearts, you share my deep concern for the welfare of our people and the brave men under your command.

Hearty greetings from your sincere friend and comrade.

I informed Washington at once of the message and received this reply from General Marshall:

It appears to the War Department that the only way to combat statements such as that issued by Aguinaldo is to have our propaganda agencies here contrast against the Aguinaldo attitude the position, example, and statements of President Quezon with the purpose of exciting admiration for the latter and contempt for the former. This effort will be undertaken immediately all over the world and in appropriate languages coupled with this will be a program of contrasting the proved record of the United States in the Philippines with that of Japan in China and Manchuria. The purpose will be to show that if Aguinaldo is sincere in his statement he is merely being deceived by insincere and worthless promises. An important part of our publicity will be the glorification of Filipino loyalty and heroism.

Our troops were now approaching exhaustion. The guerrilla movement was going well, but on Bataan and Corregidor the clouds were growing darker. My heart ached as I saw my men slowly wasting away. Their clothes hung on them like tattered rags. Their bare feet stuck out in silent protest. Their long bedraggled hair framed gaunt bloodless faces. Their hoarse, wild laughter greeted the constant stream of obscene and ribald jokes issuing from their parched, dry throats. They cursed the enemy and in the same breath cursed and reviled the United States; they spat when they jeered at the Navy. But their eyes would light up and they would cheer when they saw my battered, and much reviled in America, "scrambled egg" cap. They would gather round and pat me on the back and "Mabuhay Macarsar" me. They would grin—that ghastly skeleton-like grin of the dying—as they would roar in unison, "We are the battling bastards of Bataan—no papa, no mama, no Uncle Sam."

They asked no quarter and they gave none. They died hard—those savage men—not gently like a stricken dove folding its wings in peaceful passing, but like a wounded wolf at bay, with lips curled back in sneering menace, and always a nerveless hand reaching for that long sharp machete knife which long ago they had substituted for the bayonet. And around their necks, as we buried them, would be a thread of dirty string with its dangling crucifix. They were filthy, and they were lousy, and they stank. And I loved them.

As the days slipped by with no serious effort being made to reinforce the Philippines, Quezon became increasingly aroused. He wrote:

We are before the Bar of History and God only knows if this is the last time that my voice will be heard before going to my grave.

My loyalty and the loyalty of the Filipino people have been proven beyond question. Now we are fighting by her side under your command, despite overwhelming odds. But it seems to me questionable whether any government has the right to demand loyalty from its citizens beyond its willingness or ability to render actual protection.

The war is not of our making. Those that had dictated the policies of the United States could not have failed to see that this is the weakest point in American territory. From the beginning they should have tried to build up our defenses. As soon as the prospects looked bad to me, I telegraphed President Roosevelt requesting him to include the Philippines in the American defense program. I was given no satisfactory answer.

When I tried to do something to accelerate our defense preparations, I was stopped from doing it.

Despite all this we never hesitated for a moment in our stand. We decided to fight by your side and we have done the best we could and we are still doing as much as could be expected from us under the circumstances. But how long are we going to be left alone? Has it already been decided in Washington that the Philippines front is of no importance and that, therefore, no help can be expected here in the immediate future, or at least before our power of resistance is exhausted? If so, I want to know, because I have my own responsibility to my countrymen whom, as President of the Commonwealth, I have led into a complete war effort. I am greatly concerned as well regarding the soldiers I have called to the colors and who are now manning the firing line. I want to decide in my own mind whether there is justification in allowing all these men to be killed, when for the final outcome of the war the shedding of their blood may be wholly unnecessary. It seems that Washington does not fully realize our situation nor the feelings which the apparent neglect of our safety and welfare have engendered in the hearts of the people here.

Some time ago, I telegraphed the President of the United States about this matter. I did not receive even one word of acknowledgment. Is the sacrifice that I, members of my government, and my whole family are making here, of no value at all?

I am confident that you will understand my anxiety about the long-awaited reinforcements and trust you will again urge Washington to insure their early arrival.

I forwarded the letter immediately to Washington, and President Roosevelt replied to President Quezon as follows:

I have read with complete understanding your letter to General MacArthur. I realize the depth and sincerity of your sentiments with respect to your inescapable duties to your own people and I assure you that I would be the last to demand of you and them any sacrifice which I considered hopeless in the furtherance of the cause for which we are all striving. I want, however, to state with all possible emphasis that the magnificent resistance of the defenders of Bataan is contributing definitely toward assuring the completeness of our final victory in the Far East. While I cannot now indicate the time at which succor and assistance can reach the Philippines, I do know that every ship at our disposal is bringing to the southwest Pacific the forces that will ultimately smash the invader and free your country. Every day gained for building up the forces is of incalculable value and it is in the gaining of time that the defenders of Bataan are assisting us so effectively.

I have no words in which to express to you my admiration and gratitude for the complete demonstration of loyalty, courage and readiness to sacrifice that your people, under your inspired leadership, have displayed. They are upholding the most magnificent traditions of a free democracy.

Quezon responded to Roosevelt's noble words, and broadcast to his people: "I urge every Filipino to be of good cheer, to have faith in the patriotism of valor of our soldiers in the field, but above all, to trust America. The United States will win this war, America is too great and too powerful to be vanquished in this conflict. I know she will not fail us."

But, as no relief came to the Philippines, the constant flow of radio speeches from America telling of the enormous economic output of munitions going to Europe threw him into a state of extreme agitation. It was the Atlantic war, not the Japanese, that was bothering Washington in those days, and Quezon felt the Philippines were being given, in the slang of the day, the "brush-off." Sitting in his wheelchair and racked by tuberculosis, he felt caged and frustrated whenever he heard the barrage of voices telling Americans about the thousands of aircraft that would shortly be coming from the assembly lines and on their way—across the Atlantic. Doña Aurora, his devoted wife, tried to calm him, but with little success. Bitter denunciations began to pour from his lips. He told Colonel Charles Willoughby, my versatile G-2, who speaks fluent Spanish: "For thirty years I have worked and hoped for my people. Now they burn and die for a flag that could not protect them. I cannot stand this constant reference to Europe. I am here and my people are here under the heels of a conqueror. Where are the planes that they boast of? America writhes in anguish at the fate of a distant cousin, Europe, while a daughter, the Philippines, is being raped in the back room."

Quezon finally composed a bitter letter to Roosevelt in which he proposed that the United States grant the Philippines complete independence at once, to be followed by a protocol between the United States and Japan under which the islands would be declared a neutral area. With Filipino military forces demobilized, the Philippines would be no longer a battleground. The message said in part:

After nine weeks of fighting not even a small amount of aid has reached us from the United States. Help and assistance have been sent to other belligerent nations, viz., the Netherlands East Indies, Australia, Ireland, England, Russia and possibly others; however, not only has nothing arrived here but seemingly no attempt has been made to transport anything here. The British and American Navies, the two strongest fleets in existence, have seemingly pursued a strategy that excludes any attempt to bring aid to the Philippines. Consequently, while perfectly safe itself, the United States has practically doomed the Philippines to almost total extinction to secure a breathing space. You have assured us eventual liberation, but what is needed is present help and preservation.

I speak the undivided sentiment of my war cabinet and I am confident the equally undivided sentiment of all my fellow countrymen that conditions being what they are we should initiate measures to save the Filipinos and the Philippines from further disaster. Because of sagacious strategy two-thirds of the Philippines is up to now uninvaded.

We do not suggest that the foregoing be accomplished by a breach of faith with the United States. It appears to us that our purpose is only to battle without hope for as long a period as possible in order to aid in defending other areas. However, there is no necessity to sacrifice the Filipinos to gain final victory. Officials of your government have asserted again and again that the war against Hitler would be the determining factor in the final outcome of the world conflict. I think that the basic facts here can be evolved into a solution which will spare my native land further destruction as the arena of two mighty nations.

Then followed his proposals. The message was shown to High Commissioner Sayre, who agreed with President Quezon.

I remonstrated with Quezon as best I could against the proposals involved, and said bluntly I would not endorse them, that there was not the slightest chance of approval by either the United States or Japan. Quezon listened patiently and then revealed his true purpose in sending the message. He said he fully realized that his plan would not be accepted by either country and that it was entirely impractical. But that he felt that only something of an explosive nature could shock Washington into a realization of the importance of the Far East. He said such action was necessary to concentrate immediate attention or it would be too late, even if the Allies won the war in Europe. He explained that he did not expect me to approve his suggestions, but asked that I present the military situation in a purely professional light. This I did, and asked Washington to instruct me.

The message startled Washington and genuinely disturbed the President, Secretary Stimson, and General Marshall. Finally, I received this answer from President Roosevelt to my request for instructions:

My reply must emphatically deny the possibility of this government's agreement to the political aspects of President Quezon's proposal. I authorize you to arrange for the capitulation of the Filipino elements of the defending forces, when and if in your opinion that course appears necessary and always having in mind that the Filipino troops are in the service of the United States. Details of all necessary arrangements will be left in your hands, including plans for segregation of forces and the withdrawal, if your judgment so dictates, of American elements to Fort Mills. The timing also will be left to you.

American forces will continue to keep our flag flying in the Philippines so long as there remains any possibility of resistance. I have made these decisions in complete understanding of your military estimate that accompanied President Quezon's message to me. The duty and the necessity of resisting Japanese aggression to the last transcends in importance any other obligation now facing us in the Philippines.

I therefore give you this most difficult mission in full understanding of the desperate nature to which you may shortly be reduced. The service that you and the American members of your command can render to your country in the titanic struggle now developing is beyond all possibility of appraisement.

I immediately replied: "I have not the slightest intention in the world of surrendering or capitulating the Filipino forces of my command. I intend to fight to destruction on Bataan and then do the same on Corregidor." Quezon's message marked a change in the Pacific war. From that point, things began to get better.

General Marshall had suggested that Mrs. MacArthur and Arthur be evacuated by submarine. The tactical picture was worsening almost minute by minute; this might be the last opportunity for sure deliverance of the two human beings dearest to me. The Quezons implored me to agree; they and the Sayres planned to leave at once. It was one of the desperate moments of my life, but even before I spoke to Jean I knew the answer. When I returned to the Quezons, I said simply, "She will stay with me to the end. We drink from the same cup." I heard the convulsive gasp of Doña Aurora, and Quezon's eyes filled, but they said no word. They understood.

I answered Marshall's sympathetic suggestion: "I and my family will share the fate of the garrison." The following day he responded that he was concerned by those words. His message contained the implication that a further assignment for me could very well force me from my family, under conditions of even greater danger, and from the valiant garrison whose fate I had pledged us to share.

The High Commissioner and Mrs. Sayre left on February 20th by submarine for Australia, followed by the Quezons. Manuel slipped the signet ring he always wore from his finger to mine, and said in broken words, "When they find your body, I want them to know you fought for my country." They were my son's godparents, and I held them in deepest affection.

On February 21st—Arthur's fourth birthday—Marshall notified me that the President was considering ordering me to Mindanao to set up a new base of operations for the defense of the southern part of the Philippines. The same day the cabinet in Canberra had requested my immediate assignment to Australia as commander of the newly formed Southwest Pacific Area. When Prime Minister Curtin's recommendation reached the White House, President Roosevelt personally sent me a message to proceed as soon as possible to Mindanao. There I was to do what I could to buttress defenses, then go on to Australia.

My first reaction was to try and avoid the latter part of the order, even to the extent of resigning my commission and joining the Bataan force as a simple volunteer. But Dick Sutherland and my entire staff would have none of it. They felt that the concentration of men, arms, and transport which they believed was being massed in Australia would enable me almost at once to return at the head of an effective rescue operation. They also suggested that I might seek to delay my departure. For two days I delayed a final decision. Finally, I answered the President in a message that warned of the results that might follow the failure to adequately sustain the Philippines. Because of the very special confidence the Filipino people and army had in me, my sudden departure might set off a collapse of the Filipino defenses. I therefore requested authorization to delay my departure.

"Please be guided by me in this matter," I concluded. "I know the situation here in the Philippines and unless the right moment is chosen for so delicate an operation a sudden collapse might result. These people are depending upon me now, any idea that might develop in their minds that I was being withdrawn for any other reason than to bring them immediate relief could not be explained."

Two days later Marshall replied, advising me that the decision as to my departure was to be left up to me. I began seriously to weigh the feasibility of trying to break through from Bataan into the Zambales Mountains, to carry on intensified guerrilla operations against the enemy. For three weeks I postponed my leaving until Marshall responded with the information that the situation in Australia called for my early arrival.

My first care was the selection of those who were to accompany me. Besides my family, there were seventeen servicemen. They were chosen because of their anticipated contribution to the liberation of the Philippines and largely formed the subsequent staff of the Southwest Pacific Area. Two naval officers, Rear Admiral II. G. Rockwell and Captain Harold G. Ray, were selected on the basis of their general usefulness to the United States.

My detractors would have seized on any selection as an opportunity for further criticism. Virulent stories gained currency and grew with the telling. One, widely retailed with apparent relish, suggested that seriously ill American nurses had been left on Corregidor so that the PT boats could transport furniture (one version included the piano) from my Manila Hotel apartment. The fact is that no member of that group who left the Rock, including myself and the members of my family, was allowed more than one suitcase. There was no other baggage of any kind. Another excuse for angry criticism was the fact that Ah Cheu, the Cantonese nurse, went out with us. Few people outside the Orient know how completely a member of the family an *amah* can become, and Ah Cheu had been with us since Arthur's birth. Because of her relationship to my family, her death would have been certain had she been left behind.

I had decided to try and pierce the blockade with PT boats rather than go under with a submarine. The PT's, 77 feet of light plywood, under the command of Lieutenant John D. Bulkeley, were powered by Packard motors which had been slowed below top performance of 40 knots by long and arduous service, but were still capable of giving a Japanese cruiser or destroyer a run for its money. Bulkeley ordered the boats into roughly a diamond formation that would afford the best position for launching any of the sixteen torpedoes, each capable of sinking a destroyer or a cruiser. The plan was to attack at once if we were sighted by Japanese surface craft, sending out a co-ordinated salvo of torpedo fire. After that we would have to depend on our superior, high-speed maneuverability.

I sent for General Wainwright, who was to be left in command to tell him goodbye. He had been a plebe at West Point when I was a first classman and later became the First Captain of the Class of 1906. A fine soldierly figure, he had already done wonders in the campaign, and was popular with both officers and men. "Jim," I told him, "hold on till I come back for you." I was to come back, but it would be too late—too late for those battling men in the foxholes of Bataan, too late for the valiant gunners at the batteries of Corregidor, too late for Jim Wainwright.

It was 7:15 on the evening of March 11th when I walked across the porch to my wife. "Jean," I said gently, "it is time to go." We drove in silence to the South Dock, where Bulkeley and PT-41 were waiting; the rest of the party was already aboard. Shelling of the waterfront had continued intermittently all day. I put Jean, Arthur, and Ah Cheu on board, and then turned slowly to look back.

On the dock I could see the men staring at me. I had lost 25 pounds living on the same diet as the soldiers, and I must have looked gaunt and ghastly standing there in my old war-stained clothes—no bemedaled commander of inspiring presence. What a change had taken place in that once-beautiful spot! My eyes roamed that warped and twisted face of scorched rock. Gone was the vivid green foliage, with its trees, shrubs, and flowers. Gone were the buildings, the sheds, every growing thing. The hail of relentless bombardment had devastated, buried, and blasted. Ugly dark scars marked smouldering paths where the fire had raged from one end of the island to the other. Great gaps and forbidding crevices still belched their tongues of flame. The desperate scene showed only a black mass of destruction. Through the shattered ruins, my eyes sought "Topside," where the deep roar of the heavy guns still growled defiance, with their red blasts tearing the growing darkness asunder. Up there, in command, was my classmate, Paul Bunker. Forty years had passed since Bunker had been twice selected by Walter Camp for the All-American team. I could shut my eyes and see again that blond head racing, tearing, plunging—210 pounds of irresistible power. I could almost hear Quarterback Charley Daly's shrill voice barking, "Bunker back." He and many others up there were old, old friends, bound by ties of deepest comradeship.

Darkness had now fallen, and the waters were beginning to ripple from the faint night breeze. The enemy firing had ceased and a muttering silence had fallen. It was as though the dead were passing by the stench of destruction. The smell of filth thickened the night air. I raised my cap in fare-well salute, and I could feel my face go white, feel a sudden, convulsive twitch in the muscles of my face. I heard someone ask, "What's his chance, Sarge, of getting through?" and the gruff reply, "Dunno. He's lucky. Maybe one in five."

I stepped aboard PT-41. "You may cast off, Buck," I said, "when you are ready."

Although the flotilla consisted of only four battle-scarred PT boats, its size was no gauge of the uniqueness of its mission. This was the desperate attempt by a commander-in-chief and his key staff to move thousands of miles through the enemy's lines to another war theater, to direct a new and intensified assault. Nor did the Japanese themselves underestimate the significance of such a movement. "Tokyo Rose" had announced gleefully that, if captured, I would be publicly hanged on the Imperial Plaza in Tokyo, where the Imperial towers overlooked the traditional parade ground of the Emperor's Guard divisions. Little did I dream that bleak night that five years later, at the first parade review of Occupation troops, I would take the salute as supreme commander for the Allied Powers on the precise spot so dra-matically predicted for my execution.

The tiny convoy rendezvoused at Turning Buoy just outside the mine-field at 8 P.M. Then we roared through in single file, Bulkeley leading and Admiral Rockwell in PT-34 closing the formation.

On the run to Cabra Island, many white lights were sighted—the enemy's signal that a break was being attempted through the blockade. The noise of our engines had been heard, but the sound of a PT engine is hard to differentiate from that of a bomber, and they evidently mistook it. Several boats passed. The sea rose and it began to get rough. Spiteful waves slapped and snapped at the thin skin of the little boats; visibility was becoming poorer.

As we began closing on the Japanese blockading fleet, the suspense grew tense. Suddenly, there they were, sinister outlines against the curiously peace-ful formations of lazily drifting cloud. We waited, hardly breathing, for the first burst of shell that would summon us to identify ourselves. Ten seconds. Twenty. A full minute. No gun spoke; the PT's rode so low in the choppy seas that they had not spotted us.

Bulkeley changed at once to a course that brought us to the west and north of the enemy craft, and we slid by in the darkness. Again and again, this was to be repeated during the night, but our luck held.

The weather deteriorated steadily, and towering waves buffeted our tiny, war-weary, blacked-out vessels. The flying spray drove against our skin like stinging pellets of birdshot. We would fall off into a trough, then climb up the near slope of a steep water peak, only to slide down the other side. The boat would toss crazily back and forth, seeming to hang free in space as though about to breach, and then would break away and go forward with a rush. I recall describing the experience afterward as what it must be like to take a trip in a concrete mixer. The four PT's could no longer keep formation, and by 3:30 A.M. the convoy had scattered. Bulkeley tried for several hours to collect the others, but without success. Now each skipper was on his own, his rendezvous just off the uninhabited Cuyo Islands.

It was a bad night for everybody. At dawn, Lieutenant (j.g.) V. E. Schumacher, commander of PT-32, saw what he took for a Jap destroyer bearing down at 30 knots through the early morning fog. The torpedo tubes were instantly cleared for action, and the 600-gallon gasoline drums jettisoned to lighten the vessel when the time came to make a run for it. Just before the signal to fire, the onrushing "enemy" was seen to be the PT-41—mine.

The first boat to arrive at Tagauayan at 9:30 on the morning of March 12 was PT-34, under the command of Lieutenant R. G. Kelly. PT-32 and Bulkeley's PT-41 arrived at approximately 4 P.M. with PT-32 running out of fuel; those aboard were placed on the two other already crowded craft. A submarine which had been ordered to join us at the Cuyos did not appear. We waited as the day's stifling heat intensified, still spots on the water camouflaged as well as possible from the prying eyes of searching enemy airmen. Hours passed and at last we could wait no longer for Ensign A. B. Akers' PT-35 (it arrived two hours after we left). I gave the order to move out southward into the Mindanao Sea for Cagayan, on the northern coast. This time Rockwell's boat led and PT-41 followed. The night was clear, the sea rough and high.

Once more, huge and hostile, a Japanese warship loomed dead ahead through the dark. We were too near to run, too late to dodge. Instantly we cut engines, cleared for action—and waited. Seconds ticked into minutes, but no signal flashed from the battleship as she steamed slowly westward across our path. If we had been seen at all, we had been mistaken for part of the native fishing fleet. Our road to safety was open.

We made it into Cagayan at 7 A.M. on Friday, March 13. I called together the officers and men of both PT's. "It was done in true naval style," I told them. "It gives me great pleasure and honor to award the boats' crews the Silver Star for gallantry for fortitude in the face of heavy odds."

Brigadier General William F. Sharp, commander of the Visayan-

Mindanao Force, greeted me on landing, and reported all was well with his troops. Davao was in enemy hands, but if Bataan fell, his plans for intensified guerrilla warfare were well advanced.

Four B-17's from Australia had been scheduled to meet our party. One had crashed in the waters offshore, two never reached Cagayan, and the fourth was so dangerously decrepit that General Sharp had ordered it back empty to Australia before our arrival. Of three more planes dispatched for us, two arrived around 8 P.M. on March 16. They were in bad shape, tied together, as their pilots said, "with chewing gum and baling wire." We took off from the Del Monte strip shortly after midnight on March 17th, the plane in which I was traveling rattling down the runway with one engine sparking and missing. We would be flying over enemy-held territory, relying on darkness to help us evade Japanese patrols. Over Timor, we were spotted and they came up after us. But we changed course from Darwin, where they figured we would land, and came in at Batchelor Field, 40 miles to the south, just as they hit the Darwin field. They discovered their mistake too late, and their dive bombers and fighters roared in at Batchelor ten minutes after I had left in another plane for Alice Spring to the south.

"It was close," I remarked to Dick Sutherland when we landed, "but that's the way it is in war. You win or lose, live or die—and the difference is just an eyelash."

When we arrived at Batchelor Field, reporters pressed me for a statement. I said: "The President of the United States ordered me to break through the Japanese lines and proceed from Corregidor to Australia for the purpose, as I understand it, of organizing the American offensive against Japan, a primary object of which is the relief of the Philippines. I came through and I shall return."

I spoke casually enough, but the phrase "I shall return" seemed a promise of magic to the Filipinos. It lit a flame that became a symbol which focused the nation's indomitable will and at whose shrine it finally attained victory and, once again, found freedom. It was scraped in the sands of the beaches, it was daubed on the walls of the *barrios,* it was stamped on the mail, it was whispered in the cloisters of the church. It became the battle cry of a great underground swell that no Japanese bayonet could still.

Conditions on Bataan rapidly approached a climax, and rumors reached me of an impending surrender. I at once radioed General Marshall, informing him that under any circumstances or conditions I was utterly opposed to the ultimate capitulation of the Bataan command. If Bataan was to be destroyed, it should have been on the field of battle in order to exact full toll from the enemy. To this end, I had long ago prepared a comprehensive plan for cutting a way out if food or ammunition failed. This plan contemplated an ostentatious artillery preparation on the left by the I Corps as a feint, a sudden surprise attack on the right by the II Corps, taking the enemy's Subic Bay positions in reverse, then a frontal attack by the I Corps. If successful, the supplies seized at this base might well rectify the situation. If the movement was unsuccessful, and our forces defeated, many increments thereof, after inflicting important losses upon the enemy, could escape through the Zambales Mountains and continue guerrilla warfare in conjunction with forces now operating in the north. I told him I would be very glad to rejoin the command temporarily and take charge of this movement.

But Washington failed to approve. Had it done so, the dreadful "Death March" which followed the surrender, with its estimated 25,000 casualties, would never have taken place.

The light finally failed. Bataan starved into collapse. I knew it was coming, but actual word of the surrender came to me as a shock. Corregidor capitulated soon after. Its surrender included all our armed forces in the islands and dealt a destructive blow to the guerrilla movement. Up to then, the Japanese had been largely confined to the cities, and the countryside had been kept comparatively free. It forced me to start from the bottom again.

When word of the disaster reached me, I wrote out my final tribute to the courage and resistance of the men who had held the entrance of Manila Bay inviolate for five months. "Corregidor needs no comment from me. It has sounded its own story at the mouth of its guns. It has scrolled its own epitaph on enemy tablets. But through the bloody haze of its last reverberating shot, I shall always seem to see a vision of grim, gaunt, ghastly men, still unafraid." The bitter memories and heartaches will never leave me.

It was not until several months later, when three Americans who escaped prison with the help of the guerrillas and were later brought to Brisbane by submarine told me the story, that I received the agonizing details of the "Death March" and the atrocities of the prison camps in which its survivors were confined.

I directed the issuance of the story to the press, but that very day Washington forbade the release of any of the details of the prisoner-of-war atrocities. Perhaps the Administration, which was committed to a Europe-first effort, feared American public opinion would demand a greater reaction against Japan, but whatever the cause, here was the sinister beginning of the "managed news" concept by those in power. Here was the first move against that freedom of expression so essential to liberty. It was the introduction, under a disarming slogan, of a type of censorship which can easily become a menace to a free press and a threat to the liberties of a free people.

Not a word of the atrocities practiced by its soldiery was published in Japan itself, and when the truth came out after the surrender, it shocked the fine sensibilities of the Japanese public as much as it did those of the Americans and their allies.

I was awarded the Medal of Honor for my role in the Philippines, but the road back looked long and difficult.*

* "For conspicuous leadership in preparing the Philippine Islands to resist conquest, for gallantry and intrepidity above and beyond the call of duty in action against invading Japanese forces, and for the heroic conduct of defensive and offensive operations on the Bataan Peninsula. He mobilized, trained and led an army which has received world acclaim for its gallant defense against tremendous superiority of enemy forces in men and arms. His utter disregard of personal danger and under heavy fire and aerial bombardment, his calm judgment in each crisis, inspired his troops, galvanized the spirit of resistance of the Filipino people and confirmed the faith of the American people in their armed forces."

PART SIX

World War II:
The Allied
Offensive
1943–1944

As the train pulled into Melbourne, cheering thousands lined the streets in a tumultuous welcome. But heartening as the welcome was, it did not disguise the fact that a sense of dangerous defeatism had seized upon a large segment of Australia's 7,000,000 people. The primary problem was to replace the pessimism of failure with the inspiration of success. What the Australians needed was a strategy that held out the promise of victory.

As quickly as practicable, I arranged a conference with the man who had been instrumental in having me brought to Australia, Prime Minister John Curtin. A few days later, I drove the 300 miles through prairie grasslands and groves of native trees to Canberra for my first conference with the Australian leader.

Curtin was determined that Australia should link its hopes and plans with the United States. Aware of the Commonwealth ties between his country and Great Britain, he nevertheless stood firm in the belief that the Pacific war was primary, and Australia's needs came first.

We promptly came to a sense of mutual trust, co-operation, and regard that was never once breached by word, thought, or deed. He was the kind of a man the Australians called "fair dinkum." As I rose to leave, I put my arm about his strong shoulder. "Mr. Prime Minister," I said, "we two, you and I, will see this thing through together. We can do it and we will do it. You take care of the rear and I will handle the front." He shook me by both my hands and said, "I knew I was not wrong in selecting you as Supreme Commander."

The immediate and imperative problem which confronted me was the defense of Australia itself. Its actual military situation had become almost desperate. Its forces were weak to an extreme, and Japanese invasion was momentarily expected. The bulk of its ground troops were in the Middle East, while the United States had only one division present, and that but partially trained. Its air force was equipped with almost obsolete planes and was lacking not only in engines and spare parts, but in personnel. Its navy had no carriers or battleships. The outlook was bleak.

Having been witness to the Japanese conquest of Hong Kong, Thailand, Malaya, Rabat, and the Northern Solomons, the Australian chiefs of staff understandably had been thinking and planning only defensively. They had traced a line generally along the Darling River, from Brisbane, midway up the eastern shoreline, to Adelaide on the south coast. This would be defended to the last breath. Such a plan, however, involved the sacrifice of three-quarters or more of the continent, the great northern and western reaches of the land. Behind this so-called Brisbane Line were the four or five most important cities and the large proportion of the population—the heart of Australia. As the areas to the north fell to the enemy, detailed plans were made to withdraw from New Guinea and lay desolate the land above the Brisbane Line. Industrial plants and utilities in Northern Territory would be dynamited, military facilities would be leveled, port installations rendered useless and irreparable.

The concept was purely one of passive defense, and I felt it would result only in eventual defeat. Even if so restrictive a scheme were tactically successful, its result would be to trap us indefinitely on an island continent ringed by conquered territories and hostile ocean, bereft of all hope of ever assuming the offensive.

I decided to abandon the plan completely, to move the thousand miles forward into eastern Papua, and to stop the Japanese on the rough mountains of the Owen Stanley Range of New Guinea—to make the fight for Australia beyond its own borders. If successful, this would save Australia from invasion and give me an opportunity to pass from defense to offense, to seize the initiative, move forward, and attack.

This decision gave the Australians an exhilarating lift, and they prepared to support me with almost fanatical zeal. As a matter of fact, throughout the war, the most complete co-operation existed not only with the Australians, but with the other nationalities under my command—Dutch, British, New Zealanders, and Filipinos. Not only was there complete lack of friction and misunderstanding, but the ties of mutual respect, good will, and admiration among the commanders, staffs, and men of all branches and services, could well serve as a model for any mixed international force. The full confidence of these nations and their forces, of such marked native variance, was an important factor in the success of the Pacific war.

Just at this time, Churchill presented Roosevelt with the thought that the Japanese intended to halt their advance on Australia and, instead, launch an attack on India. He wished the American buildup in the Pacific to be transferred to the British command in Southeast Asia. Roosevelt was apparently impressed enough to send me a personal message asking my opinion. On May 8th I sent my outline of the situation to the President:

The fall of Corregidor and the collapse of resistance in the Philippines, with the defeat of Burma, brings about a new situation. At least two enemy divisions and all the air force in the Philippines will be released for other missions. Japanese troops in Malaya and the Netherlands East Indies are susceptible of being regrouped for an offensive effort elsewhere since large garrisons will not be required because of the complacency of the native population. The Japanese Navy is as yet unchallenged and is disposed for further offensive effort. A preliminary move is now under way probably initially against New Guinea and the line of communications between the United States and Australia. The series of events releases an enormously dangerous enemy potential in the Western Pacific. That the situation will remain static is most improbable.

I am of the opinion that the Japanese will not undertake large operations against India at this time. That area is undoubtedly within the scope of their military ambitions, but it would be strategically advisable for them to defer it until a later date. On the other hand, the enemy advance toward the south has been supported by the establishment of a series of bases while his left is covered from the Mandated Islands. He is thus prepared to continue in that direction. Moreover, operations in these waters will permit the regrouping of his naval and air forces from the East. Such is not the case in a movement towards India. He must thrust into the Indian Ocean without adequate supporting bases, relinquishing the possibilities of concentrating his naval strength in either ocean.

The military requirements for a decisive Indian campaign are so heavy that it can not be undertaken under those conditions. On the other hand, a continuation of his southern movement at this time will give added safety for his eventual move to the west.

In view of this situation I deem it of the utmost importance to provide adequate security for Australia and the Pacific area, thus maintaining a constant frontal defense and a flank threat against further movement to the southward. This should be followed at the earliest possible moment by offensive action.

The Japanese did not concentrate against India, and continued their drive southward, closing in on eastern Papua. They had already occupied western Papua, and were firmly entrenched at Lae and Salamaua. Their next objective was Port Moresby in New Guinea, which would become their main base of operation for the invasion of Australia. The first effort to affect its seizure was an overland advance from Lae, but the difficulty of supply over mountain and jungle trails made the effort a weak one, and it was abandoned. The second was an amphibious movement of envelopment from the east by way of the Coral Sea. This was blocked by a naval engagement which resulted in a tactical draw, but caused the withdrawal of their transports bearing the troops which were to make the landing. Their third effort was to be from the center across the Owen Stanley Mountains, using Buna as a base.*

I moved headquarters forward to Brisbane and then to Port Moresby. If I could secure Moresby, I would force the enemy to fight on ground of my selection—across the barrier of the Owen Stanley Range.

This range of mountains, over 13,000 feet high, covered with dense jungle, formed a natural barrier which ran the entire length of eastern New Guinea. Winding foot trails were the only means of crossing it. Port Moresby, to its rear, was well sheltered by its towering cliffs. The only other feasible approach by which the enemy could attack was through Milne Bay, at the southeastern tip of New Guinea. Such an attack might be blocked if adequate air bases at Port Moresby could be constructed in time. My problem was to move my center of gravity forward 1,500 miles and secure this line before the enemy could seize it. The operation involved almost insuperable obstacles of time and space. It necessitated the construction of airfields for fighter planes and bases for heavy bombers, first within range of Papua, then on Papua itself. It involved provision for supply and reinforcement of advanced areas from rear bases in Australia which were in large part merely ports for the reshipping of material from the distant West Coast of the United States. It necessitated the exploration and mapping of unfamiliar areas, the charting of unknown waters, and demanded friendly co-operation from the New Guinea natives. It required the training of our forces for combat against an experienced and numerically superior enemy. And it risked carrying out these moves by sea into areas dominated by the naval power of the Japanese.

My confidence in the success of the plan was not shared in all quarters; many believed that the difficulties made it impracticable. It is to the eternal

* On June 13th the Congress of the United States, the Parliament of Australia, and the Philippine Government in Exile, proclaimed the day, "MacArthur Day," in commemoration of my induction into the armed service forty-three years before. I was now midway between sixty-two and sixty-three years of age.

credit of the officers and men involved that they more than justified my confidence in them and successfully overcame all difficulties. The results fully vindicated my full hopes and undoubtedly saved Australia.

The Japanese themselves were taken completely by surprise. Captain Toshikazu Ohmae of the Imperial Japanese Navy, the senior staff officer of the Southeast Area Fleet at Rabaul, said:

In the spring of 1942 the Japanese did not think that General MacArthur would establish himself in New Guinea and defend Australia from that position. They also did not believe that he would be able to use New Guinea as a base for offensive operations against them. The Japanese felt that General MacArthur could not establish himself in Port Moresby because he did not have sufficient forces to maintain himself there and because the Japanese Navy was confident that it could keep him out of New Guinea. In view of the successful air attacks against Darwin and Townsville, the Japanese reasoned that General MacArthur's forces were weak or they would have staved off the attacks.

In addition to all our other difficulties, there was New Guinea itself, as tough and tenacious an enemy as the Japanese. Few areas in the world present so formidable an obstacle to military operation. The jagged mountains rear their tall peaks amid sudden plunging gorges, towering above the trackless jungle that covers nearly the entire surface of the sprawling island. Swamps of nipa and mangrove pock the lowest areas—"a stinking jumble of twisted, slime-covered roots and muddy soup." In the jungle itself, trails were a sea of mud, with little relief from the swollen rivers, and the razor-edged kunai grass that grows in treacherous bunches higher than a man's head. Offshore were dangerous reefs, most of them uncharted, and the existing harbors were poor and inadequate. Everything about the island and its approaches seemed to hamper combat efforts.

Nature did not stop with adverse terrain, however. Constant high humidity intensified the unrelenting heat that sapped human energy; the rain came as an unpredictable but frequent blinding deluge. Health conditions matched the world's worse. Malaria could be controlled only by means of an intensive constant regimen of tiresome preventive measures. Dengue fever was widespread, the quickly fatal blackwater fever was also a waiting menace. Both amoebic and bacillary dysentery were continuing threats. Tropic ulcers could develop from a scratch. For the man who relaxed his guard, even for a moment, there waited hookworm, ringworm, scrub typhus, and the dread yaws. Disease was an unrelenting enemy. And, if only to add an almost intolerable irritation, millions of insects were ever-present, always finding any unguarded spot to bite or sting—mosquitoes, flies, leeches, chiggers, ants, fleas. New Guinea was a background in which almost every threat of nature combined with the sudden and unforeseeable dangers of modern war to provide a miniature of the vast struggle in the Southwest Pacific.

The effect of the New Guinea terrain and climate on combat troops was later described in an official report: "The psychological factors resulting from the terrain and climate were tremendously important. After a man had lain for days in a wet slit trench, or in the swamp, his physical stamina was reduced materially. This reduction served to make him extremely nervous and to attribute to the unfamiliar noises of the jungle, spectres of Japanese activities. These reactions preyed on his mind until he was reduced often to a pitifully abject state, incapable of aggressive action."

None of the three elements of my command—naval, air, or ground—was adequate. The naval force was small and unbalanced. It lacked direct air support because of the absence of carriers, and was therefore suitable "only for operations of a minor and subsidiary nature." The Royal Australian Air Force would require many months for its development. The organization and training of the American air component was below the required standard; months of intensive effort would be needed for it to reach a satisfactory condition. The ground troops, too, were inadequate for the tremendous task ahead. Not only were they too few in number, but they lacked the equipment and the strenuous training necessary for combat. The shortage of water transportation for supplies and equipment, as well as for troops, was one of the most difficult problems of all. Sufficient shipping was unavailable to adequately mount operations and then to support the troops in widely dispersed locations. Allowances of supplies and equipment accompanying troops into battle, and also the amounts to be sent later for their maintenance, had to be curtailed—at times to the danger point. Factors used for the computation of these requirements in the Southwest Pacific were less than those in any other theater or area in the world—at times they were less than half the usual figure. Considerably less than 10 per cent of America's military resources came to the area.

Hazardous logistic risks had to be taken in making decisions for planning and launching operations. These risks had to be taken if the war was to be pursued aggressively, and if the Allies were to seize the initiative and hold it.

Shortages in all supplies made it urgent to prepare for every specific tactical maneuver. The lack of combat equipment and service personnel intensified the logistic difficulty of the operation. There was neither equipment nor men for construction of ports, supply points, and airstrips, which had to be hewn from the untouched jungle; these had to be in operation before an attack could effectively commence. The lack of indispensable specialized ammunition at certain critical moments added still another problem to be resolved.

The picture was not all dismal, however. New commanders of proven ability were arriving. General Sir Thomas Blamey, a veteran soldier of highest quality, was appointed to command the Allied Land Forces. He was to justify his high repute and to deserve his appointment to field marshal. Brigadier General Stephen J. Chamberlin, a West Point professional, became my operations officer, G-3. A sound, careful staff officer, a master of tactical detail and possessed of bold strategic concepts, he was a pillar of new strength. Lieutenant General Robert Eichelberger, with a Corps headquarters, arrived from the United States. He had been the secretary of the General Staff when I was its chief, a superintendent of the United States Military Academy at West Point, and was already noted for his administrative ability. He proved himself a commander of the first order, fearless in battle, and especially popular with the Australians. Major General George C. Kenney came to command the Allied Air Forces. Of all the brilliant air commanders of the war, none surpassed him in those three great essentials of combat leadership: aggressive vision, mastery of air tactics and strategy, and the ability to exact the maximum in fighting qualities from both men and equipment. Through his extraordinary capacity to improvise and improve, he took a substandard force and welded it into a weapon so deadly as to take command of the air whenever it engaged the enemy, even against apparent odds. He brought with him as a field commander a leader of similar caliber in Brigadier General Ennis P. Whitehead.

When he assumed command of the American air units in Australia General Kenney made a personal, plane-by-plane inventory of his available forces. Of bombers, he found we had sixty-two B-17s but only five of them were in condition to fly. The rest were grounded for various reasons, either damaged in combat or awaiting replacement parts. There had been a failure to solve the problem of front-area aircraft maintenance. Nothing is more useless than a plane that cannot fly. A grounded air force is no air force at all. Kenney's soundness of concept was brilliantly evidenced in his ability to keep his planes flying. The Japanese never were able to solve the problem, and it became a major contributing factor in their loss of air control. Time after time, at Wewak and Rabaul, at Hollandia and in the Philippines, our air force destroyed hundreds of their planes on the ground awaiting repairs or replacement parts. Later, after the surrender and my arrival in Japan, I inspected some 8,000 Japanese aircraft which were found on airfields in the home islands. All of these were from 95 to 98 per cent complete, but not operational because some small part was unavailable. What an inestimable difference these 8,000 planes would have made to the enemy's war effort! They were the tragic evidence of the gap between maintenance and the lack of it. The difference in extra attention to detail and extra effort is not too great, but for some reason the Japanese could not cross this line, which spells the eyelash between air victory and defeat.

The most reassuring event was the spectacular support contributed by the Australian people as a whole. This involved the heaviest sort of drain on the meager Australian population of 7,000,000. After the requirements of the armed forces had been met, the Australians had a working force of only slightly more than 2,000,000 men. But from this group, ably directed by the labor government of Prime Minister Curtin, the man I called "the heart and soul of Australia," great things came.

Australia's supply contribution throughout the war was of paramount importance. Less than 100,000 tons arrived from the United States during the critical final quarter of 1942, and supplies to the New Guinea front were kept flowing only by the strictest compliance with the War Department directive that "local resources will be exploited to the utmost." Our ground and air forces in the Southwest Pacific Area were vastly more self-sufficient than those in any other theater of operations. Local produce and materials furnished 65 to 70 per cent of the resources needed by them for the second half of 1942. To the adjacent South Pacific theater, I shipped a greater tonnage of supplies than the United States delivered to my own area. In general effect, therefore, the Southwest Pacific, far from being a drain on the United States, was self-sufficient. Curtin was the mainspring of this magnificent Australian war effort.

Despite all these obstacles, Pat Casey, my chief engineer, built the airstrips, dredged the harbors, and laid out the roads that enabled our forces to move to the north as planned.

Just at this time I received an honor from home that, in view of my devotion to my son, Arthur, moved me deeply. I was named the "Father of the Year." I accepted with a feeling of profound humility, cabling:

Nothing has touched me more deeply than the act of the National Father's Day Committee. By profession I am a soldier and take great pride in that fact, but I am prouder, infinitely prouder, to be a father. A soldier destroys in order to build; the father only builds, never destroys. The one has the potentialities of death; the other embodies creation and life. And while the hordes of death are mighty, the battalions of life are mightier still. It is my hope that my son when I am gone will remember me, not from the battle, but in the home, repeating with him our simple daily prayer, "Our Father Who art in Heaven."

Between June 3 and June 6, a naval battle was fought in the Central Pacific which considerably altered the general strategic situation. Our Navy had broken the Japanese code and was fully prepared to meet a powerful enemy concentration southwest of Midway Island. Our carrier aircraft, supported by land-based planes from Midway, sank one heavy cruiser, severely damaged a destroyer, and destroyed 250 aircraft. Our losses totaled one carrier, one destroyer and 150 aircraft. Again, as in the Coral Sea Battle, the opposing warships never once sighted each other and not a single direct shot was exchanged. The dominant role of air power in naval warfare was clearly demonstrated.

This decisive victory restored the balance in naval power in the Pacific, and removed the threat to Hawaii and the West Coast of the United States. Thereafter, except for the Aleutians, where the Japanese had landed on Attu and Kiska Islands, enemy operations were confined to the South and Southwest Pacific Areas.

After the Battle of Midway, the Japanese concentrated on the New Guinea area. Their immediate objective became Milne Bay, the strategic importance of which they suddenly realized. It would serve them not only as a base for the air support of an attack on Port Moresby, but would control coastal trails along which ground troops could infiltrate and, by a flanking movement, made in conjunction with a direct attack over the Owen Stanley Mountains, capture Port Moresby.

Our own plans included an Allied base at Milne Bay which would pave the way for a move around the end of New Guinea and along the Papuan coast to Buna, and thence to the main objectives of Lae and Salamaua, avoiding the mountains entirely. With Milne Bay in Allied hands, the east flank of Port Moresby would be secured.

Accordingly, I ordered the secret construction of an air, land, and naval base at Gili Gili, located at the head of Milne Bay. The move along the coast, to the site of the projected base, was made secretly and skillfully so that the initial execution of the plan was unhampered by enemy opposition. Had the Japanese been aware of my intention to fortify Milne Bay, they would have undoubtedly made every effort to prevent its fulfillment. This was clearly demonstrated by the fury and determination of their counterattacks as soon as they learned that we had beaten them to this all-important position.

Before I left Melbourne to go north, President Quezon, who had established his government-in-exile there, sailed for the United States on the invitation of President Roosevelt. Prime Minister Curtin and I saw him off. In his cabin he turned to me and said, "Tell me the frank truth. Can you liberate my country and free my people?" I replied immediately, "I intend to do just that. And when I stand at the gates of Manila, I want the President of the Commonwealth at my right hand and the Prime Minister of Australia at my left." He replied with deepest emotion, "So help me God." There was a general election to be held shortly in Australia which tempered the words of the Prime Minister: "I cannot pledge that the Prime Minister of Australia will be there. That depends on the people of Australia. But I can pledge that John Curtin will be." But before we could liberate the Philippines, they were both in their graves.

Even before I arrived at Port Moresby, I anticipated enemy efforts along the Kokoda Trail, the easier route across the mountains from Buna. I was convinced that the Japanese intended to employ this route to attack Port Moresby in direct assault. To forestall such a move, I requested General Blamey to prepare plans, to the degree his meager forces would permit, for the protection of Kokoda and the points along the trail. This estimate of the enemy's intentions proved correct, for within three days after the directive to General Blamey, Imperial Japanese Headquarters ordered the Commander of the Seventeenth Army, in co-operation with the Navy to "immediately make land-attack plans against Port Moresby."

Late in June, I was presented with a prepared plan from Washington, originating in the Navy Department. It required the employment of the forces of the Southwest Pacific on the south and west coasts of New Guinea, rather than, as I contemplated, on the north coast. Its first phase would be an attack on Timor. I at once pointed out the weakness of such a strategy, saying, "The action projected northwest of Australia, the attack on Timor, even if successful, cannot be supported. It is doubtful whether Timor could be held under present circumstances, in view of nearby Japanese bases and control of adjacent seas. Its capture should not be undertaken unless we are prepared to support it fully, which includes control of the sea lanes between there and Australia." Such a move would have tended to isolate my command from that of Admiral Nimitz in the Central Pacific and would have slanted it away from rather than toward the final objective—Japan. Without mutual support between the Central Pacific and the Southwest Pacific, both forces lacked strength. I opposed any diversion of the Allied effort and, rather than dissipate limited strength in various areas, I proposed a single unified drive under united command. The Navy plan was dropped, but there was to be no unified command in the Pacific. On July 2nd, the Navy's South Pacific Force under Vice Admiral Robert L. Ghormley undertook operations at Guadalcanal on the island of Bougainville.

On July 23rd, the first ground action in New Guinea took place. The Australians, determined fighters as always, were forced to give way before greatly superior forces. A series of engagements followed, and by late August the enemy had passed over the peak of the trail and was descending the slopes toward Moresby.

In the meantime, the Japanese discovered the Allied occupation of Milne Bay and, unaware of the strength we had built up there, launched a series of headlong assaults which ended in their complete destruction. They had fallen into the trap with disastrous results. By September 5th, the area was completely cleared.

The Japanese secondary advance on the Kokoda Trail increased in pressure and the Australians finally took up a stand on the heights at Imita. This ridge was the final remaining terrain hurdle before Port Moresby.

Here the line held. The Japanese, having left the comparatively smooth slopes of their initial advance from Buna, had begun to experience increasing difficulties with the terrain and their extended, tenuous lines of supply. Casualties from bombing, sickness, and shortage of food had exacted a heavy toll. A mere 20 air miles from his long-sought goal, the difficulties of the situation forced the Japanese commander to halt and consolidate his worn forces while awaiting reinforcements of men and supplies. His grim story of the battle for Kokoda Trail, told a short time before his death, is revealed by Major General Tomitaro Horii in a proclamation to his troops:

1. Repeatedly we were in hot pursuit of the enemy. We smashed his final resistance in the fierce fighting at Ioribaiwa, and today we firmly hold the heights of that area, the most important point for the advance on Port Moresby.

2. For more than three weeks during that period, every unit forced its way through deep forests and ravines, and climbed scores of peaks in pursuit of the

enemy. Traversing knee-deep mud, clambering up steep precipices, bearing un-complainingly the heavy weight of artillery ammunition, our men overcame the shortage of our supplies, and we succeeded in surmounting the Stanley Range. No pen or word can depict adequately the magnitude of the hardships suffered. From the bottom of our hearts we appreciate these many hardships and deeply sympathize with the great numbers killed and wounded.

3. We will strike a hammer blow at the stronghold of Moresby. However, ahead of us the enemy still crawls about. It is difficult to judge the direction of his movement, and many of you have not yet fully recovered your strength. I feel keenly that it is increasingly important during the present period, while we are waiting for an opportunity to strike, to strengthen our positions, reorganize our forces, replenish our stores, and recover our physical fitness.

4. When next we go into action, this unit will throw in its fighting power unre-servedly.

I decided that the moment had come for a counter-drive that would clear the enemy from eastern Papua. I was certain that General Horii had over-reached himself along the Kokoda Trail and that his advance would sputter out as it ran ahead of its supply line. My plan of attack was formulated along three axes. One would engage the enemy in a frontal action along the Kokoda Trail; the second would involve a wide flanking movement over the Owen Stanleys east of Moresby against the enemy lines of communica-tion and supply; and the third axis of advance would consist of large-scale infiltrations from Milne Bay along the north coast of Papua. All three axes were to converge upon the Buna-Salamaua-Gona area for a final simultaneous attack against this enemy coastal stronghold.

I rushed all available ground troops into New Guinea and placed them under the command of General Blamey. The American contingent con-sisted of the I Corps under General Eichelberger, and comprised the 32nd and 41st Divisions. The Australians were the 6th and 7th Divisions under the command of Lieutenant General Edmund F. Herring. Two of the regiments of the 32nd Division were transported to Moresby by air. This was "the first large scale airborne troop movement by United States forces in any theatre of operations." By the end of October, I had augmented my ground forces in Papua to something like five divisions. They struck along all three axes of advance, and by the end of November, after much savage fighting, had com-pressed the enemy into the narrow coastal strip from Gona on the east, through Buna Village and Buna Mission in the center, and on to Salamaua on the west. In the battling by the Australians on the Kokoda Trail, General Horii was drowned while attempting to escape an enveloping movement.

During this period, although hard put to it in New Guinea, I did everything possible to support the South Pacific Command in Guadalcanal, where operations were not going too well. I reported to Washington on this feature as follows:

From its inception I have been acutely aware of the critical situation in the Solomons, at Guadalcanal on Bougainville Island, and in fact anticipated it and reported it with Ghormley in July and in August. Action in South Pacific has been supported to maximum capacity of my Air Force, using all planes that can reach targets. Admiral Ghormley three times has radioed me his appreciation. Admiral Turner has also communicated to that effect. While it is impossible to assess all damage it is believed that our bombardment missions have had a vital effect upon the operations to date by pounding hostile air and supply installations. The major effort has been expended in Rabaul area, because it can be reached with full bomb loads, while planes going to Guadalcanal area must carry bomb bay tanks, reducing bomb load by fifty percent. Am in constant communication with Ghormley coordinating my reconnaissance with his and giving priority to his requests for attack. Planes capable of effecting his situation have been used exclusively to that end. Three times within the past week I have ordered missions at Ghormley's request, using every bomber available during the period. My own operations in New Guinea have been supported only by short-range aircraft.

I had hoped that a co-ordinated drive of the three Allied forces poised before the last remaining strongholds in eastern Papua would be able to gain an early victory. The Japanese, however, realizing they could no longer retreat without forfeiting the vital air bases along the northern coast, were determined to hold their positions no matter what the cost. They methodically prepared a series of well-designed and extremely strong defenses. Every contour of the terrain was exploited, and the driest stretches of land were carefully chosen to be occupied and fortified, making it impossible for the Allies to execute any lateral movement without becoming mired in swamp. All potential roads of approach were cleverly channeled into narrow corridors along tracks which led into a murderous crossfire of well-hidden machine guns. They fought with great courage and tenacity. The final phase of the struggle for Papua and the reduction of the enemy pockets on the northern coast witnessed some of the most grueling fighting of the entire campaign.

To complicate the problem of piercing the enemy defenses, the already difficult logistical situation had become even more critical. Allied lines of communication were stretched 1,700 miles from Australia to the landing strips and supply dumps along the coast of New Guinea. Rations, ammunition, and equipment were generally transported by the Fifth Air Force from Moresby forward. Flying weather was usually bad, and for days at a time supply planes were grounded, unable to penetrate the thick, low-hanging clouds which veiled the mountains. This break in the supply line at so crucial a period caused the failure of the first Allied thrust at the enemy's coastal defenses. When we attacked Japanese positions at Gona on November 19th, we were forced to withdraw because of a shortage of ammunition.

As an additional aggravation, the New Guinea jungle and swamp were unrelenting in their toll of disease and sickness. The troops were beginning to suffer from an increasing debility and lassitude engendered by the stifling climate and an insufficient food ration. The incident of illness climbed rapidly as man after man was stricken and hospitalized with at least one of the multitude of ever-present fevers which infested the entire region.

Initial assaults against the enemy entrenchments failed to achieve any appreciable gains. General Blamey, feeling that his covering artillery fire was inadequate to support a frontal attack, proposed that an amphibious landing be made at the rear of the enemy's positions at Buna. The lack of small landing craft, however, and the fact that the Navy was unwilling to risk destroyers and corvettes in the shallow, uncharted, and dangerous waters prevented his plan from being carried out.

The Allied offensive, therefore, unable to pierce the enemy's powerful positions by frontal assault, and incapable of mounting an amphibious flanking maneuver, had to give way to painstaking infiltration tactics. The situation developed into a virtual stalemate, with activity on both sides restricted to sporadic thrusts by small groups, constantly isolated from their main units and left largely to their own resources.

In order to break the existing deadlock, I sent in General Eichelberger with my last reserve. The fresh troops made their presence felt immediately, capturing Gona on December 9th. On December 14th, a heavy attack was launched against Buna Village. Despite fierce resistance and repeated attempts by the enemy to bring in waterborne reinforcements, the village was at last wrested from the Japanese. Describing this first major victory in the coastal offensive, I reported as follows:

Buna Village has been taken. It was occupied by our troops at ten o'clock this morning, December 14. In another attempt by the enemy's naval forces to reinforce their ground troops in the Buna area, the enemy launched a convoy of two cruisers and three destroyers, with a great number of barges, to make a landing. Our air force intercepted this convoy. In heavy bombing and strafing attacks the enemy's landing barges were all sunk or disabled. Survivors attempted to reach land by swimming, suffering heavy casualties. Hits were made on the war vessels which withdrew. The enemy's air force intervened unsuccessfully. It is believed that a major enemy effort was parried.

The final stage of the struggle was now at hand. The Japanese troops, severed from all reinforcement, their leaders lost in action or by suicide, their bodies worn with starvation and sickness, and their morale shattered by the unrelenting blows of their attackers, were finally forced to yield their positions. On January 2, 1943, Buna Mission fell; Sanananda followed, and on January 22nd, the Papua campaign, after six months of bitter, ceaseless struggle, ended.*

During the entire Papuan campaign, the enormous flexibility of modern air power was constantly exploited. The calculated advance of bomber lines through seizure of forward bases meant that a relatively small force of bombers operating at short and medium ranges could attack under cover of an equally limited fighter force. Each phase of advance had as its objective an airfield which could serve as a steppingstone to the next advance. In addition, as this air line moved forward, naval forces under newly established air cover began to regain the sea lanes, which had been the undisputed arteries of the enemy's far-flung positions. Ground, air, and sea operations were thoroughly co-ordinated. It

---

* I cited a number of senior officers for their conduct of the Papuan Campaign in my Order of the Day on January 9, 1943: "It is my high honor to cite to the Order of the Day, for extraordinary courage, marked efficiency and precise execution of operation during the Papuan Campaign, the following officers: General Sir Thomas Blamey, Lieutenant General Kenney, Lieutenant General Herring, Lieutenant General Eichelberger, Major General Sutherland, Major General Vasey, Brigadier General Willoughby, Brigadier General Whitehead, Brigadier General Walker, Brigadier Wooten, Brigadier Eather, Group Captain Garing. The victory which has been achieved would have been impossible of accomplishment without the invincible leadership which they have provided. I have directed that each be awarded the Distinguished Service Cross of the United States, the highest decoration at my disposal, with appropriate individual citation. This award will serve for all time and for all eyes as the outward symbol of the devotion and gallantry with which they have performed their dangerous and difficult duty. The magnificent conduct of the troops and elements of this command operating under difficulties rarely, if ever, surpassed in campaign, has earned my highest praise and commendation. In spite of inadequate means in many categories, their resourcefulness, their ingenuity, their adaptability, have produced a self-reliance that has overcome all handicaps and difficulties. Through skill and courage and an indomitable will for victory they have defeated a bold and aggressive enemy possessing a marked superiority of resources and potentialities in the areas of campaign and combat. To Almighty God I give thanks for that guidance which has brought us to this success in our great Crusade. His is the honor, the power and the glory forever."

Other senior officers who rendered outstanding service were: General Dick Marshall who administered the service of supply; General Casey, the chief engineer, and his assistant, General Sverdrup; General Byers, the chief of staff of the I Corps; and General McNider, who commanded an independent combat team.

was a new type of campaign—three-dimensional warfare—the triphibious concept.

It was the practical application of this system of warfare—to avoid the frontal attack with its terrible loss of life; to by-pass Japanese strongpoints and neutralize them by cutting their lines of supply; to thus isolate their armies and starve them on the battlefield; to, as Willie Keeler used to say, "hit 'em where they ain't"—that from this time forward guided my movements and operations.

This decision enabled me to accomplish the concept of the direct-target approach from Papua to Manila. The system was popularly called "leap-frogging," and hailed as something new in warfare. But it was actually the adaptation of modern instrumentalities of war to a concept as ancient as war itself. Derived from the classic strategy of envelopment, it was given a new name, imposed by modern conditions. Never before had a field of battle embraced land and water in such relative proportions. Earlier campaigns had been decided on either land or sea. However, the process of transferring troops by sea as well as by land appeared to conceal the fact that the system was merely that of envelopment applied to a new type of battle area. It has always proved the ideal method for success by inferior but faster-moving forces. The paucity of the resources at my command made me adopt this method of campaign as the only hope of accomplishing my task. To put it into application required a secure base from which to anchor all operations, and Australia obviously was the only logical answer.

The lack of naval aircraft carriers affected and hampered the Southwest Pacific operations most seriously. The presence of carriers would have entirely altered our potential and shortened the war materially, with a consequent saving of life and money. Prime Minister Curtin did his best to persuade Prime Minister Churchill to let us have some carriers, and I did the same with Washington, but without success. To this day I cannot imagine why the decision was in the negative. The very essence of our so-called "island-hopping" method of advance depended upon securing air control over the area covered in each forward step. In the present state of development of the art of war, no movement can safely be made of forces on sea or land without adequate air protection. The limit of such protection in our case was the possible radius of operation of our fighter planes. This radius had to be measured from the actual location of our ground air bases. This required the seizing or construction of such new bases at each forward movement. The presence of carriers, with their inherent movability, would have immeasurably increased the scope and speed of our operations. I know of no other area or no other theater where they could have been used to such advantage. The enemy's diversion of his air forces on many different islands and fields was peculiarly adapted to his piecemeal destruction, which would have been drastically assisted if we could have utilized the mobility of carriers in surprise concentrations. With our inferior air strength, I had to locate my advance air bases between those of the enemy and, by surprise, concentrate first on one side, then on the other. His combined forces could have beaten me, but I could destroy the parts individually. With carriers I would not have to creep along this way, but could strike quickly and decisively. Said Colonel Matsuichi Juio, senior intelligence officer, Eighth Area Army staff: "This was the type of strategy we hated most. The Americans, with minimum losses, attacked and seized a relatively weak area, constructed airfields and then proceeded to cut the supply lines to troops in that area. Without engaging in a large-scale operation, our strongpoints were gradually starved out. The Japanese Army preferred direct assault, after the German fashion, but the Americans flowed into our weaker points and submerged us, just as water seeks the weakest entry to sink a ship. We respected this type of strategy for its brilliance because it gained the most while losing the least." *

I was awarded my third Distinguished Service Medal.

---

* The Buna victory was a heartening tonic to the Allies, and Secretary Stimson sent me a warm message of congratulations: "The coming of the New Year, coinciding as it does with your success at Buna, impels me again to send you my warmest congratulations and good wishes. Have followed your masterly campaign with close interest and much gratification.

"Not only are you completing successfully a most difficult campaign in New Guinea, carried through with great skill and judgment, but I have been doubly pleased with the considerate diplomacy with which you have handled your difficulties with the Australians on the one side and your unfailing cooperation with the naval campaign in the Solomons on the other.

"It is a tremendous satisfaction to feel that American fortunes in SWPA are in such skillful hands. Am in constant touch with President Quezon here and we are both beginning to think with encouragement of the time, which now really seems approaching, when we shall redeem our promise to the Filipinos."

Prime Minister Curtin told the Australian Parliament near the end of the campaign: "The position of General MacArthur in Australia is unique. He is a commander of a foreign though friendly power with his headquarters located in the country of another Government which has continued to exercise all its sovereign powers, but assigned to him its combat forces which for long constituted the great bulk of his command.

"General MacArthur has also looked to the Australian Government for many of his supplies and services and the provision of his base installations and facilities.

"The Commander-in-Chief has been in close association with the Government for almost two years. His position has been one of delicacy fraught with possibilities of trouble and difficulty if tact, discretion and diplomacy were not employed on both sides, but it is my great pleasure to state that the most cordial relations have been maintained and the closest working cooperation established. General MacArthur has displayed all the qualities of an able diplomat as well as those of a great commander.

"A feature of the story of the New Guinea campaign will be the genius with which air power

The successful culmination of the Papuan campaign opened the way for a drive up the New Guinea coast, and laid the groundwork for long-range offensive planning which would disrupt Japanese strategy and destroy their war machine in the Southwest Pacific. The victory at Buna, however, which had been gained by the bold use of "shoestring" equipment, did not mean that I could immediately push my master plan of moving along the northwest axis toward the Philippines. The Japanese still occupied most of New Guinea, maintaining strong bases at Lae and Salamaua. And directly to the north they held both sides of the narrow body of water known as Vitiaz Strait, through which our convoys from Australia westward would have to pass in support of any movement toward the Philippines. Rabaul was the focal point for the protection and reinforcement by the enemy of the whole northeast area which he had seized and occupied. Allied victories in Papua and Guadalcanal had temporarily contained him, but did not threaten his main centers of power. My primary goal in 1943 was to cut off the major Japanese naval staging area, the menacing airfields, and the bulging supply bases at Rabaul.

To push back the Japanese perimeter of conquest by direct pressure against the mass of enemy-occupied islands would be a long and costly effort. My staff worried about Rabaul and other strongpoints. They were skeptical

---

was integrated with naval and land strength to render possible a new conception of offensive power in the realms of strategy, tactics and logistics. I vividly recall the critical stage of the New Guinea campaign when every civil air service in Australia was suspended to provide the Commander-in-Chief with temporary aircraft to support his operations. The incident was typical of the close cooperation existing between General MacArthur and the Government.

"With relatively little loss of life and the minimum of frontal assaults by ground forces, enemy strongholds have been by-passed and their supply lines severed first by air attacks and then by naval forces. The objective of each advance has been the seizure of air fields which determine the scope and distance of the next advance.

"General MacArthur has achieved his main objective. To hold Australia as a base for future offensive action against Japan, to check Japanese aggression in the Southwest Pacific Area and to prepare to take the offensive."

Prime Minister Churchill sent me the following message:

"The rapid movements I have been making and pressure upon me made me delay till my return my most cordial congratulations upon the capture of Buna by American and Australian forces, and important and resolute operations under your distinguished command which have resulted in the destruction of the Japanese invaders in Papua.

"I have watched with particular admiration your masterly employment of transport aircraft to solve most complicated and diverse logistical problems.

"I should like to let you know how grateful we all feel throughout the British Empire that you stand on guard over all these vital interests."

He also told the House of Commons:

"We must express our admiration for hard won successes of the Australian and American forces, who, under the brilliant commander, General MacArthur, have taken Buna, in New Guinea, and slaughtered the last of its defenders.

"Ingenious use of aircraft to solve intricate tactical problems by transport of reinforcements, supplies and munitions, including field guns, is a prominent feature of MacArthur's generalship and should be carefully studied by all concerned in the technical conduct of the war."

of the possibility of its capture unless the number of our troops and planes was increased tremendously, and predicted losses in men and matériel that would make those we had suffered in capturing Buna, or in holding Guadalcanal, seem minor. Replacements were trickling in slowly, providing only the minimum essentials with which to conduct immediate operations. At a staff meeting, one of them said, "General, I know your peculiar genius for slaughtering large masses of the enemy at little cost in the lives of your own men, but I just don't see how we can take these strongpoints with our limited forces." I thoroughly agreed with him, but said I did not intend to take them—I intended to envelop them, incapacitate them, apply the "hit 'em where they ain't—let 'em die on the vine" philosophy. I explained that this was the very opposite of what was termed "island-hopping," which is the gradual pushing back of the enemy by direct frontal pressure, with the consequent heavy casualties which would certainly be involved. There would be no need for storming the mass of islands held by the enemy. "Island-hopping," I said, "with extravagant losses and slow progress, is not my idea of how to end the war as soon and as cheaply as possible. New conditions and new weapons require new and imaginative methods for solution and application. Wars are never won in the past."

To successfully envelop the enemy called for the careful selection of key points as objectives and the choosing of the most opportune moment to strike. I accordingly applied my major efforts to the seizure of areas which were suitable for airfields and base development, but which were only lightly defended by the enemy. Thus, by daring forward strikes, by neutralizing and by-passing enemy centers of strength, and by the judicious use of my air forces to cover each movement, I intended to destroy Japanese power in New Guinea and adjacent islands, and to clear the way for a drive to the Philippines.

With the fall of Papua, the Japanese decided to consolidate their positions in the Southwest Pacific Area and retract their first line of defense. The key points along this new defensive perimeter were northern New Guinea, New Britain, and the northern Solomons. New Guinea in particular assumed special significance. Not only was it a strategic anchor on the right flank of the new defense line, but its loss would provide the Allies with an ideal springboard for a thrust into the heart of the Japanese inner zones of operations.

In emphasizing the particular importance of New Guinea to their new defensive positions, the Japanese First Demobilization Bureau *War Report* read:

New Guinea, especially, was the strategic point on the right flank of the defensive line, and if it should fall into the hands of the enemy, who had already secured firm operational bases in Australia and in one corner of the Solomon Islands, it would be a case of giving the enemy the best possible route to penetrate into the Philippines and any part of the South Co-Prosperity Sphere. This would be a great menace to the foundation of our general defense system. It was clear that the northern coastal area of New Guinea Island was of great importance to the enemy for his offensive bases and for conducting his operations, and also because of the difference in the terrain of the northern and southern areas of New Guinea. The strategic value of the Lae and Salamaua areas in the present stage of the operation was of immense importance.

Additional ground troops began to arrive from the United States, and on January 11th I wired General Marshall: "Experience indicates the necessity for a tactical organization of an American Army. In the absence of such an echelon the burden has been carried by General Headquarters. I recommend the U.S. Third Army under Lieutenant General Walter Krueger, which would provide an able commander and an efficient operating organization. I am especially anxious to have Krueger because of my long and intimate association with him." In response to my request, Headquarters Sixth Army, commanded by General Krueger, arrived in the Southwest Pacific Area, and all American combat units were assigned to it on February 16, 1943.

Walter Krueger had been my war plans chief when I was chief of staff. He became to the Sixth Army what George Kenney was to the Fifth Air Force. History has not given him due credit for his greatness. I do not believe that the annals of American history have shown his superior as an Army commander. Swift and sure in attack, tenacious and determined in defense, modest and restrained in victory—I do not know what he would have been in defeat, because he was never defeated.

Late in January, the Japanese launched an attack against Wau, held by a small contingent of Australian troops. Wau was valuable to the Allies as it was a threat to the security of the Japanese strongholds of Lae and Salamaua. At first successful, the enemy was finally repulsed and completely routed by reinforcements transported from Moresby by air. This engagement proved to any remaining skeptics that tactical movement of troops by aircraft had become a strong and trusty adjunct of the armed forces. It also marked the final effort of the enemy to extend his hold in New Guinea. Anticipating a major Allied advance, he now concentrated every effort in strengthening those areas he already held.

The defeat of the Japanese at Wau increased the danger to their general position in New Guinea. Realizing that the enemy would become increasingly apprehensive about the security of his defenses below the Huon Peninsula, I anticipated a major effort by the Japanese to reinforce their garrisons at Lae and Salamaua. This assumption was further substantiated by numerous intelligence reports of a growing concentration of shipping in Rabaul, and of a noticeable increase in activity on enemy airfields along the probable convoy route.

I accordingly alerted our forces to be ready for a large-scale effort by the enemy to transport troops through the Bismarck Sea from Rabaul to New Guinea. So certain were we of an imminent convoy movement that General Kenney's air forces carried out actual practice maneuvers under conditions similar to those expected, reconnoitering the most advantageous routes of attack so that superiority could be attained at the point of combat. In addition, special preparations were made to carry out a new technique of skip-bombing in the event of unfavorable weather and low cloud formations.

Our preparations were well taken. At this time the Japanese Eighth Area Army, with headquarters at Rabaul, was commanded by General Hitoshi Imamura, and consisted of General Haruyeshi Hyakutake's Seventeenth Army in the Solomons and General Hataze Adachi's Eighteenth Army in New Guinea and New Britain. On February 28th, a strong enemy convoy of from eight to twelve transports, and a similar number of destroyers, carrying a large part of the 51st Division, certain key personnel, and vital supplies for the New Guinea front, left Rabaul harbor. General Kenney's planes, American and Australian, struck them with deadly effect. Despite heavy overcast and rain, in the running battle that followed all transports were destroyed and all but four enemy destroyers, two of which were severely damaged. As a sea battle, it was unique—not a single Allied vessel was involved.

Most of the enemy's troops were lost. The entire load of provisions and matériel, including a large amount of airplane fuel and a four months' supply of food, was totally destroyed. The forces in eastern New Guinea were thus deprived of supplies and reinforcements necessary to withstand the forthcoming Allied blows at Salamaua and Lae. Control of the air and sea lanes had passed to the Allies, marking the end of the Japanese offensive in the Southwest Pacific.*

* Many congratulatory messages were received. From President Roosevelt: "The efficient bombardments launched by your air forces during the past few weeks and especially in the last few days in support of the situation in the Solomons and in furtherance of your own operations command our admiration. The arduous land campaign along the Papuan Coast which has decimated the enemy and now threatens him at Salamaua has made a great impression on our people and

At this time I had slightly less than 2 per cent of the total U.S. Army and Air Force. My allocation of slightly more than 100,000 gave me almost exactly 10 per cent of the more than 1,000,000 Army and Air Force personnel then stationed outside of the continental limits of the United States. My share of the total U.S. Navy forces, in both ships and men, was even smaller than my percentage of Army troops.

I urged, with all the earnestness of which I was capable, that the command in the Pacific be unified. I stated that, although I was the senior ranking officer by many years, I would be willing to accept a subordinate position, to accomplish the general good. It was in vain. Of all the faulty decisions of war perhaps the most unexplainable one was the failure to unify the command in the Pacific. The principle involved is the most fundamental

must have a demoralizing effect on Japanese confidence in the fighting efficiency of their ground troops. My thanks go to you who carried the fight to the enemy on all levels and over great distances and even greater difficulties."

From Prime Minister Curtin: "On behalf of the Commonwealth Parliament and the people of Australia, I warmly congratulate you on the magnificent victory which has been achieved by the Air Forces operating under your command in the destruction of the large enemy seaborne force in the battle of the Bismarck Sea."

From the Prime Minister of New Zealand: "Will you please convey to General MacArthur on behalf of the Government and people of New Zealand a message of warmest congratulations on the decisive victory of his forces in the Bismarck Sea. This action has undoubtedly contributed in considerable measure towards the lessening of the immediate menace threatening Australia and New Zealand and is an important step towards victory in the Pacific."

From Sir Winston Churchill: "My warmest congratulations to you on the annihilation of the Japanese convoy in the Bismarck Sea. It was a striking testimony to the proper use of air power. It is just over a year since your historic journey from Corregidor and your appointment at the head of the Allied force in the Southwest Pacific. The United Nations owe you a deep debt of gratitude for your inspiring leadership during these difficult days."

From Air Marshal Trenchard: "As an old Royal Air Force Officer, I would like heartily to congratulate you on the wonderful air victory in the sinking of the whole Japanese convoy and escort. You have shown wonderful appreciation of how air power should be used."

One that especially pleased Kenney and Whitehead was from Air Marshal Sir Charles Portal, Chief of the Air Staff of Great Britain: "On behalf of all ranks of the Royal Air Force I send you warm congratulations upon magnificent victory of Air Forces of your command in recent action in Bismarck Straits. The annihilation of the Japanese convoy by your aircraft is yet another grave defeat for the enemy. And it is proof, if such were still needed, of the devastating power of shore-based aircraft where they have secured command of the air over either land or sea."

Another was in a letter from a senior officer in the Navy Department in Washington: "My warmest congratulations on that Bismarck Strait affair. It was beautifully conceived and executed and hit the Jap hard at his most vulnerable spot—shipping. Good Lord, what a shame you were denied the land-based air power you tried so hard to get for the defense of the Philippines. It would have been a greatly different story there.

"The skip bombing appeals to me as a most clever development—eliminating the weakness of high level bombing against ships underway."

And another, which I prized highly, from one of our greatest citizens: "When we review the military situation on your side of the world we can see the remarkable versatility which has been necessary to have, on the one hand, men crawling on their bellies to cross the Owen Stanley Mountains in primitive fashion, and on the other the glorious victory of the Bismarck Sea where your land based planes took on a Japanese fleet or convoy or combination of both and simply obliterated them with the very newest weapon of warfare.

"We write you to let you know that you have heartened and inspired us not alone by your military accomplishments but by the spirituality which you have inculcated in your command. We rejoice that your wisdom has maintained the honor of the nation against odds."

one in the doctrine and tradition of command. In this instance it did not involve choosing one individual out of a number of Allied officers, although it was an accepted and entirely successful practice in the other great theaters. The failure to do so in the Pacific cannot be defended in logic, in theory, or in common sense. Other motives must be ascribed. It resulted in divided effort, the waste, diffusion, and duplication of force, and the consequent extension of the war, with added casualties and cost. The generally excellent co-operation between the two commands in the Pacific, supported by the good will, good nature, and professional qualifications of the numerous personnel involved, was no substitute for the essential unity of direction of centralized authority. The handicaps and hazards unnecessarily resulting were numerous, and many a man lies in his grave today who could have been saved.

In mid-March, 1943, The Chief of Naval Operations, Admiral Ernest King instituted the new numbered-fleet system, by which all fleets in the Pacific were to be odd-numbered and those in the Atlantic, even-numbered. Thus my old Naval Forces Southwest Pacific—strengthened by the addition of the 7th Amphibious Force and the 2nd Engineer Special Brigade—became the Seventh Fleet, under Vice Admiral Arthur S. Carpender. The amphibious force, which was to be employed for major amphibious movements, brought to the command such outstanding figures as Rear Admirals Daniel Barbey, William M. Fechteler and Arthur Struble. The old South Pacific Force, including the 3rd Amphibious Force under Rear Admiral T. S. Wilkinson, became Third Fleet under Vice Admiral William Halsey.

Near the end of the same month, Halsey's force was placed under my strategic command for the Solomons campaign, but naval units remained under Admiral Nimitz, who controlled the allocation of fleet units subject to the rulings of the Joint Chiefs of Staff.

William Halsey was one of our great sailors. He was a graduate of the Naval Academy in the class of 1904. While I had never known him personally, I was familiar with him as the fullback of the Navy eleven in its contests with West Point. Blunt, outspoken, dynamic, he had already proven himself to be a battle commander of the highest order. A strong advocate of unity of command in the Pacific, there seemed always to be an undercurrent opposed to him in the Navy Department. He was of the same aggressive type as John Paul Jones, David Farragut, and George Dewey. His one thought was to close with the enemy and fight him to the death. The bugaboo of many sailors, the fear of losing ships, was completely alien to his conception of sea action. I liked him from the moment we met, and my respect and admiration increased with time. His loyalty was undeviating, and I placed the greatest confidence in his judgment. No name rates higher in the annals of our country's naval history.

He was about my age and, gossip had it, sensitive about getting old, although I never detected anything of the sort. They tell this anecdote on him: A visiting dignitary was calling on the Admiral on his flagship, the *Enterprise*. A rough sea was running, and the Admiral's gig had difficulty in reaching the boarding platform. Twice the coxswain missed. Halsey, in his anxiety, leaned over the rail and shouted his instructions. And that was too much for the veteran coxswain's pride. He turned to a crewman and shouted, "Listen to the old bastard trying to tell us how to run this barge!" Halsey overheard and the silence was profound as he bent over the rail, shook his fist at the coxswain. In a voice trembling with rage bellowed, "How dare you call me 'old'!"

On April 18th we made one of the most significant strikes of the war. Our Air Force shot down the commander-in-chief of the Japanese Combined Fleet, Admiral Isoruku Yamamato. He had originally been opposed to war with the Allies, but when the decision was made, it was his comprehensive, plan which was put into effect so successfully at Pearl Harbor. Yamamato was in over-all charge of the Japanese operations in the Solomons and was generally regarded as the strategic brains of the Japanese naval war effort.

The Japanese code had been broken, and an intercepted radio message informed us that the Admiral was flying to Bougainville from Rabaul to reconnoiter personally the bloody ground campaign underway there. The message outlined the route to be flown, the air cover to be provided, and a rendezvous point off the west coast of Bougainville.

There was much skepticism that the message was a hoax, but I knew Yamamato as a front-line fighter who always pressed forward to the decisive points of contact. Major John W. Mitchell, commander of the 339th Fighter Squadron, was detailed to take his fighter unit and intercept at the rendezvous point.

It was a misty day, with dark clouds swirling menacingly over a turbulent sea. The hour of rendezvous was three o'clock, and when Captain Thomas G. Lanphier, a pilot of the 339th, arrived shortly before that time, nothing unusual met his anxious gaze. He waited. Nothing was stirring but the uneasy muttering of a rising storm. The order to return to base was on his lips when there—dead ahead—were two big lumbering transport planes of the enemy under an umbrella of Zeros above them.

Up went our fighters to engage the Zeros, up to intervene and cut off the two transport planes. The Zeros tried desperately to cover, but in the swirling, tangled melee of dogfights that followed the transports were forced to go it alone. The second one, bearing the bulk of the Admiral's staff, crashed, leaving Captain Lanphier and the Admiral's plane to fight it out unmolested. The Japanese pilot was no set-up. He was skilled and used every artifice to escape. Dodging behind cloud covers, zigzagging, twisting, and turning, he reached the shoreline. A quick drop and he was at tree-top height over the dense, tangled jungle of the island. It looked as though he had made it. Every gun in Lanphier's plane was blazing. And then suddenly there was a puff of black smoke from the rear of the transport—a red flame flickered into blaze, the big ship quivered and rolled, and then came a mighty crash tearing a jagged hole through the sweating jungle suddenly strewn with the smoldering debris of a wrecked plane. It was the end of Isoruku Yamamoto.

One could almost hear the rising crescendo of sound from the thousands of glistening white skeletons at the bottom of Pearl Harbor.

Washington lauded the action as one of the most important bags of the war, but labeled it top secret and forbade its publication, fearing it would jeopardize the work of the cryptanalytic division. And Lanphier became the unsung hero of an extraordinary exploit.

On May 27th, I received word from Prime Minister Curtin that I had been awarded the Grand Cross of Bath by the King of England. His message of congratulations was a warm one, indeed: "With unbounded pleasure I tender our congratulations on the high honor His Majesty the King has accorded you. It places the highest seal on your personal part in our common cause and I am certain will evoke pride in your country as you may be assured it evokes gratification to all Australians. My deep regards." *

I also received this letter from Prime Minister Winston Churchill:

---

* Lord Birdwood, the famous ANZAC commander of World War I, now senior field marshal of the British Empire, whom I had first met in India when he was Kitchener's chief of staff, wrote me as follows: "I wish I could tell you with what intense satisfaction throughout the whole British Army your appointment as G.C.B.—our highest military honor—has been received. We all feel that never has it been more deserved. As a G.C.B. myself I feel that great honor has come to all of us by your joining in our rank. May you be spared for many long years—I will not say to wear all your honors but to realize in full all the gratitude and admiration the peoples of your own great country and of the British Empire have for you."

I replied: "How very thoughtful of you to send me so splendid a note of congratulation on the G.C.B. Its bestowal moves me deeply. Out here I am continually thrusting at the enemy in the hope of keeping him in a state of unbalance and uncertainty until we can mount a sufficient force to really strike. Your name is one I constantly use in welding the fighting spirit of our troops and it has all of its old magical effect."

I was most interested to receive the account which General Dewing gave me of your views about the Pacific situation, and I wish indeed that we were in closer and more continuous contact. I can well believe that the Japanese will ensconce themselves firmly in any of the territories they have conquered, and that, apart from a collapse at the centre of their homeland, the process of ejecting them will be long and painful. I look forward indeed to the days when, having cleared up our troubles here, we can come with all our needful forces and aid you in your great task.

I am asking the President and his staff to discuss with us at our next meeting together the whole policy of the final combined attack upon Japan. Only when we know the form that is to take will it be possible to plan ahead over here for the maximum war effort against Japan. This prospect raises formidable difficulties as, obviously, there will not be the shipping available to carry more than a portion of our military forces to the Far East. Whatever is needed, and can be carried, will be sent, together with the bulk of the Navy and all possible employable Air Force. Meanwhile we shall of course bring heavy forces to bear against Burma, Malaya and other parts of the Japanese western front. If, as I hope, the operations in the Mediterranean now proceeding so successfully should neutralize or destroy the Italian fleet, we should be able to constitute a powerful British fleet in the Indian Ocean and Bay of Bengal. I hope this may happen before the year is out.

I am of opinion on the whole that once Stalin has been relieved of the pressure of the German Army—out of which he has cut a good part of the guts— he will most likely come into the war against Japan, whose hyena attitude he has thoroughly understood. This of course would open very large possibilities for the attack by air upon Japan itself. All this is rolling forward in the future. Meantime we must do our best to sustain China and to work Allied Air Forces in there.

I can assure you I am under no delusion about the Japanese. They are a terrible foe, and their military qualities extort admiration from the most reluctant minds. The progress you are making against them is remarkable, and I offer you my warmest congratulations and thanks. It gave me great pleasure to recommend His Majesty to bestow the Grand Cross of the Bath upon you as a token of the gratitude of the British Empire for all you have done for the common cause.

I was now ready to put into effect my final plans for the 1943 offensive. Briefly, the plan envisioned simultaneous operations along two lines of advance, from Guadalcanal and from Papua, securing northeast New Guinea and the Solomons group, and converging to pinch off the Japanese stronghold at Rabaul. The immediate objective was the seizure of airfields along these routes from which to whittle down the enemy's strength and at the same time provide cover for Allied assaults.

To furnish air support for operations in the two sectors of intended advance, I planned to occupy Woodlark and Kiriwina Islands with General Krueger's forces and begin immediate development of airfields there. In New Guinea, meanwhile, an initial feint would be made at Salamaua to divert enemy forces to its protection. The main drive, however, would be made against Lae, seizing its valuable airstrips by a combined assault of an airborne force operating overland through the Markham Valley and an amphibious force moving along the coast from Milne Bay and Buna. Then Finschhafen and other bases in the Huon Gulf-Vitiaz Strait area would be taken by shore-to-shore movements.

In the Solomons, the forces of the South Pacific Area under the immediate command of Admiral Halsey were assigned the capture of the New Georgia Island group. After attaining these objectives, both prongs, the Southwest Pacific and the South Pacific, covered and supported by the newly won bases, would push on to strike simultaneous blows against New Britain to the west and Bougainville to the east. Operations could then be undertaken to deprive Rabaul of naval support and airborne supply, and to eliminate it as a threat to the Allied flank as we moved west toward the Philippines.

To deceive the enemy as to the direction of the offensive, I ordered air raids to be made on Ambon, Timor, Tanimbar, and other bases in the Netherlands East Indies. False dummy signals by radio from Darwin, Perth, and Mirauke helped convince the Japanese that at least a diversionary attack was to be mounted from northwest Australia.

The offensive was initiated by General Krueger's Alamo Force, which occupied Woodlark and Kiriwina Islands with little opposition. The clearing of runways proceeded swiftly, and by July 24th the 67th Fighter Squadron was ready for operations from Woodlark, and by August 18th the 79th RAAF Fighter Squadron from Kiriwina.

In New Georgia, the Third Fleet, formerly the South Pacific Force, attacked as planned. The enemy defended his positions stubbornly, and the U.S. XIV Corps, Marine divisions, and New Zealand troops were all brought forward. From Rabaul, the enemy counterattacked both by air and sea. He used 315 aircraft, of which he lost half. In two naval engagements in the Kula Gulf on July 5-6th and July 12-13th he was defeated and lost a number of cruisers and destroyers. By October 7th, New Georgia and its adjacent islands were in Allied hands.

My plan to advance in northeast New Guinea and to seize the Huon Peninsula was entrusted to what was called the New Guinea Force. It was largely composed of Australian troops under the command of General

Blamey. My order to the Force was to seize and occupy the sector that contained Salamaua, Lae, Finschhafen, and Madang. Lae was to be the first main objective—its capture would breach the vital gate into the Huon Peninsula. The advance pushed the enemy back toward Salamaua with the purpose of deceiving him into the belief that it, and not Lae, was the prime objective. The strategem was highly successful, and under its diversionary cover the New Guinea Force completed its preparation for the drive against Lae.

Meanwhile Japanese Imperial Headquarters was pushing forward air reinforcements not only into Rabaul, but into Wewak on the north coast of New Guinea. This placed the bulk of our own air forces approximately between the enemy's air groups at these two strongholds. Their combined strength was about two to one against us, but individually we could almost match them at either place. I directed Kenney to mass first against one, and if successful, then against the other—to fight and destroy them in detail. I enjoined the greatest secrecy in his preparations so as to utilize to the full the element of surprise.

The operation was conducted by him and his field commander, Ennis C. Whitehead, with outstanding brilliance. He struck Wewak first, taking it completely by surprise, catching 100 enemy planes on the ground and destroying them. In the air battle that followed, he destroyed another 100 as the Japanese endeavored to rally their disorganized air squadrons.

Enemy air activity grew lighter and the high quality of his pilots deteriorated from this time on.

On August 15th, I received a personal letter from President Roosevelt of which these are extracts:

Dear Douglas: As you know Mrs. Roosevelt is leaving for the Southwest Pacific, and I am delighted that she will be able to see you. She is, of course, anxious to see everything, but I leave it wholly to your discretion as to where she should go and where she should not go. She is especially anxious to see Guadalcanal and at this moment it looks like a pretty safe place to visit.

I have told her that I am leaving the decision wholly up to the Area Commanders, not only in regard to Guadalcanal, but other places as well. I doubt, of course, at the present writing, whether she should go to New Georgia or to Funafuti.

I think that Mrs. Roosevelt's visit to places where we have military or naval personnel will help the general morale.

You have been doing a grand job and we are all proud of you.

I was at the front, and detached General Eichelberger in Australia to attend Mrs. Roosevelt. She wished to come to New Guinea, but I thought it too dangerous. We were old friends and she took my refusal in good part. Her visit was a warm reminder that we were not forgotten.

On September 4th, the attack on Lae was launched by the Australians moving along the coast to strike from the east. At the same time, another Australian column was being prepared to fly in overland by way of the Markham Valley to strike from the west. The success of this second column depended upon the seizure of an unused prewar airfield at Nadzab. With this field in our possession, and made usable, we could land the troops, close the gap, and completely envelop Lae and the enemy forces there.

It was a delicate operation involving the first major parachute jump in the Pacific war. The unit to make the jump was the United States 503rd Parachute Regiment. I inspected them and found, as was only natural, a sense of nervousness among the ranks. I decided that it would be advisable for me to fly in with them. I did not want them to go through their first baptism of fire without such comfort as my presence might bring to them. But they did not need me. One plane after another poured out its stream of dropping men over the target field. Everything went like clockwork. The flame-throwers ate away the tall, irregular blotches of tropical Kunai grass; holes in the field were patched up, and the follow-up transports began to discharge their loads of infantry troops. The vertical envelopment became a reality.

We closed in from all sides and entered the shambles that had been Lae on September 16th.

To my astonishment, I was awarded the Air Medal. Like all ground officers, this exceptionally pleased me, even though I felt it did me too much credit.*

But what warmed my heart even more was the comment of General Pershing, my old and beloved commander of the First World War: "It is not often given to a commander to achieve the ideal of every general—the surrounding and annihilating of his enemy. But MacArthur, with greatly inferior forces, has achieved this three times in the last eighteen months: In the Kokoda and Milne Bay campaign, in the Bismarck Sea, and now in the operations round Lae and Salamaua."

After Lae, one column from the New Guinea Force moved on Finsch-

---

* The citation read: "On September 5, 1943, General MacArthur, in a B-17 bomber called the Talisman, personally led the American paratroopers on the very successful and important jump against the Nadzab airstrip. General MacArthur flew through enemy infested airlanes and skillfully directed this historic operation which was accomplished with the greatest success and made possible the later landings of Australian airborne troops and the closing of the western inland approaches of the Markham Valley. He remained over the combat area until all paratroops had landed in initial contact with the enemy in this battle."

hafen, the strategic port at the eastern tip of the Huon Peninsula that commanded the western entrance to the vital Vitiaz Straits. Finschhafen was one of the main bastions in the enemy defense structure, and one vital to our plans. The movement took the Japanese by surprise and Allied forces occupied Finschhafen on October 2nd.* This column continued its successful drive up the New Guinea coast in spite of stubborn enemy resistance.

South of the enemy, the second column of the New Guinea Force thrust inland through the Markham Valley, slashing the center of New Guinea in a 200-mile advance. The Allies now dominated the Huon Peninsula. The twofold maneuver ringed all the important enemy positions, and left powerless his remaining installations and concentrations on the northeast New Guinea coast. Surprised by the swiftness of these movements, the enemy was forced to loosen his hold on New Guinea, with overwhelming loss of irreplaceable troops and supplies.

In the Solomons, the enemy's strength in southern Bougainville, north of Guadalcanal, was so great I told Halsey to by-pass these lines, located in the east, and jump forward 200 miles to Empress Augusta Bay on the west coast. To further this movement, I directed Kenney to strike Rabaul, the enemy's supporting stronghold, with his full power. Just as the right wing of the Japanese air force had been smashed at Wewak to help the New Guinea advance, I told him to destroy the left wing at Rabaul to help the South Pacific advance.

"Kenney struck like a cobra. On October 12, 349 planes took off against Rabaul, attacking airstrips, shipping and supply dumps and firing large areas. I cited Kenney and his command and later, when I saw him personally, I said, 'George, you broke Rabaul's back yesterday.' He shot back instantly, 'The attack marks the turning point in the war in the Southwest Pacific.'"

"From this time on, the intensity of the bombings increased, reaching a peak early in the next year. In October alone, our Fifth and Thirteenth Army Air Forces dropped 685 tons of bombs on Rabaul targets. Before the end of February, the Japanese had no air support whatsoever; some 30 naval vessels had been sunk, 23 damaged, more than 200 cargo ships plus 517 barges and four submarines destroyed."†

---

* General Marshall sent me this fine message: "Congratulations, personal and official, on campaign just completed with capture of Finschhafen. The combination of forces, tactics and speed and celerity with which the successive operations have followed are a splendid promise for the future."

† I cited Kenney and his command in the following message: "The history of warfare shows no more valiant, no more determined and no more effective battle than the one waged by your medium bombers and fighters at Rabaul. Please express to every officer and man of the force my unbounded admiration for such a magnificent performance." Later, when I saw Kenney personally, I said, "George, you broke Rabaul's back yesterday." He shot back instantly, "The attack marks the turning point in the war in the Southwest Pacific." Perhaps he was not far wrong.

On November 1st, the 3rd Marine Division of the South Pacific Force attacked Bougainville's western shores at Empress Augusta Bay, and pushed inland against weak opposition. The Japanese had not expected an attack at this point. Their main forces concentrated on the east coast were cut off by mountains, swamp, and jungle from Empress Augusta Bay and, consequently, were unable to counterattack.

The enemy continued to fall back toward the stronghold of Madang. To cut this line of retreat, I directed Alamo Force to seize Saidor in an amphibious operation on its flank. After the landing on January 2, 1944, the Force's United States troops drove toward the east to intercept the retreating enemy. The Japanese were trapped.

Caught between the closing pincers of the two advancing forces, with no sources of supply, the Japanese disintegrated and scattered in chaotic flight. That the steaming jungle finished what the Allies began was written grimly across the thousands of emaciated Japanese corpses our troops discovered along the hill trails and in the mountains. The last Japanese were routed by February 10th, when the Alamo and New Guinea Forces joined.

Rabaul was being steadily emasculated. Enemy thrusts from that once-powerful stronghold were becoming weak and ineffectual, and by the end of February 1944 had no air support whatsoever. In spite of replacements and reinforcements, the once-powerful Japanese air force in this area had been defeated almost to the point of extinction.

At the start of the year the Japanese had held an advanced line running from Salamaua and Lae across southern New Britain and the Solomon Sea to New Georgia. Now their ground forces had been pushed back to Madang, Rabaul, and Kavieng. They had lost great numbers of men and matériel, and further thousands of troops were tactically cut off on isolated islands. Allied planes and undersea craft were sending to the bottom a constantly growing toll of enemy transport and supply ships. For the Southwest Pacific Area, 1942 had been a good year.

Prime Minister Churchill suggested that a direct liaison with Britain be established with my headquarters, and sent General Lumsden to act as liaison officer.

Back in Australia, Mr. Curtin was apparently being needled as to what next. He had not been included in the great conferences held by Roosevelt and Churchill. He had visited London and Washington, but without tangible results. It is possible that a certain sense of frustration at being overlooked might have gripped him. Whatever the reason, I received on November 22nd a letter of which these extracts are the gist:

The splendid progress of your operations has been the subject of some thought on my part and discussion by the Government in relation to your future plans and the area of employment of the Australian Forces which have been assigned to you.

Australia has a special interest in the employment of its own forces in the operations for the ejection of the enemy from territory under its administration. Furthermore, it is essential that the Government should be at least broadly aware of your ideas for the employment of the Australian Forces in any areas outside Australia and mandated territory, and of what you may contemplate in regard to operations affecting the latter areas.

Although, by the most complete cooperation on your part, there has never been any need to refer to the documentary basis which governs your relationship to the Australian Government, you will be aware that the position under the set-up in the Southwest Pacific Area is so governed.

I would greatly appreciate advice of prospective plans in regard to the use of the Australian land forces, in order that the Australian Government may consider their contemplated use.

It is, of course, unnecessary for me to add that this request is not prompted by any desire to interfere in any way with your conduct of operations, or to participate in the formulation of plans. The Australian Government has at all times had the utmost confidence in your handling of these matters, and is deeply appreciative of the remarkable results you have achieved with the limited resources at your disposal. My present request arises solely from the responsibility to the Australian people which must be exercised by myself and the Australian Government.

I, at once, sent him the following message, flew to Brisbane, and set up an immediate conference:

I am in complete accord with the general position outlined in your letter of November 22. The desirability and necessity of your being informed of operational plans for the area are self-evident. At our meeting I shall give you my general concept of the campaign in such detail as you may desire. In this connection, however, I call attention to the limitations with reference to operations which are imposed upon me by higher authorities. I am constantly receiving directives which modify materially my use of the forces here and at the present time am still in doubt as to master decisions with regard to the future. In addition, you of course understand that whatever plan may be made, the vicissitudes of campaign and the reaction of the enemy may result in almost instantaneous decisions by the military commander producing comprehensive changes in the projected use of the forces. Within these limitations I shall acquaint you with everything that is within my scope and knowledge.

I conferred with him at length and the following day he broadcast to the Australian people:

I have just completed an important conference with the Commander-in-Chief. The war problem of Australia is now entering upon a new phase. A completely successful and brilliant defense is now to be followed by the attack. Australia's part will be a mighty one as from this continent, as a base, will be launched in due time one of the major offensives of the war. In the defense stage, every resource available to me was thrown in to stem the engulfing tide of enemy assault. Demands were immediate and the action taken was dictated only by the extreme urgency of the moment. We have met and absorbed this lethal shock and, in turn, are now on the offensive. This will require a redistribution of our resources, a readjustment along many lines, a calculated distribution of our effort and a minute examination of our long-range potentialities. There is no more difficult and delicate operation in war than the passage of a nation from defense to offense. It is the almost limitless ramifications of this extraordinarily complicated process that I have discussed at length with the Commander-in-Chief, who is a vital factor in all decisions to be taken not only along military lines, but those of commerce, industry and economics. In this broad field we have endeavored to fix firmly general principles which will ensure not only a maximum war effort, but the future transition to an equally successful after war effort. I am indebted to General MacArthur for the high statesmanship and breadth of world vision he has contributed to the discussion. The complete integration of our concepts, which has been a source of such strength in the past, will continue to the end.

Late in December, General Marshall, while returning from an Allied conference between Roosevelt, Stalin, and Churchill at Tehran, stopped over a day in the Southwest Pacific Area. We had a long and frank discussion. I called attention to the paucity of men and matériel I was receiving as compared with all other theaters of war. He said he realized the imbalance and regretted it, but could do little to alter the low priority accorded the area. He said:

Admiral King claimed the Pacific as the rightful domain of the Navy; he seemed to regard the operations there as almost his own private war; he apparently felt that the only way to remove the blot on the Navy disaster at Pearl Harbor was to have the Navy command a great victory over Japan; he was adamant in his refusal to allow any major fleet to be under other command than that of naval officers although maintaining that naval officers were competent to command ground or air forces; he resented the prominent part I had in the Pacific War; he was vehement in his personal criticism of me and encouraged Navy propaganda to that end; he had the complete support of the Secretary of the Navy, Knox, the support in general principle of President Roosevelt and his Chief of Staff, Admiral Leahy, and in many cases of General Arnold, the head of the Air Force.

I called Marshall's attention to the fact that all naval disasters in the Pacific—Pearl Harbor, Macassar Strait, and the four-cruiser loss to an unscathed enemy in the Solomon Sea—had been under naval commanders; that in my area we had no naval losses of such character; that the Navy and the Air Force had no greater supporter and booster than I; that I felt it fantastic, to say the least, that interservice rivalry or personal ambitions should be allowed to interfere with the winning of the war; that my naval units were among the most loyal and efficient elements of the command; and that I had publicly stated that, to secure unity of command, I would accept a subordinate assignment.

He seemed to agree, but, having been chief of staff myself, I realized how impossible it was to have professional and objective matters decided on the basis of merit and common sense. Upon his return to Washington he informed me that he had spoken to General Arnold, who promised greater air support. From that time on Washington became more generous to the SWPA.

About this time I became aware that my name was being bandied about in the United States as a possible candidate for President on the Republican ticket. I at once stated that I had no political ambitions whatsoever and only hoped to see Allied victory in the war before retiring. But in spite of this, a furor was raised by the unauthorized publication of a correspondence initiated by Republican Congressman Dr. A. L. Miller from Nebraska. I tried to clear the atmosphere by giving out this public statement:

My attention has been called to the publication by Congressman Miller of a personal correspondence with him. In so far as my letters are concerned they were never intended for publication. Their perusal will show any fair-minded person that they were neither politically inspired nor intended to convey blanket approval of the Congressman's views. I entirely repudiate the sinister interpretation that they were intended as criticism of any political philosophy or any personages in high office. They were written merely as amiable acknowledgments, to a member of our highest law-making body, of letters containing flattering and friendly remarks to me, personally. To construe them otherwise is to misrepresent my intent. I have not received Congressman Miller's third letter in which he is reported to advise me to announce candidacy for the office of President of the U.S.

But even this formal disavowal failed to pacify the angry critics, so I felt it necessary to issue a follow-up statement:

Right: General MacArthur's grandfather, Arthur MacArthur, Sr., at the time of his appointment to the Supreme Court of the District of Columbia (1870). State Historical Society of Wisconsin

Below: Douglas (left) with his parents and brother, Arthur, at Fort Selden, New Mexico (1881). Duell, Sloan & Pearce, Inc.

Right: Douglas MacArthur (fourth from left) as a member of West Texas Military Academy baseball team (1895). International N. P.

Below: Brigadier General MacArthur, General Moneher and General deBazelaire discussing American military maneuvers in France (1918). U.S. Army Signal Corps

Left: Captain MacArthur during his tour of duty in Veracruz (1914). General Douglas MacArthur Memorial Foundation

Below: MacArthur (at left) with General deBazelaire watching Rainbow Division artillery at Glonville (1918).

Right: MacArthur shortly after being promoted to brigadier general (1921). U.S. Army Signal Corps

Below: MacArthur being decorated with the Distinguished Service Cross by General Pershing (1918).

Left: General MacArthur as Superintendent of West Point. General Douglas MacArthur Memorial Foundation

Below: General MacArthur, then Chief of Staff, signs the Golden Book after laying a wreath on the tomb of the French Unknown Soldier. At left is General Henri Gouraud, the Military Governor of Paris (1931, Paris). International

Below: General MacArthur (fourth from left) as a member of the trial board at the court-martial of Billy Mitchell (1925). Charles W. Miller Studios

Right: General MacArthur, after U.S. Army troops had ousted the Bonus Army from their camp at Anacostia Flats. At left are Col. Dwight D. Eisenhower and 1st Lt. Thomas J. Davis. General Douglas MacArthur Memorial Foundation

Far right: General MacArthur with President Roosevelt and Secretary of War George Dern (1934).

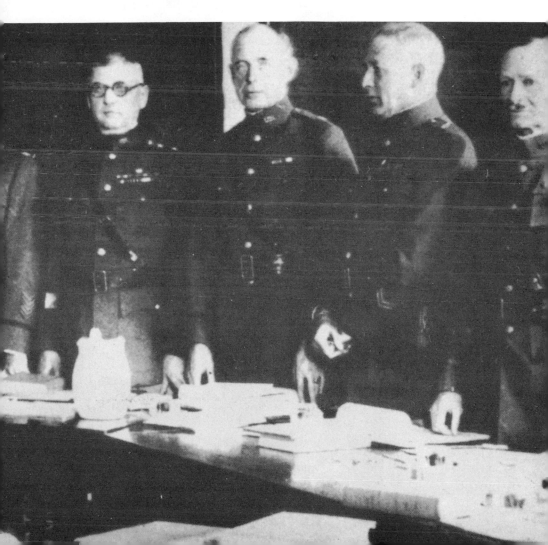

Right: Jean Marie Faircloth, Mrs. Douglas MacArthur (1941). Charles W. Miller Studios

Below: General MacArthur reviewing troops at Manila (1936). Miller Studios

I have had brought to my attention a number of newspaper articles professing in strongest terms a widespread public opinion that it is detrimental to our war effort to have an officer in high position, on active service at the front, considered for nomination for the office of President. I have on several occasions announced I was not a candidate for the position. Nevertheless, in view of these circumstances, in order to make my position entirely unequivocal, I request that no action be taken that would link my name in any way with the nomination. I do not covet it nor would I accept it.

This was a definite enough disavowal to satisfy the most skeptical critic or the worried professional politician. Along these lines, Prime Minister Curtin told me with high amusement what had transpired at the White House just before he flew back to Australia from Washington. With the state visit officially over and the required formal farewells said, Curtin went to see the President to say goodbye informally. Roosevelt greeted him warmly and the two statesmen chatted for a time. As he prepared to depart, Curtin said, "Mr. President, certainly it's none of my business and probably I shouldn't say this, but I can assure you in utter honesty and sincerity that General MacArthur has no more idea of running against you for the Presidency than I have. He has told me that a dozen times."

Roosevelt whirled in his chair, scattering papers as he roared for Steve Early. The genial and able Press Secretary came into the study and the obviously delighted President repeated the news. "I'm sure," said Curtin, "that every night when he turned in, the President had been looking under the bed to make dead sure you weren't there."

With the advent of the New Year, I prepared for a westward drive along New Guinea. Up to this time the axis of my advance had been northward, but it was now to bend sharply to the west. The route of a return to the Philippines lay straight before me—along the coast of New Guinea to the Vogelkop Peninsula and the Moluccas. I was still about 1,600 miles from the Philippines and 2,100 miles from Manila, but I was now in a position to carry out with increasing speed the massive strokes against the enemy which I had envisioned since the beginning of my campaigns in the Southwest Pacific Area.

With the Japanese confused and thrown off balance by the recent series of Allied successes, I urged Washington that the situation be exploited immediately. There were large forces available in the Pacific which, with the accretions scheduled for the current year, would permit the execution of an offensive that would place us in the Philippines in December if the forces were employed in effective combination. All available ground, air, and assault

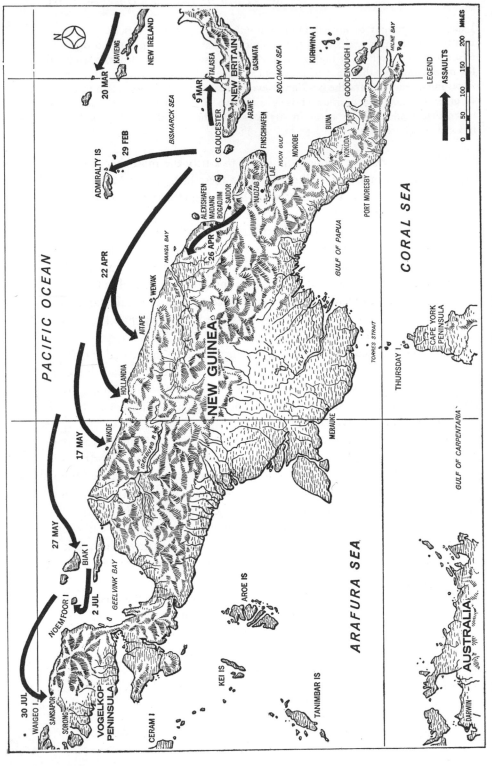

Westward Drive along New Guinea

forces in the Pacific could be combined in a drive along the New Guinea-Mindanao axis, supported by the main fleet and other facilities readily available in these waters. I proposed that the maximum force from all sources in the Pacific be concentrated in a drive up the New Guinea coast, to be co-ordinated with a Central Pacific operation against the Palaus, and the support by combatant elements of the Pacific Fleet with orders to contain or destroy the Japanese Fleet. Time pressed.

I planned to advance through western New Guinea because that route would provide the best opportunity for the complete utilization of the Allied ground-air-navy team. Such a drive, penetrating Japan's defense perimeter along the New Guinea line, would permit the by-passing of heavily defended areas. The land-based bomber line would again be moved by the successive occupation of new air sites; ground forces would be rapidly deployed forward by air transport and amphibious movements; additional plane and ship bases would be established as each objective was taken. Enemy naval forces and shipping would be eliminated along the line of advance to prevent reinforcement; then the same pattern would be repeated, neutralizing and pocketing hostile concentrations until the Allied forces were in position to make a direct attack against the Japanese in the Philippines.

As a preliminary to the coming drive, I directed the seizure of the Green Islands, north of Bougainville. On February 15th, Allied troops carried out a weakly opposed amphibious landing and captured the islands to cut off an estimated 25,000 enemy troops to the south. Starvation and disease, certain to ensue from military blockade, rendered their position hopeless. With their airfields destroyed and their barge traffic paralyzed, the relief of these scattered garrisons became no longer practicable, and their ultimate fate was sealed. For all strategic military purposes, this completed the campaign for the Solomon Islands.

During this same period, Admiral Nimitz's forces struck powerful blows in the Central Pacific, including the capture of Kwajalein and heavy raids against Truk. These attacks forced the Japanese to withdraw their navy to more secure bases.

Before launching a full-scale attack to the west, I needed an additional base near enough for staging purposes and with a harbor of sufficient size to accommodate a large amphibious striking force. At the same time, I wished to insure the protection of my right flank, and to prevent reinforcements from reaching enemy troops bottled up in the Bismarck-Solomons areas.

The Admiralty Islands in the Bismarck Archipelago filled these requirements. They possessed ideal natural harbors and airfield sites which could support subsequent operations along the New Guinea coast, and against the

Carolinas and Marianas to the north. Their occupation would put the final seal on the isolation of Rabaul.

The original plan called for an amphibious operation on April 1st by Southwest Pacific Forces, in conjunction with an attack on Kavieng by Admiral Nimitz's fleet units. In February, however, I saw reflected in the lack of opposition to Allied air and naval craft in the Bismarck area a temporary confusion and weakness of the enemy which I decided to capitalize on without delay. I felt that the situation presented an ideal opportunity for a *coup de main* which, if successful, could advance the Allied timetable in the Pacific by several months and save thousands of Allied lives.

Enemy strength on the islands was unknown, but our air observation flights reported little activity. Reports from Momote indicated the complete disuse of the main airfield, where bomb craters remained unfilled and grass was growing along the airstrip. Surrounding buildings and installations were seemingly unattended and in a bad state of disrepair.

On February 24th, I decided to make an immediate reconnaissance in force to probe eastern Los Negros, where enemy positions seemed to be weakest. My aim essentially was to strike swiftly, achieve surprise, and thus avoid bitter fighting and heavy casualties at the beachhead. If an initial foothold could be established without undue losses, the reconnaissance force would then advance, seize Momote airstrip nearby, and be promptly reinforced. If unforeseen enemy strength should be encountered at the beaches, however, and an unfavorable situation should develop, a speedy withdrawal would be made.

On the morning of February 29th, the strike was launched. The reconnaissance force was light, the 5th Calvary, which I had known so well on the frontier nearly sixty years before, commanded by Major General William C. Chase, an unsurpassed front-line fighter, and a naval convoy under Admiral Kinkaid. I was relying almost entirely upon surprise for success and, because of the delicate nature of the operation and the immediate decision required, I accompanied the force aboard Admiral Kinkaid's flagship, the light cruiser, *Phoenix*.

The landing met little opposition, the surprise being complete. General Chase rapidly established a wide perimeter around the airstrip and accompanied me on a reconnaissance of the surrounding terrain which convinced me it could be held. I immediately radioed for the auxiliary force from Finschhafen to be brought forward, and told Chase, "Hold what you have taken, no matter against what odds. You have your teeth in him now, don't let go." He didn't, although later the enemy heavily attacked, only to be bloodily repulsed.

By the end of March, all enemy resistance in the Admiralties had been over-come. Rabaul was now securely encircled—the noose was complete. More than 80,000 Japanese troops were now choked off in the Bismarck-New Britain-Solomons area.*

Meanwhile, the Australians pressed westward along the New Guinea coast. Madang was captured, and by the end of April the Japanese carried out a mass retreat toward Wewak and Aitape.

It was originally planned that Hansa Bay was to be the next objective on the Dutch New Guinea coast, but, in view of the spectacular success in the Admiralties, I was anxious to take a longer step forward. The capture of Hansa Bay would mean an advance of only 120 miles, but I now planned a maneuver which at one stroke would move us almost 500 miles forward and at the same time render some 40,000 Japanese troops ineffective. I would by-pass Hansa Bay, by-pass the enemy stronghold at Wewak, and strike well to the rear at Aitape and Hollandia. Once this area was securely ours, we would have airstrips from which our ground-based aircraft could dominate the Vogelkop, and our advance westward would be hastened by several months.

The development of the Admiralties' extensive harbor and airfield facili-ties made the capture of Kavieng and the invasion of New Ireland unneces-sary. This saving of life on our part was to me the most gratifying feature of the operation. Indeed, the greatest satisfaction I have always felt as a result of campaign successes is of the men I saved and brought back safely rather than the glory of the victories that were gained.

My plan called for landing on both sides of Hollandia, at Humboldt and Tanahmerah Bays, with a simultaneous landing by a smaller force at Aitape, midway between Hollandia and Wewak, a distance of 150 miles. The Hol-landia forces would converge on the flanks of the three airstrips inland, while the forces to the east would seize the fighter field at Aitape and prevent any junction of the enemy's Wewak and Hollandia troops. I set the target date for April 22nd. Admiral Nimitz agreed to fully support the operation with his Pacific Fleet.

---

* General Marshall sent me the following message: "Congratulations on the skill and success with which the Admiralty Islands operation has been carried through. Please accept my admira-tion for the manner in which the entire affair has been handled."

I was awarded the Combat Bronze Star with Arrowhead. Winston Churchill wrote me: "I send you my warm congratulations on the speed with which you turned to good account your first entry into the Admiralty Islands. I expect that this will help you to go ahead quicker than you originally planned. Every good wish, my dear MacArthur, and believe me we shall never forget all you have done to help us and the British Commonwealth of Nations in the defense of Austra-lia and New Zealand from mortal peril."

During March and early April, intensive air raids were launched against the Japanese fields along the coast. Large numbers of enemy planes were destroyed and shipping concentrations heavily hit. Comprehensive deception plans were put into effect to further the enemy's belief that the attack would fall on Wewak and Hansa Bay. He strengthened these positions to the neglect of the real points of attack.

The task force for the invasion rendezvoused north of the Admiralties, and I hoisted my flag on the light cruiser *Nashville*. We proceeded in a northwesterly direction. Although this course was 200 miles longer than the direct route, it was intended to mislead the Japanese and prevent them from determining the exact objective in case of discovery by aerial reconnaissance. Swinging suddenly southward, the huge convoy approached the Dutch New Guinea coast.

Just as the branches of a tree spread out from its trunk toward the sky, so did the tentacles of the invasion convoy slither out toward the widely separated beaches in the objective area. The first split was when the Aitape force turned off to port and disappeared over the horizon. Toward four o'clock of the next morning, the second group veered to starboard and sped for Tanahmerah Bay, 20 miles north of Hollandia. The main convoy continued on its course straight for Humboldt Bay.

As the first rays of dawn began to pierce the morning's dark mist on April 22nd, after heavy preliminary air and naval bombardment, the invasion troops went ashore according to plan. Complete tactical and strategic surprise was achieved. The convoys had sailed within striking distance apparently without detection. The ease of the landings exceeded even my highest hopes. No withering fire met us at the beach. Instead, there was only disorder—rice still boiling in pots, weapons and personal equipment of every kind abandoned. No more than token resistance was met at any point, and there was no interference from the enemy's air or naval forces. The painstaking deception measures had been remarkably effective.

Similar to the Solomons and Bismarck loops of envelopment, we surrounded the Japanese Eighteenth Army. To the east were the Australians and Americans, to the west, the Americans, to the north, the sea controlled by our Allied naval forces, to the south, untraversed jungle mountain ranges, and over all, our Allied air mastery. Since the start of the campaign, the Japanese had lost 110,000 men, 44 per cent of their original strength of a quarter of a million, and the remainder was now neutralized and strategically impotent. The enemy's maritime and air losses were proportionally heavy. For the first time we had recaptured Dutch territory, and present operations, if continued successfully, promised the liberation of all of New Guinea.*

The expanding nature of the tasks ahead required a substantial increase in the United States forces allocated to the Southwest Pacific Area. Accordingly, on June 15th, the Thirteenth Air Force; the XIV Corps; the 25th, 37th, 40th, 43rd, 93rd, and the American Divisions; and the 1st and 2nd Philippine Regiments were added to my command. The Eighth Army was organized and placed under the command of General Eichelberger. The XIV Corps was under Lieutenant General Oscar Griswold. United States naval forces comprised three light cruisers, twenty-seven destroyers, thirty submarines, and a number of mine-layers and PT boats. The South Pacific

---

* I received many comments on the Allied advance.

From General Marshall:

I send you my personal congratulations on the Aitape-Hollandia campaign which has completely disorganized the enemy plans for the security of eastern Malaysia and has advanced the schedule of operations by many weeks. The succession of surprises effected and the small losses suffered, the great extent of territory conquered and the casualties inflicted on the enemy, together with the large Japanese forces which have been isolated, all combine to make your operations of the past one and a half months models of strategical and tactical maneuvers.

From Admiral Nimitz:

My warmest congratulations and appreciation to you on the destruction of planes in and around Hollandia. Such proficient work is not only a serious blow to the enemy but is most effective support to ships. It is heartening to have such splendid evidence of close and successful coordination by our forces.

I replied in thanking him:

It is a matter of inspiration to this area to be fighting in cooperation with your own magnificent command.

From Lord Mountbatten, the British commander of the Southeast Asia Command:

Landing at Hollandia has been followed with admiration by all of us here and especially by the Dutch officers on my staff. We send you our warmest congratulations.

From General Pershing:

When history looks back to master strategic strokes, your capture of Hollandia will undoubtedly stand out as one of the most masterly. Seldom, if ever, in history have such important military results been obtained at such small cost to the attacker and with such surprise and disaster to the defender.

And John Curtin's comment to the press:

His devotion to duty could not have been greater had he been an Australian officer with a lifetime of service in the Australian Army. He is a great genius.

All words which cheered me in my loneliness no end.

Force was relieved from my operational control and returned to the command of Admiral Nimitz. This took with it Admiral Halsey, a great loss to me. On leaving, he sent me this moving letter, which I treasure greatly:

My dear General:

Amenities have been observed through the media of despatches and my last personal visit, but I feel impelled to add something to the requirements of official courtesy.

You and I have had tough sledding with the enemy, and we have had other complex problems nearly as difficult as our strategic problems; and I have the feeling that in every instance we have licked our difficulties. My own personal dealings with you have been so completely satisfactory that I will always feel a personal regard and warmth over and above my professional admiration.

I also know, and take great pleasure in telling you, that the members of my staff continually express their satisfaction over the way that business can be done by the South Pacific and Southwest Pacific.

I must confess to a feeling of envy as I watch the battle tempo building up in your area; but the envy is tempered by an enthusiastic appreciation of the bold and masterly manner in which you are capitalizing on enemy weakness and keeping the little devils off balance.

I sincerely hope, and firmly believe, that I will have further opportunity to join forces with you against our vicious and hated enemy. In the meantime, I shall watch with interest and pride, your progress toward your goal.

I send this last message from the South Pacific with a genuine feeling of professional and personal comradeship.

Late in June, Admiral Nimitz asked for assistance in his operation against Saipan. I threw in all my available air force to help him. He signaled me on June 26th: "Advising a successful landing on Saipan and the destruction on June 19th and 20th of the enemy fleet. Once again, Air and Naval forces in concert had overwhelmed the enemy."

The Hollandia invasion initiated a marked change in the tempo of my advance westward. Subsequent assaults against Wakde, Biak, Noemfoor, and Sansapor were mounted in quick succession, and, in contrast to previous campaigns, I planned no attempt to complete all phases of one operation before moving on to the next objective. I was determined to reach the Philippines before December, and consequently concentrated on the immediate utilization of each seized position to spark the succeeding advance.

As the Allied movement speared westward into Dutch territory, I directed that civil affairs in that region be administered by Netherlands East Indies officials accompanying the troops. This policy of immediate transfer of civil control without a preliminary military government had been instituted by me at the start of the war. This policy I had continued during the occupation of the islands north of Australia, when Australian civil officials assumed authority promptly in the wake of the operations. The success of this method was reflected in the complete lack of friction between the various governments concerned.

On April 27th, I informed the War Department that I would attack positions in the Wakde region about May 15th with the primary objective of obtaining "more airdrome space for displacement of the air forces forward." The Wakde-Sarmi region, beginning approximately 140 miles west of Hollandia, had been developed by the Japanese into a ground and air position of considerable strategic importance. There were good airfields and the enemy had established numerous bivouac and storage areas along the entire coastal road.

The attack was launched on May 17th and met stubborn resistance from a strongly entrenched enemy, but by May 20th all opposition had been overcome. This provided me with a new advance base from which all remaining enemy airdromes and harbors were within the range of our medium bombers with fighter protection.

Biak Island, 180 miles northwest of Wakde, lay next in the line of my advance. On May 27th, the 41st Division made the initial assault on Southern Biak in the face of light opposition. The light enemy resistance at the beachhead held little hint of what was to come. Utilizing the peculiar topography of the island, the enemy had devised a brilliant defense structure. His principal units were held in check until our forces moved from the shore to the hilly terrain inland, where from overhanging crags and caves the Japanese savagely counterattacked, and, behind 5-ton tanks, drove a wedge between the first waves and the main attacking force. We threw in reinforcements, and, after violent fighting, by July 22nd major resistance had been overcome. The tenacity of the enemy was shown in his casualty list of over 7,200 dead, including those killed in mopping-up operations.

Noemfoor was next, and after sporadic resistance was cleared by July 7th.

While we were leaping forward in our coastal drive from one success to another, the trapped Japanese army below Hollandia was writing the last chapters in its epic story of defeat. These pocketed Japanese waited helplessly and in vain for outside relief or some definite instructions from higher headquarters. After two months of isolated confinement, they could wait no longer. With their food running out, their nerves frazzled by frustrating inactivity, and with fresh Allied successes at Sarmi and Wakde making a withdrawal to western New Guinea impossible, the Japanese decided to act.

General Adachi, commanding the remnants of the once-powerful army, cast aside all logic and pretense at strategy and gave orders for a desperate attempt to break through at Aitape. It was a hopeless enterprise, but rather than submit passively to a situation which gave every promise of eventual starvation, General Adachi chose to chance a course of positive action which might somehow constitute an impediment to Allied strategy. In an impassioned address, he exhorted his troops virtually to destroy themselves in a blind mass attack:

I cannot find any means nor method which will solve this situation strategically or tactically. Therefore, I intend to overcome this by relying on our Japanese *Bushido*. I am determined to destroy the enemy in Aitape by attacking him ruthlessly with the concentration of our entire force in that area. This will be our final opportunity to employ our entire strength to annihilate the enemy. Make the supreme sacrifice, display the spirit of the Imperial Army.

The initial effort of the main enemy offensive took place soon after midnight on July 11th as the Japanese plunged forward in a mad suicidal rush against the Allied line. Our machine-gunners mowed down wave after wave of oncoming Japanese troops. Artillery, already placed in position and ranged beforehand, wiped out enemy assembly points, while Allied planes kept up a continuous and accurate bombardment of supply points and routes of attack.

When the Japanese were frustrated in their frontal attempt, they tried to pierce the Allied right flank to the south. For over a month they battered violently against the Allied lines in fruitless efforts to overrun the Aitape defenses, but every drive was repulsed as the toll of enemy dead mounted sharply. Finally, on July 31st, we launched a double enveloping counter-offensive which cut the Japanese into three main segments. The encircling Allied forces then hunted down and destroyed the divided enemy units in detail, virtually annihilating the remainder of General Adachi's army. By August 10th all effective resistance had ceased. As General Adachi, himself, later gloomily acknowledged: "The story of this army is tragic. We lost ten thousand killed in our first attack at Aitape."

My next strike was directed at the Vogelkop Peninsula, the last enemy stronghold in the New Guinea area. Adhering to the principle of avoiding massed enemy concentrations where feasible, I attacked the western end of the peninsula, by-passing the thousands of Japanese massed at Manokwari. We made simultaneous and unopposed landings on the mainland near Cape Opmaria, and on Middleburg and Amsterdam Islands to the northwest. A shore-to-shore landing from Cape Opmaria was then made at Sansapor. These operations advanced our forces another 200 miles to the west. We were now within 600 miles of the Philippines. The enemy garrison at Manokwari, the pivot of the defenses of the Vogelkop, was by-passed and useless; its garrison, 25,000 strong, isolated, with its only possible escape route to the south over hazardous terrain of swamp and jungle. Our air bases were now established from Milne Bay along the entire coast of New Guinea. The enemy was now no longer able to operate either by sea or air beyond the Halmahera-Philippine line, which was the main defense cover for his conquered empire in the Southwest Pacific. Should this line go, all of his conquests south of China would be imperiled and in grave danger of flank envelopment.

The capture of Sansapor marked the successful termination of the long and hard-fought New Guinea campaign. In a little more than a year, our troops, penetrating line after line of the enemy's defensive arc, had advanced 1,800 miles westward and 700 miles to the north. Compared with the Japanese, our offensive employed only modest forces and, through the maximum use of maneuver and surprise, had incurred only light losses. Untold thousands of the enemy had been pocketed and cut off from outside aid, and thus rendered unable to interfere with our main operational plans. When Washington inquired concerning these scattered enemy segments, I recommended that, since their capacity for organized offensive effort had passed and they represented no menace to current or future operations, we disregard them for the moment. I felt that the actual process of their immediate destruction by assault methods would unquestionably have involved heavy loss of life without adequate compensating strategic advantages.

One of my gravest concerns during the campaign, waged through broiling sun and drenching rain, amid tangled jungle and impassable mountain trails, was the health of my troops. Both climate and terrain were bitter. The *anopheles* mosquito, a malaria carrier, was as dangerous and deadly a foe as the enemy. On the Papuan front, it had been responsible for more noneffectives than any other single factor. But we finally conquered this everpresent menace. This remarkable achievement, comparable with the Goethals-Gorgas triumph in the building of the Panama Canal over the yellow fever, was accomplished by the splendid co-operation of everyone who served in New Guinea. The medical department surveyed, researched, lectured, demonstrated, and recommended, and general headquarters issued the necessary directives. I appointed a special committee from both the Australian and American medical services to formulate general principles to insure success of the struggle against malaria. Troops were educated to the dangers and the preventive measures with posters and pamphlets, and every man was urged to wage his own personal war against the mosquito. The result was success, and by the time we were ready to go into the Philippines it was reduced to secondary importance as a cause of disablement.

Japanese efforts along these lines were ineffective and their losses assumed enormous proportions. Nature is neutral in war, but if you beat it and the enemy does not, it becomes a powerful ally.

Another significant feature of the New Guinea campaign was the battle against enemy shipping. The wholesale destruction by our planes, submarines, and PT boats of enemy coastal vessels, transports, barges, schooners, and sailing craft gradually paralyzed Japanese efforts to supply, reinforce, or evacuate the remnants of his armies as they were cut off. More than 8,000 of these craft were destroyed. After the conclusion of the fighting in the Buna-Lae area and the Solomons, the Japanese were reluctant to risk major naval units, and, as a result of their heavy losses in cargo ships and transports, they were forced to devise a new supply technique. Submarines were too small and unmaneuverable to be of more than minor aid; moreover, they were too few in number. Accordingly, the enemy's most ambitious efforts along these lines were directed to a greatly expanded use of barge traffic. These barges were manufactured and collected in Japan, China, the Philippines, and various island posts, then routed to the New Guinea area. They had a troop capacity of from thirty-five to sixty men, and a cargo-carrying capacity of up to 20 tons, and were generally of excellent workmanship. I found it imperative to develop effective counter-tactics. The answer lay in a co-ordinated, intensive employment of PT boats, Catalinas, and low-flying planes. This combination destroyed the enemy's small craft much faster than they could be rebuilt.

Late in July, I received a summons from General Marshall to repair to Pearl Harbor for a conference. No intimation was given as to the identity of the personage with whom I was to confer or the subject to be discussed. I felt reasonably certain it was President Roosevelt, but as I had never before been invited to sit in on any of the big conferences, and in fact I never was again, I felt that something closely affecting me must be involved. I took no staff officers with me except personal aides-de-camp, and carried no plans or maps.

The President received me warmly and spoke generously of my campaigns. He was accompanied by his chief of staff, Admiral William D. Leahy, and a retinue of personages both military and civil. Admiral King had been there the day preceding, but had left before my arrival.

In the conference hall the Navy had a tremendous paraphernalia of maps, plans, manuscripts, statistics of all sorts, and other visual adjuncts. I began to realize I was to go it alone. Admiral Nimitz, with his fine sense of fair play, asked if I had been informed of the subject to be discussed, and if I had been asked to bring my important staff members. When I told him I had not, he seemed amazed and somewhat shocked.

President Roosevelt stated the general purpose of the conference, which was to determine the next phase of action against Japan. The Navy then presented its plan, which was to by-pass the Philippines and enter the Western Pacific to attack Formosa. For this purpose, all of my American forces, except a token group of two divisions and a few air squadrons, were to be transferred to the command of Admiral Nimitz, who was to continue to drive across the Central Pacific. By the summer of 1945, he would be ready to invade Formosa. Just how to neutralize and contain the 300,00 Japanese troops left in his rear in the Philippines was never clearly explained to me.

Admiral Nimitz put forth the Navy plan, but I was sure it was King's and not his own. By this time I knew why I had been included in the conference. The President apparently knew the general concept of the plan, but was evidently doubtful of it. He was entirely neutral in handling the discussion.

I was in total disagreement with the proposed plan, not only on strategic but psychological grounds. Militarily, I felt that if I could secure the Philippines, it would enable us to clamp an air and naval blockade on the flow of all supplies from the south to Japan, and thus, by paralyzing her industries, force her to early capitulation. I argued against the naval concept of frontal assault against the strongly held island positions of Iwo Jima or Okinawa. In my argument, I stressed that our losses would be far too heavy to justify the benefits to be gained by seizing these outposts. They were not essential to the enemy's defeat, and by cutting them off from supplies, they could be easily reduced and their effectiveness completely neutralized with negligible loss to ourselves. They were not in themselves possessed of sufficient resources to act as main bases in our advance.

In addition, I felt that Formosa, with a hostile population, might prove doubtful to serve as a base of attack against Japan itself. I was also critical of what I regarded as a major blunder in originally abandoning all effort to relieve the Philippines. I stated that had we had the will to do so, we could have opened the way to reinforce the Bataan and Corregidor garrisons, and probably not only saved the Philippines, but thereby stopped the enemy's advance eastward toward New Guinea and Australia. I felt that to sacrifice the Philippines a second time could not be condoned or forgiven.

I argued that it was not only a moral obligation to release this friendly possession from the enemy, now that it had become possible, but that to fail to do so would not be understandable to the Oriental mind. Not to do so, moreover, would result in death to the thousands of prisoners, including American women, children, and men civilians, held in Philippine concentration camps. Practically all of the 17,000,000 Filipinos remained loyal to the United States, and were undergoing the greatest privations and sufferings because we had not been able to support or succor them. To by-pass isolated islands was one thing, but to leave in your rear such a large enemy concentration as the Philippines involved serious and unnecessary risks. I invited attention to the fact that nothing had been said of the attitude of the War Department—that I could not understand why General Marshall's views were not presented.

The meeting adjourned until the following morning, with the President making no final decision. At this second meeting, I once again pointed out how necessary for the winning of the war was the recapture of Luzon, and how simple it would be, once Manila Bay and the northern part of Luzon were back in our hands, to deny Japan the oil, rubber, and rice she was presently draining out of the conquered areas along the shores of the South China Sea and farther south. The President interrupted: "But Douglas, to take Luzon would demand heavier losses than we can stand." "Mr. President," I replied, "my losses would not be heavy, anymore than they have been in the past. The days of the frontal attack should be over. Modern infantry weapons are too deadly, and frontal assault is only for mediocre commanders. Good commanders do not turn in heavy losses."

Then I sketched my own over-all plan for future operations in the Southwest Pacific. Once I held the Philippines, I would begin the reconquest of the Dutch East Indies, using the Australian First Army for the ground operations. Operating from the Philippines, I could sweep down on these Japanese-held islands from the rear.

I spoke of my esteem for Admiral King and his wise estimate of the importance of the Pacific as a major element in the global picture, however I might disagree with some of his strategic concepts.

Admiral Leahy seemed to support what I said, and the President accepted my recommendations and approved the Philippine plan.

At the close of the conference, I planned to fly back at once to my headquarters, but the President asked me to ride with him through the multitude of camps Lieutenant General Robert C. Richardson had established near Honolulu. We talked of everything but the war—of our old carefree days when life was simpler and gentler, of many things that had disappeared in the mists of time. He spoke briefly to the troops at each stop, and everywhere was received with enthusiasm. I asked him about the coming election, and he seemed completely confident. In turn, he inquired what I thought were the chances. I told him I knew nothing of the political situation in the United States, but that he, Roosevelt, was an overwhelming favorite with the troops. This seemed to please him greatly.

I had been shocked at his personal appearance. I had not seen him for a number of years, and physically he was just a shell of the man I had known. It was clearly evident that his days were numbered.

On August 2nd, Manuel Quezon died. I felt a stab in the heart when I thought of that gay little dinner forty years before at the Army and Navy Club in the walled city of Manila. Death was striking close to me when he took such a friend.

On August 9th, I received this letter from President Roosevelt:

I am on the last leg of my return journey to Washington. It has been a most successful, though all too short, visit and the highlight of it was the three days that you and I saw each other in Honolulu. I got a splendid picture of the whole vast area—far better than I had when I left Washington. You have been doing a really magnificent job against what were great difficulties, given us by climate and by certain human animals. As soon as I get back I will push on that plan for I am convinced that it is logical and can be done.

And to see you again gave me a particular happiness. Personally, I wished much in Honolulu that you and I could swap places and personally, I have a hunch that you would make more of a go as President than I would as General in the retaking of the Philippines.

Since I left for the Aleutians I got word of the death of Quezon, and that Osmena had taken the oath as President of the Philippines. Someday there will be a flag-raising in Manila—and without question I want you to do it. As the day comes nearer I wish you would let me know personally any thoughts you have. Maybe I will be vegetating at Hyde Park, but in any event, my heart will be with you. Give my warm regards to your wife and the youngster. Some day soon I shall hope to see them.

The President then wrote from Quebec on September 15th:

Dear Douglas:

I wish you were here because you know so much of what we are talking about in regard to the plans of the British for the Southwest Pacific. There is no question that Mr. Churchill and the British Chiefs of Staff want to send all they can to the Malay Peninsula, etc.—Army and Navy and Air—as soon as the German war ends.

In regard to our own force, the situation is just as we left it at Hawaii though there seem to be efforts to do bypassing which you would not like. I still have the situation in hand.

I formally received our old friend, Osmena, and his staff about a week ago. He wants to go out—with about a dozen others—as soon as we get a permanent foothold. I will wire you a little later to ask what your thought is on this.

I wish I could hope to come out myself for the great event but we all know there is a lot of this "in the lap of the gods stuff."

Take care of yourself.

On August 3rd, I received a farewell letter from the governor-general of Australia, Lord Gowrie:

I shall shortly be leaving for England and retiring from the Governor-Generalship of Australia and I am afraid that I shall not have the opportunity of saying goodbye to you in person, but I cannot leave these shores without expressing my gratitude for all you have done for Australia, and my admiration for the way in which you have dealt with the tremendous problems which faced you when you assumed Command of this area in the early days of 1942.

When you arrived here, a powerful and victorious enemy, flushed with success and determined on further conquests, was at our very gates. Our Defense Forces were small in number and the danger of invasion was imminent and real. In spite of these difficulties, you have succeeded in pushing the enemy back from stronghold to stronghold and opened the way to the complete conquest of lost territory, with heavy loss to the enemy but with minimum amount of loss to our own forces.

These operations will be ranked amongst the great achievements of all time and your name will be quoted amongst the greatest.

I have enjoyed greatly our association together and you have given me your complete confidence. I know too the happy relations which have existed between yourself and my Prime Minister and Ministers, and the respect and confidence in which you are held by all ranks and ratings in the Australian Forces.

So, my dear General, I say goodbye with gratitude for the great service you have rendered to Australia.

About this time I received several letters from Churchill concerning the use of British forces against Japan. He said:

The decisive question so far as Great Britain is concerned is whether we should shift the center of gravity of our war against Japan from the Bay of Bengal to the Southwest Pacific. We are sending a mission to Australia to investigate bases and logistics.

We have offered to place our whole fleet under United States command to take part with the United States fleet in the main assault on the Japanese mainland or outlying islands; but they do not feel they can service it.

I have my own ideas about a campaign across the Indian Ocean, but it would certainly not be in disharmony with your general plans. On the contrary, I think we shall work hand in hand. Naturally, the recovery of British possessions from the Japanese weighs heavily with me.

I am sure you and Mountbatten would be able to work together on any plans that are settled at our forthcoming conference.

Considering the debt that we, Australia and New Zealand owe you for your admirable conduct of our joint affairs, we shall always desire to preserve your cordial agreement. Every good wish.

I had General Lumsden send the following reply:

General MacArthur has asked me to express to you his deep personal appreciation for your message. He is delighted that there is to be a conference and is entirely confident that sound and considered opinions will be taken.

He feels that, above and beyond anything else, friction between the two Governments should not arise to imperil the future.

As you know, General MacArthur has from the beginning advocated the use of the British Fleet and any other elements of British power that could be brought to the Pacific.

There is absolutely no question of there being other than the most friendly cooperation with any plans set up for Mountbatten.

General MacArthur feels that his present campaign into the Philippines will have the strategic effect of piercing the enemy's center and permitting rapid and economic envelopment either to the north or south or preferably both. Having pierced the center he feels it would be advisable to take full advantage of the Philippines as an ideal base from which to launch these developments, rather than to pull back to stage frontal attacks, on the Japanese perimeter in any of the areas from existing bases.

He further feels that, with the Philippines captured, the entire command structure should be redesigned, abandoning the artificial area boundaries as they now exist; these areas at best were defensive in nature and will have completed their purpose and outlived their usefulness. For the final drive in the Pacific, if such becomes necessary, a much simpler and integrated combination of forces should be employed.

General MacArthur suggests that I join your staff for the conference in Washington, in view of the complete and intimate knowledge I have of local strategic concepts and tactical ideas.

Our next objective was the Halmahera-Palau line. To pierce these defenses, the Southwest Pacific was to hit at our end and the Central Pacific at the other. Simultaneous landings were carried out on September 15th. I selected Morotai Island at the northern tip of the Hamaheras as my point of attack following reports indicating it was inadequately garrisoned. A successful landing at this point would afford an excellent opportunity to secure a base within 300 miles of the Philippines without prolonged fighting or heavy losses. Strategically, the penetration of the Halmaheras would expose the enemy's conquests to the south to the threat of Allied envelopment. It would cut off in the Netherlands East Indies the Japanese Sixteenth and Nineteenth Armies, a force of 200,000 men, and would sever essential supplies of oil and other war matériels from the Japanese mainland.

I selected the XI Corps to make the landing, and because of the necessity of immediate decision whether in case of strong resistance the assault should be pressed or withdrawn, I accompanied the expedition aboard the *Nashville*.

Under cover of naval and air bombardment, our ground forces seized the Morotai beachhead. Intelligence had proved correct, and the small Japanese forces were quickly routed with little loss of our own men. We now dominated the Moluccas.

It was my feeling that the rank and file of the Japanese troops were beginning to lose some of their idolatry for their leaders. The myth of military infallibility which had dominated Japanese culture for centuries was no more. The generals and admirals were exposed as mere inheritors of a tradition, not the far-sighted and imaginative near-gods they had been proclaimed to be.

The Central Pacific had been less fortunate; while taking Palalu, its casualties numbered more than 8,000 men.

After the fall of Corregidor and the southern islands, organized resistance to the Japanese in the Philippines had supposedly come to an end. In reality, it had never ended. I had expected and laid plans long before for an underground struggle by guerrilla forces against the Japanese army of occupation. I was certain that a great number of those indomitable defenders of Bataan and Corregidor had escaped into the mountains and jungle, and that they were already at work against the enemy. Unfortunately, for some time I could learn nothing of these activities. A deep, black pall of silence settled over the whole archipelago.

Two months after the fall of the Manila Bay defenses, a brief and pathetic message from a weak sending station on Luzon was brought to me. Short as it was, it lifted the curtain of silence and uncertainty, and disclosed the start of a human drama with few parallels in military history. I knew, after that message, that my estimate of the moral fiber of the Filipino people was correct. The fire and the spirit of this indomitable nation burned as brightly as ever. I knew that the remnants of my soldiers were not abandoning the fight while they lived and had the means. The words of that message warmed my heart. "Your victorious return is the nightly subject of prayer in every Filipino home." I had acquired a force behind the Japanese lines that would have a far-reaching effect on the war in the days to come. Let no man misunderstand the meaning of that message from the Philippines. Here was a people in one of the most tragic hours of human history, bereft of all reason for hope and without material support, endeavoring, despite the stern realities confronting them, to hold aloft the flaming torch of liberty. I recognized the spontaneous movement of a free people to resist the physical and spiritual shackles with which the enemy sought to bind them. It was a poignant moment.

Unhappily, the sender of that first message, Lieutenant Colonel Guillermo Nakar, a former battalion commander of the 14th Infantry of the Philippine forces, was caught by the Japanese, tortured, and beheaded. He wasn't the first and he wasn't to be the last to die in the struggle, but for every patriot who thus went to a horrible and lonely death, a new leader rose to carry on the fight. The word passed from island to island and from *barrio* to *barrio*. From Aparri in the north to Zamboanga in the south, the fire of resistance to the invader spread. Whole divisions of Japanese troops that the Emperor badly needed elsewhere were deployed against phantom enemy units. Not many times in recorded history has the world witnessed a spectacle such as the struggle that now ensued. A strong and ruthless force, at times using barbaric methods, was never able to completely conquer this simple, brave people armed with very little more than courage and faith in the promise that we would return.

The scope of the struggle in the Philippines gradually became apparent. Four months after the message from Colonel Nakar, in November, Major Macario Peralta, Jr., formerly of the 61st Philippine Division, radioed us that he was taking command of the fighters in the Visayas.

Fourth Philippine Corps consists of 61st, strength eight thousand men fully reorganized on Panay. Only about eight hundred enemy there in all provincial capitals. Pansy outfit controls all interior and west coast. Civilians and officials ninety-nine per cent loyal. Supplies could be dropped anywhere away from towns and subs could make coast anywhere more than twenty miles distant from capitals. Puppet governor Hernandez of Capiz captured in guerrilla raid and sentenced to death by court martial. Request confirmation of sentence. I have installed Governor Confessor, who refused surrender to enemy, as governor of whole island. I have declared martial law for Panay. Request information as to general policy finances.

I replied immediately:

Your action in reorganizing Philippine Army units is deserving of the highest commendation and has aroused high enthusiasm among all of us here. You will continue to exercise command. Primary mission is to maintain your organization and to secure maximum amount of information. Guerrilla activities should be postponed until ordered from here. Premature action of this kind will only bring heavy retaliation upon innocent people. Your intelligence by covering maximum territory can perform great service. You cannot operate under provision of martial law in the Philippines, occupied as they are by the enemy. It is not practical to issue money. You should issue to your men certificates showing that the United States owes them pay as accrued. Similar certificates can be used as required showing purpose. The United States will honor them in due course of time. The enemy is now under heavy pressure and victory will come. I cannot predict the date of return to the Philippines, but I am coming.

We now began hearing from other parts of the Philippines. In January 1943, Captain Ralph Praeger, the former commander of Troop "C," 26th Cavalry, Philippine Scouts, radioed from the Cagayan Valley in North Luzon.

Am conducting government with utmost care legally and morally devoid of politics and personal considerations. Military and civil authorities in perfect accord helping one another. I have provided all needs of the army composed of scouts, constabulary, and Philippine Army in the Cagayan and Aparri. If I may be permitted I can organize five thousand additional men.

Praeger told me that two other officers, Lieutenant Colonels Arthur Nobel and Martin Moses, both Americans who had held important commands in the 11th Philippine Division, were free and were taking charge of guerrilla fighting at the north end of Luzon. I later heard from Nobel, advising that he and Moses "have unified command, and control six thousand guerrilla troops in provinces north of Manila." But the enemy snared them both. They were publicly tortured to death.

Forces came into being at Dagupan, Leyte, Panganiman, and Mindanao. Colonel Wendell Fertig, an engineer officer, reported from the big southernmost island of his activities:

Have strong force in being with complete civilian support. . . . Large number of enemy motor vehicles and bridges have been destroyed. Many telephone poles have been torn down, food dumps burned, and considerable enemy arms and ammunition captured. Thousands young Filipinos eager to join when arms available. Ready and eager to engage the enemy on your orders.

I detailed General Courtney Whitney to co-ordinate and direct the entire organization. He was ideal for such an assignment. A prominent Manila lawyer, his thirteen years there had made him thoroughly familiar with Philippine conditions and personnel. Rugged and aggressive, fearless and experienced in military affairs, his driving force found full play in charge of a guerrilla army.

His objectives were the formation of a battle detachment in every important Filipino area, alerted to strike against the enemy's rear as our battle-lines advanced; to secure fields adjacent to military objectives into which our airmen might drop with assurances of immediate rescue and protection; to arouse the militant loyalty of a whole people by forming resolute armed centers of resistance around which they could rally; to establish a vast network of agents numbering into the thousands to provide precise, accurate, and detailed information on major enemy moves and installations; to create a vast network of radio positions extending into every center of enemy activity and concentration throughout the islands; to build on every major island of the Philippines a completely equipped and staffed weather observatory to flash to my headquarters full weather data morning, afternoon, and night of every day; to implement an air-warning system affording visual observation of the air over every square foot of Philippine soil to give immediate warning of enemy aircraft or naval movement to our submarines on patrol in Philippine waters; to apply close interior vigilance so as to secure for our military use enemy documents of value; and to exploit any other aids to our military operations that might arise.

All this was done in a saga of blood and loyalty that I can never forget. The Japanese were ruthless in their frantic efforts at suppression. Innumerable cruelties were practiced. Whole villages were razed, but, try as they might, the Japanese could not overcome that indomitable spirit which seemed almost to neutralize the force of their arms. There followed a series of odysseys by individuals which included three who were to become president of the Philippine republic—Roxas, Magsaysay, and Garcia—and innumerable others—Ozamis, Kangleon, Anderson, Volkmer, Parsons, Villamor, Confessor, Datu Mindalano, Yay Panlillio. Their names run into the hundreds.

One of the most dramatic incidents of the war involved a Cebu Area Command guerrilla group under Lieutenant Colonel James M. Cushing. Admiral Mineichi Koga, successor to Admiral Yamamato as commander of the Combined Imperial Fleet, decided to move his headquarters from the Palau Islands to Mindanao to better supervise a massive plan of attack against our advancing amphibious campaign.

On March 31, 1944, he and his staff left for his new headquarters in two four-engined Kawanishe flying boats, one carrying himself, the other his chief of staff and second-in-command, Vice Admiral Shegeru Fukudome, with the plans for the attack.

The day had been heavy with the humid heat so characteristic of the region. As the breathless afternoon went into the brief dusk of the tropics, towering, black cumulus clouds swirling with a continuous play of lightning smashed the Japanese planes into the sea.

A band of Filipino guerrillas near the *barrio* of Balud moved to the rescue in a swarm of little black fishing boats. Admiral Koga's plane had been swallowed up by the sea, but the guerrillas were able to rescue and capture Vice Admiral Fukudome. The Japanese government decided to keep Koga's disappearance a secret until all hope of finding him had expired. Aware of the capture of the Japanese prisoners, the enemy started sweeping through the helpless areas of southern Cebu like an avenging scourge to secure their recovery, even if it meant the extinction of every living thing before them. Soon the countryside was under a glare by night and a shroud by day, as men, women, and children alike died in their ravaged *barrios*. Cushing then proposed to the captured admiral to surrender the captives, if the Japanese on their part would spare the civilian population. His terms were accepted. It was unorthodox and it was unique, yet it saved many innocent lives. But nothing could save Mineichi Koga, deep in the waters of the Pacific Ocean. The Emperor once again would have to name a new chief to head the Imperial fleets.

Through the understanding assistance of our Navy, I was able to send in by submarine—in driblets at first—arms, ammunition, and medical supplies. News of the first such shipment spread rapidly by the "bamboo telegraph" through the Philippines to electrify the people into full returning consciousness that America had neither abandoned nor forgotten them.

Later, as resources increased, I was able, after formalizing the guerrilla forces by their recognition and incorporation into units of our army, to send through Philippine coastal contacts vitally needed supplies in ever-increasing quantities, by four submarines committed exclusively to that purpose.

The story of the resistance of the people of the Philippines to the Japanese occupation of their land is a saga of unflinching devotion to those precepts of freedom inculcated into their hearts during forty years under the

American flag, of an indomitable will to hold aloft the torch of human liberty when little hope seemed left for its survival, of a militant and unflagging loyalty to the United States and the American people.

There is probably no better expression of this devotion and loyalty and will than is contained in the letters of two patriots from widely separated parts of the archipelago which were circulated throughout the land, copies of which I received by submarine in the early fall of 1943. The one from Governor Tomas Confessor, a Christian Filipino political leader, was in reply to a letter from Dr. Fermin Caram which urged him to collaborate with the Japanese. It was dated February 20, 1943, and read in part:

This struggle is a total war in which the issues between the warring parties are less concerned with territorial questions but more with forms of government, ways of life, and things that affect even the very thought, feelings and sentiments of every man. In other words, the question at stake with respect to the Philippines is not whether Japan or the U.S. should possess it but fundamentally it is: what system of government should stand here and what ways of life; what system of social organization and code for morals should govern our existence.

The burden of your so-called message to me consists of the entreaty that further bloodshed and destruction of property in Panay should stop and that our people be saved from further suffering and misery resulting from warfare and hostilities now existing between Japan and ourselves. The responsibility, however, of accomplishing this end does not rest upon us but entirely upon your friends who have sworn allegiance to Japan. For it was Japan that projected and created those conditions; Japan is the sole author of the holocaust in the Far East.

You may not agree with me but the truth is that the present war is a blessing in disguise to our people and that the burden it imposes and the hardships it has brought upon us are a test of our character to determine the sincerity of our convictions and the integrity of our souls. In other words, this war has placed us in the crucible to assay the metal in our being. For as a people, we have been living during the last 40 years under a regime of justice and liberty regulated only by universally accepted principles of constitutional government. We have come to enjoy personal privileges and civil liberties without much struggle, without undergoing any pain to attain them. They were practically a gift from a generous and magnanimous people—the people of the United States of America.

Now that Japan is attempting to destroy those liberties, should we not exert any effort to defend them? Should we not be willing to suffer for their defense? If our people are undergoing hardships now, we are doing it gladly; it is because we are willing to pay the price for those constitutional liberties and privileges. You cannot become wealthy by honest means without sweating heavily. You very well know that the principles of democracy and democratic institutions were brought to life through bloodshed and fire. If we sincerely believe in those principles and institutions, as we who are resisting Japan do, we should contribute to the utmost of our capacity to the cost of its maintenance to save them from destruction and annihilation, and such contribution should be in terms of painful sacrifice, the same currency that other peoples paid for these principles. . . .

You are decidedly wrong when you tell me that there is no ignominy in surrender. That may be true in the case of soldiers who were corralled by the enemy consisting of superior force, with no way of escape whatsoever. For when they gave themselves up they did not repudiate any principle of good government or of life which inspired them to fight heroically and valiantly—to use your own words. Should I surrender, however, and with me the people, by your own invitation and assurance of guarantee to my life, my family and those who follow me, I should be surrendering something more precious than life itself: the principles of democracy and justice, and the honor and destiny of our people.

I note you emphasized in your letter only peace and the tranquility of our people. I do not know whether by omission or intentionally you failed to refer in any way to the honor and destiny of our race. You seem to have forgotten those noble sentiments already, despite the fact that Japan has hardly been a year in our country. It appears clearly evident, therefore, that there is a great difference between the manner in which we are trying to lead our people during these trying days. You and your fellow puppets are trying to give them peace and tranquility by destroying their dignity and honor, without suffering, or if there is any, the least possible. On the other hand, we endeavor to inspire them to face difficulties and undergo any sacrifice to uphold the noble principles of popular rule and constitutional government, thereby holding up high and immaculate their honor and dignity at the same time. . . .

You may have read, I am sure, the story of Lincoln who held firmly to the conviction that the secession of the southern states from the northern was wrong. Consequently, when he became the President and the southern states seceded he did not hesitate to use force to compel them to remain in the union. The immediate result was civil war that involved the country in the throes of a terrible armed conflict that, according to reliable historians, produced proportionately more loss of lives, hardships and miseries than the First World War. The sufferings of the people of the south were terrible but the union was saved and America has become thereby one of the strongest and most respected nations on the surface of the earth. If Lincoln had revised his convictions and sacrificed them for the sake of peace and tranquility as you did, a fatal catastrophe would have befallen the people of America. With this lesson of history clearly before us, I prefer to follow Lincoln's example than yours and your fellow puppets. . . .

I will not surrender as long as I can stand on my feet. The people may suffer now and may suffer more during the next months. To use the words of St. Paul the Apostle: "The sufferings of the present are not worthy to be compared with the glory to come that shall be revealed in us."

The other letter was from Datu Manaleo Mindalano, a Moro leader of the Mohammedan faith, in answer to an attempt by Captain K. Takemoto, local Japanese commander, to induce him to collaborate. It was dated July 3, 1943, and read in part:

It gives me no surprise to hear from you Japanese the same old alibi that you came to the Philippines with good intentions. What have you done in Lanao that is worth appreciating anyway? When you came, you kill the natives like chicken and attack towns and barrios who are innocent. Now that you cannot force us to submission and your doomsday is in sight, your note is sorrowful. . . .

You can be very sure that I will continue to redouble my efforts in attacking places wherever I smell Japs. If I have been active when I was fighting by my own accord, you should expect a much more terrific attack from me now that I am following military orders and have taken oath reaffirming my allegiance to the Commonwealth of the Philippines and the United States of America. . . . If I were to choose between being a pro-satan and pro-Japanese, I would choose being the former just to be always against Japanism of all types in the Philippines. Had you been enlightened enough in the affairs, the psychology, the needs, and well-being of my people, the Maranaos, you would not keep on wondering why I will never be tempted by your persuasive propaganda and sugarcoated promises and why, in spite of a temporary collapse of U.S. Army resistance in the country on account of the surrender of the main USAFFE Forces in the Philippines, I have not only withstood the defense of my sector but have continued harassing your forces wherever we met until you became imprisoned in the fox holes of your garrisons. . . .

Believe me, if there is any impossibility under the sun, it is a Philippine Independence granted by Japan. . . . Before this war, America promised the Philippines her independence in 1946. We honor American promises after a close observation of their character for over 40 years. But Japan's one-year commitment does not warrant honoring her promise of independence even if the date of that promise were to take effect tomorrow.

Receipt of these letters filled me with a sense of deep pride and infinite assurance in the ultimate triumph of the cause of Philippine liberation. For they reflected a spirit of dynamic patriotism unexcelled by any patriots of any age. They gave me the measure of the internal support I might expect when the lines of battle converged on Philippine soil.

The Philippine Islands had constituted the main objective of my planning from the time of my departure from Corregidor in March 1942. From the very outset I regarded this strategic archipelago as the keystone of Japan's captured island empire, and, therefore, the ultimate goal of the plan of operations in the Southwest Pacific Area. The Japanese war records attest the decisive priority they gave the Philippines in their over-all strategic war plans:

The Philippines were the east wing of the so-called "Southern Sphere" in the Japanese operations in the southern regions [said Lieutenant General Shuichi

Miyazaki, Chief of the Operations Section, Imperial General Headquarters]. They took the shape of the main line of defense against American counter-attacks. The western wing was Burma and Malaya, and together the two wings protected Japanese access to the southern regions. Viewed from the standpoint of political and operational strategy, holding the Philippines was the one essential for the execution of the war against America and Britain. With the loss of these islands, not only would Japanese communications with the southern regions be severely threatened, but as far as supplies and reinforcements were concerned would be a paramount difficulty. The loss of the Philippines would greatly appropriate strategic bases for the enemy advance on Japan. If they were captured the advantage would be two to one in favor of the enemy and the prosecution of the war would suddenly take a great leap forward for the enemy.

As the Allies advanced westward along New Guinea and across the Central Pacific, a wide divergence of opinion developed among international planners and military strategists as to the methods of defeating Japan, but I never changed my basic plan of a steady advance along the New Guinea–Philippines axis, from Port Moresby to Manila. This plan was conceived as a forward movement of ground, sea, and air forces, fully co-ordinated for mutual support, operating along a single axis with the aim of isolating large Japanese forces that could be attacked at leisure or slowly starved into surrender. By choosing the route from Australia via New Guinea and the Halmaheras to the Philippines, I could constantly keep my lines protected, pushing my own land-based air cover progressively forward with each advance. My plan insured control of the air and sea during major amphibious operations, and was so designed that land-based air power, with its inherent tactical advantages, could be used to the maximum extent. This remained my fundamental concept of operations as I moved my forces from Port Moresby and Milne Bay to Buna and Lae, through the Vitiaz Straits to the Admiralties, on to Hollandia and the Vogelkop, until they reached their final springboard at Morotai.

My plan, called "Reno," was based on the premise that the Philippine archipelago, lying directly in the main sea routes from Japan to the source of her vital raw materials and oil in the Netherlands Indies, Malaya, and Indo-china, was the most important strategic objective in the Southwest Pacific Area. Whoever controlled the air and naval bases in the Philippine Islands logically controlled the main artery of supply to Japan's factories. If this artery were severed, Japan's resources would soon disappear, and her ability to maintain her war potential against the advancing Allies would deteriorate to the point where her main bases would become vulnerable to capture. Mindanao was selected as the tactical objective in the Philippines, and the flanks of my advance beyond the western tip of New Guinea would be safeguarded by the Central Pacific drive across the Pacific.

"Reno" enabled our forces to depart from a base closest to the objective, and advance against the most lightly organized positions of the enemy's defenses, effecting a decisive penetration. The advance would be made by a combination of airborne and seaborne operations, always supported by the full power of land-based aviation, and assisted by the fleet operating in the open reaches of the Pacific. A penetration of the defensive perimeter along this line would result in by-passing extended, heavily defended areas that would fall, practically of their own weight, enabling us to perform mopping-up operations with a minimum of loss.

Other proposals were put forth, but "Reno" finally met with general acceptance. Initial lodgements were to be effected in southern Mindanao on November 15th and at Leyte Gulf on December 20th. "Musketeer II," as the plan was renamed, had as its major objective "the prompt seizure of the Central Luzon area to destroy the principal garrison, command organization and logistic support of hostile defense against Japan." The plan envisioned the full support of the United States fleet not only to secure a foothold on the eastern coast of the Philippines archipelago, but also to assist in the invasion of central Luzon.

In conformity with this provision, carrier-based aircraft of Admiral Halsey's Third Fleet hit Mindanao on September 9th and 10th, and discovered unexpected and serious weakness in the enemy's air defenses. Few Japanese planes were encountered, and further probing disclosed that Southwest Pacific land-based bombers, operating out of New Guinea fields, had caused severe damage to enemy air installations.

On September 12th and 13th, carrier task groups of the Third Fleet hit the Visayas. Again enemy air reaction was surprisingly meager, and heavy loss was inflicted upon Japanese planes and ground installations. It became more and more apparent that the bulk of the once mighty Japanese air force had been destroyed in the costly war of attrition incidental to the New Guinea operations.

Admiral Halsey suggested that Leyte should be seized immediately. At the time he radioed this suggestion, virtually the whole strategic apparatus of the United States government had moved to Quebec in attendance at the conference then being held between Mr. Roosevelt and Mr. Churchill. My views were requested on the proposed change of the invasion date for Leyte, and I cabled my assent to Halsey's proposal. Thus, within ninety minutes after Quebec had been queried as to the change in plans, we had permission to advance the date of our invasion of Leyte by two months.

The operation to take Leyte without a preliminary landing in Mindanao was a most ambitious and difficult undertaking. The objective area was located over 500 miles from Allied fighter cover. It was at the same time in the center of a Japanese network of airfields covering the Philippines. The islands would doubtless be defended to the limit of the enemy's capabilities, probably even at the risk of losing his heretofore husbanded navy, since a successful landing on Leyte would presage the eventual reoccupation of the entire Philippine area. The Japanese could reinforce their positions by bringing in troops and supplies from their lines, whereas, without air bases in the vicinity, the Allied forces would have to rely on naval aircraft to prevent enemy supply and reinforcement convoys from reaching the area. Again, as at Hollandia, Southwest Pacific forces would advance beyond the range of their own land-based fighter cover and put themselves under the protection of carrier planes for the assault phase. The success of the operation, even after a landing was secured, would depend on the ability of Allied naval forces to keep the enemy from building up a preponderance of strength on Leyte and adjoining Samar, and to prevent enemy naval craft from attacking shipping in the beachhead area.

Careful study preceded the selection of the landing beaches and the direction of the inland thrust on Leyte. The northeastern coastal plain of Leyte was chosen as most suitable for the assault. Seizure of the 18-mile stretch between Dulag and San Jose would permit the early capture of the important Tacloban Airfield, and make possible the occupation and use of the airfield system under development at Dulag. It would permit domination of vital San Juanico Strait, and place the invading force within striking distance of Panaon Strait to the south. Intelligence reports indicated that the beach area would not be heavily defended, although some fortifications were being prepared along the inland road net.

I had no illusions about the operation. I knew it was to be the crucial battle of the war in the Pacific. On its outcome would depend the fate of the Philippines and the future of the war against Japan. Leyte was to be the anvil against which I hoped to hammer the Japanese into submission in the central Philippines—the springboard from which I could proceed to the conquest of Luzon, for the final assault against Japan itself. With the initiative in my hands, the war had reached that decisive stage where an important Japanese defeat would seal the fate of the Japanese Empire and a centuries-old tradition of invincibility.

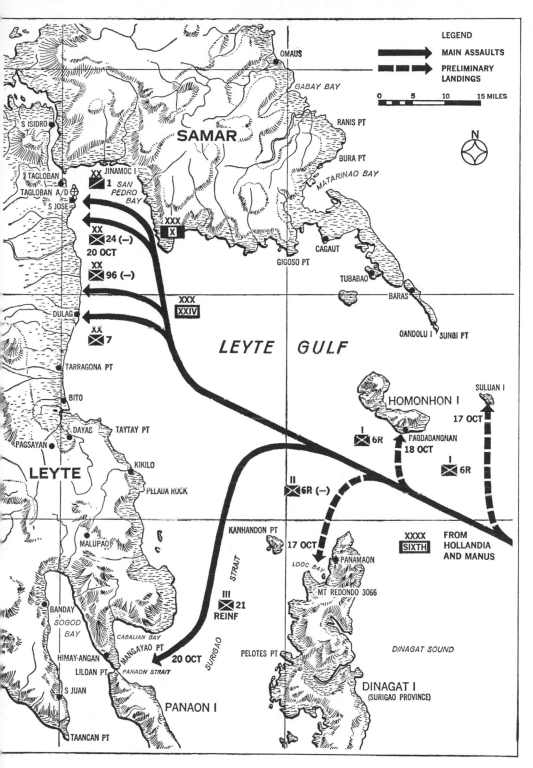

The Landings on Leyte

The plan for the ground operations in the capture of Leyte comprised four main phases. Phase one covered minor preliminary landings to secure the small islands lying across the entrance to Leyte Gulf. Phase two included the main amphibious assaults on Leyte from Dulag to Tacloban, and called for the seizure of the airstrip, an advance through Leyte Valley, and the opening of San Juanico and Panaon Straits. The third phase consisted of the necessary overland and shore-to-shore operations to complete the capture of Leyte and the seizure of southern Samar. Phase four contemplated the occupation of the remainder of Samar and the further neutralization of enemy positions in the Visayas.

On October 16th, I left Hollandia and went aboard the *Nashville,* which was to serve as my flagship. On the waters around me lay one of the greatest armadas of history. America's rebuilt strength consisted of new battleships that replaced those lying at the bottom of Pearl Harbor, and many of the veteran ships that had survived that initial assault itself; of aircraft carriers, cruisers, and destroyers in massive array; of transports and landing craft of a type that had not even existed three years before. Altogether, there were 700 of these ships of war. They carried 174,000 of America's finest fighting men, veteran soldiers now a match for any warrior the world has ever known. The size of the landing force was equal to about half the Japanese strength in the islands, but the enemy was scattered. My force was concentrated. I intended my maneuver and surprise to bring a superior force to bear at the points of actual combat and, thereby, to destroy him piecemeal.

It is difficult even for one who was there to adequately describe the scene of the next two days. Ships to the front, to the rear, to the left, and to the right, as far as the eye could see. Their sturdy hulls plowed the water, now presenting a broadside view, now their sterns, as they methodically carried out the zigzag tactics of evasion.

We came to Leyte just before midnight of a dark and moonless night. The stygian waters below and the black sky above seemed to conspire in wrapping us in an invisible cloak, as we lay to and waited for dawn before entering Leyte Gulf. Phase one of the plan had been accomplished with little resistance. Now and then a ghostly ship would slide quietly by us, looming out of the night and disappearing into the gloom almost before its outlines could be depicted. I knew that on every ship nervous men lined the rails or paced the decks, peering into the darkness and wondering what stood out there beyond the night waiting for the dawn to come. There is a universal sameness in the emotions of men, whether they be admiral or sailor, general or private, at such a time as this. On almost every ship one could count on seeing groups huddled around maps in the wardrooms, infantrymen nervously inspecting their rifles, the crews of the ships testing their gear, last-minute letters being written, men with special missions or objectives trying to visualize them again. For every man there were tons of supplies and equipment—trucks and vehicles of all kinds, and more than one ton of ammunition for every man who would storm those shores. Late that evening I went back to my cabin and read again those passages from the Bible from which I have always gained inspiration and hope. And I prayed that a merciful God would preserve each one of those men on the morrow.

The big guns on the ships opened fire at dawn. The noise, like rolling thunder, was all around us. The *Nashville,* her engines bringing to life the steel under our feet, knifed into Leyte Gulf. The ominous clouds of night still hung over the sea, fighting the sun for possession of the sky, but the blackness had given way to somber gray, and even as we saw the black outline of the shore on the horizon, the cloak of drabness began to roll back. On every side ships were riding toward the island. The battle for Leyte had already begun.

I was on the bridge with Captain C. E. Coney. His clear, keen eyes and cool, crisp voice swung the cruiser first to port, then to starboard as he dodged floating mines. An enemy periscope suddenly spouted up, only to be blotted out as destroyers closed in with roaring depth charges. And then, just as the sun rose clear of the horizon, there was Tacloban. It had changed little since I had known it forty-one years before on my first assignment after leaving West Point. It was a full moment for me.

Shortly after this, we reached our appointed position offshore. The captain carefully hove into line and dropped anchor. Our initial vantage point was 2 miles from the beaches, but I could clearly see the sandstrips with the pounding surf beating down upon the shore, and in the morning sunlight, the jungle-clad hills rising behind the town. Landings are explosive once the shooting begins, and now thousands of guns were throwing their shells with a roar that was incessant and deafening. Rocket vapor trails crisscrossed the sky and black, ugly, ominous pillars of smoke began to rise. High overhead, swarms of airplanes darted into the maelstrom. And across what would ordinarily have been a glinting, untroubled blue sea, the black dots of the landing craft churned toward the beaches.

From my vantage point, I had a clear view of everything that took place. Troops were going ashore at "Red Beach," near Palo, at San Jose on "White Beach" and at the southern tip of Leyte on tiny Panson Island. On the north, under Major General Franklin C. Sibert, the X Corps, made up of the 1st

Cavalry and 24th Infantry Divisions; to the south, the XXIV Corps, under Major General John R. Hodge, consisting of the 7th and 96th Infantry Divisions. In over-all command of ground troops was Lieutenant General Walter Kreuger of the Sixth Army.

At "Red Beach" our troops secured a landing and began moving inland. I decided to go in with the third assault wave. President Osmena, accompanied by General Basilio Valdez, the Philippine Army chief of staff, and General Carlos Romulo, my old aide, who had joined me on Bataan in 1942, had sailed with the convoy on one of the nearby transports. I took them into my landing barge and we started for the beach. Romulo, an old stalwart of the Quezon camp, was the resident commissioner for the Philippines in Washington. Noted for his oratorical ability, this popular patriot served on Bataan, and had been the radio "Voice of Freedom" from Corregidor.

As we slowly bucked the waves toward "Red Beach," the sounds of war grew louder. We could now hear the whining roar of airplane engines as they dove over our heads to strafe and bomb enemy positions inland from the beach. Then came the steady crump, crump of exploding naval shells. As we came closer, we could pick up the shouts of our soldiers as they gave and acknowledged orders. Then, unmistakably, in the near distance came the steady rattle of small-arms fire. I could easily pick up the peculiar fuzzy gurgle of a Japanese machine gun seemingly not more than 100 yards from the shoreline. The smoke from the burning palm trees was in our nostrils, and we could hear the continual snapping and crackling of flames. The coxswain dropped the ramp about 50 yards from shore, and we waded in. It took me only 30 or 40 long strides to reach dry land, but that was one of the most meaningful walks I ever took. When it was done, and I stood on the sand, I knew I was back again—against my old enemies of Bataan, for there, shining on the bodies of dead Japanese soldiers, I saw the insignia of the 16th Division, General Homma's ace unit.

Our beachhead troops were only a few yards away, stretched out behind logs and other cover, laying down fire on the area immediately inland. There were still Japanese in the undergrowth not many yards away. A mobile broadcasting unit was set up, and as I got ready to talk into the microphone, the rains came down. This is what I said:

People of the Philippines: I have returned. By the grace of Almighty God, our forces stand again on Philippine soil—soil consecrated in the blood of our two peoples. We have come, dedicated and committed to the task of destroying every vestige of enemy control over your daily lives, and of restoring upon a foundation of indestructible strength, the liberties of your people.

At my side is your President, Sergio Osmena, a worthy successor of that great patriot, Manuel Quezon, with members of his cabinet. The seat of your government is now, therefore, firmly re-established on Philippine soil.

The hour of your redemption is here. Your patriots have demonstrated an unswerving and resolute devotion to the principles of freedom that challenge the best that is written on the pages of human history. I now call upon your supreme effort that the enemy may know, from the temper of an aroused people within, that he has a force there to contend with no less violent than is the force committed from without.

Rally to me. Let the indomitable spirit of Bataan and Corregidor lead on. As the lines of battle roll forward to bring you within the zone of operations, rise and strike. Strike at every favorable opportunity. For your homes and hearths, strike! For future generations of your sons and daughters, strike! In the name of your sacred dead, strike! Let no heart be faint. Let every arm be steeled. The guidance of Divine God points the way. Follow in His name to the Holy Grail of righteous victory.

President Osmeña and I then walked off the beach, and picked our way into the brush behind the beach until we found a place to sit down. We had made our return and it was time to think of returning the government to constitutional authority. It was while we were finishing our discussion that the beachhead was subjected for the first time to an enemy bombing attack. It shook the log on which we sat, but that was all. As we finally got up to move, I noticed that the rain was no longer falling and that the only soldiers left near the beach were members of sniper patrols.

I wrote the following letter to President Roosevelt:

Near Tacloban, Philippine Islands
October 20, 1944

Dear Mr. President:

This note is written from the beach near Tacloban where we have just landed. It will be the first letter from the freed Philippines. I thought you might like it for your philatelic collection. I hope it gets through.

The operation is going smoothly and if successful will strategically as well as tactically cut the enemy forces in two. Strategically it will pierce the center of his defensive line extending along the coast of Asia from the Japanese homeland to the tip of Singapore, and will enable us to envelop to the north or south as we desire. It severs completely the Japanese from their infamous propaganda slogan of the "Greater East Asia Co-Prosperity Sphere." Tactically it divides his forces in the Philippines in two and by by-passing the southern half of the Philippines will result in the saving of possibly fifty thousand American casualties. He had expected us and prepared on Mindanao.

The Filipinos are reacting splendidly and I feel that a successful campaign of liberation if promptly followed by a dramatic granting to them of independence will place American prestige in the Far East at the highest pinnacle of all times.

Once more, on the highest plane of statesmanship, I venture to urge that this great ceremony be presided over by you in person. Such a step will electrify the world and redound immeasurably to the credit and honor of the United States for a thousand years.

Please excuse this scribble but at the moment I am on the combat line with no facilities except this field message pad.

Very faithfully

After inspecting the forward elements of our troops and the Tacloban Airfield, I returned to the *Nashville*. That evening I ordered a co-ordinated attack by guerrillas all over the Philippines.

As I dropped off to sleep that night, the vision that danced before my tired eyes was not of bayonet, bullet, or bomb, but of an old, old man, a resident of Leyte, who stepped up to me amidst the shot and shell of the afternoon, welcoming me with outstretched arms. "Good afternoon, Sir Field Marshal," he said in his Visayan dialect. "Glad to see you. It has been many years—a long, long time." *

---

* Many messages of congratulations on the landing were received by me.

From President Roosevelt: "The whole American nation today exults at the news that the gallant men under your command have landed on Philippine soil. I know well what this means to you. I know what it cost you to obey my order that you leave Corregidor in February 1942, and proceed to Australia. Ever since then you have planned and worked and fought with whole-souled devotion for the day when you would return with powerful forces to the Philippine Islands. That day has come. You have the nation's gratitude and the nation's prayers for success as you and your men fight your way back to Bataan."

From the Secretary of War: "I congratulate you heartily on the successful consummation of the first step in regaining the Philippines. I am following your progress with keenest interest."

From the Secretary of the Navy, James Forrestal: "I send the Navy's congratulations on the initial success of your operation and our confidence that under your leadership the Philippines will be restored to freedom." I replied thanking him and said: "The Navy elements as usual played their part magnificently."

From Prime Minister Churchill and Field Marshal Allanbrooke, Chief of the Imperial General Staff: "Hearty congratulations on your brilliant stroke in the Philippines. Good wishes."

From Admiral Halsey: "It was a great day for your fleet teammates when the successful landing of the 6th Army was announced. It was a beautifully conceived and executed plan. All of my staff join me in heartiest congratulations to you and your smooth working team."

PART SEVEN

*World War II:
Conquest of
Japan*

1944–1945

The next two days our forces secured both the Tacloban area in the north and the Dulag area to the south, and continued to push inland in the face of increasing resistance. The airfields at Dulag proved to be unsuitable for immediate use because of numerous small swamps, the thick, sedimentary silt of the surrounding plain, and poor drainage. I established General Headquarters at Tacloban.

The Japanese recognized that we had made the most threatening move of the war to date. They knew, all too well, that if I succeeded, a half million of their best combat soldiers would be cut off to the south, without hope of support and with ultimate destruction at the leisure of the Allies a certainty. They placed in command of their Philippine forces their most distinguished general, Tomoyuki Yamashita. In 1942, General Yamashita had directed the brilliant drive down the Malayan peninsula to Singapore, and he was as confident of success in 1944 as he was then. He boastfully informed the world that "the only words I spoke to the British Commander during negotiations for the surrender of Singapore were, 'All I want to hear from you is yes or no.' I expect to put the same question to MacArthur." He was an able commander, much like those I had known in the Russo-Japanese war, but, unlike them, he talked too much.

In their desperation, the Japanese now prepared to stake their most valuable military asset, the Imperial fleet, on a gigantic gamble to repel the invasion of Leyte and maintain their position in the Philippines. This determination to drive the Americans off the beaches was to very nearly succeed. It resulted in one of the great naval battles of modern times—actually four battles fought between October 23 and 26, 1944—the Battle of Leyte Gulf.

The Japanese fleet had been in southern waters for many months, and Admiral Suemo Toyoda, its commander, maintained his flag at Singapore. As soon as he learned that the Americans had invaded Leyte in force, he assembled every ship in his command and set sail for his rendezvous with fate in Leyte Gulf.

Since without the participation of our Combined Fleet [he stated] there was little possibility of the land based forces in the Philippines having any chance against MacArthur, it was decided to send the whole fleet, taking the gamble. If things went well we might obtain unexpectedly good results, but if the worst should happen, there was a chance that we would lose the entire fleet, but I felt that that chance had to be taken. Should we lose in the Philippines operations, even though the fleet should be left, the shipping lane to the south would be completely cut off so that the fleet, if it should come back to Japanese waters, could not obtain its fuel supply. If it should remain in southern waters, it could not receive supplies of ammunition and arms. There would be no sense in saving the fleet at the expense of the loss of the Philippines.

Impressive and far-ranging, his plan was to deliver a paralyzing blow at the U.S. Navy and, with the strategic situation in his favor, to collapse my invasion of the beaches by the same attack. To maneuver their warships within firing distance of our troops and supply transports in the Leyte Gulf, the Japanese were ready to gamble the loss of their entire mobile fleet. They felt one such chance would be decisive.

Admiral Toyoda divided the combined fleet into three distinct groups: a Central Force, under Admiral Takeo Kurita; a Southern Force, (van) under Vice Admiral Shoji Nishimura; and Southern Force (rear) under Vice Admiral Kiyohide Shima; a Northern Force, under Vice Admiral Jisabuto Ozawa. The Central Force would pass through San Bernardino Strait north of Leyte, then set a course southward for Leyte Gulf. The Southern Force would pace its approach by way of the Mindanao Sea and Surigao Strait, so that both fleets, in a co-ordinated pincer movement, would converge simultaneously on the Allied flanks and attack the vulnerable "soft shipping" unloading in Leyte Gulf. The Northern Force, in the Philippine Sea 300 miles north of San Bernardino Strait, was to decoy the powerful U.S. Third Fleet from the protection of the entrance to Leyte Gulf.

In the crucible of the coming battle, my own position was unique. The sweep of my forces along New Guinea had been consistently directed so that each operation would have available the full protection of my own land-based air force. Every step forward had been governed by the basic concept of securing airfields no more than 200 to 300 miles apart from which to

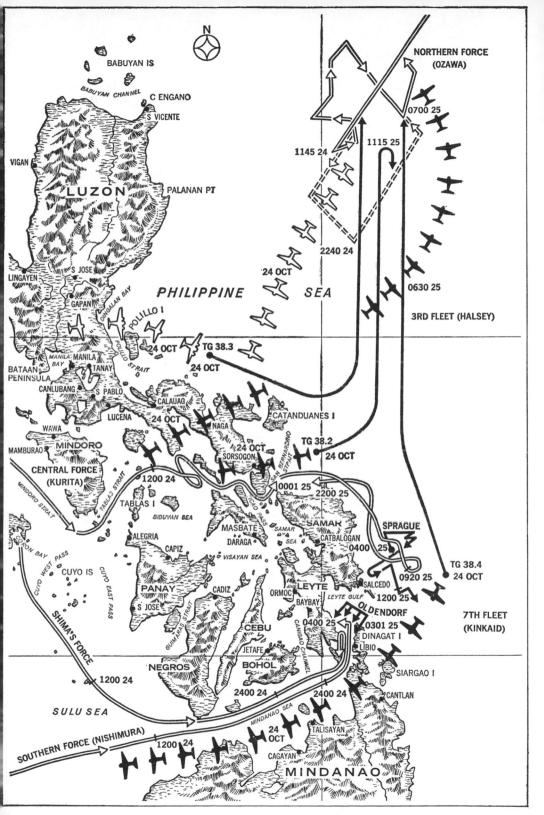

The Battle of Leyte Gulf

assure an "air umbrella" over each progressive thrust into the enemy. By invading Leyte two months in advance of the original schedule, however, it became necessary to put my units onto beachheads without my own guaranteed air protection. The U.S. Navy, therefore, had a double responsibility. Initially, it had to assist the landing itself by its usual tasks of shore bombardment, convoy escort, and plane cover. In addition, it had the important mission of giving me further air support for a period of time beyond the landing date, until I could develop local airfields and stage my own air units forward from the south.

Should the naval covering forces allow either of the powerful advancing Japanese thrusts to penetrate into Leyte Gulf, the whole Philippine invasion would be placed in the gravest jeopardy. It was imperative, therefore, that every approach to the gulf be adequately guarded at all times, and that an enemy debouchment by way of either Surigao or San Bernardino Straits be blocked with adequate naval strength.

The naval forces protecting the Leyte invasion were disposed in two main bodies. The Seventh Fleet, under Vice Admiral Thomas C. Kinkaid, protected the southern and western entrances to Leyte Gulf, while the stronger Third Fleet, under Admiral Halsey, operated off Samar to cover San Bernardino Strait and the approaches from the north and east. Admiral Halsey's immediate superior was Admiral Nimitz in Hawaii; Admiral Kinkaid was responsible to me, and was with me at Tacloban. While it was understood that such a division of command entailed certain disadvantages, it was theoretically, but wrongly, assumed in Washington that frequent consultation and co-operative liaison would overcome any difficulties in the way of proper co-ordination. The coming battle was to demonstrate the dangers involved in the lack of a unified command and the misunderstandings that can ensue during major operations in which the commander ultimately responsible does not have full control over all forces in the operation.

Up until October 24th, I had contented myself with daily expeditions ashore in order to keep in close touch with the action as it unfolded. I did not wish to add confusion on the beachhead in any way or to slow the flow of vital supplies ashore. The transportation of a large headquarters like my own, with all of its necessary communications and other equipment, was not imperative at that period. By October 23rd, it had become apparent that the Japanese intended to commit their fleet. Admiral Kinkaid wanted to use the added firepower of the *Nashville* in the coming naval battle of the Seventh Fleet to the south. When we discussed this, I concurred. When word reached the Admiral that I intended to go along, he demurred. So did my staff. For some reason they felt that a 16-inch naval shell represented a greater peril to my person than all the tons of steel that the enemy was directing at the beachhead. All my life I had been reading and studying naval combat, and the glamor of sea battle had always excited my imagination. But Kinkaid was adamant. He said, "I will not commit the *Nashville* as long as GHQ is aboard." It was to be his fight, so I moved my headquarters ashore on the 24th, and the *Nashville* moved out to take its honored position in the battleline.

For half a day on the 24th, the Japanese Central Force under Admiral Kurita's command was under constant open attack by aircraft from the Third Fleet, while the enemy nervously threaded the dangerous reefs leading to San Bernardino. The *Musashi,* one of the newest and largest of Japan's battleships, mounting 18-inch guns, was sunk; its sister ship, the mighty *Yamato,* was hit; one heavy cruiser was put out of action; other cruisers and destroyers were damaged. The increasing force of these aerial blows, together with the torpedoes of Seventh Fleet submarines, caused Admiral Kurita, who lacked air cover, to reverse his course for a time in order to reform his forces. This temporary withdrawal—executed at 3:33 in the afternoon—was later reported by hopeful airmen as a general retreat of Japanese Central Force. Admiral Kurita had no intention of abandoning his mission, however, and at 5:14 the force advanced again toward San Bernardino Strait. Shortly thereafter he received a message from Admiral Toyada in Tokyo: "All forces will dash to the attack, trusting in divine assistance."

In the meantime, Admiral Nishimura's Southern Force sailed doggedly on into the Mindanao Sea. Amply forewarned by sightings, Admiral Kinkaid had dispatched almost the whole of the Seventh Fleet's gunnery and torpedo force under Admiral Oldendorf to intercept and destroy the approaching Japanese fleet. Admiral Oldendorf deployed his PT squadrons at the entrance to Surigao Strait at a place where the Japanese would have to reform in columns to negotiate the narrow passage. Behind the torpedo boats, and covering the northern part of the strait, were posted the destroyer squadrons, cruisers, and battleships to form a curtain of vast firepower which the enemy would be forced to approach vertically as he moved forward.

The ambush worked perfectly. The Japanese fleet was practically annihilated. Only one lone destroyer escaped. The Japanese admiral went down with his flagship. This closed the southern entrance to Leyte Gulf.

In the late afternoon of the 24th, scout planes of the Third Fleet reported a large enemy task force, including several carriers, off the northeastern coast of Luzon, about 300 miles from San Bernardino Strait. Admiral Halsey apparently felt that Admiral Kinkaid's Seventh Fleet had ample strength with which to meet the Southern Force, and judging from his aviator's optimistic reports that the Central Force had been greatly damaged, had perhaps retired, and in all likelihood had been removed as a serious menace, estimated that the Northern Force constituted the most potent danger to be met, and therefore decided to move his entire force northward to intercept it.

During the afternoon, Halsey had formed Task Force 34 as a strong surface force comprising four battleships, two heavy cruisers, three light cruisers, and fourteen destroyers. It was assumed that this task force would engage Admiral Kurita's force if it advanced. In the early evening Halsey informed Admiral Kinkaid and others of the position of the Japanese Central Force, and added that he was "proceeding north with three groups to attack the enemy carrier forces at dawn." Accordingly, on the evening of the 24th, he withdrew the battleships, carriers, and supporting ships of the Third Fleet from San Bernardino Strait. It was a crucial decision, and no end of confusion and uncertainty followed his action. As the last battleships of the Third Fleet had been detached from the carrier groups and organized as Task Force 34, it was assumed that Task Force 34 was still guarding San Bernardino Strait. Although no definite statement had been made by Admiral Halsey, Admiral Kinkaid thought that the big battleships were standing by, awaiting the Japanese Central Force, and that Admiral Halsey was going after the Japanese Northern Force with carrier units. Actually, however, Admiral Halsey took his complete task groups on his run to the north, and left San Bernardino Strait open.

Unhampered movement through San Bernardino Strait was the kingpin of the enemy's strategy. Admiral Halsey did not know that Japan's carriers were to be deliberately sacrificed in a bold gamble to keep the Philippines from falling to the Allies. It was later revealed that the Northern Force of Admiral Ozawa, almost completely destitute of planes and pilots, had only one mission—to serve as a decoy and turn the most powerful units of the U.S. fleet away from the Leyte area. It was expected that the Northern Force would probably be destroyed, but it was hoped that this desperate device would enable the Japanese Central Force to pass unmolested through San Bernardino Strait and move southward into Leyte Gulf.

To accomplish his mission, Admiral Ozawa continually sent out radio messages in an effort to advertise his position to the U.S. fleet. An undetected fault in his transmission system, however, prevented the Third Fleet from intercepting these signals. Equally important to later operations, communication difficulties also prevented an exchange of information between the enemy's Northern and Central Forces.

During the night of the 24th, Admiral Kurita led his warships through the treacherous passes of San Bernardino Strait in a dash that was a spectacular display of navigational skill. Shortly after midnight, he debouched into the Philippine Sea. About 5:30 in the morning of the 25th, as he was coming down the coast of Samar, he received word of the disaster to the Southern Force of Admiral Nishimura. His was now the only Japanese force within striking distance of Leyte. The task of destroying the U.S. invasion units rested solely in his hands.

At dawn on the 25th, a group of sixteen escort carriers, nine destroyers, and twelve destroyer escorts of the Seventh Fleet, under the command of Rear Admiral Thomas L. Sprague, was disposed east of Samar and Leyte Gulf. On a northerly course, they were directly in the path of Admiral Kurita's oncoming force. It soon became apparent that Halsey was too far to the north to properly cover the Gulf of Leyte, and I so radioed Nimitz asking him to drop Halsey back. This would not only protect my base, but would insure his fleet being in the action, as the magnetic attraction of my point of landing would draw the enemy's fleet there. Three times I sent such dispatches, but without results. Nimitz repeated to Halsey, apparently without getting through, and then finally authorized me to communicate directly with Halsey, but it was then too late.

Through a series of fatal misunderstandings, directly attributed to divided command, ambiguous messages, and poor communication between the Third and Seventh Fleets, neither Admiral Kinkaid at Leyte Gulf nor Admiral Sprague off Samar realized that the exit from San Bernardino Strait had been left unguarded. During the night of the 24th, however, Admiral Kinkaid became uneasy concerning the actual situation at San Bernardino Strait and decided to check on the position of Task Force 34. At 4:12 A.M. on the 25th, he sent an urgent priority signal telling Admiral Halsey of the results in Surigao Strait and asking him the crucial question: "Is Task Force 34 guarding San Bernardino Strait?" The reply was not dispatched until 7:04, by which time Admiral Kurita's battleships had opened fire off Samar. Admiral Halsey's answer said: "Your 241912 negative. Task Force 34 is with carrier group now engaging enemy carrier force."

It was a dramatic situation fraught with disaster. The forthcoming battle of Samar between the Seventh Fleet's slow and vulnerable "jeep" carriers and the Japanese Central Force of greatly superior speed and firepower gave every promise of a completely unequal struggle. The light carriers of Admiral Sprague were no match for the great battleships and heavy carriers of the Japanese Central Force. Should the enemy gain entrance to Leyte Gulf, his powerful naval guns could pulverize any of the eggshell transports present in the area and destroy vitally needed supplies on the beachhead. The thousands of U.S. troops ashore would be isolated and pinned down helplessly between enemy fire from ground and sea. Then, too, the schedule for supply reinforcement would not only be completely upset, but the success of the invasion itself would be placed in jeopardy. The battleships and cruisers of the Seventh Fleet were more than 100 miles away in Surigao Strait, their stock of heavy ammunition virtually exhausted by the preceding shore bombardment and the decisive early morning battle with the Japanese Southern Force. Halsey's Third Fleet was some 300 miles distant, still chasing the Northern Force, and could not possibly return in time to halt the progress of Admiral Kurita.

Ashore, all I had been able to do was call for carrier air cover over the Leyte beaches. Under the divided command set-up, I had no effective control over the Third Fleet. Having advanced beyond the range of my own land-based aircraft, I was completely dependent upon carrier planes for protection —a fact which I had emphatically made clear both before and during the planning for the invasion. In October, in discussions with Admiral Halsey, I had reiterated my conception of his mission by saying: "The basic plan for this operation in which for the first time I have moved beyond my own land-based air cover was predicated upon full support by the Third Fleet; such land-based cover is being expedited by every possible measure, but until accomplished, our mass of shipping is subject to enemy air and surface raiding during this critical period. Consider your mission to cover this operation is essential and paramount." Now I could do nothing but consolidate my troops, tighten my lines, and wait the outcome of the impending naval battle.

Admiral Kurita's Central Force had suffered considerable damage, yet it was still a powerful fleet. The main force was four fast battleships backed by eighteen smaller craft—eleven destroyers, and six heavy and two light cruisers. It was in quest of big game, its guns and shell hoists brimming with armor-piercing projectiles.

The battle was joined at 6:58 A.M. The Yamato's 18-inch guns fired first, with the cruisers following as soon as they came within range. Never before had U.S. warships been subjected to such heavy caliber fire. With the world's biggest guns blazing away, Admiral Kurita pressed the attack at full speed.

As soon as the enemy was sighted, Admiral Sprague's escort carriers changed course due east and began launching all available aircraft. Scarcely had the planes been sent aloft, when large-caliber shells began falling among the units of the formation. Admiral Kurita was closing rapidly, straddling the escort carriers with dye-marker salvoes which bracketed the area of their targets with vivid splotches of red, yellow, green, and blue. The situation was critical, and at 7:42 Admiral Kinkaid received a request for support. He promptly ordered Admiral Oldendorf "to prepare to rendezvous his forces at the eastern end of Leyte Gulf." The escort carriers' planes were sent the same order, and another dispatch was transmitted to Admiral Halsey requesting immediate aid.

Kurita's ships gradually closed, and his big batteries began to find the range. Along with these surface attacks, Japanese air units based in the Philippines launched a series of Kamikaze strikes against the escort carriers. In his great distress, Admiral Kinkaid sent Admiral Halsey another dispatch: "Urgently need fast battleships Leyte Gulf at once." Meanwhile, the Third Fleet continued to steam northward in hot pursuit of the Japanese carrier group.

Admiral Sprague's escort carriers used every tactic of waterborne combat in their desperate struggle. Hit-and-run was the order of the day, heavy smokescreens were laid, temporary sanctuary sought in a providential rain squall. His destroyers and destroyer escorts fought back furiously. Interposing themselves between the carriers and their adversary, they boldly closed the range, and unleashed their fire with guns and torpedoes at cruiser and battleship targets. The planes from the escort carriers attacked continuously and put several cruisers out of action. They were greatly handicapped, however, by the damage inflicted on the carriers. The pilots, seeing their carrier decks ripped open or their ships sunk, were forced to put down on Tacloban's already jammed airstrip. With General Kenney, I watched them with aching heart as, again and again, in endless stream, they crashed in. Some also landed on the Dulag strip, while others were compelled at the last minute to ditch in Leyte Gulf.

With disaster staring him in the face, Admiral Kinkaid sent Admiral Halsey another urgent dispatch, which the latter received at nine o'clock: "Our escort carriers being attacked by four battleships, eight cruisers plus others. Request Lee cover Leyte at top speed. Request fast carriers make immediate strike." Admiral Lee commanded Task Force 34.

By this time ammunition aboard the escort carriers was running low; some of the destroyers had expended their torpedoes, and the torpedo planes were reduced to the dire expedient of making dummy runs on the enemy ships. Our losses had been very heavy. After two and a half hours of continuous battle, victory lay within Admiral Kurita's grasp.

In his desperation Admiral Kinkaid sent uncoded a last insistent plea to Admiral Halsey, this time in the clear: "Where is Lee? Send Lee." Back in Hawaii, thousands of miles away, Admiral Halsey's commander, Admiral Nimitz, had tried to contact the Third Fleet without success. He finally got through this query almost simultaneously with Kinkaid's last message: "The whole world wants to know where is Task Force 34."

Then suddenly, Admiral Kurita broke off the engagement. His units had sustained much damage, and he was apparently unaware of the true battle situation. He ordered his forces to cease firing and to reassemble to the north. For the U.S. carrier forces this retirement by the enemy meant a remarkable and completely unexpected escape. Admiral Sprague, in summing up the results of the battle shortly thereafter, stated: "The failure of the enemy main body and encircling light forces to completely wipe out all vessels of this Task Unit can be attributed to our successful smoke screen, our torpedo counterattack, continuous harassment of the enemy by bomb, torpedo and strafing air attacks, timely maneuvers, and the definite partiality of Almighty God."

The continuous and urgent dispatches from Admiral Kinkaid and the cryptic message from Admiral Nimitz caused Admiral Halsey to change course and direct the bulk of his fleet southward. He expected to arrive early the next morning. His other units caught up with Admiral Ozawa's fleet and in the battle of Cape Engano, inflicted much damage, but did not destroy it.

After regrouping his forces, Admiral Kurita decided to make one last attempt against Leyte Gulf. At 11:20, he ordered his ships to change course toward the target area to the southwest. He was en route approximately one hour, and was only 45 miles from his objective when he finally decided to give up the attempt. At 12:36, he ordered his ships about. He passed through San Bernardino Strait at 9:30 P.M. on October 25th. In the meantime, Admiral Halsey came racing down from the north with his big battleships. They were not to fire a shot, however, for when they arrived it was too late. Admiral Kurita had escaped.

I have never ascribed the unfortunate incidents of this naval battle to faulty judgment on the part of any of the commanders involved. The near disaster can be placed squarely at the door of Washington. In the naval action, two key American commanders were independent of each other, one under me, and the other under Admiral Nimitz 5,000 miles away, both operating in the same waters and in the same battle. The Seventh Fleet of my force performed magnificently, as they always had, and always would, and Admiral Kinkaid wrote his name in this engagement among the greatest leaders in our naval annals.

To Admiral Nimitz I sent this message regarding the conduct of the units of his command which had participated:

At this time I wish to express to you and to all elements of your fine command my deep appreciation of the splendid service they have rendered in the recent Leyte operations. Their record needs no amplification from me, but I cannot refrain from expressing the admiration everyone here feels for their magnificent conduct. All of your elements—ground, naval, and air—have alike covered themselves with glory. We could not have gone along without them. To you my special thanks for your sympathetic and understanding cooperation.

The defeat of the enemy's fleet meant the failure of only one phase of Japan's threefold plan for disrupting the Allied invasion of Leyte. Despite the loss of the naval battle, Japanese efforts in the air and on the ground were intensified rather than diminished. By bringing in plane reinforcements from Formosa and Japan to numerous existing bases in Luzon, they were able to maintain a continuous aerial offensive against the Allied transports and fleet units in Leyte Gulf. Vigorous enemy air assaults began on October 24th against Allied beachhead installations. Headquarters of the Sixth Army and my command post at Tacloban were special targets, but they were never quite able to hit the bullseye.

These raids marked the first serious appearance of the suicidal Kamikaze attack pilots, whose startling debut caused considerable concern to Allied naval commanders, and inflicted widespread destruction on fleet units. The necessity of dealing with the dangerous threat of these Kamikaze attacks forced the carriers to commit their planes to their own protection at the expense of furnishing support to the Leyte ground forces.

Heavy monsoon rains and difficult terrain delayed the construction of suitable airfields on Leyte. The Japanese naturally realized the importance of Tacloban, and attacked the airstrip continuously, causing severe destruction to closely parked planes. Twenty-seven of these planes were disabled in one raid alone, and ammunition dumps and oil tanks were razed almost nightly. Except for the vicious air bombardment of Corregidor, never before had the Japanese blanketed an Allied position with such powerful, sustained, and effective air action.

The land phase of the enemy's co-ordinated attack plan was also comparatively unaffected by the outcome of the naval battle. Taking full advantage of the temporary insecurity of the American air position, they poured a steady stream of reinforcements into Leyte from Luzon and the neighboring islands. Nearly 50,000 fresh troops were landed and committed to the defense of the Ormoc Corridor in the so-called "Yamashita Line." These reinforcements made it clear that the enemy intended to hold Leyte at all costs. General Yamashita commanded: "The Japanese will fight the decisive battle of the Philippines on Leyte."

Our forces on the ground continued to drive inland and along the coast in a two-pronged attack and envelopment. We met mounting resistance as the advance moved forward and enemy reinforcement increased. Allied planes from our carriers were active against these Japanese convoy movements and inflicted many heavy losses.

The heavy and continuous tropical rainfall became a serious impediment to the progress of our operation. Important roads were turned into rivers of mud, slowing and, at times, halting the movement of supplies to the advancing forces. Communication lines were constantly disrupted and contact between units was difficult to maintain. The poor drainage and swampy soil continued to delay the conditioning of the vital airstrips, leaving ground troops without adequate land-backed air support for combat operations. The dangerous shortage of air power and the rapidly increasing opposition from a greatly strengthened enemy made it necessary for me to bring in the 32nd and the 11th Airborne Divisions under Major Generals William G. Hill and Joseph M. Swing. A heavy and unremitting pressure was kept up all along the front. The Japanese continued to maintain a vigorous defense of all Ormoc Corridor approaches, strengthening the "Yamashita Line" and mounting occasional vicious counterattacks. By the end of November, despite large convoy losses and severe combat attrition, there were many thousand more enemy troops on Leyte than there had been at the end of October.

I had long recognized the decisive advantage to be gained by severing the enemy's supply lines at Ormoc. Heretofore, the lack of fighter cover to insure the safety of the convoy, and the fact that supporting naval forces did not have sufficient landing craft and resupply shipping to maintain amphibious operations had prevented the mounting of any sizable seaborne assault. These conditions were now remedied, and I decided that the time had arrived when the enemy's "back door" to Leyte could be slammed shut by a strike on the west coast. Accordingly, orders were issued for the newly arrived 77th Division to land in the Ormoc area in conjunction with a coordinated drive from the front.

On December 6th, the 77th Division, under the command of Major General Andrew D. Bruce, sailed around the southern tip of Leyte in a shore-to-shore movement from the east coast, and landed at Deposito three and one-half miles south of Ormoc. The Japanese reacted immediately to the threatening sealing-off of their main supply route, and employed their remaining planes in the Visayas in an intensive effort to cripple the convoy. In spite of this aerial opposition, which succeeded in inflicting serious damage on the ships and destroyers in the convoy, the division unloaded rapidly and established a firm beachhead. The strategic implications of the Ormoc landing were described by me in my order of the day: "By this maneuver we have seized the center of the Yamashita Line from the rear and have split the enemy's forces in two, isolating those in the valley to the north from those along the coast to the south. Both segments are now caught between our columns which are pressing in from all fronts."

The 77th Division, hammering down fierce enemy resistance, entered Ormoc on December 10th and the next day established contact with our main force.

The enemy fought valiantly, but found it impossible to cope with our three-way offensive. His forces were chopped into isolated segments, either struggling in small pockets or being scattered into the mountains. On December 26th, I reported that the Leyte-Samar campaign could be regarded as closed except for minor mopping-up. General Yamashita had sustained perhaps the greatest defeat in the military annals of the Japanese Army.*

---

* I cited our forces in a general order as follows:

"As Commander-in-Chief of the campaign, I wish to express the admiration and gratitude I feel to all commanders and to all ranks, for the determination, fortitude and courage which they have displayed under the most difficult, dangerous and complex situations.

"The magnificent coordination displayed by the Services was as marked as the special tactical efficiency of the various branches.

"The ground troops have shown a tenacity of purpose which has carried them unflinchingly through every ordeal. The local tactical skill with which the troops have been maneuvered has not only outwitted the enemy but has resulted in a relatively low casualty list that is unsurpassed in the history of war. General Krueger has written his name high in the annals of generalship.

"The naval components operating under my command have not only shown complete loyalty to a Commander-in-Chief drawn from another branch, but have exhibited an elasticity of tactical pattern and that grim unflinching courage in combat which have so characterized our Navy from its very origin. The Australian Squadron conducted itself in accordance with the highest tradition of the British Commonwealth of Nations. Admiral Kinkaid has shown himself to be one of the great Naval leaders of the day.

"The Air Forces assigned to me, both land and sea, have fought with a ferocity and intelligence never surpassed even by the brilliant performance of this Branch of the Service in the present war. General Kenney and Admiral Sprague have confirmed their high place in the annals of airmen.

"I am deeply grateful to the covering forces of the Third Fleet for their brilliant and successful advance forays and for their timely intervention at a critical moment in the decisive naval action following the initial landing.

"To the Philippine people, civil populace as well as guerilla, led by President Osmena, I wish to express my deep appreciation for their complete cooperation and help to our cause both before and during the operation.

"To my loyal staff, I thank them personally for their unfailing devotion through endless hours of toil, perplexity, and suspense when they so unflinchingly gave me of their full sustenance.

"We have our hold now and I shall not relax the grip until Bataan and Corregidor once more rise into life.

"Almighty God has blessed our arms."

A year before the assault against Leyte, my forces had been deep in the tangled jungles and swamps of New Guinea, almost 1,500 miles from the Philippines. Now we were in the very heart of the islands—in a position to become masters of the archipelago. We had met the enemy under its finest soldier, with armies and corps pitted against each other in free maneuver, and had totally destroyed them. The dark shadow of defeat was edging ever faster across the face of the rising sun of Japan. The hour of total eclipse was not far off.

Years afterwards, the Japanese Emperor told me that with the failure to hold the "Yamashita Line," the Japanese government knew the war was lost and all their subsequent efforts were to achieve peace without internal explosion.

The enemy's losses in the Leyte campaign were terrific. They refused to surrender, and had to be killed to the last man. Their counted dead numbered 80,557; their captured, only 798. Our own casualties consisted of 3,320 killed and 12,000 wounded. There were no survivors from the Japanese 16th Division, the unit which had conducted the infamous "Death March" of Bataan.

The Philippine government awarded me the Medal of Valor, the Philippine equivalent of the United States Medal of Honor.*

General Marshall sent "Congratulations on the great success of your operations," and the American government promoted me to its highest military rank, General of the Army.

But the old thrill of promotion and decoration was gone. Perhaps I had heard too often the death wail of mangled men—or perhaps the years were beginning to take their inexorable toll.

During the Leyte campaign I was faced with civic problems as well as military ones. Like all American professional soldiers, I believed that the civil power of government should be paramount to any power wielded by the military. I, therefore, restored to the duly elected Philippine government, in the person of President Osmena, the right to govern in that part of Leyte which we had recaptured. I called the president to the wrecked and devastated provincial capitol building three days after the landing and formally proclaimed the resumption of constitutional government before a gathering of Filipino citizens.

---

* In making the presentation President Osmena said: "America and General MacArthur are one. He is a singular representative of the highest and the best in the American ideal of freedom and democracy. He embodies the noblest in the American character and integrity of soul. In the building of the greater democratic Philippines, he will surely serve as the inspiration of our people. His name will be ever remembered by the Filipinos."

"On behalf of my government," I said then, "I restore to you a constitutional administration by countrymen of your confidence and choice. As our forces advance, I shall in like manner restore the other Philippine cities and provinces throughout the entire land."

I don't think the president and the other government officials expected anything like this. I had not discussed it with any of them beforehand. Indeed, I gathered that President Osmena looked upon his trip to Leyte as a ceremonial visit, and that he fully expected to go back to the United States and continue to administer a government-in-exile until the war was over, or at least until military operations in the Philippines were concluded. As fast as we freed an area, it was turned over to administration by civil authority. There never was any military government of the Philippines during and after the American recapture of the archipelago. The American and Filipino Army that ended the campaign was already subject to civil authority and never, in any sense of the word, was an army of occupation.

Serious differences along this line developed with Secretary of the Interior Harold Ickes. By virtue of the office he held, and in the absence of a high commissioner through whom he had formerly operated, Secretary Ickes argued that he should take over the running of the Philippines. It was his claim that the archipelago was a "possession" of the United States and he seemed to think of the islands as another one of his national parks. In the period before our landings at Leyte, he informed me that he would take charge as soon as we had completed the invasion. Most certainly he was opposed to giving the reins of government into the hands of President Osmena and the regularly elected authorities. He informed me that he had been advised as to who had been loyal and who had been disloyal to the United States during the period of Japanese occupation, and that he was going to try the disloyal people for treason.

The Japanese had granted independence to the Philippines and had established a puppet government, and it was quite evident to me that Ickes intended to shoot or hang any Filipino who had anything to do with this puppet government, no matter what reasons they may have had for co-operating. All of these men were well known to me and their devotion to their country was unquestionable. No *prima facie* case of treason existed against a man simply because he accepted duties under the Japanese-established government. Many men were led to do so simply by a desire to ameliorate the hardships and rigor imposed upon the people. I stated that any Filipino who had been named as a collaborator or accused of other disloyalties would be rounded up and held for trial by and under such procedures as were provided for in the Philippine constitution, and that I would guarantee the safety of such individuals until the Philippine authorities could act.

I further stated that I had complete confidence in the commonwealth government to discharge its functions and loyally co-operate as it had always done. I recalled that at the outbreak of the war it had been urged upon me that, as military commander, I should assume general charge of all Philippine administration. I had opposed this concept, feeling that these matters should be left to the Filipinos themselves, and this co-operative arrangement had been completely successful. I called attention to the fact that the personality of Secretary Ickes was such as to insure friction, especially as he had never been to the Philippines, and was utterly unacquainted with the Orient.

My position was completely supported by Secretary of War Stimson. Following a sharp disagreement in Washington, President Roosevelt decided against Ickes, and the Secretary was not permitted to inject himself into the local scene.

The collaboration issue was settled in due course by the Philippine Republic, and the Filipinos were never subjected to the domination of our irascible and eccentric Secretary of the Interior. Ickes never forgave me, and became a leader of a vengeful and abusive faction which has repeatedly misrepresented and falsified my position, opinions, and personal character.

The Communists had never ceased their violent attacks against me and, with the liberal extremists joining them, the crescendo was rising.

A vivid example of Mr. Ickes' failure to understand the facts behind the "collaborators" is the case of General Manuel Roxas, who became the first President of the Republic in 1946. The general was operating as an agent throughout the war. In 1943, President Quezon sent his personal physician, Dr. Emigidio Cruz, to me in Australia. He wished Dr. Cruz to talk with the various resistance leaders and especially with Roxas.

The story of Dr. Cruz's adventure was a thrilling one. Under cover of night, he left the submarine *Thresher,* and landed on Negros. Word of his arrival in the Philippines was reported to the Japanese, and he was immediately regarded as the most important agent to enter the islands. Every resource at the hands of the Japanese forces was utilized to catch him. Using a series of disguises and forged documents, Dr. Cruz finally reached Manila, narrowly escaping raids and ambushes on the way. He spent several days in the capital and talked with many of the guerrilla leaders, including a long conversation with Roxas. Escaping back to Australia in February 1944, he brought with him the most important information regarding the resistance movement that we then had.

There was never any question in the mind of President Quezon, or the guerrilla leaders, or myself, as to the exact role that Manuel Roxas played during the war. I was doubly certain because it was under my own personal orders that he stayed in the Philippines. Nothing more clearly proved his loyalty than the visit of Dr. Cruz. Had he revealed the movements of this personal representative of President Quezon, the Japanese government undoubtedly would have rewarded him highly, because Cruz was the man they most wanted.

In the weeks immediately after the liberation of the Philippines, General Roxas was the target of Ickes and his supporters, and because I refused to brand him as a traitor, I also became an object of the venom of the Secretary. Even after Roxas was elected President of the Philippine Republic, the false innuendos against this great patriot continued.

In the campaign for liberation of the Philippines, I now faced my final and decisive objective, the recapture of Luzon. It was a difficult and dangerous problem, for the Japanese ground forces greatly outnumbered my own. I needed one last steppingstone before a main attack could be launched. The island of Mindoro was selected. It was located just south of Luzon in a central position along the coast. Its possession would enable me to return to my strategy of never leaping ahead of my own air cover. Midway between Leyte and the Lingayen Gulf area of Luzon, an airfield on Mindoro could be used to cover a landing at Lingayen, which was to be my point of assault on Luzon.

On December 12th, a scant two weeks before the final tactical stroke of the Leyte campaign, I dispatched a task force commanded by Brigadier General William C. Dunkel, and accompanying vessels of the Seventh Fleet to Mindoro by way of Surigao Strait. Once again the Japanese misjudged our goal, this time believing it to be the beaches of Panay and Negros. They realized our destination only after our ships had anchored off the chosen beachheads. The landing phase of the operation was accomplished without the loss of a single soldier. The Kamikaze attacks which soon followed, however, did much damage to our shipping off Mindoro, and the destruction wrought by these suicidal assaults created a serious local shortage of aviation gasoline for a period. But, by December 23rd, two airfields were in operation on Mindoro.

Upon the surrender of Mindoro, Japan ceased sending additional troops to the Philippines, and no longer used Manila Bay as a transfer point for convoys from the Netherlands Indies area. I was at last ready for Luzon.

Mindoro was the gate to Lingayen—and I held the keys. General Marshall wired me:

"What you have done on Leyte and are doing on Mindoro are masterpieces. You and your command have my prayers for your continued success and safety." *

Before leaving Leyte, I had the great pleasure of decorating Major Richard Bong, Kenney's ace of aces, with the Medal of Honor. He had shot down forty enemy planes in air combat. I cited him, saying:

"Of all military attributes the one which arouses the greatest admiration is courage. It is the basis of all successful military ventures. You, who have ruled the air from New Guinea to the Philippines, I now induct into the society of the bravest of the brave, the wearers of the Congressional Medal of Honor of the United States. My dear boy, may a merciful God continue to protect you is the constant prayer of your old Commander-in-Chief." He made his last flight on August 7, 1945, as a test pilot in the United States. His jet engine had "flamed out" on take-off. He jumped, but there was not enough altitude for the parachute to function.

With our occupation of Mindoro, General Yamashita became greatly concerned over the prospect of an imminent invasion of the southern area of Luzon. Stationing the Eighth Army off the southern coast of Luzon, I planned to threaten landings at Legaspi, Batangas, and other southern ports, hoping to draw the bulk of the Japanese into the south. Our plans then called for landing the Sixth Army in an amphibious enveloping movement on the exposed northern shore, thus cutting off the enemy's supplies from Japan. This would draw the enemy back to the north, leaving the Eighth Army to land against only weak opposition on the south coast, in another amphibious movement. Both forces ashore, we would then close like a vise on the enemy deprived of supplies and destroy him. No plan ever worked better.

Every possible deceptive measure was taken to conceal our real invasion

---

* Under date of December 29th, I received a letter from Douglas Southall Freeman, our greatest living military historian at that time, reading as follows:

"Dear General MacArthur:

"Sometimes I think of myself as a voice from the tomb because, for half the day, I study your campaigns and for the other half of my waking hours, I live with General Lee.

"Now that you have driven the enemy from Leyte, may I tell you that General Lee would be proud of you. No campaigns by an American officer remind me so strongly of him as your campaigns do.

"I hail you as the inheritor of the boldness and the strategy of 'Marse Robert' and 'Old Jack.' Their immortal mantle has descended upon your shoulders. I hope I live long and learn enough about the details of what you are doing to write of you and your lieutenants as I have of Lee and his.

"Gratefully yours."

And he sent me a copy of his biography of General Lee with the inscription: "To General Douglas MacArthur, who is making a record as great."

point of assault at Lingayen. Our bombers struck unceasingly at targets in southern Luzon. Other aircraft flew photographic and reconnaissance missions over the Batangas-Tayabas region. Transport planes made dummy jumps over the same area to simulate an airborne invasion. PT boats patrolled the southern and southwestern coasts of Luzon as far north as Manila Bay. Minesweepers cleared Balagan, Batangas, and Tayabas Bays. Landing ships and merchantmen approached the beaches in these areas, only to slip away under cover of darkness when fired upon. Guerrillas in lower Luzon intensified their activities and conducted ostentatious operations designed to divert Japanese attention to the south. The Japanese, as I had hoped, were deceived, and moved troops south in anticipation of an attack there. Not until we had actually landed at Lingayen did General Yamashita move his center of gravity to the north. He established his new headquarters at Baquio. The deception of the Eighth Army had been remarkably successful.

The plan of the attack was regarded by some in Washington as too daring in scope, too risky in execution. The assault convoy was to sail on January 4th through narrow straits, by-pass the enemy-held islands, then steam up the China Sea, passing Manila, and boldly looping around fortified Bataan and Corregidor. At no time would the convoy be moving more than twenty minutes flying time from enemy airfields, which, for the past week, our air force in unrelenting sweeps was attempting to neutralize. The enemy's strength on Luzon was known to be heavy; his suicidal fanaticism, the last ditch of the defeated, was fully comprehended.

The command setup was much the same as the Leyte campaign. Under my over-all command, the ground forces comprised the Sixth Army, under General Krueger, and consisted of the I Corps of Major General Innis P. Swift and the XIV Corps of Lieutenant General Oscar W. Griswold, with a strong army reserve. The divisions in the assault waves were the 6th, 37th, 40th, and 43rd, with the 25th and other troops in reserve. The plan called for the two corps to land abreast, with I Corps on the left, the XIV Corps on the right. The naval forces comprised the Seventh Fleet and Australian Squadron, under the immediate direction of Admiral Kinkaid, whose subordinate commanders were Admirals Oldendorf, Berkey, Barbey, and Wilkinson. The Third Fleet, under Admiral Halsey, would again provide strategic support. The air forces, comprising the Fifth and Thirteenth Air Force, were under the command of General Kenney, with General Whitehead his operating deputy. To the south was the Eighth Army, under General Eichelberger, and in New Guinea was the First Australian Army under General Blaney.

On January 4th, I boarded the light cruiser *Boise,* which was to act as my flagship. She was under complete radio silence and only the pulse of her engines and the wash of the waves broke the quiet as she steamed through the deep blue waters off the west coast of the Philippines. The atmosphere was one of stillness and tension. Officers and men alike were waiting—just waiting. My own thoughts went back to that black night three years gone, when I churned through these same waters with only the determination to return. In the sporting world there is an adage among the gamblers, "They never come back," but as I filled my old corncob pipe, I had a warm feeling in my heart that sometimes the betting boys might be wrong.

The air would suddenly crackle with an ominous call to "man battle stations" as the sinister wake of a torpedo would cut through the water dead on course for the *Boise*. The cruiser would spin sharply to port or starboard, away from that deadly white streak, and depth charges from our escorting destroyers would cover the area. Midget submarines, looking for all the world like dripping black whales, would suddenly emerge only to be sent bubbling to the bottom under the crushing lunge of a destroyer. Again and again, with vicious plunge and whirling propellers, enemy planes would dive, only to be cut down in the blazing barrage of anti-aircraft fire as every ship opened in a deafening blast of flak.

I watched these attacks at a battery near the quarterdeck. Through careless publicity, the enemy had guessed rightly that the commander-in-chief was aboard the *Boise*. But other thoughts gripped me as that mighty armada —the greatest ever gathered in the Pacific—steamed close enough inshore to see the old familiar landmarks. There they were, gleaming in the sun far off on the horizon—Manila, Corregidor, Marivales, Bataan. I could not leave the rail. One by one, the staff drifted away, and I was alone with my memories. At the sight of those never-to-be-forgotten scenes of my family's past, I felt an indescribable sense of loss, of sorrow, of loneliness, and of solemn consecration.

The enemy's Kamikaze air attacks inflicted much damage to the convoy. During the invasion, the Allies suffered an irreparable loss when Lieutenant General Herbert Lumsden of the British Royal Marines was killed while accompanying Admiral Sir Bruce Fraser, Commander-in-Chief of the British Pacific Fleet, who was aboard the battleship *New Mexico* as an observer. Lumsden was on the starboard side of the flag bridge when a destroyer astern of the *New Mexico* was hit by a suicide ship. The general went up to the navigation bridge, and stood amidships in order to get a better view. Meanwhile, an enemy plane at which the *New Mexico* was firing began to close. General Lumsden started down the port ladder leading to the flag bridge just as the crash came. The explosion blew him from the ladder to his death. We buried him at sea. He was England at its best.

We arrived off the landing beaches of Lingayen before dawn on January 9, 1945. Only three years before, General Homma's transports had anchored in about the same place. The landing boats were away by 9:30. Initial opposition was limited to mortar fire from the hills fronting the I Corps. I had achieved exactly the surprise intended, and a deep beachhead 12 miles in width was firmly established.

I went ashore in a landing craft of the I Corps. As was getting to be a habit with me, I picked a boat that took too much draft to reach the beach, and I had to wade in. The scene was one of immense activity. More than 2,500 landing craft were hard at it. Since those first days at Milne Bay, the United States had developed a wide variety of amphibious types. There were tanks that could travel on both sea and land. There were trucks that were as much at home in the water as on the highway. There were tracked personnel carriers which could carry their men right up on the beach, then drop them well inland. On that morning, all of these vehicles and more were about the sands of Lingayen in the pulsing fever of a successful beachhead. Now and then an enemy Zero would whine down over the beach, but this time we had the wherewithal to handle them. Almost a solid wall of fire would go up, and swarms of American fighters from the carriers offshore would dive in to take care of the intruder. It warmed my heart to finally see the weight on our side.

Prior to the landings, President Osmena had prepared a message printed in leaflet form. As our troops came ashore, these were dropped all over the Philippines by our planes. "In a series of brilliantly conceived blows," it said, "General MacArthur's forces of liberation have successfully, in but a short span of time, destroyed the enemy army defending Leyte, seized firm control of Mindoro, and now stand defiantly on the soil of Luzon at the very threshold to our capital city. Thus are answered our prayers of many long months."

The guerrillas had been busy ever since receiving my orders to open up. They cut telephone wires and otherwise disrupted Japanese communications. They blew up bridges and mined roads; they blocked supplies to front-line troops; they smashed patrols, and burned ammunition dumps. Their shining bolos began to turn red. I estimated Colonel Russel W. Volckmann's northern Luzon guerrillas accomplished the purpose of practically a front-line division.

I established general headquarters at Dagupan. Everywhere I went jubilant Filipinos lined the roads and rent the air with cheers and applause. They would crowd around me, try to kiss my hand, press native wreaths around my neck, touch my clothes, hail me with tears and sobs. It embarrassed me no end.

As we pressed forward, Japanese resistance began to stiffen. The terrain lent itself to defense, and they used it to full advantage. They dug caves into the sides of the hills and connected them with tunnels, well supplied with ammunition and other essentials. Quite often there would be a whole series of these positions, each one covering and supporting another. Tanks, buried deep, with only their turrets showing, became, in effect, pillboxes. There was no surrendering. Every Japanese soldier fought to the death. You had to blow his head off or thrust him through with a bayonet.

It soon became evident to me that General Yamashita was concentrating strength in the hill sections to the east guarding the approaches to Baguio and the Cagayan Valley. This allowed the XIV Corps to take advantage of the highway system and unobstructed terrain of the Luzon central plain for a swift southward drive on the direct road to Manila. The I Corps would cover its flank by containing the enemy in the mountains to the northeast.

The central plain, formed by the alluvial deposits flowing from the high ranges bordering on the east and west, cuts a swath 30 to 50 miles wide through Luzon from Lingayen Gulf to Laguna de Bay—a distance of about 120 miles. A highly developed irrigation system, fed by numerous streams coursing down from the surrounding mountains, turns this vast region into an immensely fertile valley. With its extensive plantations and well-developed transportation system of railroads and motor highways, the central plain constitutes the wealthiest and most important area in the Philippines.

It took us just twelve days to cover the central plain as far as Tarlac, half-way to Manila. The speed of our advance gave the enemy little and, in some cases, no time to utilize their well-prepared defense positions. As General Yamashita sought to bring his troops up from the south, where they had been decoyed by the Mindoro operation, many units were caught before their transportation movement could be completed or while in the process of regroupment. Contact between field units and headquarters was constantly broken, and some elements were cut off entirely.

Asked later to comment on the extraordinary initial speed of the operation, I said:

There was no fixed timetable. I hoped to proceed as rapidly as possible, especially as time was an element connected with the release of our prisoners. I have always felt, however, that to endeavor to formulate in advance details of a campaign is hazardous, as it tends to warp the judgment of a commander when faced with unexpected conditions brought about by the uncertainties of enemy

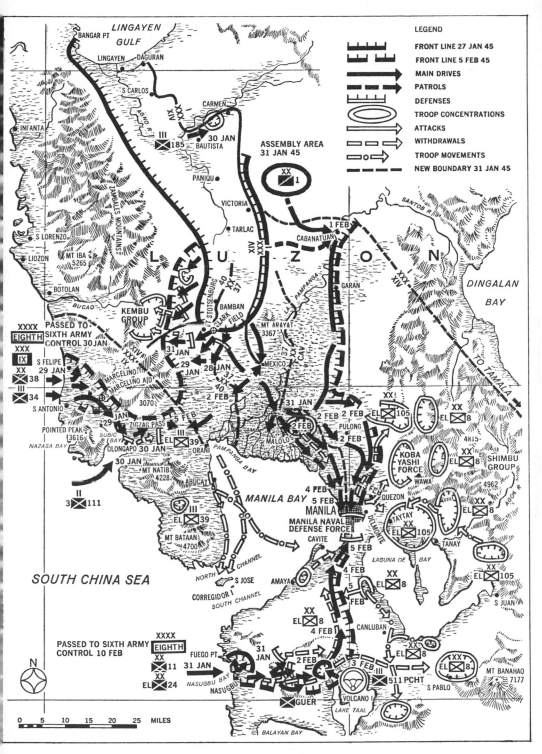

The Envelopment of Manila

reaction or enemy initiative. I therefore never attempted fixed dates for anything but the start of operations. The rate of progress in this operation was fast and more than fulfilled all hopes and expectations. No greater danger can confront a field commander than too-close "back seat driving" and too-rigid "timetables" of operations from those above. There is a natural limit on a command, due to its inherent strengths and weaknesses which place a bracket upon its operation, which only its own commander can know and which even he at times has to estimate. Any arbitrary violation either way by those not present in the theater of operations might well prove disastrous.

I moved GHQ to Tarlac. The going became harder. As the drive approached Clark Field, the rage of battle intensified.

At San Manuel, the enemy launched a savage counterattack led by a tank brigade. Our lines reeled, and I became so concerned over a possible penetration that I personally hastened to the scene of action of the 161st Infantry. Its colonel, James Dalton II, was one of my finest field commanders. I joined him in steadying the ranks. The enemy was finally stopped, and led by its gallant colonel, the 161st counterattacked and practically annihilated the Japanese attackers. I at once recommended Dalton for promotion as a brigadier general, which was done. He was killed a short time later in the Balete Pass.

Washington awarded me the Distinguished Service Cross, my third.*

At this critical juncture, I received a shocking order from Washington to release seventy of my transport ships at once. They were to return to San Francisco, and be used to carry supplies and munitions to the Soviet forces at Vladivostok. I protested violently. The abrupt removal of these transports endangered the entire Philippine campaign and threatened the loss of thousands of our men fighting in north Luzon. No heed was given my warnings. The government apparently had made up its mind that, in order to win the war against Japan, Russian help was needed. My views as to whether such

---

* I received many heartwarming messages:

From Secretary Stimson: "I congratulate you on your success in the attainment of another major step in regaining the Philippines. It greatly reflects your able leadership. I send warmest regards and wishes."

From General Marshall: "Congratulations on your presence at the head of a tremendously successful operation for the liberation of Manila, Bataan, and Corregidor. The total destruction of the Japanese forces of Leyte now to be followed by the elimination of their troops on Luzon are very satisfying repayments for the cruelty and the insolence and barbarism following the initial Japanese success."

From General Arnold: "Sincerest congratulations and good wishes as you stand within sight of Manila. Your advance toward Japanese homeland has earned the wholehearted admiration of the entire Army Air Forces."

From John Curtin: "I offer to you the best wishes of the Government and people of Australia. Your splendid success in the cause of Australia, your own country and of the United Nations has won the admiration of the world. Our thoughts will always be with you and I extend my warmest felicitations."

a step at this late date in the war would be advisable were never solicited. As it turned out, all of the supplies carried to Vladivostok by those ships, and hundreds of thousands of other tons, were eventually used in Korea by the Communist governments of North Korea and China against our own forces. So far as I know, not one shell, not one pound of food, not one stitch of clothing, not one gallon of gasoline was ever used by the Soviet Army in the brief war they finally fought—if it can be called a war.

Shortly after the transports were taken from me, I was instructed to return most of the Pacific fleet to Admiral Nimitz to be used in the attack on Okinawa. These ships comprised much of the naval forces I was using. As a result, my supply base at Lingayen would be defended only by a portion of the Seventh Fleet and would be thus exposed to attacks and raids from Formosa to the north. To meet this new and unexpected situation, I decided to bring the XI Corps of the Eighth Army, commanded by General Hall, forward by sea and throw it in on the Zambales coast of west Luzon so that if Lingayen, in its weakened naval state, became jeopardized, I could shift my supply line to a more secure geographic position. In addition, the movement, a complete surprise to the enemy, would place Hall's forces so as to threaten the flank of the enemy's resistance in the Manila plains and would effectively bar any movement of the enemy to or from the Bataan Peninsula. I then intended, when the resistance in the plains crumbled, to suddenly envelop from the other flank, with the 1st Cavalry Division, which I was bringing up by way of Lingayen for that purpose. Manila would thus be enveloped by this movement from the east, by simultaneous attack from the south by the Eighth Army, and by direct drive from the north by the main forces of the Sixth Army. The plan worked perfectly.

The XI Corps landed without losing a man, seized Olongapo, and by February 5th vital passes to Bataan were in its hands. In the face of growing resistance, it moved in to secure the remainder of Bataan Peninsula and to assist in the opening of Manila Bay. The XIV Corps, after heavy fighting, cleared Clark Field and Fort Stotsenburg, joined contact with the XI Corps at Dinalupihan, and prepared to continue its drive toward Manila. The 1st Cavalry Division, under Major General Verne D. Mudge, landed in north Luzon and was attached to the XIV Corps. The I Corps continued to contain the main body of the enemy, cooped up in the Bontoc hills and the Cagayan Valley to the northeast. The Eighth Army landed the 11th Airborne and the 24th Division at Batangas in the south, and moved forward to form the lower jaw of the Manila pincer movement.

I was fighting on ground that had witnessed my father's military triumph nearly fifty years earlier and my own campaigns at the beginning of the war. I knew every wrinkle of the terrain, every foot of the topography. I was able to avoid many a pitfall, to circumvent many an enemy trap. To have saved lives in this way is perhaps my most gratifying memory of the war. My staff did not like my front-line activity and tells this tale on me, whether in reproach or otherwise I never knew:

General Kenney dropped in late one evening to report to me near Tarlac. Although an energetic mess sergeant had cooked a hearty meal, Kenney noticed that I was scarcely eating. "What's the matter with you?" he asked. I said, "George, I'm so darn tired I can't eat." Kenney prepared to leave the next morning before daybreak. He told the orderly officer to convey his goodbyes, that he was obliged to get away very early. "Oh," said the officer, "General MacArthur left for the front two hours ago." "What," said Kenney. "The guy must be nuts. If he works overtime, he'll lose his union card."

I was deeply concerned about the thousands of prisoners who had been interned at the various camps on Luzon since the early days of the war. Shortly after the Japanese had taken over the islands, they had gathered Americans, British, and other Allied nationals, including women and children, in concentration centers without regard to whether they were actual combatants or simply civilians. I had been receiving reports from my various underground sources long before the actual landings on Luzon, but the latest information was most alarming. With every step that our soldiers took toward Santo Tomas University, Bilibid, Cabanatuan, and Los Banos, where these prisoners were held, the Japanese soldiers guarding them had become more and more sadistic. I knew that many of these half-starved and ill-treated people would die unless we rescued them promptly. The thought of their destruction with deliverance so near was deeply repellent to me. A unique operation was devised to rescue the prisoners at Cabanatuan 35 miles within the enemy lines. In a masterful action executed by picked men from the Sixth Army's Ranger Battalion, and Filipino guerrillas, we surprised the Japanese completely. Their lines were penetrated and our forces walked into Cabanatuan, liberating every last man, woman, and child. Similar raids were later made at other prison centers with equally stunning results.

In the morning hours of February 1st, the 1st Cavalry Division started down toward Manila, its exposed left flank guarded by Marine air units. Simultaneously, the 37th Division from the XIV Corps and the 11th Division of the Eighth Army closed in on the city. A flying column from the cavalry under Brigadier General William C. Chase entered Manila on February 4th, and relieved the prisoners at Santo Tomas and Bilibid. For all strategic purposes, Manila was now in our hands. A desperate element of the enemy trapped by our encirclement fought for two weeks to the death and caused numerous unnecessary casualties and much destruction of property.

I entered the city with the 37th Division. I was anxious to rescue as much as I could of my home atop the Manila Hotel, and accompanied a leading patrol of the division. It had been reported to me that the penthouse was intact, having been preserved probably because of two vases at the entrance which had been presented to my father by the former Emperor of Japan.

We reached the New Luneta, but were temporarily pinned down on Burnham Green by machine-gun fire from the hotel itself. Suddenly, the penthouse blazed into flame. They had fired it. I watched, with indescribable feelings, the destruction of my fine military library, my souvenirs, my personal belongings of a lifetime. It was not a pleasant moment.

The patrol finally worked forward to the hotel, and, flanked by submachine men, I climbed the stairs toward the top. Every landing was a fight. Of the penthouse, nothing was left but ashes. It had evidently been the command post of a rearguard action. We left its colonel dead on the smoldering threshold, the remains of the broken vases of the Emperor at his head and feet—a grim shroud for his bloody bier. The young lieutenant commanding the patrol, his smoking gun in his hand and his face wreathed in the grin of victory, sang out to me, "Nice going, chief." But there was nothing nice about it to me. I was tasting to the last acid dregs the bitterness of a devastated and beloved home.

I made my way to the concentration camps. I cannot recall, even in a life filled with emotional scenes, a more moving spectacle than my first visit to the Santo Tomas camp. It was still under bombardment. When I arrived, the pitiful, half-starved inmates broke out in excited yells. I entered the building and was immediately pressed back against the wall by thousands of emotionally charged people. In their ragged, filthy clothes, with tears streaming down their faces, they seemed to be using their last strength to fight their way close enough to grasp my hand. One man threw his arms around me, and put his head on my chest and cried unashamedly. A once-beautiful woman in tatters laboriously lifted her son over the heads of the crowd and asked me to touch him. I took the boy momentarily and was shocked by the uncomprehending look of deprivation in his eyes. They wept and laughed hysterically, and all of them at once tried to tell me "Thank you." I was grabbed by the jacket. I was kissed. I was hugged. It was a wonderful and never-to-be-forgotten moment—to be a life-saver, not a life-taker.

Conditions were even worse at Bilibid. I will never know how the 800 prisoners there survived for three long years. The food given them was generally full of worms and skimpy even by Oriental standards. The men who greeted me were scarcely more than skeletons.

The military prisoners of war had been kept separate from the civilians. The soldiers had maintained their sense of discipline all through those long years. Somehow, every man had dragged himself to his feet to stand beside his cot in some semblance of attention. They remained silent, as though at inspection. I looked down the lines of men bearded and soiled, with hair that often reached below their shoulders, with ripped and soiled shirts and trousers, with toes sticking out of such shoes as remained, with suffering and torture written on their gaunt faces. Here was all that was left of my men of Bataan and Corregidor. The only sound was the occasional sniffle of a grown man who could not fight back the tears. As I passed slowly down the scrawny, suffering column, a murmur accompanied me as each man barely speaking above a whisper, said, "You're back," or "You made it," or "God bless you." I could only reply, "I'm a little late, but we finally came." I passed on out of the barracks compound and looked around at the debris that was no longer important to those inside: the tin cans they had eaten from; the dirty old bottles they had drunk from. It made me ill just to look at them.

Manila was in a frenzy. Men, women, and children literally danced in the streets. "Mabuhay" was the joyous word I heard everywhere. I had intended to drive around the city to survey the damage, but I found myself the center of triumphal procession. For me it was the end of a 4,000-mile road. It had been a long hard journey, but in some ways that last 5 miles was the hardest.*

President Roosevelt sent me the following message:

---

*I received the thanks of the Senate and House of Representatives of the Congress of the United States.

From Prime Minister Curtin: "Heartiest congratulations on this day. One more important march towards the goal you have set yourself with such inflexible purpose has been completed. Our thoughts are with you and we pray that your great final purpose may not be long in fulfillment." It was my last message from him.

From Generalissimo Chiang Kai-shek: "The luster of your recapture of Manila sends unbounded cheer to the Chinese people who look forward to the speedy junction of American and Chinese forces in the task of driving Japan from the mainland. My government and people join me in sending you our heartiest congratulation."

From the French government, which had been in exile: "Campaign liberation Philippines most perfect in history. Congratulations."

From General Pershing: "Well done. Your latest victory has thrilled all your countrymen."

From Secretary Stimson: "My heartiest congratulations to you on your return to Manila and the culmination of one of the most brilliant campaigns in all history."

From General Arnold: "The deep personal satisfaction you must have experienced in reentering

On the occasion of your entrance into Manila, please deliver the following message to President Osmena for the Philippine people. The American people rejoice with me in the liberation of your capital. After long years of planning our hearts have quickened at the magnificent strides toward freedom that have been made in the last months, at Leyte, Mindoro, Lingayen Gulf, and now Manila. We are proud of the mighty blows struck by General MacArthur, our sailors, soldiers and airmen; and in their comradeship-in-arms with your loyal and valiant people who in the darkest days have not ceased to fight for their independence. All the Japanese and other enemies of peaceful nations take warning from these great events in your country; their world of treachery, aggression and enslavement cannot survive in the struggle against our world of freedom and peace.

And in a personal message to me:

Congratulations to you personally and to your commanders and troops on the liberation of Manila. This is an historical moment in the reestablishment of freedom and decency in the Far East, and the celerity of movement and economy of force involved in this victory add immeasurably to our appreciation of your success. Please give the men of the guerilla forces my thanks and congratulations on their gallant contribution to the campaign and especially for the years of suffering they have endured in preparation for this moment.

On February 15th, the XI Corps continued on its mission to occupy Bataan Peninsula and clear the entrance to Manila Bay. Two forces were designated to carry out simultaneous operations along both sides of the peninsula. By February 18th, the east coast had been occupied, and three days later the final stronghold at Bagae on the west coast was stormed, thus securing the entire peninsula. It had taken just seven days to retake Bataan.

Corregidor had been steadily pounded from both sea and air since late in January, and on February 16th the XI Corps launched a co-ordinated air-sea attack against this strategic rock fortress. The 503rd Parachute Infantry Regiment, of Nadzab fame, made the first assault, dropping onto the western portion of the island at "Topside." It was followed shortly by a water

---

Manila is shared by all of us. Through the long series of successes your forceful and imaginative leadership has been of primary importance."

From General George Patton: "Please accept warm congratulations from self and all members of the Third Army for your magnificent success."

From Supreme Court Justice Frank Murphy, the last governor general of the Philippines: "Your tenacity, your flawless military judgment and your grasp of our responsibilities out in the Philippines has enshrined you in every heart."

From Secretary of the Navy Forrestal: "The magnitude and scope of your accomplishments have stirred the imagination and evoked the admiration of your fellow countrymen. I may add that the Navy—and when I say the Navy I include *all* hands—share this admiration, and don't let anyone tell you to the contrary."

And scores of others.

landing to the east near Malinta Tunnel. The Japanese fought to the bitter end, blowing up many of their tunnels in suicidal desperation. By February 28th, we had cleared the island. The twelve-day fight had been vicious and bloody. Virtually the entire Japanese garrison of approximately 6,000 men was annihilated.

There are moments of drama and romance in every life, and my first visit to recaptured Corregidor was one of these. I borrowed four PT boats from the Navy and gathered all those who had originally left Corregidor with me. We went back to the Rock the same way we had left it. We had departed in the darkness of a somber night. We came back in the sunlight of a new day. In the background, the ragged remnants of our parachute dangled from the jagged tree stumps, the skeleton remains of the old white barracks of "Topside" gleamed down on us, and a smart-looking honor guard rendered us its salute.

I was greeted by Colonel George Jones, the young man who had commanded the troops that had so recently retaken the island in such gallant fashion. I congratulated and decorated him.

"I see that the old flag pole still stands," I told him. "Have your troops hoist the colors to its peak, and let no enemy ever haul them down." I then paid my tribute to the original defenders of Bataan and Corregidor:

> Bataan, with Corregidor the citadel of its integral defense, made possible all that has happened since. History, I am sure, will record it as one of the decisive battles of the world. Its long-protracted struggle enabled the Allies to gather strength. Had it not held out, Australia would have fallen, with incalculably disastrous results. Our triumphs today belong equally to that dead army. Its heroism and sacrifices have been fully acclaimed, but the great strategic results of that mighty defense are only now becoming fully apparent. It was destroyed due to its dreadful handicaps, but no army in history more fully accomplished its mission. Let no man henceforth speak of it other than as a magnificent victory.

By this time enemy casualties on Luzon had reached the tragic figure of approximately 124,000, practically all dead. My own were less than 25,000, two-thirds of whom were wounded and would recover.

The Civil Affairs Division of the War Department became concerned as to just what part it should play in the postwar administration of the Philippine Islands, and requested my views. I replied:

> It is essential in any plans for the control of civil affairs that the measure of freedom and liberty given to the Filipino people be at least comparable to that enjoyed under the Commonwealth Government before Japanese occupation. It

would be a matter of gravest concern if instructions were imposed whether by direct or by individual means, in excess of those existing before the war. If any impressions were created that the United States is curtailing rather than expanding liberties, the most unfortunate repercussions might be expected. The only restrictions which might be imposed are the minimum required by military necessity, and these should be removed as quickly as possible. I repeat, utmost care should be taken that an imperialist policy not be introduced into the situation under the guise of military operations and necessities.

This philosophy was rigidly adhered to by the War Department.

On February 27, 1945, full constitutional government was restored to the Filipinos with appropriate ceremonies at Malacanan Palace. As I passed through the streets with their burned-out piles of rubble, the air still filled with the stench of decaying unburied dead, the tall and stately trees that had been the mark of a gracious city were nothing but ugly scrubs pointing broken fingers at the sky. Once-famous buildings were now shells. The street signs and familiar landmarks were gone. One moved by sense of direction rather than sight. But Malacanan itself was virtually untouched; its stained windows, elaborate carvings, and even its richly embroidered hangings and large crystal chandeliers were still there.

Accompanied by my senior commanders and staff, I entered the state reception room, where I found President Osmena with his cabinet and other high officials of the Philippine government awaiting me. There was a feeling of tense expectancy at the unusual spectacle of a soldier voluntarily divesting himself of power in favor of a civilian.

For me, it was a soul-wrenching moment. Nearly every surviving figure of the Philippines was there, but it was the ghosts of the past—the men who used to be—who filled my thoughts: my father, Quezon, Taft, Wood, Stimson, Davis, Theodore Roosevelt, Murphy. In this city, my mother had died, my wife had been courted, my son had been born; here, before just such a gathering as this, not so long ago, I had received the baton of a Field Marshal of the Philippine Army. There was not a sound in the great room as I prepared to speak:

Mr. President, more than three years have elapsed—years of bitterness, struggle and sacrifice—since I withdrew our forces and installations from this beautiful city that, open and undefended, its churches, monuments, and cultural centers might, in accordance with the rules of warfare, be spared the violence of military ravage. The enemy would not have it so, and much that I sought to preserve has been unnecessarily destroyed by his desperate action at bay—but by these ashes he has wantonly fixed the future pattern of his own doom.

Then we were but a small force struggling to stem the advance of overwhelming hordes, treacherously hurled against us behind the mask of professed friendship and international good will. That struggle was not in vain. God has indeed blessed our arms. The girded and unleashed power of America, supported by our Allies, turned the tide of battle in the Pacific and resulted in an unbroken series of crushing defeats of the enemy, culminating in the redemption of your soil and the liberation of your people. My country has kept the faith.

On behalf of my government I now solemnly declare, Mr. President, the full powers and responsibilities under the constitution restored to the Commonwealth, whose seat is here reestablished as provided by law. Your country, thus, is again at liberty to pursue its destiny to an honored position in the family of free nations. Your capital city, cruelly punished though it be, has regained its rightful place—citadel of democracy in the East. Your indomitable . . .*

My voice broke. I could not go on. To others it might have seemed my moment of victory and monumental personal acclaim, but to me it seemed only the culmination of a panorama of physical and spiritual disaster. It had killed something inside me to see my men die.

Immediately after the fall of Manila, I began operations to clear all remaining enemy forces from the entire Philippine Archipelago, utilizing the Sixth Army in Luzon and the Eighth Army in the Visayas and Mindanao. I also began operations to secure Borneo with the Australian First Army.

On Luzon, the Sixth Army launched a three-directional offensive: the I Corps was ordered toward Baguio and the Cagayan Valley in the north and east; the XI Corps was sent to clear the Sierra Madre range north

---

* President Osmena began his administration with this speech:

"This is an historic event in an historic city. From the time our Malay ancestors founded it more than eight centuries ago, colonial powers have fought for its conquest and domination. The Spaniards, the Dutch, the English, a Chinese pirate, our Revolutionary fathers, have all vied with each other for its possession. But today's event is different from any of the previous conquests and victories. The present victory of American arms is not a victory for power, control or domination, but a victory for freedom, democracy and independence.

"To General MacArthur, this campaign has been a crusade. Friend and defender of our race, he never lost faith in the spiritual strength of our people. In this crusade, he is finishing the noble work begun by his illustrious father, General Arthur MacArthur, who on August 13, 1898, successfully led another American Army to free Manila from a European power. General Douglas MacArthur will go down in history not only for his signal military successes but also for consistently following truly democratic methods in dealing with Philippine civil affairs in areas retaken from the enemy. Instead of taking advantage of military operations to maintain military government over territories already recaptured, he has been faithful in his role as liberator in the truest American tradition."

and east of Manila; and the XIV Corps was directed to move southeast and take Batangas, Laguna, and Tayabas provinces. General Yamashita resisted stubbornly. General Muto, his chief of staff, commenting on this operation, stated:

Based on previous concepts of tactics, the terrain features of these areas provided impregnable fortification. However, the Americans started attacking in the beginning of February and kept it up incessantly. The superior enemy bombardment and shelling gradually obliterated the jungle. Bulldozers accomplished the impossible. Tanks and artillery appeared in positions where we had thought they would never penetrate. Our front-line troops destroyed bulldozers, tanks and artillery by valiant hand-to-hand fighting. However, the enemy advanced inch-by-inch, capturing this mountain, taking that hill.

Balete Pass, entrance to the Cagayan Valley, proved the toughest nut to crack, but on May 23rd the 25th Division broke through. By this time resistance in the Bicol Peninsula and the areas to the south of Manila had been overcome. The scattered remnants of General Yamashita's once powerful army were now surrounded in the hills, incapable of anything but nuisance efforts, with a choice of surrender or ultimate starvation.

On June 28th, I was able to report:

Our northern and southern columns have joined forces, securing the entire length of the Cagayan Valley. Battered enemy remnants have been driven into rugged mountain ranges to the east and west, cut off from all sources of supply. Except for isolated operations, this closes the major phases of the Luzon campaign, one of the most savage and bitterly fought in American history. No terrain has ever presented greater logistical difficulties and none has ever provided an adversary with more naturally impregnable strongholds. The entire island of Luzon, embracing 40,420 square miles and a population of 8,000,000, is now liberated.*

---

* President Truman, who had succeeded President Roosevelt, wired me: "My sincere congratulations to you and your command on the successful conclusion of the defeat of the enemy on Luzon. You have swept them from all the Philippines and redeemed the promises of the American people to the loyal Filipino people. All Americans are happy that victory has been won with the lowest possible loss of lives. I am confident the powerful base we are now fashioning in the Philippines will play its full part in the final knockout blow against Japan and restore the world to peace, freedom and sanity."

Secretary of War Stimson sent a message that reflected his long association with the islands: "Your announcement that all Luzon has been liberated marks the achievement of a great military success. It has been brought about with a minimum of casualties. My congratulations to you and to all officers and men in your command for this most skillful and heroic accomplishment. From my own service in the Islands and my close association with their government, I have retained a high respect and warm friendship for the Philippine people. They have suffered cruelly under the Japanese occupation. I share their rejoicing at the liberation of the main island of their Commonwealth. Your great victory hastens the day when the last of the oppressors will have cleared Philippine soil."

Operations in the southern islands proceeded rapidly. In his official report to the Secretary of War, General Marshall described them as follows:

Using the elements of the Eighth Army under General Eichelberger, General MacArthur instituted a series of amphibious thrusts with such lightning speed that the bewildered enemy, completely surprised, was successively overwhelmed. The islands of Panay, Cebu, Mindanao and the remainder of the Visayan and far southern groups were in rapid succession reconquered, liberated and restored to civil rule. This done, with the same brilliant tactics but using elements of General Blamey's Australian Army, he landed in succession on the north, east and south coasts of Borneo and reclaimed this great island with its almost limitless source of oil and other supplies.

The regular ground units engaged in these Philippine operations, which were conducted with much skill and gallantry, comprised the X Corps, consisting of the 24th, 31st, 40th, 41st, 77th, and American Divisions. The Air Force and the Navy and the guerrillas performed splendidly as always.

By April, Tawi Tawi Island, at the southern tip of the Sulu Archipelago, was under the control of the Eighth Army. The last link in the chain of blockading airfields which the recapture of the Philippines had made possible was now secured. Along the entire coast, from the northern end of Luzon to the southern tip of the Sulu Archipelago, a distance of more than 1,000 miles, our airfields now flanked the waters of the South China Sea between the coast of Asia and the Philippines, while our fields, stretching for 2,000 miles from New Guinea to the Philippines, covered the waters necessary for communication from Japan to Java, Borneo, Celebes, the Moluccas, and all the other islands in the Southwest Pacific. The width of the South China Sea averages only a few hundred miles, so that its expanse, as well as the coastline of the Asiatic mainland, was easily covered by our bombers, in addition to our submarines. This cut off enemy sea traffic to the conquered possessions to the south and severed the so-called Empire lifeline to the East Indies. The effectiveness of the blockade resulted from its great depth, permitting multiplicity of successive fields to bear upon the target.

The enemy could easily, under favorable weather conditions, slip through waters covered only from one set of bases, but when faced with successive belts flanked by fields extending for thousands of miles, he finds it impossible to pierce the blockade. The campaign of the Southwest Pacific area along the coast of New Guinea through the Halmaheras and throughout the length of the Philippines had this end in view as one of its primary strategic objectives. Already our blockade had sunk many hundreds of thousands of tons of enemy shipping, and with the acquisition of the Tawi Tawi base it was now in complete operation. It was now extremely difficult for Japan to ship oil, rubber, or other military commodities from the Southwest Pacific to the homeland, or military supplies from Japan to garrisons in those waters, and as the air pressure of our blockade reached its peak such traffic became practically impossible. The entire Dutch East Indies were now isolated not only for exploitation, but from enemy reinforcement and supply.

In the Borneo operations I used the Australian I Corps of Lieutenant General Sir Leslie Morshead composed of the 7th and 9th Australian Divisions. Tarakan, to the north, was taken first, followed by Brunei in the center and Balikpapan further south. The Japanese had expected the attack on the west coast and were consequently not well prepared. I accompanied the latter two operations, shipping on the *Boise* for Brunei and the heavy cruiser *Cleveland* for Balikpapan. I can still taste those chocolate ice cream sodas the Navy stewards served me and remember the movie shows each night we were not in action. No enemy aircraft, no submarines, just peace and quiet—such a delightful contrast to the savagery of the past months.

At Brunei I personally supervised the initial landing, and, with General Moorsehead and General Kenney, went ashore with the assault waves. Resistance was negligible. Rarely was such a prize obtained at such low cost.

Again at Balikpapan, enemy resistance was only sporadic. I landed with the corps commander in the last wave of the assault troops. I told General Moorsehead, "Today I think we settled the score of that Makassar Strait affair of three and a half years ago." The Australians, with skill and courage, drove inland, and by the end of July every objective of the Borneo campaign had been attained.

At Balikpapan, as the corps commander and myself were inspecting his advance elements, we ran into heavy machine-gun fire, which caused some of our group to "hit the dirt." An exaggerated account of this trivial instance was given to the press, and when I returned to Manila I was greeted by my staff, who thoroughly disapproved of my being at the front, with a big lampoon from the *Portland Oregonian* of July 16th:

Duck, General, Duck! When Japanese snipers fired eight rounds at him, as he pored over a map the other day in Borneo, General Douglas MacArthur did not take cover. The fact is, they say, he paid no least heed to his peril, although his staff members ducked. We see no reason why a civilian should not advise the brave savior of the Pacific to duck, the next time this happens, and stand not upon the order of his ducking. To the deuce with his soldierly pride, say we. We believe in General MacArthur, and have a lot of hope invested in him, not to mention a great deal of money. And distinctly we do not cotton to the possibility that, through his own soldierly foolhardiness, the general may allow some half-pint, no-account Jap private to use him for a target, and speed a bullet to its shining mark. Duck, General, duck! They say that you believe the Jap bullet never has been molded that can hit you, quite as George Washington felt about the lead of the redcoats. But as a soldier who has seen a great many of his comrades go west, you must know that such a fancy is worse than fantastic. It just doesn't make sense. They say you went into Corregidor tunnel while it was infested with Japs that wanted to die for the Emperor. You hadn't any business doing that. There are risks enough in the work you are doing without your deliberate invitation of extra hazards. They say that in the invasion of Leyte you were nine miles ahead of your own patrols. Your worried staff wanted to hightail it for the American lines. Is danger so sweet to you, is her face there so bright, that you indulge yourself? Hit the ground when common sense tells you that you should. You don't have to convince your men that you are a brave man. You don't have to convince us taxpayers and war bond buyers. So when the next time comes, as it will, duck, general, duck! You are said to be bent upon saving as many lives of your men as possibly can be saved while thoroughly whipping the enemy. Why not have a sensible regard for your own? Already you are a sort of living legend. Why take the unnecessary chance of an exit into history before your time comes? Duck, general; duck!

After the Borneo campaign, I had planned to proceed with the Australian troops to Java and to retake the Netherlands East Indies. Then, as in New Guinea, restoration of the Dutch government would have brought the return of orderly administration and law. But for reasons I have never been able to discover, the proposed movement was summarily vetoed by Washington—even in the face of my assurance that its full success was certain at minor cost. This reversal soon bore fruit in the chaos that ensued in that portion of Indonesia; it was a grave error and was the result of political meddling in what was essentially a military matter.

The Australian government awarded me its Pacific Star. I valued it highly, as I was the only foreigner to receive this decoration.

The chiefs of the Indian tribes of our Southwest, at a meeting in New Mexico, made me their Chief of Chiefs, and sent me the war bonnet of the high medicine man. I would not swap it for any medal or decoration I have ever received. They were my oldest friends, the companions of my boyhood days on the Western frontier.

In the several months immediately following the fall of Manila, a number of events occurred not directly related to the fighting. On March 14th, I received a letter from J. Edgar Hoover stating that special agents of the

Bureau of Investigation would be assigned my headquarters for counter-intelligence purposes. He said: "I trust they will be able to be of some assistance to you. I think all of us on the home front view with tremendous admiration the phenomenal success with which you have met in the battle of the Far Pacific, and to have attained that success with so little is one of the miracles of this war. Particularly is it true that those of us who had the privilege of knowing you, feel a great pride in that friendship."

On March 15th, Lord Louis Mountbatten wrote arranging a visit to Manila:

I should like once more to congratulate you on the success of your operations in the Philippines. The speed of your advance on Manila and the capture of the town were astonishing, and I must congratulate you on the brilliant display your forces put up in the face of strong Japanese resistance. I can not help feeling that when the final history of your campaign comes to be written, the landing at Lingayen Gulf and the subsequent advance will be taken as a classic example of an amphibious assault and subsequent exploitation.

His visit was a most pleasant occasion. An amazingly handsome young man, with a delightful personality, everyone at headquarters liked him. He was professionally trained in the naval art of war and showed a ready grasp of the problems of the Far East.

Churchill wrote me in April:

I am sending this letter to you by the hand of Lieutenant General Gairdner, my new Personal Liaison Officer with you. General Gairdner has had a good deal of war experience. He was Chief Staff Officer to the 7th Armored Division, the now famous "Desert Rats," in Wavell's first Libyan campaign, and later he commanded the 6th and 8th Armored Divisions, the latter at El Alamain. He has also served as Chief of Staff to Field Marshal Alexander who thinks very highly of him. I feel confident that you will find him a worthy successor to General Lumsden. We have watched your brilliant operations against the Philippines with the greatest admiration, and I send you my warmest congratulations and best wishes.

General Gairdner was all that the prime minister predicted.

The Majority Leader of the House of Representatives, John W. McCormack, later to become the Speaker, wrote me of the death of President Roosevelt:

"While I have not had the pleasure of meeting you personally," he said, "I have a profound feeling of respect for you, as well as confidence in you. On several occasions I heard President Franklin D. Roosevelt make comments of a most complimentary nature to yourself. In view of the fact that he is dead, I thought it would be appropriate to let you know of the high regard that he had for you personally and for your military leadership. I remember on one occasion when he told us of the meeting at Hawaii—in a most important conference—he gave the entire credit to you for selling the Philippine campaign. He told us that you sold it to the other Naval and Military leaders who were present at that conference in twenty-four hours, that the plans were flown back to Washington for final action and approval. I refer to this, in view of his death, as indicating the high regard that he had for you. I thought that coming from a great man like Franklin D. Roosevelt that this was one of the finest compliments I ever heard paid to anyone and in this case, yourself. I thought you might like to receive this information at this time—a statement made by the late President to myself, the Vice President, the Speaker, Sam Rayburn, and Senator Alben Barkley, giving you the full credit, and the whole credit, for selling the idea that instead of going from island to island that they could be jumped and a campaign conducted successfully in the Philippine Islands. The success of the campaign is a complete justification of your judgment at that time. The late President was most enthusiastic in his praise of you."

John Curtin, the prime minister of Australia, died early in July. His death saddened me greatly. I tried to express what I felt in my message to the Australian people: "He was one of the greatest of wartime statesmen, and the preservation of Australia from invasion will be his immemorial monument. I mourn him deeply."

On April 6th, there was a reorganization of the United States forces in the Pacific. I was given command of all ground troops and Admiral Nimitz of all Naval units in the Pacific. Under General H. H. Arnold, the Twentieth Air Force was constituted, a strategic air command that operated its own particular kind of war from Washington, literally half the world away. From this time on, three different air forces—Kenney's, Nimitz's, and Arnold's—operated in the same area, at the same time, and with the same general targets. I lost my fine little Seventh Fleet, but added Lieutenant General Robert C. Richardson's strong ground forces in Hawaii, the main unit of which was the Tenth Army, commanded by Lieutenant General Simon Bolivar Buckner.

A determined effort was made in Congress for a united command in the Pacific, but it was unavailing. An indication of this struggle was given me in a letter I received from Senator Lister Hill of Alabama, the Democratic whip of the Senate:

It seems to me, that the time is at hand when we must have a Supreme Commander of all our forces in the Pacific. I want you to know that I strongly feel that you should be the Supreme Commander, and I have urged your appointment with those in highest authority. I believe that when the history of this war is written, your campaign from New Guinea to the Philippines will be acclaimed as one of the most brilliant in all military annals. You have won so much, and yet with the smallest possible loss in the lives and bodies of our boys. I congratulate you, my dear General. More power to you.

Apparently so sure of this was Carlos Romulo that he radioed me: "Now we can be sure we will be in Tokyo on scheduled time with the greatest American soldier in history leading us."

Shortly after the fall of Manila, the Central Pacific force launched direct assault attacks, first on Iwo Jima and then Okinawa. I did everything I could to help. The Tenth Army was continued under the operational control of Admiral Nimitz and I directed Kenney to go all-out in his air assistance. Both Admiral Spruance, whose Fifth Fleet constituted the naval support of the attacks, and Admiral Nimitz expressed their gratitude.

Both places were finally taken, but at terrific loss. Total estimated casualties on Okinawa were nearly 50,000, and on Iwo Jima nearly 22,000. At Okinawa, Japanese air—largely suicide planes—sank 36 American ships, damaged 368 others, and destroyed 800 planes. These figures exceed the entire American losses in the SWPA from Melbourne to Tokyo. General Buckner was killed and General Stillwell was assigned to the command of the Tenth Army.

On July 4th, I announced the official end of the Philippine campaign. Some minor isolated action of a guerrilla nature in the practically uninhabited mountain ranges was to be expected, but the great land mass of 115,600 square miles, with its population of 17,000,000, was now freed of the invader.

The enemy, during the operations, employed twenty-three divisions, approximately 450,000 men, all of which were practically annihilated. Our forces comprised seventeen divisions. This was one of the rare instances when, in a long campaign, a ground force superior in numbers was entirely destroyed by a numerically inferior opponent.

In contrast to the New Guinea campaign, which had required two long years of uphill battle, the Philippine campaign was won in nine months of rapid operations. The intensity of the fighting had varied from area to area according to terrain conditions and the state of the Japanese defenses, but in all operations, the complete co-ordination of United States land, sea, and air forces was the keynote of our success—triphibious warfare.

During the three years of fighting that took place in the Southwest Pacific Area, eight Japanese armies had been either defeated or rendered powerless to conduct more than delaying actions. In the New Guinea–Solomons region, the Japanese Second, Seventeenth, and Eighteenth Armies had been crushed. In the Philippines, the Japanese Fourteenth Area and Thirty-Fifth Armies were annihilated. In the Borneo-Celebes area, the Japanese Sixteenth, Nineteenth, and Thirty-Seventh Armies were helplessly cut off, and constituted no threat to an Allied drive toward Japan.

These millions of enemy troops could never contract their lines to keep pace with the ever-narrowing area of conflict. They were unable to conduct an orderly retreat, in classic fashion, to fall back on inner perimeters with forces intact for a last defense of Japan's main islands. It was a situation unique in modern war. Never had such large numbers of troops been so outmaneuvered, separated from each other, and left tactically impotent to take an active part in the final battle for their homeland.

I was awarded the Distinguished Service Medal for the fourth time.

As the end of the Philippine campaign approached, plans were considered at my headquarters regarding the future of the war. Captured documents revealed a fatal degree of exhaustion of Japan's heavy and armaments industries. It was known that the Japanese ambassador to Moscow was making frantic appeals to the Soviet foreign minister to have Russia intercede as a neutral in developing a basis for an armistice and peace with the United States. My staff was unanimous in believing Japan was on the point of collapse and surrender. I even directed that plans be drawn "for a possible peaceful occupation" without further military operations.

On April 12th, General Marshall asked my views as to future Pacific operations. In Washington there were two schools of thought.

One school of thought [he said] is that much more preparation is necessary before the main operations. Hence a campaign of air-sea blockade and bombardment should be adopted which involves a Chosen operation and perhaps others such as lodgement on Shantung or Korea or the islands in the Tsushima Strait area. The other school of thought believes in driving straight into Japan proper as soon as the forces can be mounted. Russia's entry into the war would be a prerequisite to a landing in the Japanese homeland by December.

I replied on April 20th strongly recommending a direct attack on the Japanese mainland at Kyushu for the purpose of securing airfields to cover the main assault on Honshu. There was no doubt in my mind that the com-bined resources then in the Pacific were adequate for the purpose. In reitera-tion of my belief in the imminence of Japan's collapse, I recommended a target date of November 1st.

On May 25th, the joint chiefs of staff issued the directive for the "Olym-pic" operation against Kyushu, setting the target date for November 1st. Under this directive I was given the primary responsibility for the conduct of the entire operation including control, in case of exigencies, of the actual amphibious assault through the appropriate naval commander. Once there was formal establishment of my role as over-all commander for this operation, it was possible to quickly make final detailed strategy for the invasion of Japan. Code designation of the entire operation was "Downfall"; the first phase, "Olympic," was to be followed by "Coronet," the landing on Honshu —the heart of Japan. The Sixth Army would be employed for "Olympic," the Eighth, and the First Army from Europe, for "Coronet." The XXIV Corps of the Tenth Army was to be used in Korea when opportunity permitted.

Toward the end of 1944 and in early 1945 the question of Russian inter-vention in the Pacific was seriously considered in such international discus-sions as Yalta. The political, economic, and military effect of such interven-tion seemed to have become a vital factor in those secret understandings. I was never invited to any of these meetings, and my views and comments were never solicited. From my viewpoint, any intervention by Russia during 1945 was not required. The substance of Japan had already been gutted, the best of its army and navy had been defeated, and the Japanese homeland was now at the mercy of air raids and invasion. Although in 1941 I had urged Russian participation to draw the Japanese away from the South Pacific and Southeast Asia, by 1945 such intervention had become superfluous.

My astonishment over the apparent deal with Soviet Russia against al-ready near-defeated Japan is contained in a public statement made by Gen-eral William I. Ritchie, the officer in charge of the operations division of the War Department in the Southwest Pacific Area, and general staff and liaison officer between General Marshall and myself. Ritchie not only saw all dispatches to and from me, but made frequent official visits to my head-quarters.

He said:

In August of 1945, I had gone to the South West Pacific theatre to brief the General on the results of the Potsdam Conference. The subject of Yalta came up.

General MacArthur was shocked at the concessions given Russia and kept pressing for details. Again and again he asked: "What else? What other concessions
were given?" After he fully realized that the Russians had agreed definitely to
come into the war against Japan, he turned to details of participation. General
MacArthur wanted to know when they would attack, where they would attack.

In view of the projected assault on Japan, it was decided at the Potsdam
Conference to dissolve the Southwest Pacific Area on August 15th. The
Southeast Asia command of Admiral Mountbatten was expanded to include
Borneo and the Celebes. The Australian and Dutch units would garrison
the Netherlands East Indies. As the date for the transfer of responsibilities
approached, I dispatched messages to the Governments of Australia, New
Zealand, and the Netherlands in tribute to the Allied troops who had fought
under me in the arduous campaigns of the Southwest Pacific.*

On July 26th, came the Potsdam ultimatum giving Japan the single
choice of surrender or destruction. The Japanese government failed to accept
promptly the terms of the Potsdam proclamation, and as a direct consequence
Japan became the victim of the most destructive and revolutionary weapon
in the long history of warfare—the atom bomb. The first bomb of this type
ever used against an enemy was released early on August 6th from an American Superfortress over the military base city of Hiroshima, and exploded
with incomparable and devastating force. The city was almost completely
and uniformly leveled. The development of nuclear weapons had not been
revealed to me until just prior to the attack on Hiroshima.

On August 7th, President Truman shook the world with a broadcast
statement which declared:

---

* To the Australian soldiers, sailors, and airmen, I wrote:
"Since the 18th of April, 1942, it has been my honor to command you in one of the most bitter
struggles of recorded military history—a struggle against not only a fanatical enemy under the
stimulus of early victory, but the no less serious odds of seeming impenetrable barriers of nature—
a struggle which saw our cause at its lowest ebb as the enemy hordes plunged forward with almost irresistible force to the very threshold of your homeland.
"There you took your stand and with your Allies turned the enemy advance on the Owen
Stanleys and at Milne Bay in the fall of 1942, thus denying him access to Australia and otherwise
shifting the tide of battle in our favor. Thereafter, at Gona, Wau, Salamaua, Lae, Finschhafen,
the Huon Peninsula, Madang, Alexishafen, Wewak, Tarakan, Brunei Bay, and Balikpapan, your
irresistible and remorseless attack continued.
"Your airmen ranged the once enemy-controlled skies and secured complete mastery over all
who dared accept your challenge—your sailors boldly engaged the enemy wherever and whenever in contact in contemptuous disregard of odds and with no thought but to close in battle so
long as your ships remained afloat.
"These, your glorious accomplishments, filled me with pride as your commander, honored for
all time your flag, your people, and your race, and contributed immeasurably to the advancement
of the sacred cause for which we fought.
"I shall shortly relinquish this command which, throughout its tenure, you have so loyally and
so gallantly supported. I shall do so with a full heart of admiration for your accomplishments
and of a deep affection born of our long comradeship in arms. To you of all ranks, I bid farewell."

Sixteen hours ago an American airplane dropped one bomb on Hiroshima, an important Japanese army base. This bomb had more power than 20,000 tons of TNT. With this bomb we have now added a new and revolutionary increase in destruction to supplement the growing power of our armed forces. It is an atomic bomb. It is a harnessing of the basic power of the universe. We are now prepared to obliterate more rapidly and completely every productive enterprise the Japanese have above ground in any city. We shall destroy their docks, their factories, and their communications. Let there be no mistake; we shall completely destroy Japan's power to make war. It was to spare the Japanese people from utter destruction that the ultimatum of July 26 was issued at Potsdam.

On August 8th, with the world still reeling from this shattering experience, the Soviet Union formally declared war on Japan—following four years of pretentious neutrality that had allowed Japanese forces to move against and occupy New Guinea and the Philippines, instead of being tied down to guarding the Siberian frontier. The Russians attacked the Japanese Kwangtung Army in Manchuria and sent a military mission to my headquarters in Manila. It was headed by General Kuzma Derevyanko, an officer of considerable ability who later became the Soviet diplomatic representative in Tokyo.

On August 9th, a second atomic bomb destroyed the city of Nagasaki amid a cloud of dust and debris that rose 50,000 feet and was visible for more than 175 miles. The two bombs which fell on Hiroshima and Nagasaki were dropped by the 509th Composite Bomb Group based on Tinian and belonging to General Arnold's strategic command. The selection of Nagasaki as the second objective of the atomic bomb was caused by unfavorable weather conditions. After circling for fifty minutes above the smoke-obscured city of Kokura, which was the primary target, the bombing plane flew on to drop the bomb over Nagasaki, the alternate target. Kokura was spared by a blind miracle of chance, but in Nagasaki 100,000 inhabitants died within seconds.

By August 10th, Japan had had enough. After much internal struggle and argument, the Japanese government instructed its minister to Switzerland to advise the United States through the Swiss government that the terms of the Potsdam ultimatum would be accepted if Japan's national polity could be preserved. The Japanese note read in part:

The Japanese Government several weeks ago asked the Soviet Government, with which neutral relations then prevailed, to render good offices in restoring peace vis-a-vis the enemy power. Unfortunately, these efforts in the interest of peace having failed, the Japanese Government in conformity with the august wish of His Majesty to restore the general peace, and desiring to put an end to the untold sufferings entailed by war as soon as possible, have decided upon the following:

The Japanese Government are ready to accept the terms enumerated in the joint declaration which was issued at Potsdam on July 26th, 1945, by the heads of the Governments of the United States, Great Britain, and China, and later subscribed to by the Soviet Government with the understanding that the said declaration does not comprise any demand which prejudices the prerogatives of His Majesty as a Sovereign Ruler.

The Japanese Government sincerely hope that this understanding is warranted and desire keenly that an explicit indication to that effect will be speedily forthcoming.

On August 11th, the United States, acting on behalf of the United Nations, transmitted a reply which stated:

From the moment of surrender the authority of the Emperor and the Japanese Government to rule the state shall be subject to the Supreme Commander of the Allied Powers who will take such steps as he deems proper to effectuate the surrender terms.

The Emperor will be required to authorize and ensure the signature by the Government of Japan and the Japanese Imperial General Headquarters of the surrender terms necessary to carry out the provisions of the Potsdam Declaration, and shall issue his commands to all the Japanese military, naval, and air authorities and to all the forces under their control wherever located to cease active operations and to surrender their arms, and to issue such other orders as the Supreme Commander may require to give effect to the surrender terms.

Immediately upon the surrender, the Japanese Government shall transport prisoners of war and civilian internees to places of safety as directed, where they can quickly be placed aboard Allied transports.

The ultimate form of government of Japan shall, in accordance with the Potsdam Declaration, be established by the freely expressed will of the Japanese people.

The armed forces of the Allied Powers will remain in Japan until the purposes set forth in the Potsdam Declaration are achieved.

While the Japanese government pondered the Allied answer, President Truman, on August 12th, directed the strategic air force to cease its attacks. The Far East air forces of my command and the Allied fleet in Japanese waters continued their steady pounding. When no reply was received from the Japanese by August 13th, the strategic air force was ordered to renew its operations and on the same day 1,000 carrier planes from Halsey's Third Fleet made their final raid on Tokyo.

Never before in history had one nation been the target of such concentrated air power. In the last fifteen days of the war, my Fifth and Seventh Air Forces flew 6,372 sorties against Kyushu alone. Thus, with a deafening roar of blasting bombs, Kenney's Far East air forces culminated their blows against Japan. During the last seven and a half months of the war, their planes destroyed 2,846,932 tons of shipping and 1,375 enemy aircraft, dropped 100,000 tons of bombs, and flew over 150,000 sorties.

The 15th of August was an eventful date in history: Japan's notification of final surrender was received in the United States; President Truman announced the end of conflict in the Pacific; the Emperor of Japan made a dramatic and unparalleled broadcast to his people announcing the surrender. It was a notable day for me, too—I was made Supreme Commander for the Allied Powers.

The felicitations, the congratulatory messages, and the honors that were now heaped upon me were too numerous to count. They gave me far too much credit.*

To my mind the most signal honor of all were the first two joint resolutions passed by the postwar Congress of the Philippines.

The first conferred upon me honorary citizenship in the Philippines. The second read:

That in reverent appreciation of General Douglas MacArthur, his name be carried in perpetuity on the company rolls of the Philippine Army, and at parade

---

* One that I prized highly was the Navy Distinguished Service Medal, for "brilliant mastery of all phases of combined warfare of land, sea, and air forces, his conspicuously outstanding leadership and his indomitable courage." But those that moved me most, perhaps because they were the most heartfelt, were the ones from the Philippines.

Manuel Roxas, who was shortly to become the first president of the Philippine Republic, paid me this tribute: "To those who know him well, what is even more remarkable than his extraordinary physical courage is his moral courage. Every problem that faces him, he decides not on the basis of whether it will be popular or not, not because of its possible effect on his own future, not in response to influential pressures, but solely and simply on what he judges to be right or what he judges to be wrong. Meticulous in carrying out the directives he receives, he is fearless in his outspoken frankness of view in the discussion period preceding a final decision. Emotionally sensitive to the rights of the lowly and absolutely devoted to the welfare of his nation, he is the very embodiment of the West Point tradition of 'Duty, Honor, Country.' "

And before the House of Representatives in Washington, Philippine Delegate Carlos Romulo eloquently spoke: "He is a soldier, and as a soldier, he is one who apparently destroyed. He has not destroyed; he has built. Through his understanding of the simple people, he has salvaged understanding between two worlds. You of America, is it not a matter of national pride to learn that in a section of the world where white men have lost dignity and were being trampled under the advancing juggernaut of Japanese destruction, that one American remained in the hearts of eighteen million Filipinos as an emblem of all they most admired? The gulf between Orient and Occident was cleverly widened by Japanese propaganda, but Douglas MacArthur as an individual bridged that gulf, with no sudden protestation of friendship, but with a kindly faith expressed from the beginning in a nation and its people. His sympathetic understanding of the aspirations of the people—it is that that has made him a great statesman as well as a great soldier. Men like him will eventually put an end to war. To America he is the hero strategist who held the Stars and Stripes in its prideful place in the Far East. To us in the Philippines, he is you. He is America."

roll calls, when his name is called, the senior non-commissioned officer shall answer "Present in spirit," and during the lifetime of the General he shall be accredited with a guard of honor composed of 12 men of the Philippine Army. That coins and postage stamps, to be determined by the President, having the likeness of General Douglas MacArthur, shall bear the inscription—"Defender—Liberator."

It made me weep, something I had not done since my earliest childhood.

PART EIGHT

The Occupation of Japan
1945–1950

I did not participate in the original negotiations for the surrender, but after the Japanese government had agreed to terms, the task of implementation fell to me. Over the radio, I directed the Imperial government to send a delegation to Manila to receive instructions concerning the surrender ceremonies. This delegation was charged with the removal of propellers from all Japanese aircraft on Yokohama's Atsugi Airfield, with providing transportation for the Allies from Atsugi to Yokohama, and to reserve the New Grand Hotel for Allied use. Yokohama would be my temporary headquarters, the battleship *Missouri* the scene of formal surrender ceremonies.

The Japanese argued about only one thing. They made an earnest protest against the use of Atsugi Airfield for my arrival, feeling that it involved too great a risk.

Atsugi was a training base for Kamikaze pilots, and numbers of them were living in its vicinity. Many of these suicide pilots refused to surrender. They mutinied and invaded the palace grounds in protest of the Emperor's broadcast announcing the Japanese capitulation. They killed the commanding general of the Imperial Guard Division and fired on the house of Prime Minister Kantaro Suzuki before being subdued. The Japanese delegation were fearful of my landing in such an atmosphere of violence.

My staff was unutterably opposed to my projected landing. They called it a gamble. They argued that on the Kanto plain of Tokyo alone twenty-two Japanese Divisions, 300,000 well-trained fighting soldiers, remained, while numbers of well-armed troops were stationed across the enemy's homeland. For the supreme commander, a handful of his staff, and a small advance party to land unarmed and unescorted where they would be outnumbered by thousands to one was foolhardy. But years of overseas duty had schooled me well in the lessons of the Orient and, what was probably more important, had taught the Far East that I was its friend.

Small advance parties were flown in to Atsugi, and on the morning of August 30th, General Eichelberger arrived to direct the landing operations.

At two o'clock in the afternoon my C-54, *Bataan* emblazoned on its nose, soared above Kamakura's giant bronze Buddha, past beautiful Mt. Fuji, and swung down toward Atsugi. General Whitney, who was acting as my military secretary, recorded his feelings of the moment: *

We circled the field at little more than treetop height, and as I looked out at the field and the flat stretches of Kanto Plain, I could see numerous anti-aircraft emplacements. It was difficult not to let my mind dwell on Japan's recent performances. The war had been started without a formal declaration; nearly everywhere Japanese soldiers had refused to give up until killed; the usual laws of war had not been complied with; deadly traps had frequently been set. Here was the greatest opportunity for a final and climactic act. The anti-aircraft guns could not possibly miss at this range. Had death, the insatiable monster of the battle, passed MacArthur by on a thousand fields only to murder him at the end? I held my breath. I think the whole world was holding its breath. But as usual, he had been right. He knew the Orient. He knew the basic Japanese character too well to have thus gambled blindly with death. He knew and trusted that national spirit of traditional chivalry called "Bushido."

The plane nestled down on the field and MacArthur, his corncob pipe in his mouth, got out. He paused for a second or two to look about him. The sky was a bright blue, splotched with patches of fleecy clouds. The sun beating down on the airfield made the concrete runways and apron shimmer with the heat. There were several other United States planes on the field, and the few armed Allied troops in the area seemed a frighteningly small force. A handful of officers waited to greet him. The senior was General Eichelberger who strode forward to meet MacArthur. They shook hands and MacArthur said in a quiet voice:

---

* Almost a year later, under date of September 27, 1946, I was to receive the following letter from Winthrop W. Aldrich, later United States Ambassador to Great Britain:

"So many years have passed since I had the pleasure of meeting you in Washington in the days when my father was United States Senator there that I am sure you do not remember me but I have always been one of your great admirers.

"It might interest you to know that I was seated next to Winston Churchill at dinner the night before he left New York at the time of his last visit here and during the course of our conversation he asked me to guess what in his opinion was the outstanding accomplishment of any commander during the war. I naturally did not attempt to make this guess but asked him to what he referred and he said that it was your landing in Japan with such a small force of troops in the face of several million Japanese soldiers who had not yet been disarmed. I believe this opinion is shared almost unanimously by the people of this country."

"Bob, from Melbourne to Tokyo is a long way, but this seems to be the end of the road."

In the background was a string of the most decrepit vehicles I have ever seen—the best means of transportation that the Japanese could round up for the trip into Yokohama. MacArthur climbed into an American Lincoln of uncertain vintage. The other officers found their places in a ramshackle motorcade. A fire engine that resembled the Toonerville Trolley started with an explosion that made some of us jump; then it led the way as the procession headed for Yokohama. That was when I saw the first armed troops in Japan proper.

All along the roadway the fifteen miles to Yokohama they stood in a long line on each side, their backs to MacArthur in a gesture of respect. They were guarding the American Supreme Commander in the exact fashion that they guarded their Emperor. There were two divisions of them, thirty thousand men fully armed. I must say that I regarded these formidable looking troops with a wary eye. My misgivings were not put at rest by this display because I could not help wondering whether the Japanese intended it as a gesture of deference, whether they felt that a strong guard like this was really necessary, or whether there was some other deep-seated, mysterious, ulterior motive.

Yokohama seemed a phantom city. Shop windows were boarded up, blinds were drawn, and many of the sidewalks were deserted. Down empty streets we were taken to the New Grand Hotel, where we would stay until MacArthur made his formal entry into Tokyo. The New Grand Hotel is a magnificent establishment erected after its predecessor was destroyed by the earthquake of 1923, and World War II had been kinder to the second building than the earthquake had been to the first. The manager and his staff all but prostrated themselves as they greeted us and showed us to the suite selected for MacArthur. We were tired and hungry, so we lost no time in going to the dining room, where amid the other American officers and almost surrounded by solicitous hotel officials, we were seated and served a steak dinner.

I found it difficult to resist the impulse to snatch MacArthur's plate away from him that first night and make sure that his food had not been poisoned. When I voiced my misgivings to him, he merely laughed and said: "No one can live forever."

Prisoners had begun dribbling out of the Japanese camps almost as soon as the landings in Japan were made, and among the first of those liberated were General Wainwright and General A. E. Percival. They had been held in Mukden in Manchuria and had been flown back to Manila. I immediately directed that they be brought to Japan for the surrender ceremonies on the *Missouri*. I was just sitting down to dinner when my aide brought me the word that they had arrived. I rose and started for the lobby, but before I could reach it, the door swung open and there was Wainwright. He was haggard and aged. His uniform hung in folds on his fleshless form. He walked with difficulty and with the help of a cane. His eyes were sunken and there were pits in his cheeks. His hair was snow white and his skin looked like old shoe leather. He made a brave effort to smile as I took him in my arms, but when he tried to talk his voice wouldn't come.

For three years he had imagined himself in disgrace for having surrendered Corregidor. He believed he would never again be given an active command. This shocked me. "Why, Jim," I said, "your old corps is yours when you want it." The emotion that registered on that gaunt face still haunts me.

The formal ceremonies of surrender aboard the *Missouri* were fixed for September 2, 1945. I had received no instructions as to what to say or what to do. I was on my own, standing on the quarterdeck with only God and my own conscience to guide me.

I have read several accounts of what occurred and what was said that morning, but my favorite of all is that which was officially rendered to the Emperor after it was over by a Japanese member of the surrender party, Mr. Toshikazu Kase, an alumnus of Amherst and Harvard, and a Japanese diplomat of twenty years service with the foreign office. It has been published but I would like to include it here.

It was a surprisingly cool day for early September. The sky was dull gray with clouds hanging low. We left Tokyo at about five o'clock in the morning. There were nine of us, three each from the Foreign Office, and the War and Navy Departments, besides the two delegates, Shigemitsu, the Foreign Minister representing the government, and General Umedzu, the Chief of Staff of the Army representing the Supreme Command. With the two delegates leading the procession, our cars sped at full speed on the battered and bumpy road to Yokohama. Along the highway, we could see nothing but miles and miles of debris and destruction where there had once flourished towns containing a great number of munitions factories. The ghastly sight of death and desolation was enough to freeze my heart. These hollow ruins, however, were perhaps a fit prelude to the poignant drama in which we were about to take part for were we not sorrowing men come to seek a tomb for a fallen Empire? They were also a grim reminder that a nation was snatched from an impending annihilation. For were not the scenes of havoc the atomic bomb wrought a sufficient warning? The waste of war and the ignominy of surrender were put on my mental loom and produced a strange fabric of grief and sorrow. There were few men on the road and none probably recognized us. Our journey was kept in utmost secrecy in order to avoid publicity lest extremists might attempt to impede us by violence.

To begin with, there was much ado in selecting the delegates. Nobody wanted to volunteer for the odious duty. The Prime Minister, Prince Higashikuni, was the Emperor's uncle and was considered unsuitable on that account. Next choice fell on Prince Konoye, who was Vice Premier and the real power in the government, but he shunned the ordeal. Finally the mission was assigned to Shigemitsu, the Foreign Minister. On accepting the imperial command to sign the surrender document as principal delegate, he confided to me what an honor he felt it, since it was the mark of the sovereign's confidence in him. Shigemitsu, who had served twice before as Foreign Minister—namely, in the latter period of the Tojo Cabinet and through the duration of the succeeding Koiso Cabinet—is a man of confirmed peaceful views and during his twelve months' term of office did his utmost to prepare for an early termination of the war. His efforts, in which I assisted him to the best of my ability, were in fact, powerfully instrumental in expediting the restoration of peace. Such being the case, there was reason to believe that unlike others who evaded the mission, hating it as unbearably onerous, Shigemitsu regarded it as a painful but profitable task. In his mind he was determined to make this day of national mortification the starting point for a renewed pilgrimage onward toward the goal, though dim and distant, of a peaceful state. If this day marked a journey's end it must also signify a journey's beginning. Only the traveler to grief must be replaced by the traveler to glory.

Not so with General Umedzu, who reluctantly accepted the appointment as the second delegate. He had opposed the termination of hostilities to the last moment and was, moreover, a soldier born to command and not to sue. When he was recommended for the mission he grew, so it is reported, pale with anger and laconically remarked that if it was forced upon him, he would instantly commit hara-kiri in protest. It required the Emperor's personal persuasion to make him execute the duties with good grace.

It may sound somewhat silly, but as precautions were then deemed necessary, the appointment of two delegates was not intimated to the press until the last moment. The names of nine persons who accompanied them were not published at all as the service officers were against this, though these names had been communicated to and approved by the Allied authorities. Such, indeed, was the temper of the times.

This party arrived in Yokohama in less than an hour's time. It was on this day that the spearhead of the Eighth Army landed at the same port. Sentries with gleaming bayonets were heavily guarding the streets through which we rode slowly to the port area. All the cars had removed the flags on the bonnet and officers had left their swords behind, at the office of the Prefectural Governor where we rested a while. We had thus furled the banner and ungirt the sword. Diplomats without flag and soldiers without sword—sullen and silent we continued the journey till we reached the quay.

There were four destroyers with white placards hung on the mast marked A to D. We boarded the one marked B, which was the *Lansdown*, a ship which saw much meritorious service in the battle of the Pacific. As the destroyer pushed out of the harbor, we saw in the offing lines on lines of gray warships, both heavy and light, anchored in majestic array. This was the mighty pageant of the Allied navies that so lately belched forth their crashing battle, now holding in their swift thunder and floating like calm sea birds on the subjugated waters. A spirit of gay festivity pervaded the atmosphere.

After about an hour's cruise the destroyer stopped in full view of the battle-ship *Missouri,* which lay anchored some eighteen miles off the shore. The huge 45,000 tonner towered high above the rest of the proud squadron. High on the mast there fluttered in the wind the Stars and Stripes. It was this flag that has lighted the marching step of America's destiny on to shining victory. Today this flag of glory was raised in triumph to mark the Big Day. As we approached the battle-ship in a motor launch, our eyes were caught by rows of sailors massed on her broadside lining the rails, a starry multitude, in their glittering uniforms of im-maculate white.

Soon the launch came alongside the battleship, and we climbed its gangway, Shigemitsu leading the way, heavily limping on his cane. For he walks on a wooden leg, having had his leg blown off by a bomb outrage in Shanghai some fifteen years ago. It was as if he negotiated each step with a groan and we, the rest of us, echoed it with a sigh. As we, eleven in all, climbed onto the veranda deck on the starboard side, we gathered into three short rows facing the repre-sentatives of the Allied powers across a table covered with green cloth, on which were placed the white documents of surrender. The veranda deck was animated by a motley of sparkling colors, red, gold, brown, and olive, as decorations and ribbons decked the uniforms of different cut and color worn by the Allied repre-sentatives. There were also row upon row of American admirals and generals in somber khaki; but what added to the festive gayety of the occasion was the sight of the war correspondents who, monkey-like, hung on to every cliff-like point of vantage in most precarious postures. Evidently scaffolding had been specially constructed for the convenience of the cameramen, who were working frantically on their exciting job. Then there was a gallery of spectators who seemed number-less, overcrowding every bit of available space on the great ship, on the mast, on the chimneys, on the gun turrets—on everything and everywhere.

They were all thronged, packed to suffocation, representatives, journalists, spectators, an assembly of brass, braid, and brand. As we appeared on the scene we were, I felt, being subjected to the torture of the pillory. There were a million eyes beating us in the million shafts of a rattling storm of arrows barbed with fire. I felt their keenness sink into my body with a sharp physical pain. Never have I realized that the glance of glaring eyes could hurt so much.

We waited for a few minutes standing in the public gaze like penitent boys awaiting the dreaded schoolmaster. I tried to preserve with the utmost sangfroid the dignity of defeat, but it was difficult and every minute seemed to contain ages. I looked up and saw painted on the wall nearby several miniature Rising Suns, our flag, evidently in numbers corresponding to the planes and submarines shot down or sunk by the crew of the battleship. As I tried to count these markings, tears rose in my throat and quickly gathered to the eyes, flooding them. I could hardly bear the sight now. Heroes of unwritten stories, they were young boys who defied death gaily and gallantly, manning the daily thinning ranks of the suicide corps. They were just like cherry blossoms, emblems of our national character, all of a sudden blooming into riotous beauty and just as quickly going away. What do they see today, their spirit, the glorious thing, looking down on the scene of our surrender?

MacArthur walks quietly from the interior of the ship and steps to the microphones:

"We are gathered here, representatives of the major warring powers," he said, "to conclude a solemn agreement whereby peace may be restored. The issues, involving divergent ideals and ideologies, have been determined on the battlefields of the world and hence are not for our discussion or debate. Nor is it for us here to meet, representing as we do a majority of the people of the earth, in a spirit of distrust, malice or hatred. But rather it is for us, both victors and vanquished, to rise to that higher dignity which alone befits the sacred purposes we are about to serve, committing all our people unreservedly to faithful compliance with the obligation they are here formally to assume.

"It is my earnest hope and indeed the hope of all mankind that from this solemn occasion a better world shall emerge out of the blood and carnage of the past—a world founded upon faith and understanding—a world dedicated to the dignity of man and the fulfillment of his most cherished wish—for freedom, tolerance and justice.

"The terms and conditions upon which the surrender of the Japanese Imperial Forces is here to be given and accepted are contained in the instrument of surrender now before you.

"As Supreme Commander for the Allied Powers, I announce it my firm purpose, in the tradition of the countries I represent, to proceed in the discharge of my responsibilities with justice and tolerance, while taking all necessary dispositions to insure that the terms of surrender are fully, promptly and faithfully complied with."

In a few minutes' time the speech was over and the Supreme Commander invited the Japanese delegates to sign the instrument of surrender. Shigemitsu signed first followed by Umedzu. It was eight minutes past nine when MacArthur put his signature to the documents. Other representatives of the Allied Powers followed suit in the order of the United States, China, the United Kingdom, the Soviet Union, Australia, Canada, France, the Netherlands and New Zealand.

When all the representatives had finished signing, MacArthur announced slowly: "Let us pray that peace be now restored to the world and that God will preserve it always. These proceedings are closed."

At that moment, the skies parted and the sun shone brightly through the layers of clouds. There was a steady drone above and now it became a deafening roar and an armada of airplanes paraded into sight, sweeping over the warships. Four hundred B-29's and 1,500 carrier planes joined in the aerial pageant in a final salute. It was over.

MacArthur broadcast to the American people:

"Today the guns are silent. A great tragedy has ended. A great victory has been won. The skies no longer rain death—the seas bear only commerce—men everywhere walk upright in the sunlight. The entire world is quietly at peace. The holy mission has been completed. And in reporting this to you, the people, I speak for the thousands of silent lips, forever stilled among the jungles and the beaches and in the deep waters of the Pacific which marked the way. I speak for the unnamed brave millions homeward bound to take up the challenge of that future which they did so much to salvage from the brink of disaster.

"As I look back on the long, tortuous trail from those grim days of Bataan and Corregidor, when an entire world lived in fear, when democracy was on the defensive everywhere, when modern civilization trembled in the balance, I thank a merciful God that He has given us the faith, the courage and the power from which to mould victory. We have known the bitterness of defeat and the exultation of triumph, and from both we have learned there can be no turning back. We must go forward to preserve in peace what we won in war.

"A new era is upon us. Even the lesson of victory itself brings with it profound concern, both for our future security and the survival of civilization. The destructiveness of the war potential, through progressive advances in scientific discovery, has in fact now reached a point which revises the traditional concept of war.

"Men since the beginning of time have sought peace. Various methods through the ages have attempted to devise an international process to prevent or settle disputes between nations. From the very start workable methods were found insofar as individual citizens were concerned, but the mechanics of an instrumentality of larger international scope have never been successful. Military alliances, balances of power, leagues of nations, all in turn failed, leaving the only path to be by way of the crucible of war. We have had our last chance. If we do not now devise some greater and more equitable system, Armageddon will be at our door. The problem basically is theological and involves a spiritual recrudescence and improvement of human character that will synchronize with our almost matchless advances in science, art, literature and all material and cultural developments of the past two thousand years. It must be of the spirit if we are to save the flesh.

"We stand in Tokyo today reminiscent of our countryman, Commodore Perry, ninety-two years ago. His purpose was to bring to Japan an era of enlightenment and progress, by lifting the veil of isolation to the friendship, trade, and commerce of the world. But alas the knowledge thereby gained of Western science was forged into an instrument of oppression and human enslavement. Freedom of expression, freedom of action, even freedom of thought were denied through appeal to superstition, and through the application of force. We are committed by the Potsdam Declaration of principles to see that the Japanese people are liberated from this condition of slavery. It is my purpose to implement this commitment just as rapidly as the armed forces are demobilized and other essential steps taken to neutralize the war potential.

"The energy of the Japanese race, if properly directed, will enable expansion vertically rather than horizontally. If the talents of the race are turned into constructive channels, the country can lift itself from its present deplorable state into a position of dignity.

"To the Pacific basin has come the vista of a new emancipated world. Today, freedom is on the offensive, democracy is on the march. Today, in Asia as well as in Europe, unshackled peoples are tasting the full sweetness of liberty, the relief from fear.

"In the Philippines, America has evolved a model for this new free world of Asia. In the Philippines, America has demonstrated that peoples of the East and peoples of the West may walk side by side in mutual respect and with mutual benefit. The history of our sovereignty there has now the full confidence of the East.

"And so, my fellow countrymen, today I report to you that your sons and daughters have served you well and faithfully with the calm, deliberate, determined fighting spirit of the American soldier and sailor, based upon a tradition of historical truth as against the fanaticism of an enemy supported only by mythological fiction. Their spiritual strength and power has brought us through to victory. They are homeward bound—take care of them."

When the Supreme Commander finished, I wrote in my report the impression his words had made on me. He is a man of peace. Never has the truth of the line "peace has her victories no less renowned than war" been more eloquently demonstrated. He is a man of light. Radiantly, the gathering rays of his magnanimous soul embrace the earth, his footsteps paving the world with light. Is it not a piece of rare good fortune, I asked myself, that a man of such caliber and character should have been designated as the Supreme Commander who will shape the destiny of Japan? In the dark hour of our despair and distress, a bright light is ushered in, in the very person of General MacArthur.

While the destroyer sped home, I wrote down hurriedly the impressions of the surrender ceremony which Shigemitsu took to the Throne immediately after our return to the Capital, as the Emperor was anxiously waiting for his report. At the end of this report, in which I dwelt at length upon the superb address of the Supreme Commander, I raised a question whether it would have been possible for us, had we been victorious, to embrace the vanquished with a similar magnanimity. Clearly it would have been different. Returning from the audience, Shigemitsu told me that the Emperor nodded with a sigh in agreement. Indeed, a distance inexpressible by numbers separates us—America from Japan. After all, we were not beaten on the battlefield by dint of superior arms. We were defeated in the spiritual contest by virtue of a nobler idea. The real issue was moral—beyond all the powers of algebra to compute.

The day will come when recorded time, age on age, will seem but a point in retrospect. However, happen what may in the future, this Big Day on the *Missouri* will stand out as one of the brightest dates in history, with General MacArthur as a shining obelisk in the desert of human endeavor that marks a timeless march onward toward an enduring peace.

This most favorable impression of a Japanese diplomat differed completely with everything that the Japanese government had been telling its people for years. The philosophy I had expressed, based upon the truth that men may be destroyed by what they have and what they know, but that they may be saved by what they are, produced a most favorable result, immediate and unqualified. Just as I understood them, so they reacted with irresistible energy in the creation of a new Japan.

Trying to recall my emotions and impressions as I prepared to receive the surrender of the mighty warlords of the Far East, I wish that my pen were wielded by one on such intimate terms with words—those immortal heralds of thought which at the touch of genius become radiant—that at my call they would convey my feelings in terms that would satisfy the ultimate sources of reason, history, and interpretation. For I have a consciousness that in the events culminating at this immortal moment lie those truths which at last are transplanted into epics and lyrics, and those exalted terms which we find on the lips of the great seers and prophets.

Was the day beclouded by mists and trailing clouds? Were there lone trees cresting Tokyo's shores against the moving sky? Were there voices of waters falling far up within some wild ravine racing into the bay? Were there nearby fields where bees were buzzing? I cannot remember, but this I do—the all-embracing pride I felt in my country's monumental victory. Its future seemed to gleam as though seen through the optimistic gates of youth.

I told myself, the tide of world affairs may ebb and flow, old empires may die, new nations be born; alliances may arise, thrive, wither and vanish —but in its effort to build economic growth and prosperity, an atmosphere of hope and freedom, a community of strength and unity of purpose, a lasting peace of justice, my own beloved country now leads the world. It points the way to an age of evolution, in which the brain of man will abstract from the universe its fundamental secrets. Today's wonders will become tomorrow's obsolescence. We stand on the threshold of a new life. What vast panoramas will open before us none can say. They are there, just beyond the horizon, just over there. And they are of a magnificence and a diversity far beyond the comprehension of anyone here today. This new world would have no boundaries—no lost horizons. Its limits would be as broad as the spirit and the imagination of man.

But with this exhaltation of pride, my soul saddened as my thoughts turned to my faithful men-at-arms. I had seen them die at Verdun, at St. Mihiel, at Guadalcanal; in the foxholes of Bataan and the batteries of Corregidor; on land, on sea, and in the air; amidst swamp and jungle, hot sands, and frozen reaches; in the knee-deep mud of shell-shocked roads and dripping trenches. They were the driving soul of Americanism. They had given me an abiding faith in the future of this nation—a faith based on the invincible character of the American people. A faith that once again they had restored to our beloved country the serenity of hope without fear. A faith in the course of our destiny as a free, prosperous, and happy people.

Eleven months later I received from then-Prime Minister Yoshida the following missive revealing the sentiments of the ruling classes regarding the surrender and its immediate aftermath.

Dear General:

This morning I noticed in one of our newspapers,—the *Mainichi Shimbun,* August 15, page 2—a story of Japan's surrender as told by Baron Suzuki, then our Prime Minister.

What he says at the end of the narrative has my unqualified endorsement. His attitude and sentiments at the time of the momentous decision were not only the attitude and sentiments of His Majesty but also, I am quite sure, of the vast majority of the inarticulate but right-minded men in the street throughout Japan. I enclose an English translation of the particular portion of the article signed by Admiral Suzuki himself.

Yours sincerely,
Shigeru Yoshida

The enclosure read as follows:

Calm and serene was my feeling at the time of making the surrender. People about me were much worried. Some insisted that we should negotiate to get a definite guarantee from the Allies regarding the preservation of our national structure. But such a proposition seemed essentially illogical, and I did not care to go to the trouble of taking it up. My position was this: we were defeated, and as long as we admitted our defeat, the only manly thing to do was to leave everything to the victor. Such had been the military tradition from ancient times. Only I had one absolute conviction as to what to do. That was to trust the enemy commander. The "Bushido" is not a Japanese monopoly. It is an universal code. To protect your adversary who has surrendered as one enlisted on your side is the way of the warrior. I did not know about the personality of General MacArthur, but I myself as a soldier had a firm trust in this soldierly spirit. Therefore, despite all manner of disquieting rumors born of fear and uncertainty in those days I had not the least apprehension. In this respect His Majesty felt exactly the same as I did. As is well known, His Majesty never inclined to suspect others. He even commanded me to confide in the enemy and to place everything at his disposal.

The last audience I had was in the middle of June 1946, when I resigned from the presidency of the Privy Council. On that occasion His Majesty said to me that the occupation policy of Supreme Commander MacArthur was fair and just, and things were progressing quite satisfactorily. Now with the full realization that I was right in my conviction about trusting in the enemy commander, I am watching from my country place of retirement the operation of the Allied occupation policy and the progress of the democratization of Japan. I am very happy to know that the course on which I chose to steer the nation to the termination of war has proved by no means a bad thing for Japan.

Kantaro Suzuki

But the approval of the masses of the people was in sharp contrast to the chilly reaction at the State Department in Washington and in the chancelleries of some of our European Allies. In an interview with United States Senator Claude Pepper of Florida, Generalissimo Joseph Stalin expressed apprehension that our occupation of Japan may be too "soft," and Foreign Commissar Molotov used the same argument in London when he demanded that I be replaced by a four-power commission. A magnanimous approach was far indeed from preconceived plans born in hate and dedicated to vengeance. The Soviets had already divined that, though I had defeated the Japanese in battle, I intended, by means of the concepts of a free world, to win them in peace.

There was a vehement press and radio campaign within the United States against retention of the Emperor. By and large, the same media and commentators who had been loudest in demanding that German industrial potential be destroyed, were now insisting that Hirohito and his family, and the complete Japanese government, be stamped out. Not unexpectedly, the Communist *Daily Worker* spearheaded this propaganda drive; several normally responsible New York papers took the same line, and a number of news analysts with national radio audiences echoed the assaults. Those who shouted for a merciless peace had no hesitation in slandering me as the supreme commander when they felt such a tactic would further their ends.

As contingents of the Eighth Army proceeded to unload in Tokyo Bay on September 4th, an extraordinary meeting of the Diet was summoned to hear the Emperor's speech and Prime Minister Higashi-Kuni's summary of the factors that had culminated in the imperial decision to capitulate. For the first time in history the Emperor addressed his people personally, ordering them to submit to the terms of surrender and to strive to re-establish a position of trust and respect in the world. He explained that he had followed the path of submission to improve Japan's precarious position, underlining the need for self-discipline and composure. For his subjects this meant a directive to work in peace, and marked a new phase in the history of Japan.

I did not visit Tokyo for the first time until six days after the surrender ceremonies. It was just 22 miles from the New Grand Hotel in Yokohama to the American Embassy, which was to be my home throughout the occupation, but they were 22 miles of devastation and vast piles of charred rubble.

I established headquarters in the Dai Ichi Building in downtown Tokyo, across from the moat surrounding the Emperor's palace. The pattern of government was unique in modern annals. I, a professional soldier, had the civil responsibility and absolute control over almost 80-million people, and I would maintain that control until Japan had once more demonstrated that it was ready, willing, and able to become a responsible member of the family of

*Left: Arthur MacArthur in Malinta Tunnel,
Corregidor, during the Japanese attack (1942).*
General Douglas MacArthur Memorial Collection

*Below: Corregidor. With Philippine President
Manuel Quezon.* General Douglas MacArthur
Memorial Foundation

Left: With Gen. Jonathan Wainwright just before MacArthur left Corregidor by PT boat for Australia.

Below: Arriving in New Guinea with Minister Francis M. Forde, Gen. Sir Thomas Blamey, Lt. Gen. George C. Kenney, and Lt. Gen. Leslie Morshead (1942). General Douglas MacArthur Memorial Foundation

Left: General MacArthur on a visit to troops and supply lines at Port Moresby (1943). General Douglas MacArthur Memorial Foundation

Below: General MacArthur visits liberated internees at Santo Tomas in Manila. The battle for Manila was just beginning (1945). General Douglas MacArthur Memorial Foundation

Left: Wading ashore at Leyte, October 20, 1944. General Douglas MacArthur Memorial Foundation

Top right: General MacArthur with aides while directing the recapture of the Philippines (1945). General Douglas MacArthur Memorial Foundation

Bottom right: General MacArthur leaving the Bataan *at Atsugi airport to assume command of the Japanese Occupation.* U.S. Army

Below: President Roosevelt, General MacArthur and Admiral Nimitz aboard a cruiser of the U.S. Pacific fleet in Pearl Harbor (1944). Culver

Right: Reunion between MacArthur and Gen. Jonathan Wainwright in Yokohama after General Wainwright was a prisoner of the Japanese for three years. General Douglas MacArthur Memorial Foundation

Below: Japanese Foreign Minister Mamoru Shigemitsu signs the document of surrender aboard the Navy battleship Missouri, *as General MacArthur broadcasts ceremony.* U.S. Navy

free nations. Never in history had a nation and its people been more completely crushed than were the Japanese at the end of the war. They had suffered more than a military debacle, more than the destruction of their armed forces, more than the elimination of their industrial bases, more even than the occupation of their land by foreign bayonets. Their entire faith in the Japanese way of life, cherished as invincible for many centuries, perished in the agony of their total defeat. The impact of such a disaster was probably greater than had ever been experienced in modern history. The extraordinary feudalism which had prevailed in this isolated land had resulted in almost mythological and fanatical belief in the invincibility of its arms and the superiority of its culture.

Although lacking in iron, coal, metals, cotton, oil, and nearly all commodity essentials, Japan had prospered in the past century largely because of the thrift and industry of its people. By trade and barter it imported raw materials—the wool of Australia, the cotton of America, the rubber and tin and oil of Malaya and the East Indies—and with its cheap labor and transportation supplied the markets of the millions of the coolie class throughout Asia who could not afford the more costly manufactured goods of Europe and America.

Its basic policy and purpose over the years had been to secure the bases which supplied its manufacturing plants. It had absorbed Formosa, Korea, and Manchuria, and was attempting to bring China under its control. It had prospered and poured billions of its profits into these outlying areas. Indeed, one of the contributing causes of the war had been its fear of the economic sanctions of the Allies initiated by President Roosevelt. Rightly or wrongly, it felt that this course would paralyze its industry and lead to internal revolution. It had hoped to seize and hold the bases contributing to its industrial empire and thus insure for all time its so-called "Greater East Asia Co-Prosperity Sphere."

All during the war its people had been deluded into believing they were winning. Now, in one dreadful moment, all this was to change. Ruin and disaster never conceived possible had engulfed them. In their hour of agony, like all human beings, they turned to their religious faiths to bolster them. But even these failed them at the crucial moment. Shintoism and Buddhism had become so absorbed by governmental control as to be almost an integral part of the fascist hierarchy of leadership.

Because I had been given so much power, I was faced with the most difficult situation of my life. Power is one thing. The problem of how to administer it is another. My professional military knowledge was no longer a major factor. I had to be an economist, a political scientist, an engineer, a manufacturing executive, a teacher, even a theologian of sorts. I had to rebuild a nation that had been almost completely destroyed by the war. Whatever my ethical teachings had been, whatever my basic character was, whatever the concept of mankind that lay within my soul, I would have to bring into this political, economic, and spiritual vacuum concepts of honor, justice, and compassion. Japan had become the world's great laboratory for an experiment in the liberation of a people from totalitarian military rule and for the liberalization of government from within. It was clear that the experiment in Japan must go far beyond the primary purpose of the Allies—the destruction of Japan's ability to wage another war and the punishment of war criminals. Yet history clearly showed that no modern military occupation of a conquered nation had been a success.

Military occupation was not new to me. I had garrisoned the west bank of the Rhine as commander of the Rainbow Division at the end of World War I. At first hand, I had seen what I thought were basic and fundamental weaknesses in prior forms of military occupations: the substitution of civil by military authority; the loss of self-respect and self-confidence by the people; the constantly growing ascendency of centralized dictatorial power instead of a localized and representative system; the lowering of the spiritual and moral tone of a population controlled by foreign bayonets; the inevitable deterioration in the occupying forces themselves as the disease of power infiltrated their ranks and bred a sort of race superiority. If any occupation lasts too long, or is not carefully watched from the start, one party becomes slaves and the other masters. History teaches, too, that almost every military occupation breeds new wars of the future. I had studied the lives of Alexander and Caesar and Napoleon, and great as these captains were, all had erred when they became the leaders of occupation forces. I tried to remember the lessons my own father had taught me, lessons learned out of his experiences as military governor of the Philippines, but I was assailed by the gravest misgivings. With such hazards as I anticipated, could I succeed? My doubts were to be my best safeguard, my fears my greatest strength.

From the moment of my appointment as supreme commander, I had formulated the policies I intended to follow, implementing them through the Emperor and the machinery of the imperial government. I was thoroughly familiar with Japanese administration, its weaknesses and its strengths, and felt the reforms I contemplated were those which would bring Japan abreast of modern progressive thought and action. First destroy the military power. Punish war criminals. Build the structure of representative government. Modernize the constitution. Hold free elections. Enfranchise the women. Release the political prisoners. Liberate the farmers. Establish a free labor movement. Encourage a free economy. Abolish police oppression. Develop a free and responsible press. Liberalize education. Decentralize the political power. Separate church from state.

These tasks were to occupy me for the next five years and more. All were eventually accomplished, some easily, some with difficulty. But as the reforms progressed and freedom increasingly came to the Japanese masses, a unique bond of mutual faith developed between the Japanese people and the supreme commander. As they increasingly sensed my insistence upon just treatment for them, even at times against the great nations I represented, they came to regard me not as a conqueror, but as a protector. I had a deep responsibility as guardian of these people so dramatically brought under my charge. I felt they needed spiritual leadership as well as material administration. I cautioned our troops from the start that by their conduct our own country would be judged in world opinion, that success or failure of the occupation could well rest upon their poise and self-restraint. Their general conduct was beyond criticism. Many ancient customs of the Japanese, bred by isolation, gave way before the example they set, and admiration for them was aroused in Japanese hearts. They were truly ambassadors of good will.

I carefully abstained from any interferences by edict with the cultural traditions or the personal Japanese way of life. In frequent public statements I advised the Japanese people to seek a healthy blend between the best of theirs and the best of ours, and I was careful to tell them that no people or country was sufficient unto itself in these matters. I encouraged delegations of Japanese from every walk of life to travel in the West, and where it was possible, I paved the way for such visits. I have always felt that one of the things that made the occupation a success was my insistence that we wanted to learn from the Japanese as well as teach them. It had a great deal to do with restoring a sense of dignity and purpose in their people, and as they regained self-respect and pride, they approached an exchange of ideas with avidity and good will. This mutual respect became the foundation of the basic esteem our two peoples came to have for one another—and enabled the occupation to write a unique and warmly human chapter of world history.

The extent of some of our problems went far beyond anything that we could possibly have imagined at the moment of the cease-fire in the summer of 1945.

Supposedly, the Japanese were a twentieth-century civilization. In reality, they were more nearly a feudal society, of the type discarded by Western nations some four centuries ago. There were aspects of Japanese life that went even farther back than that. Although theocracy was a system of government that had been thoroughly discredited by 3,000 years of progress in the Western world, it still existed in Japan. The Emperor was considered a divine being, and the average Japanese subject dared not even lift up his eyes to view his ruler. This God-Emperor was absolute. His word was final. He was bolstered in power by a small group of families who controlled the military, the apparatus of government, and the economy. There was no such thing as civil rights. There were not even human rights. The property and produce of the average Japanese individual could be taken away from him in whole or in part as it suited the ruling cliques. Between 1937 and 1940 more than 60,000 people were thrown into prison for "dangerous thinking" by the secret police. Indeed, an American viewing Japan would be inclined to class it as more nearly akin to ancient Sparta than to any modern nation.

Let there be no mistake about the extent of Japan's defeat in the war. It was completely crushed. Part of the defeat was physical, with factories, homes, and whole cities destroyed. But another part of that defeat was spiritual. For almost four years the Japanese people had expected nothing but victory. Every bulletin blared of success. Not only that; the people had been told they were fighting a kind of holy crusade against barbarians who had no respect for anything. The war must be won to prevent rape, murder, and other unspeakable crimes. As a leader of the American forces, the Japanese government concentrated on me. When American troops landed in Japan in August 1945, the image of the sadistic commander and his rapacious soldiery was in every Japanese mind.

From the very beginning I tried to erase this false conception. In my speech aboard the *Missouri* I had very carefully tried to reassure the Japanese people, and a few days later, when I moved my headquarters into the Dai Ichi Building, I made a public statement that "SCAP is not concerned with how to keep Japan down, but how to get her on her feet again." I underlined again and again that we had several missions. It was true that we intended to destroy Japan as a militarist power. It was true that we intended to impose penalties for past wrongs. These things had been set out in the surrender terms. But we also felt that we could best accomplish our purpose by building a new kind of Japan, one that would give the Japanese people freedom and justice, and some kind of security. I was determined that our principles during the occupation would be the same principles for which our soldiers had fought on the battlefield.

So effective had been the blockade established by our air and sea forces during the war that the Japanese food supplies had become insufficient for the civil population. Starvation threatened many communities which had been severely bombed. Under Japanese armies of occupation, conquered populations, despite their poverty, had been expected to provide not only full, but even luxurious provisions for the invaders. The Japanese had no reason to expect anything better when the situation was reversed. But as soon as the complete exhaustion of Japanese food resources was confirmed, I issued an order forbidding the consumption by the occupation forces of local food and requested Washington to begin at once shipment of relief supplies. The effect was instantaneous. The Japanese authorities changed their attitude from one of correct politeness to one of open trust. The press, which had been dubious at first, now began to voice unanimous praise.

The Russians commenced to make trouble from the very beginning. They demanded that their troops should occupy Hokkaido, the northern island of Japan, and thus divide the country in two. Their forces were not to be under the control of the supreme commander, but entirely independent of his authority. I refused point blank. General Derevyanko became almost abusive and threatened that the Soviet Union would see to it that I would be dismissed as supreme commander. He went so far as to say Russian forces would move in whether I approved or not. I told him that if a single Soviet soldier entered Japan without my authority, I would at once throw the entire Russian Mission, including himself, into jail. He listened and stared as though he could not believe his own ears, and then said politely enough, "By God, I believe you would." He turned and left, and I heard nothing more of it. But the Soviet had other ways of carrying out his threat against me. It took several years, but their day finally came.

The problem of the demobilization and disarmament of the Japanese forces became an immediate objective as soon as the surrender ceremonies were completed. On September 2nd, the strength of these contingents totaled 6,983,000 troops, consisting of 154 army divisions, 136 brigades, and 20 important naval units. On the home islands were 2,576,000 soldiers, comprising 57 divisions, 14 brigades, and 45 regiments. The rest of Japan's armed might was scattered in a huge semicircle from Manchuria to the Solomons, and among the islands of the central and southwest Pacific.

Demobilization of the war machine was made the responsibility of the Japanese army and navy ministers in order to make full use of their technological and executive knowledge in the complex procedures of dismantling military installations and discharging personnel. General headquarters, Eighth Army, and the U.S. Navy supervised and co-ordinated this complicated and top-priority operation, but it was the Japanese themselves who performed the task.

The dismantling of Japanese munitions and war potential led to an unfortunate incident involving the destruction of Japanese cyclotrons. I directed that these instruments were basically scientific and should therefore be preserved. The War Department overruled my decision. I protested, but received orders in the name of the Secretary of War to destroy the machines. Their destruction called forth bitter protests from scientific circles throughout the world, and to my astonishment the War Department placed the responsibility on me. Dr. Karl T. Compton, president of the Massachusettts Institute of Technology, wrote the Secretary of War as follows:

Only my absence from the country during the past ten days, to which I have just this morning returned, has prevented my earlier participation in condemning the wanton destruction by the Army of the Japanese cyclotrons. It was an act of utter stupidity which has seriously set back public confidence in the military, which asset was built up with such great effort and considerable success during the past five years.

It will have the unfortunate effect of uselessly antagonizing those leaders of Japanese thought who were probably our best friends in that country. It has brought both censure and ridicule on us from intelligent people of other countries, if my observations in England are any criterion.

Three months ago I inspected two of these Japanese cyclotrons and participated in the drafting of the regulations under which Japanese nuclear scientists might carry on scientific work, which was adopted by General MacArthur. They were simple and wholly adequate to safeguard against any Japanese work in this field which could possibly be dangerous.

As a matter of fact, the cyclotron is not an instrument capable of producing atomic bombs. It is a scientific laboratory tool inadequate by a very large factor, to produce explosive quantities of anything. Furthermore, the largest cyclotron, Nishima's, was limited to scientific research in biology and medicine.

To science, cyclotrons are more precious than are battleships to the Navy, more difficult to procure, and of far greater value to society. We do not like to see them wasted.

I read in the London papers that the order to destroy these cyclotrons was in General MacArthur's name. I believe that I know him well enough to be confident that he was not responsible.

I feel similarly about you, Mr. Secretary. But somewhere up or down the line there is some officer or official or group whose judgment or competence is inadequate for the authority exercised, and I believe that housecleaning on the spot is called for.

Very rarely, indeed, have I been willing to make a public protest, and I greatly dislike so doing. But in this instance, I feel such action to be justified, and I am therefore releasing this letter to the press.

A short time later, Dr. Compton wrote me, saying:

I have been continually gratified at the reports in the papers over the continual progress and success of your administrative program in Japan. The one happening which has disturbed me was the episode of the Japanese cyclotrons. In fact, I had to release a certain amount of high pressure by writing to the Secretary of War. From him I had a very nice letter of the sort which I would expect, honest and straightforward. He accepted responsibility for the order as having gone out from his office. He said that it went without his personal cognizance, that it was a mistake, and that the matter should have been reported to him.

It was an unhappy affair and the attempt of the War Department to falsely shift the blame left a bad taste in my mouth. Whatever faults may be inherent in the military character, evasive misrepresentation has never been one of them.

Before the cyclotron episode, many changes had been made in the high command in Washington. General Marshall had been replaced by General Eisenhower, Admiral King by Admiral Nimitz, and Secretary of War Stimson by Assistant Secretary of War Patterson. The latter had been in close communication with me during the war and had been present at my headquarters during parts of the New Guinea campaign. He enjoyed an excellent reputation throughout the Army and was regarded with confidence by the military.

Shortly after my arrival in Tokyo, I was urged by members of my staff to summon the Emperor to my headquarters as a show of power. I brushed the suggestions aside. "To do so," I explained, "would be to outrage the feelings of the Japanese people and make a martyr of the Emperor in their eyes. No, I shall wait and in time the Emperor will voluntarily come to see me. In this case, the patience of the East rather than the haste of the West will best serve our purpose."

The Emperor did indeed shortly request an interview. In cutaway, striped trousers, and top hat, riding in his Daimler with the imperial grand chamberlain facing him on the jump seat, Hirohito arrived at the embassy. I had, from the start of the occupation, directed that there should be no derogation in his treatment. Every honor due a sovereign was to be his. I met him cordially, and recalled that I had at one time been received by his father at the close of the Russo-Japanese War. He was nervous and the stress of the past months showed plainly. I dismissed everyone but his own interpreter, and we sat down before an open fire at one end of the long reception hall. I offered him an American cigarette, which he took with thanks. I noticed how his hands shook as I lighted it for him. I tried to make it as easy for him as I could, but I knew how deep and dreadful must be his agony of humiliation. I had an uneasy feeling he might plead his own cause against indictment as a war criminal. There had been considerable outcry from some of the Allies, notably the Russians and the British, to include him in this category. Indeed, the initial list of those proposed by them was headed by the Emperor's name. Realizing the tragic consequences that would follow such an unjust action, I had stoutly resisted such efforts. When Washington seemed to be veering toward the British point of view, I had advised that I would need at least one million reinforcements should such action be taken. I believed that if the Emperor were indicted, and perhaps hanged, as a war criminal, military government would have to be instituted throughout all Japan, and guerrilla warfare would probably break out. The Emperor's name had then been stricken from the list. But of all this he knew nothing.

But my fears were groundless. What he said was this: "I come to you, General MacArthur, to offer myself to the judgment of the powers you represent as the one to bear sole responsibility for every political and military decision made and action taken by my people in the conduct of war." A tremendous impression swept me. This courageous assumption of a responsibility implicit with death, a responsibility clearly belied by facts of which I was fully aware, moved me to the very marrow of my bones. He was an Emperor by inherent birth, but in that instant I knew I faced the First Gentleman of Japan in his own right.

When he left, I started to tell my wife how he looked, but she stopped me with her rippling laugh, saying, "Oh, I saw him. Arthur and I were peeking behind the red curtains." It's a funny world, but delightful, no matter how you figure it.

The Emperor called on me often after that, our conversations ranging over most of the problems of the world. I always explained carefully the underlying reasons for occupation policy, and I found he had a more thorough grasp of the democratic concept than almost any Japanese with whom I talked. He played a major role in the spiritual regeneration of Japan, and his loyal co-operation and influence had much to do with the success of the occupation.

After demobilization had been accomplished, early in October I issued what was later called the "Civil Liberties Directive." It provided that all restrictions of political, civil, and religious rights then existing in Japan would be lifted immediately. There would be no censorship of the press, all strictly political prisoners were released, and the infamous Kempi-Tai was abolished.

A storm of criticism in the press of our European Allies greeted my action. The leader in denunciation was Russia, which insistently demanded more participation in the occupation and control of Japan. In the United States it took the form of mild criticism of my initiating local action, instead of referring problems, even of a minor nature, for a decision from the State Department, where Far East affairs were handled by the newly appointed Under Secretary of State, Dean Acheson. The general press of the United States, however, overwhelmingly applauded and many messages from the United States were received by me in support of my actions.*

But my own doubts and fears still gripped me. You do not become overnight the chief magistrate of a great state without many qualms unless your own egotistical vanity has made you a fool or a knave.

On November 27th, I received a message from Turkey which vividly brought back memories of those old days when I was chief of staff. It read: "At opening of 5th Congress of Turkist Linguistic Society at Ankara yesterday motion by Nurettin Artem proposing General Douglas MacArthur for Honorary Membership was carried. General is first foreigner so honored. In motion, Mr. Artem pointed out that General attended first Congress of Society held at Istanbul in September 1932 as guest of late President Ataturk." Little did I dream how soon this Turkish friendship was to be transplanted to the bloody fields of Korea.

Early in November, I had a visit from the chairman of the British chiefs of staff, Field Marshal Viscount Alanbrooke, England's leading soldier. He stayed for a week and I found in him the finest strategic mind I had as yet encountered during or after the war. He had been a high commander in the field as well as the chief of staff of the British Army, and was a professional soldier of the highest class. A blunt-spoken, straightforward sort of man,

---

* As samples from the United States this letter from Senator Arthur Vandenberg: "You are much too busy, magnificently busy, to read 'fan mail.' But I cannot resist the impulse to tell you that millions of Americans, including your old friend the undersigned, think you are doing a superb job; and are prepared to back you 'to the hilt.' Your speech on the deck of the *Missouri* was the greatest since Lincoln's Gettysburg Address. Your *peaceful* achievement of *total* Japanese subjugation is a real miracle of statesmanship. You continue to vindicate the great faith I have always had in you. Good luck and God bless you!"

And from the Far East, this message from Generalissimo Chiang Kai-shek in China: "I have the highest admiration for the manner in which General MacArthur has conducted the occupation of Japan and the administration of the conquered country. It has been and still is one of the greatest exploits in history."

indifferent to the roar of the crowd, he had a broad view of global strategy that had no inhibitions of service rivalry. He was none too complimentary of high American commanders and kept a diary which was later published. I was praised, so I am naturally proud of his opinion. Here is what he recorded:

I had kept a very careful watch on MacArthur's strategy in the Pacific, and the more I saw of it the more impressed I had become. The masterly way in which he had jumped from point to point leaving masses of Japs to decay behind him had filled me with admiration, whereas any ordinary general might have eaten up penny packets of Japs till he had such indigestion that he could proceed no farther. The points he selected for his jumps were always those best suited for the efficient use of the three services. In addition I had heard a great deal about MacArthur from our excellent liaison officers.

From everything I saw of him he confirmed the admiration I already had. A very striking personality, with perhaps a tinge of the dramatic, but any inclination in this direction was certainly not offensive. On the contrary, he assumed the attitude of the "grand seigneur" and did it with great dignity.

I came away with the impression that he is a very big man and the biggest general I have yet seen during the war. He is head and shoulders bigger than Marshall, and if he had been in the latter's place during the last four years I feel certain that my task in the Combined Chiefs of Staff would have been far easier.

MacArthur was the greatest general and the best strategist that the war produced. He certainly outshown Marshall, Eisenhower and all other American and British Generals including Montgomery. As a fighter of battles and as a leader of men Monty was hard to beat, but I doubt whether he would have shown the same strategic genius had he been in MacArthur's position. After his liberation of Corregidor MacArthur showed considerable political ability in the handling of the Australian Prime Minister, Curtin, and the Australians themselves. He rapidly gained their confidence in the organization of Australia as a base for operations in the Pacific. He directed the employment of Australian forces in the early days, and before adequate American forces were available, in the overland operations through New Guinea. Subsequently, with masterly genius, he proceeded to leap frog his way up to the Philippines.

In all these operations I never felt he had the full support of the American Chiefs of Staff. Certainly Ernie King bore him no friendly feelings, but this may have been part of the normal friction between the Navy and the Army in the United States. I never felt that Marshall had any great affection for MacArthur.

I am convinced that, as the war can be viewed in better perspective, it will be agreed that the strategic ability shown by MacArthur was in a class of its own.

The most distinguished of British military analysts, B. H. Liddell Hart, joined Lord Allanbrooke in saying: "MacArthur was supreme among the generals. His combination of strong personality, strategic grasp, tactical skill, operative mobility, and vision put him in a class above other allied commanders in any theatre."

Of course, in this free land of ours, no one is obliged to accept the opinions of Lord Alanbrooke or Liddell Hart. Unhappily, I, myself, have some doubts concerning their high rating in my own case. But the armchair strategists with little or no actual military experience, who write with such assured confidence on problems concerning the art of war, and who glibly analyze the pros and cons of commanders, will find much to discuss in the war diary of this great soldier, and the writings of so eminent an historian.

As winter approached, the Russians and the British intensified their pressure for a division of the unilateral power being exercised by the United States in the occupation. These two powers insisted that Japan be divided into spheres of Allied responsibility. It was already evident that the division of Germany into separate zones of occupation had been a serious mistake. I refused to allow it. In spite of my opposition, I learned that the Allies were trying to devise some kind of a plan for a commission. I pointed out that the United States was furnishing 75 per cent of the occupation force and once again voiced my most earnest objections. I also used this opportunity to underline the fact that none of these powers had been forthcoming with troops to fight the Pacific war when we needed them. We had borne the burden with Australia, and I felt strongly that we therefore should oversee the occupation and see it through a conclusion. But Secretary of State James Byrnes went to Moscow in December, and met with delegates of Russia and Great Britain to discuss the matter with the two powers who were doing most of the demanding. No representative of France or China was called to this meeting. I received no information or communication from the conference, and did not know Japan was under discussion until I saw it in the press.

It was at this Moscow conference that the Far Eastern Commission was authorized. Its membership consisted of representatives of all eleven of the nations that had been at war against Japan. The United States surrendered its unilateral authority to the commission. The Far Eastern Commission itself held its meetings in Washington and transmitted its orders to an advisory group known as the Allied Council for Japan. This consisted of four members: The United States, the British Commonwealth, China, and Soviet Russia. They met in Tokyo and were, I suppose, to oversee my supervision of the occupation.

It is difficult to reconcile this formal action taken at Moscow with President Truman's statement in his memoirs:

"Anxious as we were to have Russia in the war against Japan, the experience at Potsdam now made me determined that I would not allow the Russians any part in the control of Japan." Already the growing confusion in Washington due to a lack of co-ordination was becoming apparent.

The action at Moscow was bitterly assailed throughout the United States. The outcry became so great that, in its alarm, the Administration sought to shift the responsibility to me. On December 30th, a United States State Department officer, Mr. Thomas Blake, speaking for the Far Eastern Commission, said in answer to a question: "General MacArthur saw and did not object to the new Japan control plan before it was approved at Moscow. General MacArthur was kept informed throughout the conference on matters dealing with Japan and Far Eastern affairs."

This was a complete prevarication and I at once made the following announcement:

The statement attributed to a Far Eastern Commission officer that I 'did not object to the new Japan control plan before it was approved at Moscow' is incorrect. On October 31, before the convening of the Moscow conference, my final disagreement, to such a suggested plan, was contained in my radio to the Chief of Staff for the Secretary of State advising that the terms "in my opinion are not acceptable." Since that time my views have not been sought. Any impression which Mr. Blake's statement might imply that I was consulted during the Moscow conference is also incorrect. I have no iota of responsibility for the decisions which were made there.

The State Department thereupon acknowledged the error and confirmed the accuracy of my denial. But I realized, all too well, that the gap was growing.

The very nature of its composition and procedures eventually made the Far Eastern Commission ineffective. All four of the major powers had a veto. It took time for the commission members to convene, and it took an even longer time for them to make a decision once they had convened. As it turned out, they usually confined themselves to approving actions which the occupation had already taken on its own initiative. From the start, the Russian member tried to turn the commission into a propaganda instrument for derogatory speeches and statements designed to obstruct orderly government in Japan.

The State Department did little to counter this propaganda. The Soviet Ambassador to Washington, apparently emboldened by this silence, finally charged in an unparalleled vituperative speech, that the occupation was being mismanaged, and denounced SCAP and the Japanese government. At this period in history, Soviet rowdiness and incivility were rarely answered in kind. I knew them well and felt it a mistake not to reply in their own type of language. I therefore issued the following public reply:

I have noted the statement of the Soviet Ambassador before the Far Eastern Commission in derogation of American policy and action with reference to Japan. It has little validity measured either by truth or realism and can be regarded as mainly a continuation of the extraordinary irresponsibility of Soviet propaganda.

Its basic cause is the complete frustration of the Soviet effort to absorb Japan within the orbit of the Communistic ideology. This effort has been incessant and relentless from the inception of the occupation. It has sought by every means within its power to spread discord and dissension throughout this country reduced by the disasters of war to an economy of poverty originally threatening the actual livelihood of the entire nation. It has hoped to so mutilate the masses that there would be imposed through the resulting despair and misery a godless concept of atheistic totalitarian enslavement. It has failed, due largely to the innate common sense and conservatism of the Japanese people, the concepts of democratic freedom implanted during the occupation and a progressive improvement in living conditions. The resulting rage and frustration have produced, as in the present instance, an unbridled vulgarity of expression which is the sure hallmark of propaganda and failure.

For the Soviet to prate of brutality, of labor freedom and economic liberty, is enough to make Ananias blush. At least his sin was not compounded by provocative hypocrisy.

These were rough words, but words the Soviet understood. The Far Eastern Commission became little more than a debating society, and when a peace treaty was finally signed with Japan, it died a quiet death. Not one constructive idea to help with the reorientation and reconstruction of Japan ever came from the Far Eastern Commission or its satellite, the Allied Council. This latter body was, by its terms of reference, solely advisory and consultative. But it was neither the one nor the other, its sole contribution being that of nuisance and defamation.

Prince Higashi-Kuni, the Emperor's uncle and a member of the traditional ruling class, had been the prime minister of Japan from the surrender until well into October. This relationship was regarded by the Emperor as detrimental to the reforms being initiated by the occupation, and he was replaced by Baron Shidehara, one of Japan's most respected and experienced diplomats. When the newly appointed prime minister called on me I expressed to him the following views:

I expect you to institute the following reforms in the social order of Japan as rapidly as they can be assimilated:

1. The emancipation of the women of Japan through their enfranchisement—that, being members of the body politic, they may bring to Japan a new concept of government directly subservient to the well-being of the home.

2. The encouragement of the unionization of labor—that it may have an influential voice in safeguarding the working man from exploitation and abuse, and raising his living standard to a higher level.

3. The institution of such measures as may be necessary to correct the evils which exist in the child labor practices.

4. The opening of the schools to more liberal education—that the people may shape their future progress from factual knowledge and benefit from an understanding of a system under which government becomes the servant rather than the master of the people.

5. The abolition of systems which through secret inquisition and abuse have held the people in constant fear—substituting therefor a system of justice designed to afford the people protection against despotic, arbitrary and unjust methods. Freedom of thought, freedom of speech, freedom of religion must be maintained. Regimentation of the masses under the guise or claim of efficiency, under whatever name of government it may be made, must cease.

6. The democratization of Japanese economic institutions to the end that monopolistic industrial controls be revised through the development of methods which tend to insure a wide distribution of income and ownership of the means of production and trade.

7. In the immediate administrative field take vigorous and prompt action by the government with reference to housing, feeding and clothing the population in order to prevent pestilence, disease, starvation or other major social catastrophe. The coming winter will be critical and the only way to meet its difficulties is by the full employment in useful work of everyone.

The Prime Minister was in full and enthusiastic agreement, and acted promptly and energetically. I knew better than to present this as an order from me, or to intimate that I would be disgruntled if these reforms were not made. Nothing that was good in the new Japanese government was going to be done because I imposed it, or because of fear of me and what I represented. Any change pressed home on those grounds would last only as long as I lasted. The minute I left Japan, so would the changes. These things had to come from the Japanese themselves, and they had to come because the Japanese sincerely wanted them. Some of the changes I had proposed went to the very core of the Japanese character—institutions, myths, former policy methods were in the throes of transition, and the Japanese had to understand why new institutions and new ways of doing things were desirable. I knew that the whole occupation would fail if we did not proceed from this one basic assumption—the reform had to come from the Japanese.

During the years I was in Tokyo, I kept this concept constantly before me and before my staff. "We must scrupulously avoid interference with Japanese acts merely in search for a degree of perfection we may not even enjoy in our own country."

By January 1, 1946, progress of the occupation had been so favorable that I was able to issue the following statement to the people of Japan:

A New Year has come. With it, a new day dawns for Japan. No longer is the future to be settled by a few. The shackles of militarism, of feudalism, of regimentation of body and soul, have been removed. Thought control and the abuse of education are no more. All now enjoy religious freedom and the right of speech without undue restraint. Free assembly is guaranteed. The removal of this national enslavement means freedom for the people, but at the same time it imposes upon them the individual duty to think and to act on his own initiative. The masses of Japan now have the power to govern and what is done must be done by themselves.

The Potsdam proclamation directed specifically that, "Stern justice shall be meted out to all war criminals, including those who have visited cruelties upon our prisoners." In compliance with this directive General Yamashita was placed on trial before a military commission, found guilty and sentenced to death. He appealed to the Supreme Court of the United States, but that tribunal declined to intervene. Of the nine Justices, Justices Murphy and Rutledge alone dissented. President Truman supported the action of the commission. The case came to me for review in February 1946. Here are my findings:

It is not easy for me to pass penal judgment upon a defeated adversary in a major military campaign. I have reviewed the proceedings in vain search for some mitigating circumstances on his behalf. I can find none. Rarely has so cruel and wanton a record been spread to public gaze. Revolting as this may be in itself, it pales before the sinister and far reaching implication thereby attached to the profession of arms. The soldier, be he friend or foe, is charged with the protection of the weak and unarmed. It is the very essence and reason for his being. When he violates this sacred trust, he not only profanes his entire cult but threatens the very fabric of international society. The traditions of fighting men are long and honorable. They are based upon the noblest of human traits—sacrifice. This officer, of proven field merit, entrusted with high command involving authority adequate to responsibility, has failed this irrevocable standard; has failed his duty to his troops, to his country, to his enemy, to mankind; has failed utterly his soldier faith. The transgressions resulting therefrom as revealed by the trial are a blot upon the military profession, a stain upon civilization and constitute a memory of shame and dishonor that can never be forgotten. Peculiarly callous and purposeless was the sack of the ancient city of Manila, with its Christian population and its countless historic shrines and monuments of culture and civilization, which with campaign conditions reversed had previously been spared.

It is appropriate here to recall that the accused was fully forewarned as to the personal consequences of such atrocities. On October 24—four days following the landing of our forces on Leyte—it was publicly proclaimed that I would "hold the Japanese Military authorities in the Philippines immediately liable for any harm which may result from failure to accord prisoners of war, civilian internees or civilian non-combatants the proper treatment and the protection to which they of right are entitled."

No new or retroactive principles of law, either national or international, are involved. The case is founded upon basic fundamentals and practices as immutable and as standardized as the most natural and irrefragable of social codes. The proceedings were guided by that primary rational of all judicial purposes—to ascertain the full truth unshackled by any artificialities of narrow method or technical arbitrariness. The results are beyond challenge.

I approve the findings and sentence of the Commission and direct the Commanding General, Army Forces in the Western Pacific, to execute the judgment upon the defendant, stripped of uniform, decorations and other appurtenances signifying membership in the military profession.

General Homma was also brought to trial by military commission in Manila. The story of the "Death March" of Bataan, heretofore concealed from the Japanese public, had shocked Japan. The Emperor, when told of it, had stripped Homma of his commission as an officer, and of his medals and decorations. The commission found him guilty and sentenced him to death. The case came to me for final decision early in March.

Mrs. Homma asked for an opportunity to personally present her plea for clemency, and I agreed to see her. She was accompanied by one of the American officers who had defended Homma at his trial. She was a cultured woman of great personal charm. It was one of the most trying hours of my life. I told her that I had the greatest possible personal sympathy for her and understood the great sorrow of her situation. No incident, I said, could more deeply illustrate the utter evil of war and its dreadful consequences upon those like her who had little or no voice or part in it. I added that I would give the gravest consideration to what she had said.

My review of the case was rendered on March 21st, as follows:

I am again confronted with the repugnant duty of passing final judgment on a former adversary in a major military campaign. The proceedings show the defendant lacked the basic firmness of character and moral fortitude essential to officers charged with the high command of military forces in the field. No nation can safely trust its martial honor to leaders who do not maintain the universal code which distinguishes between those things that are right and those things that are wrong. The testimony shows a complete failure to comply with this simple but vital standard. The savageries which resulted have shocked the world. They have become synonyms of horror and mark the lowest ebb of depravity of modern times. There are few parallels in infamy and tragedy with the brutalization of troops who in good faith had laid down their arms. It is of peculiar aversion that the victims were a garrison whose heroism and valor has never been surpassed. Of all fighting men of all time none deserved more the honors of war in their hour of final agony. The callousness of denial has never been exceeded. This violation of a fundamental code of chivalry, which has ruled all honorable military men throughout the ages in treatment of defeated opponents, will forever shame the memory of the victorious troops. I can find no circumstances of extenuation although I have searched for some instance upon which to base palliation.

In reviewing this case I have carefully considered the minority views presented by distinguished justices of the United States Supreme Court in negation not only as to jurisdiction but as to method and merit. My action as well as the record in this case would be incomplete were I to fail the obligation as the final reviewing authority of frank expression on issues of so basic a nature. I do so from the standpoint of a member of the executive branch of the government in process of its responsibility in the administration of military justice.

No trial could have been fairer than this one, no accused was ever given a more complete opportunity of defense, no judicial process was ever freer from prejudice. Insofar as was humanly possible the actual facts were fully presented to the commission. There were no artifices of technicality which might have precluded the introduction of full truth in favor of half truth, or caused the slanting of half truth to produce the effect of non-truth, thereby warping and confusing the tribunal into an insecure verdict. On the contrary, the trial was conducted in the unshaded light of truth, the whole truth and nothing but the truth. Those who would oppose such honest method can only be a minority who either advocate arbitrariness of process above factual realism, or who inherently shrink from the stern rigidity of capital punishment. Strange jurisprudence it would be, which for whatever reason defeated the fundamental purpose of justice—to rectify wrong, to protect right and to produce order, safety and well-being. No sophistry can confine justice to a form. It is a quality. Its purity lies in its purpose, not in its detail. The rules of war and the military law resulting as an essential corollary therefrom have always proven sufficiently flexible to accomplish justice within the strict limitations of morality.

If this defendant does not deserve his judicial fate, none in jurisdictional history ever did. There can be no greater, more heinous or more dangerous crime than the mass destruction, under guise of military authority or military necessity, of helpless men incapable of further contribution to war effort. A failure of law process to punish such acts of criminal enormity would threaten the very fabric of world society. Human liberties, the fundamental dignities of man, the basic freedoms upon which depend the very future of civilization, all would be in peril and hazard. Soldiers of an army invariably reflect the attitude of their general. The leader is the essence. Isolated cases of rapine may well be exceptional but widespread and continuing abuse can only be a fixed responsibility of highest field authority. Resultant liability is commensurate with resultant crime. To hold otherwise would be to prevaricate the fundamental nature of the command function. This imposes no new hazard on a commander, no new limitation on his power. He has always, and properly, been subject to due process of law. Powerful as he may become in time of war, he still is not autocratic or absolute, he still remains responsible before the bar of universal justice. From time immemorial the record of high commanders, of whatever side, has been generally temperate and just. The lapses during this latest war are contrary to past trend. By universal practice such military transgressions are tried by military tribunals. No escutcheon is more unsullied of revenge and passion than that of the United States. Firmly rooted in long and noble tradition American military justice may safely be predicted to remain so.

I approve the finding of guilt and direct the Commanding General, United States Forces in the Western Pacific, to execute the sentence.

As our forces were being demobilized in the Philippines, the remaining United States cases of this kind were tried by the International Tribunal in Tokyo. The rest of the Allies tried war criminals in their own military tribunals.

The Potsdam declaration also contained a purge provision requiring all Japanese who had actively engaged in militaristic and ultra-nationalistic activities prior to the war to be removed from public office and excluded from political influence. I very much doubted the wisdom of this measure, as it tended to lose the services of many able governmental individuals who would be difficult to replace in the organization of a new Japan. I put the purge into operation with as little harshness as possible, but it was the one issue in which popular support by the Japanese people was lacking. The punitive feature of such a policy always outweighs all other attributes and invariably breeds resentments which carry the germs of future discord. Many of those involved are patriots who serve their country in the light of existing conditions, and their punishment makes personal expiation for the mistakes of the nation. As soon as the peace treaty restored Japan's full sovereignty, all prohibitions against the purgees were promptly, and properly, removed.

Before we could really do much with the Japanese governmental system, there had to be sweeping changes in the fundamental law of the land—the constitution. The political situation in Japan was desperate. Its old Meiji constitution had been so warped in interpretation, and so deprecated in public opinion by the results of the war, that a new charter was immediately imperative if the structure of Japanese self-government was to be sustained. The choice was alien military government or autonomous civil government. The pressure for the former by many of the Allied nations was intense, accompanied by many drastic concepts designed to fracture the Japanese nation.

We could not simply encourage the growth of democracy. We had to make sure that it grew. Under the old constitution, government flowed downward from the Emperor, who held the supreme authority, through those to whom he had delegated power. It was a dictatorship to begin with, a hereditary one, and the people existed to serve it. Under these conditions, the population of Japan had no basic rights, written or unwritten. Because they had never been exposed to the idea that they might have such inherent rights, they had existed for centuries without any idea of what the possession of those rights might mean to them. The fact that they were being given something that they had never experienced promised to make the task of writing and getting acceptance for a new constitution somewhat easier than it might otherwise have been.

In my efforts for a revision of the Meiji constitution, I emphasized the point that we felt a democratic regime was essential to the new Japan, and that we could only insure such a society by having a plainly written and clearly understood statement of rights. I did not, however, try to force an American version of a Japanese constitution, and order them to adopt it. The revision had to be made by the Japanese themselves and it had to be done without coercion.

The actual task of revising the old constitution was begun in October 1945 by a committee especially appointed by Prime Minister Shidehara. Its members were all prominent political leaders under the chairmanship of Dr. Joji Matsumoto, a member of the cabinet. The Constitutional Problem Investigating Committee, as it was called, began receiving advice almost at once from the rank and file of the Japanese people. This advice came in the form of editorials, letters, and even calls on the committee members. With no censorship in Japan any longer, the people discussed and debated the new constitution on every street corner, in every newspaper, and in every home. Even the Communist Party entered into the arguments with some zest. Everyone had his own ideas of what should go into the new document and lost no time in presenting them.

I took no part in the deliberations of the Constitutional Problem Investigating Committee, nor did any member of my staff. Because of my hands-off attitude, I was not aware of everything that went on in the committee. For three months, the work went on. It was not until the end of that period that I was informed of a split in the committee. There were two main groups: those who advocated the adoption of an extremely liberal constitution, and those who wanted as little change as possible. The committee reflected, however, the wishes of its chairman, Dr. Matsumoto, who, it developed, was an extreme reactionary and who ruled the deliberations with an iron hand. When the first draft of the new constitution was submitted in January 1946, it turned out to be nothing more than a rewording of the old Meiji constitution. The power of the Emperor was deleted not a whit. He simply became "supreme and inviolable" rather than "sacred and inviolable." And instead of incorporating a bill of rights, the new constitution took away some of the few rights that already existed. This was done by simply making them subordinate to statutory law. For example, it gave a man religious freedom, "except as otherwise provided by law." All that had to happen was for the old crowd of militarists or civil servants to get control of the Diet, and wipe out all the rights that were granted by the constitution. In other words, after three months of work, the constitution was the same as always—worse, perhaps.

I was now confronted with a time problem. Earlier, at my suggestion, the legislative body had revised the election laws, giving those who had been disenfranchised the right to vote. With this new law in effect, the government had called for a general election on April 10, 1946. I had expected that the new constitution would be finished by then and that the voting would, in fact, be a plebiscite. The way things stood after Dr. Matsumoto finished his work, the people would be voting on whether they wanted to keep the old constitution or one just like it.

Accordingly, I directed my staff to assist and advise with the Japanese in the formation of an acceptable draft. The prime minister himself became active and energetic in its final preparation. The Emperor was shown the draft, and at once approved, saying that "upon these principles will truly rest the welfare of our people and the rebuilding of Japan." It was a remarkable reaction, because these principles were the very ones that were to take away the power of the imperial throne and to sign over to the state the biggest part of his personal estate and that of his family.

On March 6th, I stated to the anxious people: "It is with a sense of deep satisfaction that I am today able to announce a decision of the Emperor and the government of Japan to submit to the Japanese people a new and enlightened constitution which has my full approval."

Now began the task of seeing to it that the masses of the Japanese people had a chance to read and evaluate the new document. It was circulated throughout Japan and earnestly debated for a month. Ideas for small changes were forwarded from all sections, but by and large the people liked it and approved of it in wholehearted fashion. The only dissenters, as might have been expected, were the Communists. The government carried out a large-scale educational program in the papers and on the radio, explaining all the features and answering questions. The April election was what I had wanted—a true plebiscite. The people who had publicly committed themselves to the adoption were elected to a strong and clear majority in the new Diet.

The new constitution was not immediately adopted. In what might be called the new spirit of the times in Japan, the members of the Diet spent all summer exploring the various ramifications. When it was approved by the lower house in August, there had been a great many changes, although the basic principles were intact. The following month the House of Peers approved it. The Emperor proclaimed it the law of the land on November 3rd, and it went into effect in May 1947. As can be seen, more than a year and a half had gone by since work on the new document had started, and during that whole long period it had been scrutinized by the people of Japan. I know of no similar important document that ever received so much attention and open debate, including our own Constitution.

The new Japanese constitution is really an amendment to the older Meiji one. I felt that by using this particular device we could insure a continuity, and continuity is important in Japan. It is undoubtedly the most liberal constitution in history, having borrowed the best from the constitutions of many countries. From an absolute monarch, the Emperor has turned into a constitutional one, "the symbol of the state and unity of the people." The supreme power in the state is now held by the Diet. The Japanese people, for the first time in their history, enjoy the safeguards and the protection of a bill of rights. As in our own government, it provides for a separation of powers between the three branches of government. By making the courts independent of the ministry of justice, it ends one of the great evils of the former government. There is a supreme court, and all courts are permitted to establish their own procedural rules, within the limits of the law, and they are allowed to set up their own independent budget for approval by the Diet, a fact that removes them from the influence of the legislative branch.

The form of government is a combination of the American executive system and the British parliamentary one. The prime minister serves a term of four years, but he is elected from the membership of the lower house of the legislature. If, for any reason, the prime minister is not upheld on issues that come before the Diet, he has two choices: he can resign and let the lower house elect a successor, or he can dissolve the Diet and call for new elections. This provision provides a degree of stability in the government. No group within the Diet is going to question the administration of a prime minister in an idle fashion if they are going to be forced to stand the expense of a new election campaign as a result of their capriciousness.

One of the more important amendments to the new constitution that was made as the result of the free and open debate in the Diet during the summer of 1946 was the provision for amendment by national referendum. If two-thirds of the Japanese electors decide that a change needs to be made, it goes into effect. The people themselves thus control their own constitution and are, in the final analysis, the sovereigns in their own land. One of the most interesting things about the Japanese constitution as adopted in 1946 is the fact that it has never been amended, although it has been in force for seventeen years. This speaks well for the wisdom and judiciousness that went into its final draft. Indeed, most Japanese politicians today take great pride in pointing out that they were members of the body that helped draft it or that they had worked for its adoption. It is probably the single most important accomplishment of the occupation, for it brought to the Japanese people freedoms and privileges which they had never known. And I am certain that it would never have been accomplished had the occupation been dependent on the deliberations of the Far Eastern Commission—with the Soviet power of veto!

The new Japanese constitution is not entirely free of criticism and never has been, but its critics, always extremists, do not attack the constitution on its own merits.

It has frequently been charged, even by those who should be better informed, that the "no war" clause was forced upon the government by my personal fiat. This is not true, as the following facts will show: Long before work was completed on the new document by Dr. Matsumoto, I had an appointment with Prime Minister Shidehara, who wished to thank me for making what was then a new drug in Japan, penicillin, available in aiding in his recovery from severe illness. He arrived at my office at noon on January 24th and thanked me for the penicillin, but I noticed he then seemed somewhat embarrassed and hesitant. I asked him what was troubling him, that as prime minister he could speak with the greatest frankness, either by way of complaint or suggestion. He replied that he hesitated to do so because of my profession as a soldier. I assured him soldiers were not as unresponsive or inflexible as they are sometimes pictured—that at bottom most of them were quite human.

He then proposed that when the new constitution became final that it include the so-called no-war clause. He also wanted it to prohibit any military establishment for Japan—any military establishment whatsoever. Two things would thus be accomplished. The old military party would be deprived of any instrument through which they could someday seize power, and the rest of the world would know that Japan never intended to wage war again. He added that Japan was a poor country and could not really afford to pour money into armaments anyway. Whatever resources the nation had left should go to bolstering the economy.

I had thought that my long years of experience had rendered me practically immune to surprise or unusual excitement, but this took my breath away. I could not have agreed more. For years I have believed that war should be abolished as an outmoded means of resolving disputes between nations. Probably no living man has seen as much of war and its destruction as I had. A participant or observer in six wars, a veteran of twenty campaigns, the survivor of hundreds of battlefields, I have fought with or against the soldiers of practically every country in the world, and my abhorrence reached its height with the perfection of the atom bomb.

When I spoke in this vein, it was Shidehara's turn to be surprised. His amazement was so great that he seemed overwhelmed as he left the office. Tears ran down his face, and he turned back to me and said, "The world will laugh and mock us as impracticable visionaries, but a hundred years from now we will be called prophets."

Article 9 of Chapter 11 of the Japanese Constitution provides:

Aspiring sincerely to an international peace based on justice and order, the Japanese people forever renounce war as a sovereign right of the nation and the threat or use of force as means of settling international disputes. In order to accomplish the aim of the preceding paragraph, land, sea and air forces, as well as other war potential, will never be maintained. The right of belligerency of the State will not be recognized.

There were attacks made on this article of the constitution, especially by the cynics who said that it was against the basic nature of man. I defended it, and advocated that it be adopted. Not only was I convinced that it was the most moral of ideas, but I knew that it was exactly what the Allies wanted at that time for Japan. They had said so at Potsdam and they had said so afterwards. Indeed, my directive read, "Japan is not to have an Army, Navy, Air Force, Secret Police organization, or civil aviation." And now this had been accomplished by the Japanese themselves, not by the conquering powers.

Nothing in Article 9, however, prevents any and all necessary steps for the preservation of the safety of the nation. Japan cannot be expected to resist the overweening law of self-preservation. If attacked, she will defend herself. Article 9 was aimed entirely at eliminating Japanese aggression. I stated this at the time of the adoption of the constitution, and later recommended that in case of necessity, a defense force be established consisting of ten divisions with corresponding sea and air elements.

I stated unequivocally:

Should the course of world events require that all mankind stand to arms in defense of human liberty and Japan comes within the orbit of immediately threatened attack, then the Japanese, too, should mount the maximum defensive power which their resources will permit. Article 9 is based upon the highest of moral ideals, but by no sophistry of reasoning can it be interpreted as complete negation of the inalienable right of self-defense against unprovoked attack. It is a ringing affirmation by a people laid prostrate by the sword, of faith in the ultimate triumph of international morality and justice without resort to the sword.

It must be understood, however, that so long as predatory international banditry is permitted to roam the earth to crush human freedom under its avarice and violence, its high concept will be slow in finding universal acceptance. But it is axiomatic that there must be always a first in all things. The great immediate purpose Japan can serve in the confusion which overrides all of strifetorn Asia is to stand out with striking and unruffled calmness and tranquility as the exemplification of peaceful progress, under conditions of unalloyed personal freedom. It can thus wield a profound moral influence upon the destiny of the Asian race.

In the general election of April 10, 1946, the centuries of custom and tradition in Japan were upset by the first completely free election ever held in that country. Seventy-five per cent of those eligible to vote helped to elect 466 members of the Diet. More than 13,000,000 women registered their choices for the first time, and those 13,000,000 votes changed the whole complexion of Japanese political life. Even in modern times it had been the custom of the prime minister in power to choose the majority of the Diet members who were voted on, and all of these holdovers were now voted out of office. An analysis of election returns revealed that only six of the old-line professional politicians had been sent to the legislature. Farmers, teachers, doctors, and laboring men now sat in the house once dominated by lawyers and industrialists. These were, by and large, much younger people. Best of all, they included thirty-eight women.

The election was not without its amusing aspects. The day after the results were announced, I received a call from an extremely dignified but obviously distraught Japanese legislative leader requesting an appointment with me. The caller, who was one of a numerous group of Harvard Law School graduates in Japan, immediately launched into the subject that was troubling him so deeply. "I regret to say that something terrible has happened. A prostitute, Your Excellency, has been elected to the House of Representatives."

I asked him, "How many votes did she receive?"

The Japanese legislator sighed, and said: "256,000."

I said, as solemnly as I could: "Then I should say there must have been more than her dubious occupation involved."

He burst into a gale of laughter. "You soldiers!" he exclaimed, and dropped the subject. He probably thought I was a lunatic.

The Japanese women were quick to take advantage of their new status under the constitution. They found jobs in professions where they had never been seen before. In the next five years, some 2,000 of them even became policewomen. They took an active part in the various labor unions, a million and a half of them joining workmen's organizations. For the first time in Japanese history they fought for and secured laws giving them the same pay and same hours as men. They even asked for and received maternity leave. Until the occupation there had never been co-education in Japan except in the lower grades. This was now changed and the women received exactly the same quality of education as men. Laws concerning marriage, divorce, and adultery were revised as part of the program for equality. The old custom of contract marriages was forbidden, and concubinage was abolished.

Of all the reforms accomplished by the occupation in Japan, none was more heartwarming to me than this change in the status of women.

There was much criticism of my support for the enfranchisement of women. Many Americans, as well as other so-called experts on Japan, expressed the view that Japanese women were too steeped in the tradition of subservience to their husbands to act with any degree of political independence. But I had my defenders as well.*

---

* President Truman sent this message: "Tell MacArthur that I am behind him a hundred percent, that I think he's doing an excellent job and he can be absolutely certain I'll back him to the finish."

And Secretary of State Byrnes joined in: "Tell MacArthur that I think he is doing a magnifi-

The occupation endeavors were not confined to political reforms alone, but were far more comprehensive in scope. When the war ended in 1945, Japan was a nation completely exhausted. The cities and the factories had been gutted, the entire population of the country faced starvation. With the war, she had lost her supply of raw materials, all of which had been traditionally brought in from outside her markets, and virtually her entire merchant marine. She had no place to sell anything that she made, and no ships in which to carry her trade. Of the four home islands in the Japanese archipelago, not one was capable of feeding or supplying its population with any of the necessities of life. Only 16 per cent of the land in Japan was capable of cultivation. Rice, the staple crop, was imported in large amounts, but as the war progressed the imports had ceased. Now, not even the small crops grown in Japan could be moved, as the transportation system had completely broken down. One of the first things I did was to set up our Army kitchens to help feed the people. Had this not been done, they would have died by the thousands.

I had to move fast to prevent disaster, so I immediately imported 3,500,000 tons of food from the supplies the United States Army had built up in the Pacific area. The effect upon the Japanese was electrical. The Appropriations Committee of the United States House of Representatives wanted to know how I could justify the expenditure of Army appropriations to feed our late enemy. I explained.

There is a popular misconception that the achievement of victory in modern war is solely dependent upon victory in the field. History itself clearly refutes this concept. It offers unmistakable proof that the human impulses which generated the will to war, no less than the material sinews of war, must be destroyed. Nor is it sufficient that such human impulses merely yield to the temporary shock of military defeat. There must be a complete spiritual reformation such as will not only control the defeated generation, but will exert a dominant influence upon the gen-

---

cent job and that all of us back here are and will continue to support his efforts to the limit of our ability, We are all mighty proud of him."

From Herbert Hoover: "I think I have a realization—as perhaps no one else has—of the difficulties with which you have been confronted and of the amazing service you have been to the American people."

And from the eminent scholar and historian, Dr. Mary R. Beard: "There is something in General MacArthur's determination to enfranchise the women of Japan indicative of his conception of the family as the core or heart of society, and of woman as its prime guardian, which I would almost have to go back to Confucius for comparison. That he should associate the care and nutrition of the family with political democracy—and do this in his own mind, not just by pressure from another mind—gives him a standing in my mind—which is at the top of my judgment of statecraft. The whole procedure in Japan is so superior in intelligence to the occupation in Germany that General MacArthur's leadership shines with brilliant illumination."

eration to follow as well. Unless this is done, victory is but partially complete and offers hope for little more than an armistice between one campaign and the next. The great lesson and warning of experience is that victorious leaders of the past have too often contented themselves with the infliction of military defeat upon the enemy power without extending that victory by dealing with the root causes which led to war as an inevitable consequence.

Under the responsibilities of victory the Japanese people are now our prisoners, no less than did the starving men on Bataan become their prisoners when the peninsula fell. As a consequence of the ill treatment, including starvation of Allied prisoners in Japanese hands, we have tried and executed the Japanese officers upon proof of responsibility. Can we justify such punitive action if we ourselves, in reversed circumstances but with hostilities at an end, fail to provide the food to sustain life among the Japanese people over whom we now stand guard within the narrow confines of their home islands? To cut off Japan's relief supplies in this situation would cause starvation to countless Japanese—and starvation breeds mass unrest, disorder and violence. Give me bread or give me bullets.

I got bread.

We fed the Japanese, but we didn't intend to feed them forever. I directed my staff to work out the plans we needed to make Japan self-sufficient as soon as it was humanly possible. We had to rebuild the factories that had been bombed. We had to put the machinery in working order. We had to get the trains running, and float some kind of a merchant marine. We had to get the telegraph and radio and newspapers in operation. And last of all, we had to get the overseas trade revived. One of the biggest tasks was to give Japan a balanced budget.

I've never seen a more tangled financial mess than that into which the Japanese government had fallen by the end of the war. Most of the money had gone to support the war effort. No one really knew how much. The taxes were incredibly heavy, and for some of the poor people amounted to confiscation of everything they had. There had been a tax rebellion in the later stages of the war. Some tax collectors were too frightened to even try to collect any longer. We decided to start over, and to that end we brought in tax experts from the United States government to completely revise the tax laws and methods of collection. When this revision was finally passed, it worked well. And I required the Japanese government to live within its income. The Japanese leaders and people responded splendidly to these budgetary provisions, and for my entire administration the fiscal policies of the country were an admirable model for the rest of the world to follow. The public debt of Japan was less than $2 billion at the time I left the country.

I experienced some trouble in establishing a free enterprise system. For many decades a monopolistic control of the means of production and distribution had been exercised by the so-called *Zaibatsu*—about ten Japanese families who practiced a kind of private socialism. They controlled 90 per cent of all Japanese industry. These great trusts were partially dissolved and a truly competitive free enterprise system inaugurated. We did not expropriate the stock in these industries without compensation. The stockholders, practically all belonging to the big families, were paid off. The main thing was that their influence was broken.

Japanese labor had never had the right of collective bargaining until the occupation gave it to them. It was one of the first reforms I made. Laboring men throughout the empire were quick to take advantage of this new right. By 1947 there were approximately 25,000 unions in Japan and over 5,000,000 workingmen belonged to them. The labor front soon became divided into a rightist and a leftist group. Manifestations of labor unrest promptly took forms that were peculiar to Japan. A chorus line went on half-strike by only kicking half as high as usual. One railroad union protested by blowing the whistles on all the trains in Japan for one minute at the same time. I tried to encourage a labor leadership that would have the common sense to understand that labor's conflicts were never confined to the interests of workers and management alone, but that the interest of the general public was equally great. But due to trouble with the Communists, I was only partially successful.

We had trouble with the Communists in the labor movement. They obtained control of some unions and eventually called a general strike. It was a difficult situation for me. I did not want to stand in the way of newly organized laborers attempting to assert their rights, but I was not going to let a few Communist leaders use the strike as a political weapon and in so doing wreck the whole economy. It became necessary to use the powers of my office for the general good. I therefore issued the following edict:

Under the authority vested in me as Supreme Commander for the Allied Powers, I have informed the labor leaders whose unions have federated for the purpose of conducting a general strike that I will not permit the use of so deadly a social weapon in the present impoverished and emaciated condition of Japan, and have accordingly directed them to desist from the furtherance of such action. I have done so only to forestall the fatal impact of such extreme measures upon an already gravely threatened public welfare. Japanese society today operates under the limitations of war, defeat and Allied occupation. Its cities were laid waste, its industries are almost at a standstill, and the great masses of its people are on little more than a starvation diet.

A general strike, crippling transportation and communications, would prevent the movement of food to feed the people and of coal to sustain the essential utilities, and would stop such industry as is still functioning. The paralysis which would inevitably result might reduce large masses of the Japanese people to the point of actual starvation, and would produce dreadful consequences upon every Japanese home, regardless of social strata, or direct interest in the basic issue. Even now, to prevent actual starvation in Japan, the people of the United States are releasing to them large quantities of their own food resources. The persons involved in the threatened general strike are but a small minority of the Japanese people. Yet this minority might well plunge the great masses into a disaster not unlike that produced in the immediate past by the minority which led Japan into the destruction of war.

As I expected, the Japanese people, including the rank and file of labor, understood what I was talking about. There was no general strike.

The Communists did not give up, however. They infiltrated the key transportation unions, which were primarily operating in government-owned and -operated industries. I looked upon this as a threat to the whole government, and I advised the leaders of the government to bring all workers into the civil service. A law was passed to this effect. Immediately, people in other countries condemned the action and described me as an enemy of labor. Even people in the United States government criticized the legislation. I asked the United States Civil Service Commission to review the act, and they wrote me that it was "decidedly more liberal than the statutes pertaining to the United States Civil Service System." That ended the Communists as a factor in Japanese labor.

I stated Japan's economic situation at that time as follows:

The Japanese are a proud, sensitive, and industrious race. They ask no alms from anyone and expect none. They seek only the inalienable right to live. The alternatives are as simple as they are few. Either Japan must have access to the raw materials needed to sustain its industrial plant and to markets in which to dispose of its manufactured products, or it must have provisions for voluntary migration of large masses of its population to less populated areas of the world. Either solution rests upon the good will and statesmanship of others. Lacking such good will and if statesmanship fails, Japan would be forced to desperation or to death. Men will fight before they starve.

Japan underwent a spiritual recovery along with its economic and political changes. For centuries the Japanese people, unlike their neighbors in the Pacific basin—the Chinese, the Malayans, the Indians, and others— have been students and idolators of the art of war and the warrior caste. They were the natural warriors of the Pacific. Unbroken victory for Japanese arms convinced them of their invincibility, and the keystone to the entire arch of their civilization became an almost mythological belief in the strength and wisdom of the warrior caste. It permeated and controlled not only all the branches of the government, but all branches of life—physical, mental, and spiritual. It was interwoven not only into all government process, but into all phases of daily routine. It was not only the essence, but the warp and woof of Japanese existence.

Control was exercised by a feudalistic overlordship of a mere fraction of the population, while the remaining millions, with a few enlightened exceptions, were abject slaves to tradition, legend, mythology, and regimentation. During the progress of the war, these millions heard of nothing but Japanese victories. Then they suddenly felt the concentrated shock of total defeat; their whole world crumbled. It was not merely the overthrow of their military might—it was the collapse of a faith, it was the disintegration of everything they had believed in and lived by and fought for. It left a complete vacuum, morally, mentally, and physically. And into this vacuum flowed the democratic way of life. The falseness of their former teachings, the failure of their former leadership, the tragedy of their past faith were infallibly demonstrated in actuality and realism.

A spiritual revolution ensued which almost overnight tore asunder a theory and practice of life built upon 2,000 years of history and tradition and legend. Idolatry for their feudalistic masters and the warrior class was transformed into hatred and contempt, and the hatred and contempt for their foe gave way to honor and respect. This revolution of the spirit among the Japanese people represents no thin veneer designed to serve the purpose of the present. It represents an unparalleled convulsion in the social history of the world.

Christianity, of course, is not the oldest of man's faiths. Although I was brought up as a Christian and adhere entirely to its teachings, I have always had a sincere admiration for many of the basic principles underlying the Oriental faiths. Christianity does not differ from them as much as one would think. There is little conflict between the two, and each might well be strengthened by a better understanding of the other. I asked for missionaries, and more missionaries.

From the beginning I guaranteed that every Japanese could worship as he wished. I knew however that true religious freedom could never be achieved in Japan until drastic revision was made in the ancient, backward, state-controlled subsidized faith known as Shintoism. The Emperor, himself, was the High Priest of Shinto and, by the precepts of a mythological holdover from primitive times, derived his spiritual power from his imperial ancestors who had become gods. The Japanese people were told that the Emperor was divine himself and that the highest purpose of every subject's life was death in his service. The militarists who had led Japan into war had used this religion to further their efforts, and the state still subsidized it.

In November 1945, while making no theological attack, I ordered state subsidization to cease. On New Year's Day, 1946, the Emperor, without any suggestion or discussion with me, issued a rescript in which he publicly renounced his own divinity. The Emperor's statement read:

We stand by the people and we wish always to share with them in their moments of joys and sorrows. The ties between us and our people have always stood upon mutual trust and affection. They do not depend upon mere legends and myths. They are not predicated on the false conception that the Emperor is divine and that the Japanese people are superior to other races and fated to rule the world.

I publicly commented at once: "The Emperor's New Year's message pleases me very much. By it he undertakes a leading part in the democratization of his people. He squarely takes his stand for the future along liberal lines. His action reflects the irresistible influence of a sound idea. A sound idea cannot be stopped." After this, Shinto priests were permitted to continue their teachings so long as church and state were separated.

Whenever possible, I told visiting Christian ministers of the need for their work in Japan. "The more missionaries we can bring out here, and the more occupation troops we can send home, the better." The Pocket Testament League, at my request, distributed 10,000,000 Bibles translated into Japanese. Gradually, a spiritual regeneration in Japan began to grow.

The educational system when I arrived in Japan gave me deep concern. The Japanese practiced central control over the schools. There was no such thing as a local school board or superintendent. A ministry of education in Tokyo bought standard textbooks in everything, and distributed them throughout the country. These textbooks were filled with militaristic and anti-American items, and all was under the control of Tokyo. As a matter of fact, up until the time of the occupation, the schools, newspapers, theater, radio, and motion pictures were all part of an official propaganda machine, and can be said to have existed for the purpose of "thought control" rather than for their own intrinsic purpose.

A free people can exist only without regimentation of thought, and the publication of textbooks was promptly taken out of the control of the ministry of education. I put the Japanese publishing industry on a competitive basis for the first time in the preparation and printing of school textbooks. No texts were forced upon them, but the books had to show that the previous militaristic, ultra-nationalistic propaganda was absent. In the first year of the occupation, the schoolchildren of Japan, for the first time in several generations, studied from textbooks that were primarily educational. I believe the number of such new textbooks distributed in that time was something over 250,000,000.

Uncensored textbooks are of little value without uncensored teachers. I wanted the teachers to have complete academic freedom, and I moved to insure this with my directive to the ministry of education. "Teachers and educational officials who have been dismissed, suspended, or forced to resign for liberal or anti-militaristic opinions or activities," I said, "will be declared immediately eligible for reappointment. Discrimination against any student, teacher or educational official on grounds of race, nationality, creed, political opinion or social position, will be prohibited. Students, teachers and educational officials will be encouraged in unrestricted discussion of issues involving political, civil and religious liberties."

After the new system had been in effect for some time, we tested our efforts, and the results were extremely gratifying. There was a complete reorientation in the outlook of Japanese children. In a society that had been almost completely militaristic in outlook only a few years before, it was found that most children were now most interested in the professions and the workaday world. As a matter of fact, among hundreds, there was only one child who expressed an interest in an army or navy career. He wanted to be General MacArthur! So I knew I had at least one faithful follower.

Health was another pressing problem. It had always been a popular conception in the United States that the Japanese were far advanced in the field of medicine and hygiene. This was not at all the case. Diseases such as smallpox, diphtheria, and typhoid—diseases which had all but disappeared in the United States by 1920—were still epidemic in Japan in 1945. Tuberculosis was almost a national scourge. In investigating these amazing statistics, it was not hard to find the reasons. At the close of the war, in all of Japan there were only two sanitary engineers. And the lack of personnel to handle the country's hygienic problems made the situation in a bombed-out country almost chaotic.

I sought immediately to improve this situation. I suggested to the prime minister that he set up some kind of a health department in the cabinet, something that Japan had never had. The ministry of health and welfare was the outgrowth of this suggestion, and today its activities are felt in every community in the land. I also suggested that all schools educate their children in public health. This was done. With the help and co-operation of American medical authorities, the Japanese people were given what amounted to a mass inoculation and vaccination. In three years, we vaccinated 70,000,000 for smallpox and succeeded in curbing the disease which had been rampant. We tested the population for tuberculosis, and administered 23,000,000 vaccinations for that disease. Seventy-nine per cent of the tuberculosis cases in Japan disappeared. By systematically inoculating residents of every hamlet and city in the nation against diphtheria, we reduced the number of cases by 86 per cent in three years. By a co-ordinated program of inoculation and education, we practically wiped out typhoid and paratyphoid. Through education alone we almost conquered dysentery. Our greatest triumph was over cholera, which we completely eradicated from Japan by the beginning of 1947. It was the estimate of my medical officers that we had saved 2,000,000 lives with these health measures in the first two years of the occupation. With the dreadful loss of lives in the war fresh in my mind, these statistics brought much comfort to my soul.

One of the most far-reaching accomplishments of the occupation was the program of land reform. Japan's feudalistic regime was most evident in the matter of landholding. As late as the end of the war, a system of virtual slavery that went back to ancient times was still in existence. Most farmers in Japan were either out-and-out serfs, or they worked under an arrangement through which the landowners exorbited a high percentage of each year's crops. The occupation was only a few months old when I attacked this problem. I felt that any man who farmed the land should, by law, be entitled to his crops, that there should be an end to sharecropping, and that even more fundamental, perhaps, was the need to make land itself available to the people. Under the system then in use it was practically impossible for a farmer to buy his own land.

I set up a natural resources section in the headquarters, and this group advised the Japanese government. Over the next few years, a series of laws was passed under which the government bought up land at fair prices from the big, absentee landlords, and made it available to the tenants on long-term installment purchasing plans. By 1950, more than 5,000,000 acres had been redistributed. In this period, Japan was transferred from a feudal economy of impoverished serfs and tenant farmers into a nation of free landholders. More than 89 per cent of all arable land in Japan was controlled by the people who lived on it. The redistribution formed a strong barrier against any introductions of Communism in rural Japan. Every farmer in the country was now a capitalist in his own right.

The police problem in Japan was an extraordinarily difficult one to solve. One school of thought was that Japan lent itself to the maintenance of public order by a centralized police system; this was contrasted with the view that local responsibility for exercise of the police power was inherently an aspect of local autonomy, provided for by the new constitution, without which local government could not become dynamic and grow.

I told the prime minister:

It has been a dominant characteristic of modern totalitarian dictatorships, as it was in Japan's feudalistic past, to establish and maintain a strongly centralized police bureaucracy headed by a chief executive officer beyond the reach of popular control. Indeed, the strongest weapon of the military clique in Japan in the decade prior to the war was the absolute authority exercised by the national government over the "thought police" and the Kempei-Tai extending down to prefectural levels of government. These media enabled the military to spread a network of political espionage, and suppress freedom of speech, of assembly and even of thought.

It should be borne in mind that in the final analysis police power in the preservation of law and order in a democratic society does not attain its maximum strength through oppressive controls imposed upon the people from above, but rather does it find the infinitely greater strength in the relationship of a servant of, and answerable directly to, the people. Thereby and thereby alone may it encourage respect for the people's laws through confidence and paternalistic pride in the police as the law enforcement agency of the people themselves.

The Diet, after a long debate, passed a law providing that "local public entities shall have the right to manage their property affairs and administration and to enact their own regulations within the law."

It was a knotty problem then and is still a matter of argument in Japan.

I will always take the utmost satisfaction in having introduced the writ of *habeas corpus* into Japan. It was one of the laws which were passed to bolster the bill of rights in the new constitution. This same basic right had been brought to the Philippines by my father in 1901. It is a unique provision in Anglo-Saxon jurisprudence that a great many peoples of the world still do not possess. It moves me deeply that my family helped to bring this guarantee against arbitrary arrest to the Far East as a safeguard for Asian peoples.

In these various reforms, numerous officials of the occupation distinguished themselves—Whitney, Marquat, Willoughby, Sams, Dodge, Moss,

Schenk, Shoup, Kades, and many others. Without their special talents and skill, little could have been accomplished. And the Japanese themselves truly earned the respect and faith of men of good will everywhere. Under their able Prime Minister Yoshida, they rose, in their own merit, from the ashes of destruction to a vibrant nation firmly rooted in immutable concepts of political morality, economic freedom, and social privilege evolved from a blend of ideas and ideals of the West and their own hallowed traditions and time-honored cultures.

Many distinguished visitors came to Tokyo to observe the progress of the occupation. One was my old associate, now Chief of Staff of the Army Eisenhower. It was a pleasant reunion, indeed. His is a delightful personality, and our long service together had made me regard him with deep friendship and regard. Many unwarranted and malicious efforts have been made to depict our relationship as that of jealous rivalry, but nothing could be further from the truth. He had sent me the following messages, on my birthday. They read:

My congratulations and cordial regards on your birthday. May your future years be filled with the gratitude of a thankful nation, for your astute vision, steadfast purpose, and brilliant success which contributed so heavily to the unconditional capitulation of the Japanese Empire. I send my deepest appreciation for your superb performance as Supreme Allied Commander in Japan and for your masterful approach to the manifold problems of our own forces.

And:

On this Victory Day, celebrating triumph over the Japanese War Machine, I extend to you on behalf of the Army its appreciation of your magnificent effort, both on the long and tragic road from Bataan to Tokyo and in your unprecedented task of guiding the Japanese nation toward a new way of life. During the dark days of war your military leadership, repeatedly proved against staggering odds, inspired free men the world over. Perhaps even more significant to mankind, seeking freedom from threat of war, are your achievements in your present post where you are pioneering new paths in human relations. The entire Army joins me in saluting you on this memorable day.

I have always felt for him something akin to the affection of an older man for a younger brother. His amazingly successful career has filled me with pride and admiration.

The critics kept hammering away with little regard for realism or factuality. They were answered in overwhelming force from many sources. For example, an editorial in *The New York Times* said: "Japan is the one bright spot in Allied military government. General MacArthur's administration is a model of government and a boon to peace in the Far East. He has swept away an autocratic regime by a warrior god and installed in its place a democratic government presided over by a very human emperor and based on the will of the people as expressed in free elections." It noted that the Russian delegate to the Allied Council for Japan did not share this view. The Soviet viewpoint was termed "a definite policy, the purpose of which is an attempt at Communist propaganda inspired from outside Japan and in violation of Potsdam terms. The odd feature in this picture is the more or less open support of these tactics by the Chinese and British delegates. It may be they hope to back up demands of their governments for stripping Japan economically in the same way that Russia stripped Manchuria and Northern Korea." *

On July 4, 1946, the Philippines became a sovereign state. Before a jubilant throng of a million cheering people, the republic was inaugurated at the Luneta in Manila. I represented the American Army to mark the seal of friendship between our two countries.

In the spring of 1947, I authorized the display of the national flag of Japan. There was a great resurgence throughout the nation of self-respect and self-confidence. Kozaemon Kimura, minister of agriculture and forestry, following a conference with the Emperor, commented as follows: "With tears in his eyes, the Emperor expressed his appreciation of General MacArthur's attitude and interest in the reconstruction of Japan. He said the Japanese people think of him as *Kamikaze* (divine influence). Admiral Perry opened the door of Japan to America. General MacArthur has opened the heart of America to Japan."

Japan was not the only place where change was taking place. In the

---

* And a delegation of five members from the House of Commons in England, headed by Gordon Lange, after a comprehensive investigation of the occupation, praised it in unstinted terms. Its spokesman said: "It would be just about impossible to exaggerate the good opinion the Reverend Lange and his colleagues formed of the occupation following their investigation in Tokyo and elsewhere in Japan. All members of the group were tremendously impressed with the personal leadership of SCAP and will report to the government in London that the occupation should be considered one of the great achievements of history. Members of the group felt that the British conception of parliamentary government is being implanted in Japan and that General MacArthur is an ideal man to carry on this work because of broad knowledge of the underlying principles of popular self-government as developed in British and American political experience."

And from Secretary of War Patterson: "I cannot close this letter without mention of your extraordinary achievement. I know of no brighter page in our history. The record is so strong that your support in the United States is virtually unanimous."

United States, the armed services were centralized into a Department of Defense, with James Forrestal at its head. In England, the Labour Party ousted Winston Churchill as prime minister and replaced him with Clement Attlee. I was astounded at this British action. It had been Churchill's leadership that had saved the nation in its time of gravest peril, and it was unexplainable to me at that time, and still is, how a majority of the people could vote to dismiss him just when his great wisdom and experience were so needed to shape the peace. It was democracy, surely—but democracy with a vengeance.

He wrote me from his home at Chartwell in Kent:

I have been meaning for a long time to tell you with what interest and sympathy I have followed your policy and administration in Japan. In spite of what happened in the War, I have a regard for the Japanese nation and have pondered upon their long, romantic history. To visit Japan is one of my remaining ambitions; but I can hardly hope it will be fulfilled. I am so glad you have been able to raise them up from the pit into which they had been thrown by the military castes, who only had a part of the facts before them. I admire your wise and far-sighted policy. They ought to be our friends in the future, and I feel this wish has been a key to many of your important decisions.

It would have been very easy to prevent the last war but it is not so easy to cope with the future. The peace and freedom-loving nations must not make exactly the same mistakes again. That would be too hard.

With every good wish and my sincere congratulations on your masterly achievements as a general and a statesman.

Sometime after the adoption of the constitution, the public prosecutor of the city of Tokyo dismissed charges against five individuals who had publicly criticized the Emperor. This was a unique experience for the Japanese people, and I took the opportunity to point out that neither the President of the United States nor the King of England is protected by any special laws. If the President of the United States is assassinated, his murderer is treated exactly as though he had slain a private citizen.

The decision [I said] is a noteworthy application of the fundamental concept that all men are equal before the law, that no individual in Japan, not even the Emperor, shall be clothed in legal protection denied the common man. It marks a true understanding of the lofty spirit of the new National Charter which secures to all the right to freely discuss all issues, political, social and economic of concern to the people. For the free interchange of ideas, the free expression of opinion, the free criticism of officials and institutions is essential to the life and growth of popular government. Democracy is vital and dynamic, but cannot survive unless all citizens are free to speak their minds. The legal protection accorded an Emperor should be no more or no less than the legal protection accorded a citizen.

Probably nothing during my administration of the occupation gave me deeper concern than the obligation to act upon the judgment of the International Military Tribunal of the Far East. I had approved penalties adjudged against enemy field commanders or other military personnel who had permitted or committed atrocities against soldiers or civilians who had fallen under their custody during the war, but the principle of holding criminally responsible the political leaders of the vanquished in war was repugnant to me. I felt that to do so was to violate the most fundamental rules of criminal justice. I believed, and I so recommended, that any criminal responsibility attached to Japanese political leaders for the decision to wage war should be limited to an indictment for the attack on Pearl Harbor, since this act was effected without a prior declaration of war as required by international law and custom. I was then relieved of all responsibility having to do with the actual trial procedures before the International Military Tribunal, which started sitting in Tokyo January 19, 1946. The tribunal was composed of distinguished jurists from the Allied powers nominated by their respective governments. My obligations did not even include the selection of those to be tried. My only duties were to pass on the final judgments of the tribunal and to enforce the sentences.

By the terms of the Potsdam declaration, I was to see that "stern justice shall be meted out to all war criminals." We had no trouble finding the individuals who were accused. Within a few weeks we had imprisoned such diverse characters as "Tokyo Rose" and Prime Minister Tojo. The number of such prisoners ran into the hundreds. We made a distinction between major and minor war criminals. "Tokyo Rose" was considered a minor one. So were the many guards at the various prisoner camps who had mistreated our people. They were tried and appropriate punishment was imposed. There were only twenty-eight major war criminals. These were the people in political offices and other positions who actually were responsible for taking Japan to war. Of these, only twenty-five were brought to trial, the other three dying or going insane before entering the courtroom. All twenty-five of those who stood trial were found guilty, including Prime Minister Tojo.

I was besieged with requests for permits to allow press photographers to record the actual executions. I refused on the grounds that such a spectacle would outrage the sensibilities of the Japanese, and high-minded people everywhere. The Secretary of the Army was asked to override my decision, but I refused to allow him to interfere, because in this particular case I was acting as a representative of international powers, rather than as an officer of the United States Army. The uproar soon died away, but to reassure the people of the world that the executions had actually taken place, I invited the members of the occupation advisory group—the Allied Council—to attend as official witnesses. All accepted, although reluctantly.

I was pleasantly surprised at the attitude of the Japanese people during the period of trial. They seemed to be impressed both by the fairness of the procedures and by the lack of vindictiveness on the part of the prosecutors. The prisoners themselves and their families made it a point to write letters to me and to the tribunal after their conviction to express their thanks for our impartiality and justice. No perceptible ill will was generated in Japan as a result of the trials.

While events in Japan continued to progress favorably, many happenings were occurring in other parts of the world. In the United States, my name was again precipitated into the struggle for the Republican nomination for the Presidency. I was not a candidate and declined to campaign for the office. I had not the slightest desire to become the head of state, having had more than enough of such an office in the administration of Japan. It was a great mistake on my part not to have been more positive in refusing to enter into the political picture. As might have been expected, the attempt was abortive, and its only tangible result was to bring down on my head an avalanche of political abuse from the party in power. Such derogation, coming from the opposition, means little to a politician, but it seriously hampers anyone engaged in a purely professional effort such as I was performing in the Far East. From that moment on it became only a question of time until retaliation would be visited upon me.

In Korea, the XXIV Corps, under General Hodge's able leadership, had moved in during the aftermath of the war and had occupied the country up to the 38th Parallel, to which line the Russian troops had advanced by the time of Japan's capitulation. South Korea had suffered little damage from the war and led by that fine old patriot, Syngman Rhee, had reorganized and prepared for independence. On August 15, 1948, the Republic of Korea was proclaimed, with Rhee its president. I attended the inaugural ceremonies and was warmly received.

Our troops were withdrawn from Korea, leaving only a military mission to assist in the training of Korean military forces, and Korea was removed from my command, the State Department exercising full control of United States interests, including operational command of the military mission.

In China, Generalissimo Chiang Kai-shek was gradually pushing the Communists back, being largely aided and supplied by the United States. For some unaccountable reason, the Communists were not looked upon with disfavor by the State Department, who labeled them "agrarian reformers." Instead of pushing on to the victory that was within the Generalissimo's grasp, an armistice was arranged, and General Marshall was sent to amalgamate the two opponents. He went by way of Tokyo and stayed with me at the embassy.

Mentally, he had aged immeasurably since his visit to New Guinea. The former incisiveness and virility were gone. The war had apparently worn him down into a shadow of his former self.

After months of fruitless negotiation, he withdrew without tangible results, and the war for China resumed. But in this interval of seven months a decisive change had taken place. The Generalissimo had received no munitions or supplies from the United States, but the Soviets, working day and night, reinforced the Chinese Communist armies. The great mass of military supplies we had sent them at Vladivostok during the latter stages of the war, none of which had been used, was largely transferred to the Chinese forces, so that when hostilities were resumed, the balance of power had shifted. They pressed their advantage to the fullest, and finally drove the Generalissimo's forces out of continental Asia onto Formosa. The decision to withhold previously pledged American support was one of the greatest mistakes ever made in our history. At one fell blow, everything that had been so laboriously built up since the days of John Hay was lost. It was the beginning of the crumbling of our power in continental Asia—the birth of the taunt, "Paper Tiger." Its consequences will be felt for centuries, and its ultimate disastrous effects on the fortunes of the free world are still to be unfolded.

The panorama of events which contributed so decisively to the downfall of our wartime ally, the Republic of China, has never been told to the American people. After the surrender of Japan, events and actions transpired that now seem almost incredible, brought about by ignorance, misinterpretation, and errors of judgment. One of the most accurate comments on this period was made on January 30, 1949, by a young veteran of the war in the Pacific, Congressman John Fitzgerald Kennedy, in an address at Salem, Massachusetts. He said:

Our relationship with China since the end of the Second World War has been a tragic one, and it is of the utmost importance that we search out and spotlight those who must bear the responsibility for our present predicament.

It was clearly enunciated on November 26, 1941, that the independence of China and the stability of the National Government was the fundamental object of our Far Eastern policy. That this and other statements of our policies in the Far East led directly to the attack on Pearl Harbor is well known.

During the postwar period began the great split in the minds of our diplomats over whether to support the Government of Chiang Kai-shek or force Chiang Kai-shek as the price of our assistance to bring Chinese Communists into his government to form a coalition.

Our policy in China has reaped the whirlwind. The continued insistence that aid would not be forthcoming unless a coalition government was formed was a crippling blow to the National Government. So concerned were our diplomats and their advisors . . . with the imperfections of the diplomatic system in China after twenty years of war, and the tales of corruption in higher places, that they lost sight of our tremendous stake in a non-Communist China.

This is the tragic story of China whose freedom we once fought to preserve. What our young men had saved, our diplomats and our President have frittered away.

The failure of those in authority to implement existing United States policy brought about the downfall of an ally and jeopardized the very security of our nation. We have seen the growth of a Communist enemy where we once had a staunch ally. We have watched Communist imperialism spread its influence throughout the world. We have seen thousands of our young men vainly sacrifice their lives in blind pursuit of sterile policies of appeasement based on ignorance of history and of this enemy.

By December 9, 1949, the last legions of the Generalissimo had been driven into Formosa. Shortly afterward, the American press carried a story that the State Department had notified its representatives abroad that the loss of Formosa to the Communists was to be anticipated, and that in order to prevent damage to United States prestige at home and abroad, the public must be informed that the island was of no strategic value. The directive said all available material should be used "to counter false impressions" that the retention of Formosa would save the Chinese government, and that its loss would damage seriously the interests of either the United States or of other countries opposing Communism. "Without evidencing undue preoccupation with the subject," it continued, "emphasize as appropriate any of the following points: Formosa is exclusively the responsibility of the Chinese Government. Formosa has no special military significance."

On January 12th, in an address before the National Press Club in Washington, Secretary of State Acheson declared Formosa outside "our defense perimeter." He also excluded South Korea from the American defense outposts. These policies of the Truman Administration received unfavorable publicity, being widely condemned throughout the United States. Under the pressure of public opinion, they were to be completely changed. I felt that the Secretary of State was badly advised about the Far East, and invited him to be my guest in Tokyo. I had never met Dean Acheson, but felt certain that his own survey of the Asiatic situation would materially alter his expressed views. He declined the invitation, saying that the pressure of his duties prevented him from leaving Washington. He did, however, visit Europe eleven times during his stay in office.

In the Philippines, the brilliant and gifted President Manuel Roxas died. At such a critical time, it was almost an irreparable loss. He was succeeded by an old friend of mine who had served his country faithfully both in war and peace, Elpidio Quirino.

I was now seventy years old, and the greetings I received on my birthday warmed my heart.*

The State Department sent out its own representative early in the winter to check on the progress of Japan, and the glowing reports it had received. Ambassador Philip C. Jessup was selected to make the investigation. On leaving Japan he issued this public statement:

The days I have spent in Japan have given me a vivid impression of the extraordinary progress which the Japanese people have made since the end of the war. General MacArthur has rendered a service of extraordinary distinction and of great historical significance. It has been of unique value to me to have an opportunity to meet him and to discuss problems with him. These experiences and

---

* Elpidio Quirino: "I join in my people's joy and thanksgiving upon your achievement of another milestone in a life completely given to, and so rich in creative service, not only to America and the Philippines but to the world. Because of the breadth of your sympathies it has become natural that no one single nation should limit the spacious scope of your capacity for advancing human welfare. You have become the legend and symbol of a great tradition in soldiering and statesmanship rooted in the richest American heritage of democracy and freedom. May God bless you and the great work you are doing to help insure the liberty, the peace and the stability of Asia and the world."

President Truman: "On the occasion of your birthday, I desire to express the appreciation and gratitude of your country for your services in war and peace which have made and will continue to make an important contribution to the great cause of freedom and democracy."

Secretary of State Dean Acheson: "My warm congratulations to you on this day. As you look back over other birthdays which have passed since the beginning of your career, you must find deep satisfaction in your record of splendid military achievements and statesmanship. I am joined by my associates in appreciation of the close cooperation and understanding which you have contributed to our mutual problems. You have my cordial best wishes for the years to come."

conversations have been of great value in the broad program of the Department of State for studying the problems of the Far East.

I constantly urged the leaders of Japan to visit the United States, and suggested that a representative group from the Diet go to New York. I wired Governor Thomas E. Dewey if such a visit would be agreeable, the war passions still not having entirely abated. His invitation was prompt and warm, and reflected the changing sentiment in the United States toward Japan. The temper of the American people was reflected, too, in a letter from Republican Senator Robert Taft, who wrote:

I know that you have taken an active interest in sending the Japanese legislators here, and I believe projects of this kind will contribute to a constantly improving friendship between Japan and America. I should like to know just how you feel about a Japanese peace treaty. I don't like to press for consideration or take any public position without being better advised than I am now. I hear nothing but good of your splendid administration of Japan and can only express my highest admiration for the work you have done.

I wrote him, the sooner the peace treaty and the end of the occupation, the better for everyone.

To move invincibly forward [I said] toward consummation of a just peace for Japan is one way—possibly the most dramatic and dynamic way open at this time—of asserting our leadership and regaining our lost initiative in the course of Asian affairs. We could not fail to blunt the existing trend and establish the basis for its ultimate reversal.

On May 27, 1950, Australia withdrew her troops from the occupation forces. I cited them in these words:

From their distinguished Commander-in-Chief to the last man in the ranks they have rendered model service worthy of the luster of the great nation that bred them. In peace they have emulated their conduct in war and I can pay them no greater tribute than that. I am proud indeed to have been associated with them through the long years of the past decade and will bid them a last farewell with an emotion I cannot express.

With the formation of the Republic of Korea and the withdrawal of American forces, my official connection with Korea ceased. From August 15, 1948, the doomed little country was under the sole charge of the State Department. But my intelligence section was increasingly aware of the distinct menace of an attack by the North Korean Communists in the summer of 1950.

The Joint Chiefs of Staff reiterated the Administration's unwillingness to commit itself to the defense of South Korea and had recently drawn up a plan of strategic defense in Asia which was based on the assumption that under no circumstances would the United States engage in the military defense of the Korean peninsula.

In vain were my attempts to expose the growing Communist threat in the Far East. From June 1949 to June 1950, constant intelligence reports of increasing urgency were submitted to Washington, advising of a possible North Korean thrust. But little impression was made against the general apathy and the inspired "agrarian reform" propaganda. One of these reports even suggested that June 1950 would be the likely time for North Korea to cross the 38th Parallel.

On June 19th, John Foster Dulles, as the personal representative of Secretary Acheson, visited Korea. He had come to Tokyo to discuss a Japanese peace treaty with me, the framework of which I had submitted to Washington. In Korea, he apparently reversed the previous policy enunciated by the State Department, by stating his belief before the Korean legislature that the United States would defend Korea if she were attacked. It made me wonder just what was United States policy in Asia.

Dulles took a brief motor trip from Seoul to the demarcation line between North and South Korea, and what he saw alarmed him not at all. He noted that the South Korean forces appeared quite ready if any attack should come from north of the border. With his tactical inexperience and possible lack of accurate information, Dulles clearly did not realize the inferiority in both troop strength and matériel of the forces he had seen in comparison with their Communist kinsmen above the 38th Parallel.

PART NINE

*Frustration
in Korea*

1950–1951

It was early morning Sunday, June 25, 1950, when the telephone rang in my bedroom at the American Embassy in Tokyo. It rang with the note of urgency that can sound only in the hush of a darkened room. It was the duty officer at headquarters. "General," he said, "we have just received a dispatch from Seoul, advising that the North Koreans have struck in great strength south across the 38th Parallel at four o'clock this morning." Thousands of Red Korean troops had poured over the border, overwhelming the South Korean advance posts, and were moving southward with a speed and power that was sweeping aside all opposition.

I had an uncanny feeling of nightmare. It had been nine years before, on a Sunday morning, at the same hour, that a telephone call with the same note of urgency had awakened me in the penthouse atop the Manila Hotel. It was the same fell note of the war cry that was again ringing in my ears. It couldn't be, I told myself. Not again! I must still be asleep and dreaming. Not again! But then came the crisp, cool voice of my fine chief of staff, General Ned Almond, "Any orders, General?"

How, I asked myself, could the United States have allowed such a deplorable situation to develop? I thought back to those days, only a short time before, when our country had been militarily more powerful than any nation on earth. General Marshall, then Army chief of staff, had reported to the Secretary of War in 1945: "Never was the strength of American democracy so evident nor has it ever been so clearly within our power to give definite guidance for our course into the future of the human race." But in the short space of five years this power had been frittered away in a bankruptcy of positive and courageous leadership toward any long-range objectives. Again I asked myself, "What is United States policy in Asia?" And the appalling thought came, "The United States has no definite policy in Asia."

Dulles had returned to Tokyo and wired the Secretary of State:

Believe that if it appears the South Koreans cannot themselves contain or repulse the attack, United States forces should be used even though this risks Russian counter moves. To sit by while Korea is overrun by unprovoked armed attack would start a world war.

The only immediate military obligation involving my own forces had to do with the evacuation of 2,000 American and United Nations personnel from the area of the Korean Republic. Late on Sunday, the American Ambassador to Korea, John Muccio, asked that they be brought out. I acted immediately. Within minutes, flights of transport planes were rising off runways in Japan and ships at sea were swinging about and heading full draft toward Korean ports. When enemy aircraft began to threaten, I sent in our warplanes from Japan. The operation was successfully concluded without the loss of a single man, woman, or child.

Geographically, South Korea is a ruggedly mountainous peninsula that juts out toward Japan from the Manchurian mainland between the Yellow Sea and the Sea of Japan. An uneven north-south corrridor cuts through the rough heart of the country below the 38th Parallel, and there are highways and rail links on both the eastern and western coastal plains.

The South Koreans had four divisions along the 38th Parallel. They had been well trained, and the personnel were brave and patriotic, but they were equipped and organized as a constabulary force, not as troops of the line. They had only light weapons, no air or naval forces, and were lacking in tanks, artillery, and many other essentials. The decision to equip and organize them in this way had been made by the State Department. The argument advanced by the State Department for its decision was that it was a necessary measure to prevent the South Koreans from attacking North Korea, a curiously myopic reasoning that, of course, opened the way for a North Korean attack. It was a vital and a fatal error not to prepare South Korea to meet an

Map of Korea

attack from the north. The potential of such an attack was inherent in the fact that the North Korean forces had tanks, heavy artillery, and fighter aircraft with which South Korea was not equipped.

The decision was made in Washington by men who understood little about the Pacific and practically nothing about Korea. While they idealistically attempted to prevent the South Koreans from unifying the country by force, they inevitably encouraged the North Koreans along opposite lines. Such a fundamental error is inescapable when the diplomat attempts to exercise military judgment, and the result in Korea was that 100,000 United States-trained constabulary troops, with few weapons besides their rifles, were opposed by a Soviet-trained North Korean army of 200,000 men equipped with every modern adjunct of war.

The Communists showed great shrewdness in masking their preparations for attack. Along the 38th parallel itself they deployed only a lightly armored force similar to that of their neighbors to the south. But this was only a screen for the purpose of deception. Back of this first line of offense, they concentrated a powerful striking army, fully equipped with heavy weapons, including the latest model of Soviet tanks. The thrust across the border was launched by the lightly armed first line which then swung right and left, while the heavy main force charged through the gap, moving irresistibly southward, sweeping the lightly armed South Korean defenders before it.

Even then, it was evident that this was far more than a "police action," as President Truman was to euphemistically characterize it, far more than any localized clean-up of border-raiding North Koreans. In Korea, Communism had hurled its first challenge to war against the free world. Now was the time for decision. Now it was as clear as it would ever be that this was a battle against imperialistic Communism. Now was the time to recognize what the history of the world has taught from the beginning of time: that timidity breeds conflict, and courage often prevents it.

Momentous decisions were being made in Washington and Lake Success that Sunday afternoon. At the request of the United States, United Nations Secretary-General Trygve Lie called the Security Council delegates into a special session. The Russians, who were boycotting the United Nations in protest against membership of the Chinese Nationalists, did not have a delegate present. The United States proposed a resolution condemning the action of the North Korean forces as a breach of the peace, and (1) called for the immediate cessation of hostilities and for the authorities of North Korea to withdraw forthwith their armed forces to the 38th Parallel; (2)

requested that the United Nations Temporary Commission on Korea communicate its fully considered recommendations on the situation at once, observe the withdrawal of the North Korean forces to the 38th Parallel, and advise the Security Council upon compliance with its resolution; and (3) called upon all members to render every assistance to the United Nations in the execution of the resolution and to refrain from giving assistance to the North Korean authorities.

President Truman immediately interpreted the United Nations call to "render every assistance" as an authorization to assist the South Koreans militarily. No one in Washington was quite ready to commit the United States completely, so by "telecom" I was directed to use the Navy and the Air Force to assist South Korean defenses by whatever use I could make of these two arms. I was ordered also to isolate the Nationalist-held island of Formosa from the Chinese mainland. The United States Seventh Fleet was turned over to my operational control for thus purpose, and I was specifically directed to prevent any Nationalist attacks on the mainland, as well as to defend the island against Communist attacks.

On June 27th, the United Nations Security Council met again and passed another resolution. In this one, after noting the events, and particularly the failure of the North Korean authorities to desist from the attack and withdraw their military forces to the 38th Parallel, the Security Council concluded that "urgent military measures are required to restore international peace and security," and recommended "that the members of the United Nations furnish such assistance to the Republic of Korea as may be necessary to repel the armed attack."

Thus, step by hesitant step, the United States went to war against Communism in Asia. I could not help being amazed at the manner in which this great decision was being made. With no submission to Congress, whose duty it is to declare war, and without even consulting the field commander involved, the members of the executive branch of the government agreed to enter the Korean War. All the risks inherent in this decision—including the possibility of Chinese and Russian involvement—applied then just as much as they applied later.

My immediate problems were pressing ones. Would United States air and naval forces be enough? Could the South Korean defenders, supported by these forces and supplied with armor, make a successful stand against the powerful war machine that was rolling down upon them from the north?

Or would United States ground troops have to be thrown into the battle after all South Korea was lost? In past wars there was only one way for me to learn such things. There was only one way now. I decided to go to Korea and see for myself.

The morning of June 29th was rainy and overcast as I climbed into the *Bataan*. The news from Korea seemed even more disastrous than it had the day before. The capital city of Seoul was under heavy attack, and the South Korean government had moved to temporary headquarters at Taejon. Here I was with fifty years of service behind me, over half of which had been on foreign soil—a record for American Army officers—now facing another desperate campaign. And once again it looked like a forlorn hope. Once again I was being thrust into the breach against almost insuperable odds. Once again it was Bataan—and Corregidor—and New Guinea. I confess that for a fleeting moment my heart failed me. But as the plane rose above the murk of the overcast, I pulled out my old corncob pipe and, as its smoke curled up, I was myself again. Someone said, "Haven't seen you smoke that pipe, General, for years!"

"I don't dare smoke it back there in Tokyo," I explained. "They'd think I was nothing but a farmer. The Peers Club would surely blackball me."

The gloom of the day and the even gloomier news dispatches were lightened when I received a message relayed to the plane that the British Asiatic Fleet had been placed under my command. I had long been associated with British fighting units and had the greatest admiration for them. Their professional excellence, their splendid martial bearing, and their unfailing courtesy had long since endeared them to me. I knew that come what may I could count on them to see me through.

The *Bataan* landed at Suwon, 20 miles south of Seoul, through clouds of oily smoke from some bombed and strafed transports which had just been attacked and destroyed. I commandeered a jeep and headed north toward the Han River under constant air bombardment, through the dreadful backwash of a defeated and dispersed army. The South Korean forces were in complete and disorganized flight. We reached the banks of the Han just in time to be caught up in the last rearguard action to defend its bridges.

Seoul was already in enemy hands. Only a mile away, I could see the towers of smoke rising from the ruins of this fourteenth-century city. I pushed forward toward a hill a little way ahead. It was a tragic scene. Across the Han, Seoul burned and smoked in its agony of destruction. There was the constant crump of Red mortar fire as the enemy swooped down toward the bridges. Below me, and streaming by both sides of the hill, were the retreating, panting columns of disorganized troops, the drab color of their weaving lines interspersed here and there with the bright red crosses of ambulances filled with broken, groaning men. The sky was resonant with shrieking missiles of death, and everywhere were the stench and utter desolation of a stricken battlefield. Clogging all the roads in a writhing, dust-shrouded mass of humanity were the refugees. But among them there was no hysteria, no whimpering. Here were the progeny of a proud and sturdy race that for centuries had accepted disaster imperturbably. As they painfully plodded south, carrying all their worldly belongings on their backs, and leading their terror-stricken but wide-eyed, uncrying children, I watched for an hour the pitiful evidence of the disaster I had inherited. In that brief interval on the blood-soaked hill, I formulated my plans. They were desperate plans indeed, but I could see no other way except to accept a defeat which would include not only Korea, but all of continental Asia.

The scene along the Han was enough to convince me that the defensive potential of South Korea had already been exhausted. There was nothing to stop the Communists from rushing their tank columns straight down the few good roads from Seoul to Pusan at the end of the peninsula. All Korea would then be theirs. Even with air and naval support, the South Koreans could not stop the enemy's headlong rush south. Only the immediate commitment of ground troops could possibly do so. The answer I had come to seek was there. I would throw my occupation soldiers into this breach. Completely outnumbered, I would rely upon strategic maneuver to overcome the great odds against me. It would be desperate, but it was my only chance.

And what of Japan? Japan was where my primary responsibility lay. Only a few hours before, my most recent directive from Washington had reiterated that no action I took to protect South Korea should prejudice the protection of Japan. Could I denude this great bastion of troops without inviting Soviet entry from the north? Could I improvise native forces in Japan sufficient to deter any abortive seizure of that country by an enemy if I took elements of the pitifully thin American forces there and committed them in Korea? Could I salvage the time necessary to bring my forces to Pusan? Could I find the transportation to carry the troops to Korea, the munitions and supplies to sustain them in combat, the minimum equipment to create and organize a Japanese protective force? Could I rally, reorganize, and reinspire the defeated Korean army? Could I, if all this were accomplished and the enemy's tenuous supply lines extended to dangerous limits, cut these lines, then envelop and destroy his main forces with only a handful of troops available? I would be outnumbered almost three to one. But in these reflections the genesis of the Inchon operation began to take shape—a counter-stroke that could in itself wrest victory from defeat. I immediately wired Washington:

The South Korean forces are in confusion. Organized and equipped as a light force for maintenance of interior order, they were unprepared for attack by armor and air. Conversely they are incapable of gaining the initiative over such a force as that embodied in the North Korean Army. The South Koreans had made no preparation for defense in depth, for echelons of supply or for a supply system. No plans had been made, or if made were not executed, for the destruction of supplies or materials in the event of a retrograde movement. As a result they have either lost or abandoned their supplies and heavier equipment and have absolutely no system of intercommunication. In most cases the individual soldier in his flight to the south has retained his rifle or carbine. They are gradually being gathered up by an advanced group of my officers I sent over for the purpose. Without artillery, mortars and anti-tank guns, they can only hope to retard the enemy through the fullest utilization of natural obstacles and under the guidance of leadership of high quality. The civilian populace is tranquil, orderly and prosperous according to their scale of living. They have retained a high degree of national spirit and firm belief in the Americans. The roads leading south from Seoul are crowded with refugees refusing to accept the Communist rule.

It is essential that the enemy advance be held or its impetus will threaten the over-running of all of Korea. The South Korean Army is incapable of counter-action and there is a grave danger of a further breakthrough. If the enemy advances continue much further, it will threaten the Republic.

The only assurance for holding the present line and the ability to regain later the lost ground is through the introduction of United States ground combat forces into the Korean battle area. To continue to utilize the forces of our air and navy without an effective ground element can not be decisive. Unless provision is made for the full utilization of the Army-Navy-Air team in this shattered area, our mission will at best be needlessly costly in life, money and prestige. At worst, it might be doomed.

Within twenty-four hours, President Truman authorized the use of ground troops. The number of combat elements which might be withdrawn from Japan without impairing that country's safety was left to my discretion. Thus the United States accepted Communism's challenge to combat in Korea. The risk that the Soviet or the Chinese Communists might enter the war was clearly understood and defiantly accepted. The American tradition had always been that once our troops are committed to battle, the full power and means of the nation would be mobilized and dedicated to fight for victory—not for stalemate or compromise. And I set out to chart the strategic course which would make that victory possible. Not by the wildest stretch of imagination did I dream that this tradition might be broken.

In Japan, I had four occupation divisions, the 7th, 24th, 25th, and 1st Cavalry, comprising the Eighth Army, with garrisons extending from Kyushu to Hokkaido. The army commander was General Walton Walker, a seasoned and experienced officer who had been one of George Patton's corps commanders in the European war. The Air Force was under Lieutenant General George E. Stratemeyer, and the Navy under Admiral C. Turner Joy, both able and efficient veterans of the war. All of my old commanders and most of my staff had long since returned to the United States.

The occupation infantry in Japan was one-third below strength. The regiments had only two instead of three battalions, light tanks instead of heavy, 105-mm. howitzers instead of 155-mm. cannon. The Korean War meant entry into action "as is." No time out for recruiting rallies or to build up and get ready. It was move in—and shoot. This put the bulk of the burden on the G.I. The story of the infantry soldier is an old and honorable one. He carries his home with him—and often his grave. Somehow, he has to bring along the whole paraphernalia of fighting, as well as domesticated living: the grocery store, the ration dump; the hospital, the Medical Corps; the garage, the motor pool; the telephone, the Signal Service. He must sleep and eat and fight and die on foot, in all weather, rain or shine, with or without shelter. He is vulnerable day and night. Death has his finger on him for twenty-four hours, in battle, going toward it, or retreating from it. It is a wonder that the morale of those uniformed gypsies never falters.

The North Koreans had advanced across the 38th parallel in an estimated strength of six infantry divisions and three constabulary brigades, spearheaded by nearly 200 Soviet tanks, with supporting units of heavy artillery, all under cover of an air umbrella. The main attack was along the central corridor, with simultaneous attacks to the west and down the east-coast road, and amphibious landings at various South Korean coastal points. They crossed the Han River, and South Korean resistance became increasingly unsuccessful.

The immediate necessity was to slow down the Red advance before it enveloped all of Korea. My only chance to do this was to commit my forces piecemeal as rapidly as I could get them to the front, relying upon the stratagem that the presence of American ground forces in the battle area would chill the enemy commander into taking precautionary and time-consuming methods. By this method of buying time for space I could build up a force at Pusan, which would serve as a base for future operations. Speed in getting the troops to Korea was of the essence. Every ship, every plane, every train was commandeered. Never had I known such a fast mobilization to a battle front. Elements of the 24th Division were first in by air. Roadblocks were thrown up and defended desperately. Every artifice of harassment and deception was practiced, and the stratagem worked.

The effect of American ground troops, however small in number, resisting the enemy advance confirmed my hopes. The enemy commander at once brought his advance to a stop to permit the laborious bringing up of artillery from across the river without benefit of the regular bridges, which our air force by then had destroyed. He had no way of knowing either the strength of the American forces already committed, and in their immediate support, or what change in the battle situation their presence presaged. He decided, as I had anticipated, against taking any chance. So, instead of continuing to drive his tank columns forward, he deployed all of his forces across the difficult terrain in conventional line of battle. This was his fatal error. It had exacted a painful sacrifice from my men committed to this unequal battle, but it paid off in precious time, so essential if any tactic in the prevailing situation was to be successful.

During those first days of American fighting in South Korea, I threw in troops by air in the hope of establishing a locus of resistance around which I could rally the fast-retreating South Korean forces. I had hoped by that arrogant display of strength to fool the enemy into a belief that I had greater resources at my disposal than I did. We gained ten days by this process before the enemy had deployed in line of battle along the 150-mile front, with Suwon as the pivotal point. By that time, I had brought forth the rest of the 24th Division, under Major General William F. Dean, with orders to delay the enemy until I could bring the 1st Cavalry Division and the 25th Division over from Japan. Dean fought a very desperate series of isolated combats in which a large part of that division was destroyed.

By the time this had happened, the enemy commander had realized his mistake. He had been stopped not by a massive American defensive force, but merely by the appearance of force—by that arrogant display of strength. He moved rapidly to make up for the time he had lost, but it was too late. I had by this time established the Eighth Army in Korea. The enemy, though, still had an enormous superiority in manpower and weight and quality of arms. Aided by this preponderance of numbers and weapons, he was able simultaneously to exert heavy pressure against General Walker's men in the center and flow around them on both sides.

On July 7th I made my first call to Washington for reinforcements. In a message to the Joint Chiefs of Staff I explained that we were facing "an aggressive and well trained professional army operating under excellent top level guidance and demonstrated superior command of strategic and tactical principles." My immediate need was for not less than five full-strength divisions and three tank battalions, together with reinforcing artillery and service elements. My ultimate purpose, I said, was "fully to exploit our air and sea control and, by amphibious maneuver, strike behind his mass of ground forces." Should Soviet Russia or Communist China intervene, I added, "a new situation would develop which is not predictable now."

I was amazed when this message of desperate need for the necessary strength to implement a Washington decision was disapproved by Washington itself. The reasons given were that: (1) no increase in any part of the armed services had been authorized; (2) a suitable United States military posture in other parts of the world had to be maintained; and (3) there was a shortage of shipping. What all this amounted to actually was the old faulty principle of "priorities," under which the Far East was again at the bottom of the list. That it reaffirmed a principle that had lost us the Philippines and immeasurably retarded the defeat of Japan was surprising enough in itself, but the circumstances under which the decision was being formulated made it almost unbelievable. The all-important difference, of course, was that while during World War II we had been fighting in Europe, now we were not. And it could not fail to be obvious even to the non-military mind that Soviet military dispositions in eastern Europe were defensive rather than offensive. I repeated my original request. It was again disapproved.

The Security Council of the United Nations on July 7th, directed the establishment of a unified Korean command. The United States was to be the U.N.'s operative agent, and was instructed to appoint the over-all commander. The next day President Truman named me commander-in-chief, and (the Republic of Korea was not a U.N. member) President Syngman Rhee signified his government's approval of the appointment.

On July 8th, I authorized Japan to increase its defense force by approximately 100,000 men, and in Korea brought our units up to full strength by integrating Koreans into the ranks. This was the so-called "buddy system" which proved so successful. While I could obtain only a trickle of soldiers from Washington, under the plea that they were needed in Germany where there was no war, the local governments, just as in the Pacific war, supported my efforts with every fiber of their being.

My appointment as commander-in-chief was generally well-received in the United States, despite the usual clamor of my leftist enemies. I was more than gratified at the editorial of *The New York Times:*

As American people watch eagerly for news from Korea one constantly recurring cause for satisfaction and assurance surely to be found is the fact that it is Douglas MacArthur who directs this effort in the field. Fate could not have chosen a man better qualified to command the unreserved confidence of the people of this country. Here is a superb strategist and an inspired leader; a man of infinite patience and quiet stability under adverse pressure; a man equally capable of bold and decisive action. His long years of experience in the Orient, his thorough grasp of fundamentals of organization and supply, the immense prestige which he enjoys not only in this country but throughout the whole Pacific world, all these are assets of unmeasurable value.

In every home in the United States today there must be a sure conviction that if any man can carry out successfully the task which Truman and the Security Council of the United Nations have given him, and carry out this task honorably, efficiently and with no waste of life and effort, that man is the good soldier in Tokyo who has long since proved to the hilt his ability to serve his country well.

I felt it would be difficult indeed to live up to such extravagant encomiums.

Gloomy and doubtful as was the situation at this time, the news reports painted it much worse than it actually was. I felt obliged to issue an explanatory release:

This is the result of an experiment being tried perhaps for the first time in modern combat; that of avoiding any military censorship or undue restriction of the movements of war correspondents. Reports of warfare are, at any time, grisly and repulsive and reflect the emotional strain normal to those unaccustomed to the sights and sounds of battle. Exaggerated stories obtained from individuals wounded or mentally shocked have given a distorted and misrepresentative picture to the public. Probably the most flagrant of these exaggerated reports dealt with the so-called "lost battalion" of the 34th Infantry which was reported as being completely annihilated whereas its actual losses amounted to only 2 killed, 7 wounded, and 12 missing.

American ground units in Korea are fighting one of the most skillful and heroic holding and rearguard actions in history. Their excellent peacetime training is reflected in the combat record they are now compiling. They have been overwhelmingly outnumbered, in some instances more than 20 to 1, and the casualties inflicted on the enemy have been immeasurably greater than those they have sustained. They have filled a breach without which the North Korean forces would have, long ere this, completely overrun and destroyed South Korea. This has provided time for the rapid movement of reinforcements forward. Each day we reduce the enemy's relative superiority in numbers and weapons.

Two days later I received a message from the managing editor of the Chicago *Sun-Times,* stating that his paper had imposed self-censorship. Once again a free press exhibited its fullest commitment to the burdens of a free society.

By July 20th, the period of piecemeal entry into action was over, the painful rearguard type of retreat under pressure of overwhelming numbers was ended, the fight for time against space was won. The enemy's plan and great opportunity depended upon the speed with which he could overrun South Korea once he had breached the Han River line. This chance he had now lost through the extraordinary speed with which the Eighth Army had been deployed from Japan to stem his rush. When he crashed the Han line, the way seemed entirely open and victory was within his grasp. The desperate decision to throw in piecemeal American elements as they arrived by every available means of transport from Japan was the only hope to save the situation. The skill and valor thereafter displayed in successive holding actions by the ground forces in accordance with this concept, brilliantly supported in complete co-ordination by air and naval elements, forced the enemy into continued deployments, mostly frontal attacks, and confused logistics which so slowed his advance and blunted his drive that we bought the precious time necessary to build a secure base. With the issue fully joined, our future action could be predicated on choice. We now held South Korea, and, in the face of overwhelming numbers, had relatively few casualties.

The area in which I had military responsibility having been enlarged to include Formosa and the Pescadore Islands, I felt it necessary, late in July, to visit the island in order to determine its military capabilities for defense.

Among the problems which were discussed was the prompt and generous offer of the Nationalist Chinese to send troops to join the United Nations forces in Korea. The belief of all concerned, however, was that such action at this time might so seriously jeopardize the defense of Formosa that it would be inadvisable. Arrangements were completed for effective co-ordination between the American forces under my command and those of the Chinese Nationalists, the better to meet any attack which a hostile force might be foolish enough to attempt. Such an attack would, in my opinion, stand little chance of success. It was a great pleasure for me to meet my old comrade-in-arms of the last war, Generalissimo Chiang Kai-shek. His indomitable determination to resist Communist domination aroused my sincere admiration.

To my astonishment, the visit to Formosa and my meeting with Chiang Kai-shek was greeted by a furor. My habitual critics, including those within the United Nations who advocated appeasement of the Soviet Union and Red China, naturally set in with their cudgels, but I was somewhat startled to find myself attacked by certain groups within the United States itself. It did not dawn on me that my visit to Formosa would be construed as political or in any way undesirable. I was merely trying to make my own military estimate of the situation. There was such a frenzy of irresponsible diatribe, some of the misrepresentations so gross and obviously malicious, that I felt it necesssary to make a further statement:

There have been so many misstatements made with reference to my trip to Formosa that in the public interest at this critical moment I feel constrained to correct them. This trip was formally arranged and coordinated beforehand with all branches of the American and Chinese Governments. It was limited entirely to military matters, as I stated in my public release after the visit, and dealt solely with the problem of preventing military violence to Formosa as directed by the President—the implementation of which directive is my responsibility. It had no connection with political affairs and, therefore, no suggestion or thought was ever made from any source whatsoever that a political representative accompany me. The subject of the future of the Chinese Government, of developments on the Chinese mainland, or anything else outside the scope of my own military responsibility was not discussed or even mentioned. Full reports on the results of the visit were promptly made to Washington. This visit has been maliciously misrepresented to the public by those who invariably in the past have propagandized a policy of defeatism and appeasement in the Pacific. I hope the American people will not be misled by sly insinuations, brash speculations and bold misstatements invariably attributed to anonymous sources, so insidiously fed them both nationally and internationally by persons ten thousand miles away from the actual events, which tend, if they are not indeed designed, to promote disunity and destroy faith and confidence in American institutions and American representatives at this time of great world peril.

The Administration apparently became somewhat alarmed at our deteriorating prestige in the Orient, and President Truman issued a public statement saying: "The occupation of Formosa by Communist forces would be a direct threat to the security of the Pacific area and to the United States forces performing their lawful and necessary functions in that area."

I received the following message from President Truman: "At my direction, my assistant, W. Averell Harriman, will leave here Friday 4 August by air to confer with you in Tokyo on political aspects of Far Eastern situation. Announcement of mission will be made here. Warm regards."

As special envoy from President Truman, Averell Harriman was sent to Tokyo to advise the President on political aspects of the Far Eastern situation. Harriman and I were friends of long standing. While superintendent of West Point I had hunted ducks on his preserve near Tuxedo. We discussed fully global conditions. I found him careful and cautious in what he said, but gained these very definite impressions: that there was no fixed and comprehensive United States policy for the Far East; that foreign influences, especially those of Great Britain, were very powerful in Washington; that there was no apparent interest in mounting an offensive against the Communists; that we were content to attempt to block their moves, but not to initiate any counter-moves; that we would defend Formosa if attacked, just as we had done in Korea; that President Truman had conceived a violent animosity toward Chiang Kai-shek; and that anyone who favored the Generalissimo might well arouse the President's disfavor. He left me with a feeling of concern and uneasiness that the situation in the Far East was little understood and mistakenly downgraded in high circles in Washington.

On August 17th, I received an invitation from the commander-in-chief of the Veterans of Foreign Wars to send a message to be read at their forthcoming annual encampment. I had sent messages to many other organizations in the past and regarded it as a matter of routine. The message expressed my personal opinion of the strategic importance of Formosa and its relation to our defensive position in the Pacific. There was nothing political in it. I sent it through the Department of the Army ten days before the encampment. The officials of that Department apparently found nothing objectionable in it. It was in complete support of the President's announced policy toward Formosa. It actually contained this paragraph:

The decision of President Truman on June 27th lighted into a flame a lamp of hope throughout Asia that was burning dimly toward extinction. It marked for the Far East the focal and turning point in this area's struggle for freedom. It swept aside in one great monumental stroke all of the hypocrisy and the sophistry which has confused and deluded so many people distant from the actual scene.

A week after sending the message I received a wire in the name of the "President of the United States" directing that I withdraw the message to the Veterans of Foreign Wars. The reason given was that "various features with respect to Formosa are in conflict with the policy of the United States." I was utterly astonished. I sent for a copy of the message and re-examined it, but could find no feature that was not in complete support of the President.

I replied, "My message was most carefully prepared to fully support the President's policy position. My remarks were calculated only to support his declaration and I am unable to see wherein they might be interpreted otherwise. The views were purely my personal ones and the subject had previously been freely discussed in all circles, governmental and private, both at home and abroad." To this day I do not know who managed to construe my statement as meaning exactly the opposite of what it said, and how this person or persons could have so easily deceived the President. Were his political advisers playing strategist, and his military advisers playing politics?

On August 30th, only two days later, I received this letter from the President: "I am sending you for your information the text of a letter which I sent to Ambassador Warren Austin (U.S. Ambassador to the United Nations) addressed to Trygve Lie on August 25. You will understand why my action of the 26th in directing the withdrawal of your message to the Veterans of Foreign Wars was necessary." The letter contained seven points:

1. The United States has not encroached on the territory of China, nor has the United States taken aggressive action against China.

2. The action of the United States in regard to Formosa was taken at a time when that island was the scene of conflict with the mainland. More serious conflict was threatened by the public declaration of the Chinese Communist authorities.

3. The action of the United States was an impartial neutralizing action addressed both to the forces on Formosa and to those on the mainland. We have no designs on Formosa and our action was not inspired by any desire to acquire a special position for the United States.

4. The action of the United States was expressly stated to be without prejudice to the future political settlement of the status of the island. The actual status of the island is that it is territory taken from Japan by the victory of the Allied Forces in the Pacific. Like other such territories, its legal status cannot be fixed until there is international action to determine its future. The Chinese Government was asked by the Allies to take the surrender of the Japanese forces on the island. That is the reason the Chinese are there now.

5. The United States has a record through history of friendship for the Chinese people. We still feel the friendship and know that millions of Chinese reciprocate it.

6. The United States would welcome United Nations consideration of the case of Formosa.

7. Formosa is now at peace and will remain so unless someone resorts

to force. If the Security Council wishes to study the question of Formosa we shall support and assist that study.

What was significant about the letter was that its basic premise, as set forth in item 4, was simply not correct. At Cairo on December 1, 1943, an agreement was entered into between the United States, China, and the United Kingdom, represented respectively by President Roosevelt, General-issimo Chiang, and Prime Minister Churchill. The agreement which they all signed reads in part as follows:

It is their purpose that Japan shall be stripped of all the islands in the Pacific which she had seized or occupied since the beginning of the first World War in 1914, and that the territories Japan has stolen from the Chinese, such as Man-churia, Formosa, and the Pescadores, shall be restored to the Republic of China.

That, and only that, was the reason why Formosa was given to China at the end of World War II. There was no further need to settle the question of who owned Formosa; as far as we were concerned, the Republic of China owned Formosa by the terms of the agreement at Cairo.

My opinion of the strategic importance of Formosa was shared by the Joint Chiefs of Staff. On September 1st, they officially recommended that the island and its disposition be kept out of any political bargaining at a forth-coming meeting of the foreign ministers. "The strategic consequences of a Communist-dominated Formosa," the Joint Chiefs advised, "would be so seriously detrimental to United States security that in the opinion of the Joint Chiefs of Staff, the United States should not permit the disposition of Formosa to be recommended in the first instance or decided by any com-mission or agency of the United Nations."

But the pressure against our Nationalist Chinese ally of World War II did not cease. It had started immediately after the war's end, with the argu-ment, mentioned before, that the Chinese Communists were really only "agrarian reformers"—a claim that has become one of modern history's bit-terest jests. It was, of course, given its greatest impetus when General Mar-shall made the tragic mistake of using American prestige as a lever for attempting to force a coalition government on Chiang Kai-shek. And it manifested itself most vocally when I tried to implement the President's directive to defend Formosa by strengthening the alliance between Nation-alist and United States military forces.

The arguments took many forms. At first, the claim was that Chiang's government was corrupt. Somehow, the reasoning ran, rule by the Kuomintang was even worse than a Communist police state, and, therefore, any change would be for the better. Why they would ally with the same Chiang against the Japanese, but not against the Communists, was never clear. But it was perfectly clear to me now that it was only a question of time when my head would roll.

On August 20th, the atrocities being committed by the North Koreans on prisoners caused me to advise the enemy's commander-in-chief that unless immediate orders were given for the cessation of such brutality, I would hold each and every enemy commander criminally accountable under the rules and precedents of war.

From this time on there was a marked decrease in such atrocities and a noteworthy improvement in the enemy's handling of prisoners.

As supreme commander for the Allied powers, I issued the following statement to the Japanese people on the occasion of the fifth anniversary of V-J Day:

Five years have passed since the nations of the world entered into solemn covenants designed to restore and preserve the peace. All men then looked forward with new hope and a new resolve to achieve a relationship based upon a mutuality of purpose, a mutuality of understanding, and a mutuality of dedication to higher human and spiritual ideals. Hope found its genesis in the determination enunciated by the major powers that irresponsible militarism, the scourge of mankind since the beginning of time, be driven from the world.

This hope has not materialized. While militarism in Japan, largely through the self-dedicated efforts of the Japanese people themselves, has been banished and no longer exists even as a debatable concept, elsewhere imperialistic militarism, marching under different banners but unified direction, is leaving in its wake the stark tragedy of human and spiritual wreckage. Many peoples have fallen under its savage and merciless assaults and fear of conquest and enslavement grips much of the earth.

In the universal atmosphere of doubt and uncertainty generated by the clash of opposing forces—good and evil—the Japanese people with calmness and resolution have written a record of political reorientation, economic reconstruction and social progress which attests to Japan's unconditional qualification to resume membership in good standing in the family of free nations.

From the ashes left in war's wake there has arisen in Japan an edifice dedicated to the primacy of individual liberty and personal dignity, and in the ensuing process there has been created a truly representative government committed to the advance of political morality, freedom of economic enterprise, and social justice. Thus oriented, Japan may be counted upon to wield a profound influence over the course of events in Asia.

The basic objectives of Occupation have been achieved. Politically, economically, and socially, Japan at peace will not fail the universal trust.

I had a premonition as I wrote the message that this would be the last time I would address Japan.

On September 8th, I received this letter from John Foster Dulles:

We have been making progress on the Japanese Peace Treaty matter and now finally the State and Defense Departments are in agreement to proceed, and on the general goals to be sought. I expect that we shall take the occasion of the forthcoming New York meetings of the Foreign Ministers and of the delegates at the United Nations Assembly to feel out informally the views of some of our friendly allies as to future procedure. Our present conclusions here coincide with the views which you put forward to Secretary Johnson and to me and I feel that your position created the bridge over which we can now make constructive progress.

In view of the tendency of the United Nations Assembly, probably no major steps, certainly of a formal nature, can be taken for two or three months yet. But some useful preliminary work can perhaps be done so that the time will not really be lost. I hope that someone from the Department will shortly again be in Tokyo to talk over future steps with you.

With my best wishes and admiration for the magnificent way in which you are carrying your new responsibilities, I am

Faithfully yours

The month of August in Korea witnessed repeated and savage attacks on our forces. But the South Koreans had now been rallied and reorganized, and five small R.O.K. divisions—the 1st, 3rd, 6th, 8th, and Capital—were with General Walker. A brigade of the 1st United States Marine Division had also joined the Eighth Army. Our forces made a planned withdrawal from Taejon and accepted battle along the Naktong River. At Yongdong, after a bitter four-day struggle, the enemy overwhelmed our position and forced our withdrawal further south to what amounted to an extended beachhead around Pusan.

The North Koreans now had thirteen divisions at the front. They were fighting not on a continuous line of deployment, but in a series of columns of battalion and regimental size, probing roads and mountain trails in a continuous effort to penetrate and outflank our position. For a time, it was touch and go. The Cassandras of the world gloomily speculated on a vast Asiatic Dunkirk.

The pattern and density of the enemy's supply and reinforcement movement showed that heavy tonnage was coming from Chinese Manchuria and
Russian Siberia, through Seoul, in spite of our bombing and strafing. It
moved habitually by night. The ingenuity and tenacity in repair of bridges
and tracks was of the highest order. Fresh divisions and tank brigades from
North Korea arrived constantly. Supply, food, and ammunition went forward without a letup, by train, by truck and motor, by oxcart, and cargodoes.
But Walker, his back to the sea, with great skill and courage by all commands and ranks, slowed the enemy to a walk, and by the end of the month
had established a fairly stable line of defense. The order was "to stand or die."

With a Japanese force of 100,000 men mustered and well on the road
toward securing the safety of Japan from sudden seizure by Russia, with
Japan proving its utter loyalty by its well-ordered conduct, with my air and
naval forces unopposed, I was now finally ready for the last great stroke to
bring my plan into fruition. My Han River dream as a possibility had begun
to assume the certainties of reality—a turning movement deep into the flank
and rear of the enemy that would sever his supply lines and encircle all his
forces south of Seoul. I had made similar decisions in past campaigns, but
none more fraught with danger, none that promised to be more vitally con-
clusive if successful.

The target I selected was Inchon, 20 miles west of Seoul and the second
largest port in South Korea. The target date, because of the great tides at
Inchon, had to be the middle of September. This meant that the staging for
the landing at Inchon would have to be accomplished more rapidly than that
of any other large amphibious operation in modern warfare. On July 23rd
I had cabled Washington:

Operation planned mid-September is amphibious landing of a two division
corps in rear of enemy lines for purpose of enveloping and destroying enemy
forces in conjunction with attack from south by Eighth Army. I am firmly convinced that early and strong effort behind his front will sever his main lines of
communication and enable us to deliver a decisive and crushing blow. The alternative is a frontal attack which can only result in a protracted and expensive
campaign.

My plan was opposed by powerful military influences in Washington.
The essence of the operation depended upon a great amphibious movement,
but the chairman of the Joint Chiefs of Staff, General Omar Bradley, was of
the considered opinion that such amphibious operations were obsolete—that
there would never be another successful movement of this sort. He had stirred

up a storm in calling Navy personnel, which included Marines, "Fancy Dans." President Truman also was not in favor of using the Marines as a major military unit of our armed forces. In a letter to Congressman McDonough of California he said: "The Marine Corps is the Navy's police force and as long as I am President that is what it will remain. They have a propaganda machine that is almost equal to Stalin's."

After a silence of three weeks, the Joint Chiefs of Staff wired me that General Joseph Collins, Army Chief of Staff, and Admiral Forrest Sherman, Chief of Naval Operations, were coming to Tokyo to discuss this maneuver with me. It was evident immediately upon their arrival that the actual purpose of their trip was not so much to discuss as to dissuade.

On August 23rd, I called a strategic conference to debate the problem at the Dai Ichi Building in Tokyo. The conferees included General Collins and Admiral Sherman, as well as Marine Chief Lieutenant General Lemuel C. Shephard Jr.; my air commander, Stratemeyer; my chief of staff, Almond, whom I had already designated commander of the X Corps, which was to make the Inchon landing; my Navy commander, Joy; my fleet commander,

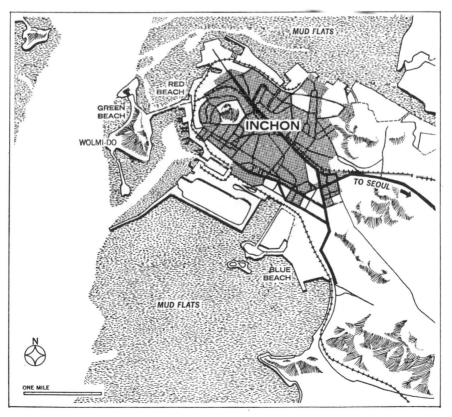

Inchon and Its Harbor: Low Tide

Struble; my amphibious expert, Admiral James T. Doyle; and a gathering of other staff officers and aides making up a veritable constellation of silver stars.

As at the Pearl Harbor conference with Roosevelt and Nimitz in 1944, the Navy presented its case first. A naval briefing staff argued that two elements—tide and terrain—made a landing at Inchon extremely hazardous. They referred to Navy hydrographic studies which listed the average rise and fall of the tides at Inchon at 20.7 feet—one of the greatest in the world. On the tentative target date for the invasion, the rise and fall would be more than 30 feet because of the position of the moon. When Inchon's tides were at full ebb, the mud banks that had accumulated over the centuries from the Yellow Sea jutted from the shore in some places as far as 2 miles out into the harbor. And during ebb and flow these tides raced through "Flying Fish Channel," the best approach to the port, at speeds up to 6 knots. Even under the most favorable conditions "Flying Fish Channel" was narrow and winding. Not only did it make a perfect location for enemy mines, but any ship sunk at a particularly vulnerable point could block the channel to all other ships.

On the target date, the Navy experts went on, the first high tide would occur at 6:59 in the morning, and the afternoon high tide would be at 7:19, a full thirty-five minutes after sunset. Within two hours after high tide most of the assault craft would be wallowing in the ooze of Inchon's mud banks, sitting ducks for Communist shore batteries until the next tide came in to float them again. In effect, the amphibious forces would have only about two hours in the morning for the complex job of reducing or effectively neutralizing Wolmi-do, the 350-foot-high, heavily fortified island which commands the harbor and which is connected with the mainland by a long causeway.

Assuming that this could be done, the afternoon's high tide and approaching darkness would allow only two and a half hours for the troops to land, secure a beachhead for the night, and bring up all the supplies essential to enable forces to withstand counterattacks until morning. The landing craft, after putting the first assault waves ashore, would be helpless on the mud banks until the morning tide.

Beyond all this, the Navy summed up, the assault landings would have to be made right in the heart of the city itself, where every structure provided a potential strong point of enemy resistance. Reviewing the Navy's presentation, Admiral Sherman concluded by saying: "If every possible geographical and naval handicap were listed—Inchon has 'em all."

General Collins then presented his arguments. The Army, its chief of staff said, felt that Inchon was too far in the rear of the present battle area to have the necessary immediate effect on the enemy. To accomplish this big maneuver successfully with the limited resources available would require withdrawing the 1st Marine Brigade, which was then holding a sector in Walker's hard-pressed defense line, and would thus further endanger that position. Collins was not at all sure, in fact did not believe, that even if I captured Seoul I could make contact with Walker to the south. And furthermore, he said, I might well run into overwhelming enemy force in the area of the capital city and suffer complete defeat.

Collins had an alternate proposal to abandon the plan of the Inchon landing and instead aim for the west-coast port of Kunsan. This port was much further south and presented few of Inchon's physical obstacles. At this point Sherman spoke up and seconded Collins in urging me to give up Inchon in favor of Kunsan.

Sherman and Collins finished their argument. I waited a moment or so to collect my thoughts. I could feel the tension rising in the room. Almond shifted uneasily in his chair. If ever a silence was pregnant, this one was. I could almost hear my father's voice telling me as he had so many years ago, "Doug, councils of war breed timidity and defeatism."

The bulk of the Reds [I said] are committed around Walker's defense perimeter. The enemy, I am convinced, has failed to prepare Inchon properly for defense. The very arguments you have made as to the impracticabilities involved will tend to ensure for me the element of surprise. For the enemy commander will reason that no one would be so brash as to make such an attempt. Surprise is the most vital element for success in war. As an example, the Marquis de Montcalm believed in 1759 that it was impossible for an armed force to scale the precipitous river banks south of the then walled city of Quebec, and therefore concentrated his formidable defenses along the more vulnerable banks north of the city. But General James Wolfe and a small force did indeed come up the St. Lawrence River and scale those heights. On the Plains of Abraham, Wolfe won a stunning victory that was made possible almost entirely by surprise. Thus he captured Quebec and in effect ended the French and Indian War. Like Montcalm, the North Koreans would regard an Inchon landing as impossible. Like Wolfe, I could take them by surprise.

The Navy's objections as to tides, hydrography, terrain, and physical handicaps are indeed substantial and pertinent. But they are not insuperable. My confidence in the Navy is complete, and in fact I seem to have more confidence in the Navy than the Navy has in itself. The Navy's rich experience in staging the numerous amphibious landings under my command in the Pacific during the late war, frequently under somewhat similar difficulties, leaves me with little doubt on that score.

As to the proposal for a landing at Kunsan, it would indeed eliminate many of the hazards of Inchon, but it would be largely ineffective and indecisive. It would be an attempted envelopment which would not envelop. It would not sever or destroy the enemy's supply lines or distribution center, and would therefore serve little purpose. It would be a "short envelopment," and nothing in war is more futile. Better no flank movement than one such as this. The only result would be a hookup with Walker's troops on his left. It would be better to send the troops directly to Walker than by such an indirect and costly process. In other words, this would simply be sending more troops to help Walker "hang on," and hanging on was not good enough. No decision can be reached by defensive action in Walker's perimeter. To fight frontally in a breakthrough from Pusan will be bloody and indecisive. The enemy will merely roll back on his lines of supply and communication.

But seizure of Inchon and Seoul will cut the enemy's supply line and seal off the entire southern peninsula. The vulnerability of the enemy is his supply position. Every step southward extends his transport lines and renders them more frail and subject to dislocation. The several major lines of enemy supply from the north converge on Seoul, and from Seoul they radiate to the several sectors of the front. By seizing Seoul I would completely paralyze the enemy's supply system— coming and going. This in turn will paralyze the fighting power of the troops that now face Walker. Without munitions and food they will soon be helpless and disorganized, and can easily be overpowered by our smaller but well-supplied forces.

The only alternative to a stroke such as I propose will be the continuation of the savage sacrifice we are making at Pusan, with no hope of relief in sight. Are you content to let our troops stay in that bloody perimeter like beef cattle in the slaughterhouse? Who will take the responsibility for such a tragedy? Certainly, I will not.

The prestige of the Western world hangs in the balance. Oriental millions are watching the outcome. It is plainly apparent that here in Asia is where the Communist conspirators have elected to make their play for global conquest. The test is not in Berlin or Vienna, in London, Paris or Washington. It is here and now—it is along the Naktong River in South Korea. We have joined the issue on the battlefield. Actually, we here fight Europe's war with arms, while there it is still confined to words. If we lose the war to Communism in Asia, the fate of Europe will be gravely jeopardized. Win it and Europe will probably be saved from war and stay free. Make the wrong decision here—the fatal decision of inertia—and we will be done. I can almost hear the ticking of the second hand of destiny. We must act now or we will die.

If my estimate is inaccurate and should I run into a defense with which I cannot cope, I will be there personally and will immediately withdraw our forces before they are committed to a bloody setback. The only loss then will be my professional reputation. But Inchon will not fail. Inchon will succeed. And it will save 100,000 lives.

I finished. The silence was complete. Then Sherman, an old associate of the Pacific war, rose and said, "Thank you. A great voice in a great cause."

And on August 29th I received a wire from the Joint Chiefs of Staff: "We concur after reviewing the information brought back by General Collins and Admiral Sherman, in making preparations and executing a turning movement by amphibious forces on the west coast of Korea—at Inchon."

I planned to use the 7th Division, until this time retained in Japan, and the 1st Marine Division to make the Inchon landing. They were to form the X Corps under Almond. This involved the withdrawal of the 1st Marine Brigade from the perimeter. To compensate to some extent for this withdrawal, a regimental combat team of the 7th Division was to be in floating reserve off Pusan. It could be rushed into any gap that might develop in Walker's line, and, if not, would be the last element to land at Inchon.

No operation of this size could be performed without taking the chance of disclosure. It is to the credit of the many news correspondents at the front who could not fail to witness these troop dispositions and surmise the reason for them, as well as to the credit of their editors back home, that the projected counterattack was a well-kept secret.

By a week before the target date, all the details of the master plan had been worked out. The troops that had come from Japan, the United States, and even the Mediterranean had virtually all arrived. Each unit had been assigned its separate responsibility, and those Marines and soldiers who were not already afloat along Korea's west coast were in the final stages of embarkation. It was at this eleventh hour that I received a message from the Joint Chiefs of Staff which chilled me to the marrow of my bones.

The message expressed doubt of success and implied the whole movement should be abandoned. It read in part: "We have noted with considerable concern the recent trend of events in Korea. In the light of the commitment of all the reserves available to the Eighth Army, we desire your estimate as to the feasibility and chance of success of projected operation if initiated on planned schedule." What could have given rise to such a query at such an hour? Had someone in authority in Washington lost his nerve? Could it be the President? Or Marshall, who had just become Secretary of Defense? Or Bradley? Or was it merely an anticipating alibi if the operation should run into trouble? Whatever lay behind this last-minute hesitancy, it clearly suggested the possibility that even after the millions of man-hours already expended, I might be ordered to abandon it.

I immediately penciled a reply:

I regard the chance of success of the operation as excellent. I go further in belief that it represents the only hope of wresting the initiative from the enemy and thereby presenting the opportunity for a decisive blow. To do otherwise is to commit us to a war of indefinite duration, of gradual attrition and of doubtful result, as the enemy has potentialities of buildup and reinforcements which far exceed our own. Our stroke as planned would prevent any material reinforcements in buildup of the enemy in the present combat zone. The situation within the perimeter is not critical. It is possible that there may be some contraction, and defense positions have been selected for this contingency. There is not the slightest possibility, however, of our forces being ejected from the Pusan beachhead.

The envelopment from the north will instantly relieve the pressure upon the south perimeter and, indeed, is the only way that this can be accomplished. The success of the enveloping movement from the north does not depend upon the rapid juncture of the X Corps with the Eighth Army. The seizure of the beach of the enemy's distributing system in the Seoul area will completely dislocate the logistical supply of his forces now operating in South Korea and therefore will ultimately result in their disintegration. The prompt juncture of our two forces, while it would be dramatically symbolic of the complete collapse of the enemy, is not a vital part of the operation.

The embarkation of the troops and the preliminary air and naval preparations are proceeding according to schedule. I repeat that I and all of my commanders and staff officers, without exception, are enthusiastic for and confident of the success of the enveloping movement.

After dispatching my reply, I waited with growing concern an answer. Was it possible, I asked myself, that even now, when it was all but impossible to bring this great movement grinding to a halt, timidity in an office thousands of miles away, even if by a President himself, could stop this golden opportunity to turn defeat into victory? Finally, a short cryptic message arrived from the Joint Chiefs of Staff, announcing that in view of my reply they had approved the operation and "so informed the President." I interpreted this to mean that it had been the President who had threatened to interfere and overrule, on a professional military problem, his military advisers.

On September 12th I boarded the *Mount McKinley* at Sasebo. A typhoon was blowing and we were hit with its full force. The second day out, the seas smoothed, the weather became bright and clear, and we headed for our rendezvous with the rest of the assault fleet. That evening I stood at the rail of the *Mount McKinley* and watched the sun go down beyond China over the horizon. I had made many landings before, but this was the most intricately complicated amphibious operation I had ever attempted. Next morning we would have to thread our way over the shifting bars of "Flying

Fish Channel," under the guns of Walmi-do, and skirt the edges of the deadly mud banks that stretched for 2 miles across the harbor.

All over the ship the tension that had been slowly building up since our departure was now approaching its climax. Even the Yellow Sea rushing past the ship's sides seemed to bespeak the urgency of our mission. That night, about half past two, I took a turn around the deck. The ship was blacked out from stem to stern. At their posts and battle stations the crew members were alert and silent, no longer exchanging the customary banter. At the bow I stood listening to the rush of the sea and watched the fiery sparklets of phosphorescence as the dark ship plowed toward the target, the armada of other craft converging on the same area, all now past the point of no return. Within five hours, 40,000 men would act boldly, in the hope that 100,000 others manning the thin defense lines in South Korea would not die. I alone was responsible for tomorrow, and if I failed, the dreadful results would rest on judgment day against my soul.

Then I noticed a flash—a light that winked on and off across the water. The channel navigation lights were on. We were taking the enemy by surprise. The lights were not even turned off. I went to my cabin and turned in.

I could not have been asleep more than a couple of hours when a sudden thunder woke me. Our guns had opened up on Wolmi-do. I went to the bridge. This harbor island was now rocking under the bombardment of naval guns and aerial bombs. As I watched, blue Corsairs swooped down from the clouds and added their strafing to the destruction. Wreaths of dirty gray smoke were rising. Against this falling curtain the arching, fiery trails of thousands of rockets could be seen as they streaked toward Inchon's beaches. Immense explosions were erupting all along the shores. The endless circles of little landing craft churned around and around the mother assault ships.

The guns on Wolmi-do were silenced, and the first assault waves were going in. If the Marines who were leading were beaten off or even pinned down for too long, it would mean the enemy was in force. It would take only a few defenders to slaughter that first wave of invaders while the rest were held back by the enormous mud banks. At 8 A.M. an orderly climbs up to the bridge and hands me a slip of paper. It says the first wave of Marines have landed and secured a beachhead without a single fatality. I turned to Admiral Doyle and said: "Please send this message to the fleet: 'The Navy and the Marines have never shone more brightly than this morning.' Let's go down and have breakfast."

By the time the tide had gone out of Inchon's harbor, only an hour later, leaving some of the landing craft squatting on the mud banks, Wolmi-do had been fully secured. And late that afternoon, as soon as the tides rolled back in, I climbed into the gig of Admiral Struble and we went in to oversee the operation. At Wolmi-do I found that the enemy had started an intense fortification of the island. Had I listened to those who had wanted to delay the landing until the next high tides, nearly a month later, Wolmi-do would have been an impregnable fortress.

I directed the prompt seizure of Seoul to be followed by an advance toward the south. This would place the bulk of the enemy's army between the two giant prongs of my forces—the X Corps from the north, the Eighth Army from the south. This would forge the pincers, both the anvil and the hammer, for the stroke of complete annihilation of the North Korean armies.

The X Corps moved inland rapidly. One column headed for Seoul with the immediate mission to cut communications to the south and to seize Kimpo Airfield, the largest in all Korea. This would sever the jugular vein of the enemy. The other column moved on toward Suwon, its mission being to recapture the air base there and to move on as the northern area of the pincer movement. Events moved with great rapidity. Kimpo Airfield was captured, and signs of weakness began to be evident in front of Walker. I directed him to attack, and he promptly crossed the Naktong River in savage assault. The enemy resisted desperately, but with his supplies gone, caught between the pincers, and without retreat routes available, he gave way at an accelerated rate. Precipitate withdrawal carried him rapidly northward over 70 miles. Soon, complete disintegration set in. He was cut off from supply, command, and communications. Red regiments ceased to exist as organized units. Arms and equipment were abandoned; tanks, artillery, mortars, and small arms littered the highways and trails. Prisoners surrendered or were captured by the thousands. Within a month, the total of Red captives rose to 130,000. The enemy fought fiercely for Seoul, but by September 28th it had been cleared.*

I moved at once to have the government of Korea re-established in Seoul. But at this juncture I received an astonishing message from Washington. In

---

* Two messages arrived whose senders, more than any Western politician, understood the psychological importance of victory. The first was from President Syngman Rhee. "On this historic occasion of the liberation of Seoul," he wired, "I wish to express to you on behalf of the Korean government and people deepest gratitude and everlasting warm memory for your brilliant leadership which has made this victory possible against great odds. Of all your great achievements in a long life of extraordinary public service, I believe history will record your leadership of the United Nations forces in Korea as the most magnificent."

The second message was from another Asian leader, Generalissimo Chiang Kai-shek. He wired: "It gives the Chinese government as well as myself great gratification indeed to learn that under your magnificent planning and command the United Nations forces have recaptured Seoul. Your personal participation at the front to conduct the great victory at Inchon inspires my highest admiration and heartfelt congratulations."

an order, undoubtedly instigated by the State Department, and reflecting its antagonism toward President Rhee, the Joint Chiefs of Staff admonished me that any plan for the restoration of his government "must have the approval of higher authority."

I replied instantly:

Your message is not understood. I have no plan whatsoever except scrupulously to implement the directives I have received. These directives envision support of the resolutions of the United Nations Security Council of 25 and 27 June, calling upon member governments to furnish "such assistance to the Republic of Korea as may be necessary to repel the armed attacks and to restore international peace and security in the area."

The existing government of the Republic has never ceased to function. The position of the United States is stated in your message of July 7, Government of Republic of Korea is recognized by U.S. as responsible governing authority and only lawful government in Korea and is only Korean government whose legality has been recognized by U.N. authority; with the concurrence of the cabinet, senior members of the legislature, the United Nations Commission, and perhaps other or similar official, it will domicile in Seoul as soon as conditions there are sufficiently stable to permit reasonable security. This of course involves no reestablishment of government, nor indeed any change in government, but merely a restoration of the existing government to its constitutional seat in order to facilitate the resumption of the civil process, and to promote prompt and effective restoration of law and order in areas liberated from enemy control. Such action is not only very much desired by the American Ambassador and all others concerned, but appears to be implicit in my directives.

I ordered that on September 29th the city of Seoul be formally restored as the seat of the existing government.

At the capital building I pinned the Distinguished Service Cross on General Walker and General Almond, citing them for their marked skill and courage in exploiting the decisive pincer movement of Inchon. The scene was impressive as the ceremony of handing back the capital city began. In the war-shattered assembly room sat row on row of heavily armed officers and men of both the U.N. and R.O.K. armies. On both sides of the room, the windows gaped brokenly, and the smell of death drifted through them. My thoughts went back to that day in Malacanan Palace in Manila when I handed the seat of government over to the authorities of the Philippines. I asked that all present rise and join me in reciting the Lord's Prayer. The steel helmets and mud-caked fatigue caps came off as everyone rose to his feet. Together we recited the Lord's Prayer, and I remember particles of glass tinkling down from the shattered roof of the assembly room as I concluded,

". . . Thine is the Kingdom, the Power and the Glory, for ever and ever, Amen."

I turned to Syngman Rhee and said virtually the same words I had spoken five years before to Sergio Osmena: "Mr. President, my officers and I will now resume our military duties and leave you and your government to the discharge of the civil responsibility." President Rhee seemed deeply moved by it all. He rose and clasped my hand.

"We admire you," he said with tears flowing down his cheeks. "We love you as the savior of our race." And, when the ceremony was over, the people of Seoul lined the streets and clapped and waved their little paper flags. I returned to Tokyo.*

---

* Many were the congratulatory messages waiting for me at the Dai Ichi Building. The text of some of them is particularly interesting because of what was soon to take place.

President Truman wired: "I know that I speak for the entire American people when I send you my warmest congratulations in the victory which has been achieved under your leadership in Korea. Few operations in military history can match either the delaying action where you traded space for time in which to build up your forces, or the brilliant maneuver which has now resulted in the liberation of Seoul. I am particularly impressed by the splendid cooperation of our Army, Navy and Air Force. The unification of our arms established by you has set a shining example. My thanks and the thanks of the people of all the free nations go out to your gallant forces— soldiers, sailors, marines and air men—from the United States and the other countries fighting for freedom. I salute you, and say from all of us at home, 'Well and nobly done.' "

From the Joint Chiefs of Staff: "The Joint Chiefs of Staff are proud of the great successes you have achieved. We realize that they would have been impossible without brilliant and audacious leadership and without the full coordination and the fighting spirit of all forces and all arms. From the sudden initiation of hostilities you have exploited to the utmost all capabilities and opportunities. Your transition from defensive to offensive operations was magnificently planned, timed and executed. You have given new inspiration to the freedom-loving peoples of the world. We remain completely confident that the great task entrusted to you by the United Nations will be carried to a successful conclusion."

From the British chiefs of staff in London: "We send you our warmest congratulations on your brilliant victory. We have admired not only the skill with which you have conducted an extremely difficult rear guard action against great odds over many anxious weeks, but equally the bravery and tenacity with which the forces under your command have responded to your inspiring and indefatigable leadership. We believe that the brilliant conception and masterly execution of the Inchon counter-stroke which you planned and launched whilst holding the enemy at bay in the south will rank amongst the finest strategic achievements in military history."

From Secretary of Defense Marshall: "Accept my personal tribute to the courageous campaign you directed in Korea and the daring and perfect strategical operation which virtually terminated the struggle."

From former Secretary of Defense Johnson: "Congratulations to you on the magnificent successes achieved to date in the brilliantly conceived and perfectly executed offensive you have just launched. The hope of achieving a lasting peace has been materially advanced."

From Secretary of the Army Pace: "While the record of our Army throughout our national history is one of unfailing response to true leadership regardless of odds and obstacles, I doubt that the response of our forces in the crucible of Korea to your inspired, courageous leadership has ever been surpassed. May God grant to you the full fruits of victory which unfailing courage and determination so richly merit."

From Prime Minister Yoshida of Japan: "The bold stroke in your strategy has changed overnight the whole picture of the Korean situation. To you, the indomitable and inspiring Commander-in-Chief, the world owes an infinite debt of gratitude."

From General Eisenhower, then President of Columbia University: "I can not stay the impulse to express the conviction that you have again given us a brilliant example of professional leadership. Your fortitude in patiently gathering up the necessary reserves to make a significant counterstroke at a time when everyone of those soldiers must have been desperately wanted on the front

Even as these messages of extraordinary praise came pouring in, I began to have misgivings as to the concepts by higher authority regarding the future of Korea. The golden moment to transmute our victory at Inchon into a political peace had arrived. Yet, it appeared that diplomatic inertia had set in, and we were failing to grasp the possibilities of ending the war and moving towards a decisive peace in the Pacific. The rule of the day was timidity and appeasement, which would not end the war, but increase the military efforts against us. I discussed my fears with General Walker, who agreed completely.

When, after Inchon, no diplomatic action looking toward peace seemed to be forthcoming, diverse views began to appear among the members of the United Nations. The United States took the position that if the North Korean Army was not completely destroyed, and peace and order restored in the northern half of the peninsula, South Korea would live indefinitely beneath the threat of renewed Communist aggression. Many others, led by the British, were opposed to sending United Nations Forces into North Korea. Their argument seemed to be that more could be accomplished in Asia by appeasement than by moral resolution. They seemed to believe that the leaders of Communism would temporize too, that they would upset the

---

lines, and your boldness in striking deep into the enemy's vitals with your counter-offensive were particularly shining examples of the kind of thing I mean."

I replied: "The way in Korea has been hard and bitter and we are still not out of the woods. I have never known more savage fighting nor a more determined, tenacious and able enemy. Whatever he may lack in spirituality and ideology, he is a first class fighting man.

"I often think of you at Columbia University and especially in connection with my own experience with the faculty at West Point. University professors sometimes present problems that are puzzling to soldiers."

From former Secretary of State Byrnes, now governor of South Carolina: "I am sure that all Americans would like to have the opportunity to show their appreciation of your magnificent services. Those of us who know some of the difficulties under which you have labored, have increased admiration for you as a soldier and as a statesman."

From Admiral Halsey: "Characteristic and magnificent. The Inchon landing is the most masterly and audacious strategic stroke in all history."

From General Spaatz: "My highest admiration, as an old-time soldier myself, of the way our inadequate military forces have been applied in an impossible situation and achieved victory. One of the most, if not the most, significant military operations in history—the change from what appeared to us in the United States a helpless situation into victory. We all pay tribute to the greatest general of all times."

From Senator John Foster Dulles: "Congratulations—you have done it again."

By Winston Churchill: "I never was apprehensive of a Dunkirk in Korea. In trading space for time and in the counter-attack MacArthur did a perfect job."

By Douglas Southall Freeman: "It has been a great campaign and a great credit to American arms under the leadership of the Old Master himself."

grand Communist design of eventual world domination, and follow a policy of expediency rather than long-range planning. A world-wide public debate erupted whether or not United Nations troops should cross the 38th Parallel to mop up the shattered remnants of the armed forces of North Korea. If not, would North Korea, behind the sanctuary of the 38th Parallel, be permitted to organize, train, and equip another army ready for battle?

The Joint Chiefs of Staff settled the question. Late in September, they sent me what they called "amplifying instructions as to further military action to be taken by you in Korea." These instructions stated unequivocally:

> Your military objective is the destruction of the North Korean armed forces. In attaining this objective, you are authorized to conduct military operations north of the 38th parallel in Korea. Under no circumstances, however, will your forces, ground, air or sea, cross the Manchurian or USSR borders of Korea and, as a matter of policy, no non-Korean ground forces will be used in the North East provinces bordering the Soviet Union, or in the areas along the Manchurian border. Furthermore, support of your operations, north or south of the 38th parallel, will not include air or naval action against Manchuria or against U.S.S.R. territory. When organized armed resistance by the North Korean Forces has been brought substantially to an end, you should direct the R.O.K. forces to take the lead in disarming remaining North Korean units and enforcing the terms of surrender. Circumstances obtaining at the time will determine the character of occupation of North Korea. Your plans for such an occupation will be forwarded for approval to the Joint Chiefs of Staff.

I replied:

> Briefly, my plan is: (a) Eighth Army as now constituted will attack across the 38th parallel with its main effort on the Pyongyang axis with the objective of seizing Pyongyang; (b) X Corps as now constituted will effect amphibious landing at Wonsan, making juncture with the Eighth Army; (c) 3rd Infantry Division will remain in Japan in GHQ reserve initially; (d) R.O.K. Army forces only will conduct operation north of the line Chungjo-Yongwon-Hungnan; (e) tentative date for the attack of the Eighth Army will not be earlier than 15 October and not later than 30 October.

On September 30th, the Joint Chiefs of Staff officially approved the plan. And six days later, their approval was confirmed by a resolution of the United Nations General Assembly. Later statements which flooded the newsstands of the world that the purpose of the United Nations was merely to drive the enemy across the 38th parallel and that I had gone beyond my authority in crossing the 38th parallel were pure fiction.

This decision presented me with problems of the gravest import. It immediately raised the shadow of Red Chinese intervention. Actually, the possibility of such an intervention had existed ever since the order from Washington, issued to the Seventh Fleet in June, to neutralize Formosa, which in effect protected the Red China mainland from attack by Chiang Kai-shek's force of half a million men. This released the two great Red Chinese armies assigned to the coastal defense of central China and made them available for transfer elsewhere. They were reported to be moving north toward Manchuria. It was undoubtedly this concept of sanctuary which tipped the scales in Red China's future decisions. Red China would represent for me new conditions and a totally new war. The United Nations chose to ignore this uncomfortable problem. No means were ever furnished or even considered to meet it, although the sinister implications were perfectly understood by all governments concerned. Unquestionably the failure, through inertia, of our diplomacy to utilize the victory of Inchon as the basis for swift and dynamic action to restore peace and unity to Korea was one of the greatest contributing causes to the subsequent war initiated by Red China.

On October 1st, in the hope of terminating the struggle, I called upon the commander-in-chief of the North Korean forces to cease hostilities "in order that the decisions of the United Nations may be carried out without further loss of life and destruction of property." I stipulated that "North Korean forces, including prisoners of war in the hands of the United Nations Command, will continue to be given the care dictated by civilized custom and practice and permitted to return to their homes." I received no response.

The Eighth Army then pressed rapidly forward toward Pyongyang, while the X Corps landed at Wonsan. The supply situation at Seoul was insufficient to maintain both the Eighth Army and the X Corps, and it was essential to establish a new port of supply entrance on the east coast. Due to tide difficulties at Inchon, where only 5,000 tons a day could be landed, and the destruction of the railroad from Pusan to Seoul during the campaign, limiting overland transportation to a minimum, Wonsan was selected as the new supply base. Tactically, it could bring flank pressure if necessary, for the capture of Pyongyang. It was essential also to secure the eastern corridor of the peninsula.

The so-called "waistline" between the east and west coasts of Korea is cut by a spinal mountain range which renders lateral communication extremely difficult between the two coastal areas, and the movement of supplies across the peninsula completely unpredictable. It was essential to secure both areas thus separated by the mountainous divide, as otherwise the entire eastern sector of the peninsula would have been left unguarded against an enemy flanking movement to the southeast, and the entire northeastern section of the peninsula would have been left open for maneuver against the Eighth Army's right. The terrain was such that there was little prospect that an enemy might drive an effective wedge between the two forces and initiate flanking operations against either or both, and no such attempt was ever made. Both the Eighth Army and the X Corps were under direct control and central co-ordination of general headquarters until they were to meet in the north, when the united command would pass to General Walker. Until these two forces could unite, it would have been impossible for Walker in the west area to attempt command responsibility and co-ordination of the east coastal area. The logistical maintenance of an entirely separate and different supply line from Japan to the east coast would have been beyond him.

On October 9th, I addressed the head of the North Korean government, inviting attention to a resolution by the United Nations General Assembly, passed the day before, "to ensure conditions of stability throughout Korea" and to take "all constituent acts, including the holding of elections, under the auspices of the United Nations for the establishment of a unified, independent and democratic government in the sovereign state of Korea."

I called "upon all North Koreans to cooperate fully with the United Nations, assured that they would be treated justly and that the United Nations would act to relieve and rehabilitate all parts of a unified Korea." My summons was ignored.

On October 12th, I received two messages, one from Averell Harriman, the other from Secretary of Defense Marshall. Harriman's read: "I am looking forward keenly to seeing you shortly and to expressing to you personally my profound admiration for your magnificent campaign. Warm regards."

The other stated that President Truman would like to have a conference with me. The President suggested Honolulu on the 15th, but "if the situation in Korea is such that you feel you should not absent yourself for the time involved in such a long trip, I am sure the President would be glad to go on and meet you at Wake Island."

I replied: "I would be delighted to meet the President on the morning of the 15th at Wake Island."

I knew nothing of the purpose of the meeting, my only information being that Averell Harriman would be there. A number of American correspondents in Tokyo requested permission to accompany me. In view of the number of Washington correspondents announced as coming, I assumed that the

Tokyo representatives would be permitted to attend also, especially as my plane could accommodate a large representation. I passed their requests along to the Pentagon, recommending approval, and was surprised when the request was promptly and curtly disapproved.

The President's party arrived in three planes with thirty-five reporters and photographers. As I shook hands with Mr. Truman, he remarked, "I've been a long time meeting you, General."

I replied, "I hope it won't be so long next time." But there was never to be a next time.

I had been warned about Mr. Truman's quick and violent temper and prejudices, but he radiated nothing but courtesy and good humor during our meeting. He has an engaging personality, a quick and witty tongue, and I liked him from the start. At the conference itself, he seemed to take great pride in his historical knowledge, but, it seemed to me that in spite of his having read much, it was of a superficial character, encompassing facts without the logic and reasoning dictating those facts. Of the Far East he knew little, presenting a strange combination of distorted history and vague hopes that somehow, some way, we could do something to help those struggling against Communism.

His advisers were numerous and distinguished: Admiral Arthur Radford, commander of the Pacific Fleet; Army Secretary Frank Pace; Press Secretary Charles Ross; U.N. Ambassador Philip Jessup; Joint Chiefs Chairman Omar Bradley; State Department Far Eastern Chief Dean Rusk; Special Adviser Averell Harriman; and Legal Adviser Charles Murphy. There were numerous other Truman aides and aides' aides. I had with me my military secretary, my aide-de-camp, and my pilot. Press Secretary Ross announced that no record was to be made of the talks.

Wake Island's heat caused the President to remove his coat. I pulled out a new briar pipe and inquired: "Do you mind if I smoke, Mr. President?"

Truman replied, "No. I suppose I've had more smoke blown in my face than any other man alive." He seemed to enjoy the laugh that followed.

The conference itself was innocuous enough. The sketchy agenda contained nothing upon which Washington did not already have my fullest views as they affected my responsibilities either as supreme commander for the Allied powers in Japan or as commander-in-chief for the United Nations in Korea. They dealt with such matters as the administration of Korea when united, its rehabilitation, the treatment of prisoners of war, the economic situation in the Philippines, the security of Indo-China, the progress of a treaty of peace with Japan, routine details of supply logistics for Japan and

Korea—nothing on which my views were not known. No new policies, no new strategy of war or international politics, were proposed or discussed. Formosa was not on the agenda.

Near the end of the conference, the possibility of Chinese intervention was brought up almost casually. It was the general consensus of all present that Red China had no intention of intervening. This opinion had previously been advanced by the Central Intelligence Agency and the State Department. General Bradley went so far as to bring up the question of transferring troops in the Far East to Europe, and said he would like to have two divisions from Korea home by Christmas for this purpose.

My views were asked as to the chance of Red China's intervention. I replied that the answer could only be speculative; that neither the State Department through its diplomatic listening posts abroad, nor the Central Intelligence Agency to whom a field commander must look for guidance as to a foreign nation's intention to move from peace to war, reported any evidence of intent by the Peiping government to intervene with major forces; that my own local intelligence, which I regarded as unsurpassed anywhere, reported heavy concentrations near the Yalu border in Manchuria whose movements were indeterminate; that my own military estimate was that with our largely unopposed air forces, with their potential capable of destroying, at will, bases of attack and lines of supply north as well as south of the Yalu, no Chinese military commander would hazard the commitment of large forces upon the devastated Korean peninsula. The risk of their utter destruction through lack of supply would be too great. There was no disagreement from anyone. This episode was later completely misrepresented to the public through an alleged but spurious report in an effort to pervert the position taken by me. It was an ingeniously fostered implication that I flatly and unequivocally predicted that under no circumstances would the Chinese Communists enter the Korean War. This is prevarication.

The entire conference lasted only an hour and thirty-six minutes, and I then drove with the President to the airfield to see him off. The discussion of Far Eastern problems was at an end. Instead, he turned the conversation to American politics. Rather impertinently, I asked him if he intended to run for re-election. The Emperor had asked me about this in a recent visit in Tokyo. The President, long accustomed to dodging this question in press conferences, immediately countered by asking me if I had any political ambitions along such lines. I had no need to duck the question, and I replied: "None whatsoever. If you have any general running against you, his name will be Eisenhower, not MacArthur."

The President chuckled. He expressed friendship for Eisenhower personally, but he said: "Eisenhower doesn't know the first thing about politics. Why, if he should become President, his Administration would make Grant's look like a model of perfection." The President seemed ready to continue at length in this vein, but I swerved the conversation into less dangerous channels.

At the airstrip, Truman surprised me by stepping up to the microphones that had been set up by the newsreel photographers, and reading to the assemblage that had gathered, a citation awarding me, by the President of the United States, the Distinguished Service Medal—the fifth time I had received this decoration.*

The conference at Wake Island made me realize that a curious, and sinister, change was taking place in Washington. The defiant, rallying figure that had been Franklin Roosevelt was gone. Instead, there was a tendency toward temporizing rather than fighting it through. The original courageous decision of Harry Truman to boldly meet and defeat Communism in Asia was apparently being chipped away by the constant pounding whispers of timidity and cynicism. The President seemed to be swayed by the blandishments of some of the more selfish politicians of the United Nations. He seemed to be in the anomalous position of openly expressing fears of over-calculated risks that he had fearlessly taken only a few months before.

This put me as field commander in an especially difficult situation. Up to now I had been engaged in warfare as it had been conducted through the ages—to fight to win. But I could see now that the Korean War was developing into something quite different. There seemed to be a deliberate underestimating of the importance of the conflict to which the government had committed—and was expending—the lives of United States fighting men.

What had been the purpose of the conference was difficult to diagnose. Many regarded it as largely a political gimmick. The Congressional elections were but two weeks away, and in this way the President could identify his party with the favorable results of the Inchon victory. Such reasoning, I am

* "... for distinguished service to the peoples of the United States and the Republic of Korea, and to the peoples of all free nations. Having been designated as the first field commander of the United Nations armed forces, and directed in the common interest, to repel an armed attack upon the Republic of Korea and to restore international peace and security in the area, he has given these forces conspicuously brilliant and courageous leadership and discerning judgment of the highest order. Having been compelled to commit his troops to combat under extremely adverse conditions and against heavy odds in order to obtain the time so imperatively needed for the buildup of his forces for the counter-offensive, he has so inspired his command by his vision, his judgment, his indomitable will and his unshakeable faith, that it has set a shining example of gallantry and tenacity in defense and of audacity in attack matched by but few operations in military history. His conduct is deserving of the enduring gratitude of the freedom-loving peoples of the world."

sure, does Mr. Truman an injustice. I believe nothing of the sort animated him, and that the sole purpose was to create good will and beneficial results to the country. My opinion along this line was strengthened by the letter he wrote me in longhand on his return to Washington. It read:

The meeting at Wake Island was a most satisfying one to me. I was pleased with the chance to meet and talk to you about Japan, Korea, and other Far Eastern countries. I was happy to have your views on all the Asiatic situations with which we are faced.

Our meeting has had a splendid reaction here in the United States, and I think it was well worthwhile if for no other reason than that we became personally acquainted.

Sincerely

I replied in part:

I left the Wake Island conference with a distinct sense of satisfaction that the country's interests had been well served through the better mutual understanding and exchange of views which it afforded. I hope that it will result in building a strong defense against future efforts of those who seek for one reason or another, none of them worthy, to breach the understanding between us.

With expressions of deep respect.

But my hope was futile. Propaganda and prejudice reigned supreme.

On October 20th, the Eighth Army hit Pyongyang. The ground troops assaulted from the south and a parachute drop by the 187th Regimental Combat Team 25 miles north of the city completed its envelopment. The move was almost a duplicate of the one that "closed the gap" at Nadzab, in New Guinea. I watched the capture of the city from my plane, which then landed me on its spacious airfield.

Pyongyang was the enemy's capital, and its fall symbolized the complete defeat of North Korea. Practically all organized resistance came to an end, leaving only a type of guerrilla warfare in its place. Aggressive Communism had been decisively defeated at a time and place of its own choosing. The prestige of the United Nations, and especially the United States, was again high in all of Asia.*

---

* President Truman wrote me at once: "The progress the forces under your command have made since we met at Wake continues to be most remarkable, and once again I offer you my hearty congratulations. The military operations in Korea under your command will have a most profound influence for peace in the world."

But at Pyongyang, both General Walker and myself were greatly disturbed by the supply situation which faced the Eighth Army. Supply is the nerve system of any military operation. The rail lines from Pusan, our naval base for overseas deliveries, had been thoroughly worked over by our air force during the months of our perimeter defense. The port of Inchon, the sea harbor of Seoul, was restricted by the same adverse tidal conditions which had aroused such violent opposition to our initial amphibious attack there. The port of Chinnampo, the sea harbor of Pyongyang, had a very limited capacity. The net result of all these adverse logistical factors was materially to slow down the advance northward. We were worried, too, by the growing indication of a startling buildup of Red Chinese troops in Manchuria, just north of the Yalu.

I was even more worried by a series of directives from Washington which were greatly decreasing the potential of my air force. First I was forbidden "hot" pursuit of enemy planes that attacked our own. Manchuria and Siberia were sanctuaries of inviolate protection for all enemy forces and for all enemy purposes, no matter what depredations or assaults might come from there. Then I was denied the right to bomb the hydroelectric plants along the Yalu. The order was broadened to include every plant in North Korea which was capable of furnishing electric power to Manchuria and Siberia. Most incomprehensible of all was the refusal to let me bomb the important supply center at Racin, which was not in Manchuria or Siberia, but many miles from the border, in northeast Korea. Racin was a depot to which the Soviet Union forwarded supplies from Vladivostok for the North Korean Army. I felt that step-by-step my weapons were being taken away from me.

Leading elements of the X Corps reached the Yalu River by November 21st, but General Walker began to experience difficulties. His report to me stated:

The Eighth Army was advancing on a broad front in widely separated columns in pursuit of the defeated North Korean forces. The advance north from Pyongyang was based on a calculated logistical risk involving supply almost entirely by airlift. Available supplies were sufficient only for bare maintenance of combat operations against light opposition, with no possibility of accumulating reserves to meet heavier opposition. An enemy attack against the II South Korean Corps threw it into confusion and halted the advance. There is no intention to take up or remain on the defense. Every effort is being made to retain an adequate bridgehead to facilitate the resumption of the attack as soon as conditions permit. All units continue to execute local attack. Plans have been prepared for resumption of the offensive to meet the new factor of organized Chinese Communist forces. These plans will be put into execution at the earliest possible moment.

The most disquieting feature of the situation was the indication that an estimated three fresh divisions, apparently consisting of Red Chinese troops, had joined the battle. The obvious questions began to assume significance. Was this a Red Chinese reconnaissance in force made across the Yalu as a defensive maneuver to obtain information of Eighth Army intentions? Was it the commitment of fresh North Korean units organized, trained, and equipped in Manchuria with a sprinkling of Chinese "volunteers"? Was it merely Red bluff? Or did it represent the jabs of a full-scale Red Chinese offensive?

The Red Chinese government had a ready explanation for the situation, which it announced to the world—the Chinese in North Korea were merely individual volunteers who had gone to the assistance of their Korean comrades. I brushed aside this subterfuge and reported to Washington: "Recent captures of soldiers of Chinese nationality and information obtained from their interrogations, together with increased resistance being encountered by United Nations forces, remove the problem of Chinese intervention from the realm of the academic, and turns it into a serious immediate threat." I felt that I could not ignore the assumption that Red China had determined upon a commitment of some kind, and at the same time I certainly could not yet assume from the evidence at hand that the decision had been made in Peiping for all-out war in Korea. The logical source for information on any such policy decisions made in Peiping was, of course, Washington, and not the front line in Korea. But neither through the State Department, the Defense Department, the Central Intelligence Agency, nor even the United Nations neutrals, who usually professed authoritative knowledge of the goings-on inside China, was there any reliable or useful knowledge on the subject. I was left in a No-Man's Land of indecision.

On November 3rd, I furnished Washington a Communist battle order, listing in complete numerical detail strength and locations in Manchuria of fifty-six regular army divisions, in sixteen corps—a total of 498,000 men. In addition, there were district service forces of 370,000, or an aggregate of 868,000 in all. Meanwhile, other forces were still converging northward from central China. This intelligence was furnished not only to Washington, but to the United Nations, either of whom could have stopped our troops at any point in North Korea if they had taken the mounting Chinese threat seriously. But the order I received was:

In the event of the open or covert employment anywhere in Korea of major Chinese Communist units, without prior announcement, you should continue the action as long as, in your judgment, action by forces now under your control offers a reasonable chance of success. In any case, prior to taking any military action against objectives in Chinese territory, you will obtain authorization from Washington.

I tried to arouse higher authority to the emergency by attempting to explain to Washington

the aggressive belligerency of the Chinese—their activities in Korea have been offensive, never defensive. In order to understand their motivating influences, one must examine the changes in Chinese character and culture. Up until fifty years ago, China was decompartmented into groups divided against each other. Their war-making tendency was almost non-existent. Not until the turn of the century did China's nationalist urge begin. This was further developed under the leadership of Chiang Kai-shek, but has been brought to its greatest fruition under the present regime, to the point that it has now taken on the character of a united nationalism of increasingly dominant aggressive tendencies.

Through these past fifty years the Chinese people have thus become militarized in their concepts and in their ideals. They now make first class soldiers and are developing competent commanders and staffs. This has produced a new and dominant power in Asia, which for its own purposes has allied with Soviet Russia, but which in its own concepts and methods has become aggressively imperialistic, with a lust for expansion and increased power normal to this type of imperialism.

There is little of the ideological either one way or the other in the Chinese makeup. The standard of living is so low, and the capital accumulation has been so thoroughly dissipated by war, that the masses are desperate and avid to follow any leadership which seems to promise alleviation of local stringencies. I have from the beginning believed that the Chinese Communists' support of the North Koreans was the dominant one. Their interests at present are parallel to those of the Soviet, but I believe that the aggressiveness now displayed, not only in Korea but in Indo-China, and Tibet pointing toward the south, reflects predominantly the same lust for the expansion of power which has animated every would-be conqueror since the beginning of time.

Quezon once said to me in the darkest days of Bataan, "I have no fear that we will not ultimately defeat the Japanese, nor do I feel any dread of ultimate conquest by them. My great fear is the Chinese. With their increasing militarism and aggressive tendency, they are the great Asiatic menace. They have no real ideologies, and when they reach the fructification of their military potential, I dread to think what may happen."

At this time such confusion existed in the public mind, due to biased and misleading news accounts, that I felt a clear explanation of the situation at hand was needed in order that both the American people and the peoples of the other United Nations, whose troops were fighting under my command, would understand what confronted their soldiers, sailors, marines, and air-men. I therefore issued a special communique on November 6th.

The Korean War was brought to a practical end with the closing of the trap on enemy elements north of Pyongyang and seizure of the east coastal area, re-sulting in raising the number of enemy prisoners-of-war in our hands to well over 135,000 which, with other losses mounting to over 200,000, brought enemy cas-ualties to above 335,000, representing a fair estimate of North Korean total mili-tary strength. The defeat of the North Koreans and destruction of their armies was thereby decisive. In the face of this victory for United Nations arms, the Communists, without any notice of belligerency, moved elements of Chinese Communist forces across the Yalu River into North Korea and massed a great concentration of possible reinforcing divisions, with adequate supply behind the privileged sanctuary of the adjacent Manchurian border. The present situation therefore is this: While the North Korean forces with which we were initially engaged have been destroyed or rendered impotent for military action, a new and fresh army faces us, backed up by a possibility of large reserves and adequate sup-plies within easy reach of the enemy but beyond the limits of our present sphere of military action. Whether, and to what extent these reserves will be moved forward remains to be seen and is a matter of gravest international significance. Our pres-ent mission is limited to the destruction of those forces now arrayed against us in North Korea with a view to achieving the United Nations' objective to bring unity and peace to the Korean nation and people.

Despite the welter of restrictions placed upon me by Washington, I felt there remained one weapon I could use against massive Chinese intervention. I ordered General Stratemeyer to employ ninety B-29's on the following morning to destroy the Yalu bridges and cut this easy line of communication between Manchuria and North Korea, over which large armies of Chinese Reds could swarm. Up to now I had avoided doing so because of the danger of accidentally missing the targets and dropping bombs in Manchuria, which had been forbidden.

An immediate dispatch came from Secretary Marshall countermanding my order and directing me "to postpone all bombing of targets within five miles of the Manchurian border." It seemed to me incredible that protection should be extended to the enemy, not only of the bridges which were the only means they had for moving their men and supplies across that wide natural river barrier into North Korea, but also for a 5-mile-deep area on this side of the Yalu in which to establish a bridgehead. It would be impossible to exaggerate my astonishment, and I at once protested.

I called attention to my previous warnings that there was a substantial movement across the bridges.

The only way to stop this reinforcement of the enemy is the destruction of the bridges by air attack and air destruction of installations in North Korea which would facilitate the movement. I feel that the operation is within the scope of the rules of war and the resolutions and directives which I have received. And I can accept the instructions rescinding my orders only under the greatest protest, as I feel that they might well result in a calamity of gravest proportions, for which I could not accept the responsibility. Urgently request reconsideration of your decision, or that the matter be brought to the attention of the President for his review.

All that resulted was a modification of the order to permit the bombing of the "Korean end of the Yalu bridges."

I asked Stratemeyer to study the conditions under which the bombing of the Yalu bridges was to be permitted. He reported: "It cannot be done—Washington must have known it cannot be done."

The head of the Far East Bomber Command, Major General Emmett (Rosey) O'Donnell, made the following estimate of the situation:

We were not allowed to violate Manchurian territory, and by violation of the territory I mean we were not allowed to fly over an inch of it. For instance, like most rivers, the Yalu has several pronounced bends before getting to the town of Antung, and the main bridges at Antung we had to attack in only one manner —in order not to violate Manchurian territory, and that was a course tangential to the southernmost bend of the river. As you draw a line from the southernmost bend of the river to the bridge, that is your course. These people on the other side of the river knew that and put up their batteries right along the line, and they peppered us right down the line all the way. We had to take it, of course, and couldn't fight back. In addition to that, they had their fighters come up alongside and join our formation about two miles to the lee and fly along at the same speed on the other side of the river while we were making our approach. And just before we got to bomb-away position, they would veer off to the north and climb up to about 30,000 feet and then make a frontal quarter attack on the bombers just about at the time of bomb-away in a turn. So they would be coming from Manchuria in a turn, swoop down, fire their cannons at the formation, and continue to turn back to sanctuary.

One of those bomber pilots, wounded unto death, the stump of an arm dangling by his side, gasped at me through the bubbles of blood he spat out, "General, which side are Washington and the United Nations on?" It seared my very soul.

I at once asked for immediate relief from assignment to duty in the Far East. In my bitterness I told my able chief of staff, General Doyle Hickey:

For the first time in military history, a commander has been denied the use of his military power to safeguard the lives of his soldiers and safety of his army. To me it clearly foreshadows a future tragic situation in the Far East and leaves me with a sense of inexpressible shock. It will cost the lives of thousands of American soldiers and place in jeopardy the entire army. By some means the enemy commander must have known of this decision to protect his lines of communication into North Korea, or he never would have dared to cross those bridges in force.

Hickey protested that the army would not understand my leaving at such a critical moment, and might become demoralized and destroyed; that it was my duty to the country and to my own honor not to go at such a crisis. I tore up my dispatch. It is interesting to know that several years later General Eisenhower was reported in the press to have said that had he been in my place and received such an order, he would have ignored it. That would have at least assured his immediate relief from command.

On the day following this extraordinary directive, and my protest, Secretary Marshall sent me a message conciliatory in tone which stated that my concern over the alarming developments was shared by the authorities in Washington. Truman was vacationing at this time in his home in Missouri. Marshall said:

The discussions and decisions here are heavily weighted with the extremely delicate situation we have before the Security Council of the United Nations, whose meeting tomorrow may have fateful consequences. We all realize your difficulty in fighting a desperate battle in a mountainous region under winter conditions and with a multinational force in all degrees of preparedness. I also understand, I think, the difficulty involved in conducting such a battle under necessarily limited conditions and the necessity of keeping the distant headquarters, in Washington, informed of developments and decisions. However, this appears to be unavoidable. We are faced with an extremely grave international problem.

I could not have agreed more that the situation in Korea was fraught with disaster. The danger was that by meeting naked force with appeasement we would not only perpetrate military disaster in Korea, but would enable Communism to make its bid for most of Asia. This was a far larger, more complex, long-range problem than Washington seemed to comprehend.

At about this time, the British Labour government suggested a strange solution to the problem of combating Red Chinese intervention—give the Communists a slice of North Korea to serve as a "buffer" area and as evidence of the United Nations' good intentions.

In protesting the short-sightedness of the British proposal, I compared it with the ceding of the Sudetenland to Germany in 1938. Besides violating the spirit of the United Nations decision of June 25th, this so-called "buffer" zone would be a signal to further aggression on the part of the Chinese, and perhaps most important, would bankrupt our political, military, and psychological position in the Far East.

There were but three possible courses. I could go forward, remain immobile, or withdraw. If I went forward, there was the chance that China might not intervene in force and the war would be over. If I remained immobile and waited, it would be necessary to select a defense line and dig in. But there was no terrain with natural obstacles to take advantage of, and with my scant forces it would be impossible to establish a defense in depth against the overwhelming numbers of Chinese. They had enough divisions to surround the army if it remained stationary, and every day they would increase their force by fresh divisions from Manchuria. This would mean the ultimate annihilation of our entire command. I estimated our forces would have to be at least tripled to cope with such a situation, but no promise of reinforcements by Washington was forthcoming. If the Chinese intended to intervene, this is exactly what they would want me to do. If I withdrew, it would be in contradiction to my orders and would destroy any opportunity to bring the Korean War to a successful end.

If I went forward and found the Chinese in force, my strategy would be to immediately break contact and withdraw rapidly, so as to lengthen and expose the enemy's supply lines. This would result in a pyramiding of logistical difficulties for the Reds and an almost astronomical increase in the destructiveness of our air power. Every step forward, his strength would decrease as compared with mine, until a degree of parity would be reached between the opposing forces. I would then rely upon maneuver, with my objective his supply lines. I would withdraw the X Corps to Pusan by sea when it had completed its covering of the right flank of the Eighth Army, build up my communications northward, and estimate the new situation that would develop.

I reviewed my orders from Washington: "In the event of the open or covert employment anywhere in Korea of major Chinese Communist units, without prior announcement, you should continue the action as long as, in your judgment, action by forces now under your control offers a reasonable chance of success." I concluded that the best "posture of security" was to go forward. This would deny the enemy the selection of the time and place of his attack, and the accumulation of additional forces from Manchuria. It would be simultaneously a mopping-up of the defeated North Korean forces, and a reconnaissance in force to probe the intentions of the Chinese. If our forward movement should prematurely expose Chinese involvement, my troops would have the necessary freedom of action to escape its jaws. In anticipation of such a situation, I directed Walker to prepare complete operational plans for disengagement and withdrawal from action in the event it developed that Red China was entering the Korean War in determined force. The field commander and staffs all agreed with my basic plan. It was submitted by me to, and approved by, the Joint Chiefs of Staff in Washington.

Meanwhile, behind the curtain of fright and frustration thrown up along the Yalu by Washington, the Chinese Communists, over a period of twenty days, were stealthily surging over the Yalu bridges into position for an attack. Under cover of darkness, and the deadly pattern of anti-aircraft defense permitted by the United Nations restrictions, they poured more than 200,000 fresh troops into North Korea between November 6th and November 26th. The order not to bomb the Yalu bridges was the most indefensible and ill-conceived decision ever forced on a field commander in our nation's history.

On November 24th, I flew to Eighth Army headquarters on the Chongchon River. Walker's advance had been originally set for November 15th, but supplies had not yet caught up, and the date had been postponed. The supply system was still unsatisfactory, but both Walker and myself felt we could wait no longer. Every day allowed more thousands to cross the Yalu bridges, and every day brought closer the winter weather, which would freeze the Yalu and let thousands more across. It was essential to move before Chinese superiority in numbers became overwhelming.

For five hours I toured our front lines. In talking to a group of officers, I told them of General Bradley's desire and hope to have two divisions home by Christmas provided there was not intervention by Red China. This remark was twisted by the press into a prediction of the success of our movement, and this false misinterpretation was later used as a powerful propaganda weapon with which to bludgeon me.

What I had seen at the front worried me greatly. The R.O.K. troops were not yet in good shape, and the entire line was deplorably weak in numbers. If the Chinese were actually in heavy force, I decided I would withdraw our troops at once and abandon any further attempt to move north. I decided to reconnoiter and try to see with my own eyes, and interpret with my own long experience what was going on behind the enemy's lines. I boarded my plane and instructed the pilot, Major Tony Storey, to head for the mouth of the Yalu River. The plane was unarmed and would be an easy target for anti-aircraft fire or air interception, but I hoped that the very audacity of the flight would be its own protection.

When we reached the mouth of the Yalu, I told Story to turn east and follow the river at an altitude of 5,000 feet. At this height we could observe in detail the entire area of international No-Man's Land all the way to the Siberian border. All that spread before our eyes was an endless expanse of utterly barren countryside, jagged hills, yawning crevices, and the black waters of the Yalu locked in the silent death grip of snow and ice. It was a merciless wasteland. If a large force or massive supply train had passed over the border, the imprints had already been well-covered by the intermittent snowstorms of the Yalu Valley. I decided to have Walker await withdrawing until actual combat might indicate its necessity.

To my astonishment, I was awarded the Distinguished Flying Cross, and later the honorary wings of a combat pilot. The Air Force's partiality toward me is one of my most grateful memories.

On my return from the Eighth Army to headquarters, I found a message from the Joint Chiefs of Staff waiting for me. It said:

There is a growing concern within the United Nations over the possibility of bringing on a general conflict should a major clash develop with Chinese Communist forces as a result of your forces advancing squarely against the entire boundary between Korea and Manchuria. Proposals in United Nations may suggest unwelcome restrictions on your advance to the north. The consensus of political and military opinion at a meeting held Thursday with the Secretaries of State and Defense, the Joint Chiefs of Staff and other officials, was that there should be no change in your mission, but that immediate action should be taken at top governmental level to formulate a course of action which will permit the establishment of a unified Korea and at the same time reduce risk of more general involvement.

Then came a suggestion that after advancing to a position near the Yalu, I should secure the position using R.O.K. forces to "hold the terrain dominating the approaches from the Valley of the Yalu." The limit of my advance in the northeast would be fixed at Chongjin. It went on to say: "Exploratory discussions were had to discover what military measures might lend themselves to political action which would reduce the tension with Peiping and the Soviet Union." I informed Washington that, in my opinion, we would never alter Chinese plans by being timid.

On November 27th, the Red commander, General Lin Piao, launched his full forces across the Yalu and into battle. Red China thus entered into open war against United States forces and those allied with us. Two Chinese Army Groups, the Fourth, operating against Walker, the Third, against Almond, attacked with overwhelming force.

The blow by the Fourth Army Group was on the South Korean II Corps, which broke, exposing the flank of the American Eighth Army troops. Walker immediately directed a rapid withdrawal, as had been planned. The 2nd Division and the Turkish contingent conducted notable rearguard actions which enabled the Eighth Army to break contact and avoid any enemy flanking movement.

The X Corps faced even greater odds than the Eighth Army. Almond, in accordance with instructions, withdrew toward Wonsan at once. The 1st Marine Division had been almost completely enveloped and had to fight its way back under its valiant commander, General Oliver Smith.

The withdrawal of both our forces was made with great skill. I regarded the professional part of the whole operation with the greatest satisfaction. I felt that the hard decisions I had been forced to make, and the skill displayed by my field commanders had saved the army. The movement north had upset the enemy's timetable, causing him to move prematurely, and to reveal the surreptitious massing of his armies. He had hoped to quietly assemble a massive force till spring, and destroy us with one mighty blow. Had I not acted when I did, we would have been a "sitting duck" doomed to eventual annihilation.

Our losses in the entire Yalu operations were comparatively light. In the Eighth Army, the number of troops killed, wounded, and missing amounted to 7,337, and in the X Corps to 5,638. This was about half the loss at Iwo Jima, less than one-fifth of that at Okinawa, and even less in comparison with the Battle of the Bulge.

That there was some leak in intelligence was evident to everyone. Walker continually complained to me that his operations were known to the enemy in advance through sources in Washington. I will always believe that if the United States had issued a warning to the effect that any entry of the Chinese Communists in force into Korea would be considered an act of international war against the United States, that the Korean War would have terminated with our advance north. I feel that the Reds would have stayed on their side of the Yalu. Instead, information must have been relayed to them, assuring that the Yalu bridges would continue to enjoy sanctuary and that their bases would be left intact. They knew they could swarm down across the Yalu River without having to worry about bombers hitting their Manchurian supply lines.

An official leaflet by General Lin Piao published in China read:

> I would never have made the attack and risked my men and military reputation if I had not been assured that Washington would restrain General MacArthur from taking adequate retaliatory measures against my lines of supply and communication.

I reported to the Joint Chiefs of Staff, advising that the Chinese military forces were committed in North Korea in great and ever-increasing strength. Interrogation of prisoners of war and other intelligence information established that exclusive of North Korean elements, the thirty-eighth, thirty-ninth, fortieth, forty-second, sixty-sixth, fiftieth, and twentieth Chinese Communist Field Armies were now in action. No pretext of minor support under the guise of volunteerism or other subterfuge had the slightest validity. We faced an entirely new war.

It was quite evident that our present strength was not sufficient to meet this undeclared war by the Chinese, especially with the advantages gained through our own timidity. The opportunity of initial onslaught in overwhelming force of undeclared belligerency, which so frequently occurred in the past, is inherent in war itself. It could not be avoided under present conditions of international relationship. The resulting situation presented an entirely new picture which broadened the potentialities to world-embracing considerations beyond the sphere of decision by the theater commander. The issues must find their solution within the councils of the United Nations and chancelleries of the world. This command did everything humanly possible within its capabilities, but was now faced with conditions beyond its control and strength. The limitless capabilities of the entire Chinese nation, with Soviet logistical support, were arrayed against it. My strategic plan for the immediate future was to pass from the offensive to the defensive, with such local adjustments as may be required by a constantly fluid situation. The Joint Chiefs of Staff approved, and a new war thus started in Korea.

On November 29th, I wired Washington urgently recommending that "the theater commander be authorized to negotiate directly with the Chinese government authorities on Formosa for the movement north and incorporation into United Nations command of such Chinese units as may be available and desirable for reinforcing our position in Korea." My recommendation, Washington replied, was under consideration, but a firm answer would be delayed because it involved "world-wide consequences. We shall have to consider the possibility that it would disrupt the united position of the nations associated with us in the United Nations, and leave the United States isolated. It may be wholly unacceptable to the Commonwealth countries to have their forces employed with Nationalist China. Our position of leadership in the Far East is being most seriously compromised in the United Nations. The utmost care will be necessary to avoid the disruption of the essential Allied line-up in that organization."

Long after the event, some sources mistakenly tried to adduce additional reasons as to why Chiang Kai-shek's offer of help was not accepted. Spurious claims were made that the troops were of doubtful value, that not only were they overage and poorly trained, but they were untrustworthy and at the first contact with the Red Chinese would probably defect to the enemy. During my trip to Taiwan, I had an opportunity to observe troops of the Nationalist Army, and I gained the distinct impression that they were well-equipped and well-trained and of the same general quality as the soldiers of Red China. They were certainly trustworthy, free men in the Nationalist Army by choice, and would have been undoubtedly effective in battle. To the best of my knowledge, no one ever questioned this fact at the time.

United Nations member governments refused to consent to the use of the eager, fresh troops offered by Chiang Kai-shek, nor were sizeable reinforcements forthcoming from any other source. In a press conference, President Truman threatened once that he might make atomic weapons available to the United Nations command in this uneven battle, but within forty-eight hours Prime Minister Attlee hurried to Washington, and nothing more was heard of it. Actually, after the entry of China into the war, the American forces were compelled to face odds never before encountered in the military history of the nation. It is impossible to understand on a professional basis how we could have placidly accepted the disadvantages piled on the Eighth Army in Korea.

Early in January, I stabilized the lines of the Eighth Army at a position midway in South Korea. The progressive deterioration of the enemy's supply potential was working with deadly effect. Walker's skillful withdrawal had been accomplished with such speed that it led to many comments by ignorant correspondents that the troops were in flight.* Nothing could have been

* The success of this hazardous maneuver was due to the unsurpassed co-ordination of ground, sea and air forces. I received many messages of congratulations—from President Truman; Secretary of the Army Pace; Army Chief of Staff Collins; Chief of Naval Operations Sherman. Truman said: "It is the best Christmas present I ever had. My personal thanks." Secretary Pace called it a "magnificent achievement." General Collins remarked, "This brilliant achievement of the combined arms is a tribute to sound planning and efficient execution by commanding officers and men of all ranks. The entire Army joins me in admiration." Admiral Sherman praised "this masterful cooperation of all services which has brought a most difficult military operation to a brilliant conclusion."

As Supreme Commander (1946).

Below: Emperor Hirohito is received by General MacArthur at the United States Embassy. Gae Faillace

Right: General MacArthur at the Russian Embassy in Tokyo. Acme

Far right: General MacArthur and Korean President Syngman Rhee at the South Korean government inauguration (1948). General Douglas MacArthur Memorial Foundation

Below right: General MacArthur seated on the bridge of the USS McKinley *on his arrival at Inchon harbor. Standing left to right are: Vice Adm. Arthur D. Struble, Commander of the U.S. Seventh Fleet; Brig. Gen. E. K. Wright, Assistant Chief of Staff G-3 Far East Command; Maj. Gen. Edward M. Almond, Commanding General, 10th Corps.* Department of Defense

Right: Part of the campaign to draft General MacArthur as a Republican nominee for President. International

Below: Cigar in hand, Gen. Douglas MacArthur shakes hands with President Eisenhower as they pose outside the White House after lunch. Among the other guests are, left to right: Sen. Leverett Saltonstall (R., Mass.); Sen. William Knowland (R., Calif.); Gen. Matthew Ridgway, Army Chief of Staff, and Rep. Dewey Short (R., Mo.).

General MacArthur's first visit to Inchon. General Douglas MacArthur Memorial Foundation

Lt. Gen. Walton H. Walker, Commander of the Eighth Army, greets General MacArthur at Pyongyang Airport, Korea, 85 miles south of the Manchurian border. Acme

Observing the landings at Inchon, Korea (1950). General Douglas MacArthur Memorial Foundation

Far upper left: General MacArthur with Lt. Gen. Matthew Ridgway and Ninth Corps Commander Maj. Gen. William Hoge (1951). General Douglas MacArthur Memorial Foundation

Far lower left: President Truman bestows a Distinguished Service Cross on General MacArthur prior to his leaving the Wake Island Conference. General Douglas MacArthur Memorial Foundation

Left: During a visit to the front line in Korea, approximately 15 miles north of the 38th parallel. International

Below: Shortly after being called home by President Truman, General MacArthur leaves Haneda Airport in Tokyo for the last time. International

General MacArthur's triumphant homecoming (San Francisco, 1951). General Douglas
MacArthur Memorial Foundation

left: General MacArthur on his seventy-fifth birthday (1955). International

Lower left: General MacArthur's return to the Philippines (1961). General Douglas MacArthur Memorial Foundation

Upper Right: General MacArthur and President John F. Kennedy at the White House (1961). General Douglas MacArthur Memorial Foundation

Lower right: General MacArthur on the steps of the Capitol for ceremonies honoring him for his services to the country (1962). General Douglas MacArthur Memorial Foundation

Below: General MacArthur on his eighty-fourth birthday at the Waldorf-Astoria Hotel in New York (1964). General Douglas MacArthur Memorial Foundation

General MacArthur's boyhood home in Milwaukee, Wisconsin (1964).

further from the truth. The troops moved in good order and with unbroken cohesion among the various components. They were in excellent spirit and good condition.

As soon as the X Corps had completed its mission of protecting Walker's right flank from envelopment, I directed its withdrawal by sea to Pusan to join the Eighth Army. Almond's three divisions, the 1st Marine, 2nd and 7th Infantry, fought brilliant actions that stopped three Chinese corps in their tracks. The evacuation from Hungnan was a classic. General Almond's report on December 24th read:

The X Corps has completed evacuation by air and sea from Hungnan. 350,000 tons of supplies and equipment have been withdrawn. Nothing has been left to the enemy. 105,000 troops, including South Korean units and approximately 100,000 refugees, have been evacuated to safety in South Korea. Structures of possible military value to the enemy have been destroyed. The enemy paid heavily for his attempt to interfere with our operations. The losses of our forces were comparatively light.

When the X Corps arrived at Pusan, it was in excellent shape, with high morale and conspicuous self-confidence.

I myself felt we had reached up, sprung the Red trap, and escaped it. To have saved so many thousands of lives entrusted to my care gave me a sense of comfort that, in comparison, made all the honors I had ever received pale into insignificance.

The basic policies and decisions which had governed operations against the North Korean Army were still in effect, but the situation had entirely changed. This was a new war against the vast military potential of Red China. What I needed, as much as more men and arms and supplies, was a clear definition of policy to meet this new situation. Washington, however, again seemed uncertain and doubtful as to what course to pursue. I received this message from the Joint Chiefs of Staff:

It appears from all estimates available that the Chinese Communists possess the capability of forcing United Nations forces out of Korea if they choose to exercise it. The execution of this capability might be prevented by making the effort so costly to the enemy that they would abandon it, or by committing substantial additional United States forces to that theatre, thus seriously jeopardizing other commitments including the safety of Japan. It is not practical to obtain significant additional forces for Korea from other members of the United Nations. We believe that Korea is not the place to fight a major war. Further, we believe that we should not commit our remaining available ground forces to action against Chinese Communist forces in Korea in face of the increased threat of general war. However, a successful resistance to Chinese-North Korean aggression at some position in Korea and a deflation of the military and political prestige of the Chinese Communists would be of great importance to our national interest, if they could be accomplished without incurring serious losses.

Your basic directive required modification in the light of the present situation. You are now directed to defend in successive positions, subject to the primary consideration of the continued threat to Japan, and to determine in advance our last reasonable opportunity for an orderly evacuation. It seems to us that if you forced back to position in the vicinity of the Kum River a line generally eastward therefrom, and if thereafter the Chinese Communists mass large forces against your positions with an evident capability of forcing us out of Korea, it then would be necessary under these conditions to direct you to commence a withdrawal to Japan. Your views are requested as to the above outlined conditions which should determine a decision to initiate evacuation, particularly in the light of your continuing primary mission of defense of Japan, for which only troops of the Eighth Army are available.

This message seemed to indicate a loss of the "will to win" in Korea. President Truman's resolute determination to free and unite that threatened land had now deteriorated almost into defeatism. Washington planning was not directed toward methods of counterattack, but rather toward the best way to run; no solution was advanced as to the problem of reinforcement, even with Nationalist Chinese troops, but toward unrealistically expecting the impossible from men who had gone in to fight one war, had won it, and were now trying to fight a much bigger one. What seemed especially fantastic was to expect the Eighth Army, already facing a vastly superior Chinese force, to accept the additional responsibility, in case of Russian intervention, for the defense of Japan. The thought of defeat in Korea had never been entertained by me. It was my belief that, if allowed to use my full military might, without artificial restrictions, I could not only save Korea, but also inflict such a destructive blow upon Red China's capacity to wage aggressive war that it would remove her as a further threat to peace in Asia for generations to come.

Late in the evening of December 30th, I sat down to compose my reply to the Joint Chiefs of Staff's message on the evacuation of Korea.

Any estimate of relative capabilities in the Korean campaign appears to be dependent upon political-military policies yet to be formulated regarding Chinese military operations being conducted against our forces. It is quite clear now that the entire military resources of the Chinese nation, with logistic support from the Soviet, is committed to a maximum effort against the United Nations Command. In implementation of this commitment, a major concentration of Chineses force in the Korean-Manchurian area will increasingly leave China vulnerable to areas from which troops to support Korean operations have been drawn. Meanwhile, under existing restrictions, our naval and air potential are being only partially utilized and the great potential of Chinese Nationalist force on Formosa and guerilla action on the mainland are being ignored. Indeed, as to the former, we are preventing its employment against the common enemy by our own naval force.

Should a policy determination be reached by our government or through it by the United Nations to recognize the state of war which has been forced upon us by the Chinese authorities and to take retaliatory measures within our capabilities, we could: (1) blockade the coast of China; (2) destroy through naval gunfire and air bombardment China's industrial capacity to wage war; (3) secure reinforcements from the Nationalist garrison on Formosa to strengthen our position in Korea if we decided to continue the fight for that peninsula; and (4) release existing restrictions upon the Formosan garrison for diversionary action, possibly leading to counter-invasion against vulnerable areas of the Chinese mainland.

I believe that by the foregoing measures we could severely cripple and largely neutralize China's capability to wage aggressive war and thus save Asia from the engulfment otherwise facing it. I believe furthermore that we could do so with but a small part of our overall military potential committed to the purpose. There is no slightest doubt but that this action would at once release the pressure upon our forces in Korea, whereupon determination could be reached as to whether to maintain the fight in that area or to effect a strategic displacement of our forces with the view to strengthening our defense of the littoral island chain while continuing our naval and air pressure upon China's military potential. I am fully conscious of the fact that this course of action has been rejected in the past for fear of provoking China into a major effort, but we must now realistically recognize that China's commitment thereto has already been fully and unequivocally made and nothing we can do would further aggravate the situation as far as China is concerned.

Whether defending ourselves by way of military retaliation would bring in Soviet military intervention or not is a matter of speculation. I have always felt that a Soviet decision to precipitate a general war would depend solely upon its own estimate of relative strengths and capabilities with little regard to other factors. If we are forced to evacuate Korea without taking military measures against China proper as suggested in your message, it would have the most adverse effect upon the people of Asia, not excepting the Japanese, and a material reinforcement of the forces now in this theatre could be mandatory if we are to hold the littoral defense chain against determined assault. Moreover, it must be borne in mind that evacuation of our forces from Korea under any circumstances would at once release the bulk of the Chinese forces now absorbed by that campaign for action elsewhere—quite probably in areas of far greater importance than Korea itself.

I understand thoroughly the demand for European security and fully concur in doing everything possible in that sector, but not to the point of accepting defeat anywhere else—an acceptance which I am sure could not fail to insure later defeat in Europe itself. The use of force in the present emergency in the Far East could not in any way prejudice this basic concept. To the contrary, it would ensure thoroughly seasoned forces for later commitment in Europe synchronously with Europe's own development of military resources.

So far as your tactical estimate of the situation in Korea is concerned, under the conditions presently implied, namely—no reinforcements, continued restrictions upon Chinese Nationalist action, no military measures against China's military potential, and the concentration of Chinese military force solely upon the Korean sector, would seem to be sound.

I received this answer from the Joint Chiefs of Staff:

The retaliatory measures you suggest have been and continue to be given careful consideration. There is little possibility of policy change or other eventuality justifying strengthening of our effort in Korea. Blockade of China coast, if undertaken, must await either stabilization of our position in Korea or our evacuation from Korea. However, a naval blockade off the coast of China would require negotiations with the British in view of the extent of British trade with China through Hong Kong. Naval and air attacks on objectives in Communist China probably can be authorized only if the Chinese Communists attack United States forces outside of Korea and decision must await that eventuality. Favorable action cannot be taken on the proposal to obtain Korean reinforcements from the Chinese Nationalist garrison on Formosa, in view of the improbability of their decisive effect on the Korean outcome and their pobable greater usefulness elsewhere.

In the light of the foregoing and after full consideration of all pertinent factors, defend in successive positions as required by the Joint Chiefs of Staff's message, inflicting maximum damage to hostile forces in Korea, subject to primary consideration of the safety of your troops and your basic mission of protecting Japan. Should it become evident in your judgment that evacuation is essential to avoid severe losses of men and materiel you will at that time withdraw from Korea to Japan.

I shot a query right back, asking for clarification in view of the self-evident fact that the strength of my command, as presently constituted, was insufficient to hold a position in Korea and simultaneously protect Japan against external assault. I suggested that strategic dispositions must be based upon an overriding political policy establishing the relativity of American interests in the Far East. There was no doubt but that a beachhead line could be held by our existing forces for a limited time, but this could not be accomplished without losses. Whether such losses were to be regarded as "severe" or not would to a certain extent depend upon the connotation one gives the term. After completing a long and difficult campaign, the troops were embittered by the shameful propaganda which had falsely condemned their courage and fighting quality. Their morale threatened to become a serious threat to their battle efficiency unless the political basis on which they were asked to trade life for time was quickly delineated, fully understood, and so impelling that the hazards of battle could be cheerfully accepted.

The issue really boiled down to the question of whether or not the United States intended to evacuate Korea, and involved a decision of highest national and international importance, far above the competence of a field commander guided largely by incidents affecting the tactical situation developing upon a very limited field of action. Nor was it a decision which should be left to the initiative of enemy action, which in effect would be the determining criterion under a reasonable interpretation of the Joint Chiefs' message. My query therefore amounted to this: was it the present objective of the United States political policy to maintain a military position in Korea indefinitely, for a limited time, or to minimize losses by the evacuation as soon as it could be accomplished?

I received no direct answer. A series of messages followed dealing with the details of a possible evacuation. Then on January 14th, I received a personal message from President Truman.

I wish in this telegram to let you have my views as to our basic national and international purposes in continuing the resistance to aggression in Korea. We need your judgment as to the maximum effort which could reasonably be expected from the United Nations forces under your command to support the resistance to aggression which we are trying to rapidly organize on a world-wide basis. This present telegram is not to be taken in any sense as a directive. Its purpose is to give you something of what is in our minds regarding the political factors. A successful resistance in Korea would serve the following important purposes: (a) to demonstrate that aggression will not be accepted by us or by the United Nations and to provide a rallying point around which the spirits and energies of the free world can be mobilized to meet the world-wide threat which the Soviet Union poses; (b) to deflate dangerously exaggerated political and military prestige of Communist China which now threatens to undermine the resistance of non-Communist Asia and to consolidate the hold of Communism on China itself; (c) to afford more time for and to give direct assistance to the organization of non-Communist resistance in Asia both outside and inside China; (d) to carry out our commitments of honor to the South Koreans and to demonstrate to the world that the friendship of the United States is of inestimable value in time of adversity; (e) to make possible a far more satisfactory peace settlement for Japan and to contribute greatly to the post-treaty security position of Japan in relation to the continent; (f) to lend resolution to many countries not only in Asia but also in Europe and the Middle East who are now living within the shadow of Communist power, and to let them know that they need not rush to terms with Communism on whatever terms they can get, meaning complete submission; (g) to inspire those who might be called upon to fight against great odds if subject to a sudden onslaught by the Soviet Union or by Communist China; (h) to lend urgency to the rapid buildup of the defenses of the Western world; (i) to bring the United Nations through its first great effort in collective security and to produce a free world coalition of incalculable value to the national security interests of the United States; (j) to alert the peoples behind the Iron Curtain that their masters are bent upon wars of aggression, and that this crime will be resisted by the free world.

Our course of action at this time should be such as to consolidate the great majority of the United Nations. This majority is not merely part of the organization, but is also the nations whom we would desperately need to count on as allies in the event the Soviet Union moves against us. We recognize, of course, that continued resistance might not be militarily possible with the limited forces with which you are being called upon to meet large Chinese armies. Further, in the present world situation, your forces must be preserved as an effective instrument, for the defense of Japan and elsewhere. However, some of the important purposes mentioned above might be supported, if you should think it practical and advisable, by continued resistance from off-shore islands of Korea, particularly Cheju-Do, if it becomes impracticable to hold an important position in Korea itself. In the worst case it would be important that, if we must withdraw from Korea, it be told to the world that that course was forced upon us by military necessity and that we shall not accept the result politically or militarily until the aggression has been rectified.

The entire nation is grateful for your splendid leadership in the difficult struggle in Korea, and for the superb performance of your forces under the most difficult circumstances.*

I replied at once: "We will do our best." And I told my staff: "That, gentlemen, finally settles the question of whether or not we evacuate Korea. There will be no evacuation."

A mission headed by Ambassador John Foster Dulles came to Tokyo on January 22nd, to work out final details of the peace treaty with Japan. They stayed until February 9th, and, with the complete co-operation of the Japanese, appeared to make firm progress. I worked hand-in-hand with Dulles, continu-

---

* The message from President Truman arrived on my seventy-first birthday. President Truman wired his "hearty greetings and best wishes." Secretary Acheson sent felicitations from the State Department, saying, "We are all sincerely appreciative of your close cooperation and outstanding efforts in defending the cause of freedom." My old friend William Randolph Hearst quite outdid himself in his "happy returns of the day to the greatest General and American of all times." In reply to my classmate and long-time buddy, Colonel Charles Patterson, I wrote: "Thank you so much for your fine birthday letter which has just reached me. It brought back so vividly the life-long affection which has united us. The going in Korea is tough. We had almost cleaned up the North Koreans when suddenly China hurled her entire military might at our relatively small force. With the handicaps and delimitations imposed upon us, we have had a difficult time to maintain the integrity of our troops and some degree of stability in the general situation. Just what is in store I do not know, but the confusion which exists in the political ramifications which have determined military actions have perhaps never been equalled in American history. My best to you, Pat, as always, and if you hear of my last round-up at the end of a rope, from an oriental telephone pole, don't be surprised or shocked."

ally stressing the fact that Japan deserved the treaty and that its realization would restore a defeated people to their place among the nations of the world. The treaty itself would show the people of Asia that the United States was not a conqueror but a friend.

Not too long afterward, a peace treaty was signed in San Francisco amid great pomp and ceremony. I was not invited to attend. Perhaps someone just forgot to remember.

On December 23rd, General Walker was killed in a freak jeep accident. It was a great personal loss to me. It had been "Johnny" Walker who had held the line, with courage and brilliant generalship, at the very bottom of Korea, until we could save him by slicing behind the enemy's lines at Inchon. It had been Walker who, even in the darkest hours, had always radiated cheerful confidence and rugged determination.

It was a difficult time to change field commanders, but I acquired one of the best in General Matthew Ridgway. An experienced leader with aggressive and fighting qualities, he took command of the Eighth Army at its position near the 38th parallel. After inspecting his new command, he felt he could repulse any enemy attempt to dislodge it. On New Year's Day, however, the Reds launched a general offensive in tremendous force, making penetrations of up to 12 miles. It forced the Eighth Army into further withdrawal. By January 4th, the enemy had recaptured Seoul, and by January 7th, the Eighth Army had retired to new positions roughly 70 miles south of the 38th parallel.

The press of Europe and much of that of the United States cried hysterically that the United Nations forces "are going to be pushed into the sea"—a dire prediction that was solemnly repeated on the floor of Congress. But I figured it differently. The strategy of progressive weakness, because of stretched supply lines, was beginning to tell on the enemy, and disease was commencing to ravage his ranks. Typhoid fever and other widespread epidemics, which the Chinese did not know how to control, decimated their lines. At Ridgway's headquarters, I told the correspondents:

There has been a lot of loose talk about the Chinese driving us into the sea, just as in the early days there was a lot of nonsense about the North Koreans driving us into the sea. No one is going to drive us into the sea. This command intends to maintain a military position in Korea just as long as Washington decides we should do so.

I ordered Ridgway to start north again. His first probing patrols struck in battalion strength. They met only light to moderate resistance, and the

Eighth Army flowed forward. My plan was to push on until we reached the line where a balance of strength was achieved which was governed by the relativity of supply. I directed Ridgway: "Keep advancing until contact with the main line of resistance is established." By February 3rd, he had reached Haengsong, with the next stop the Han River just short of Seoul. By mid-February, I was able to report:

I am entirely satisfied with the situation at the front. The enemy has suffered a tactical reverse. His losses are amongst the bloodiest in modern times. He is finding it an entirely different problem fighting 350 miles from his base than when he had sanctuary in his immediate rear. He is paying now for the illusion so falsely but effectively propagandized that he had defeated the Eighth Army decisively. I note that Marshal Stalin has just predicted the annihilation of our forces in Korea—but his comrades will have to do lots better to prove him a prophet. Until I develop the enemy's main line of resistance, or the fact that there is no such line south of the 38th parallel, it is my purpose to continue ground advances. It is evident that the enemy has lost his chance for achieving a decisive military decision in Korea.

I now began to formulate long-range plans for destroying the Chinese forces in Korea. My decisive objective would be their supply lines. By constant, but ubiquitous ground thrusts at widely scattered points with limited objectives, I would regain the Seoul line for a base of future operations. I would then clear the enemy rear all across the top of North Korea by massive air attacks. If I were still not permitted to attack the massed enemy reinforcements across the Yalu, or to destroy its bridges, I would sever Korea from Manchuria by laying a field of radioactive wastes—the by-products of atomic manufacture—across all the major lines of enemy supply. The destruction in North Korea had left it bereft of supplies. Everything the Chinese used in the way of food or munitions had to come across the border. The Reds had only ten days' supply of food in their North Korean dumps to feed nearly a million troops, and their ammunition was equally limited. Then, reinforced by Nationalist Chinese troops, if I were permitted to use them, and with American reinforcement on the way, I would make simultaneous amphibious and airborne landings at the upper end of both coasts of North Korea, and close a gigantic trap. The Chinese would soon starve or surrender. Without food and ammunition, they would become helpless. It would be something like Inchon, but on a much larger scale.

The first phase of this strategy went well. By the middle of March, we had retaken Seoul and reached the 38th parallel. The Joint Chiefs of Staff recommended to the Secretary of Defense that a naval blockade be imposed upon China, with the joint removal of restrictions on both air reconnaissance over China's coastal areas and those of Manchuria, and restrictions on Allied use of Chinese Nationalist forces. They also urged that logistic support be given to effectuate operations against the Communists.

General Ridgway wrote a strong personal note to General Collins, as one old friend to another, urging him to allow Chinese Nationalist troops to reinforce his Eighth Army. But, again, nothing was done. The Joint Chiefs of Staff's recommendation was turned down. And so was Ridgway's personal request for Nationalist reinforcement.

The old debate whether or not the United Nations forces should cross the 38th parallel was again renewed. The scapegoat hunters, both abroad and in the United States, concentrated their fire upon me personally. Their propaganda charged that I had caused the Chinese Communists to enter the Korean War by arbitrarily crossing the 38th parallel. This was more than a mere rumor started by a few correspondents. It was a carefully outlined campaign exploited by anonymous sources high in governmental circles, and propagated by certain elements of the American press. The truth, of course, was that the decision to cross had been made in Washington.

The authorities made little effort to present the true and full picture of events in the Far East to the public. No information was taken from the dispatches recorded in these pages. Only information regarded as favorable to those in power was released. A muzzling order was issued that "no speech, press release, or other public statement concerning foreign policy or military policy will be released without clearance from the Department of the Army." I issued frequent communiques of the campaign and of the occupation of Japan, and sent the next one to Washington for clearance. It was returned to me stating it would not be necessary to clear such reports with Washington. The President confirmed this in a press interview in Florida.

On March 8th, Congressman Joe Martin, Minority Leader of the House of Representatives, wrote me as follows:

In the current discussions on foreign policy and overall strategy many of us have been distressed that although the European aspects have been heavily emphasized we have been without the views of yourself as Commander-in-Chief of the Far Eastern Command.

I think it is imperative to the security of our nation and for the safety of the world that policies of the United States embrace the broadest possible strategy and in our earnest desire to protect Europe we not weaken our position in Asia.

Enclosed is a copy of an address I delivered in Brooklyn, N. Y., February 12, stressing this vital point and suggesting that the forces of Generalissimo Chiang Kai-shek on Formosa might be employed in the opening of a second Asiatic front to relieve the pressure on our forces in Korea.

I have since repeated the essence of this thesis in other speeches and intend to do so again on March 28 when I will be on a radio hook-up.

I would deem it a great help if I could have your views on this point, either on a confidential basis or otherwise. Your admirers are legion and the respect you command is enormous. May success be yours in the gigantic undertaking which you direct.

I have always felt duty-bound to reply frankly to every Congressional inquiry into matters connected with my official responsibility. This has been a prescribed practice since the very beginning of our nation, and is now the law. Only in this way, and by personal appearance, can the country's law-makers cope intelligently with national problems.

In due course, I replied to Congressman Martin on March 20th.

My views and recommendations, with respect to the situation created by Red Chinese entry into war against us in Korea, have been submitted to Washington in most complete detail. Generally these views are well known and clearly under-stood, as they follow the conventional pattern of meeting force with maximum counter-force as we have never failed to do in the past. Your view with respect to the utilization of the Chinese forces on Formosa is in conflict with neither logic nor this tradition. It seems strangely difficult for some to realize that here in Asia is where the Communist conspirators have elected to make their play for global conquest, and that we have joined the issue thus raised on the battlefield; that here we fight Europe's war with arms while the diplomats there still fight it with words; that if we lose the war to Communism in Asia the fall of Europe is inevitable; win it and Europe most probably would avoid war and yet preserve freedom. As you point out, we must win. There is no substitute for victory.

I attached little importance to the exchange of letters, which on my part was intended to be merely a polite response couched in such general terms as to convey only a normal patriotic desire for victory. My critics took particular exception to the statement that in war "there is no substitute for victory." The absurdity of such a complaint is apparent. As subsequent events so clearly demonstrated, the only substitute for victory lies in appeasement. A great nation which enters upon war and does not see it through to victory will ultimately suffer all the consequences of defeat. Stalemate may end the casualties on the battlefield, but marks the military collapse of the purpose which induced entry into combat.

On March 21st, I received the following message from the Joint Chiefs of Staff:

Presidential announcement planned by State shortly that, with the clearing bulk of South Korean aggressors, United Nations now preparing to discuss conditions of settlement in Korea. Strong United Nations feeling persists that further diplomatic efforts towards settlement should be made before any advance with forces north of the 38th parallel. Time will be required to determine diplomatic reaction and permit new negotiations that may develop. Recognizing that parallel has no military significance, State has asked Joint Chiefs of Staff what authority you should have to permit sufficient freedom of action for next few weeks to provide security United Nations forces and maintain contact with the enemy. Your recommendations desired.

I replied with an urgent request that "no further military restrictions be imposed upon the United Nations Command in Korea."

Before receiving this message, I had prepared the following routine communique to be issued from Tokyo as I left for the front:

Operations continuing according to schedule and plan. We have now substantially cleared South Korea of organized Communist forces. It is becoming increasingly evident that the heavy destruction along the enemy's lines of supply, caused by our round-the-clock massive air and naval bombardment, has left his troops in the forward battle area deficient in requirements to sustain his operations. This weakness is being brilliantly exploited by our ground forces. The enemy's human wave tactics have definitely failed him as our own forces have become seasoned to this form of warfare; his tactics of infiltration are but contributing to his piecemeal losses, and he is showing less stamina than our own troops under the rigors of climate, terrain and battle.

Of even greater significance than our tactical successes has been the clear revelation that this new enemy, Red China, lacks the industrial capacity to adequately provide many critical items essential to the conduct of modern war. He lacks at this time the manufacturing and those raw materials needed to produce, maintain and operate even moderate air and naval power, and he cannot provide the essentials for successful ground operations, such as tanks, heavy artillery and other refinements science has introduced into the conduct of military campaigns. Formerly, his great numerical potential might well have filled this gap but with the development of existing methods of mass destruction, numbers alone do not offset the vulnerability inherent in such deficiencies. Control of the sea and the air, which in turn means control over supplies, communications and transportation, are no less essential and decisive now than in the past. When this control exists, as in our case, and is coupled with an inferiority of ground fire power as in the enemy's case, the resulting disparity is such that it cannot be overcome by bravery, however fanatical, or the most gross indifference to human loss.

These military weaknesses have been clearly and definitely revealed since Red China entered upon its undeclared war in Korea. Even under the inhibitions which now restrict the activity of the United Nations forces and the corresponding military advantages which accrue to Red China, it has shown its complete inability to accomplish by force of arms the conquest of Korea. The enemy, therefore, must by now be painfully aware that a decision of the United Nations to depart from its tolerant effort to contain the war to the area of Korea, through an expansion of our military operations to his coastal areas and interior bases, would doom Red China to the risk of imminent military collapse. These basic facts being established, there should be no insuperable difficulty in arriving at decisions on the Korean problem if the issues are resolved on their own merits, without being burdened by extraneous matters such as Formosa or China's seat in the United Nations.

The Korean nation and people, who have been so cruelly ravaged, must not be sacrificed. That is a paramount concern. Apart from the military area of the problem where issues are resolved in the course of combat, the fundamental questions continue to be political in nature and must find their answer in the diplomatic sphere. Within the area of my authority as the military commander, however, it should be needless to say that I stand ready at any time to confer in the field with the Commander-in-Chief of the enemy forces in the earnest effort to find any military means whereby realization of the political objectives of the United Nations in Korea, to which no nation may justly take exception, might be accomplished without further bloodshed.

On my return from the Korean battle front on the evening of March 24th, I made the following comments:

Everything goes well at the front. All elements of our forces are in fine spirit and fettle. The enemy supply lines are taking terrific punishment from our implacable air and naval bombardments, conducted under the field commands of General Partridge and Admiral Struble. There is no heavy ground fighting. Our troops maintain the initiative and the enemy continues to withdraw. South Korea is now substantially cleared of enemy forces and everywhere there is a quickening effort at rehabilitation and reconstruction. Seoul is beginning to resume some evidence of life. No further comment would seem to be necessary with reference to the 38th parallel, the status of which has been so thoroughly discussed in recent statements from Washington, London and other capitals. As a matter of fact it has never had any military significance. Our naval and air forces cross it at will and both ground forces have done so in the past.

While I did not know it at the time, this statement, addressed to my troops, to Korea, to Japan, and to the world at large, was to be my last as a commander.

A tirade of criticism was raised against my last communiques. The section that was seized upon was my offer to the enemy field commander to talk military terms. The argument was made that I had disrupted some magic formula for peace on which the United States had already secured international agreement and which it was about to announce. This was utter nonsense. No such plan was even in draft form. And what I said would entirely support any peace effort that might be made. Under any interpretation, it was only the local voice of a theater commander who carefully limited his own responsibilities by stating "the fundamental questions continue to be political in nature and must find their answer in the diplomatic sphere." Twice before, I had called upon the enemy commander to surrender and stop further bloodshed—after the Inchon victory and after our capture of Pyongyang. In neither instance had there been the slightest whisper of remonstrance from any source—indeed, quite the contrary. From the beginning of warfare, it has not only been a right, but a duty for a field commander to take any steps within his power to minimize bloodshed of the soldiers committed to his command. Complaint was made of my emphasizing China's weakness, but my statement was not only factual, but intended to present to the enemy the basic reasons why he should agree to stop the war. Actually, less than four months later the Russian initiation of a proposal for a conference to arrange an armistice was avidly accepted.

At this critical juncture, Congressman Martin, for some unexplained reason and without consulting me, released my letter. There was an instant hue and cry that I wanted to spread the war. This put the cart before the horse—I only wanted to end the war, not to spread it. I had not started it, and many times had stated, "Anyone in favor of sending American ground troops to fight on Chinese soil should have his head examined."

At one o'clock in the morning of April 11th, President Truman summoned the press to the White House and announced my relief from command in the Far East. His action was fraught with politics, as he was apparently of the belief that I was conspiring in some underhanded way with the Republican leaders. This was completely erroneous. I had no part whatsoever in the political situation. Although nominally Republican, probably because of my attraction to Abraham Lincoln, I had always expressed admiration for the basic accomplishments of the Democratic Party, and appreciation of its many great leaders. Such criticisms as I have made have never been of parties, but of what I regarded as concrete instances of mistakes and failures by the parties.

My relief was important, not because of the personalities involved, but as a symbol of a basic change in attitude toward Asia since our entrance into the Korean War. Of even greater significance were the calamitous events which resulted thereafter. A chain of reactions was set off which has prejudiced to its very foundation the struggle between the free and the Red world. The decision to meet Communist aggression in its military effort to seize Korea would have been a noble one, indeed, had it been implemented with unswerving courage and determination. But the United Nations proved unequal to the task. After Red China entered the conflict, it yielded to counsels of fear, and abandoned pledged commitments to restore to the people of Korea a nation which was unified and free.

Such abandonment of principles by the United Nations, in whose solemn declaration the peoples of Asia had placed such trust and faith, was a catastrophic blow to the hopes of the free world. Its disastrous consequences were reflected throughout Asia. Red China promptly was accepted as the military colossus of the East. Korea was left ravished and divided. Indochina was partitioned by the sword. Tibet was taken almost on demand. Other Asian nations began to tremble toward neutralism. Sadly, we wasted the opportunity to retrieve the basic mistake of the 1946-1947 Marshall Mission in offering appeasement to the Red Chinese at the expense of Nationalist China, under the naive concept that the Reds were only agrarian reformers. It confirmed Red control of continental China, and fostered the growth of a powerful ally of Soviet Russia which well might become a balance of military power in the struggle for the world. It signalized the artificial restraint of our forces in Korea, which could have attained victory without recourse to other than conventional warfare and with much less than actually occurred under protracted negotiations. Approximately three-fifths of our casualties took place during the indecisive aftermath which followed my recall. It reversed United States military doctrine of a century and a half, from the attack to the defense, although the history of warfare shows the latter never attained more than an indecisive stalemate. It accepted at tragic cost the policy of indecision that in war there can be a substitute for victory; that enemy leaders who violate the conventional laws of warfare by savage brutalities need not be held to ultimate responsibility; that the rights of honorable prisoners of war are no longer a sacred national trust. All of this destroyed Oriental faith in Western fortitude, in Western determination, and in Western interest in Asia. This largely cost the free world its psychological gains which were the result of our World War II victory in the Far East.

There was an abysmal failure to comprehend the Soviet strategy in the latter's continuing and relentless effort to control the world, although that strategy is clearly expressed and delineated in the public writings of the Soviet leadership. There was a failure to understand that the global panorama has long encompassed three great areas of potential struggle: in the center, Europe; in the flanks, Asia to the north and Africa to the south. The free world apparently conceived of the center as the area of supreme interest and potential struggle; that if it could be held safely, all else would fall into place. This concept was fostered and encouraged by the constant propaganda pressures of the Soviet designed to convey the clear impression of aggression there and thus concealing his real objective to the flanks.

What the Soviets sought were the economic frontiers of the world, Asia to the north, Africa to the south—frontiers which possessed a mighty reservoir of the world's potential wealth in raw resources. The center represented little in economic advance, the flanks everything. The Soviet strategy was merely to defend in the center, but to advance by way of the flanks, to cause the free world to concentrate its resources at the center to the neglect of the vital ends. It has worked even beyond wildest expectations. The free world's main priority, even with war waging on the north flank in the Far East, has been the center; although practically free from battle combat, and now, with the north flank turned in Asia, the Soviet has started to envelop the southern flank. All this and more has followed from the United Nations' fatal decision not to see it through in Korea. The free world plunged from an invincible position of moral strength into the confusion of uncertain bewilderment. We fostered a practice of doubtful expediency and the eventual misery of timid appeasement. The result was a tragic and precipitous loss in prestige.

I was chided for regarding the Korean conflict as a war and not as a "police action." How could Red China have been more at war against us? Every ounce of her military and economic force was thrown into the Korean struggle. Lacking naval and air power, she was incapable of anything more. She was already strained to the breaking point, a 100 per cent war effort against us. How can one reasonably say it is not war when approximately 150,000 Americans and many times that of our ally, South Korea, were killed or maimed? The preponderance of these casualties were inflicted by Red China.

Attempts have been made to justify the extraordinary military policy which placed our arms in a straitjacket, based on the possibility that if we followed our tradition and fought to win, it might precipitate Soviet Russia's entry into the war. But the entry of Soviet Russia, or Red China, was a risk inherent in the original decision to intervene in Korea. At that time the possible consequences should have been weighed, and the decision taken with full acceptance of all the circumstances involved. Even had Russia desired to actively intervene, she would have found it militarily almost impossible to do so. Her position in Siberia was of necessity defensive and highly vulnerable because of her limited and tenuous supply line. This consisted of a single railroad system which could be cut by air interdiction almost at will. There was little local supply in eastern Siberia, and its military needs depended entirely upon this sole transportation system. At no place in the world would she have been weaker for battle. At this time, while we had the atomic bomb, she had not yet developed its manufacture. There was never serious danger of active Soviet intervention. The Russian policy is not to sacrifice its own troops, but to use those of its friends. The enormous expansion of Soviet influence since the end of World War II has been brought about without the Russian soldier firing a shot in battle. Basically, the problem was the indeterminate question of whether the Soviet contemplated the conquest of the world by military means or by more peaceful persuasion. If it intended to use force, the time and place would be at its own choice and initiative, and any action we might have taken to resolve the Korean situation could not have been a controlling factor in the precipitation of a world conflict.

Several years after my abrupt relief just when victory was within my grasp, the charge was made that I had been insubordinate. Nothing could have been more grotesque. It was completely repudiated by all members of the Joint Chiefs of Staff, my immediate military seniors in the conduct of the Korean War, who specifically denied under oath before the Senate Committee investigating the reasons for my recall, that I had ever committed such a breach of regulations. The committee itself was unanimous in its agreement. It was stated that General Bradley had charged me with such an offense. But General Bradley, in answer to direct questions by Senators George, Byrd, and Morse, three times swore that there had been no such dereliction on my part. Later, in an article carried in the *Saturday Evening Post,* Bradley went so far as to say he thought that I "might have been right" in the Korean problem.

Field Marshal Lord Alanbrooke, the famous chairman of the British chiefs of staff, gave this estimate:

The decisions MacArthur finally arrived at as regards the war in Korea were, I think, based on a Pacific outlook and, as such, in my opinion were right. He has been accused of taking actions without previous political approval, but he had been unable to obtain the political policy and guidance he had sought. To my mind a general who is not prepared to assume some responsibility on his own, when unable to obtain political direction, is of little value.

And even President Truman's relief order contained this contradictory paragraph:

General MacArthur's place in history as one of our greatest commanders is fully established. The nation owes him a debt of gratitude for the distinguished and exceptional service which he has rendered his country in posts of great responsibility.

The legal authority of a President to relieve a field commander, irrespective of the wisdom or stupidity of the action, has never been questioned by anyone. The supremacy of the civil over the military is fundamental to the American system of government, and is wholeheartedly accepted by every officer and soldier in the military establishment. It was not an issue in this case. Since the beginning of time, commanders have been changed, some through whim, some through cause, but never in history was there a more drastic method employed than in my relief—without a hearing, without an opportunity for defense, with no consideration of the past. Up to the moment of my recall, I had been receiving laudatory commendations from the President, publicly and through his liaison officer at my headquarters. No slightest opportunity was given me to explain my position, to answer allegations or objections, to present my future concepts and plans.

I had heard much of President Truman's violent temper and paroxysms of ungovernable rage, and had noted with growing concern his increasingly indecisive handling of the Korean situation. From strength in his original decision to free and unite Korea, he had, step by step, weakened into a hesitant nervousness indicative of a state of confusion and bewilderment. He had never been to Korea, and his ignorance of the Far East and its peoples had become a dangerous failing in one responsible for final decisions. It was quite apparent his nerves were at the breaking point—not only his nerves, but what was far more menacing in the Chief Executive of a country at war—his nerve.

But prepared as I was by the creeping appeasement which was gradually engulfing the campaign, I was shocked by the article which was published in *The New York Times* of Saturday, December 9, 1950. It read in part:

President Truman has threatened to beat up a critic who had criticized the singing of his daughter, Margaret, at a concert here Tuesday night. The story came out today in a Presidential letter that leaked out to the newspapers.

The missive, to Paul Hume, music critic of the *Washington Post,* caused almost as great a sensation as the letter Mr. Truman wrote to a member of Congress a few months ago in which he referred to the Marine Corps as the Navy's police force.

What was learned of the latest letter appeared as a bowdlerized version published by the *Washington Daily News.* "Margaret Truman sang here the other day. Paul Hume, the *Washington Post's* music critic, panned her. He is now showing around a letter, on White House letterhead, which goes like this: 'I have just read your lousy review buried in the back pages. You sound like a frustrated old man who never made a success, an eight-ulcer man on a four-ulcer job, and all four ulcers working.

" 'I never met you, but if I do you'll need a new nose and plenty of beefsteak and perhaps a supporter below. Westbrook Pegler, a guttersnipe, is a gentleman compared to you. You can take that as more of an insult than as a reflection on your ancestry.'

"The letter was initialed, 'H.S.T.'

"It was soon acknowledged at the White House that the letter had been written by Mr. Truman. The language was reported to be even earthier than the expurgated version. The letter was written in longhand on a scratch pad bearing the White House imprint."

I am free to confess that this article dismayed me. I realized that I was standing at the apex of a situation which could make me the next victim of such an uncontrolled passion. It came with suddenness and violence. What a contrast with the calm dignity and self-control of President Lincoln in a somewhat comparable circumstance with General Grant. He wrote him on April 30, 1864, as follows:

Not expecting to see you again before the spring campaign opens, I wish to express in this way my entire satisfaction with what you have done up to this time, so far as I understand it. The particulars of your plan I neither know or seek to know. You are vigilant and self-reliant; and, pleased with this, I wish not to obtrude any constraints or restraint upon you. While I am very anxious that any great disaster or capture of our men in great numbers shall be avoided, I know these points are less likely to escape your attention than they would mine. If there is anything wanting which is within my power to give, do not fail to let me know it. And now, with a brave Army and a just cause, may God sustain you.

The great gap between Lincoln and Truman was not of time only. As one of Truman's most prominent critics summed it up: "Among President Truman's many weaknesses was his utter inability to discriminate between history and histrionics."

The actual order I received was so drastic as to prevent the usual amenities incident to a transfer of command, and practically placed me under duress. No office boy, no charwoman, no servant of any sort would have been dismissed with such callous disregard for the ordinary decencies.

I was first appraised of the action through a press dispatch over the public radio. It is claimed that Washington tried to inform me, before announcing my relief to the public, through the Secretary of the Army, Mr. Pace, then on a visit to Japan and Korea, but could not reach him. This is incredible. Secretary Pace had been with me in my office just before, and had reflected a most complimentary attitude in Washington. He was in Korea at the moment in immediate message contact with my headquarters, which had similar contact with Washington.

But if every allegation made by my detractors had been justified, they would all together have been but trivia compared with the great issues involved in the Far East. There could not have been a more distorted perspective, a more complete inability to put first things first.

The order for my relief reached Tokyo on the afternoon of the 11th as the radios broke through their normal programs to announce a special bulletin from Washington: "President Truman has just removed General MacArthur from his Far Eastern and Korean Commands and from the direction of the occupation of Japan." In the embassy we had just finished luncheon, and I was preparing to leave for the front in Korea. The bulletin had been heard by one of my faithful aides, Colonel Sidney Huff, who had been with me for many years. He informed my wife by telephone that I had been removed from command, with the only reason given a doubt that I would be able to "support the policies of the Administration." I saw the look of distress on her face as she told me, but as for myself I had long ago become shockproof. "Jeannie," I said, "we're going home at last." It had been a long tour—fifteen consecutive years of foreign service since I had left Washington to become military advisor to the Philippines.

Moscow and Peiping rejoiced. The bells were rung and a holiday atmosphere prevailed. The left-wingers everywhere exulted. But in the Far East, there was bewilderment and shock. I had been there so long in supreme command that I had become a kind of symbol of the free world— a bulwark against the spread of Communism. The removal of the symbol was not understood, and tended to shake faith in our ways and methods.

The Japanese Diet and the Korean Parliament passed a resolution of tribute and thanks. The Emperor made a farewell call of sorrow. Prime Minister Yoshida broadcast for the nation saying:

The accomplishments of General MacArthur in the interest of our country are one of the marvels of history. It is he who has salvaged our nation from post-surrender confusion and prostration, and steered the country on the road of recovery and reconstruction. It is he who has firmly planted democracy in all segments of our society. It is he who has paved the way for a peace settlement. No wonder he is looked upon by all our people with the profoundest veneration and affection. I have no words to convey the regret of our nation to see him leave.*

I received letters from Natokesato,** the president of the House of Councillors; Kotaro Tanaka,† the chief justice of the Supreme Court of Japan; President Syngman Rhee of Korea,‡ and a joint tribute published in the two leading Japanese newspapers, the *Asahi Shimbun* and the *Mainichi Shimbun*.§

---

* And in a personal note to me he wrote: "Words fail me to tell you how shocked and how grieved I am at your precipitous departure from our shores. In this personal note it would be superfluous of me to duplicate the resolutions and testimonials of appreciation and thanks which are being sent to you from both Houses of the Diet and many other quarters, and which constitute a spontaneous tribute of the nation to the monumental task you have accomplished as Supreme Commander for the Allied Powers in rebuilding and revitalizing our country. All Japanese from the Emperor to the man on the street regret your going."

** "The sudden news was so shocking to me that I have not yet recovered from its effects. The feeling of a great regret together with an irrevocable loss and bewilderment is shared by the people of entire Japan. They sorrow from the bottom of their hearts to have to part with the great leader whom they have loved and trusted. Since my appointment as the President of the House of Councillors, your wise counsel gave me courage and now the prospect of your departure saddens me profoundly."

† "It is with the deepest regret that I learned of the sudden departure of Your Excellency, who has gained the everlasting respect and admiration of the Japanese people by your great leadership in the reconstruction and democratization of Japan. The fruit of the great achievements of Your Excellency, rarely seen in the annals of history, are ready to be crowned with the signing of the Peace Treaty. I am sure that you must feel great satisfaction in the healthy progress of a peaceful and democratic Japan, established by the ideals of your noble and farsighted policies based on your firm religious faith. On your departure, I wish to express my deepest sorrow and my hearty gratitude on behalf of the Supreme Court, and the entire judicial branch of the Japanese Government, for your great material and spiritual aid and advice, especially the benevolent advice and assistance given the Japanese Courts, and also the precious achievements left by Your Excellency."

‡ President Syngman Rhee had written: "The entirely unexpected news of your relief from your commands came as a shock to us and I do not know how to express my feelings. I so well remember how you told me that you would defend Korea as you would defend California in the event that we were attacked and so you did. This fact no Korean patriot will ever forget. I know how you have worked to find a solution to our problems and how you have labored in the cause of a unified and independent Korea. All our people will remember forever all that you have done for Korea and your staunch, enduring friendship for us. I believe, dear General, that the ultimate solution of our problems will be in accordance with your plans, for there is no other honorable result which can come from this war. As time unfolds your name will gain added luster as the outstanding leader and statesman of this period in World history."

§ The two leading papers, the *Asahi Shimbun* and the *Mainichi Shimbun*, had spoken: "The removal is a great disappointment to the Japanese, especially when the peace settlement is so near. We feel as if we had lost a kind and loving father. His recall is the greatest shock since the end of the war. He dealt with the Japanese people not as a conqueror but as a great reformer. He was a noble political missionary. What he gave us was not material aid and democratic reform alone—but a new way of life, the freedom and dignity of the individual. We shall continue to love and trust him as one who best understood Japan's position. We wanted his further help in nurturing our green democracy to fruition. We wanted his leadership at least until a signed peace treaty had given us a sendoff into the world community."

PART TEN

Soldier's Return
1951–1964

W e left for Atsugi Airfield at daybreak
on the 16th. Two million Japanese lined the route from the embassy to
Atsugi, waving and some weeping. All the dignitaries of Tokyo and its full
garrison of troops were at the airfield. We took off as the sun rose with the
breath of early spring in the air. Beneath us lay this land of the chrysanthe-
mum, with its deep shadows and brilliant hues, with its majestic peaks and
low-lying valleys, its winding streams and inland seas, its cities and towns
and rolling plateaus. We circled Fuji for a last look and then we were gone.

But Japan did not forget. On the centennial of the first American-
Japanese Treaty of Friendship, I was decorated with the Grand Cordon of the
Order of the Rising Sun with Paulownia Flowers, one of the highest awards
of the nation and reserved for monarchs and heads of government.*

This honor moved me deeply, because I could recall no parallel in the
history of the world when a great nation recently at war had so distinguished
its former enemy commander. This feeling was intensified in that it came,

---

* The citation read: "This high decoration for distinguished service is awarded you in recognition especially of your great contribution to the postwar reconstruction of Japan and to the development of the immense reservoir of good will that exists between our two nations today. Your
role as Supreme Commander for the Allied Powers in Japan will certainly go down in history as
the greatest of all examples of enlightened occupation administration; and it will for all time be
remembered with devoted gratitude by the Japanese people. In the trying days after the war, you
instilled hope and a sense of direction into the Japanese people. You helped them regain their
self-respect and rebuild their economic life. Under your leadership, Japan became a nation of free
men, thereby laying the basis for her membership in the free world. Both the Japanese Government and the Japanese people are entering the second century of their relations with the United
States with the conviction that their future lies with the nations of the free world, and particularly
in friendship and cooperation with the United States."

not during my proconsulship, but only after time and thought, study and analysis had carefully evaluated the results of the occupation.

Our welcome home was tumultuous. It seemed to me that every man, woman, and child in San Francisco turned out to cheer us. I had been invited by Congress to address it at a joint session on the 19th, and flew on to Washington, where it looked as though the whole District of Columbia greeted our arrival. I mounted the rostrum and delivered the following speech.

Mr. President, Mr. Speaker, and distinguished Members of the Congress:

I stand on this rostrum with a sense of deep humility and great pride—humility in the wake of those great American architects of our history who have stood here before me, pride in the reflection that this forum of legislative debate represents human liberty in the purest form yet devised. Here are centered the hopes and aspirations and faith of the entire human race.

I do not stand here as advocate for any partisan cause, for the issues are fundamental and reach quite beyond the realm of partisan consideration. They must be resolved on the highest plane of national interest if our course is to prove sound and our future protected. I trust, therefore, that you will do me the justice of receiving that which I have to say as solely expressing the considered viewpoint of a fellow American. I address you with neither rancor nor bitterness in the fading twilight of life with but one purpose in mind—to serve my country.

The issues are global and so interlocked that to consider the problems of one sector, oblivious to those of another, is but to court disaster for the whole.

While Asia is commonly referred to as the gateway to Europe, it is no less true that Europe is the gateway to Asia, and the broad influence of the one cannot fail to have its impact upon the other.

There are those who claim our strength is inadequate to protect on both fronts—that we cannot divide our efforts. I can think of no greater expression of defeatism. If a potential enemy can divide his strength on two fronts, it is for us to counter his effort.

The Communist threat is a global one. Its successful advance in one sector threatens the destruction of every other sector. You cannot appease or otherwise surrender to Communism in Asia without simultaneously undermining our efforts to halt its advance in Europe.

Beyond pointing out these simple truisms, I shall confine my discussion to the general area of Asia. Before one may objectively assess the situation now existing there, he must comprehend something of Asia's past and the revolutionary changes which have marked her course up to the present. Long exploited by the so-called colonial powers, with little opportunity to achieve any degree of social justice, individual dignity, or a higher standard of life such as guided our own noble administration of the Philippines, the peoples of Asia found their opportunity in the war just past to throw off the shackles of colonialism and now see the dawn of new opportunity, a heretofore unfelt dignity and the self-respect of political freedom.

Mustering half of the earth's population and 60 per cent of its natural resources, these peoples are rapidly consolidating a new force, both moral and material, with which to raise the living standard and erect adaptations of the design of modern progress to their own distinct cultural environments. Whether one adheres to the concept of colonization or not, this is the direction of Asian progress and it may not be stopped. It is a corollary to the shift of the world economic frontiers, as the whole epicenter of world affairs rotates back toward the area whence it started. In this situation it becomes vital that our country orient its policies in consonance with this basic evolutionary condition rather than pursue a course blind to the reality that the colonial era is now past and the Asian peoples covet the right to shape their own free destiny. What they seek now is friendly guidance, understanding, and support, not imperious direction; the dignity of equality, not the shame of subjugation. Their prewar standard of life, pitifully low, is infinitely lower now in the devastation left in war's wake. World ideologies play little part in Asian thinking and are little understood. What the peoples strive for is the opportunity for a little more food in their stomachs, a little better clothing on their backs, a little firmer roof over their heads, and the realization of the normal nationalist urge for political freedom. These political-social conditions have but an indirect bearing upon our own national security, but form a backdrop to contemporary planning which must be thoughtfully considered if we are to avoid the pitfalls of unrealism.

Of more direct and immediate bearing upon our national security are the changes wrought in the strategic potential of the Pacific Ocean in the course of the past war. Prior thereto, the western strategic frontier of the United States lay on the littoral line of the Americas with an exposed island salient extending out through Hawaii, Midway, and Guam to the Philippines. That salient proved not an outpost of strength but an avenue of weakness along which the enemy could and did attack. The Pacific was a potential area of advance for any predatory force intent upon striking at the bordering land areas.

All this was changed by our Pacific victory. Our strategic frontier then shifted to embrace the entire Pacific Ocean which became a vast moat to protect us as long as we hold it. Indeed, it acts as a protective shield for all of the Americas and all free lands of the Pacific Ocean area. We control it to the shores of Asia by a chain of islands extending in an arc from the Aleutians to the Marianas held by us and our free allies. From this island chain we can dominate with sea and air power every Asiatic port from Vladivostok to Singapore and prevent any hostile movement into the Pacific. Any predatory attack from Asia must be an amphibious effort. No amphibious force can be successful without control of the sea lanes and the air over those lanes in its avenue of advance. With naval and air supremacy and modest ground elements to defend bases, any major attack from continental Asia toward us or our friends of the Pacific would be doomed to failure. Under such conditions the Pacific no longer represents menacing avenues of approach for a prospective invader—it assumes instead the friendly aspect of a peaceful lake. Our line of defense is a natural one and can be maintained with a minimum of military effort and expense. It envisions no attack against anyone nor does it provide the bastions essential for offensive operations, but properly maintained would be an invincible defense against aggression.

The holding of this littoral defense line in the western Pacific is entirely dependent upon holding all segments thereof, for any major breach of that line by an unfriendly power would render vulnerable to determined attack every other major segment. This is a military estimate as to which I have yet to find a military leader who will take exception. For that reason I have strongly recommended in the past as a matter of military urgency that under no circumstances must Formosa fall under Communist control. Such an eventuality would at once threaten the freedom of the Philippines and the loss of Japan, and might well force our western frontier back to the coasts of California, Oregon and Washington.

To understand the changes which now appear upon the Chinese mainland, one must understand the changes in Chinese character and culture over the past fifty years. China up to fifty years ago was completely non-homogeneous, being compartmented into groups divided against each other. The war-making tendency was almost nonexistent, as they still followed the tenets of the Confucian ideal of pacifist culture. At the turn of the century, under the regime of Chan So Lin, efforts toward greater homogeneity produced the start of a nationalist urge. This was further and more successfully developed under the leadership of Chiang Kai-shek, but has been brought to its greatest fruition under the present regime, to the point that it has now taken on the character of a united nationalism of increasingly dominant aggressive tendencies. Through these past fifty years, the Chinese people have thus become militarized in their concepts and in their ideals. They now constitute excellent soldiers with competent staffs and commanders. This has produced a new and dominant power in Asia which for its own purposes is allied with Soviet Russia, but which in its own concepts and methods has become aggressively imperialistic with a lust for expansion and increased power normal to this type of imperialism. There is little of the ideological concept either one way or another in the Chinese makeup. The standard of living is so low and the capital accumulation has been so thoroughly dissipated by war that the masses are desperate and avid to follow any leadership which seems to promise the alleviation of local stringencies. I have from the beginning believed that the Chinese Communist's support of the North Koreans was the dominant one. Their interests are at present parallel to those of the Soviet, but I believe that the aggressiveness recently displayed not only in Korea, but also in Indo-China and Tibet, and pointing potentially toward the south reflects predominantly the same lust for the expansion of power which has animated every would-be conqueror since the beginning of time.

The Japanese people since the war have undergone the greatest reformation recorded in modern history. With a commendable will, eargerness to learn, and marked capacity to understand, they have, from the ashes left in war's wake, erected in Japan an edifice dedicated to the primacy of individual liberty and personal dignity, and in the ensuing process there has been created a truly representative government committed to the advance of political morality, freedom of economic enterprise, and social justice. Politically, economically and socially, Japan is now abreast of many free nations of the earth and will not again fail the universal trust. That it may be counted upon to wield a profoundly beneficial influence over the course of events in Asia is attested by the magnificent manner in which the Japanese people have met the recent challenge of war, unrest and confusion surrounding them from the outside, and checked Communism within their own frontiers without the slightest slackening in their forward progress. I sent all four of our occupation divisions to the Korean battlefront without the slightest qualms as to the effect of the resulting power vacuum upon Japan. The results fully justified my faith. I know of no nation more secure, orderly and industrious—nor in which higher hopes can be entertained for future constructive service in the advance of the human race.

Of our former ward, the Philippines, we can look forward in confidence that the existing unrest will be corrected and a strong and healthy nation will grow in the longer aftermath of war's terrible destructiveness. We must be patient and understanding and never fail them, as in our hour of need they did not fail us. A Christian nation, the Philippines stand as a mighty bulwark of Christianity in the Far East, and its capacity for high moral leadership in Asia is unlimited.

On Formosa, the Government of the Republic of China has had the opportunity to refute by action much of the malicious gossip which so undermined the strength of its leadership on the Chinese mainland. The Formosan people are receiving a just and enlightened administration with majority representation on the organs of government, and politically, economically and socially they appear to be advancing along sound and constructive lines.

With this brief insight into the surrounding areas I now turn to the Korean conflict. While I was not consulted prior to the President's decision to intervene in support of the Republic of Korea, that decision, from a military standpoint, proved a sound one, as we hurled back the invader and decimated his forces. Our victory was complete and our objectives within reach when Red China intervened with numerically superior ground forces. This created a new war and an entirely new situation—a situation not contemplated when our forces were committed against the North Korean invaders—a situation which called for new decisions in the diplomatic sphere to permit the realistic adjustment of military strategy. Such decisions have not been forthcoming.

While no man in his right mind would advocate sending our ground forces into continental China and such was never given a thought, the new situation did urgently demand a drastic revision of strategic planning if our political aim was to defeat this new enemy as we had defeated the old.

Apart from the military need as I saw it to neutralize the sanctuary protection given the enemy north of the Yalu, I felt that military necessity in the conduct of the war made mandatory:

1. The intensification of our economic blockade against China;

2. The imposition of a naval blockade against the China coast;

3. Removal of restrictions on air reconnaissance of China's coastal area and of Manchuria;

4. Removal of restrictions on the forces of the Republic of China on Formosa with logistic support to contribute to their effective operations against the common enemy.

For entertaining these views, all professionally designed to support our forces committed to Korea and bring hostilities to an end with the least possible delay and at a saving of countless American and Allied lives, I have been severely criticized in lay circles, principally abroad, despite my understanding that from a military standpoint the above views have been fully shared in the past by practically every military leader concerned with the Korean campaign, including our own Joint Chiefs of Staff.

I called for reinforcements, but was informed that reinforcements were not available. I made clear that if not permitted to destroy the enemy buildup bases north of the Yalu; if not permitted to utilize the friendly Chinese force of some 600,000 men on Formosa; if not permitted to blockade the China coast to prevent the Chinese Reds from getting succor from without; and if there were to be no hope of major reinforcements, the position of the command from the military standpoint forbade victory. We could hold in Korea by constant maneuver and at an approximate area where our supply line advantages were in balance with the supply line disadvantages of the enemy, but we could hope at best for only an indecisive campaign, with its terrible and constant attrition upon our forces if the enemy utilized his full military potential. I have constantly called for the new political decisions essential to a solution. Efforts have been made to distort my position. It has been said that I was in effect a war monger. Nothing could be further from the truth. I know war as few other men now living know it, and nothing to me is more revolting. I have long advocated its complete abolition as its very destructiveness on both friend and foe has rendered it useless as a means of settling international disputes. Indeed, on the 2nd of September 1945, just following the surrender of the Japanese nation on the battleship *Missouri*, I formally cautioned as follows: "Men since the beginning of time have sought peace. Various methods through the ages have been attempted to devise an international process to prevent or settle disputes between nations. From the very start, workable methods were found insofar as individual citizens were concerned; but the mechanics of an instrumentality of larger international scope have never been successful. Military alliances, balances of power, leagues of nations, all in turn failed, leaving the only path to be by way of the crucible of war. The utter destructiveness of war now blots out this alternative. We have had our last chance. If we will not devise some greater and more equitable system, Armageddon will be at the door. The problem basically is theological and involves a spiritual recrudescence and improvement of human character that will synchronize with our almost matchless advances in science, art, literature, and all material and cultural developments of the past 2,000 years. It must be of the spirit if we are to save the flesh."

But once war is forced upon us, there is no other alternative than to apply every available means to bring it to a swift end. War's very object is victory—not prolonged indecision. In war, indeed, there can be no substitute for victory.

There are some who for varying reasons would appease Red China. They are blind to history's clear lesson. For history teaches with unmistakable emphasis that appeasement but begets new and bloodier war. It points to no single instance where the end has justified that means—where appeasement has led to more than a sham peace. Like blackmail, it lays the basis for new and successively greater demands, until, as in blackmail, violence becomes the only alternative. Why, my soldiers asked of me, surrender military advantages to an enemy in the field? I could not answer. Some may say to avoid spread of the conflict into an all-out war with China; others, to avoid Soviet intervention. Neither explanation seems valid. For China is already engaging with the maximum power it can commit and the Soviet will not necessarily mesh its actions with our moves. Like a cobra, any new enemy will more likely strike whenever it feels that the relativity in military or other potential is in its favor on a world-wide basis.

The tragedy of Korea is further heightened by the fact that as military action is confined to its territorial limits, it condemns that nation, which it is our purpose to save, to suffer the devastating impact of full naval and air bombardment, while the enemy's sanctuaries are fully protected from such attack and devastation. Of the nations of the world, Korea alone, up to now, is the sole one which has risked its all against Communism. The magnificence of the courage and fortitude of the Korean people defies description. They have chosen to risk death rather than slavery. Their last words to me were, "Don't scuttle the Pacific."

I have just left your fighting sons in Korea. They have met all tests there and I can report to you without reservation they are splendid in every way. It was my constant effort to preserve them and end this savage conflict honorably and with the least loss of time and a minimum sacrifice of life. Its growing bloodshed has caused me the deepest anguish and anxiety. Those gallant men will remain often in my thoughts and in my prayers always.

I am closing my fifty-two years of military service. When I joined the Army even before the turn of the century, it was the fulfillment of all my boyish hopes and dreams. The world has turned over many times since I took the oath on the Plain at West Point, and the hopes and dreams have long since vanished. But I still remember the refrain of one of the most popular barrack ballads of that day which proclaimed most proudly that—

"Old soldiers never die, they just fade away."

And like the old soldier of that ballad, I now close my military career and just fade away—an old soldier who tried to do his duty as God gave him the light to see that duty.

Good-by.

M y welcome throughout the entire land defies description. America took me to its heart with a roar that will never leave my ears. Everywhere it was the same—New York, Chicago, Boston, Cleveland, Detroit, Houston, San Antonio, Manchester, Fort Worth, Miami, Los Angeles, Little Rock, Seattle, Norfolk, Austin, Dallas, Portland, Murfreesboro, Honolulu, Milwaukee. Men, women, and children, rich and poor, black and white, of as many different origins as there are nations on the earth, with their tears and smiles, their cheers and handclaps, and, most of all, their heart-lifting cries of, "Welcome home, Mac." In New York, where I settled down to live, the crowd was estimated by city officials to be the largest up to that time. I found 20,000 telegrams and 150,000 letters waiting for me. They came from all over the world, from the high and mighty to the lowly and downtrodden. But of all those messages perhaps the one I most cherished was from my old chief, former President Herbert Hoover:

There is no way to measure the service General MacArthur has given the American people. He is the greatest general and one of the greatest statesmen of our nation's history. He is the greatest combination of statesman and military leader that America has produced since George Washington. It was his military genius which won the war with Japan. It was his statesmanship which turned away the natural enmity of the Japanese people. When at the time of the Japanese surrender, he marched his victorious men down the streets of Tokyo, the Japanese, breathing hate, turned their backs upon him. Six years later, when he went through the streets on his way home, the people bade him good-bye in tears. General MacArthur may say, "Old soldiers never die, they just fade away." Physically they will. But the great deeds of men live forever after them.

I was shortly asked to appear before a hearing to be conducted by a joint session of the Senate Committee on Armed Services and Foreign Relations, to inquire into the military situation in the Far East and my relief from assignment in that area. For three days the committee bombarded me with questions covering the whole scope of Asian history and United States foreign policy and military power. It reminded me of the many appearances I had made years before. But this one was to be my last. It was pleasant, therefore, to have the chairman, Senator Richard Russell, of Georgia, end my hearing on a happy note of cordiality.

General MacArthur, [he said] I wish to state to you that the three days you have been here with us are without parallel in my legislative experience. I have never seen a man subjected to such a barrage of questions in so many fields and on so many varied subjects. I marvel at your physical endurance. More than that, I have been profoundly impressed by the vastness of your patience and the thoughtfulness and frankness with which you have answered all the questions that have been propounded. We have certainly drawn freely on your vast reservoir of knowledge and experience, not only as a great military captain, but as a civilian administrator of 80 million people.

The committee shortly divided along political lines, and its final report was of little value. The Congress, itself, however, when passions had cooled and the calamitous results of the appeasement policy in the Far East had become increasingly evident, rendered its own verdict by conferring upon me its highest award, the thanks of Congress.

A joint resolution to that effect was submitted to the House of Representatives by Congressman Lucius M. Rivers.* He had been in Tokyo at the time of my relief as a member of a Congressional committee investigating conditions in the Far East.

It was passed unanimously. The Senate followed with a similar unanimous approval.

The joint resolution was presented on the steps of the Capitol by the Speaker of the House of Representatives, John McCormack. It read: "That the thanks and appreciation of the Congress and the American people are hereby tendered to General of the Army Douglas MacArthur, in recognition of his outstanding devotion to the American people, his brilliant leadership during and following World War II, and the unsurpassed affection held for him."

---

* Another member of the same Committee, Congressman Dorn, outlined the resolution from the floor, saying:

"Mr. Speaker, of course this resolution will be adopted unanimously. Douglas MacArthur is one of the greatest military captains of all history. His superlative strategy during World War II and in Korea saved this nation and the free world many thousands of lives.

"The genius of a truly great general is marked by his ability to accomplish the objective with a minimum loss of lives and resources—also by his ability to prevent war altogether. Douglas Mac-Arthur possessed to a maximum degree this genius. General MacArthur could foresee the coming of World War II and desperately, as Chief of Staff, provided for a bare nucleus around which our magnificent armies of World War II were built. If we had listened to MacArthur in the 1930's on preparedness, we might have prevented war through strength. Had we listened to MacArthur's warnings in the Pacific, we would not have been caught unprepared and might have prevented war with Japan through strength.

"General MacArthur could see in the 1920's and 1930's the advantage of controlling the air in the next war. I have always believed that General MacArthur was a great admirer of General Billy Mitchell. They were beneath the surface kindred spirits in that they had the ability to look ahead and the courage to point the way.

"If General MacArthur's recommendations had been followed during the early stages of the Korean war, the world would not be in such critical condition today. If General MacArthur had been permitted to win the Korean war conclusively, Red China would have been destroyed in a matter of months and the balance of world power would have been tipped heavily today in favor of the cause of freedom. The North Korean attack and the subsequent entrance of Red China into the war was a God-given opportunity for the United States to correct with little cost the tragic mistakes of Yalta and Potsdam. Red China's only armies were ground to pieces in North Korea. The Russians were recuperating from World War II and did not have nuclear weapons in mass production. MacArthur noted with regret and much sadness the passing of this unbelievable opportunity.

"Some day we will have to fight Red China on her terms at a time of her choosing. She will have atomic power backed by the entire Eurasian land mass. This issue could have been resolved forever in our favor in 1951 had those of us in Washington had the foresight to give MacArthur the green light in Asia. This great general could have secured the peace and could have assured the ascendency of the Western democratic world. MacArthur was right and many of us here in Washington, in London, and in the United Nations were wrong.

"The Committee report speaks eloquently of MacArthur's magnificent career. We can add little to the report. The least we can do now is to adopt this resolution unanimously expressing the appreciation of the Congress and the American people to General of the Army Douglas MacArthur."

The Speaker spoke of "countless exploits and unparalleled military accomplishments;" the Vice President, Lyndon Johnson, the President of the Senate, of "a career never equalled in American military annals, a towering intellect, right in his decisions."

And later it passed another joint resolution directing that a special gold medal be struck in my honor, bearing my likeness and inscribed, "Protector of Australia; Liberator of the Philippines; Conqueror of Japan; Defender of Korea."

It was all quite overwhelming and I could but tell the Congress it "had rendered an opinion of my services that I felt did me too much honor."

I was showered with countless awards and medals and decorations and made many speeches before state legislatures, universities, veterans organizations, civic bodies, and even the keynote address at the Republican National Convention in 1952. I found the liberties of private life refreshing and exhilarating. I entered the business world and became an executive of one of the larger manufacturing companies. I saw my boy graduate from Columbia University, and in peace and tranquillity I have enjoyed to the full the relaxation of release from the arduous responsibilities of high national command.

On December 5, 1952, I made the following remarks on the Korean conflict at the annual dinner of the 57th Congress of American Industry, sponsored by the National Association of Manufacturers:

In Korea, the principle of collective security is now on trial. If it fails there—and thus far it shows few signs of success—it will fail everywhere. It is not the least of the strange anachronisms of these strange times that those who advocate most strongly the principle of collective security in the protection of Western Europe are either lukewarm or actually opposed to the successful application of the same principle in the protection of Korea and the Far East.

Indeed, if we would frankly face and review our own weaknesses we need go no further than the great tragedy of Korea. While it is well known that my own views have not been sought in any way, yet I am confident that there is a clear and definite solution to the Korean conflict. There has been a material change in conditions from those of twenty months ago when I left the scene of action, and the solution then available and capable of success is not now entirely applicable. A present solution involves basic decisions which I recognize as improper for public disclosure or discussion, but which in my opinion can be executed without either an unduly heavy price in friendly casualties or any increased danger of provoking universal conflict. Until a solution is forthcoming, hundreds of thousands of the flower of American youth must continue their fight with only an occasional uneasy rest before re-entering the valley of the shadow of death.

So it has been these endless weeks and months which have grown into years since Red China initiated war against us in Korea and the indecision of our leaders committed us to the terrible blood tribute exacted by this type of stalemated attrition. Never before has this nation been engaged in mortal combat with a hostile power without military objective, without policy other than restrictions governing operations, or indeed without even formally recognizing a state of war.

Two days later, on December 7th, I received the following message from President-elect Eisenhower who was returning from an inspection trip to Korea:

Have just received aboard the *USS Helena* excerpts of your speech before NAM and am gratified by your continued interest in the Korean War which so vitally affects the United States and our Allies. Naturally I and my associates in the new administration, particularly the Secretaries of State and Defense, are vitally concerned about Korea and the Far East. We are now in the process of outlining a future program to be based upon the best interest of our country and the free world. It will aim, of course, at ultimate peace in that section of the world. I appreciate your announced readiness to discuss these matters with me and assure you that I am looking forward to informal meeting in which my associates and I may obtain the full benefits of your thinking and experience. With personal regards. Eisenhower.

I immediately replied as follows:

Dear Ike:

I have just received your message. I am grateful for your interest in my views concerning solution of the problems involved in the Korean War and the Far East. This is especially so because, despite my intimate personal and professional connection and well known concern therewith, this is the first time that the slightest official interest in my counsel has been evidenced since my return. A failure of policy there might doom indefinitely the progress of civilization. A successful solution on the other hand might well become the key to peace in the world. You know, without my saying, that my service is, as it always has been, entirely at the disposition of our country. My best to you, Ike, as always.

MacArthur

On December 10, I received this message:

Thanks for your prompt answer to my cable. Because of persistent press speculation, I wonder if you would have any objection to my release of our two cables. Eisenhower.

I replied at once: "No objection whatsoever. MacArthur"

A meeting was held at the residence in New York City of Secretary of State designate John Foster Dulles on December 17. Those present were

Eisenhower, Dulles and myself. In order that there be no misunderstanding or confusion as to my views and recommendations, I prepared and gave to Eisenhower a written memorandum reading as follows:

Memorandum on Ending the Korean War.

A successful solution of the problem of Korea involves political as well as military considerations. For the sacrifice leading to a military victory would be pointless did we not translate it promptly to the political advantage of peace. As a matter of historical record, the failure through inertia of our diplomacy to utilize the victory of Inchon and destruction of the North Korean Armies as the basis for swift and dynamic political action to restore peace and unity to Korea is one of the great contributing causes to the subsequent new war into which we were later plunged by Red China.

In April 1951, when I left the scene of action, the enemy, although well supplied with excellently trained infantry with adequate small arms and light equipment, had practically no supporting air power and was markedly deficient in artillery, anti-aircraft guns, transport and communications equipment. This permitted our own air to operate strategically and tactically with little or no opposition and made possible an early and inexpensive military victory through destruction of the enemy's bases of attack and supply north of the Yalu, conventional targets never before provided sanctuary in the history of war. Indeed, it is self-evident that the Red Chinese Commander would not have risked the entry of major forces into the Korean Peninsula without the knowledge previously gained, through indiscretion or leakage, of the extraordinary and unprecedented protection our military policy restrictions would afford his supply lines and bases north of his point of entry which otherwise would have been at the complete mercy of our then largely unopposed air power.

Now after 20 months the situation as it then existed is markedly changed. The enemy reportedly has appreciable air forces with an arc of air bases extending from Port Arthur to Vladivostok to challenge our own air operations within the general area of the Yalu. He probably now has artillery superiority and through greatly increased motor equipment has largely solved the logistical problems which then confronted him. His communications now permit far more efficient tactical control of his front line units. But a change of even greater significance lies in the fact that through the ensuing 20 months the Korean war has grown to symbolize in the eyes of the world the struggle between the Soviet and the United States in which every facet of disagreement in every sector of the world is a part of the correlated whole. That this is so may well prove to our advantage if we utilize the fact with skill, courage and vision. For the capability which we still possess to destroy Red China's flimsy industrial base and sever her tenuous supply lines from the Soviet would deny her the resources to support modern war and sustain large military forces in the field. This in turn would greatly weaken the communist government of China and threaten the Soviet's present hold upon Asia. A warning of action of this sort provides the leverage to induce the Soviet to bring the Korean struggle to an end without further bloodshed. It would dread risking the eventuality of a Red China debacle and such a threat would consequently prove a powerful, possibly an all-powerful weapon in our hands.

To such end our consideration of the Korean problem should be broadened in the search for peace. A general outline of procedure might be as follows:

(a) Call a two-party conference between the President of the United States and Premier Stalin to be held at a mutually agreed upon neutral point. (The inclusion of the heads of other States would but enhance the possibility of disagreement and failure. Indeed, the President of the United States has every right to so confer on settlement of the Korean War by virtue of the designation of the United States as the agent of the United Nations in that conflict);

(b) That such a conference explore the world situation as a corollary to ending the Korean War;

(c) That we insist that Germany and Korea be permitted to unite under forms of government to be popularly determined upon;

(d) That thereafter we propose that the neutrality of Germany, Austria, Japan and Korea be guaranteed by the United States and the Soviet with all other nations invited to join in as co-guarantors;

(e) That we agree to the principle that in Europe all foreign troops should be removed from Germany and Austria, and in Asia from Japan and Korea;

(f) That we urge that the United States and the Soviet undertake to endeavor to have incorporated in their respective constitutions a provision outlawing war as an instrument of national policy, with all other nations invited to adopt similar moral limitations;

(g) That at such conference, the Soviet be informed that should an agreement not be reached, it would be our intention to clear North Korea of enemy forces. (This could be accomplished through the atomic bombing of enemy military concentrations and installations in North Korea and the sowing of fields of suitable radio-active materials, the by-product of atomic manufacture, to close major lines of enemy supply and communication leading south from the Yalu, with simultaneous amphibious landings on both coasts of North Korea);

(h) That the Soviet should be further informed that, in such eventuality, it would probably become necessary to neutralize Red China's capability to wage modern war. (This could be accomplished by the destruction of Red China's limited airfields and industrial and supply bases, the cutting of her tenuous supply lines from the Soviet and the landing of China's Nationalist forces in Manchuria near the mouth of the Yalu, with limited continuing logistical support until such time as the communist government of China has fallen. This concept would become the great bargaining lever to induce the Soviet to agree upon honorable conditions toward international accord. Should all efforts to arrive at a satisfactory agreement fail, then this phase of the plan should be considered in the light of conditions then existing).

It is obvious that American public opinion will not indefinitely countenance the present indecision and inertia. Underlying the whole problem is the indeterminate question as to whether the Soviet contemplates further military conquest or not. If it does, the time and place will be at its initiative and could not fail to be influenced by the fact that in the atomic area the lead of the United States is probably being diminished with the passage of time. So likewise is the great in-dustrial potential of the United States as compared with that of the communist world. In short, it is not believed that any action we might take to resolve the Far Eastern problem now would in itself be a controlling factor in the precipita-tion of a world conflict. It is my own belief that the Soviet masses are just as eager for peace as are our own people. I believe they suffer the delusion that there are aggressive intentions against them on the part of the capitalistic world, and that they would welcome an imaginative approach which would allay this false impression. The Soviet is not blind to the dangers which actually confront it in the present situation, and it might well settle the Korean War on equitable terms such as those herein outlined, just as soon as it realizes we have the will and the means to bring the present issues to a prompt and definite determination.

This memorandum is intended to present in broadest terms a general concept and outline without the encumberance of detailed discussion. If its basis is accept-able, I shall be glad indeed to present my views as minutely as may be desired.

Douglas MacArthur

New York, New York
December 14, 1952

While Eisenhower was studying the memorandum I asked Dulles his own reaction. He said:

"Your premature relief has resulted tragically for the free world. I regard it as the greatest mistake Truman ever made. Your present plan is a bold and imaginative one and could well succeed. I believe, however, that Eisenhower should first consolidate his position as President before attempt-ing so ambitious and comprehensive a program. It might take him a year to do so."

I replied that Eisenhower would be at the peak of his power and prestige the day he was sworn in as President; that every day after his inauguration his power with the people would diminish, the first three months arithmeti-cally, the second three geometrically, and the final six months astronomically; that by the end of a year he would be just the leader of his party fighting for the programs of his administration; that the plan represented action, to wait inaction; that he was the one American the Soviet esteemed highly; that if he did not act at once he could never do so, that it would then become too late.

On December 16 I received the following letter from the Chairman of the Joint Chiefs of Staff:

Dear General MacArthur:

The Joint Chiefs of Staff have discussed many possible courses of military action in Korea and we are interested in any new idea or suggestion that could possibly end this conflict on honorable terms acceptable to the people of this nation and to the United Nations.

We have been informed of your statement that there is a clear and definite solution which might end the Korean conflict. We would appreciate meeting with you at your earliest convenience to discuss this matter, or to receive your views on this matter by letter should it not be practicable for you to meet with us.

For the Joint Chiefs of Staff

> Omar N. Bradley
> General of the Army
> Chairman

I replied at once:

December 16, 1952

Dear Mr. Chairman:

I have just received your note of the 16th and appreciate the invitation of the Joint Chiefs of Staff to confer with them on the Korean conflict.

I do have certain views concerning basic general policies differing materially from those now in effect, which I believe would produce favorable results. These views, however, involve predominant political decisions which are more vital than are the related military phases. To initiate implementation, action would require a longer period of time than is left to the present administration. This time factor makes it essential that the incoming administration make the fundamental decisions involved.

Prior to receipt of your note, I had accepted an invitation to confer on December 17 with the President-elect on the solution of the Korean problem. I am confident that he will bring to the attention of the Joint Chiefs of Staff anything suggested by me which he believes appropriately requires their consideration. If this necessitates a coordinated discussion of the matter with the Joint Chiefs of Staff, I should, of course, be glad to participate. Any solution could hardly be of such military immediacy as could be reflected in an instantaneous cessation of daily casualties.

> Very sincerely,
> Douglas MacArthur

General Bradley replied on December 29:

Dear General MacArthur:

Thank you very much for your prompt reply to my recent letter. I have informed the Joint Chiefs of Staff of its contents and they appreciate, as I do, your position.

May I take this opportunity to wish you a happy and prosperous New Year. I hope it will find many good things coming your way.

With kindest personal regards.

> Sincerely,
> Omar N. Bradley

And from that day to this I have never been further approached on the matter from any source.

Great changes have taken place in our military establishment, some good, some not so good. Materially the improvement has been spectacular, psychologically yet to be proven. The men in the ranks are largely citizen soldiers, sailors or airmen—men from the farm, the city, from school, from the college campus—men not dedicated to the profession of arms; men not primarily skilled in the art of war; men most amazingly like the men you know and see and meet each day of your life.

If hostilities come these men will know the endless tramp of marching feet, the incessant whine of sniper bullets, the ceaseless rustle of sputtering machine guns, the sinister wail of air combat, the deafening blast of crashing bombs, the stealthy stroke of hidden torpedoes, the amphibious lurch over perilous waves, the dark majesty of fighting ships, the mad din of battle and all the tense and ghastly horror and savage destruction of a stricken area of war.

These men will suffer hunger and thirst, broiling suns and frozen reaches, but they must go on and on and on when everything within them seems to stop and die. They will grow old in youth burned out in searing minutes, even though life owes them many tranquil years. In these troublesome times of confused and bewildered international sophistication, let no man misunderstand why they do that which they must do. These men will fight, and, perchance die, for one reason only—for their country—for America. No complex philosophies of world intrigue and conspiracy dominate their thoughts. No exploitation or extravagance of propaganda dims their sensibilities. Just the simple fact, their country called.

But now strange voices are heard across the land, decrying this old and proven concept of patriotism. Seductive murmurs are arising that it is now outmoded by some more comprehensive and all-embracing philosophy, that we are provincial and immature or reactionary and stupid when we idealize our own country; that there is a higher destiny for us under another and more general flag; that no longer when we send our sons and daughters to the battlefields must we see them through all the way to victory; that we can call upon them to fight and even to die in some halfhearted and indecisive war; that we can plunge them recklessly into war and then suddenly decide that it is a wrong war or in a wrong place or at a wrong time, or even that we can call it not a war at all by using some more euphemistic and gentler name; that we can treat them as expendable, although they are our own flesh and blood; that we, the strongest military nation in the world, have suddenly become dependent upon others for our security and even our welfare.

Listen not to these voices, be they from the one political party or from the other. Be they from the high and the mighty or the lowly and forgotten. Heed them not. Visit upon them a righteous scorn, born of the past sacrifices of your fighting sons and daughters. Repudiate them in the market place, on platforms, from the pulpit. The highest encomium you can still receive is to be called a patriot, if it means you love your country above all else and will place your life, if need be, at the service of your Flag.

Great changes, even more comprehensive than in the military field, have taken place in industry. In its massive and almost limitless potential, the rugged determination of its leaders, the skill and energy of its workers, there has been welded an industrial supremacy such as the world has never before known. It comprises not only a power in being but a reserve power capable of being quickly mounted to meet and overcome any eventuality that might arise. This not only insures a continuity of human progress but imposes an almost impassable barrier against any who would threaten the security of the American continent. It has thus become a leavening influence in a world where war and the threat and fear of war would otherwise so distort the minds of men as to threaten the progress of the human race.

It represents a condition of preparedness born of American enterprise and vision, nurtured upon American energy and incentive, and depending for its ultimate strength upon American will and determination. It is the result and fruition of the capitalistic system—a system embracing every segment of American society—the owners of industry, the workers in industry, the public served by industry. This free enterprise based upon the right to work and the right to possess the fruits of that work has created an economic freedom which is the basis of all other freedoms.

But this very success has created its own perils and harassments, both from without and within. For from one end of the world to the other there is a titanic struggle to seize control of industry and of the economics. Whether this be in the masquerade of Communism or Socialism or Fascism the purpose is the same—to destroy a primary element of Freedom and preempt it for the State.

The capitalistic system has hence become the great target, although it has never failed to provide the resource for an ever increasing standard for human life, has never failed to maximize the fruits of human energy and creative enterprise, has never failed to provide the sinews for victory in war. It has built this nation far beyond the wildest dreams of its architects; it has through the scientific advance of means of communication closed the international geographic gap to permit rapid and effective trade and commerce among the peoples of the world, has elevated the laborer, the farmer and the tradesman to their rightful station of dignity and relative prosperity, and has established the pattern for modern industrialization and scientific development.

The first prominent opponent of capitalism was Karl Marx who shunned the use of violence and sought the voluntary acceptance of the principle of communal ownership of the sources and means of production. The innate common sense of the human race, however, rejected this principle and the element of force was injected by the Bolshevik after the close of the first World War. Then was combined the theory of Karl Marx with the principle of Nihilism under which the control of public policy was sought through terrorism and violence. This combination known as Communism has had many successes. The minority, the Communist Party, in many sectors of the globe has been able to establish its rule over the majority. Only where the concept of human liberty was most deeply rooted and greatly advanced were such minority pressures decisively thrown back.

Such was the case in this nation where our economy, built upon the principle of private capitalism, became recognized as the great barrier to the universal enforcement of the theories of modern Communism. There followed repeated and diversified efforts to reduce and destroy it. Resort was had to the control of private profit by the Marxism-inspired device of confiscatory taxation and the levies upon privately accumulated resources.

It began in this country with the Federal Income Tax Law of 1914 which gave unlimited access to the people's wealth, and the power for the first time to levy taxes not for revenue only but for social purposes. Since then the sphere of government has increased with a kind of explosive force.

Karl Marx, while planning the destruction of all constitutional government, said: "The surest way to overturn the social order is to debauch the currency." And the Russian dictator, Lenin, that implacable foe of the free enterprise system, predicted as early as 1920 that the United States would eventually spend itself into bankruptcy.

Karl Marx referred, of course, to the process of inflation, induced by extreme taxation; the process of "planned economy"; the process of controlling economic conditions and thereby controlling the lives of individuals —a control of fiscal, monetary and general economic forces which produce higher prices and a gradual devitalizing of the purchasing power of money. The continuing rise in the cost of living is due to our drift deeper and deeper into inflation until today our whole economic, social and political system is infected by an inflationary mentality. "Taxation, with its offspring inflation," said Lenin, in support of the basic thesis of Karl Marx, "is the vital weapon to displace the system of free enterprise."—the system on which our nation was founded—the system which has made us the most prosperous people of all history—the system which enabled us to produce over half of the world's goods with less than one-seventeenth of the world's area and population—the system which gave our people more liberty, privileges and opportunities than any other nation ever gave its people in the long history of the world. To destroy it is the sure road to Socialism. And by Socialism is meant the forcing of a centrally controlled economic life upon all persons in the nation under an authoritarian monopoly that is politically managed. Actually, there has been through the direction of our own public policy an incessant encroachment upon the capitalistic system. Most officials of our government over the past years will deny, and justifiably, any intent to establish in this nation the basis for the emergence of a Socialistic, much less a Communistic State, but the course of fiscal policy has done just that. The fact is unmistakeable and clear that if the capitalistic system—free enterprise—is to be preserved to the future generations of our people, the course of government must be oriented to foster and preserve adequate incentive to encourage the thrift, the industry and the adventure which brought our nation to its present pre-eminence among all of the other nations of the earth and which alone can carry it forward in peace and security and progress.

I realize full well that the restless spirit of the times seeks change. But change should not be made for the sake of change alone. It should be sought only to adapt time tested principles which have been proven in the crucible of human experience to the new requirements of an expanding society. To do otherwise is not true liberalism. The Constitution is not to be treated as an instrument of political expediency. Every move that is made to circumvent its spirit, every move that is made to over-centralize political power, every move that is made to curtail and suppress individual liberty is reaction in its most extreme form. For the framers of the Constitution were the most liberal thinkers of all the ages and the Charter they produced out of the liberal revolution of their time has never been and is not now surpassed in liberal thought.

The object and practice of liberty lies in the limitation of governmental power. Through the ages the constantly expanding grasp of government has been liberty's greatest threat. Daniel Webster once said on the floor of the Senate:

"Our security is in our watchfulness of executive power. It was the Constitution of this department, which was infinitely the most difficult part in the great work of creating our present government; to give to the executive department such power as should make it useful, and yet not such as should render it dangerous; to make it efficient, independent and strong, and yet to prevent it from sweeping away everything by its union of military and civil authority, by the influence of patronage, and office, and force. . . . I do not wish to impair the power of the President as it stands written down in the Constitution. But, I will not blindly confide, where all experience admonishes me to be jealous; I will not trust executive power, vested in the hands of a single magistrate, to keep the vigils of liberty."

He spoke those words 129 years ago; but they could as well have been spoken but yesterday.

There are many who have lost faith in this early American ideal and believe in a form of socialistic, totalitarian rule, a sort of big brother deity to run our lives for us. They no longer believe that free men can successfully manage their own affairs. Their thesis is that a handful of men, centered in government, largely bureaucratic not elected, can utilize the proceeds of our toil and labor to greater advantage than those who create it. Nowhere in the history of the human race is there justification for this reckless faith in political power. It is the oldest, most reactionary of all forms of social organization. It was tried out in ancient Babylon, ancient Greece and ancient Rome; in Mussolini's Italy, in Hitler's Germany, and in all communist countries. Wherever and whenever it has been attempted, it has failed utterly to provide economic security, and has generally ended in national disaster. It embraces an essential idiocy, that individuals who, as private citizens, are not to manage the disposition of their own earnings, become in public office supermen who can manage the affairs of the world.

The fundamental and ultimate issue at stake is liberty, itself—liberty versus the creeping socialization in every domestic field. Freedom to live under the minimum of restraint! A least common denominator of mediocrity against the proven progress of pioneering individualism! The free enterprise system or the cult of conformity! The result will determine the future of civilization. It will be felt on every human life. It will be etched in blazing rainbow colors on the very arch of the sky.

I had a rough bout with illness, and treasure highly the note of sympathy that came from BBC in London:

The illness of General Douglas MacArthur dominates the news of America here in Europe, especially in Britain. Throughout England, where memoir-writing

Field Marshals tend to be heavily critical of American commanders in World War II, General MacArthur is a highly regarded and non-controversial figure. While even President Eisenhower's command decisions in Europe are considered fair game for postwar critics, military men here have unreserved praise for General MacArthur's conduct of the Pacific and Korean wars. Hence his illness is major and depressing news here as well as in the United States.

While I was convalescing I received a request from a distinguished minister in Chicago asking my favorite text from the scriptures at my moment of crisis. I replied:

I have received your letter asking that I indicate a passage in the Bible which has been most helpful to me. It would be difficult, indeed, for me to select a single verse as the most inspirational from the myriad passages which are so immutable and everlasting in that greatest of books. But perhaps one example will suffice. I was once given but thirty-six hours of life. I remembered the Gospel of St. John where it says a certain man named Lazarus of Bethany, the town of Mary, was desperately sick even unto death. When Jesus was told he said this sickness was not unto death, and he called upon Lazarus to come forth. And Lazarus arose from the dead. And Jesus said, 'I am the resurrection and the life; he that believeth in Me, though he were dead, yet shall he live.' And so, I came through.

My illness left me gaunt and haggard. One of my Rainbow soldiers visited me and said, "I haven't seen you, General, for nearly forty years. You have changed since being our young 'Hell-to-breakfast baby.' How does it seem to be old?" I told him I liked it, and when he expressed amazement, I said, "With my date of birth, if I were not old, I would be dead." But he just scratched his head and went away puzzled.

And shortly afterward a kindly passerby stopped me with congratulations on how much better I looked than the local pictures depicted me. "You seem bigger and stronger," he said, "and much younger without eyeglasses. Yes, sir," he exclaimed, "your pictures do you a great injustice, Mr. Truman." I didn't know whether to laugh or to cry.

I made one further trip to the Far East, a sentimental journey to the Philippines as a guest of the nation on the fifteenth anniversary of its independence. I visited again the old historic spots—the white beaches of Leyte, the great central thoroughfare through Luzon, now named the MacArthur Highway, the rugged slopes of Corregidor gone back to jungle, the hills of Bataan under the shadows of the setting sun beyond Marivales. When last I had been there, the scene had been one of desolation and destruction. The war still raged. The crash of guns roared. The sputter of rifle fire filled the air. The acrid smell of smoke, the stench of death was everywhere. There was sorrow and bereavement in countless Philippine homes. Fire and sword had taken a toll of personal tragedy, searing the hearts and souls of every Filipino citizen.

But now their cities had been restored, their economy revived, their farm shortages turned into surpluses, their commerce expanded. Their products now reached the markets of the world. They had taken their place in the counsels of the nations with dignity and universal respect. All was light and laughter. And as I saw the happiness in their faces, as I saw the prosperity of the community, a great weight was lifted from my heart, and I thanked God that I was one of those who had helped them to freedom. Once again the fragrance of the ilang-ilang and the sampaguita filled the air as millions of devoted Filipinos greeted me with their welcoming shouts of "Mabuhay."

I tried to speak to them words of wisdom, but in my heart was only affection and remembrance. Their leaders praised me saying:

The world has paid a terrible price since the Korean War when you were prevented from taking action against the planes and bases of China at the Yalu. Someone bears a tremendous responsibility for this retreat from victory. If you had been allowed to do your military job there would not have been the disaster of Indo-China; Tibet would not be slave; Laos would not be in the melting pot; Castro would be an unknown man; and Berlin would not figure so prominently as it does at present.

I told them:

The tide of world affairs ebbs and flows in and out. Old empires die, new nations are born, alliances arise and vanish. But through all this confusion the mutual friendship of our two countries shines like a beacon in the night. Together we suffered in war. Together we seek the way of peace. And in this long twilight era, that is neither war nor peace, we stand as firmly as before, together.

Senator Thomas J. Dodd of Connecticut made the following flattering statement on the floor of the Senate on my return from the Philippines, and added an assessment of my impact upon American history:

Today General MacArthur returns to the United States after once more successfully completing an important mission for our country. His trip to the Philippines has been called a sentimental journey; and it has been that, not only for him and the people of the Philippines but for all of us. The sight of General MacArthur in uniform, as of old, receiving the plaudits of admiring millions, recalls vividly to our minds the picture of our nation as we would always hope to see it, a nation that had kept its promise, a nation victorious on all fronts, a nation at the pinnacle of worldly power and esteem, a nation triumphantly dedicated to the cause of freedom. To millions of people at home and around the globe, Douglas MacArthur has seemed a symbol and almost a personification of America in its finest aspects. Outwardly there was the unforgettable surface picture, the striking countenance, the confident stride, the legendary hat and glasses and corncob pipe, the resonant, authoritative voice, the grand phrase, the dramatic gesture, and behind this surface picture were all the attributes of excellence, the supreme competence, the serene confidence, the intellectual power, the noble purpose, the complete commitment to the vision of an America that was unconquerable in the service of a just cause. General MacArthur must always have felt in his bones that electric current of excitement which America and things American brought to the world two centuries ago; and he has had the rare capacity to radiate that current to the people of his time. Here is a man with a sense of history, with a flair for what is honestly and genuinely dramatic, with an ability to surround himself with an aura of romance and mystery, all effectively and wisely used to advance our national interest.

The name of Douglas MacArthur causes to flash through the mind unforgettable images which are an essential part of the American story; the gallant, magnificent defense of Bataan and Corregidor against hopeless odds; the promise to return and the depth of conviction that made men believe the promise would be kept; the vast, brilliant, island-hopping campaign stretching from Australia to Tokyo which will ever remain a marvel of military genius; the wading ashore at Luzon; the incomparable scene on the Battleship *Missouri* where General MacArthur accepted the surrender of our enemy, appropriately concluding a victory so awesome, so complete, so seemingly final; and then the restoration of that fallen enemy to freedom, social justice and prosperity.

But if the name of Douglas MacArthur recalls to each of us the supreme hour of national triumph, so too it compels us to face up to the tragic and anguishing picture of our national retreat from that triumph. If General MacArthur was the most eminent spokesman of the American tradition of victory, so also was he the pre-eminent and perhaps the pivotal casualty of our departure from that tradition.

He has told us, "In war there is no substitute for victory." And that statement was not only an expression of military certainty, but an affirmation of the indomitable spirit which this nation had historically displayed. The Korean War and the events surrounding it ruptured that tradition. It ushered something new into American policy. From then on, fear, indecision, vacillation, the counsels of defeat, of weakness, of appeasement gained a beachhead that has since spread and grown.

The controversy which resulted in the relief of General MacArthur and the ensuing loss of the Korean War may prove to have been the turning point in American history, for it marked the first conscious decision by this nation to accept defeat rather than run the necessary risks of victory. If the cause of those who support an unyielding policy against Communist aggression could not prevail then, we may well ask ourselves: When can it prevail? For then, all of the elements were favorable to it. The United States alone possessed nuclear power.

We were engaged in active, open warfare against the Communist criminals and, therefore, our leaders and our people had every reason to be fully aware of the nature of the enemy.

Tens of thousands of our sons were casualties in a war which was being fought with one hand tied behind their back. There was a wave of national protest and disgust at our failure to push the Korean fighting to the victorious conclusion that was within our grasp. And in General MacArthur, those who stood for victory had as their champion, not only one of the most revered and respected figures of American history, but one of the most articulate spokesmen that any cause has ever had. Who can forget the outpouring of sentiment for MacArthur and the cause he represented that swept this country from end to end when he returned to the United States in the spring of 1951? I have always been convinced that the overwhelming majority of the American people supported the policies which he then outlined as a means of winning the Korean War.

In a decision for which we as a nation can truly be held responsible, the opportunity to crush the aggressive power of Communist China at its outset was lost by default and America proceeded upon a policy of vacillation and retreat from victory which, with each passing year, brings its harvest of shame and defeat.

For almost a decade General MacArthur has remained aloof from the storm center of political controversy. His return to the scene of his greatest hours has deeply stirred this nation and the world. The universal acclaim for General MacArthur which has swept through the Philippines is in my mind more than just a deserved tribute to a very great hero. It is as well the symptom of a yearning there and throughout the world for that dynamic, resolute, indomitable American leadership of which General MacArthur was and is the symbol.

The soldier is home once more. The esteem and love and thanks of a grateful nation go out to him for what he has done, for what he is, and for what he means to our generation and to all generations.

A ny lingering doubt which may have existed as to the durability of reforms instituted during the occupation in Japanese economic and political life was effectively erased by the evaluation of former Prime Minister Shigeru Yoshida in a recent letter dated February 20, 1964, wherein he said:

. . . Fondly and gratefully I cherish the memories of those years of our intimate contact—you as Supreme Commander for the Allied Powers and I as executor of your directives. You were so good to me, so kind and gracious that I was able to perform my duty to the best of my ability, and thereby contribute my mite to the making of the new Japan. I wonder if you might be interested to see with your own eyes how firmly your epochal reforms have taken root in Japanese soil. . . .

This letter moved me deeply and encouraged in me an assurance that the design I left for the new Japan would endure long, long into the future.

On May 12, 1962, I was awarded the Sylvanus Thayer Medal, the highest honor of the United States Military Academy. That day, I reviewed the Corps of Cadets on the Plain at West Point, lunched with them at the mess hall, and then responded to the presentation. I had no prepared address, but my remarks were recorded as follows:

As I was leaving the hotel this morning, a doorman asked me, "Where are you headed for, General?" And when I replied, "West Point," he remarked, "Beautiful place. Have you ever been there before?"

No human being could fail to be deeply moved by such a tribute as this. Coming from a profession I have served so long, and a people I have loved so well, it fills me with an emotion I cannot express. But this award is not intended primarily to honor a personality, but to symbolize a great moral code—the code of conduct and chivalry of those who guard this beloved land of culture and ancient descent. That is the meaning of this medallion. For all eyes and for all time, it is an expression of the ethics of the American soldier. That I should be integrated in this way with so noble an ideal arouses a sense of pride and yet of humility which will be with me always. . . .

Duty–Honor–Country. Those three hallowed words reverently dictate what you ought to be, what you can be, what you will be. They are your rallying points; to build courage when courage seems to fail; to regain faith when there seems to be little cause for faith; to create hope when hope becomes forlorn. Unhappily, I possess neither that eloquence of diction, that poetry of imagination, nor that brilliance of metaphor to tell you all that they mean. The unbelievers will say they are but words, but a slogan, but a flamboyant phrase. Every pedant, every demagogue, every cynic, every hypocrite, every troublemaker, and, I am sorry to say, some others of an entirely different character, will try to downgrade them even to the extent of mockery and ridicule.

But these are some of the things they do. They build your basic character; they mold you for your future roles as custodians of the nation's defense; they make you strong enough to know when you are weak, and brave enough to face yourself when you are afraid. They teach you to be proud and unbending in honest failure, but humble and gentle in success, not to substitute words for actions, not to seek the path of comfort, but to face the stress and spur of difficulty and challenge; to learn to stand up in the storm but to have compassion on those who fail; to master yourself before you seek to master others; to have a heart that is clean, a goal that is high; to learn to laugh yet never forget how to weep; to reach into the future yet never neglect the past; to be serious yet never to take yourself too seriously; to be modest so that you will remember the simplicity of true greatness, the open mind of true wisdom, the meekness of true strength. They give you a temper of the will, a quality of the imagination, a vigor of the emotions, a freshness of the deep springs of life, a temperamental predominance of courage over timidity, an appetite for adventure over love of ease. They create in your heart the sense of wonder, the unfailing hope of what next, and the joy and inspiration of life. They teach you in this way to be an officer and a gentleman.

And what sort of soldiers are those you are to lead? Are they reliable, are they brave, are they capable of victory? Their story is known to all of you; it is the story of the American man-at-arms. My estimate of him was formed on the battlefield many years ago, and has never changed. I regarded him then as I regard him now—as one of the world's noblest figures, not only as one of the finest military characters, but also as one of the most stainless. His name and fame are the birthright of every American citizen. In his youth and strength, his love and loyalty, he gave all that mortality can give. He needs no eulogy from me or from any other man. He was written his own history and written it in red on his enemy's breast. But when I think of his patience under adversity, of his courage under fire, and of his modesty in victory, I am filled with an emotion of admiration I cannot put into words. He belongs to history as furnishing one of the greatest examples of successful patriotism; he belongs to posterity as the instructor of future generations in the principles of liberty and freedom; he belongs to the present, to us, by his virtues and by his achievements. In twenty campaigns, on a hundred battlefields, around a thousand campfires, I have witnessed that enduring fortitude, that patriotic self-abnegation, and that invincible determination which have carved his status in the hearts of his people. From one end of the world to the other he has drained deep the chalice of courage.

As I listened to those songs of the glee club, in memory's eye I could see those staggering columns of the First World War, bending under soggy packs, on many a weary march from dripping dusk to drizzling dawn, slogging ankle deep through the mire of shell-shocked roads, to form grimly for the attack, blue-lipped, covered with sludge and mud, chilled by the wind and rain, driving home to their objective, and, for many, to the judgment seat of God. I do not know the dignity of their birth but I do know the glory of their death. They died unquestioning, uncomplaining, with faith in their hearts, and on their lips the hope that we would go on to victory. Always for them—Duty–Honor–Country; always their blood and sweat and tears as we sought the way and the light and the truth.

And twenty years after, on the other side of the globe, again the filth of murky foxholes, the stench of ghostly trenches, the slime of dripping dugouts; those broiling suns of relentless heat, those torrential rains of devastating storm, the loneliness and utter desolation of jungle trails, the bitterness of long separation from those they loved and cherished, the deadly pestilence of tropical disease, the horror of stricken areas of war; their resolute and determined defense, their swift and sure attack, their indomitable purpose, their complete and decisive victory—always victory—always through the bloody haze of their last reverberating shot, the vision of gaunt, ghastly men reverently following your password of Duty–Honor–Country.

The code which those words perpetrate embraces the highest moral laws and will stand the test of any ethics or philosophies ever promulgated for the uplift of mankind. Its requirements are for the things that are right, and its restraints are from the things that are wrong. The soldier, above all other men, is required to practice the greatest act of religious training—sacrifice. In battle and in the face of danger and death, he discloses those divine attributes which his Maker gave when He created man in His own image. No physical courage and no brute instinct can take the place of the Divine help which alone can sustain him. However horrible the incidents of war may be, the soldier who is called upon to offer and to give his life for his country is the noblest development of mankind.

You now face a new world—a world of change. The thrust into outer space of the satellites, spheres and missiles marked the beginning of another epoch in the long story of mankind—the chapter of the space age. In the five or more billions of years the scientists tell us it has taken to form the earth, in the three or more billion years of development of the human race, there has never been a greater, a more abrupt or staggering evolution. We deal now not with things of this world alone, but with the illimitable distances and as yet unfathomed mysteries of the universe. We are reaching out for a new and boundless frontier. We speak in strange terms: of harnessing the cosmic energy; of making winds and tides work for us; of creating unheard-of synthetic materials to supplement or even replace our old standard basics; of purifying sea water for our drink; of mining ocean floors for new fields of wealth and food; of disease preventatives to expand life into the hundreds of years; of controlling the weather for a more equitable distribution of heat and cold, of rain and shine; of space ships to the moon; of the primary target in war, no longer limited to the armed forces of an enemy, but instead to include his civil populations; of ultimate conflict between a united human race and the sinister forces of some other planetary galaxy; of such dreams and fantasies as to make life the most exciting of all time.

And through all this welter of change and development, your mission remains fixed, determined, inviolable—it is to win our wars. Everything else in your professional career is but a corollary to this vital dedication. All other public purposes, all other public projects, all other public needs, great or small, will find others for their accomplishment; but you are the ones who are trained to fight; yours is the profession of arms—the will to win, the sure knowledge that in war there is no substitute for victory; that if you lose, the nation will be destroyed; that the very obsession of your public service must be Duty–Honor–Country. Others will debate the controversial issues, national and international, which divide man's minds; but serene, calm, aloof, you stand as the nation's war guardian, as its life-guard from the raging tides of international conflict; as its gladiator in the arena of battle. For a century and a half, you have defended, guarded, and protected its hallowed traditions of liberty and freedom, of right and justice. Let civilian voices argue the merits or demerits of our processes of government; whether our strength is being sapped by deficit financing, indulged in too long; by federal paternalism grown too mighty; by power groups grown too arrogant; by politics grown too corrupt; by crime grown too rampant; by morals grown too low; by taxes grown too high; by extremists grown too violent; whether our personal liberties are as thorough and complete as they should be. These great national problems are not for your professional participation or military solution. Your guidepost stands out like a tenfold beacon in the night—Duty–Honor–Country.

You are the leaven which binds together the entire fabric of our national system of defense. From your ranks come the great captains who hold the nation's destiny in their hands the moment the war tocsin sounds. The Long Gray Line has never failed us. Were you to do so, a million ghosts in olive drab, in brown khaki, in blue and gray, would rise from their white crosses thundering those magic words—Duty–Honor–Country.

This does not mean that you are war mongers. On the contrary, the soldier, above all other people, prays for peace, for he must suffer and bear the deepest wounds and scars of war. But always in our ears ring the ominous words of Plato, that wisest of all philosophers, "Only the dead have seen the end of war."

The shadows are lengthening for me. The twilight is here. My days of old have vanished tone and tint; they have gone glimmering through the dreams of things that were. Their memory is one of wondrous beauty, watered by tears, and coaxed and caressed by the smiles of yesterday. I listen vainly, but with thirsty ear, for the witching melody of faint bugles blowing reveille, of far drums beating the long roll. In my dreams I hear again the crash of guns, the rattle of musketry, the strange mournful mutter of the battlefield. But in the evening of my memory, always I come back to West Point. Always there echoes and re-echoes in my ears—Duty–Honor–Country.

Today marks my final roll call with you. But I want you to know that when I cross the river my last conscious thoughts will be of the Corps—and the Corps—and the Corps.

I bid you farewell.

Index

Abucay, 132
Acheson, Dean, 289, 322, 322 fn., 324, 382 fn.
Adachi, Hataze, Gen., 173, 193, 194
Admiralty Islands, 187, 189
Aguinaldo, Emilio, 20–23, 26, 134–135
Ah Cheu (nurse), 141, 142
Aitape, 189, 194
Aker, A.B., Ens., 144
Alanbrooke, Lord, Field Marshal, 218 fn., 289–290, 291, 392
Aldrich, Winthrop W., 270 fn.
Aleutians, 112, 159
Alexander, King (Yugoslavia), 98
Alexishafen, 262 fn.
Alice Spring, Australia, 145
Allied Council for Japan, 291, 293, 316, 319
Almond, Edward N., Maj. Gen., 327, 347, 349, 351, 355, 374, 377
Ambon, 176
American Olympic Committee, 86
Amsterdam Island, 194
Andaman Islands, 112
Aparri, 123
Argonne Forest, 64, 65
Arnold, H. H., Gen., 183, 184, 244 fn., 248 fn., 258, 263
Artem, Nurettin, 289
Asahi Shimbun, 396
Ataturk, Mustapha Kemal, 98
Atlanta, Ga., 84
Atom bomb, 262–263
Atsugi Airfield, 269, 270, 399
Attlee, Clement, 317, 376
Austin, Warren, 342
Australia, 110, 120, 128, 140, 141, 151–160, 166, 181–183

Baguio, 252
Baker, Newton D., 43–44, 45, 46, 47, 67
Balete Pass, 253

Balikpapan, 255, 262 fn.
Ball, William G., Capt., 40
Baltimore, Md., 85
Baquio, 239
Barbey, Daniel, Rear Adm., 172, 239
Barstow, William A., 4
Bataan, 29, 84, 107, 124–127, 129, 130, 135, 139, 142, 145–146, 202, 249, 250
Bataan (C-54), 270, 332
Batangas, 238, 245
Batchelor Field, 145
Baton Rouge, La., 14
Bazelaire, Georges de, Gen., 54
Beard, Mary R., tribute to MacArthur, 306 fn.
Belcher, Aurelia, see MacArthur, Aurelia
Berkey, Admiral, 239
Biak Island, 192, 193
Bibles, 311
Bicol Peninsula, 253
Bilibid, concentration camp at, 246, 248
Birdwood, Lord, 174 fn.
Bismarck Sea, 172
Black, Lieutenant, 69
Blake, Thomas, 292
Blamey, Sir Thomas, 157, 160, 162, 164, 165 fn., 178, 239, 254
Blood, Sir Bindon, 32
Bois de la Sonnard, 63
Boise (light cruiser), 240, 255
Bong, Richard, Maj., 238
Bonus March, 92–97
Borneo, 112, 121, 254, 255, 262
Bougainville, 161, 163, 176, 177, 180
Bradley, Omar, Gen., 346, 351, 361, 362, 372, 392, 412–413
Brady, "Diamond Jim," 27
Bragg, Braxton, Gen., 8
Breckinridge, Henry, 43
Brereton, Lewis H., Maj. Gen., 113, 117, 120
Brisbane, Australia, 154

Brisbane Line, 152
Brown, Eddie, Col., 88, 89
Brown, Lytle, Maj. Gen., 89, 100
Bruce, Andrew D., Gen., 232
Brunei, 255, 262 fn.
Bryan, William Jennings, 19
Buckner, Simon B., Gen., 258, 259
Buddhism, 281
"Buddy system," 337
"Buffalo Bill," 13
Bulkeley, John D., Lieut., 141–144
Buna Mission, 162, 165
Buna Village, 162, 164
Bundy, Omar, Gen., 84
Bunker, Paul, 142
Burbank, Luther, 86
Burlesoa, Rev. Allen, 17
Burma, 106, 112, 153, 175
Burnside, W. A., Capt., 40
Butler, Benjamin, Maj. Gen., 14
Byers, General, 165 fn.
Byrd, Harry F., 392
Byrnes, James, 291, 306 fn., 357 fn.

Cabanatuan, 246
Cabra Island, 143
Cagayan, 144
Cagayan Valley, 252, 253
Cairo agreement, 343
California Debris Commission, 30
Camp, Walter, 142
Camp Mills, 51, 53
Camp Robinson, 12
Camp Stanbough, 12
Cannon, Joe, 33–34
Capitalism, 415–417
Caram, Fermin, 207
Carol II, King (Romania), 98
Carolinas, 188
Casey, Charles J., Capt., 55–56
Casey, Hugh (Pat), Brig. Gen., 113, 125, 126, 158, 165 fn.
Cebu, 254
Celebes, 112, 254, 262
Censorship, 146–147
Central Intelligence Agency, 362, 366
Chalons, France, 58
Chamberlin, Stephen J., Brig. Gen., 157
Chase, William C., Maj. Gen., 188, 246
Chateau Thierry, 59
Chattanooga, 52

Cheatham, Benjamin F., 10
Chenoywith, General, 113
Chiang Kai-shek, Generalissimo, 320, 321, 339–340, 341, 343–344, 359, 367, 376, 386
  messages to MacArthur, 248 fn., 289 fn., 354 fn.
Chicago Sun-Times, 339
Chicopee Falls, Massachusetts, 4
China
  Communists in, 320–321
  Japanese invasion of, 106
China, Red, intervention in Korean War, 359, 362, 365, 366, 370
Chinnampo, 365
Chongchon River, 372
Chongjin, 373
Christianity, 310, 311
Chulalongkorn, King, 32
Churchill, Sir Winston S.
  Cairo agreement, 343
  messages to MacArthur, 168 fn., 173 fn., 174–175, 189 fn., 218 fn., 257, 317
  Pacific war and, 166, 199
  Roosevelt and, 121, 153, 181, 211
  succeeded by Attlee, 317
  Tehran Conference, 183
  tribute to MacArthur, 270 fn.
"Civil Liberties Directive," 289
Civil Service Commission, U.S., 309
Civil War, 4, 6–11, 14, 36, 84
Clark Field, 110, 113, 117, 120, 244, 245
Clay, Henry, 5
Cleveland, 255
Cleveland, Grover, 19
Coetquidon, France, 53
Collins, Joseph Lawton, Gen., 347, 348–349, 351, 376 fn., 385
Communist Party, U.S., 93, 95, 96
Communists and Communism, 416
  in China, 320–321
  in Japan, 308–309
  in North Korea, 324, 327, 330
Compton, Karl T., 286–287
Concentration camps, 146, 147–148
Coney, C. E., Capt., 215
Confessor, Tomas, 205, 207–208
Congress, U.S., MacArthur's speech before, 400–405
Connor, Fox, Gen., 68
Constitution, Japanese, 299–304, 314

Constitution, U.S., 417–418
Constitutional Problem Investigating
 Committee (Japan), 299–300
Coral Sea, 154, 159
Corbett, Sergeant Major, 35
Cordier, Constant, Capt, 40–41
Corregidor, 29, 84, 107, 113, 125n, 126, 127,
 128–129, 135, 139, 141, 142, 146, 153,
 202, 247–249
Côte-de-Chatillon, 65, 66, 67
Covington, 52, 53
Cronyn, William J., 36
Cruz, Emigidio, Maj., 236–237
Cuba, 18, 39
Curley, James B., 107
Curtin, John, 140, 151, 158, 160, 166, 167 fn.,
 173 fn., 174, 181–183, 185, 191 fn.,
 244 fn., 248 fn., 258, 290
Curzon-Kitchener feud, 32
Cushing, James M., Lt. Col., 205–206
Cuyo Islands, 144
Cyclotrons, Japanese, destruction of, 286

Dade, Alexander, Maj., 40, 42
Dagupan, 204, 241
Daily Worker, 280
Dalton, James II, Col., 244
Daly, Charley, 142
Darling River, 152
Davao, 88, 145
Davis, Jefferson, 16
Davis, Thomas J., 1st Lieut., 88
Dean, William F., Maj. Gen., 336
"Death March," 146, 234, 296
Defense Department, U.S., 317, 366
Degoutte, Jean, Gen., 59
Delmonte Field, 113
Deposito, 233
Derevyanko, Kusma, Gen., 263, 285
Dern, George, 100, 101
Dewey, George, Adm., 18
Dewey, Thomas E., 323
Dewing, General, 174
Dickman, Joseph T., Gen., 68
Diet (Japan), 301–302, 304, 314, 323, 395
Dodd, Thomas J., 420
Dollar Steamship Line, 107, 108
Doolittle, Senator (Wisconsin), 6
Dorn, Congressman, 407 fn.
Douglas, Stephen, 6
Doyle, James T., Adm., 348, 353

Drum, Hugh A., Gen., 62, 100
Duffy, Father, 61
Dulag, 212, 214, 221, 229
Dulles, John Foster, 324, 328, 345, 382, 409,
 412
 message to MacArthur, 357 fn.
Dunkel, William C., Brig. Gen., 237
Duport, Pierre-Georges, Gen., 56
Dutch Borneo, 112
Dutch East Indies, 106, 110, 111, 120, 128,
 153, 176, 198, 255, 256, 262
Dutch New Guinea, 190

Early, Stephen A., 185
Eather, Brigadier, 65 fn.
Eichelberger, Robert, Lt. Gen., 157, 162, 164,
 165 fn., 178, 191, 239, 254, 270–271
Einstein, Albert, 27
Eisenhower, Dwight D., Gen., 95, 287, 290,
 370, 409–412
Eisenhower
 messages to MacArthur, 315, 356 fn., 409
Empress Augusta Bay, 180
Enterprise, 172
Erickson, Colonel, 69
Essey, France, 63

Faircloth, Jean Marie, *see* MacArthur, Jean
"Fancy Dans," 347
Far Eastern Commission, 291–293, 302
Fechteler, William M., Rear Adm., 172
Federal Bureau of Investigation, 94, 257
Federal Income Tax Law (1914), 416
Feiberger, Colonel, 27
Fertig, Wendell, Col., 204
Fiji, 112
Finschhafen, 176, 179–180, 262 fn.
Fisher, Fred, 23
Flagler, Clement, Maj. Gen., 71
"Flying Fish Channel," 348, 352–353
Foch, Ferdinand, Marshal, 57, 63 fn.
Ford, James, 95
Ford Island, 121
Formosa, 31, 106, 112, 113, 120, 197,
 231, 245, 320, 321, 322, 339–343, 359,
 375
Forrestal, James, 218 fn., 249 fn., 317
Fort Bridges, 12
Fort Fred Steele, 12
Fort Knox, 91
Fort Leavenworth, 16, 34, 35, 39

Fort MacArthur, 28
Fort Mason, 28, 89
Fort McNair, 32
Fort Myer, 90
Fort Putnam, 18
Fort Rawlins, 12
Fort Riley, 34
Fort Sam Houston, 17
Fort Selden, 14, 15
Fort Stotsenburg, 245
Fort Wingate, 14
Fraser, Bruce, Adm., 240
Free enterprise system, 415–417
Freeman, Douglas Southall, 238 fn., 357 fn.
Frontier, 12–13
Fukudome, Shegeru, Vice Adm., 206
Funafuti, 178
Funston, Frederick, Gen., 22, 40, 46
Funston, Mrs. Frederick, 47

Gairdner, Lt. Gen., 257
Gamelin, Maurice, Gen., 97
Garing, Group Captain, 165 fn.
Garrison, Lindley M., 40, 43
George, Harold L., Gen., 120
George, Walter F., 392
Geronimo, 14, 39
Ghormley, Robert L., Vice Adm., 161, 163, 171
Gili Gili, 159
Gitlow, Benjamin, 96
Glassford, Pelham, 94
Goering, Hermann, 98
Goethals, George, Col., 34
Gona, 164, 262 fn.
Gorgas, William C., Col., 34
Gouraud, Henri, Gen., 57–58, 70 fn.
Gowrie, Lord, 200
Grant, Ulysses S., Gen., 4–5, 394
Green Islands, 187
Griswold, Oscar, Lt. Gen., 191, 239
Guadalcanal, 161, 163, 168–169, 175, 178
Guam, Japanese seizure of, 122
Guimaris Island, 29

Haba, Hikaru, 111
Haengsong, 384
Haig, Douglas, Field Marshal, 47, 63 fn., 92
Hall, Charles P., Gen., 245

Halmaheras, 201–202
Halsey, William F., Adm., 171–172, 176, 180, 192, 211, 218 fn., 224–230, 239, 264
    message to MacArthur, 357 fn.
Han River, 332–333, 335, 339, 346, 384
Hansa Bay, 189–190
Hara, Kensaburo, Rear Adm., 123
Harbord, James G., Capt., 29
Hardy, Mary Pinkney, see MacArthur, Mary
Hardy, Thomas, 13
Harrell, Colonel, 69
Harriman, E. H., 28
Harriman, W. Averell, 340–341, 360, 361
Hart, Thomas C., Adm., 128
Hasbrouck, Captain, 52
Hawaii, 107, 113, 159
Hearst, William Randolph, 382 fn.
Henry, Prince of Mecklenburg-Schwerin, 86
Herring, Edmund F., Gen., 162, 165 fn.
Hickey, Doyle, Gen., 369–370
Hickok, "Wild Bill," 13
Higashi-Kuni, Prince, 272, 280, 293
Hill, Lister, 258–259
Hill, William G., Maj. Gen., 232
Hindenburg, Paul von, Field Marshal, 98
Hindenburg Line, 63, 65
Hirohito, Emperor, 234, 277, 280, 284, 287–288, 293, 296, 300–301, 310–311, 316–317, 395
Hirose, Sueto, Rear Adm., 123
Hiroshima, atom bomb attack on, 262–263
Hitler, Adolf, 91, 108
Hodge, John R., Maj. Gen., 216, 319
Hokkaido, 285
Hollandia, 189, 192, 214
Homma, Masaharu, Lt. Gen., 123–124, 132–133, 216, 241, 296–298
Homma, Mrs. Masaharu, 296
Hong Kong, Japanese seizure of, 122
Honshu, 261
Hoover, Herbert, 88, 89, 94–97, 99, 306 fn.
    message to MacArthur, 406
Hoover J. Edgar, 256
Horii, Tomitaro, Maj. Gen., 161–162
Horthy, Miklós, Adm., 98
Hough, Colonel, 70 fn.
Howe, Fred, 105–106
Huerta, Victoriano, Gen., 39
Huff, Sidney, Col., 395

Hughes, William, 15, 61
Hull, J. A. T., 30
Humboldt Bay, 189–190
Hume, Paul, 394
Hungnan, 377
Huon Peninsula, 262 fn.
Hurley, Patrick, 89, 94–95, 128
Huron Peninsula, 178, 180
Hyakutake Haruyeshi, Gen., 173

Ickes, Harold, 110, 235–237
Iloilo Harbor, 29
Imamura, Hitoshi, Gen., 173
Imita, 161
Inchon, 334, 346–351, 353, 354 fn., 355, 357, 359, 365
India, 153
Indians, 12–13, 14
Indochina, 390
Indonesia, 121
Industry, changes in, 415
Interior Department, U.S., 110
Isolationism, 18–19
Iwo Jima, 197, 259

Jackson Barracks, 13
James boys, 13
Japan, 30
  budget, 307
  Communists in, 308–309
  conditions in, at end of war, 281, 306, 307
  conquest of, 260–265
  constitution of, 299–304, 314
  demobilization of armed forces, 285
  Diet, 301–302, 304, 314, 323, 395
  dismissal of charges against individuals criticizing the Emperor, 317
  economy of, 308–309
  educational system, 311–312
  elections in, 300, 302, 304–305, 316
  free enterprise system in, 308
  health problems, 312–313
  Korean War and, 333–335, 346
  labor in, 308–309
  land reform in, 313–314
  MacArthur's departure, 399
  occupation of, 269–324
  peace treaty with, 324, 345, 382–383
  police problem in, 314

Japan, position of, after the war, 281
  spiritual revolution, 309–311
  surrender of, 265, 269
  trials of war criminals, 318–319
  women of, 305
  writ of *habeas corpus* introduced in, 314
Java, 112, 120, 128, 254, 256
Jenkins, Paul B., 36
Jessup, Philip C., 322, 361
Johnson, Louis A., message to MacArthur, 356 fn.
Johnson, Lyndon, 408
Jones, General, 113, 129
Jones, George, Col., 250
Joy, C. Turner, Adm., 335, 347
Juio, Matsuichi, Col., 167

Kamikaze attacks, 231, 237, 240
Kase, Toshikazu, 272
Kavieng, 181, 188–189
Kawabe, Torashiro, Lt. Gen., 111
Keeler, Willie, 166
Kelly, R. G., Lieut., 144
Kelly, William, Col., 61
Kempi-Tai, 289
Kennedy, John Fitzgerald, quoted on China, 320–321
Kennedy, Joseph P., 108
Kennesaw Mountain, 9, 84
Kenney, George C., Maj. Gen., 157, 168 fn., 170, 172, 173, 173 fn., 178, 180, 229, 233 fn., 238, 239, 246, 255, 258, 259, 265
Kilmer, Joyce, Sgt., 61
Kimpo Airfield, 354
Kimura, Kozaemon, 316
King, E. J., Adm., 121, 183, 196, 198, 287
King, General, 113
Kinkaid, Thomas, Adm., 172, 188, 224, 225, 226, 227, 229, 233 fn., 239
Kiriwina Island, 175, 176
Knox, Frank, 183
Koga, Mineichi, Adm., 205–206
Kokoda Trail, 160, 161, 162
Kokura, 263
Konoye, Prince, 273
Korea, 31, 106, 327–396
  Communists in, 324
  evacuation of U.S. and U.N. personnel from, 328

Korea, MacArthur's plan for ending war in, 410–412
map of, 329
occupation of, 319
Republic proclaimed in, 319, 323
topography, 328
U.S. troops withdrawn from, 319, 323
war in, 327–396
Krueger, Walter, 170, 175–176, 216
Krunhilde Stalling, 65, 67 fn.
Kula Gulf, 176
Kum River, 378
Kunsan, 349
Kurita, Takeo, Adm., 222, 224, 226, 230
Kuroki, Commander, 30
Kwajalein, 187
Kyushu, 260, 261, 265

La Guardia, Fiorello, 110, 111
Lae, 154, 159, 168, 170–173, 175, 178–179, 262 fn.
Landon, Margaret, 32
Lange, Gordon, 316 fn.
Lanphier, Thomas G., Capt., 177
Lansdown (destroyer), 273
Laurson, "Dotty," 27
Lawton, Henry Ware, Capt., 39
Leach, George E., Col., 62
Leahy, William, Adm., 106, 183, 196, 198
Lee, Admiral, 229, 230
Legaspi, 123, 124, 238
Lemnitzer, Lyman L., Gen., 83
Lenin, Nikolai, 416, 417
Levin, Emmanuel, 95
Lewis, J. Hamilton, 93
Leyte, 204, 211–218, 221–234
Leyte Gulf, 211, 214, 215
Battle of, 221–231
Leyte Valley, 214
Liberty, 417–418
Liddell Hart, B. H., 290–291
Lie, Trygve, 330, 342
Liggett, Hunter, Lt. Gen., 61, 68
Lincoln, Abraham, 6, 9, 394
Lingayen, 237, 238–239, 241, 245
Lingayen Gulf, 113, 117, 123–124, 237
Little Rock, Ark., 14
Los Angeles, Calif., 28
Ludendorff, Erich von, Gen., 56, 98
Lumsden, Herbert, Gen., 181, 201, 240–241
Lusitania, 45

Luzon, 198, 202, 204, 211, 212
Japanese attack on, 123–124
recapture of, 237–253

MacArthur, Arthur (brother), 14–15, 17, 52, 102
MacArthur, Arthur, Gen. (father), 4, 6–19, 21–25, 26, 28–31, 34, 35–36, 39, 44, 45, 47, 84, 86, 89, 103, 314, 349
MacArthur, Arthur (grandfather), 4–6, 9
MacArthur, Arthur (great grandfather), 4
MacArthur, Arthur (son), 107, 139–142, 158–159, 288, 408
MacArthur, Aurelia (grandmother), 4
MacArthur, Douglas
aide-de-camp to T. Roosevelt, 33
American Olympic Committee president, 86
ancestors, 3
appointed Commander-in-Chief of U.N. forces in Korea, 337
appointed Commanding General, U.S. Army Forces in Far East, 109
appointed Supreme Commander for the Allied Powers, 265
awards bestowed on, 55, 56, 58, 61, 63, 64, 67, 69, 72, 103, 134, 147, 168, 174, 179, 189 fn., 234, 244, 256, 260, 265, 363, 373, 399, 408, 423
birth, 14
Bonus Marchers and, 92–97
Chief of Staff, 89–102
Congressional hearing, 406–407
considered as Presidential candidate, 184–185, 319
early years, 15–36
education, 15–18, 25, 32, 34
Engineer Board member, 39
Engineer School student, 32–34
father's death, 36
first memories, 14–15
first military assignment, 28
Formosa visit, 340
General Staff member, 39, 43
Japanese surrender ceremonies, 269–279
Joint (Army-Navy) Board member, 102
Korean War and, 327–396
marriage, 83
Memorandum on Ending the Korean War, 410–412
mother's death, 103

MacArthur, Douglas, occupation of Japan, 280–324
opinion of Eisenhower, 315
Pacific war and, 117–275
parents, 6–14
Pittsburgh University speech (1932), 90
promotions, 30, 34, 43, 46, 47, 67, 89, 127, 234 265
relations with F. D. Roosevelt, 101
relations with the Navy, 101–102
relieved of command by Truman, 389–395
request for relief from command, 369–370
retirement from Army, 107
return to U.S., 399 ff.
sentimental journey to the Philippines, 419–422
speech before Congress, 400–405
speech before National Association of Manufacturers, 408–409
Truman's conference with, at Wake Island, 360–364
Vera Cruz assignment, 40–43
West Point address (1962), 423–426
West Point cadet, 25–28
West Point Superintendent, 73–83, 86
World War I and, 51–73
MacArthur, Douglas (nephew), 17, 102
MacArthur Frank (uncle), 4, 5
MacArthur, Jean (wife), 106–107, 139, 142, 288, 395
MacArthur, Malcolm (brother), 14
MacArthur, Mary (mother), 13–14, 15, 18, 19, 25, 35, 39, 89, 90, 103
MacArthur, Sarah (great grandmother), 4
"MacArthur Day," 154 fn.
Macassar Strait, 183, 255
Madang, 181, 189, 262 fn.
Magellan, Ferdinand, 19
Maginot, André, 97
Maginot Line, 98
Magsaysay, Ramón, 205
Mainichi Shimbun, 396
Malaya, 106, 110–112, 153, 175
Japanese invasion of, 121
Manchuria, 106, 263, 365–366, 368–369, 372, 384–385
Manila, 18–23, 29, 84, 88, 112
declared an open city, 126
liberation of, 246–252
Mann, William A., Brig. Gen., 46, 51, 53, 54
Manokwari, 194, 195

March, Peyton, Gen., 46, 77, 79
Marianas, 188
Maritime Commission, 107, 108
Marshall, Dick, 165 fn.
Marshall, George C., Gen.
China mission, 320, 343
compared with MacArthur, 290
MacArthur's message to, 122, 146
messages to MacArthur, 108–109, 127 fn., 133 fn., 135, 141, 180 fn., 189 fn., 191 fn., 196, 234, 238, 244 fn., 260, 356 fn., 360, 368, 370
Pacific war and, 121, 127, 139, 140, 198, 261
replaced by Eisenhower as Army chief of staff, 287
reports to Secretary of War, 254, 327
Secretary of Defense, 351
visits MacArthur in Southwest Pacific Area, 183–184
World War I and, 68
Martin, Joe, 385–386, 389
Marx, Karl, 416, 417
Mascardo, Tomas, Gen., 22–23
Matsumoto, Joji, 299–300, 302
Mauban, 132
McCook, Alexander, Maj. Gen., 16
McCormack, John W., 257, 407
McCoy, Frank, Col., 61
McDonough, Gordon, 347
McKinley, William, 19, 25
quoted on the Philippines, 19–20
McLanagan, Professor, 18
McNider, General, 165 fn.
Melbourne, Australia, 151
Menoher, Charles T., Maj. Gen., 54, 55, 56 fn., 61, 67, 70 fn., 71
Merchant Marine, American, 108
Merchant Marine Act (1938), 108
Metz, France, 63–64
Meurcy Ferme, 59
Meuse-Argonne, 64, 65
Mexico, 39–43
Mézières, France, 65
Middleburg Island, 194
Midway, 112, 159
Miles, Perry L., Gen., 95
Military establishment, U.S., changes in the, 414–415
Mill Creek, Tenn., 6, 7
Miller, A. L., 184

Milne Bay, 154, 159, 161–162, 262 fn.
Milwaukee, Wis., 4, 18
Mindalano, Datu Manaleo, 205, 208–209
Mindanao, 88, 109–110, 113, 121, 140, 204, 210–212, 252, 254
Mindanao Sea, 222, 225
Mindoro, 237–238
Missionary Ridge, Battle of, 8–9, 36
Missouri, 269, 271, 272, 274
Mitchell, William, Brig. Gen., 85–86
Miyazaki, Shuichi, Lt. Gen., 209–210
Molotov, Vyacheslav, 280
Moluccas, 185, 202, 254
Momote, 188
Mongkut, King, 32
Montcalm, Marquis de, 349
Moore, Ernest M., Gen., 113
Morotai Island, 201, 202
Morse, Wayne, 392
Morshead, Sir Leslie, 255
Moselle Valley, 64
Moses, Martin, Lt. Col., 204
Mount McKinley, 352
Mountbatten, Lord Louis, 191 fn., 201, 257, 262
Muccio, John, 328
Mudge, Verne D., Gen., 245
Murfreesboro, Battle of, 7, 36
Murphy, Charles, 361
Murphy, Frank, 249 fn., 295
Musashi (Japanese battleship), 225
"Musketeer II," 211
Muto, Akira, Lt. Gen., 111, 253

Nadzab airfield, 179
Nagasaki, atom bomb attack on, 263
Nakar, Guillermo, Lt. Col., 203
Naktong River, 345, 350, 354
Nashville, 190, 202, 214, 215, 218, 224, 225
National Association of Manufacturers, MacArthur's speech before, 408–409
National Guard, 44–45
Navy Department, U.S., 85, 106, 160
Negroes, 188, 236, 237
Netherlands East Indies, *see* Dutch East Indies
New Britain, 112, 169, 173, 176
New Grand Hotel (Yokohama), 269, 271
New Georgia Island group, 176, 178
New Guinea, 112, 152, 153, 154–164, 168–195, 263
New Ireland, 189

New Mexico, 240
New York City, welcome extended to MacArthur upon return to U.S., 406
New York Times, The, 96, 316, 338, 393
New Zealand, 173 fn.
Newton, General, 9
Nihilism, 416
Nimitz, C. W., Adm., 161, 187–189, 191 fn., 192, 197, 224, 227, 230–231, 245, 258–259, 287
Nishimura, Shoji, Vice Adm., 123, 222, 225, 227
Nobel, Arthur, Lt. Col., 204
Noemfoor, 192–193
Nogi, Commander, 30
Norfolk, Va., 14
Norris, Ravee, Maj., 67

O'Donnell, Emmett, Gen., 369
Ohmae, Toshikazu, Capt., 155
Okinawa, 197, 245, 259
Oku, Yasukata, Gen., 31
Oldendorf, J. B., Adm., 225, 229, 239
Olongapo, 245
Olympic Games, 86–87
Order of the Purple Heart, 102–103
Ormoc, 233
Ormoc Corridor, 232
Osmena, Sergio, 30, 199, 216, 233 fn., 234–235, 241, 249, 251
Ostfriesland (German dreadnaught), 85
Otis Ewell, Maj. Gen., 21
Otjen, Theobald, 18
Owen Stanley Range (New Guinea), 152, 154, 159, 162, 262 fn.
Oyama, Commander, 30
Ozawa, Jisabuto, Vice Adm., 222, 226, 230

Pace, Frank, 356 fn., 361, 376 fn., 395
Pace, John T., 95, 96
Palalu, 202
Palaus, 187
Panama Canal Zone, 34
Panaon Strait, 212, 214
Panay, 237, 254
Panganinan, 204
Panson Island, 215
Papua, 152–154, 162–163, 165, 169, 175
Pardee, George C., 28
Paris, Treaty of, 19

Parker, George M., Jr., Gen., 113, 124, 125, 129

Parsons, E. B., Capt., 9, 10, **36**

Partridge, Earl, Gen., 388

Patriotism, 414

Patterson, Charles H., Col., 88, 382 fn.

Patterson, Robert P., 287, 316 fn.

Patton, George S., Gen., 62, 95, **249** fn.

Pearl Harbor, attack on, 112, 114, 117, 120, 121, 318

Pegler, Westbrook, 394

Peninsula de Fengo line, 132

Pepper, Claude, 279

Peralta, Macario, Jr., Maj., 203

Percival, A. E., Gen., 271

Perryville, Ky., 6

Pershing, John J., Gen., 47, 53, 54, 59, 63 fn., 67, 71, 92
    MacArthur's opinion of, 48
    messages to MacArthur, 133 fn., 191 fn., 248 fn.
    Mexico and, 43
    tributes to MacArthur, 103 fn., **179**
    World War I and, 68, 70, **72**

Pescadore Islands, 339

Pétain, Henri, Marshal 57

Philippine Defense Plan, 111–112

Philippine Sea, 22, 227

Philippines, 18–24, 28, 29, 83, 84, 87, 102, 103–114, 197, 202–254, 263
    Japanese attack on, 117–121, 123
    liberation of, 215–254
    MacArthur's return to, 216–218
    MacArthur's sentimental journey to, 419–422
    republic established, 316
    resistance of people of, Japanese occupation, 202–209
    restoration of civil government, 234–237, 250–251
    retreat from the, 115–147

Phoenix, 188

Piao, Lin, Gen., 374, 375–376

Pilsudski, Jósef, 99

Pocket Testament League, 311

Port Moresby, 154–155, 159–162

Portal, Sir Charles, Air Marshal, 173 fn.

Portland Oregonian, 255–256

Potsdam Conference, 261–262, 263, 264, 295, 298, 304, 318

Praeger, Ralph, Capt., 204

President Hoover, 103, 107

Prince of Wales (British battleship), 121

Prout, William C., 86

Pusan, 333, 336, 345, 350–352, 359, 365, 371, 377

Pyongyang, 358–359, 364, 365

Quezon, Doña Aurora, 138, 140

Quezon, Manuel, 22, 30, 84, 88, 104, 105, 106, 107, 113 123 129 130, 131–132, 135, 137, 139, 140, 160, 217, 236, 237, 367
    death of, 199
    letter to F. D. Roosevelt, 138
    message to MacArthur, 131–132, 136–137
    Washington visit, 102

Quirino, Elpidio, 322

Rabaul, 168–169, 171–174, 175–176, 178, 180–181, 188–189

Racin, 365

Radford, Arthur, Adm., 361

Rainbow Division, 46, 47, 51–73

Ray, Harold G., Capt., 141

"Red Beach," 215, 216

Reddy, Colonel, 88

Reed, George, Gen., 84

Reed, Walter, Maj., 39

Reilly, Henry J., Col., 64

"Reno," 210–211

Repulse (British battle cruiser), 122

Rhee, Syngman, 319, 355–356, 396
    message to MacArthur, 354 fn.

Richardson, Robert C., Lt. Gen., 198, 258

Richelderfer, L. H., 94

Rickenbacker, Eddie, Capt., 59

Ridgway, Matthew, Gen., 383–384, **385**

Ripley, Peter, 1st Sgt., 15, 34, 127

Ritchie, William I., Gen., **261**

Riveredge, 14

Rivers, Lucius M., 407

Robenson, John A., Col., 128

Rockwell, H. G., Rear Adm., 128, 141, 143

Rolampont, France, 53

Rommel, Erwin, Field Marshal 122

Romulo, Carlos, 216, 259
    tribute to MacArthur, 265

Roosevelt, Eleanor, 177–178

Roosevelt, Franklin D., 363
    Bonus Marchers and, 93–94
    Churchill and, 121, 153, 181, 211
    Curtin's conference with, 185

Roosevelt, Franklin D., death of, 257
  letter to Quezon, 137
  MacArthur's letter to, 217–218
  MacArthur's opinion of, 99–100
  message to MacArthur, 107, 127 fn., 133 fn.,
    153, 171 fn., 177–178, 199–200, 218 fn.,
    249
  opinion of MacArthur, 96
  Pacific war and, 123, 128, 133, 140
  Quezon invited to U.S. by, 160
  Quezon's letter to, 138–139
  relations with MacArthur, 101–102
  Tehran Conference, 183
  tribute to MacArthur, 258
Roosevelt, Theodore, 30, 33
Root, Elihu, 28
Ross, Charles, 361
Ross, Lloyd, Maj., 67
Roxas, Manuel, 205, 236–237
  death of, 322
  tribute to MacArthur, 265 fn.
Rusk, Dean, 361
Russell, Richard, 406
Russia, 31
  attitude toward occupation of Japan, 285,
    291
  objectives of, 390–391
  Pacific war and, 122, 261–262, 263
Russo-Japanese War, 30, 221
Rutledge, Wiley B., 295

Saidor, 181
St. Benoit, France, 63, 64
St. Mihiel, 62
St. Nazaire, France, 52
Saipan, 192
Salamaua, 154, 159, 168, 170–173, 175, 178–
  179, 262 fn.
Sam (Negro messenger), 45
Samar, 214, 227, 233
Samoa, 112
San Antonio, Tex., 18, 34–35
San Bernardino Strait, 222, 224, 225, 226,
  227, 230
San Francisco, Calif., 28, 30, 89, 400
San Jose, 215
San Juanico Strait, 212, 214
San Manuel, 244
San Tomas concentration camp, 246, 247–248
Sanananda, 165
Sansapor, 192, 194, 195

Saturday Evening Post, 392
Sayre, Francis, 110, 138, 140
Sayre, Mrs. Francis, 140
Schumacher, V. S., Lieut. (j.g.) 144
Scott, Hugh, Maj. Gen., 45
Sedan, France, 65, 67, 68, 69–70
Seeckt, Hans von, Gen., 98
Seoul, 332–333, 346, 349–350, 354–355,
  359, 365, 383–384
Sergy, 59–60
Seringes, 59–60
Severson, Charles, 27
Sharp, William F., Gen., 113, 145
Shenandoah (Navy dirigible), 85
Shephard, Lemuel C., Jr., C.P.O., 347
Sheridan, Philip, Gen., 6–7, 8, 13
Sherman (transport), 29
Sherman, Forrest, Adm., 347, 348–351,
  376 fn.
Sherman, William T., Gen., 9, 14
Shidehara, Baron, 293–294, 299, 302–303
Shigemitsu, Mamoru, 272–275
Shima, Kiyohide, Vice Adm., 222
Shintoism, 281, 310
Siam, 32, 106
Siberia, 122, 263, 365, 392
Sibert, Franklin C., Maj. Gen., 215
Sierra Madre range, 252
Singapore, 112, 221, 222
  Japanese seizure of, 122
Sino-Japanese war, 108
Smith, Oliver, Gen., 374
Socialism, 417
Soerabaja, 112
Solomons, 163, 169, 175–176, 180, 187
South China Sea, 121, 254
Spaatz, C. A., Gen., message to MacArthur,
  357 fn.
Spanish-American War, 18–19, 39
Sprague, Thomas, Adm., 227–230, 233 fn.
Spruance, R. A. Adm., 259
Stalin, Joseph, 175, 183, 279, 384
Stanley, David S., Gen., 9, 10
Stark, Harold, Adm., 106
State Department, U.S., 105, 279, 289, 292,
  320, 321, 323, 324, 328, 345, 355, 366
Still, General 7
Stilwell, Joseph W., Gen., 259
Stimson, Henry L., 88, 108, 139, 167 fn., 236,
  244 fn., 248 fn., 253 fn., 287
Stone River, Battle of, 7

Storey, Tony, Col., 373
Stratemeyer, George E., Gen., 335, 347, 368, 369
Strawberry Valley, 30
Struble, Arthur, Rear Adm., 173, 347, 354, 388
Subic Bay, 120
Sumatra, 112
Summerall, Charles Pelot, Gen., 47, 66–68, 86–89
Surigao Strait, 222, 224, 225, 227, 228, 237
Sutherland, Richard, Gen., 113, 120, 140, 145, 165 fn.
Suwon, 332, 354
Suzuki, Kantaro, 269, 279
Swift, Innis P., Maj. Gen., 239
Swing, Joseph M., 232
Syerdrup, General, 165 fn.

Tacloban, 29, 215, 221, 224, 231
Tacloban Airfield, 212, 214, 218, 229
Taejon, 332, 345
Taft, Robert, 323
Takemoto, K., Capt., 208
Tanahmerah Bay, 189, 190
Tanaka, Kotaro, 396
Tanimbar, 176
Tarakan, 255, 262 fn.
Tarlac, 242, 244
Tawi Tawi Island, 254, 255
Taylor, Maxwell, Gen., 83
Texas, 17–18
Thomas, 30, 84
Thomas, George H., Gen., 9
Thresher, 236
Tibet, 390
Timor, 145, 160, 177
Tinian, 263
Togo, Heihachiro, Adm., 30
Tojo, Hideki, Gen., 318
Tokyo, 280
"Tokyo Rose," 130, 143, 318
Totalitarianism, 418
Toyoda, Suemo, Adm., 222, 225
Trenchard, Air Marshal, 173 fn.
Trimble, Ford, 88
Truk, 187
Truman, Harry S., 264–265, 292, 295
    atom bomb disclosed by, 262–263
    Korean War and, 330–331, 334, 337, 340–341, 347, 351–352, 360–364, 376

Truman, Harry S., MacArthur relieved of command by, 389–395
    meeting with MacArthur at Wake Island, 360–364
    messages to MacArthur, 253 fn., 305 fn., 322 fn., 340–342, 356 fn., 364 fn., 376 fn., 381–382
    personality of, 393–394
Truman, Margaret, 394
Tuilières Ferme, 67
Turner, Kelly, Vice Adm., 163
Tydings-McDuffie Act, 111
Tyndell, Robert H., Col., 64
Tynley, Colonel, 69

Umedzu, General, 272–273, 275
United Nations
    Korean War and, 330 ff.
    Temporary Commission on Korea, 330
United States Military Academy, *see* West Point

Valdez, Basilio, Gen., 216
Vandenberg, Arthur, 289 fn.
Vandenberg, Hoyt, Gen., 83
Vasey, Major General, 165 fn.
Vaucouleurs, France, 53, 61
Vera Cruz, Mexico, 40–41, 43
Veterans of Foreign Wars, 341
Vigan, 123
Villa, Pancho, 43
Visayas, 203, 211, 214, 252
Vitiaz Strait, 168, 180
Vogelkop Peninsula, 194, 195
Volckmann, Russel W., Col., 241
Von Richthofen, Baron Manfred, 65

Wainwright, Jonathan M., Gen., 113, 124–125, 129, 132, 142, 271–272
Wakde, 192–193
Wake Island
    Japanese seizure of, 122
    Truman-MacArthur conference at, 360–364
Walker, Walton, Brig. Gen., 165 fn., 335, 336, 345, 346, 349, 350, 351, 354, 355, 357, 360, 365, 372, 373, 374, 376, 377
    death of, 383
War criminals, 318–319
War Department, U.S., 40, 42, 43, 44, 44 fn., 85, 106, 109, 128, 135, 193, 198, 250–251, 261, 286

Washington, D.C., 16, 39
Washington, George, 18, 102
Washington Daily News, 394
Washington Post, 394
Waters, Walter W., 93
Wau, 171, 172, 262 fn.
Wayne, Anthony, Gen., 18
Weaver, James R.N., Brig. Gen., 126
Webster, Daniel, 5, 417
West, the, 12–13
West Point, 18, 25–28, 77–83, 86
West Texas Military Academy, 17
Wewak, 178, 189–190, 262 fn.
Weygand, Maxime, 97
White, Thomas, Gen., 83
"White Beach," 215
Whitehead, Ennis P., Brig. Gen., 157, 165 fn.,
    173 fn., 178, 239
Whitney, Courtney, Gen., 205, 270, 314
Whole of Their Lives, The (Gitlow), 96
Wilhelm, Crown Prince, 56, 58
Wilhelmina, Queen, 86–87
Wilkinson, Theodore S., Adm., 173, 239
Willoughby, Charles, Col., 113, 138, 165 fn.
Wilson, Woodrow, 40, 43, 45, 46, 47
Wisconsin, 4, 34
Wolfe, James, 349
Wolfe, Walter, Maj., 63, 69
Wolmi-do, 348, 353, 354
Women, Japanese, 305

Wood, Leonard, Gen., 39, 40, 43, 84
Wood, Robert E., 34
Woodlark Island, 175, 176
Wooten, Brigadier, 165 fn.
World War I, 15, 17, 35, 44–48, 51–73
World War II, 91
    allied offensive, 149–218
    conquest of Japan, 219–266
    retreat from the Philippines, 115–147
Wosan, 359, 374

Yalta Conference, 261–262
Yalu River, 365, 366, 368, 372, 373, 374–375
Yamamato, Isoruku, Adm., 176–177 205
Yamashita, Tomoyuk, Gen., 122, 221, 232,
    233, 238, 242, 253 295–296
Yamashita Line 232, 233, 234
Yamato (Japanese battleship), 225, 228
Yellow Sea, 353
Yokohama, 269, 271, 272, 273
Yongdong, 345
Yoshida, Shigeru, 278–279, 315, 395–396
    letter to MacArthur, 422–423
    message to MacArthur, 356 fn.
Youngers, the, 13
Younghusband, Sir Francis, 32

Zaibatsu, 308
Zambales, 130